T HE N E   *4 2 9 4

A SURVEY OF BRITISH

CLIMATE AND WEATHER

This book is due for return on or before the last date shown below.

THE NEW NATURALIST LIBRARY

CLIMATE
AND
WEATHER

JOHN A. KINGTON

Collins

This edition published in 2010 by Collins,
An imprint of HarperCollins Publishers

HarperCollins Publishers
77–85 Fulham Palace Road
London W6 8JB
www.collins.co.uk

First published 2010

A CIP catalogue record for this book is available
from the British Library.

Set in FF Nexus by
Martin Brown

Printed in Hong Kong by Printing Express

Hardback
ISBN 978-0-00-718501-6

Paperback
ISBN 978-0-00-718502-3

All reasonable efforts have been made by the author
to trace the copyright owners of the material quoted in this book and of any
images reproduced in this book. In the event that the author or publishers are
notified of any mistakes or omissions by copyright owners after publication of
this book, the author and the publishers will endeavour to rectify the
position accordingly for any subsequent printing.

Contents

Editors' Preface

GILBERT WHITE OBSERVED IN HIS CLASSIC BOOK *The Natural History of Selborne*, that 'since the weather of a district is undoubtedly part of its natural history I shall make no further apology for the four following letters . . .' The Editors of the New Naturalist Library took the same view with the publication in 1952 of Gordon Manley's *Climate and the British Scene*. This successful book reflected the wide field experience of the author and ran into several impressions, finally becoming out of print in 1980.

Since the publication of Manley's book, much has happened in our knowledge of climate and weather. The recording of relations between weather and natural history has continued to be of constant interest to natural history societies, local and national, with the weather a continual and essential backdrop to accounts of natural history. But the significance of this backdrop has been very much widened by our increased knowledge of climate change and its nature, the effects of such change in terms of flora, fauna and biodiversity and also by the increased knowledge of historical climates and weather events, a field greatly advanced by the pioneer contributions of Hubert Lamb.

The author of *Climate and Weather*, John Kington, has had a long involvement with these developments, with experience as a synoptic meteorologist in the Meteorological Office, and later researching historical climatology in the renowned Climatic Research Unit in the University of East Anglia.

This book is divided into two very different but related parts, the first describing and discussing the significant topics which determine our climate and weather, the second a chronology of climatic history since the 1st century BC. The notable year-by-year account puts our present experience of weather into striking perspective, and of course reflects circumstances that will have affected our fauna and flora in times past. This book is a welcome and timely addition to the New Naturalist Library.

Author's Foreword and Acknowledgements

Lying throughout within the domain of the westerlies, beneath the sinuosities of that upper wave-pattern that girdles the Northern Hemisphere, the moist and temperate climate of the British Isles has been described by many authors. Indeed, no climate in the world has been more provocative of comment. By some, it has been described as the best in the world. For others, the astonishing variety of small-scale effects that it can and does repeatedly provide, induces resigned tolerance, irritation, or downright dislike, accompanied by declarations that the British Isles have no climate, but merely weather.

Gordon Manley, *The Climate of the British Isles*, 1970

THE TWENTY-SECOND VOLUME IN THE NEW NATURALIST LIBRARY, Professor Gordon Manley's *Climate and the British Scene*, was published almost 60 years ago, and the enduring qualities of that renowned text have stood the test of time. The purpose of this new book is to present subsequent developments and discoveries made in the study of the climate and weather of the British Isles, with particular reference to the research that I carried out at the Climatic Research Unit (CRU), School of Environmental Sciences, University of East Anglia, Norwich, following studies under Manley at the University of London.

Besides the outstanding work of Manley, our knowledge and understanding of the climate and weather of the British Isles owes much to the efforts of Professor Hubert Lamb, founding Director of the CRU in 1971.

For instance, his study of historic storms presents a definitive account of the great windstorms that have affected the region and surrounding sea areas over the past 500 years. As one of the first meteorologists to be invited to join the staff of the CRU, I had the privilege to work with Lamb and benefit from his wide expertise in historical and synoptic climatology, particularly with the reconstruction of past circulation patterns and the classification of British Isles weather types.

I am grateful to HarperCollins for the opportunity to write this book, and to the Senior Editor, Julia Koppitz, Professor Richard West FRS and my wife, Beryl, for their advice and encouragement in seeing it through to publication. Mike Salmon (CRU) is thanked for preparing Figures 17–19.

PART I

Principal Acts in the Climatic Drama

CHAPTER 1

The Climate and Weather of the British Isles

It is commonly observed, that when two Englishmen meet, their first talk is of the weather; they are in haste to tell each other, what each must already know, that it is hot or cold, bright or cloudy, windy or calm.

Samuel Johnson, 1758

INTRODUCTION

THIS BOOK IS ABOUT THE CLIMATE AND WEATHER OF THE BRITISH ISLES, and the subject is essentially treated in the light of the author's experience as a synoptic meteorologist in the Meteorological Office, and as a historical climatologist in the Climatic Research Unit at the University of East Anglia. Developments made in climatology since Gordon Manley wrote his New Naturalist volume on *Climate and the British Scene* (Fig. 1) in 1952 are featured, together with the increasing concern, in both public and scientific circles, about the impact of climatic change on our way of life today and in the future. The book closes in the year 2000.

Part I comprises chapters on the properties of the atmosphere and its circulation, the key players in the climate and weather of these islands, seasonal characteristics, sources of meteorological data, historical weather mapping, cloud study, phenology, climatic trends, anomalies and extremes, and climatic change.

Chapter 9 provides a general overview of climate trends, but in Part II a great deal more information is given, amounting to a detailed year-by-year account of what is known about the weather and climate experienced in the British Isles during historical times. Each year's weather is related, wherever possible, to

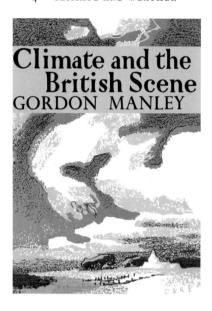

FIG 1. Cover of the New Naturalist *Climate and the British Scene*, by Gordon Manley, M.A., M.Sc., Collins, London, 1952.

actual or inferred situations in a way that has not been previously attempted for any period prior to the mid 19th century. As a result, a fuller synoptic record becomes available, and this should prove invaluable when the outlook is being considered.

However, first, it is desirable that a clear distinction should be made between the study of *climate* and that of *weather*. While climate is a summary of the weather conditions over an extended period of perhaps 30 or 40 years, weather is the state of the atmosphere at any one time, or over a short spell such as a day or a week. Climate is sometimes defined as average weather – but a straightforward mean can conceal notable occurrences. For example, while a very warm summer may have been the most memorable weather event during a year, its thermal anomaly can be lost in that year's average statistics of temperature.

In addition to examining weather as experienced in the British Isles on a daily to weekly basis and its characteristics related to large-scale synoptic situations, the book also reviews the many ways that people have observed and recorded weather conditions down the ages, using ever more sophisticated methods and instruments. It is a story based on a rich and varied resource stretching back 2000 years. This approach has allowed climatic trends, anomalies and extremes to be identified over the past two millennia.

As discussed in Chapter 4, the weather of the British Isles is basically influenced by the movement of major air masses. Situated in mid latitudes, the region lies in the path of air-mass convergence between warm subtropical and cold polar airflows. At this convergence zone, the polar front, the less dense warm air rises over the denser cold air, producing the typical weather phenomena associated with this situation, that is, fronts, depressions and rain. As a result, the climate of the British Isles can be very changeable, and various types of weather may be experienced even within the short time span of a single day. In general, however, the climate of the region is relatively mild for its latitude, since it is influenced by the North Atlantic Drift that has its origin as the Gulf Stream, the warm ocean current that develops in the Gulf of Mexico and then flows northeast across the Atlantic. In contrast, Newfoundland, on the west side of the North Atlantic at similar latitude to the British Isles, can be up to 10 °C (18 °F) colder in winter.

Although in geography textbooks the British Isles region is said to fall into the cool temperate maritime type with overall uniformity and limited range, actual experience can prove it to be very different. The region usually lies in the westerly wind belt – that is, it is in the path of travelling depressions which progress eastwards along the polar front. However, there are considerable variations in the weather, with conditions depending to a large extent upon the dominating pressure system in the circulation. For instance, the cold winter of 1947 was due to the influence of a blocking continental anticyclone, whereas the warm dry summer of 1959 was the effect of an extension of the Azores high over the British Isles, diverting away the depressions that sometimes bring unsettled conditions to the region at this time of the year.

The British Isles comprise only a relatively small geographical area of the earth's surface, but, nevertheless, differences in climate do exist across the region. For instance, while the climate of the western half of the region is dominated by maritime air masses, that further east is often influenced by more continental situations. In addition to air masses, the intensity of insolation received at different locations, which varies according to latitude, also has an effect on climate.

Consequently, the region can be divided into four climatic subdivisions. The northwest quarter, including north Ireland, northwest England and west Scotland, is characterised by mild winters and cool summers, while the northeast quarter, comprising east Scotland and northeast England, has cold winters and cool summers. The southwest quarter, containing south Ireland, Wales and southwest England, experiences mild winters and warm summers, while central and southeast England has cold winters and warm summers. In general, the western half of the British Isles experiences a more maritime climate during winter, while the east is affected by a cold air stream from mainland Europe. In summer, climatic differences are dominated more by latitude.

The greater influence of maritime air masses in the western half of the British Isles means that it receives considerably more rainfall than the east. The generally higher ground in the west forces incoming air to rise, further enhancing precipitation; parts of the Scottish Highlands, for example, can receive over 250 cm (100 inches) of precipitation per year. In some parts of northern Britain it can rain or snow on as many as 300 days in a year. The east, by contrast, is lower and flatter, lying in the rain shadow of the Scottish Highlands, the Welsh mountains and the Pennines, and is consequently much drier; some parts of southeast England may receive only 50 cm (20 inches) of rainfall per year.

THE ELEMENTS AT PLAY

Pressure

In general, pressure decreases from south to north throughout the year over the British Isles, with isobars running from southwest or west to east or northeast. The chances that the normal pressure gradient will be reversed are greatest in the spring; with higher pressure now to the north, easterly or northeasterly winds may blow for some time, and in April the frequency of winds from the northeast almost equals that from the southwest at most locations. The likelihood that the Azores high will spread over west and south Britain reaches its maximum in June with accompanying highest sunshine durations, decreased cloud amounts, and the lowest frequency of rain. July and August bring, in general, rather more unsettled cloudy conditions, but September's slightly weaker pressure gradients reflect the tendency for a spell of relatively quiet, dry weather during that month with slightly less cloud. Extremes of pressure range from 1054 mb at Aberdeen on 31 January 1902 to 926 mb at Ochtertyre (Perthshire) on 26 January 1884.

Temperature

The distribution of mean temperature in the British Isles is governed by latitude, distance from mainland Europe (from which drier air may spread, giving exceptional warmth in summer, cold in winter), proximity to or distance from the coast, and altitude. In addition, local modifications may come into play ascribed to aspect and the effects of minor relief features, soil, proximity to water bodies, and the works of man in the form of drainage, shelter-belts, building and, most markedly, the ongoing extension of built-up areas to towns and cities.

In midwinter, the coasts are a little warmer than the interior. Within England, the coldest winter temperatures occur in the centre of the country, but altitude is sufficient to ensure that central Scotland at higher levels is considerably colder. In spring, there is a sharp fall in mean temperature towards coasts adjacent to the cool waters of the North Sea. The most forward spring growth is found in the sheltered inland valleys of southwest England. In summer, the effects of inland location become marked, as shown, for example, by the relative coolness of the Isle of Man in July in comparison with the warmth of Yorkshire. In autumn, the effect of the coastal waters ensures that seaside locations remain warmer than those inland, especially towards the southwest.

The warmest summers are found in the Thames valley and inland parts of southeast England (Fig. 2). Hence London, with its additional urban effect, which raises the mean summer temperature in central parts of the capital by about 0.5–0.7 °C (c.1 °F), invariably has the highest mean and extreme temperatures in the British Isles.

FIG 2. Fair-weather cumulus clouds forming overland on a sunny day; buoyant bubbles of air (thermals) rising from the warm surface give nearly horizontal bases to the clouds on reaching the condensation level. (Nick Spurling/FLPA)

FIG 3. A frost-covered lane with rime accretion on the hedgerows and trees, one of the most beautiful but relatively rare scenes to occur in winter. Following the clearance of freezing fog, a deposit of white ice crystals is revealed which had previously formed when supercooled water droplets comprising the fog impinged on solid objects from ground to tree-top level. (Nick Spurling/FLPA)

The highest temperatures recorded in the British Isles are comparable to those observed in nearby mainland Europe. For example, 38.1 °C (100.5 °F) was reported at Tonbridge (Kent) in July 1868. There have been a number of occasions with temperatures between 35 and 37 °C (95–99 °F) at inland stations in southeast England and the east Midlands, notably in August 1911 and August 1932. Such extremes are not likely in Scotland and Ireland: 32 °C (90 °F) has rarely been recorded in these countries over the past century or so.

The lowest temperatures on record under standard conditions come from valley stations in the eastern Scottish Highlands: –27.2 °C (–17 °F) at Braemar (Aberdeenshire) in February 1895 and January 1982, and at Altnaharra (Sutherland) in December 1995. Earlier unofficial observations indicate that –30 °C (–22 °F) may have been recorded in some upland Scottish glens during the past. For England, –24 °C (–11 °F) was observed at Buxton (Derbyshire), also in February 1895, with –23 °C (–9 °F) in central Wales in January 1940. From records kept before the introduction of Stevenson screens, in combination with what is known regarding the location of unusually severe frost hollows, it is possible that values of –25 °C (–13 °F) may have occurred at times in southern England (Fig. 3). For Ireland, the lowest temperature on record is –20 °C (–4 °F), but minimum values at inland stations in the country have rarely fallen below –15 °C (5 °F).

Frost hollows

During long, clear nights in upland valleys, air cooled by contact with the ground moves downslope to form a katabatic flow. This cold air accumulates in low-lying parts, resulting in the formation of either dew or hoar frost. Thick hedges and railway embankments lying across slopes can dam the cold air and in the same way act as traps for dew or frost. Such frost hollows are widespread and are not limited to upland areas. At the bottom of many valleys in the Chilterns, the Cotswolds and the Downs, ground frost occurs throughout the year, even in midsummer, on as many as three nights in five. A small valley in the Chilterns near Rickmansworth (Hertfordshire) was one of the best-known frost hollows in the British Isles, with exceptionally low temperatures recorded in all seasons of the year. However, the former extreme microclimate of the valley has probably been affected by expanding suburban development that began during the late 1940s.

Urban climate and heat islands

Created by man, urban climate is one of the most distinctive types of local climate. By modifying the thermal, hydrological and roughness properties of the surface, distinctive changes are made to the atmospheric conditions between and above buildings, and a regionally distinct local climate can be created in towns and cities. It is at times of light winds, clear skies and inversions in the boundary layer that the greatest modifications are made.

The high heat capacity of brick and concrete, along with the reduction of wind speed by buildings, helps to raise the mean annual temperatures in towns and cities above those in the suburbs and neighbouring country. The actual increase in warming often amounts to about 2 °C (3–4 °F) and may on occasions be a 5 °C (9 °F) increase for people living or working in built-up areas. Night-time minima during winter are especially affected by these factors. In summer, evening cooling is also slower in the city than outside, although maximum temperatures may be equal. After the extensive brick- and concrete-covered areas have absorbed heat all day, they radiate strongly through the night. Although temperature inversions may form shortly after sunset in the suburbs to bring relief from the heat, temperatures inside the city remain near maximum until late evening, and if combined with high humidities become most oppressive. A city then becomes a heat island, and only when the wind increases above 25–30 km/h (15–19 mph; Beaufort force 4–5) is ventilation strong enough to make this effect disappear. Heat islands become hottest under anticyclonic conditions when winds are very light and sunshine is prolonged. Heat-island effects are lessened under windy unstable conditions, because any excess heat is transported away by turbulence.

Growing season

In lowland England the length of the growing season – that is, the period during which the mean temperature exceeds 6 °C (43 °F) – is about eight months. But the slow rise of mean temperature through the spring months implies that in open rural districts there is a considerable risk of frost, given a clear radiation night, until far on into May. Moreover, the incidence of frost varies so greatly in different locations that the average length of the frost-free period in lowland England ranges from only about two and a half months on the sandy heathlands to six months on favourable slopes and to upward of seven months within built-up areas of the larger towns and cities. Frost in this instance refers to air frost – that is, a screen minimum temperature of 0 °C (32 °F) or below at 1 m (c. 3.5 feet) above a grass surface.

An outstanding feature of the climate in upland Britain is the rapid fall of temperature with height, and the associated rapid rate of change in the length and effective warmth of the growing season with altitude. This results in a remarkably low altitude of the tree line compared with many other temperate-climate countries – between 600 and 700 m (2,000–2,300 feet).

FIG 4. Heavy seas in a gale off a British coast; moderately high waves with crests breaking into spindrift; the wind-blown foam is indicative of Beaufort wind force 7 to 8. (Gary K Smith/FLPA)

No feature is more vivid in the writer's mind than that of a well-known Swiss professor of geology who, confronted at 1,680 feet [512 m] – the level of Berne – with a wide stretch of the Pennines between Teesdale and Weardale, surprisingly declared 'this is the tundra.'

Gordon Manley, *Climate and the British Scene*, 1952

Wind

While surface winds are often influenced by local factors such as nearby relief and proximity to the sea, there is a general probability that the prevailing wind direction will be from the south to west on six days out of ten, and from the north to east on rather more than two days (Fig. 4). It will be calm on considerably less than one day, and on the remaining few occasions winds will be from the south to east, or north to west.

The strength of the wind is not so easy to generalise. In open country free from obstacles, such as on a large airfield, the average speed throughout the year is considerably greater than it would be in a built-up area, although funnelling effect between tall buildings can noticeably increase wind speeds. At representative open-country sites by day, wind strength is commonly of the order of Beaufort force 3 (12–19 km/h; 8–12 mph). At coastal sites the strongest winds tend to blow from seaward, in whichever direction that may be; winds off the land are much less strong overall.

Sea and land breezes

These are local winds, caused by the unequal heating and cooling of adjacent land and water surfaces due to solar radiation by day and terrestrial radiation by night, which produces a pressure gradient near the coast.

Onshore sea breezes are normally associated with the warmer months of the year, when the difference in temperature between the sea and the adjacent land is sufficient, and convection is not suppressed by the presence of anticyclonic subsidence. In general, a sea breeze is unlikely to develop if the pressure gradient is such that the wind comes directly off the land and exceeds Beaufort force 3.

The distribution of sea surface temperature in the waters surrounding the British Isles shows that in summer a tongue of relatively cool water extends southward off the east coast of Britain and, as a result, if suitable conditions occur, sea breezes will develop along this coastal margin. In June, July and August the water temperature off the North Sea coast is a little lower than that off the shores of the Irish Sea. At the same time, westerly winds off the land, due to friction, are likely to be less strong on the east coasts, whereas on the west coast the sea breeze merely intensifies the strength of the prevailing wind. With light westerly winds, skies inland are usually less cloudy on the eastern side of the country, day-time temperatures inland rise a little higher and the temperature gradient across the coast is greater. It is quite common to find that on summer days, when the maximum temperature a few kilometres inland rises to between 27 °C (80 °F) and 30 °C (86 °F), it will not exceed 20 °C (68 °F) along most of the east coast.

The distance to which the afternoon sea breeze will penetrate depends on the extent to which it is favoured or oppressed by the overall pressure gradient. On the east coast, if the westerly land wind does not exceed Beaufort force 3, summer sea breezes will undercut it for several hours in the afternoon and may penetrate 5–8 km (3–5 miles) or more from the coast.

Occasionally, when the pressure gradient reinforces the thermal effect, sea breezes may become perceptible on warm afternoons many kilometres inland provided there are no hills to act as a wind break. For instance, there is evidence that in warm summer weather with light easterly winds, the sea breeze from the southern North Sea, accompanied by a welcome freshening of the air, can be felt in London about five hours after noon; also at Norwich, 32 km (20 miles) from the coast, a weak sea breeze can sometimes be detected in the early evening.

Offshore land breezes are usually less developed than sea breezes, except on occasions during clear, very cold winter nights, especially when the ground is snow-covered.

Mountain breezes or drainage winds

On a radiation night of clear skies and a weak pressure gradient, terrestrial radiation from the earth's surface causes a layer of cold air to form near the ground with an associated temperature inversion. If the ground is sloping, air close to the ground is colder than that at the same level but some horizontal distance away. Downslope gravitational flow of the colder, denser air beneath the warmer, lighter air results in a mountain breeze or drainage wind. I regularly experienced this effect on night duty at Croydon Airport, when a light katabatic flow down the northern slope of the North Downs kept fog from forming at this aerodrome when other London airports such as Northholt and Heathrow became fog-bound in the Thames valley.

Föhn effects

The term *föhn* (which originates from the Alps) refers to a warm dry wind that occurs to leeward of mountains. Föhn effects are most common in the British Isles when an anticyclone has become centred to the east of the region so that the flow over the country lies between south and southeast. In this situation subsidence leads to the formation of a medium-level inversion. Under these conditions standing-wave phenomena develop over and in the lee of the mountains. In the regions where the warm dry air is descending, the temperature unexpectedly rises, accompanied by a characteristic gusty wind and very low humidities. The most frequent developments of this kind affect coastal districts along the southern shore of the Moray Firth in northeast Scotland. Temperatures exceeding 15 °C (59 °F) have been known in December and January; a maximum of 22.3 °C (72.1 °F) was observed at Kinloss and Forres on 9 March 1948. Further south, highest midwinter maxima have been recorded under similar circumstances along the north Welsh coast – for example, 17.8 °C (64 °F) in December and 17.2 °C (63 °F) in January.

Lee wave effects

Under certain meteorological conditions, severe damaging gales can occur on the normally sheltered lee side of hill ranges. For example, an extraordinary amount of damage to Scottish forests was caused by severe northerly gales during the great storm on 31 January 1953, which was the more remarkable as it was much greater on the south-facing slopes. Similarly, the Sheffield gale of 16 February 1962 caused a large amount of structural damage: this was a storm-force westerly gale whose effects were mainly confined to the eastern slopes of the Pennines. The explanation in both cases lay in the rapid spread of an anticyclone that followed the passage of a depression and the development of upper-level stability with a subsidence inversion, giving the situation that favours the production of standing waves and severe downslope winds on the lee side of hill ranges.

Helm wind

A notable phenomenon of Manley's beloved uplands is the helm wind, which he studied using data collected in the field. This local wind (condemned by John Ruskin as one of the 'plague winds' of the world), long recognised as a characteristic feature of the Crossfell district in the Pennines, most frequently occurs in late winter and spring when a northeasterly situation over the British Isles (see *Lamb weather types*, Chapter 6) produces a strong pressure gradient over northern England. If this effect is combined with an upper-level inversion layer, the strong northeasterly wind blowing down the western slope of Crossfell can produce a bank of cloud (the 'helm') that rests along or just above the summit together with a slender, nearly stationary roll of whirling cloud (the 'helm bar'), parallel with the helm, above a point 2–6 km (1–4 miles) from the foot of the fell. Local folk assert that 'the bar never crosses the Eden', the river in the leeward valley. During the mornings the bar usually moves slowly downwind, towards the southwest, but later in the day, just as the cloud seems to cross the river, it retreats back towards the escarpment, hence the old saying. Translating the story into meteorological terms, there is a tendency for lee wavelength to increase during the morning and decrease later in the day. The helm wind is very gusty and often violent as it blows down the steep fell sides but ceases under the helm-bar cloud, and west of this point a light surface westerly wind may prevail over a short distance.

Humidity

There is usually sufficient moisture in the atmosphere throughout the British Isles to ensure that the relative humidity is comparatively high and the evaporation rate by day is rarely excessive. In fact, from early November to the beginning of March, evaporation of moisture from the ground is so slow that in many years the soil and vegetation remain perceptibly damp almost throughout late autumn to early spring.

Inland in Ireland, the average daytime values of relative humidity throughout the year, even in the drier warmer southeastern counties, are well above those in central England. This gives a further objective climatic basis for the popular 'Emerald Isle' image of the country, together with the diminished evaporation, slightly less sunshine, and increased cloud and rain compared with much of England.

FIG 5. Fine conditions in a polar airstream over upland Britain; partly snow-covered slopes. (Chris Mattison/FLPA)

Precipitation

In general, precipitation over the greater part of the British Isles is relatively frequent but not heavy. About three-quarters of the English lowlands receive less than 750 mm (c. 30 in) as an annual average. With this can be included a narrow strip forming the lowland fringe of eastern Scotland and a very small coastal area around Dublin in eastern Ireland.

The uplands and mountains receive a great deal more than this amount (Figs 5 & 6). For example, in the western Scottish Highlands the summit of Ben Nevis receives upwards of 3,800 mm (150 inches) per year, and further westward it is believed that the average may locally exceed 5,000 mm (200 inches) among the mountains at the head of the sea lochs; it may also attain this figure around the summit of Snowdon in north Wales.

The prevailing intensity of rainfall in the lowlands of the British Isles is not great, with an overall value of about 1.3 mm (0.05 inches) per hour. This is about one-third of the intensity that is characteristic of the Mediterranean or eastern North America. However, heavy falls in short periods do occur, mainly in summer thunderstorms; local intensities have frequently been observed in excess of 50 mm (2 inches) per hour. Several stations have recorded falls within one hour of 75–100 mm (3–4 inches). Almost every county in Britain has recorded one or more downpours of 100 mm (4 inches) in a day. The greatest fall in one day on record (up to 2000) occurred at Martinstown (Dorset) on 18 July 1955 when 280 mm (11 inches) was measured in a prolonged series of thunderstorms over a small area close to the coast. A series of heavy summer thunderstorms converging over high ground can give rise to severe flooding in steeply falling streams and narrow valleys, with consequent devastation. Notable events of this kind occurred in Exmoor on 15 August 1952, when upwards of 230 mm (9 inches) fell over a period of a few hours in the afternoon, causing the Lynmouth (Devon) floods. Similar catastrophic upland thunderstorms have been known elsewhere in which falls of the order of 150–200 mm (6–8 inches) have been recorded, including a number in the Pennines causing much damage.

Falls exceeding 100 mm (4 inches) in a day occur among the mountains as long-continued orographic rainstorms, generally in association with strong winds and marked convergence ahead of slow-moving warm fronts of deep depressions. Most of these have taken place among the mountains towards the west coast, where several stations have reported falls of between 180 and 220 mm (7–9 inches). It is, however, noteworthy that, firstly, the most prolonged orographic falls of this type have not quite attained in one day the amount recorded in occasional thunderstorms and, secondly, that hitherto the heaviest falls of this type have all been recorded towards southwest England (Dorset, Somerset and Devon).

FIG 6. Snow shower over the Eden Valley, Cumbria. (Wayne Hutchinson/FLPA)

Very heavy orographic rains intensified by the effects of surface convergence have been recorded on the east side of Britain. Over 150 mm (6 inches) fell in one day on the uplands of Berwickshire on 12 August 1948. Probably the greatest series of floods on record in northeast Scotland were the 'Moray floods' of 2–4 August 1829, associated with cyclonic convergence over a period of three days into the Moray Firth.

The effects of the uplands and mountains lying athwart the prevailing southwesterly winds are considerable. For example, Liverpool, to leeward of the Welsh mountains, and Edinburgh and Inverness, to leeward of the Scottish mountains, record fewer days of rain than would be the case if the mountain barriers did not exist; Dublin is similarly favoured by the Wicklow mountains.

Droughts and dry spells

Absolute drought is defined as a spell of 15 days or more without measurable rain on any day – that is, less than 0.2 mm (0.01 inches). On average, at least one such spell can be expected each year in southeast England (Fig. 7), but they are much rarer in the far northwest of Britain, where as many as 20 dry days in succession have so far not been recorded. South of the Scottish Highlands, most of Britain has experienced a spell of more than 30 days without rain, rising to 40 locally. In a narrow strip along the coasts of Kent and Sussex, a spell of over 60 days without rain was recorded in the spring of 1893. Droughts in Ireland are less likely, although a total of 30 days without rain has been slightly exceeded over parts of the east and southeast.

FIG 7. A dried-up river bed due to a prolonged drought. (Erica Olsen/FLPA)

Snow and snow cover

Snow or sleet is likely to occur whenever a sufficient depth of cold air is present in the lower atmosphere with a wet-bulb temperature (temperature of saturated air) not exceeding 3 °C (37 °F). Associated surface winds are usually from some point between southeast through northeast to north, although they can occasionally be from the northwest. Westerly winds, with a longer Atlantic track, are rarely cold enough for snow, except at high altitudes in Scotland.

Due to the wide range of mean monthly temperatures during the autumn, winter and spring, it will be evident that from October to May exceptionally wide variations occur in the frequency with which snow falls, both from month to month and from year to year. At quite low altitudes in southern England, snowflakes have been observed in every month from September to June, and there are credible reports that melting snowflakes, rather than hail, were observed in northern central England on one occasion in July 1888.

The frequency of snowfall increases from south to north, from west to east, and with altitude. It also increases on all uplands that lie exposed either to unstable Arctic airstreams, or to continental airstreams, if cold, that become unstable as they cross the relatively warm North Sea. Snow and sleet showers are therefore more frequent adjacent to the North Sea coast, and sometimes in north Wales, north Norfolk and east Kent. Eastern and northern Ireland are similarly affected – but less often, as the additional crossing of the Irish Sea, which remains slightly warmer than the North Sea, means that such showers may be of cold rain or hail rather than sleet or snow.

The occurrence of snowfall has been recorded since 1668 by a long succession of observers in the London area, whose reports up to the year 1970 were standardised and meticulously analysed by Manley. Fluctuations in the total number of days for each winter can be stated in terms of percentage of the average. For instance, the 1695 winter (1694/95) gave over three times the normal total, and the 1785, 1879, 1917 and 1963 winters almost three times. By way of contrast, there have been winters during which some observers did not record any snow, although Manley's analysis did not reveal a completely snow-free winter when account was taken of the overall London area. Nevertheless, there have been occasional winters with not more than three days of snowfall, such as 1863, and the 1686, 1734, 1943 and 1957 winters were almost free of snow. As well as providing local interest in the climate of London, this long-term series of snowfall observations is of further general value, since the fluctuations in the record are broadly representative of those that occurred over the country in general.

Ireland lies at a greater distance from the continental source regions from which some of the colder air masses of winter arrive. As a result, there will be many occasions when snow falls in Scotland or England, but precipitation merely in the form of sleet or cold rain will occur in Ireland. Another factor is that the Irish Sea is generally a degree or so warmer than the North Sea throughout the winter months.

Since the mean temperature of the coldest month in the British Isles is a little above the freezing point, snow cover in the region is in general intermittent and of brief duration but exceedingly variable from season to season.

A day with snow lying is recorded when at 0900 h more than half the ground in sight at the level of the observer is covered. Hence in the milder parts of the country this will not always imply a whole day's duration of snow cover. Much depends on how far the ground surface may already have been chilled. But in the uplands, the total of days with snow cover at 0900 h is probably very close to the number of days on which snow lay for the duration of the day. Along the south English coast the average decreases from about four mornings a year in Sussex to fewer than two in Cornwall. At lower altitudes around London, though not within the closely built-up area, this rises to about seven mornings a year but with wide inter-annual variations. Over much of central England and as far north as York and Lancaster, between eight and twelve mornings a year is characteristic, and the Scottish lowlands lying by the Forth and Clyde are very similar. The effect of the sea is felt everywhere, even in Shetland, where although snow can be expected to fall on 40 days a year it only lies on average on about 12 mornings. Much of central Ireland has an average of about five mornings a year, but on its southwest coasts snow cover is quite rare and short-lasting.

FIG 8. Clear conditions over upland Britain in a polar airstream; patchy snow cover over high ground but thicker accumulations in the horseshoe-shaped corries formed during the Ice Age. Cirrus in more or less straight delicate filaments. (Michael Durham/FLPA)

FIG 9. A snow-covered gorge in upland Britain; the partly frozen waterfall has formed an impressive display of icicles on the rock-stepped sides. (John Eveson/FLPA)

The number of days with snow cover rises rapidly with altitude, not only because of lower temperatures but also because of the greater quantity that falls, especially on hills and mountains that lie exposed to easterly or northeasterly winds (Fig. 8). Orographic snowfall can occasionally be extremely heavy and prolonged on these northern uplands, and two or three such falls in succession can give very great accumulations capable of lasting for some time. Furthermore, on the open windswept uplands such falls are accompanied by severe drifting. On 4–6 March 1947, 150 cm (60 inches) fell in upper Teesdale (Fig. 9) and also on the uplands of north Wales. On 18–20 February 1941, 110 cm (44 inches) fell at Durham during a single fall lasting 56 hours.

Extremely heavy orographic snowfall can accumulate on the uplands of southwest England. With a depression centred over western France and a strong easterly wind blowing down the Channel, Dartmoor presents a barrier across which severe snowstorm-blizzards can occur. Even on the uplands of west Cornwall heavy drifting snowfalls, though rare, are not unknown, as in February 1955. For similar reasons, occasional heavy snow may fall along the south coast of Ireland.

However, apart from in the uplands and mountains, upon which orographic uplift adds to the precipitation, the maximum depth of snow that can accumulate is considerably less for a variety of reasons. It appears that 60 cm (24 inches) of level snow is probably about the largest fall that can generally be expected on low ground, and this perhaps would occur only once in 50–100 years. Much of lowland Lancashire received a snowfall approaching this depth at the end of January 1940. There are reports of falls of the same order in London on 14–20 February 1579, over East Anglia on 25–27 December 1836, and over parts of Oxfordshire on 18–19 January 1881.

In round figures, the rate of increase with altitude in the average annual number of days with snow cover can be put at about eight per 100 metres (333 feet) of rise. It is rather more rapid (about eleven) in northeast Scotland, less rapid in south Wales and Devon (about five). There are considerable variations, as some hill slopes and summits are likely to carry less snow on account of drifting, so that the local duration may be less. Hence such generalised figures must only be considered approximate.

It is probable that the most serious snowfalls from the standpoint of the disruption they cause are those that occasionally affect the whole of southern England bordering the Channel. Memorable snowstorm-blizzard conditions of this type occurred in January 1814, January 1881, March 1891, January 1963 and February 1970. In each case, a depression moving eastward into central France was associated with a cold continental flow on its northern flank.

These extremes are mentioned because although in many years snowfalls are of quite negligible importance over most of the British Isles, no part of the region is wholly free from the possibility of very heavy falls, and they can occur at unusual seasons such as those produced in a polar low developing in an Arctic maritime airstream in the spring. Exceedingly heavy snowfall was reported in northwest Ireland in April 1917, in Suffolk in April 1919, in Lancashire and west Yorkshire in May 1935, and in northern Scotland in June 1749.

On extreme and rare occasions, as in 1963, continuous snow cover can last for two months over much of lowland England and perhaps one month in central Ireland, but the probability of such an event seems to be of the order of once, possibly twice, in a century.

On the mountains, the probability of an average of 100 days with snow cover is attained at 600 m (2,000 feet) in the eastern Scottish Highlands. Snow cover at this altitude is therefore fairly reliable from early January to the end of March, and winter skiing based at Aviemore became a fairly regular event, with further developments at several other centres. It is, however, quite common for an influx of warm maritime tropical air with heavy rain to remove all the snow up to 1,000 m (3,300 feet) or so. Even on the summit of Ben Nevis (1,343 m/4,406 feet) the temperature has been known to rise to 9 °C (48 °F) in January, although the mean for the month is –4.5 °C (24 °F).

Small snowdrift accumulations may last throughout the year in the steep, narrow and heavily shaded north-facing gullies both on Ben Nevis and on Braeriach in the Cairngorms, where they persist at an altitude of 1,150 m (3,800 feet). Up until 1933 these had not been known to completely disappear, but in the September of that year they did, and since then there have been at least seven occasions when the last of them has melted completely in the late summer, sometimes in September. This response is in accordance with the recent warming trend in northwest Europe and resulting glacier retreat in Norway. As a result, the commercial skiing enterprise in the Scottish Highlands became a less viable concern during the late 20th century. Knowledge of the overall fluctuations of temperature in the British Isles since 1670 led Manley to believe that no true glaciers had developed in the Scottish Highlands during historic times.

CLIMATE AND MAN

Climatic extremes, anomalies and variations have both direct and indirect impacts on human society. Throughout the history of mankind innumerable case studies have shown that societies, nomadic as well as sedentary, industrialised as well as agrarian, recent as well as past, have been constantly engaged with atmospheric processes.

Ingenuity has allowed many societies to cope with climatic extremes, anomalies and variations as best they could. Societies have developed various ways to deal with the climatic characteristics in their respective regions. For instance, they have developed irrigation schemes and fertilisers to enhance food production, transportation and storage facilities, even air conditioning and refrigeration, as ways to deal with the natural constraints imposed on them by their regional climatic conditions.

While acknowledging, like Manley, the controversial nature of the effect of climate on human affairs, certain climatic extreme conditions down the ages have had a detectable impact on people's way of life: heat-related deaths and social unrest in very warm summers; increased death rates amongst vulnerable people, old and homeless, in severe winters; and bad harvests and famine, especially in northern Britain, in very cool wet summers. Also, there are several extreme weather events that directly affect man such as heavy snowfall, freezing rain, fog and severe floods. Widespread heavy snowfall can be one of the most disruptive and paralysing events to affect extensive areas of the country, and the rapid removal of snow is vital during and after snowstorms, since its drifting is liable to fill up previous clearances made in snow banks to allow road travel. Although relatively rare, the occurrence of freezing rain forming glazed frost ('black ice') on roads and pavements slows down traffic and causes many accidents, with the greatest danger on hills. Adequate warning of the approach of an ice storm allows highway authorities to organise manpower and equipment to grit dangerous surfaces. Poor visibility caused by fog leads to slowing down of traffic on roads and rail networks and disruption to air travel. Severe floods can cause great damage to property, especially in flood plains.

Climate and health

The way in which climate may influence people most directly – that is, by affecting their physical condition – can be critical. Most people are aware that certain days and places are more invigorating and stimulating to mental and physical activity than others. In the 1920s, the American climatologist, Ellsworth Huntington, a leading exponent of the theory that climatic change is a key factor in the history of civilisation, proposed that a monotonous climatic regime is more enervating than one having changeable conditions. According to Manley, Huntington had controversially expressed the view that the climate of southeast England might even be more advantageous than that of Yale (his university) with regard to the development and progress of civilisation.

Temperate cyclonic climates were therefore considered particularly stimulating, whereas tropical and continental interior climates were thought to encourage physical and mental lethargy. It appears that physical efficiency is highest when temperatures are around 18 °C (64 °F) and relative humidities between 75 and 80 per cent, though ideally both should fluctuate, as should pressure. Human mental capacity appears to be stimulated by living in a changeable climate and by colder weather outside than conditions in a workroom. To maintain comfortable indoor conditions, thermostats on central heating and air conditioning systems are usually set at about 20 °C (68 °F).

The key factor concerning the impact of climate on people is the capacity of the body to regulate its temperature. When the relative humidity is high and the temperature above 20 °C (68 °F), natural cooling by radiation and evaporation from the skin and lungs is insufficient to stop the body temperature rising above normal. Vigorous exercise is then followed by discomfort and a sense of oppression, and in extreme cases by heatstroke. Air movement helps to increase the body's cooling power, even when temperatures and humidities are still high. As a result, fans, or, better still, air conditioning, are almost essential for indoor comfort in the humid tropics and subtropics. The author, as a forecaster in Bahrain, experienced such conditions to the extreme when, in summer, the wet-bulb temperature rose above body heat, 37 °C (98.4 °F). It was then impossible to cool down naturally in non-air-conditioned areas due to perspiration not evaporating from one's skin.

> *The ideal warmth is that which permits the waste heat of the body to be dissipated as soon as developed, neither too fast nor too slowly, in order that the body's temperature may be maintained at the required 98.4 °F. Dry air mitigates heat by accelerating evaporation from the skin, but very dry air produces in the human being excessive excitability and sleeplessness. Moist climates have the opposite effect of producing nervous depression and lethargy. Now, whilst the complicated human mechanism of heat elimination will adjust itself to a considerable range of external temperature or moisture, it adjusts itself at the expense of energy and efficiency.*
>
> S. F. Markham, *Climate and the Energy of Nations*, 1942

In temperate climates, more than half the heat loss from the body is due to radiation. In the tropics radiation losses are small, but in polar regions they may rise to more than two-thirds when the air is calm. In cold, windy conditions, a great deal of heat is also lost by conduction and convection, but much less by evaporation, since the body perspires very little at low temperatures. Actual physical injury from intense cold occurs when the body loses more heat than it can produce; this occurs when the body is immersed in cold water or exposed to cold air. Water has a cooling power over 20 times greater than that of air, and at near-freezing temperatures may kill a person in less than 15 minutes.

The climate inside buildings, and to some extent in the streets and even the parks of urban areas, is partly man-made – but it is not always well designed for comfort. In most parts of the world traditional forms of architecture have evolved through long experience to provide the basic necessities. For example, in temperate latitudes, windows were made large enough to provide light where it was needed but they were traditionally not so large as to cool or warm the interior excessively, while pitched roofs help to dispose of rain and snow. Certain developments in architecture and building techniques made in the late 20th and early 21st centuries have often failed to provide these basic needs and safety measures without resort to expensive heating and cooling apparatus. For instance, in some so-called 'state of the art' new buildings – including, unbelievably, hospitals – large glass frontages have created huge greenhouses that become uncomfortably hot and oppressive in sunny weather.

Age Concern, the largest charity in the country providing health advice to the elderly, has taken a more enlightened approach to monitoring thermal conditions in the home by issuing temperature alert cards with critical limits highlighted: 24–27 °C (75–80 °F) – too hot, reduce your heating; 18–21 °C (65–70 °F) – ideal, do not adjust your heating; 15 °C (60 °F) – warning, turn your heating up; 10–13 °C (50–55 °F) – danger of hypothermia.

During the early 18th century, the Dutch physician Herman Boerhaave examined the possible relationship between weather and public health. One of his students at Leiden University was the English physician James Jurin, who, in 1723, was instrumental in setting up meteorological observing for the Royal Society. In the 1770s, medical authorities in France decided to make a systematic study of climate and public health. As a result, the Société Royale de Médecine was established, under the patronage of Louis XVI, to maintain a regular correspondence on meteorological and medical matters with doctors throughout the realm in order to determine whether illnesses and epidemics were influenced by weather conditions and the seasons.

Today, it is clear that many illnesses and diseases have an association with certain types of weather. In some cases there is a direct physical relationship between climate and illness – for example, the close connection between bronchitis and polluted, foggy conditions. Often the association is less direct but still unmistakable – for example, certain climates obviously foster the development and spread of particular viruses, organisms and disease-carrying insects such as the malarial mosquito and the tsetse fly. Research also shows that even old wives' tales about the weather may sometimes be based on fact. Some experts believe that old wounds, corns and aching joints can, as claimed by many sufferers, foretell the weather, especially rain, by reacting to static electrical effects that may herald the arrival of frontal systems.

Climate also plays a crucial role in the development and spread of animal and plant pests and diseases. For example, research shows that potato blight is extremely likely to develop about two weeks after a 48-hour period during which minimum air temperatures have not fallen below 10 °C (50 °F) and the relative humidity has remained above 75 per cent. Such conditions often occur in the summer during a spell of overcast, wet weather associated with a slow-moving depression over the British Isles.

Some diseases that are not of local origin depend even more directly on the weather. For instance, germs, spores and insect pests can be carried by the wind over hundreds of kilometres; the spores of black rust, a disease of cereal crops, can reach southern England from as far away as north Africa. The widespread movement of such material negates the argument, made by some members of the scientific community, that genetically modified (GM) crops could be prevented from contaminating surrounding natural arable farming by placing relatively narrow strips of neutral ground between them and normal crops.

CHAPTER 2

The Atmosphere and its Circulation

It is strange what weather we have had.

Samuel Pepys

THE ATMOSPHERE

T HE EARTH'S ATMOSPHERE COMPRISES A MIXTURE OF GASES, approximately 78 per cent nitrogen and 21 per cent oxygen with small amounts of other gases including argon, ozone and carbon dioxide. While the proportion of these gases remains constant (apart from an increasing man-made input of carbon dioxide), there is in addition a constantly varying amount of water vapour. Since the condensation of water vapour leads to the formation of cloud and precipitation, as well as surface effects such as dew, frost and fog, this gas is a vital constituent of the atmosphere in determining the character of the earth's weather and climate.

The presence of aurora indicates that the atmosphere is at least 1,000 km (600 miles) deep, but over half by weight is concentrated in the lowest 6.5 km (4 miles), and at greater heights the atmosphere is extremely tenuous.

The atmosphere is made up of several distinct layers. In the lowest layer, the troposphere, there is usually a lapse rate, that is, a decrease of temperature with height, which, on average, has a value of about 6 °C per kilometre (3.5 °F per 1,000 feet). Most of the water vapour is in the troposphere, and at any one time the variable amount of this gas decreases with height mainly due to the decrease of temperature with height. All 'normal' weather phenomena take place in this layer of the atmosphere.

The next layer, the stratosphere, is mostly isothermal in its lower part – that is, there is little change of temperature with height. There is little or no water vapour and therefore no weather occurs in the normal sense. The narrow boundary layer between the troposphere and stratosphere is termed the tropopause. On average, its height is 16–19 km (10–12 miles) over the equator, falling to about 11 km (7 miles) in the latitude of the British Isles and to about 6 km (4 miles) at the poles. A variation in height occurs seasonally and also diurnally with changes in surface temperature. For example, over the British Isles the tropopause varies in height from 8 km to 13 km (5–8 miles). As the tropopause is highest over the equator, the lowest temperatures of this boundary layer are found there. Also, as the temperature of the tropopause is comparatively high over the poles, the temperature rises in the stratosphere from the equator to the poles in any horizontal plane.

Water vapour

In meteorology, water vapour is the most important constituent of the atmosphere, as well as being the most variable in space and time. Supplied to the atmosphere by the evaporation of water at the earth's surface, water vapour decreases fairly steadily with height throughout the troposphere and into the lower stratosphere, with about 90 per cent lying below 6.5 km (4 miles). Its average mass the world over is such that if it were condensed it would be equivalent to a layer of water about 2.5 cm (1 inch) deep over the entire surface of the earth.

One of its main effects is that it acts as the main greenhouse gas in the control of the long-wave radiation balance in the atmosphere. Recent research also shows that although relatively small in amount, water vapour in the lower stratosphere plays a key role in temperature variations at the earth's surface. For instance, although almost one-third of the global warming recorded during the 1990s appears to have been due to an increase in stratospheric water vapour, the subsequent slowdown in warming since 2000 can be attributed to the decrease in water vapour at high levels after that year.

Atmospheric pressure

Pressure is the weight of the atmosphere per unit area, measured in hectopascals (hPa) or millibars (mb). The millibar, familiar from long-term use, was introduced by Sir Napier Shaw in 1909 and internationally adopted in 1929. A hectopascal is formally defined as a pressure of 100 newtons per square metre, and it is exactly equal to 1 mb. Over the British Isles the average mean sea-level pressure is about 1,014 hPa (mb); the highest and lowest values on record are 1,055 and 925 hPa (mb). At higher levels the weight of air above a particular surface will be less, and therefore pressure decreases with height. Near the surface of the earth pressure decreases with height at about 1 hPa per 9 m (30 feet). As air is compressible, it is densest and therefore heaviest at lower levels, and thus the decrease in pressure with height becomes less the higher one goes. As the horizontal variation of pressure is thousands of times smaller than the vertical variation, a correction of pressure readings to mean sea level is necessary for purposes of comparison between surface weather stations.

PRESSURE SYSTEMS

When isobars, lines of equal pressure, are drawn on a synoptic weather map several distinctive patterns such as depressions, anticyclones, troughs and ridges can usually be recognised.

Depressions

A depression, or low, is a pressure system of closed isobars with low pressure at its centre. The wind circulation in the northern hemisphere is anticlockwise. The term *cyclone*, coined by Henry Piddington in 1848 essentially for tropical revolving storms, is sometimes used for a depression. If pressure is falling at the centre, the depression is said to be deepening or intensifying; if pressure is rising, the low is filling up or weakening. When a depression is deepening, the resulting convergence of air at low levels must be more than compensated by the removal of air aloft, leading to ascending motion, clouds and precipitation.

Bombs and sting jets

Winds in a cyclonic circulation strengthen as the central pressure of the depression falls during its intensification, that is, cyclogenesis. In rare circumstances, the pressure may fall at an extremely rapid rate, resulting in the formation of a system of violent winds known as a *bomb*. The stronger the cyclogenesis the greater the risk of a bomb formation. A hook-shaped tip in the cyclonic cloud pattern, known as a *sting jet* and indicating the location of the bomb, tends to appear on the southern edge of the low. This localised feature, typically only a few tens of kilometres wide and about 1 km (0.6 miles) deep, descends towards the surface over a period of three to four hours from a distinctive cloud-top formation at a height of about 5 km (3 miles).

A sting jet is essentially the process in which part of the upper jet stream is brought down to near ground level. Precipitation falling into the bomb evaporates and cools it as it descends, helping to accelerate wind speeds in the sting jet within the bomb to values of over 160 km/h (100 mph). The band of extreme winds making up the sting jet typically lies about 150 km (90 miles) from the storm centre and can cause great devastation – such as in October 1987, when the bomb that struck southern England and northern France caused millions of trees to be flattened.

Secondary depressions

A secondary depression is a low that develops within the circulation of a larger depression, the primary low, usually in its southern periphery. Normally only one or two secondaries form around a primary, but on some occasions there can be as many as five or six. A secondary often develops along the trailing cold front of an occluded low, especially where the isobars open out in a way resembling the point at which the primary depression originally formed along the polar front.

Secondaries vary in depth and initially are much shallower than the primary. At this stage they merely circulate anticlockwise around the primary. However, a secondary may deepen enough to be as intense as the primary, and then the circulation becomes more complex. Occasionally, the secondary may become deeper than the primary and the position is reversed, with the primary circulating around the secondary. While deep primary lows only move slowly, shallow secondary depressions initially move quickly – and their formation and movement can present timing problems in forecasting. The weather associated with a secondary can be violent, with strong winds and heavy rainfall. Steep pressure gradients may form on the southern flank of a secondary, and this development can result in exceptionally destructive winds over southern districts of the British Isles.

Families of depressions

Occasionally a series of depressions may form along the polar front to give a spell of unsettled weather over the British Isles. The separate lows in the family may all become quite large depressions. At any one time, those lows in the east are more developed than those in the west, and the track of each succeeding depression is usually to the south of its predecessor. The family ends when the polar air engaged in the cyclonic family finally breaks through into the subtropical high-pressure belt to feed the northeast trade winds. These lows should not be confused with secondary depressions, as each member of the family is a distinct cyclonic system with its own circulation. The average number of depressions in a family is about four.

Non-frontal depressions

There are two main types of non-frontal depressions, orographic lows and instability lows. *Orographic depressions* form in the lee of hills and mountains when the wind is blowing across the high ground. To compensate a tendency for the compression of air to the windward, rarefaction on the lee side can produce a shallow depression. While orographic cloud and rain may occur over the windward slope, descending air to the lee may prevent any cloud formation in this type of depression. They may occur over eastern parts of the British Isles when westerly winds blow across the Pennines, Welsh mountains and Scottish Highlands. When isobars are drawn every 4 or 5 millibars only a trough may be detected in the pressure pattern, rather than a closed circulation. Lows or troughs caused purely by the orographic effect are usually only shallow features with little or no significant weather.

Non-frontal depressions associated with unstable air that produce bad weather are termed instability lows. There are two subtypes, polar lows and thermal depressions (or heat lows). The former affect the British Isles from the north, the latter from the south.

Polar lows are marked by widespread intense instability that results in deep cumuliform clouds with embedded cumulonimbus cells, heavy rain or showers, and frequently heavy snowfall, and they may be accompanied by thunderstorms. They often form over the North Atlantic near Iceland and move south and southeast to affect the British Isles – normally in winter, when an Arctic or Polar maritime airstream (see below) covers the country. Although their direction of movement is often difficult to forecast, they usually travel within the general air flow, frequently in the direction of the strongest winds in their circulation, and with a maritime track being a favoured path of motion.

Thermal depressions or heat lows are the summer equivalent of polar lows. They are also caused by localised and intense surface heating in a slack pressure gradient. These depressions are usually shallow and do not have any typical weather, but if associated with instability then thundery activity can occur. They often form in slack pressure gradients over mainland Europe when there is strong surface heating during the summer, especially if there is a cooler air current above leading to unstable conditions. They are typically features of a tropical continental airstream. When this airstream flows over the Mediterranean Sea moisture will be picked up and extra heating over the European landmass gives rise to thermal depressions. Although the clouds are often layered, each layer is unstable: altocumulus castellanus clouds commonly form initially in these lows and may give rise to outbreaks of heavy rain. When the instability is fully released, massive cumulonimbus clouds and thunderstorms develop, and these can continue for several hours over affected localities, as the winds are usually light.

Troughs of low pressure

A trough has steady movement usually round a depression. It may be cloudy and produce rain if there is sufficient inflow of air – that is, convergence. Troughs are marked by a sharp bend in the isobars away from the centre of low pressure. Fronts are always marked by troughing but not all troughs contain fronts. If a trough is non-frontal and associated with unstable air, the weather is similar to that of a polar low but along a line instead of over an area.

Anticyclones

An anticyclone, or high, is a pressure system of closed isobars with high pressure at its centre. The term *anticyclone* was coined by Sir Francis Galton in 1861. If pressure is rising at its centre an anticyclone is said to be intensifying (anticyclogenesis), whereas if pressure is falling it is declining in intensity (anticyclolysis).

An anticyclone is characterised by small horizontal pressure gradients and calm or light winds, especially in the inner part of the system (winds can be stronger in the outer parts). In the northern hemisphere there is a clockwise diverging motion of air in lower layers and an inflow of air in upper layers, especially when intensifying. There is therefore a general subsidence, that is, a gradual sinking and compressing of a large mass of air, causing dynamical warming; this usually occurs in the middle and upper levels of the troposphere, and as a result the temperature of subsided air becomes higher than that of the air below, forming an *inversion*. Subsidence results in diverging surface air and generally dry weather conditions, since clouds and precipitation require upward motion. Since the centre of an anticyclone is a region of light winds, conditions are favourable for the formation of radiation fog overnight if the air is cloudless. In winter a layer of cloud may form beneath the subsidence inversion giving rise to 'anticyclonic gloom'; impurities trapped in the lower layer are sometimes dense enough to form a smoke fog.

Anticyclones can be divided into cold and warm types. Cold types can be subdivided into two forms, cold semi-permanent and cold moving. Examples of cold semi-permanent anticyclones include the highs that develop over extensive continental regions such as northern Eurasia and Canada in winter. During this season the earth's surface in these regions becomes extremely cold and, as a result, the intensely chilled air in contact with the ground becomes very dense and heavy and forms high pressure; surface cooling more than outweighs dynamical warming due to subsidence. These anticyclones are usually shallow in depth; with pressure falling off rapidly with height they are not usually recognisable above about 2 km (6,000–7,000 feet). The weather is very cold, with sub-freezing surface temperatures and fine conditions with little or no precipitation, except when the system is invaded by travelling depressions and fronts. Fog or low cloud may form if sufficient moisture is available.

Cold moving anticyclones develop in northwesterly or westerly airstreams in the rear of depressions. Unlike other types of anticyclones, these have definite movement, travelling in the cold air between members of a family of depressions. Again such systems are usually shallow in depth and often resemble a ridge rather than a closed anticyclone. They give a short spell of fine weather, perhaps lasting 24–36 hours, between the showers of the preceding depression and the rain of the succeeding low. When the polar airstream finally breaks through to lower latitudes, bringing an end to the family of depressions, the final ridge may build into a closed anticyclone of moderate intensity with a tendency to become a quasi-permanent feature. A cold anticyclone can gradually change into a warm type by dynamical warming.

Examples of permanent warm anticyclones include the closed cells of the subtropical high-pressure belt such as the Azores high. They are extensive over subtropical sea areas throughout the year. Because warm air is less dense, pressure falls off more slowly with height in warm air than in cold air. Therefore a warm anticyclone normally extends to great heights in the troposphere, making it more persistent than a cold high. The weather is fine and warm with good visibility, but its air masses may be considerably modified at the surface when moving northward to give low cloud, fog and drizzle. The subtropical Azores high can extend northeast over the British Isles from its home region in summer. The weather will be fine and warm overland in summer, but fog and low cloud can occur at any season, especially over the sea and near coasts – radiation fog and mist particularly in autumn and winter. In summer substantial convective clouds may occur by day, especially if humid air is advected overland from the sea. Long spells of warm settled weather in summer are often associated with warm blocking anticyclones (see below).

Extreme ranges of temperature are often associated with high pressure. For example, anticyclones give warmest days in summer and coldest nights in winter. Anticyclones are usually larger and slower-moving systems than depressions, often just appearing to expand or contract. They are far more irregular than depressions both in behaviour and shape.

Blocking

This is a term that is applied to a large-scale synoptic situation when the normal eastward movement of depressions and anticyclones in mid latitudes is interrupted for at least a few days. A blocking situation is dominated by a warm anticyclone whose circulation extends from the surface to the upper troposphere. The zonal circulation to the west (see *Zonal index and zonal flow*, Chapter 3) is transformed into a meridional pattern with branches extending polewards and equatorwards. The annual course of blocking over the British Isles is marked by a maximum in spring (April and May) and a minimum in late summer to early autumn (August and September). The frequency of blocking in this region varies somewhat from year to year.

Ridges of high pressure

These are indicated by an outward curve in the isobars away from high pressure. The curve is usually less pronounced than that associated with a trough of low pressure. As with the anticyclone, a ridge is a region of descending air and hence good weather, but fog commonly occurs. If the air is initially unstable a ridge will reduce showery activity. They may swing clockwise about a centre point but can be almost stationary.

A ridge generally produces a spell of fine dry weather, and any cumulus clouds tend to flatten out due to subsidence. The ridge normally extends over a somewhat greater horizontal distance than a trough, and it usually has a definite movement, travelling between two depressions.

Cols

A col comprises a slack pressure region of light and variable winds between two depressions and two anticyclones. Air is drawn in from the anticyclones and given out to feed the depressions. As a meeting ground of different airstreams, frontogenesis (see below) may occur in a col. It also forms a suitable track for a depression to take between two anticyclones. No typical weather is associated with a col, but they often appear to intensify the weather type that is currently prevailing – this is noticeable in a thundery situation as the stagnant air allows heat lows to form. Foggy weather is common in a col during winter.

AIR MASSES AND FRONTS

A great revolution of ideas, the concept of air masses and fronts, occurred in meteorology during the early 20th century. The Bergen School, under the father and son Norwegian meteorologists Vilhelm and Jakob Bjerknes, who had conceived the theory, put the ideas into practice during the First World War when their country was cut off from international synoptic weather data due to the hostilities. The original theory was a simple and grand concept based on the movements and interactions of two distinctive air masses, polar and tropical, but it later became more detailed, as described below.

It is no coincidence that the theory had been introduced into weather analysis and forecasting during a period when the circulation over the North Atlantic–European sector was predominantly zonal. Subsequent rules formulated to predict the development and movement of pressure systems and fronts in this type of circulation proved to be invaluable tools for forecasters, but they become less effective when non-progressive patterns such as blocking highs become established in the circulation.

The term air mass applies to an extensive body of the atmosphere in which the two main meteorological properties, temperature and humidity, are relatively uniform both in the horizontal and vertical dimensions. These features have been acquired by the air mass remaining over an extensive and relatively homogeneous surface, termed a source region, for sufficient time to acquire the distinctive characteristics of the region.

Source regions of air masses

The requirements of a source region are a large surface area, uniform physical nature, and uniform surface temperatures and humidities. For air to stagnate and for outside factors to have little effect there must be little or no wind. Therefore, source regions are mostly located in the centres of large semi-permanent anticyclones, especially those of the polar and subtropical high-pressure belts; these large-scale weather systems produce either polar or tropical air masses, respectively. The main source regions of air masses affecting the British Isles are the Arctic Basin, northern parts of the North Atlantic (Greenland), northern Eurasia (Siberia), the subtropical North Atlantic (Azores), and North Africa (Sahara Desert).

When they leave source regions, changes in air masses take place initially from below. For example, polar air travelling over a warm surface is warmed in lower levels, and tropical air over a cold surface is cooled in lower levels. The effect of passage of cold air over a warm surface is to heat the lower layers and so set up convection – that is, the air is made unstable. If in addition the surface is water, then evaporation takes place in surface layers and convection currents spread this moisture through a more or less deep layer. The degree of modification of the air depends firstly on the temperature of the underlying surface and secondly on the length of track over the surface and the time taken to travel over it.

Classification of air masses

When, due to being disturbed by a travelling depression, an air mass eventually moves away from its source region, the original properties acquired will be modified, particularly at lower levels, by the type of new surface, sea or land, and its temperature, warm or cold. Accordingly, air masses can be classified according to their source region – Arctic (A), subpolar (P) and subtropical (T) – and their subsequent track – maritime (m) and continental (c). This produces designations such as Am, Pc and Tm, with the first letter essentially defining air-mass temperature and the second its humidity.

Arctic maritime (Am)

This air mass comprises cold air from the surface up to a great height. As its track is more or less at right angles to sea-level isotherms this gives rise to rapid and intense surface heating. It is therefore a very unstable air mass with a large lapse rate of temperature with height.

Typically, this extreme variation of a polar maritime air mass (see below) breaks out behind a depression in winter and early spring, but it is not usually a persistent type. Owing to its instability, convection clouds (cumulus and cumulonimbus) develop, giving frequent wintry showers of rain, sleet or snow and occasional thunderstorms. The showers may continue both day and night in exposed coastal districts. The winds are fresh to strong northerly, sometimes gusty in showers, and the visibility is good except in any precipitation.

Arctic continental (Ac)

This air mass circulates around a Scandinavian high-pressure system. On reaching the British Isles it will have an inversion in its lower layers, but in summer the air mass will be warmed over the European mainland. Arctic continental air masses mostly give dry weather with moderate visibility.

Polar maritime (Pm)

In its many varieties this is a very frequent air mass over the British Isles, being prevalent on about 40 per cent of the days during the year. Over the sea, surface heating is normally very effective. As the air travels towards the British Isles the lapse rate increases, the surface layer becomes unstable, and ascending moist surface air produces cumulus and occasional cumulonimbus clouds, giving occasional showers and perhaps thunderstorms, and good visibility outside any precipitation. The diurnal variation in these conditions is virtually nil. As the largest difference between air and sea temperatures occurs in winter and spring, the maximum showery activity occurs at this time of the year.

The effect of a coastline of some relief is to provide additional impetus to rising currents. As a result, showery activity may be intensified, producing, for example, winter thunderstorms in the western Highlands of Scotland.

Overland the diurnal variation of cumulus and cumulonimbus development depends on surface heating, and maximum showery activity therefore occurs in the afternoon. After sunset the land cools quickly, and hence clouds disperse to give a clear night.

With regard to seasonal variation, solar heating in winter may be insufficient to produce showers or even perhaps cumulus cloud. In summer, however, the surface heating effect is greater and consequently the development of convectional cloud and the probability of showers and thunderstorms is more intense at this season over the land than over the sea.

Returning polar maritime (rPm)

This air mass occurs when a large depression is more or less stationary in the North Atlantic, making the Polar maritime air mass travel well to the south before moving over the British Isles from the southwest. Its associated weather is likely to be variable, but cooling on its northeast track may be sufficient to give tropical maritime conditions in the lower layers – that is, low stratiform cloud, coastal and hill fog, but sea fog is rather unlikely. However, overland during summer, when the low cloud may be dispersed during the day by surface heating, the inherent instability of the air mass may be revealed by convectional cloud development and showery activity, since temperatures in the upper layers still remain quite low.

Polar continental (Pc)

This air mass originates over high-latitude continental sources such as northern Russia and Siberia and reaches the British Isles from an easterly direction in association with a blocking-high situation over Scandinavia and the Baltic region.

Although it may become fairly warm during the summer over inland Britain, cool conditions are more likely along North Sea coasts. However, winter is the more typical season for this air mass, with mainly dry but cold conditions, although individual situations depend on its track over the North Sea: if sufficient moisture is picked up, low turbulent stratiform clouds, stratus or stratocumulus, may form. These clouds may develop sufficiently to give occasional sleet or snow showers, especially along the east coast. If a more continental route occurs, the weather will still be bitterly cold but with bright periods and little or no cloud. Winds are easterly and visibility is often only moderate, owing to stability preventing the dispersal of any smoke or dust particles picked up en route over mainland Europe.

Tropical maritime (Tm)

The source region of this air mass is the subtropical Atlantic anticyclone – that is, the Azores high. It is a fairly common air mass both in summer and winter that arrives over the British Isles from the southwest.

As it travels northwards its relative humidity is increased in the lower layers due to surface cooling. At the same time the cooling increases its stability so that low stratiform clouds, stratus and stratocumulus, are formed. The weather is overcast with occasional drizzle especially over exposed coasts and windward slopes. The visibility is poor especially in drizzle and hill fog. This air mass gives the region its typical muggy days in winter when temperatures may even reach 10–12 °C (50–54 °F).

In summer the cloud layer often breaks up into detached small cumulus and may eventually disperse completely to give very warm clear afternoons. In winter, however, when the land is generally colder than the sea, low cloud persists and thickens; indeed, mist or even fog may prevail at ground level, especially if the surface has been previously chilled by overnight radiation or recently melted snow.

Tropical continental (Tc)

The source region in winter is North Africa; in summer the source region covers a larger area extending from North Africa to southeast Europe. It is a relatively rare air mass over the British Isles, even in southeast England, and usually occurs only during the summer.

A favourable synoptic situation sometimes occurs in summer, with pressure relatively high over the European mainland as a shallow depression approaches slowly from the Atlantic. South to southeast winds over England advect air that has perhaps been progressively warmed for several days over southeast Europe. The dry clear air is capable of giving a spell of very high temperatures, but prolonged heat waves rarely occur.

The weather is generally very warm and dry with hazy conditions due to its long land track. The skies are mainly clear, but the breakdown of these conditions is often heralded by the formation of unstable medium-level clouds, altocumulus castellanus, followed by an outbreak of thunderstorms. This type of situation is typically heralded by a large-scale convective cloud system, a 'Spanish plume', developing over the Bay of Biscay and graphically depicted on meteorological satellite images. This feature occurs when hot, dry air from the Sahara Desert is lifted over the Spanish plateau ahead of an upper-level trough moving east from the Atlantic. The potential instability released when low-level moist air is capped by medium-level relatively dry air can lead to 'explosive' convection causing severe thunderstorms and heavy rain.

Although the Channel is not wide enough to affect more than a shallow surface layer of air, the North Sea can be a more effective cooling agent, sometimes resulting in sea fogs along the east coasts of the British Isles, termed 'haars' in east Scotland, 'sea-frets' further south, and 'sea-rokes' in Yorkshire and Lincolnshire.

The polar front

When two air masses meet, the boundary between them is called a *frontal surface*. It is marked on surface weather maps as a line where it intersects the earth's surface. The polar front develops in the northern hemisphere between polar and tropical air masses. Its mean position varies seasonally by 10–20 degrees of latitude, lying on average south of Iceland in summer and over southern England in winter.

Observations show that travelling depressions of middle latitudes generally originate as a result of the interaction between two different air masses along the polar front where vast amounts of potential energy occur due to discontinuities in temperature and wind. As a result, the original polar front, with the two air masses flowing undisturbed side by side, is rarely maintained as waves or bulges usually develop along its line. Baroclinic conditions set up between the two dissimilar air masses – that is, where both temperature and pressure gradients are steep – cause instability resulting in a wavelike bulge. At the wave, warm air protrudes and ascends over cold air, resulting in local fall of pressure; convergence will occur to replace the lost surface air and ultimately a complete cyclonic circulation is set up. A warm-sector depression has now formed, in which the disturbed section of the polar front has two parts, a warm front and a cold front, each of a different character.

Polar-front jet stream

The character of the weather over the British Isles is mainly determined by the position and strength of the polar-front jet stream. A strong jet stream usually means the circulation over mid latitudes is in a mobile or zonal mode in which a series of depressions moves progressively east across the North Atlantic allowing westerly patterns to prevail over the British Isles. A weak jet stream implies that the circulation is in a blocked or meridional mode in which the pressure systems are more slow-moving, allowing northerly, southerly and occasionally easterly patterns to persist over the region.

WEATHER ASSOCIATED WITH FRONTS AND FRONTAL DEPRESSIONS

Most clouds are formed by the lifting of air with consequent cooling by expansion and the condensation of excess water vapour. Rainfall of any intensity needs a substantial depth of cloud, and thus to produce rain an effective lifting agency is required. In a frontal depression the pressure system itself is the most efficient lifting agency, because of low-level convergence and the release of potential energy. Thus, the rain area or rain shield is most extensive and intense near the depression. The sloping frontal surfaces are also lifting agencies, with the warm air being forced to rise up the slope. Whatever the type of front, warm or cold, it is the warm air that is lifted. The resulting rain shield moves with the fronts and depression. The closer to the depression centre and fronts, the thicker the cloud and lower its base. In the warm sector well away from the low there is no lifting agency in the upper levels, so little or no medium or high cloud occurs above a typical low layer of stratiform clouds.

Frontogenesis and frontolysis

The process leading to the development and intensification of fronts is termed frontogenesis. The most important factor in this process is the concentration of the horizontal temperature gradient by the convergence of air masses – for example, when a tropical air mass moving poleward meets a polar air mass moving equatorward. As the two air masses do not readily mix, the cold air will tend to undercut the warm and the warm air override the cold. The process that causes the opposite effect, the weakening of fronts, when the airflow is such that the horizontal temperature gradient becomes more diffuse, is termed frontolysis.

If the directions of the air masses are such that warm air is advancing and replacing cold air in a given region, then a warm front occurs, but if cold air is replacing warm, then the result is a cold front. In both cases the isobars will cut across the fronts. When practically no isobars cross a front it will have little or no horizontal motion and is termed quasi-stationary.

Warm fronts

As the speed of the warm air normal to the front is usually greater than that of the cold air ahead, active upslide motion occurs within the warm air. This causes the air to be cooled, leading to condensation and resulting in the formation of widespread cloud and precipitation ahead of the front. However, as the slope is generally inclined at a gentle angle to the surface, between 1:100 and 1:200, violent vertical motion is not usually associated with a warm front.

The typical sequence of weather elements associated with a warm front is as follows: the clouds comprise cirrus (up to 800 km/500 miles ahead of the front), cirrostratus (with halo and related optical phenomena), altostratus, nimbostratus and pannus (ragged low clouds of bad weather), followed by stratus in the warm sector; the wind backs and increases ahead and veers as the front passes; the rain may start up to about 250 km (150 miles) ahead, ceasing as the front passes but with occasional drizzle in the warm sector; the visibility decreases steadily in the rain; the dew point rises slowly in the rain to become highest in the warm sector; the pressure falls at an increasing rate ahead of the front, but becomes more or less steady in the warm sector.

Cold fronts

The frontal surface of a cold front slopes back behind the front at a steeper angle than that of the warm front slopes forward. The cold air behind the cold front tends to overtake the warm air ahead, and therefore the latter is forced to ascend. Because of the steeper slope, between 1:50 and 1:75, the vertical motion is usually more pronounced than that at the warm front. This vigorous lifting of warm air results in a cloud and precipitation system resembling that of the warm front in reverse. However, the horizontal extent of this system is generally smaller than the warm front, and the precipitation is therefore of shorter duration. The weather comprises moderate to heavy precipitation with occasional thunderstorms and squalls.

Anafronts and katafronts

There are two main types of cold front, anafronts (*ana*: upward) and katafronts (*kata*: downward). In an anafront the warm air generally ascends up the frontal surface with a cloud and weather sequence similar to that of a warm front but in reverse. Rain occurs on and behind the surface front followed by a slow clearance of upper cloud. This is the more usual type of cold front to affect the British Isles. In a katafront there is little ascent of warm air up the frontal slope. As a result, the cloud and weather are concentrated into a fairly narrow belt. The clouds are more cumuliform than at an anafront, with cumulonimbus and thunderstorms possibly developing. A squall line may also occur with a particularly active katafront. As the clouds develop in the warm air, the precipitation occurs on or slightly ahead of the front. However, after the passage of the front the clouds usually break and clear quickly.

Both types of cold front have certain features in common, for example, the wind backs a little ahead and veers fairly sharply as the front passes. Once the frontal cloud and weather have passed, convective clouds develop in the Pm air;

the vertical extent of the cumulus, and hence the possibility of showers, depends on the depth of cold air, which increases the further away from the front; the visibility improves in the cold air away from rain; the dew point falls fairly quickly behind the front, especially after the rain ceases; the pressure falls a little ahead but rises fairly sharply behind the front.

Secondary cold fronts

Sometimes the temperature change across the main cold front may be rather weak. The sinking motion (subsidence) of the cold air immediately behind the front can explain this effect. Thus, a real change to cold air conditions may occur 80–160 km (50–100 miles) behind, with a secondary cold front marking the boundary between the adiabatically warmed cold air and the unaffected horizontally moving cold current well to the rear.

Occlusion

The occluding, or closing, process marks the decline of a depression. Usually, due to surface friction, the cold front moves more rapidly than the warm front. As a result, the warm sector becomes narrower and eventually the warm air is lifted completely from the surface. The depression then weakens, slows down, and turns off to the left. Its centre leaves the tip of the warm sector and is usually located at the end of the occlusion. Occasionally, when the trough from the original low is very long and sharp, a new depression may form at the tip of the warm sector.

Back-bent occlusion

Sometimes the centre of the main depression will move south with the point of occlusion. In such situations the occlusion is often caught up in the circulation of the low to double back on itself, forming a back-bent occlusion. Such an occlusion often produces prolonged cloud and precipitation following a cold front when otherwise improved conditions would be expected. This situation typically affects eastern Britain when a depression has moved east into the North Sea. While clearing conditions affect the rest of the country, eastern districts can remain cloudy with rain for some time afterwards.

THICKNESS

This is the difference in height at a given place between two specified pressure levels. Thickness values, measured in decametres (dam) relating to two selected standard pressure levels, are plotted on thickness charts. The analysis of such charts plays an important role in synoptic meteorology with the development and movement of surface pressure systems.

Contour lines on thickness charts, mostly drawn for the 1,000–500 hPa layer, are usually drawn every 6 dam, at 528, 534, 540, etc. Their values are directly related to the mean temperature of the layer – that is, high thickness corresponds to warm air and low thickness to cold air. As such, they act as useful indicators of thermal conditions in the lower half of the troposphere where most of the significant weather processes take place. It has been shown that cold polar air has low thickness, and that values of 528 dam or less frequently bring snow to the British Isles. Conversely, warm tropical air has high thickness, and values in excess of 564 dam often indicate a very warm spell over the region. On average, the polar front near the centre of a depression usually lies between thickness lines 534 and 540 dam in winter, and 546 and 552 dam in summer.

Together with isobars and fronts, standard thickness lines, for example, 510, 528 and 564 dam, are shown on forecast surface weather charts issued daily on the internet by the Meteorological Office (www.weathercharts.org/ukmomslp.htm).

Thermal wind

This is a concept devised in association with thickness charts whereby a theoretical wind, the thermal wind, is considered to 'blow' parallel to the thickness lines with low thickness values (that is, low mean temperatures of the layer) to its left in the northern hemisphere, and with a speed directly proportional to the thermal gradient – that is, inversely proportional to the spacing of the thickness lines.

Thickness chart features

Some of the contours on a thickness chart will be complete curves enclosing areas of relatively low or high thickness values, that is, indicating areas of relatively low or high temperature, respectively, in the thickness layer concerned.

A centre of low thickness is termed a cold pool. This distinctive feature of a thickness chart occurs when at least one closed contour line can be identified around an area of low thickness. A cold pool typically occurs in association with an old depression, and it is kept under careful watch by forecasters, especially in winter, as it can be associated with severe weather conditions such as frequent heavy showers and thunderstorms. Although the presence of a cold pool does not always mean the air is unstable, mass ascent is likely if this feature is carried southwards over a warm surface, such as the sea areas around the British Isles in winter. While convection tends to warm up and dissipate a cold pool, this is usually a slow process allowing the severe conditions to persist for some time. Other features identified on thickness charts, such as cold troughs, warm domes and warm ridges, are also associated with distinctive weather conditions.

Sutcliffe development theory

In 1947 a major breakthrough in forecasting the weather over the British Isles was made when Reginald Sutcliffe, first Director of Research in the UK Meteorological Office, presented his development theory. This concept, based on dynamical considerations, demonstrated that the analysis of thickness patterns could be an effective means of predicting the development and movement of surface pressure systems.

In the application of these ideas the 1,000–500 hPa thickness is taken to be representative of the atmospheric layer in which such effects take place. Developments occur where there are sharp changes in the direction and spacing of the thickness lines, and the development is proportional to the strength of the thermal wind. Accordingly, thickness charts are examined for well-marked troughs and ridges and for the spreading out or closing together of the thickness lines. These features may occur in a variety of combinations, anticyclonic development being expected to occur where there is divergence in the thickness pattern and cyclonic development where there is convergence. Essentially, the theory demonstrates that surface pressure systems are likely to develop where certain characteristic features are present in the thickness pattern, with the thermal wind acting as a steering agent for the movement of depressions and anticyclones both in speed and direction.

By effectively integrating upper air analysis with the conventional surface methods, the Sutcliffe development theory revolutionised forecasting at all levels in the post-war period from the Central Forecast Office, then at Dunstable, down to the scores of out-stations scattered at airfields all over the country at that time. Today, this earlier method of weather analysis by human interpretation has been superseded by modelling using computers.

METEORS

In meteorology a meteor is a phenomenon, other than a cloud, observed in the atmosphere or on the surface of the earth. A meteor may be a precipitation, a suspension or a deposit of aqueous or non-aqueous liquid or solid particles, or a phenomenon such as an optical or electrical manifestation.

Meteors are classified into four groups: hydrometeors, lithometeors, photometeors and electrometeors.

Hydrometeors

A hydrometeor is a meteor consisting of an ensemble of liquid or solid water particles suspended or falling through the atmosphere.

Fog

When the horizontal visibility is reduced to less than 1,000 m (3,300 feet) and the air is moist with very small water droplets, the obscurity essentially becomes a cloud resting on the ground, that is, a fog. There are three main types of fog: radiation fog, advection fog, and upslope or hill fog.

The most common kind of fog in the British Isles is radiation fog (Fig. 10). This is caused by cooling air in contact with the surface of the earth on a clear night when intense long-wave radiation has been cooling the ground, hence the name. A certain amount of turbulence is necessary to spread this cooling through a reasonable depth of air. If cooling is confined to the lowest few metres only dew or possibly slight ground mist will form when the air is cooled below its dew point. On the other hand, if the wind is strong the cooling will be distributed over a much greater depth of air by the increased turbulence and final cooling may not take the air below its dew point. Three conditions are therefore necessary: clear sky at night, reasonably moist air, and slight turbulence. The upper surface of the fog is marked by an inversion of temperature, caused partly by cooling at the earth's surface and partly by radiation from the upper surface of the fog itself. The maximum density of radiation fog usually occurs soon after dawn when turbulence is increasing but air is not yet sufficiently warmed to evaporate fog. As the earth's temperature increases after dawn the fog will slowly be evaporated from the surface upwards, forming 'lifted fog'.

FIG 10. Misty conditions in a river valley and over its wide flood plain. (Robin Chittenden/ FLPA)

Advection fog is caused by comparatively warm moist air moving over a cold surface, and it may form over land in winter or over the sea at any time of the year. If formed over sea it may drift inland, where its duration will be determined by the temperature of the land.

Upslope fog forms when moist air flows up over a hill or mountain. As the air rises it expands, becomes cooler, and, if sufficiently moist, upslope or hill fog forms over the high ground.

Drizzle

Water droplets composing cloud are maintained in the air by the upward force of the rising current of air in which the cloud is formed. If the force of the rising current decreases, or if the water droplets become too heavy to be supported, then precipitation will take place. Drizzle occurs when the upward current is weak and therefore its parent cloud is thin or tenuous.

Rain

Rain forms in stronger up-currents, so its parent cloud is denser and thicker and water droplets will become much larger before their weight exceeds the upward force of the air (Fig. 11). The distinction between rain and drizzle is entirely one of size of drops and is not based on intensity.

FIG 11. Rain clouds over a field of sugar beet, Norfolk. (David Burton/FLPA)

Showers

Showers are associated with cumulonimbus clouds and are therefore of short duration, since convection clouds are usually isolated in formation. Convection currents are much stronger than vertical currents due to turbulence and frontal or orographic uplift. The water drops therefore grow much larger and precipitation is heavier. As convection currents vary in strength from time to time in the cloud a cumulonimbus cloud does not necessarily produce showers at all times.

Snow

Very tiny water drops may exist above the freezing level in a super-cooled state – that is, they remain liquid although below freezing point. If they are disturbed in any way they will immediately freeze as ice crystals. Alternatively, if water vapour condenses at temperatures below the freezing point, condensation may be in the form of ice crystals without an intermediate liquid state. These ice crystals

FIG 12. Partly snow-covered farmland; cumulonimbus giving wintry showers and low ragged cumulus clouds have formed under the main cloud base. (Erica Olsen/FLPA)

amalgamate to form snowflakes, and when they are sufficiently heavy they will fall as snow (Fig. 12). If the temperature at the earth's surface is still below the freezing point snow will fall on the ground. If the temperature is above the freezing point snowflakes will tend to melt before reaching ground. A mixture of snowflakes, partially melted snowflakes and water drops is called sleet. Snow is unusual if the ground temperature is above about 3 °C (37 °F).

Hail

Any large cumulus or cumulonimbus cloud can be divided into three regions: region 1 comprises water droplets below the freezing level; region 2 comprises a mixture of super-cooled water droplets and ice crystals; and above this layer is region 3, of predominantly ice crystals. A nucleus of soft opaque white ice forms in regions 2 or 3. When this is allowed to fall below the freezing level water droplets will freeze on it forming a layer of smooth clear ice. Further movement with varying convection currents up and down in the cloud will cause formation of further alternate opaque and clear ice layers, until the hailstone becomes too heavy to be supported by convection currents and is therefore precipitated.

Dew

The temperature to which air has to be cooled for it to become saturated is termed the dew point. If air is cooled below this point condensation will take place in the form of dew.

Hoar frost

If the dew point of air is below the freezing point, 0 °C (32 °F), condensation will take place on objects or on the ground in the form of opaque white ice crystals. If the temperature falls below the freezing point without condensation taking place a 'black' frost is said to have occurred.

Rime

If a fog appears when the temperature is below 0 °C (32 °F), the water droplets will be super-cooled. On impact with any surface, opaque white ice crystals will form (Fig. 13). The rime builds outwards on the windward side of objects as a rough deposit.

Glazed frost

When super-cooled rain falls on sub-freezing surfaces the precipitation immediately freezes to form a clear smooth deposit of glazed frost or clear ice (so-called 'black ice'). This type of frost usually lasts only for a few hours before a

FIG 13. A bleak wintry frost-covered landscape with a thick accretion of rime on the fields and trees. (Paul Hobson/FLPA)

thaw sets in as advancing warm air replaces cold air at the surface. However, under exceptional situations the conditions can persist when the underlying cold air remains in place for several days. Glazed frost is comparatively rare in the British Isles, but when it does occur it can cause traffic chaos, injuries to people falling on pavements, and considerable damage to objects such as trees, telegraph wires and power lines due to weighty deposits.

Lithometeors

A lithometeor is a meteor comprising an ensemble of particles most of which are solid and non-aqueous. The particles are more or less suspended in the air, or lifted by the wind from the ground.

Haze
A suspension in the air of extremely small, dry particles invisible to the naked eye but sufficiently numerous to give the atmosphere an opalescent appearance.

Dust haze
A suspension in the air of dust or small sand particles, raised from the ground by a dust storm or sandstorm.

Smoke
Over industrial areas a concentrated collection of small carbon particles, produced by combustion, may be suspended in the air below an anticyclonic inversion. If cloud is also present the mixture of water droplets and smoke particles will cause the formation of high fog, that is, fog not actually at the surface. It is also referred to as 'anticyclonic gloom' and is usually confined to the winter months. The more harmful smoke fog ('smog') occurs when smoke particles combine with and intensify an already formed radiation fog at the surface.

Photometeors
A photometeor is a luminous phenomenon produced by the reflection, refraction, diffraction or interference of light from the sun or moon.

Halo phenomena
A group of optical phenomena in the form of rings, arcs, pillars or bright spots, produced by the refraction or reflection of light by ice crystals suspended in the atmosphere in formations such as cirriform clouds and ice fogs.

Corona
One or more sequences of coloured rings of relatively small diameter, centred on the sun or moon shining through a cloud layer.

Irisation
Colours appearing on clouds, sometimes mingled, sometimes in the form of bands nearly parallel to the margin of the clouds; green and pink predominate, often with pastel shades.

Glory
One or more sequences of coloured rings, seen by an observer around his or her shadow on a cloud or fog or, very rarely, on dew.

FIG 14. Double rainbow, Cumbria. (John Eveson/FLPA)

Rainbow
A group of concentric arcs with colours ranging through the spectrum from violet to red, projected on a cloud 'screen' by light from the sun or moon being refracted through rain drops. The primary rainbow shows violet on the inside and red on the outside whereas a secondary much less bright bow, if visible, shows the colours in reverse (Fig. 14).

Bishop's ring
A dull reddish-brown ring seen round the sun in a clear sky, attributed to the diffraction of light by fine dust in the high atmosphere.

Electrometeors
An electrometeor is a visible or audible manifestation of atmospheric electricity.

Lightning
A luminous manifestation accompanying a sudden electrical discharge which takes place from inside a cloud or, less often, from high structures on the ground or from mountains (Fig. 15).

Thunder
A sharp or rumbling sound which accompanies lightning.

FIG 15. A spectacular display of lightning, the most powerful electrometeor in nature. The complex pattern of flashes would have been accompanied by a sudden and huge electrical discharge – a giant spark, commonly of the order of 10,000 amps, within the cumulonimbus cloud. A lightning flash links areas of positive and negative static electricity and the current travelling at 300,000 kps (186,000 mps) heats the surrounding air to 15,000 °C (27,000 °F), resulting in its sudden expansion causing a thunderclap. (ImageBroker/ImageBroker/FLPA)

Saint Elmo's fire

A more or less continuous luminous electrical discharge of weak or moderate intensity in the atmosphere, emanating from elevated objects at the earth's surface such as lightning conductors, wind vanes and ships' masts, or from aircraft in flight (wing tips, propellers, etc).

Polar aurora

A luminous phenomenon which appears in the high atmosphere in the form of arcs, bands and draperies.

CHAPTER 3

Key Players in the Drama over the British Isles

The hollow winds begin to blow,
The clouds look black, the glass is low,
'Twill surely rain – I see with sorrow
Our jaunt must be put off to-morrow.

From the poem 'Signs of Rain',
attributed to Erasmus Darwin, 1731–1802

THE WESTERLIES: LEADING ROLE PLAYERS

SINCE THE BRITISH ISLES ARE CENTRALLY PLACED in the mid-latitude westerly wind belt, as well as being located in one of the sectors around the northern hemisphere most frequently affected by blocking action in this flow, variations in the circulation over the more extensive eastern North Atlantic–European region are also well registered by the Lamb classification of weather types (see Chapter 6). Accordingly, the incidence of westerly situations over the British Isles can be directly linked with larger-scale indicators of the circulation over the Atlantic–European sector, such as the North Atlantic Oscillation. Furthermore, it appears that the number of westerly situations recorded over the British Isles during a period such as a year or a decade provides a useful index of the state of the circulation even further afield. In effect, the Lamb classification keeps a finger on the pulse of world climate.

When the frequency of westerly situations is low over the British Isles, blocking patterns tend to dominate the circulation, resulting in more frequent meridional and easterly weather types. These are situations when opposite extremes can occur within a few or even succeeding years, as only a slight shift in the longitude of the controlling centres of action, highs and lows, can result in airstreams of distinctly different source regions being advected over the same geographical area. This is the key to understanding why contrasting extremes, cold or warm, wet or dry, can occur when the circulation is non-progressive.

Such fluctuations in the wind flow over the British Isles, and by inference the strength of the circulation further afield, may be related to comparable temporal variations in the behaviour of the sun.

By extracting wind data from a select group of weather journals and meteorological registers kept both in England and nearby mainland Europe, a series of southwesterly surface wind frequencies for 'England' has been reconstructed from the mid 14th century (Lamb 1972). Since southwesterly winds over England are closely related to the westerly weather type over the British Isles, it may be inferred that a high frequency of southwesterly winds indicates a zonal or high index situation (see *Zonal index and zonal flow*, below), whereas a low frequency indicates a generally blocked or low index situation. Thus a record of changes in the circulation over the British Isles may be traced for more than six centuries, from the Little Ice Age to the present day (Fig. 16).

The most significant feature of this wind record is an oscillation of close to 200 years, with maxima in the 1340s, 1520s–1530s, 1730s and 1920s–1930s, followed in each case by a relatively abrupt decline to minima around 1440, 1610, 1810 and possibly 2000, with a 30–50 per cent lower frequency of the westerlies. These low points in the westerlies have in turn been succeeded by a much slower and irregular recovery to the next peak in zonality; the curve is not sinusoidal, with the rate of change of frequency during periods of decline being greater than that in the subsequent recoveries.

Following an initial decline in the westerlies over the British Isles during the first two decades of the continuous series based on the classification of daily synoptic weather maps from 1861, the westerly day count steadily increased, and

FIG 16. Frequency of southwesterly winds over England since the mid 14th century. (H. H. Lamb)

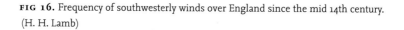
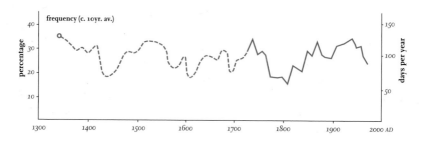

for several decades in the early part of the 20th century it averaged about 100 days per year. For example, a decadal value of 109 days occurred in the 1920s, with an annual value of 129 days being recorded in 1923. Following this maximum, the values decreased, and during the four decades since the 1950s the number of westerly wind days steadily decreased, averaging 80 days per year in the 1960s, 73 days in the 1970s and 72 days in the 1980s, with 1980 having the second lowest annual count (52 days) in the series from 1861 to 2000. The 1990s are particularly interesting, as although the westerlies were initially at a relatively high level, a notable decline soon set in and an abrupt mid-decade changeover from high to low index situations ushered in the severe winter of 1996; in this year only 50½ westerly days were recorded, the lowest annual count in the series from 1861. The low values of 52 and 50½ in 1980 and 1996 provided notable analogues with the early 1780s, when the period value fell to about 65 days per year, with only 45 days recorded in 1785 (the lowest known annual value on record). In all three cases, that is, 1980, 1996 and 1785, there were compensating variations in the frequency of blocked or stationary situations with atypical wind flows over the British Isles compared with the more normal westerlies.

With a sequence of only four complete oscillations from the mid 14th century, caution should prevail in extrapolating this cycle into the 21st century. Nevertheless, it does provide a possible dynamical tool for predicting possible future changes in the flow over the British Isles and associated situations. Accordingly, as the general decline in the westerlies over the British Isles during the late 20th century seems to have formed part of this fundamental cycle in the circulation, it may be inferred that the current low frequency of the westerlies with related extremes will continue for several more decades yet.

The extremely low annual count of westerly situations (50½ days) in 1996 was followed by a slight increase in zonality during the late 1990s. At the time, this seemed to suggest the start of a long-term irregular increase in the westerlies, with associated warming, into the 21st century (the 1990s, one of the warmest decades on record, was nearly 0.6 °C (1.0 °F) warmer than the 1961–1990 average). However, signals from the early years of the present century, concerning both the behaviour of the westerlies and the direction of a possible thermal trend, are becoming less clear, with the westerlies continuing to perform well below their normal frequency. The second lowest annual count in the record since 1861 was recorded in 2001 (51 days), and an apparent stalling or even reversal in global warming.

There are several notable features in the record of westerly situations (Figs 17–19), including the substantial variation in the frequency from year to year referred to above. Long-period changes in this circulation can also be clearly identified in the record – for example, the slow increase in the westerlies from

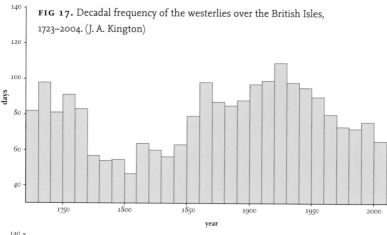

FIG 17. Decadal frequency of the westerlies over the British Isles, 1723–2004. (J. A. Kington)

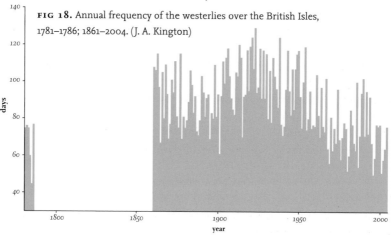

FIG 18. Annual frequency of the westerlies over the British Isles, 1781–1786; 1861–2004. (J. A. Kington)

the low values in the 1880s (85 days on average per year) to a peak in the 1920s (109 days). A further decline occurred during the 1970s, but a short-lived period of zonality seems to have set in from the late 1980s into the early 1990s. It appeared at the time that the renewed warming in the late 20th century had halted the dominance of blocked situations from the 1940s and reintroduced increased zonality in the flow. However, as mentioned above, in 1996 there was an abrupt return to a low incidence of westerly situations, and values continued at a low level for the first five years of the 21st century – comparable to the decadal mean of the 1810s when the zonal flow over the British Isles was also at weak ebb.

This tendency suggests that once a generally non-progressive mode of circulation becomes established, a factor comparable to 'persistence of type' in

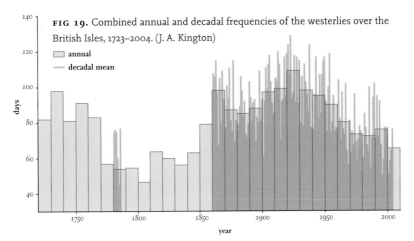

FIG 19. Combined annual and decadal frequencies of the westerlies over the British Isles, 1723–2004. (J. A. Kington)

synoptic meteorology appears to operate on a climatological time scale, whereby meridional or easterly weather patterns become more frequently recurring features of the circulation for seasons, years, decades or even longer.

The decline of the westerlies since the mid 20th century and the more recent, less clear-cut, signal raises the question: 'Is our climate as equable as it was in the early part of the last century?' The review of climatic history since the last Ice Age given in Chapter 9 shows that the British Isles have been subjected to some wide fluctuations in the prevalence of wind flow from different directions. Although the westerly type has probably been the most frequent circulation pattern over the region during the past 10,000 years or so it has undergone great variations with regard to its degree of dominance.

This is where we stand today (2010) – that is, in the latter part of a decline in the westerlies. All the signs are that the present weak zonal flow over the British Isles, with frequent blocking and an associated increase of extremes, will continue for several more decades yet. Stationary circulation patterns during periods of blocking can maintain prolonged warmth or coldness, wetness or dryness in mid-latitude regions such as the British Isles and lead to anomalous conditions at the surface over which airstreams flow. These situations ultimately produce extremes of temperature and rainfall, and, in addition, increased temperature differentials provide the potential energy for the development of severe storms.

The intriguing question arises of whether an eventual slow increase in zonality with perhaps renewed global warming will occur later in the 21st century. Such a query needs to be addressed when it is claimed that changes of climate are mainly caused by human activities and that computer modelling can provide realistic future scenarios – without taking into account the causes of past climatic behaviour due to a complex array of physical and dynamical processes including, not least, the effect of volcanic dust veils – which can either reverse any warming trends or intensify cooling periods. For example, the frequent occurrence of volcanic dust veils between 1780 and 1840 prolonged the Little Ice Age, which otherwise probably would have given way to warmer conditions much earlier than what actually happened at the start of the 20th century.

ZONAL INDEX AND ZONAL FLOW

Normally there is a broad westerly wind flow over the temperate belt in which the British Isles region is situated. The strength of this circumpolar circulation depends on the mean pressure differences between two latitudes, 30° N and 55° N, which is termed the zonal index.

The circumpolar circulation varies between two distinct modes, *high zonal index* and *low zonal index*. The high zonal index mode is more or less zonally orientated, and long waves in the upper flow, associated with progressive weather systems at the surface, are of small amplitude and transient in nature. The low zonal index mode is marked by a strongly meandering configuration forming a pronounced meridional flow with large-amplitude long waves which once established have a tendency to persist.

In the high zonal index mode the pressure difference between the Icelandic low and the Azores high is large, and this results in strong westerly winds in the intervening latitudes (*zonal flow*) with associated families of depressions travelling rapidly from west to east. This vigorous westerly circulation over the Atlantic causes distinctive maritime characteristics of temperature and humidity to be advected across the British Isles, giving rise to mild wet winters and cool damp summers. Maritime and Cyclonic weather types usually prevail over the British Isles during high index decades.

In the low zonal index mode the westerly circulation is weakened and broken up by persistent anticyclones (low zonal flow). As such anticyclones may hold up the movement of depressions, they are termed blocking highs. If the westerlies drop out completely, persistent east to northeast winds may remain over the region for some time. Continental and to some extent anticyclonic weather types usually prevail over the British Isles during low index decades.

It appears that during cooling phases of the earth's climate, the circumpolar circulation expands into a persistent and intense form of the low zonal index mode. Climatic zones such as those of the Mediterranean and subtropical regions are then compressed more tightly around the tropics, allowing the polar-front jet stream and its attendant depressions to meander more widely north and south over an expanded temperate climatic zone that includes the British Isles.

MAIN WEATHER TYPES

The maritime type (Fig. 20), and to some extent the cyclonic type (Fig. 21), correspond to high zonal index progressive westerly situations. Mild winters and an increase in the westerlies are associated with the maritime type, wet decades with the cyclonic (or frontal) type.

The continental type (Fig. 22), and to some extent the anticyclonic type (Fig. 23), correspond to low zonal index non-progressive easterly situations. Cold winters and a deficit in the westerlies are associated with the continental type, dry decades with the anticyclonic type.

FIG 20. Maritime weather type. The numbered lines, −15, −9, etc, are isopleths of pressure anomaly showing the direction of additional air flow superimposed on the normal circulation. (D. J. Schove)

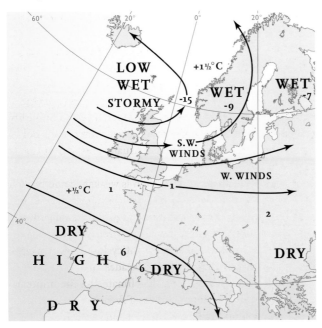

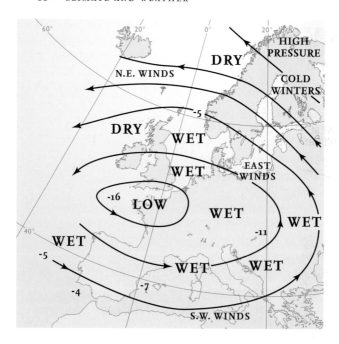

FIG 21. Cyclonic weather type. Key as in Figure 20. (D. J. Schove)

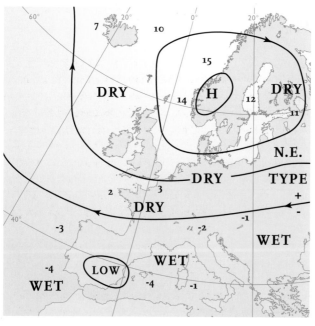

FIG 22. Continental weather type. Key as in Figure 20. The pressure anomalies represent blocking conditions or low index situations with the dry area of pressure above normal over Scandinavia and the wet area of pressure below normal over the Mediterranean. (D. J. Schove)

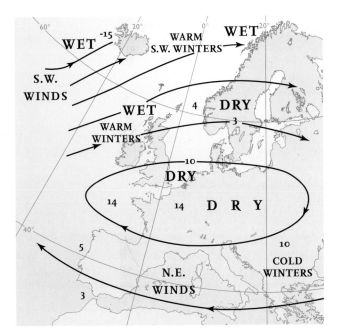

FIG 23.
Anticyclonic weather type. Key as in Figure 20. Dry anticyclonic conditions affect south Britain and much of mainland Europe, wet cyclonic conditions affect Iceland. (D. J. Schove)

DEPRESSION TRACKS

Depression tracks are controlled by the flow of the polar-front jet stream in the upper troposphere. The depressions that commonly affect the British Isles are sometimes shifted further north and south of their more usual tracks over the region when large-scale meanders develop in the long waves of the generally upper westerly flow. A northward shift allows either the Azores anticyclone to extend northeastwards over the British Isles, to give warm dry conditions, or a continental high to extend westwards, resulting in either exceptionally cold winters or very warm summers. When the depression tracks are displaced further south than usual, the British Isles are subjected to spells of unsettled wet and windy conditions, mild in winter, cool in summer. Such displacements may persist for a week, a month, or even a whole season.

BLOCKING

Depending on the location of the controlling stationary circulation pattern, the disruption of the westerlies by blocking highs can result in either cold or warm,

wet or dry extremes, which explains why relatively short-term extremes of
warmth may occur in periods of general cooling. The warm summers of 1665 and
1666, which were respectively instrumental in the outbreak of the Great Plague
and the Fire of London, occurred at the peak of cooling during the Little Ice Age.

CLUSTERING PHENOMENON

This refers to the occurrence, in a rather close but not necessarily unbroken
succession, of seasons or years in groups with some specific similar, but
otherwise quite exceptional, character. Examples include the series of cold
Marches and severe winters in the 1780s. Another notable example, the three 'war
winters', 1940, 1941 and 1942, caused the freezing of rivers in west and central
Europe accompanied by heavy snowstorms.

THOUSAND-YEAR CYCLE

Analysis of climatic oscillations over the last three millennia indicates the presence
of a fluctuation having a significant magnitude that affects middle latitudes with a
periodicity of close to 1,000 years. This effect is associated with colder periods and
glacial advances that have developed in mid latitudes of the northern hemisphere in
the middle centuries of each of the last three millennia – that is, around AD 1500, AD
500 and 500 BC. There is also some degree of parallelism with developments in these
regions around 1500 BC, 3500 BC and perhaps in even earlier millennia.

FIFTY-YEAR OSCILLATION

The data derived by Lamb from the early Middle Ages onwards have also shown a
remarkably regular and consistent oscillation of approximately 50 years. This is
an oscillation in the frequency of blocking in the eastern Atlantic–European
sector, as detected in the sequences of summer and winter character indices of
decade-by-decade frequency of markedly warm or cold, wet or dry months.
Accordingly, drier summers and colder winters have broadly been more
prevalent around the thirties and eighties decades of many centuries, such as the
870–880s, 930s and 980s, 1040s and 1070s, 1120–1130s and 1170–1180s, 1240s and
1260s, 1320–1330s and 1380–1390s, 1430s and 1470s, 1540s and 1580s, 1630s and
1680s, 1740s and 1780s, 1830s and 1880s, 1940s and 1980s.

STORM SURGES AND SEA FLOODS

Climatic research has shown that a general increase in storminess in the North Sea is directly linked to a rapid cooling of the Arctic. As the Arctic Ocean becomes colder, so the temperature differential between its waters and those of the North Atlantic Drift increases, creating a stronger thermal gradient in the sea-surface temperatures between 50° N and 65° N, leading to increased storminess in the North Sea basin.

Great inundations of coastal regions around the southern North Sea arise from storm surges associated with northwest to northerly gales in the circulation of intense depressions moving into the area. Notable examples were the severe storms of 1099, 1236, 1251, 1286, 1362, 1421, 1604, 1663, 1697, 1703, 1736, 1897, 1921, 1928, 1953 and 1987 (Fig. 24).

In a critical cyclonic situation, a storm surge generated by a deep depression in the Atlantic may track eastwards north of Scotland and then be driven into the

FIG 24. Coastal flooding in north Norfolk, 2006. (Robin Chittenden/FLPA)

relatively shallow waters of the North Sea. The rapid and intense lowering of air pressure causes the sea level to rise, resulting in a massive body of water being sucked up over an area of the order 1,000 km (600 miles) in diameter to form the storm surge. As this feature moves south its waters are funnelled and compressed between the landmasses of southeastern England, the Netherlands and northern France, which finally narrow to a strait only 35 km (22 miles) wide between Dover and Calais. Owing to their greater tidal range, these southern coastal areas are especially vulnerable to severe inundations during North Sea storm surges.

Should the arrival of such a storm surge coincide with a high spring tide, the sea level may rise by as much as 4–5 m (13–16 feet) over predicted levels, sea defences are topped and disaster follows. This situation, combined with downstream flows in the Thames, provides the trigger for flood defence operations to be put into action – and if the river is already swollen by heavy rain and thawing snow in its catchment area the situation can be made even more severe.

In 1953, the storm surge arrived before the high tide but the level still rose 1.8–2.4 m (6–8 feet) above normal and was held at that level for some hours, sufficient to cause great devastation.

Storm Tide Forecasting Service (STFS)

Following the 1953 disaster a continuous sea wall was built along the Norfolk coast from Eccles to Winterton, and a more general outcome was the introduction of a flood warning service in September 1953. Today, meteorologists and hydrographers at the Storm Tide Forecasting Service (STFS) of the Central Forecasting Office in Exeter receive reports from a number of key ports around the coast and consider these in relation to predicted weather conditions. As a further line of sea defence, construction of the Thames Flood Barrier downstream of central London at Woolwich Reach was started in 1974.

Thames Flood Barrier

An analysis of storminess over the British Isles from the 1920s shows there has been a significant increase in the frequency of severe storms since the 1950s. Although this is not above the level which occurred in the 1920s, if the trend continues there is a real threat that any storm surges in the future will be capable of producing unprecedented high tides that could breach the present sea defences and cause widespread floods in eastern and southeastern England. This trend is notably reflected in the closures of the Thames Flood Barrier since its construction was completed in 1982. Before 1990, the number of barrier closures was, on average, only one to two per year, but since 1990 the number has increased to an average of about four per year, and in 2003 the barrier was closed on 14 consecutive tides. On 9 November 2007 the barrier was closed twice after a storm surge in the North Sea comparable to that which occurred during the 1953 severe storm.

The threat of flooding from severe storms is also increasing over time because of a slow but continuous secular rise in high water level (20 cm/100 years) and the slow north–south tilting of Britain caused by a postglacial rebound. In view of this it has been suggested that it might become necessary to supersede the present Thames Barrier with a much longer 16 km (10 miles) barrier across the estuary from Sheerness in Kent to Southend in Essex.

THE THAMES: LONDON'S CLIMATIC INDICATOR

No British river is better documented than the Thames in London, and its historical record includes valuable indicators about the past climate of England. Droughts, for example, can be inferred when accounts record that the river level was exceptionally low. The occurrence of very cold winters can also be deduced from occasions when the Thames froze: the freezing of the river in London probably indicates that the mean temperature of one of the winter months (December, January or February) fell below 0.5 °C (32.9 °F) over southern England.

A critical event in the history of the Thames was the construction of the old London Bridge in 1209. This structure slowed down the flow of the river, which, in very cold conditions, allowed ice to form more readily, piling up against the bridge and then freezing right across the river. By acting as an early form of barrage it also had an effect on Thames flooding: the difference between water levels on either side of the bridge was sometimes several feet, with water pouring through like cataracts. Incoming tides were mainly expended against the bridge, and the tidal rise and fall upriver was greatly reduced. However, the bridge held up the flow of the river and therefore increased the danger of flooding above the bridge during or following heavy rain in its catchment area.

Many frost fairs were held on the frozen river in London during the Little Ice Age. These events provided various amusements and diversions to counter the severe conditions for the inhabitants of the city. Even after a thaw, ice carried downstream from its upper reaches would sometimes jam against the piers of the old London Bridge. Also, in the 17th century and earlier, ice would often spread from stagnant channels in the extensive Lambeth marshes.

The last frost fair was held on the Thames during the severe winter of 1814. Since then the river has never been completely frozen over, because of a series of man-made changes to the river, such as the construction of embankments and the channelling of tributary streams into pipes. Nevertheless, in the severe winter of 1895 the Thames became so filled with ice by February that it was almost frozen over completely, with only a narrow stream mid-channel remaining free of ice. Had the river not been embanked, increasing the tidal flow, there is little doubt that it would have been completely covered as in 1814.

During the 20th century the increasing influx of warm industrial waters has made the freezing of the Thames in London even more unlikely. For instance, although the very cold winter of 1963 was more severe than that of 1895, no trace of floating ice was seen on the river in central London. Nevertheless, only a few kilometres upstream, at Hampton Court, it was possible to cross the Thames on ice.

VOLCANIC ERUPTIONS

Perhaps a violent volcanic eruption might, by its dust, produce dislocation of the general circulation of the atmosphere.

Sir Napier Shaw, *Forecasting Weather*, 1923

Dust veil index (DVI)

A numerical indicator, the dust veil index (DVI), was devised by Lamb in 1970 to assess the probable impact of volcanic eruptions on climate and weather, as well as to construct a chronology of eruptions and their magnitudes back to 1500. The DVI is computed by employing formulae comprising factors dependent on the greatest depletion of solar radiation, the maximum extent of the dust veil, and the time between the eruption and the last observation of the dust veil; the formulae are scaled so that the Krakatau eruption of 1883 produces a DVI value of 1,000 units.

The first effect of the global spread of volcanic material by upper winds after an eruption is for the general circulation to be weakened. Later, however, after about two years, the flow reverts to a more vigorous state, as by then the dust veil only effectively covers higher latitudes, thus increasing the difference in heating between low and high latitudes. The whole cycle takes typically three to four years after the eruption, but occasionally it is up to seven years before conditions return to normal. With high-latitude eruptions generally only the enhanced-circulation phase occurs.

Eruptions which inject such massive quantities of minutely fine dust particles and gases into the upper atmosphere as to cause major volcanic dust veils that can dim the sun and moon and affect global temperatures are termed Plinian, after Pliny the Younger, who was the first to record such an event during the eruption of Vesuvius in AD 79.

There is also a tendency for the zone of main cyclonic activity in the Atlantic, associated with the polar front, to be shifted south in summer after great eruptions. This effect accounts for many, perhaps most, of the coldest wettest summers that have occurred over the years in the British Isles. Also, it is in summer, rather than winter, that the result of the earth's surface being screened by the dust veil from incoming solar radiation becomes most prominent with regard to temperature.

The historical record certainly shows that many of the coldest wettest summers in the British Isles, such as 1695, 1725, 1760s, 1784, 1816, 1845, 1860, 1879, 1903 and 1912, occurred during times when a large amount of volcanic dust had been injected into the upper atmosphere. Furthermore, the warming in the northern hemisphere that occurred during the 1920s and 1930s coincided with a period when there was a relative absence of major eruptions, suggesting the possibility that the absence of volcanic dust veils was one of the factors in the warming process. However, the risk remains that a series of violent eruptions in the future could produce dense volcanic dust veils and subsequent cooling that have not been experienced since the early 19th century. Owing to the ever-increasing developments in our way of life, the implications of a modern Tambora (the greatest known eruption in historic times) could be even more disastrous than the dire effects suffered by the world in 1816. Although less severe, the unexpected 1991 eruption of Mount Pinatubo and its impact on climate by lowering the global temperature by about one degree for two years provided a timely warning that such events, or larger ones, could occur at any time in the future.

A study of the DVI and climate from 1725 to 1950 has shown that there is a seven- to eight-year cycle in both variables, which supports the idea that variations in volcanic activity may affect climate. Furthermore, it has also been found that, like variations of climate and solar activity, there is a 180-year rhythm of activity in volcanic eruptions.

During the Little Ice Age there was a notable increase in volcanic activity, with an average of five major eruptions per century that equalled the intensity of the 1883 Krakatau eruption. In contrast, the ash content of a Greenland ice core shows that the years of the Medieval Warm Epoch, between 1100 and 1250, were volcanically quiet. However, between 1250 and 1500 and between 1550 and 1700 there were many eruptions, including a massive event in 1600 at an unknown location.

Super-volcanic eruptions

There have been volcanic eruptions in the last million years which dwarf all those that have occurred during historic times. From measurements of ash displacement it has been estimated that these super-eruptions, such as that of Mount Toba on Sumatra (Indonesia) about 70,000 years ago (the greatest known eruption in the last million years), were several orders of magnitude greater than Pinatubo and Tambora. Although they have not been experienced in historic times, they are quite common in geological terms, and it is inevitable that another such eruption will occur at some time in the future.

If Tambora caused the so-called 'year without a summer' in 1816, Toba could have been responsible for a six-year-long volcanic winter and a 1,000-year-long instant ice age. Attempts are being made to quantify the impact of such super-eruptions on the atmosphere, using measurements both from previous and from simulated events. These studies will provide us with a better understanding of the stresses that could occur on world society following the next super-eruption, and how they may be mitigated – for such an event would have not only a major effect on global climate but also the potential to change the course of human history.

COSMIC RAYS

In 1996 the Danish physicist Henrik Svensmark proposed that variations in the cosmic radiation entering the earth's atmosphere could play a role in climatic change, with, in particular, the formation of clouds in the troposphere.

The magnetic field of the sun normally shields the earth from cosmic radiation by repelling many of the particles that arrive from outer space. However, during a spell of low solar activity, as indicated by a decline in sunspots, the magnetic activity of the sun is weakened, allowing a greater influx of cosmic rays into the earth's atmosphere. Svensmark observed that such a change in cosmic radiation brought an increase in global cloudiness which, in turn, led to a greater cooling of the earth – as, for example, during the Little Ice Age, when the coldest phase coincided with the Maunder Minimum.

During the past century or so cosmic radiation has declined, because unusually vigorous action by the sun has deflected much of it away from the earth. Fewer cosmic rays and associated charged particles in the earth's atmosphere have meant, as argued by Svensmark, fewer clouds and hence a warmer world. He claims that cosmic rays have a greater effect on climate than man-made carbon dioxide emissions.

CHAPTER 4

Seasonal Characteristics

The spring, the summer,
The chiding autumn, angry winter, change
Their wonted liveries, and the mazed world
By their increase, now knows not which is which.
            William Shakespeare, *A Midsummer Night's Dream*

SEASONAL VARIATIONS IN THE CIRCULATION AFFECTING THE BRITISH ISLES

IN WINTER, THE AZORES HIGH, OR A RIDGE from this anticyclone, often extends over Spain and sometimes southwest France, while low pressure is centred to the southeast of Greenland or in the Icelandic area. Atlantic depressions associated with the polar front move east, with their most frequent tracks crossing the British Isles before reaching mainland Europe. However, sometimes activity along the polar front is deviated to the southeast owing to deep depressions over the northwest Mediterranean. A great variety of situations can arise over the British Isles if an anticyclone persists over Scandinavia, north Russia or central Europe which tends to block and deflect the movement of Atlantic depressions on their approach to the continent.

In spring, the Azores high frequently extends over the ocean. The Icelandic low is still present but its centre is further south than in winter and mean pressure gradients are weaker. Atlantic depressions from the west are least frequent, and meridional circulation patterns are the most vigorous of the year. In western Europe, the weather is often controlled by a low-pressure area covering either the British Isles and France or central Europe, and by the movement of deep troughs extending from the Icelandic low. The low-pressure area of the Mediterranean is often maintained, as is also the ridge extending southwest from high pressure over Scandinavia.

In summer, the pressure of the Azores high reaches its maximum value. Although the centre of the anticyclone is further to the north, its position with regard to longitude is rather variable; a strong ridge may extend over west and central Europe and even over the eastern Mediterranean. The Icelandic low is still present but is displaced even more towards the north and its associated activity is greatly diminished: pressure gradients are weak and fewer troughs affect the British Isles. Although the westerlies predominate, the flow is less subject to disturbances.

In autumn, the Azores high and the Icelandic low are on average in the same positions as in the spring, but the westerlies are rather more frequent. Pressure may be high over mainland Europe, being usually centred over southwest Russia. Occasionally, especially towards the end of this season, the western ridge of this European anticyclone is very well developed, extending over the Alps and joining up with the Azores high. In other situations, instead of this bridge of high pressure, Atlantic depressions may be steered southeast or south towards low pressure over the Mediterranean.

CHARACTERISTICS OF THE SEASONS OVER THE BRITISH ISLES

Because of its typical variability from one year to another, it is difficult to determine a completely ordered pattern for the seasons over the British Isles. Even the conventional system of dividing the year into four more or less equal seasons has its problems, and a survey made over an extended period during the 20th century suggests that there are in fact five distinctive seasons rather than the conventional four.

P index

Despite these reservations, a study of the circulation over the British Isles employing one of the four synoptic climatological indices devised by Murray and Lewis, the P index, shows that a fundamental pattern of progressiveness can be recognised, even during years when the westerlies are at low ebb. This supports the view that a general description of the seasons that could be expected to occur in an average year has some validity.

This yearly pattern of variations in the P index indicates that, on average, a rapid increase in progressiveness during the early to midwinter period is followed by a more gradual decline from January to February. This decreasing tendency in progressiveness becomes more marked in March, and although it is slightly checked in April it continues into May, resulting in the yearly maximum of blocking occurring in most years during late spring. A subsequent rapid increase in progressiveness in June and July results in the yearly maximum of zonal flow occurring in midsummer. A subsequent decline in progressiveness during August continues to the secondary peak of blocking in the year during October after which progressiveness increases again towards early winter to complete the annual cycle.

ANNUAL ROUND OF THE SEASONS (LIMITING DATES ONLY APPROXIMATE)

Early winter (20 November to 19 January)

Long spells of one type of weather or another affect about half the years during this period, and they are mostly cases when mild westerly types become firmly established, the sequences usually being wet and stormy but in a few cases rather anticyclonic and dry. Although any cold spells occurring during this period in recent decades have seldom lasted much more than a week, some longer severe spells were recorded in the past, notably in the 17th and 18th centuries. Apart from 1962–1963, none of the long spells established in this part of the winter during the last two centuries seems to have persisted without a break into the later part of the winter after mid January. This early winter period is occasionally affected by a brief foretaste of severe weather – which, however, does not usually set in until February.

Late winter and early spring (20 January to 31 March)

Long spells affect half the years during this period, but they are of such widely different types that sometimes this is the main period of winter, and in other years it has the nature of an early spring. Nevertheless, persistent mild westerly weather is probably slightly less common than the sum of long spells of the various cold types, though these affect only a minority of winters. The increasing power of the sun becomes very noticeable from late February onwards unless defeated by cold winds, cloudiness or deep snow. The decreasing frequency of the westerly type drops more sharply after about 9 March and westerly weather then becomes more uncommon than at any other time except for late April to early June.

Spring and early summer (1 April to 17 June)

This season contains the most changeable weather of all, with occasional northerly winds breaking out to produce wintry showers, often with hail, squalls and thunder. During the early part of summer, there is a transition from dry continental air to a moist maritime flow. This change is marked by the collapse of high pressure over mainland Europe that had extended west over the British Isles, to be replaced by occasional Atlantic depressions moving east across the country towards the Baltic or Scandinavia.

High summer (18 June to 9 September)

As a result of the notable change in the circulation during early June, the westerlies return as the predominant winds over the region. This occurs after about three months in which the zonal flow has been less frequent than easterly and northerly winds. The season is then marked by persistent westerly and northwesterly winds, occasionally interrupted by spells of more settled anticyclonic conditions when a ridge from the Azores extends towards Biscay and the Alps and, in a minority of years, towards the British Isles and Scandinavia to give the finest warm dry summers in the region.

The return of the westerlies in June marks the onset of the so-called European summer monsoon. On average, the height of this feature occurs from mid July to mid August. Slow-moving depressions are common in the British Isles–Baltic–south Scandinavian region, and Atlantic depressions are steered towards this area. In some British districts the wettest week of the year occurs in late July.

The end-of-summer turning point occurs sometime between 17 August and 2 September. The summer development of the westerlies reaches its climax, with invigoration of Atlantic depressions by colder air than formerly arriving from Arctic Canada; in some years this gives an autumnal-like strength to the winds. Another rather notable wet period occurs from 20 August to 2 September.

Autumn (10 September to 19 November)

This season generally includes at least one spell of wet and stormy weather. But the early part of the period is often characterised by mild day temperatures and occasional summer-like conditions due to high pressure extending across the country from the south or southwest.

Thoughts then turn to the forthcoming winter and whether or not there will be a white Christmas.

WEATHER LORE

All sorts of irregularities intrude themselves [into the annual round of the seasons] and the various experiences become proverbial; and so we get cold weather in April known as the borrowing days, a blackthorn winter or ice-saints in May, the

tradition of St Swithin for July and August, dog days, the days of the dog-star, a
very ancient tradition of heat in August, St Luke's summer for warm weather in
October and St Martin's summer for similar conditions in November. These are
the things which interested folk in days gone by and are even now the incidents
about which newspapers are curious.

Sir Napier Shaw, *The Drama of Weather*, 1934

Medieval farm lore

Whan that Aprill with his shoures soote
The droghte of March hath perced to the roote,
And bathed every veyne in swich licour
Of which vertu engendred is the flour.

Geoffrey Chaucer, *The Canterbury Tales*, c.1386

A dry spell in March had long been a recognised feature in the medieval farm lore of England, when it was believed ploughing and sowing could successfully begin after the winter season.

Singularities

Weather lore includes beliefs suggesting a regular tendency for abnormalities to occur at certain seasons. The Scottish meteorologist Alexander Buchan, who was instrumental in setting up the Ben Nevis Observatory and maintaining its meteorological records, published a paper in 1869 on 'Interruptions in the regular rise and fall of temperature in the course of the year'. He suggested that cold periods occur around 7–14 February, 11–14 April, 9–14 May, 29 June to 4 July, 6–11 August and 6–13 November, and that warm periods occur around 12–15 July, 12–15 August and 3–14 December. However, his suggestions were based on data for southeast Scotland, mainly during the 1860s, and subsequent analysis has found that their reliability may well be questioned. Nevertheless, further research was carried out on singularities (a term coined by the German climatologist August Schmauss in 1938) by several climatologists including C. E. P. Brooks and H. H. Lamb. Singularities are recurrent weather patterns that are said to occur on about the same day or days every year, at least with a greater-than-chance frequency, and over 20 key periods were identified when the climate of the British Isles deviated markedly from the 'normal' seasonal progression, such as a fine spell in November, analogous to the 'St Martin's summer' of weather lore, between 15 and 21 November.

Thus the subject of singularities, with its roots in weather lore, still has a key role to play in long-range weather forecasting.

CHAPTER 5

Sources of Meteorological Data

The meteorologist is impotent if alone; his observations are useless; for they are made upon a point, while the speculations to be derived from them must be on space.

John Ruskin

MEDIEVAL ANNALS AND CHRONICLES

A RICH STORE OF HISTORICAL WEATHER DATA IS CONTAINED in medieval annals and chronicles. The writing of such manuscript records was an art which developed after the fall of Rome, and medieval Ireland provided the ideal environment for an early example of this practice to develop. The recording of religious and secular events in the form of annals dates back to the final establishment of Christianity in Ireland by St Patrick during the 5th century. It is generally acknowledged that Ireland possesses the finest and most voluminous historical annals of any country in Europe. These records were made, as Dr Johnson observed, 'when Ireland was the school of the West, the quiet habitation of sanctity and literature', and some of the earliest recorded information about weather and climate in Europe is to be found in these annals.

Irish annals

Descriptions of outstanding events – droughts, floods, storms and frosts – dating back to pre-Christian times are contained in six major collections. The *Annals of Tigernach* are the oldest of the Irish annals and comprise a record from 305 BC to AD 1407 compiled by an abbot of that name in the 11th century. The *Annals of Ulster*, sometimes called *Annales Senatenses*, come next in succession, both in antiquity and in authenticity. It is believed they were compiled on the island of

Seanadh, now called Belle-Isle, in Upper Lough Erne; comprising a record from
AD 431 to 1541, they include reports of eclipses and other natural phenomena. The
Annals of Clonmacnoise were compiled in the celebrated monastery beside the
Shannon at Clonmacnoise (Co. Offaly) and extend from earliest times to AD 1408.
The *Annals of Inisfallen*, like the latter, comprise a monastic chronicle compiled in
the Abbey of Inisfallen on the island in Lough Leane at Killarney (Co. Kerry). The
Annals of Kilronan extend from AD 1014 to 1561. Finally, the *Annals of the Four
Masters* cover the years from earliest times to 1616 and were originally compiled
at the Abbey of Donegal between 1632 and 1636; this splendid national work,
published in five volumes, probably contains the richest store of historical
source material possessed by any country in Europe.

Following this scholastic tradition established by Irish monasteries, a class of
professional families emerged from the 12th to the 17th centuries who became
custodians of the purely secular writings prior to the mid 1600s, when
instrumental meteorological registers began to be made in Ireland.

European chronicles

Returning to mainland Europe, Gregory of Tours recorded major meteorological
features and occurrences for each year in his *History of the Franks* during the late
6th century. From the time of Charlemagne in about 800, the chronicles of
Europe are continuous, and from about 1090 the prevailing meteorological
conditions of almost every season can be determined from the information so
provided. The sum of all references to phenomena such as floods, droughts, cold
winters and warm summers from a number of available monastic chronicles of
medieval Europe for each decade can form the data for deriving basic statistics –
and from these definite deductions can often be made about the raininess or
warmth, for example, of a particular decade.

Documentary evidence from nearby mainland Europe, in particular from
France and the Low Countries, has been used to partly fill any gaps during the
early medieval period. However, as entries in many of these early documents
relating to natural phenomena were often coloured by the belief that the affairs
of man were subject to divine intervention, their authenticity has to be critically
examined.

English estate records

Valuable sources of historical weather data are contained in the manorial
account books, chronicles of the abbeys, and government papers from the
Middle Ages onwards (Fig. 25). However, these documents need to be critically
studied and calendar dates worked out with great care. Corrections to the

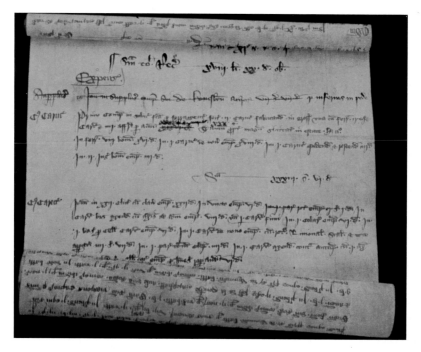

FIG 25. An extract from the scroll record of the Manor of Knightsbridge reporting a summer drought in 1342. (J. A. Kington)

modern (Gregorian) calendar are required, and account must be taken of which date marked the beginning of a new year – for example, 1 January, 15 or 25 March, and so on.

Estate records such as manorial accounts provide evidence about weather and climate over a period of more than two centuries in the later Middle Ages. In two main studies, the historians John Titow and P. F. Brandon have compiled weather chronologies from the estate records of the Bishopric of Winchester and the Sussex manors of Battle Abbey, respectively.

The task of interpreting the evidence presents many difficulties, but there is a strong incentive to establish a weather chronology so that climatic trends can be delineated. For instance, the historical climatologists Kathleen Pribyl and Christian Pfister at the University of Bern have extracted dates of the grain harvest in Norfolk from the manorial accounts of Norwich Cathedral Priory as a proxy for reconstructing average temperatures for early spring and summer in East Anglia. Preliminary results suggest that there was a cooling trend in mean

April–July temperatures in the period from 1270 to 1430, possibly indicating the onset of the Little Ice Age.

References from the Westminster Abbey accounts are most abundant from about 1290 to 1350. Weather is mentioned to explain the cost of repairing ploughshares (which were worn out quickly in dry seasons), insufficient herbage and crop failures, extra corn given to the livestock, haymaking and harvest expenses, structural damage to buildings, and uprooted trees. A type of reference which was common until the Black Death appeared in connection with seeding rates: when the fields were in a muddy condition, a denser seeding was required in order to compensate for wastage. However, sometimes the amount of seed corn was less than usual when the weather was more favourable.

Attention is also paid by historical climatologists to corn yields, since these may reflect the extent and seasonal distribution of rainfall. Harvest failures could be caused by too little rain as well as too much. For instance, the worst yields for wheat and oats on the Westminster manor of Kinsbourne in Hertfordshire occurred in the 1300s, a decade of exceptional dryness. Wheat did not do well when very wet weather prevailed during the growing season (as in 1315 and 1363), but oats often thrived. The best results were achieved in the 1290s, when conditions were dry in the summer months, but often wet in autumn and winter.

Astrometeorological roots

An important strand in the story was introduced into Europe during the 12th century when texts from ancient Greek via Arab sources became accessible to scholars through Latin translations. Amongst these volumes were manuscripts claiming to predict human destiny, as well as the weather, from the motions of the stars, planets, sun and moon. To provide data for such studies, dedicated meteorological observing began to be made on an increasing scale in Europe during medieval times.

The earliest known record of daily weather observations in England was made during a brief period from 1269 to 1270: these reports were included in a volume by Roger Bacon (c.1214–1294), one of the forerunners of the empirical method in scientific studies.

An outstanding example of a more continuous type of record is the journal of the Reverend Father William Merle, Rector of Driby (Lincolnshire) and Fellow of Merton College, Oxford. Merle has the distinction of being the keeper of the earliest known systematic continuous register of the weather. His journal, *Temperies aeris Oxoniae pro septennio scilicet a Januario MCCCXXXVII* AD *Januario MCCCXLIV*, is now housed in the Bodleian Library, Oxford (Fig. 26). This journal

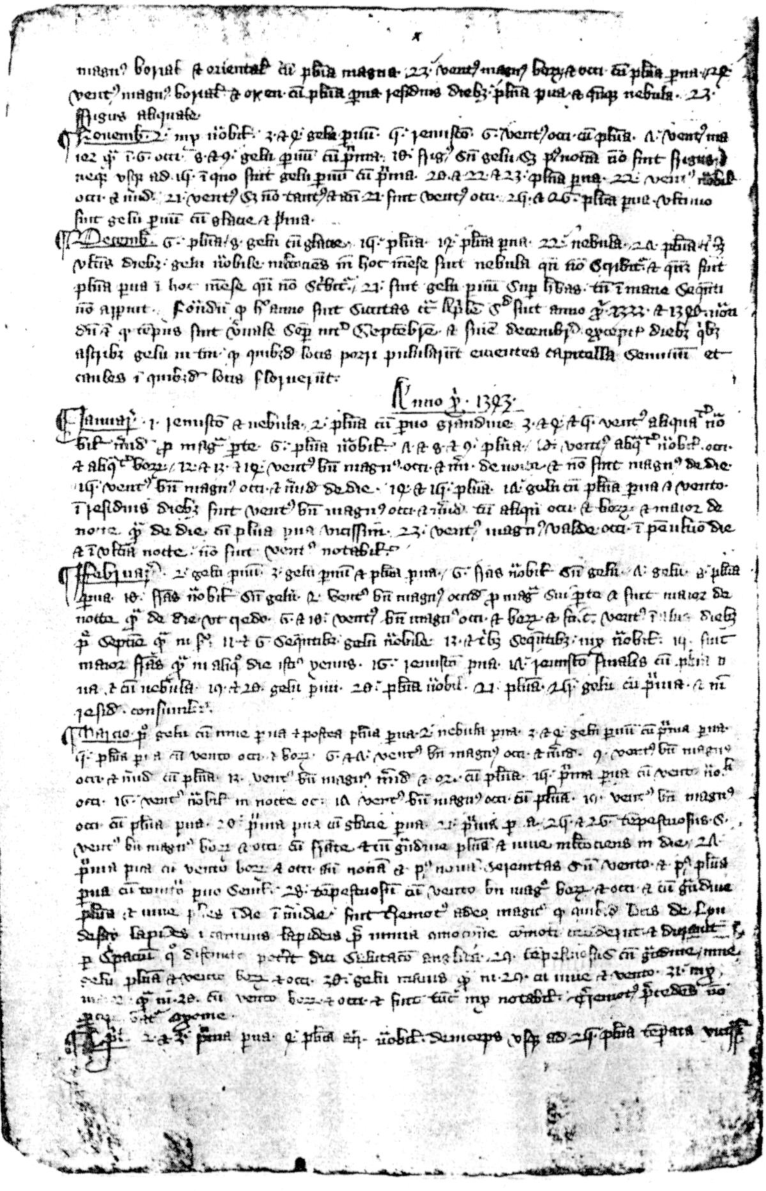

FIG 26. An extract from William Merle's weather journal (1337–1344), comprising monthly accounts in Latin including details about individual days. (E. N. Lawrence)

describes the weather from 1337 to 1343. At first the entries made by Merle were rather sketchy – for example, the journal opens with the remark, 'January 1337 was warm and partly dry. There were no severe cold spells during the past winter, and it was also rather warm and dry'. However, by the end of 1337 he was already beginning to give descriptions of individual weeks, and from 1339 he noted the weather for individual days. For instance, there is the entry, '1343, July. Considerable heat the first five days, especially the third and fourth. On the fourth of July, two or three hours before sunset, a violent thunderstorm came up, with very bright flashes of lightning which I saw at times. It continued, with heavy rain falling until midnight. The sixth and the whole of following week were overcast, with sometimes a little fog.' Merle's wind observations were analysed in 1933 by the British climatologists C. E. P. Brooks and T. M. Hunt.

As mentioned earlier, such observations on weather and attempts to predict it, partly with an agricultural interest, were being made from the 12th century onwards. However, Merle based his attempts not only on the state of the heavenly bodies but also on signs nearer to earth such as the deliquescing of salt, the carrying of sound from distant bells, and the activity of fleas and the extra pain of their bites, all of which indicated increased humidity.

Merle's example was more or less followed during the subsequent three centuries, with the result that even before the basic observing instruments were invented in the 17th century there were many learned people who were laying the foundations of meteorology as an exact science, by making systematic reports of visually observable weather elements such as the state of the sky, wind direction and precipitation.

This procedure was promoted by three main factors: the growing use of astrometeorology as a means of weather prediction, the mass publication of astronomical calendars known as *Ephemeredes*, and the growing interest in meteorological elements known to affect grain production and food prices. From the mid 16th century the *Ephemeredes* were somewhat altered to better fulfil the function of memorandum books. Daily astrometeorological prognoses combined with instructions on agricultural activities and personal hygiene appeared on one page, while on the opposite page an entire line per day was left vacant for making possible notes such as personal observations of the weather. However, because the space was restricted, weather diarists had to limit their notes to a few keywords or they had to resort to abbreviations; thus early procedures for using weather codes were being established as used in synoptic observing today.

By the 16th century, planetary astronomy had risen to be the leading hypothesis of science, and the keeping of daily weather observations was promoted to improve and test the reliability of astrometeorological predictions. Astronomical calendars provided a suitable medium in which such observations could be set down. The manner of recording weather conditions, sometimes in the margins of astronomical tables and almanacs, appears to suggest that at first there was not a great concern about keeping detailed meteorological records in their own right, but rather that they were kept simply to establish possible links between certain astronomical phenomena – such as eclipses, planetary conjunctions and phases of the moon – and particular types of weather, as well as to assess the success or failure of previous astrometeorological predictions.

However, a gradual change can be detected in the manner of recording, with the astrological entries becoming less frequent while the meteorological observations become more continuous and orderly in content. Nevertheless, the former practice was continued by some authorities well into the 17th century. For example, the text *Astro-meteorologica, or Aphorisms and Discourses of the Bodies Coelestial, their Natures and Influences*, published by John Goad in London in 1686, included his astrometeorological observations from 1652 to 1685.

METEOROLOGICAL RECORDS FROM THE 16TH CENTURY TO THE MID 19TH CENTURY

We have enough information from about 1560 onward to be able to give a connected account of our English weather. With a little trouble I think we could give the meteorological character of every week since about 1570, and every day since about 1670.

Gordon Manley, 'On British climatic fluctuations since
Queen Elizabeth's day', 1950

Many people kept meteorological records in the British Isles before the advent of official observing in the mid 19th century, and Manley's pioneering research in this field has shown how rich the region is in such data, ranging from dedicated daily meteorological journals to personal diaries containing occasional comments about the weather.

From about 1500 the weather reported in printed books and tracts is sufficient to provide about 500 items for every ten-year period. These data formed the basis of a statistical investigation by D. J. Schove of climatic variations in Europe during the late historical period, and they have provided one of the main sources used to compile the decadal accounts presented in Chapter 9 and Part II.

The sophistication of weather observations made prior to the establishment of official meteorological records in the mid 19th century can be an unexpected bonus to the student of past climates. But the practice of watching and reading the skies has a long history, and all down the ages many people, especially mariners and farmers, whose lives and livelihoods depend upon the behaviour of the atmosphere, have observed the weather. As a result, a large body of empirical knowledge, known as weather lore, gradually evolved, which attempted to relate approaching weather to such items as the face of the sky, the behaviour of flora and fauna, and many other natural phenomena.

The reconstruction of the climate of the British Isles is based on the direct observations made by a large number of observers and recorded in their weather diaries. Many such weather diaries were discovered and evaluated by Manley. His well-founded baseline of the year 1659 for the beginning of his Central England Temperature (CET) series was derived on the basis of both instrumental and non-instrumental weather diaries.

Before the 17th century, weather diaries are among the most valuable sources of non-instrumental evidence. In comparison with other kinds of proxy data, weather diaries have a number of strengths: they have an absolute dating control, they provide direct eye observations of meteorological elements, they have a daily resolution, and they are seasonally continuous. However, only two manuscripts containing daily meteorological observations are so far known in England prior to the late 15th century. The bulk of documentary evidence for determining the weather and climate for the medieval period is contained in narrative or literary sources – and there is a large quantity of such material, as described above.

There is evidence that, in common with countries in mainland Europe, an increasing number of systematic pre-instrumental daily weather records were being made in England during the 16th century, although unfortunately in many cases only fragmentary notes remain. However, during the course of the 17th century the number of known and more complete records substantially increases (Table 1).

INSTRUMENTAL RECORDS

During the 17th century, the age of science, instrumental measurement and objective comparison was dawning. By the 1660s, elements of the atmosphere were beginning to be counted and measured that when assembled would allow a truer assessment of climate to be made.

As indicated in Table 1, the increasing availability of barometers and thermometers from the early 1700s, following their invention a century or so

TABLE 1. Notable weather observers in the British Isles from the 14th century to the early 19th century.

The Reverend William Merle, Oxford and Driby (Lincolnshire): 1337–1343

John Dee, mathematician and Royal Astrologer, London: various almanacs, besides notes about significant events in his life and work, and weather observations, 1547–1551

Anon: officials at the Admiralty, London, maintained a 'Wind Book' from the reign of Queen Elizabeth I, 1558–1603

Dr Napier, Great Linford (Buckinghamshire): weather journal, 1598–1635; he also recorded the movement of planets and stars

John Evelyn, London and Wotton (Surrey): personal diary with occasional weather comments, 1620–1706

Sir Humphrey Mildmay, Danbury (Essex): weather journal, 1633–1652

Ralph Josselin, Earl's Colne (Essex): country diary with weather comments, 1644–1681

John Goad, astrometeorologist: astronomical journal with comments on daily weather conditions, 1652–1685

Robert Boyle, London: weather journal, 1656, 1670–1671

Samuel Clarke, Raynham (Norfolk): weather diary, 1657–1686

Samuel Pepys, London: personal diary with occasional weather comments, 1659–1669

Robert Hooke, 'A History of the Weather': instrumental weather journal, 1664, 1672–1681, 1695–1696

John Locke, Oxford, London and Essex: various journals with weather observations, 1666–1703

John Gadbury, Westminster: weather journal, 1668–1700

1670s: barometers available in London

Sir Philip Skippon, Wrentham (Suffolk): weather journal, 1672–1674

J. A. Conyers: instrumental weather journal, 1673–1681

Elias Ashmole, South Lambeth: weather journal, 1677–1685

Richard Towneley, Towneley, near Burnley (Lancashire): weather journal, 1677–1704

John Downes, London: weather journal, 1680–1694

Sir John Wittewronge, Rothamsted (Hertfordshire): instrumental meteorological register, 1684–1689

Sir Daniel Fleming, Rydal (Cumberland): instrumental meteorological register, 1689–1693

William Derham, Upminster (Essex): instrumental meteorological register, 1696–1705

The Reverend Say, Lowestoft (Suffolk): weather journal, 1698–1724

Thomas Short, Sheffield (Yorkshire): weather journal, 1709–1755

Thomas Hoy et al., London: instrumental meteorological register, 1723–1805

Anon, Edmundsbury/Bury St Edmunds (Suffolk): weather diary of a Roman
Catholic cleric, 1731–1743

Thomas Barker, Lyndon Hall (Rutland): meteorological instrumental register,
1733–1795

Robert Marsham, FRS, Stratton Strawless (Norfolk): meteorological/phenological
register, 1736–1797

D. Hastings, Alnwick (Northumberland): weather diary, 1739–1746

J. Fenton, Nacton (Suffolk): weather diary, 1757–1801

Janet Burnett, Kenmay and Disblair (Aberdeenshire): weather diary,
1758–1795

W. Hutchinson, Liverpool (Lancashire): instrumental meteorological register,
1768–1793

Gilbert White, Selborne (Hampshire): instrumental meteorological journal,
1768–1793

J. Houston, Johnstone (Renfrewshire): weather diary, 1768–1805

Thomas Hughes, Stroud (Gloucestershire): instrumental meteorological
journal, 1771–1813

S. Barrington, Mongewell (Oxford): instrumental meteorological register,
1771–1823

James Woodforde, Weston Longville (Norfolk): personal diary with weather
comments, 1776–1802

William Youell, Norwich and Great Yarmouth (Norfolk): weather diary, 1778–1815

M. Faviere, Dublin: weather diary, 1781–1811

James Hoy, Gordon Castle (Morayshire): instrumental meteorological register,
1781–1827

T. Heberden, Bridestowe (Devon): instrumental meteorological register,
1782–1784

C. Ashworth, Halifax (Yorkshire): weather diary, 1782–1786

Godschell Man, Albury (Surrey): instrumental meteorological register,
1782–1796

J. S. Mackenzie, Belmont Castle (Perthshire): instrumental meteorological
register, 1782–1796

J. Atkins, Minehead (Somerset): instrumental meteorological register, 1783–1784

Earl of Fife, Mar (Aberdeenshire): weather diary, 1783–1792

Thomas Pennant, Downing Hall, near Holywell (Flintshire): instrumental
meteorological register, 1784–1790

S. James, Truro and Redruth (Cornwall): instrumental meteorological register,
   1785–1788
James Meek, Cambuslang (Lanarkshire): instrumental meteorological register,
   1785–1809
A. E. Powell, Aylsham and Buxton (Norfolk): instrumental meteorological
   register, 1786–1791
T. Passant, Harleston (Norfolk): weather diary, 1786–1832
J. Andrews (father and son), Modbury (Devon): weather diary, 1788–1868
David Pennant, Downing Hall, near Holywell (Flintshire): instrumental
   meteorological register, 1793–1835

---

earlier, signalled a transition from purely visual to instrumental observing,
through which the study of weather was to be transformed into a more exact and
quantifiable science. Natural philosophers at this time showed a great interest in
these new meteorological instruments, for they appeared to provide the means to
investigate causes of weather changes using the scientific method of induction
based on systematic observations advocated by Francis Bacon in the early 1600s.

Scientific societies

It was soon realised that the value of instrumental observations would be greatly
enhanced if readings at various places could be made simultaneously. Observers
in Paris, Clermont-Ferrand and Stockholm carried out the earliest documented
experiment of this kind in about 1650.

The first attempt to establish a more permanent network of meteorological
stations was made in Italy in 1653 under the patronage of the Grand Duke of
Tuscany, Ferdinand II, member of the Medici family and founder of the
Accademia del Cimento (Academy of Experiments) in Florence. Standardised
instruments were dispatched from Florence to about a dozen academic institutes
mostly situated in northern Italy, and a standard procedure for making the
observations was devised. This included the recording of pressure, temperature,
humidity, wind direction, and state of the sky. The reports were entered on
specially prepared forms and sent later to the Academy in Florence for perusal
and analysis. Although the network ceased to function after the Academy was
disbanded in 1667, it had set the pattern for many future attempts in this field.

As an example of the many coincidental advances in science, the idea of
making standardised meteorological observations in concert was taken up in
1667 by the Royal Society of London (founded in 1662) when Robert Hooke, its
first Curator, proposed 'A Method for Making a History of the Weather' (Fig. 27).

ROYAL SOCIETY. 179

A
S C H E M E

At one View reprefenting to the Eye the Obfervations of the Weather for a Month.

Dayes of the Month and place of the Sun. Remarkable houfe.	Age and fign of the Moon at Noon.	The Quarters of the Wind and its ftrength.	The Degrees of Heat and Cold.	The Degrees of Drinefs and Moyfture.	The Degrees of Preffure.	The Faces or vifible appearances of the Sky.	The Notableft Effects.	General Deductions to be made after the fide is fitted with Obfervations: As,
14 ♊ 12.46	4 8 12 4 8 12	27 ♂ 9. 46. Perigeu.	W. 2. 3. 3. W.S W.1	9 12 16 10 7	½ 2 ½ 2 ½ 2 ½ ½	1 2 9	5 8	29 1⁄10 29 1⁄8 29 3⁄8	Clear blew but yellowifh in the N. E. Clowded toward the S. Checker'd blew.	A great dew. Thunder, far to the South, A very great Tide.	From the laft Q.of the *Moon* to the Change the Weather was very temperate, but cold for the feafon; the Wind pretty conftant betweenN.&W. A little before the laft great Wind,and till the Wind rofe at its higheft, the Quick-filver continu'd defcending til it came very low;after wch it began to re afcend, &c.
15 ♊ 13.40	8 4 6 10	18 ♂ 24.51.	N. W. 3 4 N. 2 1 7	9 8	½ 2	28 ½ 2 10	29 9	29 1⁄16 29	A clear Sky all day, but a little Checker'd at 4. P. M. at Sunfet red and hazy.	Not by much fo big a Tide as yefterday. Thunder in the North.	
16 ♊ 14 37	1c 11	N.Moon. it 7. 25' A. M. ♊ 10. 8.	S. 1	10	1 10	28 ½	Overcaft and very lowring.	No dew upon the ground, but very much upon Marbleftones, &c.	
		&c.	&c.	&c.	&c.	&c.	&c.	&c.	

Z 2   D I.

FIG 27. An extract from the Royal Society scheme for recording meteorological observations, as proposed by Robert Hooke in the 1660s. (N. Shaw)

Hooke formulated instructions for daily observations and drew up a standardised sheet for recording reports. He also designed a number of instruments for this purpose, including barometers for use on land and at sea, a thermometer graduated with zero corresponding to the freezing point of water, and a pressure-plate anemometer for measuring wind force.

The call for a network of meteorological observatories equipped with standardised instruments began in England during the 1680s with Hooke, Robert Boyle, Martin Lister and John Woodward attempting to make an exhaustive 'natural history of meteors'. The objective was either to establish a relationship between weather and public health, or to confirm astral influences on changes in the 'sublunar regions of air'. John Locke, Robert Plot, Lister, Richard Towneley and others began registers but expressed regret concerning the lack of enthusiasm among their correspondents.

Nevertheless, the aim to establish a network of meteorological observatories was further pursued by the Royal Society in 1723 when its Secretary, James Jurin, issued an invitation to the scientific community at large to participate in a worldwide scheme for making weather observations. Jurin's interest in this undertaking was both meteorological and medical; earlier, as a student at the University of Leiden, he had studied medicine under the Dutch physician, Hermann Boerhaave, who had speculated on the effect weather and climate might have on public health.

The observations organised by the Royal Society in 1723 were recorded in specially printed 'Weather Journals' having pages divided into columns for entering the day and hour of the report, the height of the barometer reading in inches and tenths, the temperature in degrees and tenths, the direction and strength of the wind, the state of the sky, a brief description of the weather, and finally the amount of rain or melted snow collected since the previous observation, measured in inches and tenths. The wind strength was estimated on a five-point scale in which 0 denoted a flat calm, 1 a light air, 2 a moderate wind, 3 a strong wind, and 4 a most violent wind. Observers were requested to send copies of their journals every year to the Royal Society in London for publication in the *Philosophical Transactions*, and for a few years reports were received from correspondents not only in Britain but in mainland Europe, America and Asia. Thus the pattern was set for recording meteorological observations that has been continued ever since at manned weather stations.

In addition to the Royal Society's efforts, a large number of private observers were recording daily meteorological observations during the 18th century. In the British Isles these more individualistic efforts were mostly made by physicians, country parsons and landed gentry. It is characteristic of the British Isles that

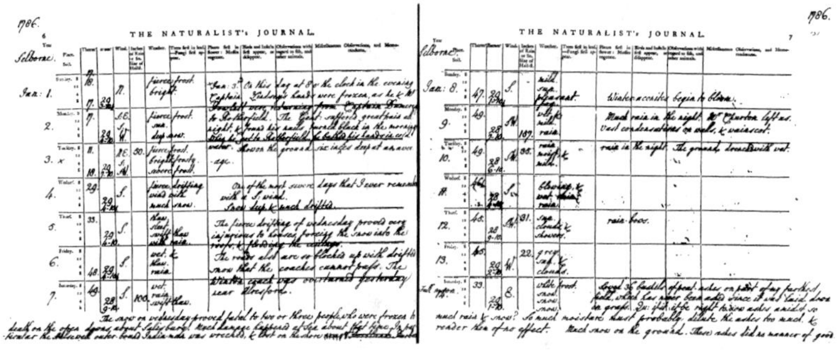

FIG 28. An extract from the meteorological journal for January 1786 kept at Selborne (Hampshire) by Gilbert White. (J. A. Kington)

almost all of these earlier observations were kept by amateurs. Official meteorology can only be said to have begun very tardily, with the establishment of observations at Greenwich Observatory in 1840. This was largely in order to provide basic data in relation to public health and welfare.

Although working in isolation, these people sometimes corresponded with one another about their mutual interests in meteorology and natural philosophy, with the Royal Society in London providing a centre for the more formal discussion and exchange of ideas. In fact, the efforts of Hooke and Jurin to establish meteorological stations in the 1660s and 1720s had not been forgotten, and by the end of the 18th century comparable methods of recording weather elements at more or less standard times every day were being carried out by a substantial number of people in the British Isles. One of the best examples of these individual 18th-century meteorological observers was the Rutland squire, Thomas Barker, who, beginning in the 1730s, kept a weather journal for over 60 years at Lyndon Hall near Oakham (Rutland). His brother-in-law, Gilbert White, also kept a meteorological journal with naturalist notes at Selborne (Hampshire) (Fig. 28). Another of Barker's contacts, Robert Marsham, kept a fine record including phenological observations at Stratton Strawless in Norfolk (see Chapter 8).

SHIPS' LOGBOOKS

One further source of historical weather data is the large collection of British naval logbooks housed in the archives of the Public Record Office, London, and the National Maritime Museum, Greenwich (Fig. 29). Initially, the weather reports contained in these logbooks were not instrumental, but, made with a

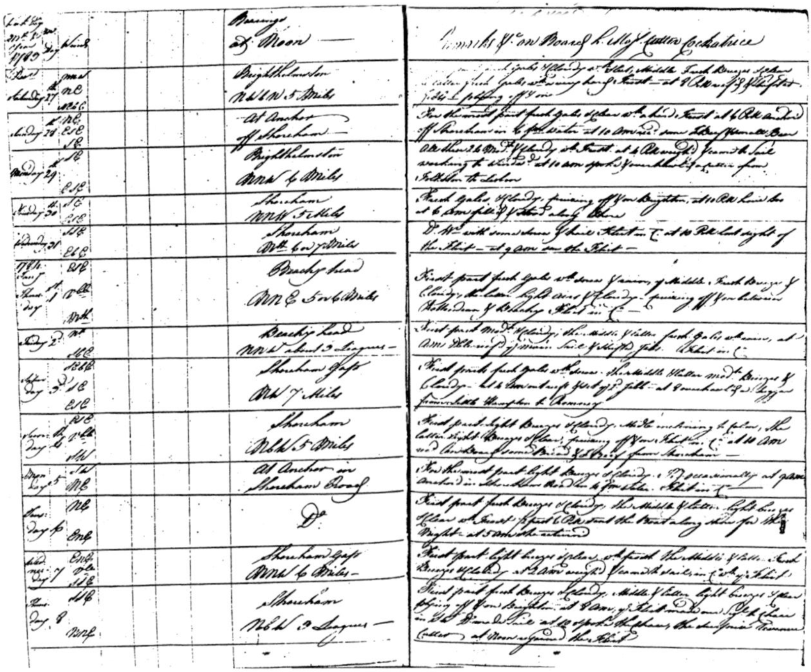

FIG 29. An extract from the logbook of HM Cutter *Cockatrice*, 27 December 1783 to 8 January 1784, cruising off the Sussex coast. (J. A. Kington)

disciplined experience of watch-keeping dating back to the 1670s, they comprise a large source of quantifiable data about daily wind and weather conditions over sea areas and coastal regions of the British Isles. The vessels were frequently anchored in the Port of London, the Thames or Medway, and other ports and anchorages such as Portsmouth, Harwich, Yarmouth and the Downs, as well as patrolling sea areas around the British Isles.

MISSING LINK

Although these sources of data are interesting enough in themselves, a link was yet to be forged that would allow individually made observations to be collected together and then analysed on a daily basis. After many promising starts, the process was very slow and erratic to develop. During the Enlightenment, for example, hopes had been raised in scientific circles that a systematic study of meteorological observations would show that the seemingly disordered spatial and temporal array of weather events was subject to predictable forms of behaviour. Consequently, scientific institutions such as the Société Royale de Médecine (founded in 1778) and the Societas Meteorologica Palatina (1780) established extensive networks of observing stations centred on Paris and Mannheim, respectively. Unfortunately, tangible results proved to be elusive by the statistical approach then applied, which earlier had been so successful in predicting the motion of the stars and planets. However, the collections of reports from these two societies, together with further data from private observers and ships' logbooks, means that a large array of daily instrumental and quantitative data became available for the late 18th century over Europe.

Regrettably, the early blossoming of meteorology at this time was brought to a halt by the political confusion and social unrest that followed the outbreak of the French Revolution. The two main scientific societies in mainland Europe that had been promoting international cooperation in the collection and exchange of weather data were disbanded in the mid 1790s. After a lapse of two decades, was it 1816 – 'the year without a summer', with exceptionally cold wet weather and disastrous harvests – that provided the stimulus for a revival of efforts to better understand and predict weather patterns? In any event, the idea of mapping simultaneously made daily observations of meteorological elements such as pressure, wind and temperature over an extended area, the concept upon which synoptic weather analysis is based, was presented at about this time by the German meteorologist Heinrich Brandes (see Chapter 6). As a network of weather stations did not exist at this time, Brandes made use of data collected in the 1780s by the Societas Meteorologica Palatina. The first observations to be subjected to the synoptic method were those made on 6 March 1783, a day on which there had been stormy weather over western and central Europe.

In 1820, Brandes published the results of his analysis of the 1783 weather using synoptic mapping methods in his *Beiträge zur Witterungskunde* (Contributions to Meteorology). However, it was not until several decades later that his method was put into practice. This was because it had to await the invention of the electric telegraph by Samuel Morse in 1832, and about eight years later he had made it possible for the system to be used as a workable apparatus for rapid communications. This, together with its almost immediate application by meteorologists, revolutionised meteorology as dramatically as the invention of the thermometer and barometer had done some 200 years earlier. In 1848, James Glaisher used observations collected by telegraphy from a network of stations in the British Isles to produce newspaper weather reports, and three years later synoptic maps were printed at the Great Exhibition in London.

UK Meteorological Office

In 1854, Robert FitzRoy was appointed Head of the Meteorological Department of the Board of Trade, the first official meteorological service in the British Isles. Three years later a series of daily weather maps was being prepared, based on simultaneous observations made at a number of stations over western Europe. During the spring of 1859 it was decided to increase the number of observations and to enlarge the area to be analysed on a trial basis. In addition to the established observatories, ships' captains, lighthouse keepers and private individuals were invited to assist in the scheme by sending their daily registers at monthly or quarterly intervals to FitzRoy in London. The project was planned to last for about a year, ending in October 1860. In America, the marine meteorologist Matthew F. Maury offered to cooperate, and he arranged for observations made along the Atlantic and Gulf coasts of the United States to be collected for this purpose.

It was quite remarkable that not long after this project had been put into operation two severe storms in close succession passed directly over the British Isles, on 25–26 October and 1 November 1859. The former became known as the 'Royal Charter Storm', after the steam clipper of that name, on a voyage from Melbourne to Liverpool, was driven ashore on the coast of Anglesey and over 400 people drowned. Between 21 October and 2 November 1859 over 200 vessels were wrecked in the sea areas around the British Isles in severe gales with a loss of 800 lives.

In the wake of these disasters, FitzRoy published a series of synoptic maps using data collected from his earlier appeal. These maps, covering the eastern North Atlantic–European sector from 21 October to 2 November 1859, well illustrate early techniques in synoptic weather mapping. In these trials, and in his recognition of the existence of polar and tropical air masses, FitzRoy anticipated developments in weather analysis and forecasting that were to occur in the early 20th century.

The British Association for the Advancement of Science indicated the importance of using telegraphic reports for transmitting warnings of the approach of storms to the Board of Trade in 1859. In the following year, FitzRoy arranged to receive daily weather reports by telegraphy from fifteen British stations and to exchange the data via Paris for reports from continental mainland stations. From 5 September 1860 official meteorological summaries began to be published in *The Times*, and several other newspapers soon followed. These have been continued to the present day. In February 1861, storm warnings began to be transmitted by telegraphy to coastal stations, whereby a system of 'cautionary signals', using cones and drums by day and lanterns by night, was hoisted from a mast and yard.

The founding of the UK Meteorological Office under FitzRoy in 1854 led to the setting up of a number of telegraphic stations, while climatological stations, still often manned by amateurs, came under the aegis of the Royal Meteorological Society and the Scottish Meteorological Society, founded in 1850 and 1855 respectively. Since the adoption of standardised exposure and observing techniques in 1881, the number of reliable sources of data upon which climatic statistics must be founded has become large. The British Rainfall Organisation, founded in 1859 and originally a mainly amateur body, is now associated with the UK Meteorological Office, and the story is taken up to the present by an official network of weather stations manned by professional meteorologists.

CHAPTER 6

Historical Weather Mapping

If one could collect very accurate meteorological observations, even if only for the whole of Europe, it would surely yield very instructive results. If one could prepare weather maps of Europe for each of the 365 days of the year, then it would be possible to determine, for instance, the boundary of the great rain-bearing clouds, which in July [1816] covered the whole of Germany and France ... In order to initiate a representation according to this idea, one must have observations from 40 to 50 places scattered from the Pyrenees to the Urals. Although this would still leave very many points uncertain, yet by this procedure, something would be achieved, which up to now is completely new.

Heinrich Brandes, Breslau, 1819

INTRODUCTION

THE APPLICATION OF MAPPING METHODS TO THE STUDY of climatic change on various time scales, both regionally and globally, forms an integral part of the work carried out by the Climatic Research Unit (Figs 30–32). The general circulation of the atmosphere above the earth's surface layer, as depicted on upper-air charts such as at the 500 hPa/mb surface level (approximately 5.5 km/18,000 feet), becomes a smoother and mostly westerly flow blowing round an upper low over the Arctic in the northern hemisphere. Variations in this upper-air flow determine the development and movement of depressions and anticyclones as depicted on surface weather charts. Jet streams occur where the upper flow becomes stronger and concentrated into narrow bands, typically 500 km (300 miles) wide and 3–5 km (2–3 miles) deep.

Although this mostly zonal current extends all round the North Polar region,

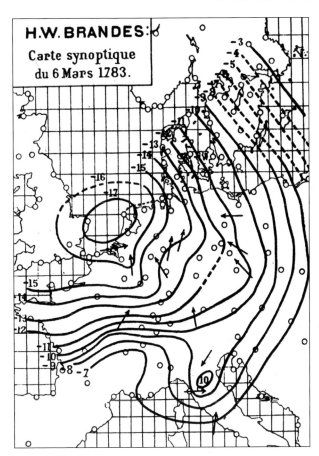

FIG 30. The first synoptic presentation of meteorological observations in relation to the surface pressure on 6 March 1783 was devised by Heinrich Brandes in 1820. The chart illustrated was later reconstructed by the Swedish meteorologist, Hildebrand Hildebrandsson, according to Brandes' original scheme. (F. H. Ludlam)

it is by no means a completely uniform flow and is usually marked by wavelike excursions north towards the pole and south towards the equator. These oscillations extend some 3,000 km (2,000 miles) or more from crest to trough and are known as long waves in the westerlies.

On some occasions the northward and southward oscillations become very large meanders, and completely closed oxbow-lake-like circulations or eddies may become cut off from the main stream. The westerly flow is then divided into two parts, one branch flowing to the north and the other to the south of the eddy. In its most contorted form, extending, for example, from the Mediterranean to the Arctic, the flow as depicted on meteorological satellite cloud images may resemble the Greek letter omega (Ω), and it is known as an omega block. Such situations, which effectively impede the normal track of the westerlies over

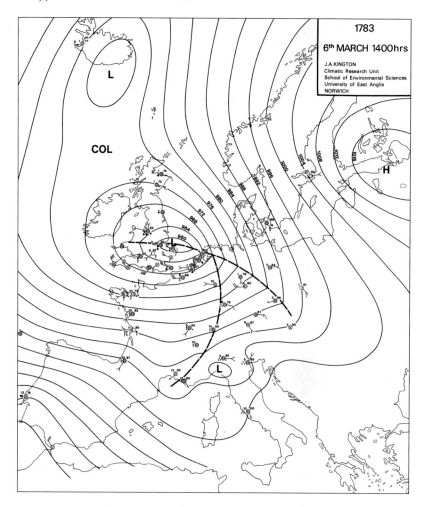

FIG 31. Historical synoptic weather map for the same day as Brandes' chart (6 March 1783), reconstructed by the author according to current methods of analysis. (J. A. Kington)

temperate latitude regions such as the British Isles, often last for a number of days, weeks or even months and are associated with persistent spells of weather. These can have outstanding characteristics, bringing some of the coldest spells in winter as well as the warmest spells in summer over the British Isles.

Thus this circumpolar circulation varies between two distinct types of mode. One is characterised by a more or less west–east orientation in which the long

FIG 32. Historical synoptic weather maps being reconstructed by the author at the Climatic Research Unit. (J. A. Kington)

waves are of small amplitude and transient nature, denoting a high zonal index associated with progressive weather systems, while the other shows a strongly meandering configuration with the long waves of large amplitude, a pronounced meridional flow, and a tendency for persistence, denoting a low zonal index associated with blocking action.

BRITISH ISLES LAMB WEATHER TYPES

It is convenient to reduce the mass of meteorological information depicted on daily weather maps into a less unwieldy form by classifying the analysed synoptic situations according to defined weather types and circulation patterns.

This opens up the way for the situations to be investigated according to statistical methods that have been developed in synoptic climatological studies.

The application of Lamb's classification of British Isles weather types to past meteorological situations demonstrates that the behaviour of the westerlies provides a vital key to a better knowledge and understanding of the region's weather and climate. This highly regarded classification of circulation patterns comprises seven main weather types, which are defined as outlined below.

W. Westerly

There is high pressure to the south, sometimes also to the southwest and southeast, and low pressure to the north of the British Isles. Sequences of depressions and ridges travel eastwards across the North Atlantic and further eastward. This can be taken as the most mobile, or progressive, of all the types.

The weather associated with this type is generally unsettled or changeable, usually with most rain in northern and western districts of the British Isles. Winds shift rapidly between south and northwest, occasionally southeast or even east for a short time. It is cool in summer, mild in winter with frequent gales.

NW. Northwesterly

The Azores anticyclone is displaced northeast towards the British Isles or northwards over the Atlantic west of Ireland. Depressions, often forming near Iceland, travel southeast or east-southeast towards the North Sea and reach their greatest intensity over Scandinavia or the Baltic Sea.

N. Northerly

There is high pressure to the west and northwest of the British Isles, particularly over Greenland, and sometimes extending as a continuous belt south over the Atlantic towards the Azores. There is low pressure over the Baltic Sea, Scandinavia and the North Sea. Depressions move south or southeastwards from the Norwegian Sea.

E. Easterly

There are anticyclones over Scandinavia; ridges may extend from there to Iceland or northern Britain. Depressions occur over the western North Atlantic and in the Azores–Spain–Biscay area.

S. Southerly

There is high pressure over central and northern Europe. Atlantic depressions are blocked west of the British Isles or travel north or northeastwards off western coasts. The southerly is less persistent than other types, occurring mainly as a variant between the westerly and easterly types; it is very rare in summer.

A. Anticyclonic

Anticyclones are centred over, near, or extending over the British Isles. Cols over the region between two anticyclones may be included.

C. Cyclonic

In this weather type there are depressions stagnating over, or frequently passing across, the British Isles.

Certain hybrids between wind direction types and either cyclonic or anticyclonic types are also recognised. These are abbreviated as follows:

SW, NE and SE
CW, CNW, CN, CE, CS, CSW, CNE and CSE
AW, ANW, AN, AE, AS, ASW, ANW and ASE
U = Unclassifiable days

The most important result to emerge from the classification of daily weather maps employing this system from 1861 (the beginning of the official synoptic record) is the wide variation in the incidence of the westerly type, with its predominantly southwesterly flow of winds, over the British Isles (see Chapter 3). Blowing off the North Atlantic, these winds have a warming effect in winter and a cooling one in summer, and accordingly the climate of the region has long been regarded as temperate with few extremes of heat or cold.

HISTORICAL WEATHER MAP SERIES

Climatic Research Unit

A series of daily synoptic weather maps centred on the 1780s has been reconstructed by the author in the Climatic Research Unit. The synoptic situations depicted on these charts have been classified according to the British Isles Lamb weather types and *Grosswetterlagen* (large-scale weather situations). This has made it possible to determine circulation patterns associated with the trends, anomalies and extremes which occurred during this period.

A full account of this project is given in the author's book, *The Weather of the 1780s over Europe* (Kington 1988).

Grosswetterlagen

This classification is comparable in approach to that of the British Isles Lamb weather types – that is, the aim is to determine the characteristics of the circulation over a given region by examining synoptic analyses portrayed on daily weather maps. The scheme comprises a set of distinctive large-scale weather situations, *Grosswetterlagen*, in which the positions of the primary steering centres and main features of circulation affecting central Europe remain essentially the same for several days. Its principles, first stated by the German meteorologist Franz Baur in the 1930s, extended an earlier approach made by Ernest Gold in 1920 concerning the classification of circulation patterns over England based on the positions of dominant anticyclones and depressions.

For general climatic studies *Grosswetterlagen* can be grouped into three main circulation forms:

> *zonal*, comprising westerly patterns
> *mixed*, comprising patterns in which the Atlantic subtropical anticyclone has shifted northwards to about 50° N but is not blocking
> *meridional*, comprising northerly, northeasterly, easterly, southeasterly and southerly situations with blocking highs lying between 50° N and 65° N over the eastern North Atlantic–European sector.

The *Katalog der Grosswetterlagen Europas* from 1881 is published by the Deutscher Wetterdienst, Offenbach am Main (www.dwd.de).

Wetterzentrale

A series of historical daily surface pressure charts from 1 December 1880 to 31 December 1949 has been made available on the internet by the Wetterzentrale Meteorological Service, Bad Herrenalb (www.wetterzentrale.de). Several of these weather maps have been selected to illustrate figures in the present volume.

UK Meteorological Office

Daily synoptic weather charts have been published in the *Daily Weather Reports* of the UK Meteorological Office from 1861.

SYNOPTIC CLIMATOLOGY

1901–1940

For comparative studies the climatic record is divided into 40-year periods in which averages of meteorological elements such as temperature, humidity and precipitation are determined. Being the first such period for which a continuous series of daily synoptic weather maps was available for the northern hemisphere, 1901–1940 came to be regarded as the standard datum for comparative studies in synoptic climatology. However, subsequent investigations have shown that the characteristic behaviour of the circulation during the early 20th century, previously thought to be normal, was, in fact, exceptionally vigorous with an unusual level of zonality. This remarkable flow reached its peak in the 1920s when the prevailing westerlies over the British Isles attained a dominance that has not been repeated in any of the following decades up to the present.

1781–1820

The earlier 40-year period of 1781–1820 falls within a notable phase from about the 1760s to the mid 19th century when the frequency of the westerlies over the British Isles appears to have been comparatively low. This period, centred on 1800, is of particular interest since investigations have shown that the weather and climatic conditions then prevalent over the British Isles were distinctly different from those that occurred during the first 40 years of the 20th century, that is, the standard period of 1901–1940. As a result of applying synoptic weather-mapping techniques to historical instrumental data, it is clear that this notable decline in the zonal circulation over the region was compensated by an increase in blocking action – which in turn led to more frequent extremes, colder, warmer, drier and wetter, than usual.

At the start of the period 1781–1820 the weakening in the zonal flow over the British Isles during the 1780s and its resulting effect on the weather and climate of the region is of particular relevance to current studies of climatic change, since a similar trend has occurred in recent years.

Solar activity and terrestrial weather

Sunspots and blocking action

A study of the climatology of blocking action by the German meteorologists H. Brezowsky, H. Flohn and P. Hess, employing *Grosswetterlagen*, has shown that during the 70-year period 1881–1950, a periodicity of 22–23 years, comparable in length to the double sunspot cycle, was apparent in the frequency of blocking anticyclones over the eastern North Atlantic–European sector, with maxima in 1892, 1915 and 1937 occurring close to the sunspot maxima in 1893, 1917 and 1937.

A forward extension in time of this study by the author shows that although the oscillation in the blocking action appeared to continue, there was a notable downward shift in the general frequency level, resulting in the minimum and maximum values of 1949 and 1958, respectively, being less pronounced than the former extreme values.

Although shorter in length and with more limited data, a similar project was undertaken by applying *Grosswetterlagen* to daily weather situations for the 1780s. This showed that frequent blocking action in 1781 closely followed the sunspot maximum in 1778, and that infrequent blocking action in 1784 corresponded to the sunspot minimum in the same year.

These results further underline the possible link between solar activity and terrestrial circulation patterns. For example, in some parts of the world wet seasons have failed about every 22 years, causing droughts such as those that occurred in North America during the 1930s, 1950s and 1970s.

Sunspot maxima and the westerlies

The frequency maxima of southwesterly winds in England, which probably correspond to maximum vigour of the westerlies in the general circulation (apparent around 1310–1350, 1530, 1730 and the 1920s), occur in a similar phase relationship to the more or less 200-year cycle of major sunspot maxima.

The search for analogues

As given above, circulation patterns over Europe in the 1780s have been determined by the reconstruction of a series of daily historical synoptic weather maps. The classified situations depicted on these charts and their subsequent analysis have revealed some notable features in the flow when, as now, the prevailing westerlies over the British Isles were in decline. In particular, this study has revealed distinctive features of the circulation over two centuries ago which closely match trends, anomalies and extremes that have occurred in recent years, thus providing useful analogues for further research.

The search for analogues in the historical instrumental period is of vital concern to improve our knowledge and understanding of present atmospheric behaviour, as circulation patterns in recent years have been presenting meteorologists with situations that are unmatched in the official synoptic record back to the mid 19th century. For example, an examination of five-year periods in the synoptic record shows that two of the five-year periods having the lowest mean frequency of the westerly type occurred over a time span of nearly 200 years. The most recent one, 1976–1980, with a value of 67 days per year, was almost as low as that of 1781–1785, with 66 days per year. A comparison of the frequencies of the other weather types in these two periods shows that there were further similarities in the circulation patterns that accompanied the decline in the westerly type two centuries ago and in more recent times. Both of the five-year periods, 1781–1785 and 1976–1980, include a year with an extreme minimum value of the westerly type, namely, 1785 with 45 days, the lowest known value on record, and 1980 with 52 days, the second lowest value in the continuous series from 1861 to 2000. In both periods the decline in the westerly type was partly compensated by almost equal increases in the frequencies of northwesterly and easterly weather types. The cyclonic type was also more frequent than usual in both periods, especially 1781–1785, when three out of the five years were very cyclonic.

Greenland Ice Sheet Project Two (GISP2)

Large-scale features of the circulation during the first millennium AD have been deduced from proxy indicators determined from the Greenland Ice Sheet Project Two (GISP2), an investigation of an ice core over 3,000 m (10,000 feet) deep through the ice sheet into the underlying bedrock. Analysis of the core provides a proxy record of palaeoenvironmental changes over thousands of years. For example, peaks in sulphate concentrations correspond to major volcanic eruptions over the past two millennia, which, in turn, affected global circulation patterns and temperatures (www.gisp2.sr.unh.edu). This study has shown that the Icelandic low weakened after about AD 200, and that this change in the pressure field over the Atlantic was followed by a decline in the westerlies around AD 400. The GISP2 indicators also show that about two centuries later the Icelandic low deepened again, which, in association with an inferred developing Azores high, resulted in one of the strongest westerly-wind periods in historical times between 600 and 1330. This notable zonal epoch, in which maritime types would have become more frequent over the British Isles, includes the onset of the Medieval Warm Epoch, the warmest known period in the last 2,000 years – that is, apart from the warming trend that occurred during the late 20th century.

CHAPTER 7

Cloud Study

It is a strange thing how little in general people know about the sky. It is the part of all creation in which nature has done more for the sake of pleasing man, more, for the sole and evident purpose of talking to him and teaching him, than in any other of her works, and it is just the part in which we least attend to her.

John Ruskin, 'Of the open sky',
Modern Painters, 1843

EARLY HISTORY

C LASSICAL WORKS AND THE BIBLE REVEAL THAT CLOUDS have always interested man and were sometimes regarded as manifestations of the supernatural. According to Homer (8th century BC), it was Poseidon who gathered the clouds and troubled the waters. In the Book of Job it is the Lord who speaks from the whirlwind, and the cloud is used to exemplify the mystery of creation.

By watering he wearieth the thick cloud ... Can any understand the spreadings of the clouds? ... Dost thou know the balancing of the clouds? ... Who can number the clouds by wisdom?

Book of Job, c.500 BC

Clearly at that time clouds were held in awe, and were completely beyond human understanding. Today the theory of air masses and fronts allows their 'spreadings' and 'balancing' to be understood, and they can be 'numbered by wisdom' by means of the *International Cloud Atlas* (Bleeker et al. 1956).

Nevertheless, this scientific approach to cloud study is not a new concept, and nor is the significance of cloud formation a modern discovery. In the 4th century BC Aristotle (384–322 BC) wrote his famous treatise *Meteorologica*, the first literary work to deal more or less systematically with meteorology, and in it he included a section relating types of clouds and weather to wind direction. Later, Theophrastus (c.373–286 BC), a pupil of Aristotle, distinguished between 'streaks of cloud from the south' (cirrus) and 'clouds like fleeces of wool' (cumulus) in his treatise on weather lore, the *Book of Signs*.

After the times of Aristotle and Theophrastus there was little progress in any branch of meteorology, and during the medieval period the ancient Greek sciences were only known to the Western world through the works of Roman poets and writers such as Virgil and Lucretius of the 1st century BC. The real inheritors of Greek learning in the medieval period were the Arabs, who preserved the remains of the original classical writings in libraries outside the frontiers of Europe. Notable writings about the science of weather made in the Arab world during the 9th and 10th centuries show that the meteorology of the ancient Greeks was understood, taught and further developed at Islamic centres such as Baghdad and Basra.

In Europe, on the other hand, original thought on many branches of science, including meteorology, was generally blocked by religious dogma for several centuries until the 17th-century French philosopher and scientist René Descartes attempted to explain the nature and cause of weather phenomena, including the formation of clouds and rain in 'Les méteors', an appendix to his book *Discours de la Méthode*.

On the practical side, recognising distinctive forms of clouds had developed alongside man's first observations of the skies. In particular, farmers came to identify certain cloud types that brought rain while mariners became aware of those forms that presaged coming storms. However, clouds had not been generally named down the ages, and it was only in the early 19th century that systematic attempts were made to classify them according to their forms. There were two key factors that had led to this situation, one of internal significance to the progress of meteorology, and the other more an external pressure from the allied subjects of natural history.

NINETEENTH-CENTURY DEVELOPMENTS

By 1800, the nature of many atmospheric processes had been sufficiently investigated to permit meteorologists to attempt a distinctive recognition of cloud forms. For instance, in 1788 the scientist and poet Erasmus Darwin (grandfather of Charles) explained how clouds could be formed by the adiabatic cooling of moist air. The second, external, factor of influence was that the study of natural history in the 18th century had been greatly affected by the work of the Swedish taxonomist Carl von Linné (Linnaeus), and many leading naturalists at the turn of the century were sufficiently interested in meteorology to keep detailed records of the weather, including clouds. Thus it was probably not by chance that the first recorded attempt to devise an ordered system of cloud forms was made in 1802 by the French biologist Jean-Baptiste Lamarck.

Jean-Baptiste Lamarck (1744–1829)

Lamarck became interested in meteorology while studying medicine in Paris. It became clear to him in his work that although clouds have an infinite variety in detail, certain general forms were not at all dependent on chance but rather 'on a state of affairs which it would be useful to recognise and determine'. Lamarck introduced his scheme for clouds in his meteorological journal of 1802. However, his system did not receive much attention, and Lamarck's reputation as a meteorologist was damaged after a slighting and rather contemptuous rebuke from Napoleon concerning some ill-fated attempts at weather prediction. Although Lamarck's classification, published in French, is not now remembered, his method of dividing the troposphere into three *étages*, or levels, is still used in the present International Classification of Clouds.

Luke Howard (1772–1864)

In contrast to and independent of Lamarck, the English pharmacist and Quaker Luke Howard proposed a classification which met with great success. The exceptionally colourful skies over London due to a volcanic dust veil following the eruption of Asama Yama in Japan during 1783 no doubt impressed the youthful Howard, and he developed a lively interest in meteorology while studying for his apprenticeship in chemistry.

About two decades later this interest led to the preparation of his historic paper, 'Essay on the Modification of Clouds', which he read before a small group of scientists known as the Askesian Society in 1802. He quickly gained recognition for this advance, and his paper was published the following year in the *Philosophical Magazine*. By using the four Latin terms, *cirrus* ('lock of hair'), *cumulus* ('heap'), *stratus* ('sheet') and *nimbus* ('cloud'), together with compounded forms of the first three, he defined seven main modifications or cloud forms, which he divided into three groups: 'simple modifications' (cirrus, cumulus and stratus), 'intermediate modifications' (cirrocumulus and cirrostratus) and 'compound modifications' (cumulostratus and cumulocirrostratus vel nimbus). Howard's keen sense of observation had resulted in the recognition of three fundamental cloud forms, whether judged on the basis of appearance or formation – that is, fibrous or cirriform clouds, heaped or cumuliform clouds, and layered or stratiform clouds.

The use of classically based terms was probably a significant factor in allowing Howard's scheme to become generally accepted in scientific circles of the 19th century. Howard employed Latin rather than Greek terms, as he considered the literal meaning in the former language would be more readily understood; this practice also concurred with the already well-established botanical nomenclature of Linnaeus. Howard compiled a collection of cloud studies, both sketches and watercolours executed in his own hand, to illustrate the nomenclature he had introduced. The suitability of this system illustrates the excellent judgement of Howard, and it later became accepted as the basis for the International Cloud Classification in use today.

In 1821 Howard was elected a member of the Royal Society, and the following year he was in correspondence with the German poet and philosopher Johann Wolfgang von Goethe. Throughout his life Goethe had also been a keen observer of the atmosphere, and he was delighted to have knowledge of Howard's classification of clouds. Goethe's scientific writings contain a section on meteorology including an article on 'The Shape of Clouds According to Howard', which closes with the poem, 'Howards Ehrengedachtnis' [To the Honoured Memory of Howard]; this work contains the verse:

> *Er aber, Howard, gibt mit reinem Sinn*
> *Uns neuer Lehre herrlichsten Gewinn:*
> *Was sicht nicht halten, nicht erreichen lässt,*
> *Er fasst es an, er hält zuerst es fest,*
> *Bestimmt das Unbestimmte, schränkt es ein,*
> *Bennennt es treffend! – sei die Ehre dein! –*
> *Wie Streife steigt, sich ballt, zerflattert, fällt,*
> *Erinnre dankbar deiner sich die Welt.*

But with pure mind Howard gives us his new doctrine's most glorious prize: he grips what cannot be held, cannot be reached, he is the first to hold it fast, he gives precision to the imprecise, confines it, names it tellingly! Yours be the honour! Whenever a streak [of clouds] climbs, piles itself together, scatters, falls, may the world gratefully remember you.

The Painters: John Constable (1776–1837) and J. M. W. Turner (1775–1851)

The early half of the 19th century also witnessed artists, such as John Constable and J. M. W. Turner, painting landscapes in which skies and clouds were

FIG 33. 'Study of Cirrus Clouds', John Constable, Victoria & Albert Museum. Constable's superb portrayal of cirrus clouds with cumulus in patches below. It is believed that he inscribed 'cirrus' on the reverse of this oil sketch confirming that he was familiar with the classification of clouds by his contemporary, Luke Howard. (The Bridgeman Art Library)

prominently depicted. Although Turner was a Londoner, his real and constant inspiration was the British countryside. During the second decade of the 19th century Constable proved himself to be a 'natural' painter in a class of his own.

After reading Howard's work, Constable became convinced that clouds must be identified and classified. He regarded the sky as 'the keynote, the standard of scale and the chief organ of sentiment' in landscape painting, and he made hundreds of cloud studies noting the month, time of day and wind direction on the reverse of the sketches.

By about 1819, Constable was working in London during the winter, but in the summer was making sketches both in Suffolk and on Hampstead Heath. Between 17 October 1820 and 31 September 1822 he made over 50 cloud studies on Hampstead Heath with actual weather inscriptions (Fig. 33). These indicate that Constable was then fully familiar with Howard's cloud classification. It was the meteorologist E. L. Hawke who, on the centenary of the painter's death, was the first to draw attention to the link between Constable and Howard:

FIG 34. *Staffa, Fingal's Cave*, by J. M. W. Turner, Agnew Gallery. Turner's dramatic portrayal of his visit to Fingal's Cave, as described in his own words, 'The sun getting towards the horizon, burst through the rain-cloud [cumulonimbus], angry . . .' (The Bridgeman Art Library)

It was when Constable was about twenty-six that Luke Howard, FRS,
inaugurated the systematic analysis of cloud-forms.
E. L. Hawke, *The Times*, 8 April 1937

The beauty of sky-colours is sometimes accentuated by volcanic dust veils that travel over immense distances in the upper air after major eruptions. Following the catastrophic eruption of Tambora in 1815 there were some remarkable sunsets in London that were portrayed by Turner. He made many studies of skies and clouds at this time with, for example, over 70 being contained in one sketchbook, dated about 1818. Turner regarded clouds as having symbolic meanings in which skies of peace and discord could be identified. He was also particularly fascinated by the line where the sky and sea join each other, where he believed the mingling of the elements and its harmony of tone led to a general reconciliation of opposites. He was not concerned, like Constable, with systematically identifying cloud types, but concentrated more on their infinite variety of moving shapes and tonal modulations.

Turner travelled further afield than Constable for his subject matter, including visits to mainland Europe and Scotland. One of Turner's most atmospheric paintings must surely be *Staffa, Fingal's Cave* (Fig. 34). In July 1831, the artist had set off for Scotland, and after visiting Glasgow he went on to Oban in September. From here Turner sailed by steamer for Staffa. Strong winds and heavy seas made it dangerous to land on the island, and the majority of the ship's passengers decided not to land – but not Turner, who climbed over the rocks to see Fingal's Cave. In his description of the incident Turner later wrote, 'The sun getting towards the horizon, burst through the rain-cloud, angry, and for wind; and so it proved, for we were driven for shelter into Loch Ulver, and did not get back to Tobermoray [Tobermory] before midnight'. From this exciting experience came *Staffa, Fingal's Cave* with its awesome portrayal in oils of heavy rain-washed clouds and rough seas. The painting was exhibited at the Royal Academy in 1832, and the following lines from Scott's *Lord of the Isles* appeared in the catalogue:

> ... *nor of a theme less solemn tell,*
> *That mighty surge that ebbs and swell,*
> *And still, between each awful pause,*
> *From the high vault an answer draws.*

This was the first painting by Turner to go to the United States. When asked if he would let a picture go to America, Turner replied, 'No, they won't come up to scratch.' But he was told there was somebody (James Lennox) who was prepared to give £500 for anything Turner would part with, and finally the stormy sunset rendering of Staffa was chosen. After the picture had arrived in New York Turner enquired of his contact, 'Well, and how does he like the picture?' 'He thinks it indistinct,' was the answer. Turner replied, 'You should tell him that indistinctness is my forte.'

John Ruskin (1819–1900)

The 19th century also saw John Ruskin describing clouds with dramatic language and detailed drawings in his book *Modern Painters*. Despite occasional inconsistencies, Ruskin presented original visions of the sky and atmosphere in his writings and drawings. He devoted a complete section to the open sky, describing cloud forms not only in artistic terms but also with scientific insight. The following passage on the classification ('outlining') of clouds contains clear references to cumulus ('heap'), cirrus ('web') and cumulonimbus ('domes of marble') clouds, as well as to their formation from water vapour ('the incense of the sea'):

How is a cloud outlined? Granted whatever you choose to ask, concerning its
material, its loftiness and luminousness, – how of its limitation? What hews it
into a heap, or spins it into a web? On what anvils and wheels is the vapour
pointed, twisted, hammered, whirled, as the potter's clay? By what hands is the
incense of the sea built up into domes of marble?

John Ruskin, *Modern Painters*, 1843

The Reverend W. Clement Ley (1840–1896)

Another 19th-century pioneer of cloud study was the Reverend W. Clement Ley.
Born in Bristol, Ley attended Magdalen College, Oxford, graduated BA in 1862,
MA in 1864, and was Vice-President of the University Meteorological Society. In
1873 he was elected Fellow of the Meteorological Society, later the Royal
Meteorological Society, and the following year became Rector of Ashby Parva,
near Lutterworth, Leicestershire.

Ley was particularly concerned with determining, by means of nephanalysis,
the relations between upper circulation patterns and the surface pressure
distribution. He was convinced that the analysis of observations of the motion of
cirrus clouds would lead to a better knowledge and understanding of winds in
the upper troposphere. In his efforts to establish a network of cirrus cloud
observers, Ley made requests to meteorological observatories and societies in
both the British Isles and mainland Europe. He later presented findings based
on his analysis of cirrus motion which show that he had identified distinctive
properties of upper-air flow that are now related to the jet stream, in particular
the strong northwesterly upper currents that frequently occur over the British
Isles ahead of frontal cyclonic weather systems.

Later, in his book *Cloudland: a Study on the Structure and Characters of Clouds*,
published in 1894, Ley presented some of the most original proposals regarding
cloud study to appear since those presented by Howard in 1803.

Observations of the motion of cirrus clouds, collected and analysed by Ley in
the late 19th century, indicated the existence of strong and predominantly zonal
winds in the upper troposphere. On many occasions it was observed that cirrus
clouds streaming out ahead of an approaching depression gave the first warning
of its approach. Ley also laid the ground for the concept of the upper-air steering
of depressions when, in his 1894 book, he commented:

And, on the whole, we may arrive at the conclusion, so far as our present
knowledge extends, that the path of a cyclone is partly dependent upon the
prevailing direction of the great upper currents.

INTERNATIONAL CLASSIFICATION OF CLOUDS

During the course of the 19th century, further genera were introduced to supplement Howard's four basic cloud genera of cirrus, cumulus, stratus and nimbus, namely, *stratocumulus* by Kämtz in 1840, *altocumulus* and *altostratus* by Renou in 1877, and *cumulonimbus* by Weilbach in 1880.

With the development of synoptic weather observing in the latter half of the 19th century, it became clear that there should be one overall system of cloud classification. Following the first International Meteorological Congress of 1873, efforts were made to introduce an International Classification of Clouds. Ralph Abercromby and the Swedish meteorologist H. Hildebrand Hildebrandsson were particularly active in this field, and in 1887 they jointly published an expanded version of Howard's original system comprising ten main types – which, apart from a few slight modifications, is still in use today. The first *International Cloud Atlas* was published in 1895.

THE TEN BASIC CLOUD GENERA

The ten basic cloud genera recognised today are cirrus, cirrocumulus, cirrostratus, altocumulus, altostratus, nimbostratus, stratocumulus, stratus, cumulus and cumulonimbus. They are illustrated in Figures 35 to 44, along with the etymologies of their Latin names.

THE ROLE OF CLOUD STUDY IN METEOROLOGY

Clouds are manifestations of complex physical processes occurring in the atmosphere that visually portray to the trained eye present and coming weather conditions. One of the objectives of cloud study is to sharpen the eye so that the face of the sky can be read with an increased degree of understanding. Present and approaching weather is indicated by the appearance of the sky, and the various forms of clouds provide visual guides to the physical and dynamical processes at work in the atmosphere. With an unobstructed skyline it is possible to see high clouds above the horizon at a distance of 240 km (130 miles). In addition to those discussed in this chapter, several other meteorologists have made major contributions to cloud study. Table 2 lists some of the more prominent among them.

FIG 35. Cirrus: from the Latin *cirrus*, which means a lock of hair, a tuft of horsehair, a bird's tuft. Composed of ice crystals, cirrus form in the upper troposphere and are the highest clouds. (J. A. Kington)

FIG 36. Cirrocumulus: from the Latin *cirrus* and *cumulus*. Cirrocumulus are a heaped-up formation of cirrus which typically make a striking fish-scale-like pattern called a mackerel sky. (J. A. Kington)

FIG 37. Cirrostratus: from the Latin *cirrus* and *stratus*. Cirrostratus is a layer of cirrus clouds that appears like a transparent white veil high in the sky and often indicates that wet weather is on the way. (J. A. Kington)

FIG 38. Altocumulus: from the Latin *altum*, which means height, upper air, and *cumulus*. Altocumulus clouds are composed of a mixture of ice and super-cooled water forming a layer of flattened white and grey globules. (J. A. Kington)

FIG 39. Altostratus: from the Latin *altum* and *stratus*. Altostratus clouds form a thin, watery sheet, thin enough for the sun to weakly appear as through ground glass. (J. A. Kington)

FIG 40. Nimbostratus: from the Latin *nimbus*, which means rainy cloud, and *stratus*. Nimbostratus clouds can cover the whole sky and completely block out the sun; they are always associated with rain or snow. (J. A. Kington)

FIG 41. Stratocumulus: from the Latin *stratus* and *cumulus*. Stratocumulus are probably the most common clouds in skies over the British Isles, forming a low layer of grey or white rounded cloudlets. (J. A. Kington)

FIG 42. Stratus: from the Latin *stratus*, past participle of the verb *sternere*, which means to extend, to spread out, to flatten out, to cover with a layer. Stratus are the lowest clouds, typically forming at about 300–500 m (1,000–1,600 feet) above the ground. (J. A. Kington)

FIG 43. Cumulus: from the Latin *cumulus*, which means an accumulation, a heap, a pile. Cumulus are clouds with rounded white tops and flat grey bases. (J. A. Kington)

FIG 44. Cumulonimbus: from the Latin *cumulus* and *nimbus*. Cumulonimbus are massive storm clouds with anvil-like tops that typically extend vertically from about 1,000 m (3,300 feet) to 10,000 m (33,000 feet) or more. (J. A. Kington)

TABLE 2. Further meteorologists who have made major contributions to cloud study.

L. C. W. Bonacina: author of 'Constable as a painter of weather', 1937; 'Turner's portrayal of weather', 1938

Arthur W. Clayden: author of *Cloud Studies*, John Murray, London, 1903

C. J. P. Cave: compiled a photographic collection of cloud types; author of *Clouds and Weather Phenomena*, Cambridge University Press, 1926

C. K. M. Douglas: took some of the first cloud photographs from the air while serving in the Royal Flying Corps during the First World War

G. A. Clarke: author of *Clouds*, Constable, London, 1920

F. H. Ludlam: co-author of *Cloud Study: a Pictorial Guide*, John Murray, London, 1957

R. S. Scorer: co-author of *Cloud Study: a Pictorial Guide*, John Murray, London, 1957

B. J. Mason: author of *Clouds, Rain and Rainmaking*, Cambridge University Press, Cambridge, 1962

J. E. Thornes: author of *John Constable's Skies: a Fusion of Art and Science*, University of Birmingham Press, Edgbaston, Birmingham, 1999

CHAPTER 8

Phenology

If the oak is out before the ash, 'Twill be a summer of wet and splash;
If the ash is out before the oak, 'Twill be a summer of fire and smoke.

Traditional phenological proverb

INTRODUCTION

P HENOLOGY INVOLVES THE OBSERVATION AND RECORDING of annually recurring events in nature, such as the leafing and flowering of plants, migration of birds and behaviour of insects. Being manifestations of prevailing climatic conditions, phenological events generally occur in a seasonal order that is substantially constant. However, the individual dates can vary widely from year to year according to the vicissitudes of the current weather. Phenological records kept over a number of years can provide valuable data from which the lateness or earliness of a series of seasons can be compared and analysed.

Various weather and climatic elements combine to affect the distribution of vegetation and influence the life cycles of plants and animals in the British Isles. For example, phenological observations have shown that the average date of flowering of a group of selected plants in spring is earlier along the coasts of southwest England than over higher ground inland, and generally earlier in the southwest than in northern regions of the country.

By providing natural indicators of atmospheric conditions, phenological observations can be applied to studies relating agriculture to weather and climate. Long-period records, comprising data from groups of mature plants and trees growing in select localities, can provide valuable information about annual variations in the onset and duration of the seasons, and in doing so they can complement studies of climatic variations based on other data sources.

NOTABLE OBSERVERS AND SOURCES OF PHENOLOGICAL DATA

Robert Marsham FRS and descendants

Stratton Strawless Hall (Norfolk), 1736–1947

One of the most famous phenological records in the British Isles was kept by Robert Marsham and his descendants. Dates of flowering of the snowdrop, wood anemone, hawthorn and turnip, and of the leafing of 13 different kinds of tree, along with other notable events such as the first observation of the swallow, cuckoo and nightingale, were recorded each year. The present author has shown that the long-term average leafing date for a select group of trees, namely, hawthorn, birch, horse chestnut, lime, beech and oak, is strongly related to the mean February to May temperatures in the CET series (Kington 1974).

Thomas Barker

Lyndon Hall (Rutland), 1736–1748

In addition to his renowned weather journals, a phenological record was maintained by Thomas Barker, which he entitled 'Birds of Passage and Forwardness of Seasons'.

Janet Burnet

Kemnay and Disblair (Aberdeenshire), 1758–1795

Janet Burnet kept a record of both weather and phenological events in her diary, with the latter providing a valuable insight regarding the recurring natural phenomena of the area during the late 18th century.

Gilbert White

Selborne (Hampshire), 1758–1793

Beside weather reports, Gilbert White also included occasional phenological observations in his meteorological journals, such as the times of flowering and the earliness or the lateness of harvest. For example, on 19 January 1759 he observed that snowdrops and some crocuses were in bloom before the end of December 1758 (the 1759 winter was very mild).

David Pennant
Downing Hall, near Holywell (Flintshire), 1793–1835

In his weather diary, David Pennant also included occasional phenological reports. For example, in January 1825 he recorded: 'The extraordinarily mild winter of the air during the present winter season was adverted to in our notices for December [1824] and are now unavoidably renewed for the past month ... The natural effects of this mildness are evidenced in our flower gardens, by the China Rose, the sweet-scented Coltswart, the Polyanthus, the Primrose, the Laurestina, all in bloom in the window of the writer of this article, and the Clematis and Lilac putting forth their buds.'

Henry Cox
Farningham (Kent), 1808–1861

Henry Cox's phenological observations included the latest 'wheat in ear' and 'harvesting finishing' dates. For example, in 1816 (the 'year without a summer') the former event occurred on 15 July (compared to an average date of 25 June) and the latter on 13 October (compared to an average date of 3 September).

Charles March Phillipps
Garendon Hall, near Loughborough (Leicestershire), 1811–1825

Charles March Phillip's recorded meteorological and occasional phenological observations in his diaries.

Orlando Whistlecraft
Thwaite (Suffolk), 1819–1864

Besides his instrumental meteorological observations, Orlando Whistlecraft compiled a record of phenological events.

John Shepheard
Erpingham, near Aylsham (Norfolk), 1819–1860

John Shepheard kept a record of agricultural-phenological events. For example, in 1834 he noted:

> 1 *January*: The most extraordinary season ever known. The wind SW ever since the gale on 31 August [1833]. Neither frost nor snow, but a great deal of rain; much damage done by wind. The hedge-banks covered with primroses, broad beans in full blossom, young rooks and young thrushes in nests, wild strawberries ripe. Plants in flower: hollyhock, crocus, snowdrop, anemone, aconite, roses, polyanthus, stock, wallflower,

heartsease, marigold, mignonette, hepatica and many others.

7 February: Some gentle rime frosts have checked vegetation.

8 February: Apricot trees and turnips in blossom.

22 February: Whitethorn hedges in full leaf on the south sides.

30 April: This, after all, was the backwardest spring for several years. Wind NE all April, and often frost and snow.

Royal Meteorological Society
British Isles, 1875–1947

Due to the initiative of the Reverend Thomas A. Preston, the Royal Meteorological Society established a national network of phenological stations in 1875. Reports covering a wide range of events were published annually for over 70 years.

A. Brewin
City of London, 1888–1903

A. Brewin kept a record of lime trees leafing and defoliating in a rare urban environment.

Edward Mawley
British Isles, 1899–1910

Edward Mawley recorded the flowering dates of thirteen plants selected for reporting by the Royal Meteorological Society.

John H. Willis
Norwich (Norfolk), 1913–1942

Following the lead of Robert Marsham and John Shepheard, the meteorologist John H. Willis compiled a unique phenological record in the form of a series of photographs of the same clumps of snowdrops and daffodils, and the same branches of chestnut and beech. It is of interest that only in the very mild winter of 1913 were snowdrops comparable in development to those observed by Gilbert White at Selborne in the similarly exceptionally mild winter of 1759. Willis noted that December 1912 was the warmest of the series: 'no subsequent January has seen vegetation so amazingly advanced nor a New Year's Day so carnivalled with flowers.' In contrast, another notable winter season commented on was the very cold wet winter of 1940, 'one of the most terrible winters ever known, the frost penetrating the soil more deeply than ever before in the records of my station.'

Frederick Lowe

Tenbury (Hereford and Worcester), 1915–1931
Frederick Lowe recorded several dates for many trees.

HISTORICAL PHENOLOGICAL RECORDS

Further sources of phenological data continue to be discovered from the investigation of historical documents. For example, information of this type has come to light in the records dealing with the royal forests dating back to the 13th century.

Pannage records

Forest laws decreed by the Norman kings allowed commoners living in the New Forest to turn out their pigs for pannage (payment for the right to pasture swine grazing on mast and acorns) only from late September to November. Acorns are green during these months, and although excellent for fattening pigs they can poison other animals, including deer. Once the acorns have turned brown, they are safe for deer and winged game to eat, so the pannage pigs had to be removed.

Charges were made for use of the forests for swine pasture. In a good year, when a mild spring allowed the trees to set fruit and a good summer promoted ripening, the income to the Crown from the forests was large. For example, £17 16s 3½d was paid in 1246–1247, indicating good weather, whereas in 1257–1258 the income was only 3s 8d, probably because of unfavourable, possibly wet, conditions. Details given in Part II. confirm that the summers of 1247 and 1258 were indeed 'very dry' and 'wet', respectively.

The pannage season still applies, though commoners are now allowed, as a privilege, to graze breeding sows in the forests all year round.

Miscellaneous historical phenological reports

1117
Mild winter: premature appearance of vegetation.

Anon, Belgium

1342
Mild autumn and early winter with unusual vegetative growth.
It is also to be noted that there was spring-like weather for the whole time between September and the end of December, except on those days to which frost is ascribed, so much so that in certain places the leeks burst forth into seed, and in certain places the cabbages blossomed.

William Merle, Oxford

1661

Mild winter with unusual phenological events.

It is strange what weather we have had all this winter; no cold at all, but the ways are dusty, and the flies fly up and down, and rosebushes are full of leaves, such a time of year as was never known in this world before.

Samuel Pepys, London, 21 January 1661

1667

Very cold winter: known in mainland Europe as the 'double winter' because many rivers froze twice. Although this season was not so severe in England, it was followed by a very cold spring.

The cold so intense that there was hardly a leaf on a tree.

John Evelyn, London, 14 April 1667

1675

Mild early January: mildness reflected in early phenological events.

Warm dry calm Christmas [4 January], grass springing, herbs budding, birds singing.

Ralph Josselin, Earl's Colne (Essex),
13 January 1675

1734

Very mild wet winter; 11 January: start of month-long mild spell, no frost or snow, primroses in hedges, flowers in garden in north England. Very mild wet spring; forward spring, trees in full leaf, hedges green in northern England.

1759

I believe it is as mild a time, considering the season of the year, as hath been known in the memory of man, everything having the appearance and carrying with it the face of April rather than of February (the bloom of trees only excepted). The meadows now are as verdant as sometimes in May; the birds chirping their melodious harmony, and the foot walks dry and pleasant.

Thomas Turner, East Hoathly (Sussex), 11 February 1759

1814 *(Jane Austen)*

Her meteorology frequently has a near-scientific exactness, like the cloud-studies, which John Constable was sketching on Hampstead Heath about this time ... hot weather has a deplorable effect on her characters. Winter turns them into moles. Snow makes them panic. The weather is never ignored or forgotten and in all the

great scenes of Emma, particularly where the heroine and Mr Knightley are united, there is a glory in the way it forms an atmospheric parable behind the action.
Ronald Blythe, notes on Jane Austen's *Emma* (1966)

Jane Austen began her novel *Emma* in January 1814 and completed it in March the following year. As in many of her books, it appears that the story and the moods of her characters are set against the changing aspects of nature, including the weather.

The year 1814 was very cold, colder than 1816, the so-called 'year without a summer', and in her novel it seems likely that Jane Austen used certain weather events that occurred during that year as background to her story. For instance, when describing an outing to Surrey she wrote, 'It was now the middle of June, and the weather fine ... It was hot ... English verdure, English comfort, seen under a sun bright, without being oppressive ... orchard in blossom'.

Why Jane Austen, that most precise of writers, should have referred to apple trees being in blossom as late as mid June has always puzzled literary scholars, and this apparent slip became known as her famous error. However, it is suggested that Jane Austen's description of the orchard, far from being a mistake, was derived from her acute powers of natural history observation, reflecting the delayed effect on plant growth of the extreme weather conditions. It is known that phenological events were two to three weeks later than usual during the spring and summer of 1814, and apple trees would very likely still have been in blossom during mid June. Perhaps Jane Austen, in her description of the picnic incident in *Emma*, recalled such a display in Surrey on the two rare very warm days in mid June, before the weather broke again.

PHENOLOGY IN THE 21st CENTURY

Observations of phenological events are most valuable, since the behaviour of plants and animals gives in many respects a more integrated indication of meteorological conditions with time than various other more conventional parameters. Thus, despite modern aids enjoyed by professional meteorological services, such as satellite imagery and computer analysis, the role of the amateur observer remains important in this and other fields.

It was a pity that a period of neglect and loss of interest in the subject followed the demise of the Royal Meteorological Society Phenological Network in the late 1940s. However, phenology has recently undergone a welcome revival, associated with the increased awareness of man's destruction of our fragile and irreplaceable natural environment. As a result, the Woodland Trust and the Centre for Ecology and Hydrology re-established a national network of phenological observers in the late 1990s to monitor and evaluate changes occurring in a select group of natural events. Access to this organisation can be made by visiting the website at www.naturescalendar.org.uk.

CHAPTER 9

Climatic Trends, Anomalies and Extremes

There is a story, which I have heard, and I would not have it given over, but waited upon a little. They say it is observed in the Low Countries (I know not in what part), that every five and thirty years the same kind and suit of years and weathers comes about again; as great frosts, great wet, great droughts, warm winters, summers with little heat, and the like ... it is a thing I do the rather mention, because, computing backwards, I have found some concurrence.

Francis Bacon,
Of Vicissitudes of Things, c.1625

INTRODUCTION

B Y EMPLOYING EVIDENCE FROM A WIDE RANGE OF SOURCES, such as palaeoclimatic data, historical documentary records and direct meteorological observations, the main course of British Isles climatic history has been traced during postglacial and historic times, that is, during the period in which man was making an ever-increasing impact on the environment.

The climatic trends, anomalies and extremes reviewed in this chapter are set within the context of distinctive periods, such as the Climatic Optimum, the Medieval Warm Epoch and the Little Ice Age, into which the climatic history of the British Isles can be divided.

DATING

Before about 10,000 BC, dates are given only as rough indications. From then on to about 2000 BC they are simple approximations, after which they gradually become more accurate until the start of exact historical dating following the expeditions of Julius Caesar to Britain in 55 and 54 BC and the final Roman conquest in AD 43.

LAMB'S LEGACY

During the 1950s, that is, well before systematic evidence of climatic change began to emerge, Lamb extended our knowledge and understanding of past climate by analysing a wide variety of documentary and proxy data, ranging from recent historical records to the earliest radiocarbon dating. By reconstructing patterns and timescales of past climate, he established that change is the norm. In the early 20th century, textbooks had given the impression that prevailing planetary patterns had become stabilised, and that notable events such as ice ages, the creation of deserts and the melting of polar ice were things either of the distant past or some time in the future. In the 1960s, Lamb shed light on current shifts in prevailing winds and temperatures, pointing to possible consequences; in the 1970s, he calculated that by the early 21st century atmospheric changes resulting from human activities would begin to affect the course of natural climatic change; and in the 1980s he stated that, whatever its cause, climatic change has a major impact on human affairs.

EARLY POSTGLACIAL TIMES

During the ice age, which lasted about 1.5 million years, there were many periods of tens of thousands of years when the ice sheets that covered Britain melted and the climate became as warm as it is today. It was during these interglacials that primitive people first came into Britain as hunters and food-gatherers. However, comprising large family groups or small clans, they were limited in numbers and scattered widely over the southern half of Britain. During this Palaeolithic ('old stone') period, Britain was still, at least at times, part of the European mainland. Each time the climate became colder and ice sheets re-formed over the high ground, animals and their human hunters moved south. Relics of former low sea levels during severe stages of the ice age persist in the form of old moraines on the beds of the Irish Sea and the Dogger Bank.

The reconstruction by Lamb of circulation patterns in early postglacial times brought to light two main points. First, up to about 1000 BC, Atlantic depressions in the westerlies appeared to have taken a more northerly track in the warmer periods such as the Climatic Optimum (5000–3000 BC), which would have meant decreased storminess and probably sunnier conditions generally over the British Isles. Second, the deterioration of climate that occurred during the last millennium BC seems to have been marked by an increase in windiness when Atlantic storm tracks shifted south. This caused various effects such as the retreat of forests from upland areas and the shifting of sands on exposed coasts, particularly in southwest England and south Wales. While there is also evidence of prolonged and extreme wetness in west Wales, as the winds were mainly westerly, it may have been drier in more sheltered eastern regions such as East Anglia.

Although glaciation ended with relatively rapid warming, there were large fluctuations of temperature while substantial amounts of ice remained in northern Europe and over the Arctic Ocean. The northward advance of flora and forests from their refugia, in some cases south of the Alps, took place over several thousand years. However, around 14,000 BC the climate over the British Isles generally became less severe. As the ice sheets of the most recent glaciation receded over much of the region, albeit with occasional halts and re-advances, the landscape underwent fundamental changes. In the north, the ice left a legacy of smooth, bare mountains and U-shaped valleys devoid of soil or vegetation, while in the south, moraine-strewn lowlands were covered with tundra vegetation and heath. Palaeolithic hunter–gatherers followed the animals that once again migrated into this region.

In about 13,000 BC the climate became rapidly warmer, and the subsequent speedy recession of the ice sheets was accompanied by an equally swift rise of sea level. However, Britain for a time continued to be joined to the continental mainland by a broad land bridge, so-called 'Northsealand', and before this was finally inundated there was a rapid spread of fauna and flora westward across the area. Although summer temperatures rose to values comparable with those of today, winters remained cold, and it was generally much drier than now.

Despite occasional setbacks, Palaeolithic people emerged from the ice age with a more diverse way of life. For instance, better conditions for shelter and survival were discovered in the caves of the limestone belt that stretches southwest–northeast across England, such as those of Cheddar Gorge (Somerset) and Creswell Crags (Derbyshire). From such home bases small bands of Old Stone Age people would have ventured out to hunt, fish and gather wild plants on the lowlands nearby. With the recession of the ice, a more friendly park-like landscape had been established over southern Britain, with scattered trees and numerous lakes.

12,000 to 11,000 BC

Following this period of improved climate there were two major setbacks when it appears that the changeover from warm to cold conditions occurred within a matter of decades. The relative rapidity of these reversals suggests a sharp trigger action at work in the ocean–atmosphere system such as the closing down of the warm-water conveyor belt in the Atlantic comprising the Gulf Stream and North Atlantic Drift. The first setback took place around 12,000 BC when intensely cold conditions, persisting for a thousand years or so, resulted in ice sheets returning to the Lake District and Scotland.

Allerød period: c.10,000 BC

By about 10,000 BC there was a return to milder conditions, the Allerød period, and the ice sheets again receded. Although initially much of Britain remained covered by tundra vegetation, temperatures eventually rose high enough for birch flora to become re-established and extend north and west into the Lake District, the Borders and central Ireland.

Younger Dryas event: c.9000 BC

Around 9000 BC the second major setback occurred in the form of the short-lived Younger Dryas event, when again, after centuries of warming, a sudden deterioration in the climate resulted in a return to near-glacial conditions. This post-Allerød temperature reversal was a climatic disaster of notable severity that occurred within a few decades. Again this suggests a sharp shut-down of the warm-water conveyor belt of the North Atlantic, due perhaps to a sudden and massive inflow of glacial meltwater from the North American ice sheets. This process caused the return of small glaciers to the Lake District, north Wales and the Wicklow Mountains, as well as glacial re-advances in the Scottish Highlands. Although these severe conditions only lasted for about five or six centuries there was a wholesale loss of forest cover, birch flora receded south, and harsh tundra conditions returned to southern Britain.

Pre-Boreal period: c.8000 BC

By about 8000 BC the massive amount of fresh glacial meltwater in the North Atlantic that had shut down the warm-water conveyor belt during the Younger Dryas period had dispersed, and the previous cold dry climate was replaced by milder moister conditions within a few decades. Nevertheless, the climate was initially severe enough to allow ice and snow to remain all the year round in some exposed areas. Eventually, however, glaciers finally disappeared from southern districts and the last glacial to affect Britain can be said to have finally ended.

BOREAL PERIOD: 8000 TO 6000 BC

The dramatic increase in warmth continued after about 8000 BC. The circulation over the British Isles was probably more anticyclonic than today, with warmer drier summers. Although winters were initially severe they later turned milder, but were still generally colder and drier than those experienced today. With any remaining mountain glaciers finally melting away, the British Isles became free of permanent ice. The conditions again became favourable for tree growth, and birches, followed by pine, spread north and west again, as well as over high ground; deciduous trees such as oak and elm also followed later in the period. Sea level was lower than at present, and although the area now covered by the North Sea was less extensive than when Britain was mostly under an ice sheet, it was still passable as marshland studded with lagoons. The 'English Channel' remained dry land, and Mesolithic groups were able to cross into Britain by foot.

ATLANTIC PERIOD: 6000 TO 3000 BC

Although the Fennoscandian ice sheet finally disintegrated around 6000 BC, the larger Laurentide feature in North America still covered about half of its original area at that time. It later collapsed, following a cataclysmic marine incursion into Hudson Bay. However, separate, smaller ice sheets remained, and the ice cover over Labrador only disappeared after about 2500 BC. These out-of-step events created asymmetrical circulation patterns over the North Atlantic, with Eurasia, including the British Isles, experiencing warm conditions, while eastern North America remained relatively cold. During this period, a strong zonal circulation became prevalent over the North Atlantic, accompanied by an intensification and northward shift of the Gulf Stream–North Atlantic Drift flow. As a result, from about 6000 BC a milder wetter climate developed over the British Isles, associated with an increased frequency of maritime types and westerly winds.

Climatic Optimum: 5000 to 3000 BC

Towards the close of the Atlantic period, anticyclonic westerly types probably became more prevalent in latitudes between 50°N and 60° N, and the warmest climatic period of postglacial times, the Climatic Optimum, developed under these situations between 5000 and 3000 BC. Most glaciers disappeared in Europe and even the Greenland and Antarctic icecaps decreased by a few hundred metres in thickness. It would appear that a sustained combination of radiation and advection heating associated with the distinctive weather situations of the period produced a level of warming which has remained unmatched until the present day. It is estimated that mean annual temperatures, for example, were probably 2–3 °C (3.6–5.4 °F) higher than at present.

The greatest postglacial spread of forest in the British Isles occurred during this most favourable period, with woods extending down to the Atlantic coast and to higher altitudes than any found today. A combination of mildness and moisture allowed the tree line to extend to higher limits than today, and in wetter areas there was a widespread growth of peat. Even more remarkable was that tree cover, comprising woods or thickets of birch and willow, and even oak, elm, hazel, and perhaps pine, extended to the now virtually treeless Orkney and Shetland. Pines also grew close to some of the most exposed parts of the Atlantic coast of the Scottish mainland. All this indicates a generally more settled and less windy anticyclonic climate, with the storm tracks of the westerlies running across higher latitudes than they do today.

As the ice sheets continued to melt there was a rise in sea level, and in about 5000 BC the North Sea broke through the Strait of Dover to make Britain an island. This event was important not only because of the direct effect of breaching the land bridge between Britain and the continental mainland but also because of its indirect effect in allowing the free circulation of ocean water round the British Isles. It is likely that the change from the colder climate of the Boreal to the milder conditions of the Atlantic period was enhanced by this fundamental shift in oceanic circulation and its consequent effect on air movements. At regional levels, the present distinctive coastal climates of the British Isles, affected at times by maritime effects such as sea fogs and low clouds, began to be established. Around 4000 BC the Neolithic Age witnessed the introduction of agriculture into the British Isles by immigrants from the coastlands of the west European mainland, whose tools were commonly made of flint.

SUB-BOREAL PERIOD: 3000 TO 500 BC

From about 3000 BC the predominating anticyclonic circulation seems to have intensified, leading to frequent blocking patterns. This effect would be in keeping with the fine weather and smoother seas that allowed Bronze Age people to sail all round the British Isles as far north as 60° N. Temperatures fell a little below the high values that occurred in the Atlantic stage but, more notably, it was drier and less windy, especially in northern Britain. In fact, from about 1200 to 1000 BC there is evidence of considerable traffic between Ireland and Scandinavia, which is probably indicative of a minimum of storminess. There is further evidence that the climate of Ireland during the Bronze Age was dry and favourable, and that a high level of civilisation developed both there and in Scandinavia.

A warmer climate than today continued to affect the British Isles until about 1000 BC. However, less settled conditions might have set in during the second millennium BC, with greater variations from century to century. These fluctuations were probably more pronounced with regard to rainfall rather than temperature, with some centuries being very dry and others quite wet. Volcanicity may also have played a notable role, with, for example, the Santorini eruption in the eastern Mediterranean producing a major dust veil (estimated DVI ≥2750) in 1450 BC.

It was probably largely due to such variations that forests receded from exposed places near the Atlantic coasts of Scotland around 2000 BC, and the tree line lowered over high ground in northern Britain. However, further south, in Cornwall, Wales and Ireland, forests still extended to the Atlantic shores and to greater heights over high ground than any present woodland.

While vegetation changes in the British Isles owed little or nothing to human interference prior to Neolithic times, the recession of forests in the Sub-Boreal was increasingly brought about by the activities of man. For instance, the first signs of extensive burning and clearance by humans are shown in the remains of former deciduous forests.

The separation of Britain from the continental mainland did not stop the migration of people into the region, and Neolithic groups from North Sea coastlands and the Mediterranean arrived during the 3rd and 2nd millennia BC. The late Stone Age witnessed steps forward toward agriculture and animal husbandry. A favourable climate allowed the former hunters to become herdsmen and then tillers of their man-made fields. Their burial sites, marked by long barrows, are widely scattered over the chalk uplands of southern England.

About 2000 BC the Neolithic implements of stone gave way slowly to instruments cast in copper and bronze. Large stone circles were built at sites from Wiltshire through Wales to the Outer Hebrides and Orkney. The most famous of these megalithic monuments, Stonehenge on Salisbury Plain, was erected in a remarkably well-organised long-term operation; about 80 bluestones from the Preseli Hills in southwestern Wales, each weighing up to four tonnes, were transported to Milford Haven, from where they were floated on rafts across the Bristol Channel and up the Bristol Avon to complete a journey of nearly 400 km (250 miles) to Stonehenge. The fact that meteorological conditions were apparently more often favourable for large-scale feats to be undertaken, such as the transportation by land and sea of huge stones and the erection of megalithic monuments in exposed sites, seemingly confirms the favourable climatic conditions of the Sub-Boreal period – that is, generally clearer skies, lighter winds and smoother seas than are mostly experienced nowadays.

During the first millennium BC copper and bronze were increasingly replaced by iron, and the next great invasion of Britain was made by the Celts, people skilled in the use of this metal. This movement of people was probably initiated by a distant but possibly related climatological event. Around 1000 BC the climate of central Asia had become drier, and waves of people, deprived of grasslands for their herds, moved westward into Europe. During their movements across the continent the Celts discovered iron, a stronger material than bronze for making tools and weapons.

From about 700 BC Celtic groups began crossing the English Channel. Initially they mostly settled in the climatically more favourable southeastern parts of Britain. Later, however, these Iron Age people moved further west and north into upland Britain when they themselves were displaced from the lowlands by subsequent invaders.

A cold episode that began about 900 BC and which lasted with internal fluctuations for about six centuries heralded the cooler conditions of the Sub-Atlantic period and provides a notable analogue with the Little Ice Age. The earlier climatic decline appears to have been characterised by abnormal wetness, especially in western parts of the British Isles, probably therefore frequent cyclonic westerly circulation patterns and a highly maritime climate with cool wet summers and mild winters. In mainland Europe there was a marked growth of Alpine and Scandinavian glaciers, many of which had disappeared at the time of the Climatic Optimum.

From these times the British Isles region became known to the chroniclers of the Classical world, centred on the Mediterranean, as a distant land at the uncertain boundary of their known world. However, it was not long before these islands attracted many more migratory movements of people from the continental mainland.

SUB-ATLANTIC PERIOD: POST 500 BC

After about 500 BC there was a rapid deterioration in the climate, with the onset of cooler, wetter and windier conditions. Summers were cloudy and damp and about 2 °C (4 °F) cooler than in the Sub-Boreal; winters, on the other hand, remained mild due to increased cloudiness and wind.

It appears that the mid-latitude westerlies had shifted southwards and the track of their associated depressions had also moved over or to the south of the British Isles, leading to increased storminess. Because of the cooler conditions there was a great reduction of evaporation, and wetter surfaces than before, even in summer. In Britain, the Somerset Levels and other English lowlands first became miry and later were flooded. Wooden trackways had previously been laid across the Somerset Levels to maintain access, but by the mid 4th century BC, owing to flooding, some of these trackways had been abandoned in favour of using boats, and around 250 BC several lake villages such as at Glastonbury and Meare were built in the swamps (the area today is drained by a web of rhines or ditches that were dug between the 17th and 19th centuries). Due to this particularly wet period, other groups of Iron Age people moved out of the low-lying flood-vulnerable areas and resettled the chalk uplands. As a result, larger areas were tilled on the downs than had been cultivated before. It seems that the plateau had remained mostly clear of trees.

This deterioration of climate also led to a rapid growth of peat over the previously forested uplands, especially where the soil was less well drained. Evidence of differential peat growth between western and eastern parts of England indicates that westerly winds were predominant, and unequalled in frequency compared with any other known period. The tree line was lowered by 300 m (1,000 feet). Birch trees increased in the lowlands, while alders and willows flourished on the wetter soils.

These unfavourable conditions did not go by unnoticed in the Classical world, and on his visit in 325 BC the Greek explorer Pytheas commented on the lack of sunshine, designating the Pretanic Isle (as Britain was then called), 'that land of clouds and rain'.

A severe storm seems to have occurred in about 350 BC. In an inferred cyclonic situation, with a North Sea storm and storm surge, severe sea floods inundated the North Sea coastlands and, according to Pytheas, German tribes such as the Cymbrians and Teutons were forced to leave their settlements.

After about 150 BC, the cold wet conditions of the early Iron Age were followed by a shift to a milder climate, which, by the time of the Roman conquest, came to more or less resemble that of today. Roman writers recorded the improvement in terms of changes in the southern limit of the beech tree and the northern limits of the vine and olive culture, as well as in the increasing rarity of severe winters and frozen rivers. Nevertheless, in about 120–114 BC there was one last bout of severe storminess in the North Sea, the Cymbrian flood, which caused severe flooding of the German Bight coastlands, gave the Jutland

and northwest German coasts their present form, and led to the southward migration of the Cymbrian and Teutonic peoples.

With historic records becoming increasingly more available from the Roman Period, the Sub-Atlantic marks the end of the postglacial climatic history of the British Isles. From this point on this chapter outlines the larger-scale trends, while a detailed year-by-year account is to be found in Part II.

EARLY ROMAN COOL PHASE: 1ST CENTURY BC TO AD 200

As the climate at the close of the Sub-Atlantic phase had continued to become milder, drier and less stormy, by the time of the Roman conquest in the 1st century AD conditions in Britain were probably not greatly different from those of today. Nevertheless, people who had been accustomed to the generally more favourable conditions of the Mediterranean region would have experienced some striking differences from their homeland. For instance, in the early 1st century the Greek geographer Strabo (64/63 BC – AD c.23) described the British climate as being wet and misty, and later in the century a summary of conditions relating to weather and agriculture in the new province of the empire was made by a Roman historian:

> *Their sky is obscured by continual rain and cloud. Severity of cold is unknown. The days exceed in length those of our world; the nights are bright, and in the extreme north so short that between sunset and dawn there is but little distinction. With the exception of the olive and vine, and plants, which usually grow in warmer climates, the soil will yield all ordinary produce in plenty. It ripens slowly, but grows rapidly, the cause in each case being excessive moisture of soil and atmosphere.*
>
> Tacitus, AD c.56 – c.120

During the years following their invasion, the Romans changed the local climates of many parts of the region by partly clearing the remaining forests, draining marshes, and extending the area for the cultivation of grain. They also established numerous vineyards in southeast England, a few more in central England and East Anglia, and even some as far north as Yorkshire. However, other warmth-loving crops were not successfully introduced, which suggests that the summers were generally no warmer than they are today. On the other hand, evidence indicates that the winters at that time were, if anything, sometimes colder than today, with more frequent frost and snow. It appears that the main track of the Atlantic depressions may have shifted northwards and, as a result, winter storminess and associated mildness were suppressed.

LATE ROMAN WARM PHASE: 3RD AND 4TH CENTURIES

While the climate of Britain was broadly similar to that of today during the early part of the Roman occupation, conditions appear to have become generally drier and warmer, with temperatures perhaps exceeding those of the present day by about 1 °C (1.8 °F), by the late 3rd century and early 4th century. This amelioration was related to a period of warming; evidence from coastal effects indicates that there was a high sea-level stand by around AD 400, a retreat of Alpine glaciers, and a reduction of storminess, especially in summer. The rise in sea level led to the Fens and Broads in East Anglia being inundated, probably in the late 3rd century. A great estuary or Danish-type fjord extended inland from the North Sea to Norwich, and places such as Great Yarmouth and Lowestoft did not exist.

Almost in parallel with the first recordings of droughts, the frequency of river floods appears to have declined sharply after about AD 270, and it seems likely that the suitability of river meadows and marshes in English lowland sites for settlements, such as the early Saxon village of West Stow in Suffolk, gradually improved over the next 130 years or so. However, conditions became wetter again in the 5th and 6th centuries.

From about AD 374 droughts were recorded at intervals of about 40–100 years until AD 676. A series of severe droughts then began that recurred annually for six or seven years, probably marking a minimum in the rainfall record, at least until the first half of the 18th century.

DARK AGES COOL PHASE: AD 400 TO 900

The mostly favourable climate of the Roman period was followed by colder wetter conditions during the 5th and 6th centuries. There were major advances of glaciers comparable with those attained both a thousand years earlier and again a thousand years later during the Little Ice Age.

Proxy indicators derived from the GISP2 show that there was a decline in the westerlies around AD 400, which, by inference, would have led to an increase in continental weather types and associated extremes. In fact, after about AD 400 there was a relatively sudden shift to colder winters and wetter summers;

these conditions affected most of Europe during the early 5th century and more or less coincided with the withdrawal of Roman armies from territories north and west of the Alps. In Britain this abrupt climatic deterioration also coincided with the departure of Roman forces, together with an increasing threat of invasion from mainland Europe by the Angles and Saxons.

Some of the settlements of these new arrivals to eastern England were soon under the threat of desertion due to the downturn in the climate during the 6th century, especially when cold episodes were also exceptionally wet. For example, it is believed that the Saxon village at West Stow in Suffolk was abandoned due to increased marshy conditions. However, in the west of the British Isles a second period of high culture, centred on Tara (Co. Meath), began in Ireland around AD 500, in which Irish learning was to become greatly esteemed in Europe. The establishment of the Irish annals provides valuable evidence of this high point in Irish history.

Elsewhere the early 7th century was marked by a rapid cultural decline in Christendom which was reflected by a virtual hiatus in mainland European annals up until about AD 660. There appear to be no adequate climatic factors that can explain either this effect or the Arabic advances into the continent which occurred at this time. However, despite this anomaly, Christianity became established in England during the 7th century and a number of priories, abbeys and churches were built. The establishment of monasteries, with their attendant schools, had already begun in western Europe during the late 6th century, following the foundation of Monte Cassino by St Benedict in AD 529. The monastic annals that were written from that time onward contain valuable references to meteorological and related events. Such compilations of knowledge, including the works of the Venerable Bede in Northumbria, helped to keep scientific learning inherited from the Greeks alive in west Europe during the 'Dark Ages'.

The first decade of the 7th century was notable for several cold winters. The succession of exceptionally cold years that occurred during the mid 7th century may have been due either to the reduction of solar radiation by volcanic dust veils or to the impact of a small asteroid.

A more continental type of climate appears to have mostly prevailed during the 8th century, with drier probably warmer summers and colder winters. The most notable example of the latter is the very cold winter of 764 (AD is now omitted from the text), for which a sizeable collection of matching data is available for the first time in the historical record. Accounts from about a dozen or so sources, some of which were contemporary, provide valuable evidence about the impact of the exceptional severe conditions over much of Europe, such as the destruction of olive and fig trees in the Balkans and the freezing of the northern Black Sea out to a distance of 160 km (100 miles). For such exceptional effects to have occurred it may be inferred that there was a persistent blocking-high situation over northern Europe that resulted in a prolonged westward flow of very cold polar continental airstreams over the continent, comparable to the situation that occurred in the severe winter of 1963. The summer drought that followed the 764 severe winter further indicates the probable dominance of blocking-high situations and the weakness of any zonal flow during that year.

In contrast with the 8th century, only one notable drought, that of 822–823, occurred in the 9th century, after which there was a gap of over 160 years before the next series of droughts was recorded in the late 10th century.

The GISP2 indicators show that the Icelandic low deepened sometime after 600, which, in association with an inferred intensification of the Azores high, may have resulted in one of the strongest westerly periods in historic times. Although four very cold winters occurred in the 9th century, a warming trend can be detected towards the close of this century that heralded the forthcoming Medieval Warm Epoch.

MEDIEVAL WARM EPOCH (LITTLE OPTIMUM): 900 TO 1300

A more settled climate with warmer drier summers and colder winters appears to have set in during the 10th century, indicating an increase in low index situations with more frequent continental and anticyclonic types; a series of severe droughts occurred later in the century. With the melting of glaciers, sea levels rose, including that of the North Sea. In about 1000, for example, the sea came up to Norwich (which today is 30 km/19 miles from the coast) via a Danish-type fjord inlet; water levels seem to have been as high as they were around AD 400.

This period of relatively warm conditions, possibly linked to increased solar activity, was also a time of glacial retreat in mainland Europe. While several very cold winters occurred in the 9th century, their frequency fell to a level of only one to three per century during the Medieval Warm Epoch.

Archaeological findings of Anglo-Danish Norwich support the idea that less progressive weather types were more prevalent during the 10th century. For instance, the positioning of the industrial Pottergate site in the western part of the city indicates provision for a possible pollution problem that would have arisen with persistent easterly winds associated with blocking highs in winter.

It may therefore be inferred that while cold anticyclonic conditions frequently occurred in winter, summers tended to be warm and dry. Looking further afield, it appears that the more favourable climate during the late 10th century coincided with a period of expansion in western Europe.

The analysis of decadal values of indices, devised by Lamb, which measure the relative proportions of dry to wet summer months and of mild to cold winter months in England, strongly indicates that during the early Middle Ages, particularly between 1100 and 1300, the British Isles enjoyed a greater and more sustained period of warmth than even that which occurred in the early 20th century. It may be inferred that during the period 1100–1300 there was a more frequent influence of subtropical anticyclones extending over temperate Europe, and a correspondingly enhanced frequency of westerly and anticyclonic weather in the British Isles, as compared with other less favourable centuries.

Traces of medieval tillage – namely, ridge and furrow patterns – extending up to over 300 m (1,000 feet) can still be seen today in upland areas of northeast England. There is also evidence of cultivation being carried out during this period up to 400 m (1,300 feet) on Dartmoor. Today, no farmer, not even in dire emergency conditions, would consider tilling up to this level, yet this type of ploughing was apparently carried out long enough in medieval times to leave its distinctive mark on the ground for centuries to come. Documentary evidence of dates and periods at which this tilling was carried out shows that it was actively continued for 200 years or so into the late 13th century.

This favourable climatic period was at its peak, with warm dry summers and mild winters, at the turn of the 12th century. It also included a number of droughts due to the combined effect of decreased rainfall and increased evaporation. Trees grew on sites where today they have not yet had time, or the necessary conditions, to grow again.

There were many productive vineyards. Besides those owned by the Crown, 38 others were maintained, according to the *Domesday Book* (1086), without the benefit of protecting walls in England south of about 53° N, that is, approximately 500 km (300 miles) further north than the present limit of commercial viticulture in mainland Europe.

The great period of cathedral building in England also coincided with this warm phase, and it is probably no coincidence that there was a great upsurge of activity in both science and the arts, including the flowering of medieval music, the flourishing of monastic farms, gardens and fish farms, the wide establishment of vineyards in the drier sunnier southeast parts of the country, and the bringing back by Crusaders of exotic fruits and vegetables from the Mediterranean with hopes, perhaps, of growing such crops on their estates in England.

However, there was a temporary downturn in the climate during the mid 11th century which brought about an economic decline, with famine, in many parts of Europe. In England, following three successive cold winters, 1067, 1068 and 1069, famine was particularly severe in the north, and there was great loss of life. In addition, much distress followed the 'harrying of the north' by the forces of William I in 1069. Little or no attempt was made to till the wasteland for several years, and this man-made scarcity was further exacerbated by several cold springs.

After a gap of over half a century without any droughts apparently being recorded, a decade or so of dry years occurred from 1075, which would have probably encouraged farming on former flood-risk lands: former fen marshes, for example, were certainly put under cultivation at Croyland Abbey in Lincolnshire.

1077: a very cold winter

Beside England, this extremely severe winter, associated by inference with a large-scale positive pressure anomaly, affected much of mainland Europe. Frozen rivers in northern and central parts of the continent indicate recurring cold-air advection and strong radiative heat losses during the long winter nights. Occurring at a time when conditions of people had begun to recover from the more severe climate of the 9th century, the significance of such an extreme event underlines the fragile nature of medieval economies based on agriculture. A decade later, heavy rain was the main cause of the famine that broke out during 1086 and 1087, which, by 1095, had become chronic.

1086: the Domesday Book

William I rewarded his supporters in the Norman Conquest by giving them control of estates known as manors, comprising a number of villages; other manors were held by bishoprics and monasteries. Reports on the size of every manor and its contents, including the number of peasants, animals, pools, mills and ploughs, were collected and recorded in the *Domesday Book*. These reports set the pattern for subsequent manorial accounts, which have provided most valuable information for determining medieval weather and climate.

1096: the First Crusade

It appears that both inclement weather and food shortages played key roles in the popularisation of the First Crusade in 1096. The connection, the previous year, between the dearth and the appeal made by Pope Urban II for the First Crusade would not have been lost on his audience. As a result, a large number of desperate people abandoned their impoverished lands, mainly in France, and set out on the People's Crusade in 1096. A contributory factor that exacerbated this dire situation was the increasing population in western Europe during the 11th century, which had resulted in a large number of land-hungry people.

The 12th century: climatic amelioration

Conditions improved in the early 12th century. The mostly mild winters probably indicate that maritime types became more prevalent over the British Isles, with increasing westerlies. Also, the golden age of medieval viticulture that began during this century shows that warmer summers generally became more frequent. It is notable that the first universities were established in Europe during the 12th century. Oxford University, for example, was founded in 1168.

The dryness of much of the 12th century is indicated both by pollen and tree-ring analysis, and the remarkable mildness during the later part of the century is related to the northern limit of wine production. Further afield, trade routes between the West and China developed rapidly by sea.

Nevertheless, after over two centuries of mostly benign climate there were signs that changes were on the way. For instance, the 1120s decade was cold, at least in winter, with three successive severe winters, 1124, 1125 and 1126, in mainland Europe and also perhaps England. This sequence provides a historic analogue with the three successive very cold winters of the early 1940s.

Furthermore, while the Thames had only frozen eight times during the first millennium, that is, less than once on average every century, the severe winter of 1150 marked the beginning of a period when such an event became more frequent. Although isolated, these events effectively heralded the decline of the Medieval Warm Epoch. Wetness and floods were notable features of the 1150s, and the cold 1160s decade was marked by five severe winters and a possible decline in the westerlies.

Very warm dry summers are evident in mainland Europe and probably also England during the 1170s, as it was a decade of agricultural prosperity with good harvests. However, because of the prevailing dryness, outbreaks of fire were widespread in tinder-dry towns and cities, such as Canterbury in 1174.

Rapid warming occurred after 1180, and it is believed to have been greater than that which occurred during the early 20th century. Dry seasons prevalent in the 1170s also persisted, and outbreaks of fire continued, such as in Winchester (1180), Glastonbury (1184), Chichester (1187) and Worcester (1202). In London the risk of fire led to an order issued in 1187–1188 that roofs should be constructed of slate or tile.

There was rapid economic and cultural progress, including a notable development in architecture from 1170 to 1190. Harvests must have yielded surplus crops at this time, since a Norwegian need for grain was supplied from England. Meanwhile in mainland Europe a notable series of wine harvests was recorded. However, an abrupt change from dry to wet conditions around 1193 to 1194 caused harvest failures and rain famines. These effects, together with several cool summers and mostly mild winters, indicate an increased frequency of maritime and cyclonic weather types. Also a very stormy period occurred in the North Sea in the late 12th century and 13th century, and many sea floods were reported in the annals.

The 13th century: signs of a downturn

There were several droughts in the opening decades of the 13th century, but a distinct change occurred in the climate from about 1250 which effectively brought the Medieval Warm Epoch to a close.

Mean annual rainfall rose significantly in the late 13th and early 14th centuries, a period which is acknowledged as one of extreme weather conditions. Throughout the 14th and 15th centuries, coinciding with a period of agricultural depression, English summers became wetter and cooler on average, thus shortening the growing season for grain crops.

Rapid cooling around 1200 was a forerunner of the more prolonged and severe chill to occur in the forthcoming Little Ice Age. Viticulture declined in England in the early 13th century, and although the influx of French wines was a major factor in this downturn, the onset of adverse climatic conditions would also have affected home yields. The fairly dry 1200s were followed by a decade notable for seven cold winters; around 1215 there was an advance of Alpine glaciers which was to continue until 1350.

Famines in mainland Europe during the 1220s were probably due to coldness. A series of unfruitful years in the early 1230s was described by the chroniclers Matthew Paris and Roger Wendover, although a period of mild winters was evident in England during the late 1230s.

Anticyclonic blocking of the westerlies may be inferred from the dry decade of the 1240s, which included the abundant years from 1246 to 1250. With warmth, notably in summer, being the main feature of the 1250s, persistent blocking of the westerlies may be inferred; a sudden temporary change from wet to dry conditions occurred in 1252. Records of vineyards in England indicate summer warmth around the mid 13th century. However, this situation was abruptly interrupted in 1258: sudden cooling and anomalous circulation patterns during this year without a summer were linked to the effect of a volcanic dust veil caused by a major eruption in the tropics earlier in the year. Data from polar ice cores suggest that this event was one of the greatest volcanic eruptions of the past two millennia, exceeding in magnitude all the greatest known historic eruptions of post-medieval times, such as Laki (1783) and Tambora (1815).

Despite this setback, warm dry conditions mostly returned in the 1260s, with good wine harvests in mainland Europe. However, the circulation turned cyclonic in the 1270s, a decade of mixed seasons with wetness now being the main feature. These conditions may have accounted for a murrain-type disease in sheep that was most severe during this decade; it appears that this disease was sheep-rot, an indicator of wetness. Various negative references were also made to viticulture in the 1270s: apparently costs were high and the wine was sour.

Warmth and dryness were features of the 1280s; the very warm summers of the period 1284 to 1291 are frequently mentioned in the manorial accounts. Warmth and dryness, again notably in summer, mostly continued during the 1290s, although autumns and winters were often wet.

LATE MIDDLE AGES RECESSION: 1300 TO 1540

The mostly favourable conditions of the Medieval Warm Epoch were followed by a distinct climatic recession during the Late Middle Ages. This downturn in the climate also included the Spörer Minimum, a 90-year span of low solar activity from about 1460 to 1550, providing evidence for a possible link between solar activity and terrestrial climate.

It has been claimed ... that the first half of the 14th century provides a remarkably clear instance of the culmination of a period of abnormal climate which prevailed throughout the northern hemisphere. Storms of great violence and destructiveness raged in the North and Baltic seas. The coastlands of England, Holland, Frisia, and Jutland were inundated many times, and changes were effected in the physical and human geography. The Frisian Islands, off the coast of Holland, were reshaped at this time, and the Zuider Zee then assumed its familiar form. In England, villages on the coasts of Holderness and Lincolnshire, and Ravenser Odd, a seaport hard by the Humber, were washed away by high seas ... The great European rivers, including the Thames and the Po, froze over for weeks and even months at a time; they were subject, too, to exceptional floods, whilst in a few summers they almost dried up ... The open-sea routes between Norway, Iceland, and Greenland, which were well frequented by the Vikings between the 10th and 12th centuries, became obstructed by ice, and by the 14th century had been forced along a more southerly course.

Gordon East, *The Geography Behind History*, 1965

The downturn in the climate which set in during the 14th century was probably linked with an expansion of the circumpolar vortex that caused the tracks of Atlantic depressions to be shifted further south. This change in the circulation occurred at a time when the seas surrounding the British Isles were still relatively warm and the atmospheric moisture content high. These two factors led to increased cyclogenesis and the development of severe storms, such as those of 1328, 1347 and 1362, together with an increase in sea flooding. After several centuries of warmer climate with melting glaciers, sea levels during the 14th century may have been generally higher than today by about 0.5 m (1.6 feet).

FIG 45. Breaking waves along a British seashore. A faint and barely visible rainbow has formed against the dark backdrop of a retreating cumulonimbus. This phenomenon was the result of sunlight behind the observer being reflected and refracted as it passed through raindrops falling ahead. (Andrew Bailey/FLPA)

A stormy episode centred on the 13th century occurred in the North Sea, with an exceptionally high frequency of wet years together with a large number of storm surges. A series of severe sea floods struck the sea defences of the Netherlands until they were overwhelmed and, as a result, a large area of fertile ground was submerged to form the Zuider Zee. Also, contemporary annals often referred to the severity of the winters, pointing, as with the high tides, to frequent northerly winds. Increased roughness of the North Sea can be linked with decreased westerlies over the British Isles. Such a decline would be partly compensated by increases in the frequency of northwest to northerly winds blowing over long fetches of Arctic waters into the northern part of the North Sea. The whole ensemble of possible circumstances suggests that during this period deep depressions tended to become located over the southern North Sea. While this type of situation brings heavy rainfall over much of Britain, its strongest effects tend to be concentrated in eastern parts of the country.

Besides the Zuider Zee, these conditions caused the Norfolk Broads to be established due to flooding of earlier peat-diggings, which had probably reached a height during the 13th century. Erosion of the eastern coast of England (Fig. 45) resulted in the loss of many coastal settlements including two great ports, Ravenspur (or Ravensburgh), which was sited on former land east of Hull beyond the present Spurn Point, and Dunwich on the coast of Suffolk. Situated between these two regions, Fenland settlements around the Wash would also have been vulnerable to increased storminess and marine inundations during this period.

From the increased reports of shifting sand burying roads, buildings and pastures along the coasts of south Wales, it may be inferred that southwesterly winds became more frequent and stronger during the early 14th century. Where the coasts faced west or southwest, sand dunes had formed over a long period in this region. This suggests that there had been an increase in the westerlies and associated severe southwesterly storms during this period which continued to around the mid 16th century.

During this downturn in the climate, summers became generally cooler and wetter, leading to a shortening of the growing season for grain crops. The impact on medieval agriculture was felt most intensely in upland regions, where even small negative changes in the climate had an exponential effect on cereal production. In the previous more benign climatic period it had been possible to cultivate up to 300–400 m (1,000–1,300 feet) in upland England. But now the increase in summer wetness was a significant factor in steadily reducing the potential for successful cereal cultivation in these vulnerable areas.

The unsettled climate during this period was also subject to a number of sharp changes from year to year as well as from decade to decade. This increased variability of the climate had a severe impact on the agriculturally based medieval economies, including the decline of formerly viable vineyards. It is also no coincidence that the onset of the Late Middle Ages Recession coincided with the Wolf Sunspot Minimum (1300–1360), when solar activity was at low ebb.

1300s

Although essentially dry, a tendency towards increasing wetness and coolness became evident in the 1300s. This decade was followed by one of the most unfavourable ten-year periods on record.

1310s

Apart from the summer drought of 1318, the decade of the 1310s was exceptionally cold and wet with unusually cool rainy cyclonic summers due to Atlantic depressions tracking further south than usual.

The excessively wet years of 1315 and 1316 dealt a catastrophic blow to agriculture that resulted in famine and death on an unprecedented scale. Further heavy rainfall and bad harvests in the following six years were the main factors that caused the Great Famine that affected many parts of Europe. Such adverse conditions may have been precipitated by a volcanic dust veil which lasted for about five years, perhaps caused by the Kaharoa (New Zealand) eruption.

1320s to 1330s

However, the unfavourable conditions of the 1310s did not indicate a lasting trend in wet summers. In fact, a notable change in the circulation set in during the 1320s and 1330s and, in contrast with the two previous decades, it was fairly dry but with several cold winters and cool unsettled summers in the latter decade.

There were several minor droughts in the 1320s. The main one, which began in 1324, continued through 1325 and culminated in 1326. Fire precautions were still being taken against dry conditions in London during 1327, but no comparable drought occurred until at least 1352.

1340s

Mostly mild winters and cool northwesterly summers prevailed in the 1340s. The decade was fairly wet, especially the period from 1343 to 1348 when a catastrophic decrease in the population (from 4 million to 2.5 million) occurred due to the Black Death.

1350s to 1360s

The mostly dry 1350s was a decade of mixed seasons associated with the onset of a sharp decline in the westerlies (the first such known event on record from the mid 14th century) and a trend towards wetter summers and colder winters. The maritime and cyclonic decade of the 1360s was one of mild winters, wet summers and bad harvests. The decline in the westerlies continued towards a minimum during the 1430s. Many gales were reported in the 1360s, and this may account for the fashion for installing weather vanes that developed in this decade.

1370s

The period of bad harvests in the 1360s was followed, apart from 1370, by the so-called 'good seventies' decade. However, with the exception of 1375, the 1370s were not particularly dry.

1380s to 1390s

Apart from the 1381 and 1389 cold winters, warmth was the outstanding feature of the 1380s, and blocking probably became more frequent. Warm dry summers prevailed from about 1384 into the early 1390s. These favourable seasons allowed a brief revival of prosperity and outlook, as reflected in Chaucer's portrayal of English life. A minimum stand of Alpine glaciers around 1400 also appears to have reflected the more benign conditions of the late 14th century.

1400s to 1410s

Weather variability greatly increased after 1400. Although the cyclonic 1400s were wetter than the 1360s, they did not approach the extremes of the rain-famine years, 1315–1321. The years 1400–1404, 1413, 1415 and 1422–1428 were notable for unfavourable weather and floods.

1420s to 1430s

The westerlies continued to decline during the 1420s, with generally mild cyclonic winters and cool progressive summers, and it is no coincidence that a period of cultural and economic decline set in about 1420. Although the related decrease in population was primarily linked to recurrent plague, a period of bad seasons from about 1430 to 1470 would not have improved the situation.

The 1430s decade, with the 1690s, is one of the coldest on record. The Thames in London froze several times, including during the severe winter of 1435. The decade was notable for northeasterly winters and cyclonic summers. The unfavourable combination of severe winters and wet summers caused an economic depression, famine and the abandonment of settlements especially in upland areas. The exceptional series of cold winters during the 1430s is unmatched for severity in western Europe, and the cluster that affected England during the early 1430s provides a striking analogue to those that occurred during the early war years from 1939 to 1942.

After fluctuating widely from about 1400 to 1430, winter temperatures rose steadily during the 70 years or so from 1435, and there were no further reports of the Thames freezing.

The wet summers and bad grain harvests of 1437, 1438 and 1439 caused a dearth almost as disastrous as the Great Famine (1310s), and thousands died of hunger in England. Although corn was imported from Prussia, it was apparently only available for the inhabitants of London; elsewhere people were reduced to making a substitute kind of bread from ivy berries and fern roots, and many starved.

1440s to 1450s

The 1440s witnessed the onset of an increase in the westerlies following a minimum around 1440, and relatively favourable conditions prevailed during this decade. It seems to have been dry in nearby mainland Europe, but owing to a lack of data conditions over England are less certain. Nevertheless, as authorities in London from 1440 to about 1456 appeared to have been concerned about the risk of fire and the supply of water, an increased incidence of droughts can be inferred.

1460s

The remarkable improvement in people's way of life during the second half of the 15th century in Europe, the waxing of the Renaissance, was possibly related to the onset of more favourable climatic conditions and good harvests. Cold winters became more frequent during the 1460s, but apparently the Thames did not freeze during any of these seasons, remaining unfrozen until 1506.

1470s to 1480s

In the warm dry anticyclonic 1470s, blocking can be inferred from the incidence of droughts in mainland Europe. For example, during the very warm summer of 1473, forest fires were sparked off in the mountains of central Europe and it was possible to wade across the Danube. Although England was not so intensely affected, dryness was clearly a predominating feature of the decade. For instance, apart from 1476 and 1478, droughts were recorded in every year from 1473 to 1479. The revival of trade in western Europe must certainly have been helped by these favourable weather conditions, and in England increased prosperity was reflected in an upturn in the artistic world.

1490s

The mainly cyclonic 1490s were the opposite in many respects to the previous 20 years. Apart from the dry years, 1490 and 1498, wetness was a prominent feature in most seasons and had its worst effect in Ireland by causing rain-famines. In mainland Europe these wet seasons led to a number of abortive peasant revolts. A spell of generally wet summers in England suggests that a series of depressions moved across the region.

1520s to 1530s

During the 1520s and early 1530s the westerlies probably increased to a level comparable to the 1920s. Besides mildness, the exceptional wetness of the cyclonic 1520s suggests that a strong negative pressure anomaly persisted over the British Isles for much of the decade. The wetness culminated in the years 1527 and 1528, probably the wettest two consecutive years on record. Although the floods that must have followed in the Fens are not recorded, they would appear to supply the reason for the early schemes of drainage in the region, first discussed during the period 1529–1531.

Already by 1524 the recurring frequency of wet years had made people fearfully receptive to the prediction that year of a second biblical-type flood by the German astrometeorologist, Johann Stöffler. This flood was forecast to arrive in February when Saturn, Jupiter and Mars were in conjunction in the sign of Pisces – but in the event the month was dry, much to the embarrassment of the astrologers!

The 1530s were generally a more favourable decade than the 1520s. This was a mostly warm dry decade, almost as dry as the 1520s had been wet. The changeover from cyclonic wet to anticyclonic dry conditions occurred around 1532, and the scarcities initially caused by rain were now due to drought. This change in conditions would help to explain why the Fen drainage schemes mooted in 1529–1531 were suddenly dropped. A notable drought that began in 1538 continued into the 1540s.

LITTLE ICE AGE: 1540 TO THE 1890s

The overall period generally known by historians of climate as the Little Ice Age is characterised by three main effects: first, a higher frequency of extremes; second, an increased seasonal, annual and decadal variability; and third, a lowering of annual temperatures up to a maximum of about 1–1.5 °C (1.8–2.7 °F) below present values. It was, however, not a continuous period of depressed temperatures but rather one comprising three colder phases separated by more variable, sometimes warmer spells.

It appears that there were no approaches to glaciation in the Scottish Highlands from the last Ice Age to about 1540, which indicates that there were not any intervening periods in postglacial times as cold as the Little Ice Age.

1540 TO 1700: LITTLE ICE AGE, PHASE I

Following the relatively warm conditions from the 15th century into the early 16th century, the coldness that set in during the late 16th century marked the onset of a severe phase in the Little Ice Age with glacial advances in Scandinavia, the Alps and Iceland. During this period the climate of the British Isles may have been at its coldest level since the last ice age; it is remarkable that in each of the last three, four and possibly earlier millennia, a cold stage occurred in or about the middle centuries which in each case appears to rival the severity of this phase of the Little Ice Age, the so-called 'climatic pessimum'.

1540s

Apart from 1540, the decidedly severe decade of the 1540s marks a downward step in the climate from the warmth of the Middle Ages to the chill of the Little Ice Age. Continental weather types dominated the circulation, and the notable dry conditions that began in 1538 continued into the latter part of the decade.

There are various indications of the zonal circulation over the British Isles weakening at about this time; almost every decade from the 1540s to the 1890s had at least one winter in which there is evidence of anticyclonic patterns persisting for a month or so over Scandinavia, with the usual consequence of severe spells occurring in mainland Europe and Britain.

1550s

With only one cold winter, 1554, the 1550s stand out as an anomalous milder interlude during the otherwise more severe conditions that set in during the 1540s. Winters and springs were definitely mild in western Europe, and summers dry. In England, fine summers appear to have lasted until at least 1556, when a drought became so severe that springs and wells ran dry.

After about 1550 previously shifting sand dunes in south Wales became more stable, which possibly suggests that southwesterly gales became either less severe or less frequent. The dunes, however, were also becoming more stable fixtures because of increasing plant cover.

1560s

The 1560s were notable for cold wet anomalies associated with a sharp decline in the westerlies (the second such known event since the mid 14th century), although the midsummer zonal flow remained strong. Colder conditions were particularly marked in the winters, associated with an increased frequency of northeasterly winds. Another indication of the more severe conditions was the floods following the 1565 cold winter, which were due to melting snow and ice rather than heavy rain.

1570s

The decline in the zonal flow continued during the cyclonic 1570s, although the midsummer westerlies remained strong. While the increased frequency of floods is the most notable characteristic of the 1570s, drier conditions that developed in southwest England from about 1571 generally extended across the rest of the country after 1574, and the period from 1575 to at least 1581 seems to have been dry over all parts of England. For example, by 1578 the Manchester Conduit, supplied by water brought by elm pipes from a spring, occasionally ran dry, and water rationing was imposed on the townspeople in 1578, 1581 and 1586.

The explanation of the notable variations during the 1570s lies in a change of weather type within the decade, with a tendency towards more settled weather from 1575 to at least 1581. It may be no coincidence that 1577 saw the rise of the so-called 'English Sea Dogs', and that Sir Francis Drake made his voyage round the world in 1580. The high frequency of northeasterly winds during the winter seasons continued.

1580s to 1590s

The mostly anticyclonic decade of the 1580s was mainly dry during the ongoing decline in the westerlies. A trend towards colder winters was associated with the continued high frequency of northeasterly winds.

The decline in the zonal flow continued during the cold wet 1590s, although the midsummer westerlies remained strong. However, the summers of 1591 and 1592 were dry, and it may be inferred that while the Azores high strengthened and extended northeast so that its northern flank lay close to southern England, there was little change of position or intensity in the Icelandic low. In this situation, Atlantic depressions move rapidly along the main track north of Scotland without secondary lows forming on their southern flanks. As a result, the westerly flow over the British Isles would have been strong but stable, and although there was probably a good deal of orographic rain over high ground in the north and west, little cyclonic rain would have fallen in the more sheltered eastern areas of lowland England and Ireland. The high frequency of northeasterly winds during the winters continued.

The overall coldness of the period was reflected in a rapid advance of Alpine glaciers during the 1590s and 1600s, and a volcanic dust veil may be inferred from reports of the sun and moon becoming dimmed.

The wetness of the 1590s was as unfavourable as the cold. For instance, reports of water rationing at Manchester between 1578 and 1585 were now replaced by remarks about a succession of bad harvests from 1593 due to the exceptional rainfall. Crop failures from 1593 to 1597 were so severe that grain had to be imported from the Baltic. Owing to the bad grain harvests, wheat became so scarce and dear that food riots broke out in many counties of England. The famine and crisis in the 1590s was followed by the return of plague in 1603.

> *Bad harvests, interrupted trade, and plague caused much distress in Yorkshire in the 1590s; distress led to much unrest and rioting.*
>
> Anon

Another contemporary description was made in verse:

> *A colder time in world was never seene*
> *The skies do loure, the sun and moon wax dim*
> *Summer scarce known, but the leaves are greene*
> *The winter's vast drives water o'er the brim ...*
> *Nature thinks scorn to do his duties right*
> *Because we have displeased the Lord of Light.*
>
> Anon

Shakespeare too would have experienced the wretched conditions of the 1590s, and he might well have had the cool wet summer of 1594 in mind when he gave Titania her evocative speech on foul weather and the dislocation of the seasons in *A Midsummer Night's Dream*:

> *Therefore the winds, piping to us in vain, as in revenge have sucked up from the sea contagious fogs; which, falling in the land, hath every pelting river made so proud that they have overborne their continents. The ox hath therefore stretched his yoke in vain, the ploughman lost his sweat; and the green corn hath rotted ere his youth attained a beard; the fold stands empty in the drowned field, and crows are fatted with the murrain flock; the nine men's morris is filled up with mud.*

1600s

The cold wave of the late 16th century generally continued into the early 1600s and was especially marked by several severe winters. Nevertheless, with more favourable conditions during the spring and summer seasons, there was a revival of viticulture in England. Also, with the growth of towns and cities during the 17th century, the risk of fires, as reported in various records such as parish registers and journals, increased especially during the droughts which occurred in the dry decades, the 1610s and 1630s. Apparently by 1633 the incidence of fires in England was so great that 'fire engines' had been brought into the country from Germany, where the danger of urban and forest fires was even greater. These devices were forgotten about in the wet years from 1660 to 1664, but a renewed period of dryness arrived with the plague year of 1665 and the Great Fire of London year of 1666.

The continental-type decade of the 1600s was marked by a minimum in the westerlies; a decrease in rainfall was probably linked with this weakened zonal flow. There are several pieces of evidence which may be connected with the weak zonal flow: for example, some of the Fen floods that prompted drainage schemes in 1606 and 1613 were due to northeasterly gales, and erratic fishing for herring off the east Scottish coast may have been due to the decreased frequency of the westerlies.

1610s

The anticyclonic 1610s were notable for warmth, dryness and good harvests. The warmth was most effective in the summers and was reflected in the continuing revival of viticulture. There were strong midwinter westerlies. A tendency towards droughts that began in the previous decade became more evident during the 1610s.

1620s

A return to cool wet conditions occurred during the mostly cyclonic 1620s, with strong midsummer westerlies. This was the decade when the English herbalist John Parkinson, in his work *Theatrum Botanicum*, ascribed the decline of English viticulture to the deterioration of the climate. Famine was prevalent throughout the 1620s, and people from both England and France emigrated in increasing numbers, many settling in the territories of the decaying Spanish Caribbean Empire. With the recurrent scarcity of food in Ireland, the potato became the staple crop of the country from 1630.

Severe weather also occurred in Scotland during the 1620s, as recorded in Scottish chronicles and diaries. For example, in 1621 a devastating flood, comparable with that of January 1993, highlighted the vulnerable location of the old town of Perth, situated beside the flood plain of the Tay.

1630s to 1640s

By contrast, dryness was the dominating characteristic of the anticyclonic 1630s, and a series of dry summers occurred from 1634 to 1638. The cool conditions of the previous decade continued; midsummer westerlies remained strong. The reclamation of the Fens began in 1630 under the Earl of Bedford, who employed the Dutch engineer Vermuyden. However, the dryness of the 1630s may partly explain the Fen revolts and opposition to reclamation, when Fenmen deliberately reflooded the Bedford Level. After three dry years, 1634, 1635 and 1636, it was reported that:

> The country is ruined everywhere by an excessive drought causing the greatest suffering. Everyone declares that there is no memory of such a misfortune in England, whose usually damp climate is so changed that the trees and the land are despoiled of their verdure as if it were a most severe winter.
>
> Anon

Difficulties arose even in the western wetter parts of England, where water power was normally more than sufficient. However, the situation was soon resolved as wetness was the dominating feature of the cyclonic 1640s, with a climax in 1648. It was also a decade of increasing zonal flow, and the midsummer westerlies remained strong.

1645 to 1715: the Maunder Minimum

There were few, if any, sunspots during the years from 1645 to 1715, a period of low solar activity (the Maunder Minimum) that coincided with the coldest phase of the Little Ice Age. In order to investigate a possible link between solar activity and terrestrial climate, a series of monthly mean pressure charts was reconstructed by a team of climatologists (including the author) employing direct and proxy historical meteorological reports held in the Euro-Climhist Data Base at the University of Bern (Wanner et al. 1995). The subsequent analysis of these charts illustrated in synoptic terms for the first time how rapid circulation changes involving the advection of both tropical maritime and polar continental airstreams had brought about many of the extreme climatic events of this period.

1650 to 1700: continental interlude

Cold, often northeasterly, winters, warm summers and dry springs during the continental 1650s were indicative of enhanced blocking. Incidentally, the spread of skating into England at this time may have been due not only to the severe winters but also to an admiration of the Dutch way of life. The return of warm dry summers was reflected by further attempts to re-establish viticulture, but late changeable springs and moist autumns lowered expectations. Because of the dry conditions that mostly prevailed during this decade, many springs and streams dried up, and the risk of fires again increased. The link between dryness and outbreak of fires was particularly notable in mainland Europe: in 1654, for example, even marshes in Hungary were burning.

1660s

The continental types of the 1650s appear, after a short break, to have continued into the 1660s. One of the features of this decade seems to have been a notable frequency of thunderstorms, since reports of their violent effects were quite common. Winters were cold and dry, springs showery and autumns dry. In London the 1660s were noted for fogs, but this was probably due to an increased use of coal rather than being indicative of a particularly anticyclonic decade, although there appears to have been a decrease in windiness. The phrase, 'to carry coals to Newcastle' occurs for the first time during this decade, and in his 1661 pamphlet, *Fumifugium: Or the Inconvenience of the Aer, and Smoak of London Dissipated*, John Evelyn wrote that a hellish and dismal cloud of sea-coal hangs perpetually over London.

A group of continental-type years with cold dry winters and mainly warm dry summers prevailed in England from about 1663 to about 1669. Warm summers also appear to have been a feature of the 1660s in Scotland, where a succession of fine seasons occurred from about 1663, notably in 1668, when the harvest was described as the best in Scotland for 60 years.

1664 to 1665: the Great Plague of London

Although London had for some time been almost free from bubonic plague, an intense outbreak, spread from Holland, occurred in the autumn of 1664. By May 1665 the epidemic had become more noticeable, and although the total number of reported deaths was over 68,000, many thousands more went unreported. At the time, the population of London was less than half a million, and of these two-thirds fled from the capital to escape the contagion, causing it to spread widely over the country. It was not until the cold weather of November and December 1665 that the plague abated and the refugees returned to the city.

12 September 1666: the Great Fire of London

The droughts of the 1660s had notable effects, particularly in 1666, when the weather in southeast England was warm and dry. The Thames became so low that it adversely affected the boat trade on the river, and in September the wood that many of the houses in London were built of became so dry that it only needed a spark to make it go up in flames. According to Samuel Pepys the exceptional heat and dryness of the spring and summer of 1666 were two reasons why the Great Fire of London took hold so easily on 12 September and rapidly spread, with the result that St Paul's Cathedral, together with 13,000 houses, 400 streets and over 80 churches, was burnt down.

During the summer of 1666 dry easterly winds had affected England for some time, associated with a persistent blocking high over northern Europe. This situation caused the drought in August and September that preceded the conflagration. A combination of drought and strong wind is a precondition for unintended fires. When the fire started, the easterly winds drove the flames forward and caused it to spread rapidly; the smoke cloud extended to Oxford and probably even further westward. On 12 September Pepys recorded, 'Everything, after so long a drought, proving combustible, the wind great.' It is ironic that only a week before St Paul's Cathedral was burnt down, Sir Christopher Wren had made a structural examination of the old Gothic building, which had been allowed to fall into a bad state of disrepair.

The dryness in the Breckland of East Anglia in 1668 is evident from an incident when sand from Lakenheath Warren was blown 10 km (6 miles) and blocked the Little Ouse at a place then known as Downham. To commemorate the event, the village has ever since been known as Santon Downham.

1670s

With an increase in the westerlies, a strong zonal flow generally prevailed during the 1670s, with strong midwinter and midsummer westerlies. However, a consistent picture does not emerge, with signs that both maritime and continental types were prevalent. For instance, while it was wet in the Low Countries, the absence of drainage schemes in the Fens and precautions against fires being taken in Lincolnshire from 1675 to 1682 both appear to suggest that it was probably dry in east England, because of the rain-shadow effect.

1680s

After a period of zonality in the 1670s there was a sharp decline in the westerlies during the 1680s to a more blocked or meridional mode by about 1690 with an associated abrupt deterioration in the climate. However, midwinter and midsummer westerlies remained strong. The resulting extreme conditions during the 1684 winter allowed a Frost Fair to be held on the frozen Thames.

1684: a very cold winter

Besides the characteristic features of this severe season, the winter of 1684 also stands out as one of the most remarkable in the climatic history of the British Isles due to an unusual and extensive amount of ice that drifted west along the English Channel. Belts of sea ice appeared off the coasts of both southeastern England and northern France, and it was also reported that ice lay 30–40 km (20–25 miles) off the Dutch coast. Many ports and harbours in the region were blocked by the ice, and shipping traffic was halted throughout the North Sea. The scene off the coast of Kent was graphically described by an eyewitness at the time:

> *The ice lay some miles off in the sea against Romney and that there was upon the tops of the steeples to be seen islands of ice, one to the west of the Light many miles long ... Old Quick observed some flakes to begin to come about 12 days before from eastward which increased every day and upon the fall of the tide went always towards west, which by reason of the wind never returned again ... I observed that when the wind and tide went together, then all the ice moved as fast as I could ride foot pace along by the side of it. I judge it must come from Holland or other eastern parts, which by reason of a continued easterly wind was brought this way. All ships were blocked in the harbours.*
>
> Richard Freebody, Lydd (Kent), February 1684

It is unlikely that such a large amount of drift ice could have formed independently in the North Sea, not only because of its huge quantity but also because the constant wave and current motion in that body of water would not have allowed it time to have developed to such a degree. Instead, northerly or northwesterly gales may have broken off a large mass from the main body of pack ice further north and forced it south into the northern North Sea. There, it probably broke up further and dispersed, but it would have been forced to converge and compact again by funnelling action towards the southern end of the North Sea and the Strait of Dover. A great influx of cold polar water could also have accompanied the ice, which, because of its lower salinity and density in comparison with Atlantic water, would have facilitated freezing.

1688: the Glorious Revolution

Stepping aside for a moment from the climatic story, 1688 was an extraordinary year in British history. The Catholic king, James II of the House of Stuart, was deposed by his Protestant daughter, Mary, and her Dutch husband, William of Orange. As on so many other occasions down the ages, the weather conditions in the English Channel and southern North Sea played a crucial role in determining the course of the country's history. On 29 October 1688, the Dutch fleet under William, comprising 52 men-of-war and 500 transports, set sail from Holland but soon encountered winds in an unfavourable quarter. The following day a strong westerly wind, the so-called 'Catholic wind', drove the Dutch fleet back into port; several hundred horses were lost and some men drowned, but apparently no vessels were wrecked.

Using undisclosed methods, Jesuit priests, acting as long-range weather forecasters, had promised James II that westerly winds would continue until Christmas, and at first it looked as though they might well be correct as the winds remained westerly during the following week. However, on 9 November the flow turned easterly, the so-called 'Protestant wind', and the Dutch fleet set sail again on the 11th. Two days later it passed through the Strait of Dover unmolested, as the same easterly wind kept the English fleet cooped up in the Gunfleet off the Essex coast. On 15 November, William landed at Brixham in Devon, from where he and his forces advanced with little or no opposition to London.

1690s

The Little Ice Age was at its most severe in Britain during the 1690s. Sea ice had advanced furthest south in the Atlantic; in 1695, one of the coldest years on record, Iceland was cut off for most of the year, with the ice sheet extending south as far as Shetland.

Londoners may well have enjoyed Frost Fairs, but elsewhere there was a great loss of life and many hill farms were abandoned in England; in highland Scotland the grain harvest failed for seven years between 1693 and 1700. These setbacks well illustrate that when the climate changed for the worse, the first people to suffer were those in marginal areas where the crops fail almost immediately. The number of people who died of starvation and disease in Scotland during the 1690s exceeded the death toll of the Black Death.

The low level of temperature values affected all seasons in the 1690s, but mostly winter and spring, of which nine of the ten combined seasons in this decade were extremely cold. The cooling began in the spring of 1690, after which there was an unbroken sequence in which every season was colder than average until the autumn of 1695. Warming set in during the summer of 1699 following the last of the cold years, 1698. The sharp decline in the zonal flow from the 1670s to the 1690s indicates an increased incidence of blocked or meridional circulation patterns. Mean pressure maps for the Januarys and Julys of the 1690s indicate that the blocking of the westerlies mostly occurred in the winters of that decade.

This was a most unfavourable decade for weather, in which cold and often wet conditions gave rise to several food crises. One of these in mainland Europe was among the worst famines in the 17th century: the failed harvest of 1693 caused a disastrous dearth in which millions died of starvation in France and neighbouring countries.

In general, while pressure values were initially below normal over much of mainland Europe, especially in the east, they were higher than normal in the Iceland–Greenland and north Scandinavian regions, suggesting a dominance of continental types over the British Isles; later in the decade the circulation appears to have become partly cyclonic maritime. Thus, while dry cold winters and warm summers occurred during the early 1690s, conditions became more generally wet from 1695.

The 1690s, together with the 1430s, was one of the coldest decades on record, and it included a decline in the westerlies (estimated average of 77 westerly situations per year) and possibly an approach to glaciation in the Scottish Highlands. Like the 1590s (a recession decade), the 1690s were years of scarcity mainly due to cold late springs. Notable low temperatures during the period 1694–1698 may have been due to a reduction of solar radiation by a volcanic dust veil.

> The last half-dozen years of William's reign (1693–1700) had been the 'dear years' of Scottish memory, six consecutive seasons of disastrous weather when the harvests would not ripen. The country had not the means to buy food from abroad, so the people had laid themselves down and died. Many parishes had been reduced to a half or a third of their inhabitants.
>
> G. M. Trevelyan, *Illustrated English Social History*, 1966

These disastrous years were long remembered as the 'ill' or 'hungry' years. A run of wet summers and early and severe winters prevented grain from ripening and blighted crops. As a result, food supplies failed or could only be procured at exorbitant prices. The poorer classes suffered intensely and many died from lack of bread. A pestilence seems to have succeeded the famine. Fodder was as scarce as grain, and thousands of cattle perished. The cool wet summer of 1695, with its widespread harvest failures, was one of the most wretched seasons experienced in Scotland, and it may even have contributed to the movement that eventually led to Union with England in 1707. In Ireland, as the potato had been introduced to meet the problem of a country where summers were generally too cool and wet for corn to ripen properly, these disasters appear to have been less severe. Nevertheless, famine was recorded in Ireland during 1690 due to unfavourable conditions.

There was an increased frequency of severe storms in the late 17th century and early 18th century. Besides the Great Storm of 1703 there were at least eight others that affected the British Isles between 1688 and 1702, all in the autumn and winter seasons. This increased intensity of storms was probably linked to the greater amount of potential energy in an enhanced thermal gradient of sea-surface temperatures between Iceland and the Atlantic Ocean south of 50–55° N and the Bay of Biscay. It is remarkable that two of the most outstanding anomalies of the period, the Great Winter of 1684 and the Great Storm of 1703, were no doubt linked with processes in the ocean, in particular, the formation of colder sea-surface temperature between Iceland and the British Isles.

The warm dry summer of 1699, the first of several favourable summers after seven successive cool summers, heralded the warming trend that set in during the early 18th century.

1700 TO 1740: WARM DRY INTERLUDE

The record of the prevailing southwesterly winds over England shows that following a decline in the late 17th century the flow increased around 1700 to culminate in a peak during the 1730s. This is in accord with variations in the CET series that are generally related to the frequency of southwesterly winds. When the prevailing southwesterly winds were at low ebb in the 1690s there was a high frequency of cold winters, namely 1691, 1692, 1694, 1695, 1697 and 1698, whereas in the 1730s, when the westerly flow was more dominant, only one severe winter occurred, in 1731. Furthermore, although there were no warm summers in the 1690s, no less than 11 occurred in the first four decades of the 18th century.

The rapid warming that occurred around 1700 well illustrates the remarkable shifts that can occur in the climate of the British Isles within a decade or so, from one mode of circulation to another. By the 1730s, only 40 years after one of the coldest decades on record, a remarkable peak of warmth was attained. Whereas there had been six cold winters in England during the 1690s, only four occurred during the following four decades. However, after the 1730s there was an abrupt reversion of temperature levels that resulted in conditions only a little less severe than those in the late 17th century. This sharp downturn was ushered in by the very cold winter of 1740, which affected much of Europe from the British Isles in the west to the Ukraine in the east.

1700s

A reminder of the earlier chill of the 1690s occurred during the 1709 winter, with January being one of the coldest winter months on record; wintry conditions were more severe and continued longer than in any year since 1698. The combined volcanic dust veil from the Vesuvius, Santorini and Fujiyama eruptions in 1707 was most likely responsible for the large negative temperature anomaly during this severe winter, which well illustrates how unpredictable volcanic activity can temporarily reverse a warming trend or intensify an ongoing cooling phase. Extremely low temperatures in England and mainland Europe were related to a blocking anticyclone over the Gulf of Bothnia that caused a very cold easterly polar airstream to affect most of Europe; Venetian lagoons were frozen and the Baltic remained ice-bound until early April. By way of contrast, temperatures in Greenland were above average because of a warm southwesterly tropical airstream, illustrating the so-called seesaw effect in winter temperatures between Greenland and central Europe.

Two years after the Union with England (1707), harvest failures in Scotland produced famine comparable to the 'dear years' of the 1690s. Farms and hamlets were abandoned, and villages filled with beggars. Until agricultural methods improved, such a disaster could always result from just one season of bad weather in northern Britain.

1710s to 1720s

Anticyclonic blocking of the westerlies is inferred during the 1710s, although the midsummer westerlies remained strong. With an estimated average of 80 westerly situations per year, a fairly normal zonal flow prevailed during the 1720s; midwinter and midsummer westerlies were strong.

1730s

The circulation over the British Isles gradually became more progressive during the early 18th century and attained a peak of zonality in the 1730s. With an estimated average of 98 westerly situations per year, zonal flow increased in this decade to a maximum comparable to that of the 1930s; midwinter and midsummer westerlies were also strong. One of the warmest decades on record, the 1730s, like the 1990s, were notable for exceptionally warm conditions – well indicated by the absence, apart from 1731, of any cold winters.

1740 TO THE EARLY 1770S: LITTLE ICE AGE, PHASE II

1740s

An approach to glaciation occurred in the Scottish Highlands during the easterly continental decade of the 1740s; the exceptional warmth of the 1730s had been abruptly terminated by the very cold winter of 1740. During a great frost, *bliain an áir* ('year of the slaughter'), in December (1739), thousands died in Ireland, stored winter food supplies were destroyed, and the cold drought and harvest failure of 1740 precipitated mass starvation. It is estimated that by the time the crisis came to an end in 1741, a higher proportion of the Irish population had died or emigrated than during the potato famine of the 1840s.

With an estimated average 81 westerly situations per year, the 1740s were notable for the onset of a sharp decline in the westerlies (the third such event in the England wind record from the mid 14th century); nevertheless, the midsummer zonal flow remained strong. In Scotland there are signs of more frequent snow and frost around this time. As the predominating winds were often easterly in the 1740s, it is certainly likely that snow occurred more frequently in eastern Scotland and rain less frequently in the west.

The high incidence of cold winters and droughts indicates more frequent blocking. This was an exceptionally dry decade, with the years from 1740 to 1743 being the driest four-year period in the instrumental record, 1741 and 1743 being comparable in dryness to 1921 (the driest year on record in the 20th century).

1750s

The rapid decline of the westerlies around 1750 to 1770 was similar to that which occurred in the 1950s.

The climax of the Little Ice Age occurred around 1750, when glaciers in the Alps, Scandinavia and Iceland reached their maximum extent during postglacial times. With an estimated average of 91 westerly situations per year, the 1750s, a decade of transition, witnessed a slight increase in the zonal flow; the westerlies were generally at about normal strength in winter and strong in midsummer.

1760s to early 1770s

With an estimated average of 83 westerly situations per year, the wet 1760s witnessed a return to the downward tendency in the westerly flow that attained an absolute record minimum in the early 1800s; midwinter westerly flow was also fairly weak in the 1760s, although midwinter westerlies remained strong.

An abrupt change in the circulation some time after 1770 brought the second phase of the Little Ice Age to an end.

1773 TO 1781: BRIEF WARM INTERLUDE

The years 1773–1781 represent a short but clearly defined warm interlude between two severe phases of the Little Ice Age. Nevertheless, there were six cold winters, and although the midsummer westerlies were strong, midwinter westerlies remained fairly weak or at normal strength.

With an estimated average of 57 westerly situations per year, the decline in zonal flow continued during the 1770s; this decade was essentially one of transition from the cyclonic situations that prevailed in about 1770 to anticyclonic situations around 1780. The year 1774 was the last in a series of wet years from the 1760s, and during this period the water table of the chalk uplands in south England had risen considerably:

> *The land springs, which are called lavants, break out much on the downs of Sussex, Hampshire and Wiltshire ... Land springs have never obtained more since the memory of man than during that period [the past decade or so] ... such a run of wet seasons, a century or two ago, would, I am persuaded, have occasioned a famine.*
> Gilbert White, Selborne (Hampshire), 1774

The following year Gilbert White's brother-in-law, Thomas Barker, reflected on some notable climatic variations he had experienced during the 18th century:

> *For a good many years past, since the seasons have been in general wet, the nature of east winds has been very different from what it formerly was. For several years after the great frost in 1740 there were many northeasterly winds in spring, but they were generally cold and dry, stopping vegetation; but for the last ten years the east winds have been often very wet; many of the greatest summer floods came by rains out of that quarter; and many times it came rain almost as certainly as the wind turned east.*
> Thomas Barker, Lyndon Hall (Rutland), 1775

The summers of the period 1772–1781 were remarkably warm in Europe, and glaciers were generally in retreat. This short but clearly defined period of warmth encouraged some positive developments, including an economic boom and the start of Alpine tourism (Fig. 46).

FIG 46. Eighteenth-century tourists viewing the Mer de Glace glacier near Mont Blanc in the French Alps.

In England, the warm dry summers centred on 1775 were long remembered, and if this trend had persisted viticulture on a commercial scale might have been possible again in the southeastern parts of the country. The lightness and elegance of fashion may also have been a reflection of these more favourable conditions, although the change in clothing from wool to cotton was also linked to the rise of the East India Company and other changes in world trade. In mainland Europe, abundant harvests relieved previous food shortages and brought an end to the emigration boom to the New World, which culminated in 1774–1775. On the downside, the very warm summers of this period led to rare outbreaks of malaria in Scotland.

1782 TO 1800: LATE 18TH-CENTURY RECESSION

During the period of 40 years or so from about 1780, there was a southward displacement of the warming waters of the North Atlantic Drift, which, unlike today, tended to turn away southwards before reaching the coasts of west Europe. This effect was no doubt associated with the corresponding shift in the latitude of the prevailing westerlies. Another factor that may have contributed to the cooling trend was the rather abrupt transition from very high to low solar activity following the major sunspot maximum in 1787.

1780s

With an estimated average of 54 westerly situations per year, the notable decline in zonal flow continued during the 1780s. However, while midwinter westerlies were also fairly weak, midsummer westerlies remained strong. The decrease in westerly situations during the 1780s was compensated by increased blocking, especially in early spring and early winter; a cluster of cold Marches and the generally early onset of wintry conditions in autumn were symptomatic features of this enhanced blocking action.

Placed at a critical phase during the closing stages of the Little Ice Age, the 1780s contain a number of outstanding temperature and rainfall extremes. Then, as now, an apparent increase in the variability of climate from season to season and year to year was causing concern. It appears that due to increased volcanic activity from about 1780, repeatedly replenished dust veils ejected into the upper atmosphere had the effect of prolonging the Little Ice Age into the first half of the 19th century, whereas purely meteorological trends suggest there would have been an earlier reversal to warmer conditions. Like today, it seems that the climate of the late 18th century had entered a less stable mode, owing to a complex interaction of various factors.

Returning to the present, it appears that man-made warming, due to the growth of industrial-produced heat and an increasing emission of carbon dioxide, is modulating to an arguably lesser or greater degree a long-term cooling trend attributable to natural causes. By showing that even without the effect of man, atmospheric behaviour can unexpectedly and abruptly shift from a benign to an unfavourable mode, the 1780s provide a valuable case study for today's concern about present and future climate.

1781

This was the last in a run of four successive favourable years for agriculture, 1778–1781, marked, for example, by a series of good wine harvests in France. In England John Fenton (Suffolk) recorded, 'grapes in ordinary places were ripe in August, the harvest was began betimes, and ended by the time in some other years that they had but just begun.' In Scotland, due to the collapse of imports from America, the growing of tobacco on a commercial basis was attempted in southern areas during these favourable seasons. However, in view of what was in store, 1781 can be regarded as a turning point both for climate and agriculture.

1782 to 1789

Although much of the 1781 grain crop was still in hand, widespread alarm broke out in Scotland when it became clear early in the summer of 1782 that owing to late bad harvests the crops would be inadequate to feed people over much of the country; grain prices rose by over 40 per cent and committees were formed in various counties to estimate the probable harvest and take steps to supplement it. In December shearers in Scotland ploughed through snow to cut frost-blackened unripe oats, but as it became clear before Christmas that crops would not suffice to feed the population, a million pounds was expended to buy grain from England.

As in 1782, conditions in 1783 were unfavourable for farmers. However, rather than cool wet conditions, harvest failures this time were due to crops being damaged by a volcanic dust fallout and heavy thunderstorms in July; also there was a lack of seed-corn owing to the disastrous harvest of 1782. In June, volcanic ash emitted from an enormous lava eruption at Laki, Iceland, produced an extensive dust veil; carried along by upper winds, this volcanic material affected much of Europe, including the British Isles, obscuring the sun and moon during the summer and autumn of 1783. This extraordinary dust haze caused great concern and speculation, and global temperatures fell by about 1 °C (1.8 °F) during the two or three years following 1783. Benjamin Franklin suggested that the resulting reduction in solar radiation was the reason for the very cold winter of 1783–1784:

> During several of the summer months of the year 1783, when the effect of the sun's rays to heat the earth in these northern regions should have been greatest, there existed a constant fog over all Europe, and great part of North America. This fog was of a permanent nature; it was dry, and the rays of the sun seemed to have little effect towards dissipating it, as they easily do a moist fog, arising from water. They were indeed rendered so faint in passing through it, that when collected in the focus of a burning glass, they would scarce kindle brown paper. Of course, their summer effect in heating the earth was exceedingly diminished. Hence the surface was early frozen. Hence the first snow remained on it unmelted, and received continual additions. Hence the air was more chilled, and the winds more severely cold. Hence perhaps the winter of 1783–4, was more severe, than any that had happened for many years.
>
> Benjamin Franklin, Passy, May 1784

The so-called 'Ill Years of 1782 and 1783' ruined many farmers in northern Britain, with some being induced to emigrate to America. Food riots occurred in some places, and distilleries were attacked in Scotland.

Another of the frequent extremes in the 1780s was a prolonged drought from August 1784 to July 1785. This was the driest period of any consecutive 12 months on record until the drought of 1975–1976. The classification of daily weather maps for the period shows that the drought was characterised by an exceptional decrease in the westerly type, combined with increased frequencies of the northwesterly, northerly, easterly and anticyclonic types.

> *For it continued a remarkable dry time all spring [1785], so that grass was very short, and hay very scarce, yet the grain continued particularly fine coloured, and eared well, though some of the winter grain was rather thin; yet these were much brought on by some refreshing showers in May and June, which were enough to freshen things but not to make much grass. During this drought there were great numbers of little whirlwinds, sometimes many in a day.*
>
> Thomas Barker, Lyndon Hall (Rutland)

1790s

With an estimated average of 55 westerly situations per year, the overall decline in zonal flow continued during the 1790s, although midwinter westerlies increased in strength.

1800 TO THE 1890s: LITTLE ICE AGE, PHASE III

The third and final phase of the Little Ice Age began in the early 19th century and continued to 1890. Increases in Arctic sea ice, glacial advances in the Alps and Scandinavia, and a near approach to glaciation in Scotland during the 1830s, all indicated a return to the more severe conditions of the Little Ice Age. It is also notable that the early decades of this period coincided with the Dalton Minimum (1790–1830), a 40-year span of low solar activity.

1800s

With an estimated average of 47 westerly situations per year, the decline in zonal flow over the previous four decades reached an absolute record minimum in the 1800s. Frequent blocking gave rise to several extreme seasons, with dryness as the outstanding feature. A ten-year series of cool summers began in 1809.

1810s

With its high frequency of cold seasons (most likely intensified by the increased amount of volcanic dust in the atmosphere), the 1810s marked a nadir of chill during the last severe phase in the Little Ice Age. Glacial advances restarted in the Alps, and there was an approach to glaciation in the Scottish Highlands. Charles Dickens was a boy during this exceptionally cold decade, and the frequent white Christmases of the 1810s would later feature in his books.

The 1810s comprised the coldest decade in England since the 1690s (one of the most severe in the Little Ice Age). With an estimated average of 64 westerly situations per year there was a slight increase in the still weak zonal flow, while midwinter westerlies were at normal strength, and midsummer westerlies were strong.

1816: the year without a summer

During this cold wet year conditions were possibly severe enough for incipient glaciation in the Scottish Highlands. Low temperatures and heavy rainfall led to widespread crop failures and famine.

The Tambora eruption during April 1815 in Indonesia and its resulting volcanic dust veil affected global climate, with mid-latitude regions of the northern hemisphere, such as western Europe and eastern North America, being much cooler than usual the following year. 1816 has become well known in the history of climate as 'The Year Without a Summer'.

There is a striking parallel with the 1780s, when the annual mean temperatures in mid latitudes fell by 1.3 °C (2.3 °F) after volcanic eruptions in Iceland and Japan in 1783. However, there appear to be two major points of difference in the timing and length of cooling following tropical and high-latitude eruptions. It seems that, unlike in 1815–1816, the cooling signal in the mid 1780s was strongest not in the year immediately following the eruptions but in 1785, two years after the event. Nevertheless, there were some notable similarities in the circulation patterns of the two cold years, 1816 and 1785. The marked increase in cyclonicity over the British Isles in July 1816 is in accordance with the finding that there is a tendency for the Icelandic low to be displaced southwards over the British Isles during the first July after a major eruption, resulting in typically cool wet summers over the region. However, the volcanic signal apparently soon died away, with temperatures recovering to above normal values by 1818. On the other hand, after high-latitude eruptions such as those of 1783, pressure and related temperature anomalies tend to persist longer.

The circulation over the British Isles during the summer of 1816 was dominated by cyclonic and northwesterly weather types, and the Azores high that often extends northeastwards over Europe during good summers hardly affected the region at all. Polar maritime airstreams, associated with quasi-stationary depressions over central Europe, were advected further south than usual and, as in 1316 and 1675, the British Isles experienced unusually cool wet conditions.

However, during brief fine spells exceptionally good visibilities were reported due to the rain-washed clear atmosphere.

During the whole of this singular summer the atmosphere has been particularly clear. This evening I observed from the Tower a range of lofty hills stretching eastwards and apparently forming two divisions, which I had never seen before.

David Pennant, Downing (Flintshire), 31 July 1816

The year 1816 saw one of the worst harvests on record, and the autumn was marked by famine. Due to the dire conditions there was a mood of social unrest in the country: in rural areas farmers were under threat and rickyards were set on fire as a protest against any remedy for the distress; in the towns there was an outbreak of machine-breaking even more violent than that of the better-known Luddite movement four years earlier.

The wretched conditions also affected people in East Anglia and were recorded in the local annals. For example, in May, farm workers in Soham (Cambridgeshire) and Downham Market (Norfolk) rioted. The Soham confrontation was the most serious, with a large group of workers clashing with soldiers. Several were killed, five men were hanged and many more transported to Australia. Besides farm workers, the urban poor also suffered. In Norwich, for instance, working people, many of them weavers struggling to make a living in the economic downturn, rioted over the cost of bread and took direct action to seize flour. 'A crowd of people gathered in the Market Place, threw fire balls and broke the windows of the Guildhall. They then broke into the New Mills ... and carried some away in sacks'. Twice in the next few days the Riot Act was read and the Royal Dragoons were called out of their barracks to disperse the crowd (Sargent 2010).

After a week's continuous rain, which greatly impeded the hay harvest, a severe thunderstorm occurred [18 July]. On the 31st the crops were beaten down, acres of turnips were washed away and in several villages the lanes were full of water. On August 12 there was another heavy rain, and on the 31st a hurricane blew, wrecking many colliers between Blakeney and Mundesley. The rains continued to the month of October, when, in consequence of the low lying lands being under water, all hopes were abandoned for the favourable termination of the harvest.

Peter Sargent, 'A moment in time', 2010

1820s

In the 1820s with an estimated average of 60 westerly situations per year, the zonal flow remained weak. Although midwinter westerlies were also very weak, midsummer westerlies were fairly strong. There was a large variability from year to year but with generally warm springs and autumns. An outbreak of malaria occurred in Scotland due to summer warmth. It may be no coincidence that Charles Macintosh invented the waterproof material that bears his name during the milder wetter 1820s.

1830s

With an estimated average of 56 westerly situations per year, the zonal flow remained very weak in the colder 1830s. Although the midsummer westerlies remained fairly strong, an easterly flow partly replaced the weaker midwinter westerlies. Due to the cool summers a near approach to glaciation again occurred in the Scottish Highlands, and there were glacial advances in the Alps and Norway. The notable series of cold years from 1836 to 1840 may have been due to the presence of a lingering volcanic dust veil caused by the eruption of Coseguina, Nicaragua, in 1835.

1840s

With an estimated average of 63 westerly situations per year, a slight increase in the zonal flow occurred in the maritime 1840s. Although the midwinter westerlies remained fairly weak, the midsummer zonal flow was strong. Further afield, there was a remarkably ice-free period in Iceland, and it may be no coincidence that cod moved north to the Davis Strait and the population of Greenland increased.

1846 to 1851: potato blight

By the 1840s the Irish population was almost totally reliant on the potato as its staple food crop, which proved to be catastrophic. Ireland had been one of the first countries in Europe to adopt the potato in the 17th century; the import from South America yielded four times as much carbohydrate per acre as wheat. It was also resilient to climatic stress and much more reliable than the then ubiquitous rye, which was often afflicted by ergot blight. The potato had been an important factor in Ireland's prosperity, as it allowed the population to increase at a rate greater than that of its European neighbours during the 17th and 18th centuries.

Potato blight arrived in Europe from the Americas in 1845 and spread rapidly from Flanders across western Europe, reaching Ireland in September. The weather, with high temperatures and abundant rainfall, was the key to the spread, but Ireland's peculiar dependence on the potato left its native population uniquely vulnerable, since there was no other source of food. While the poor only grew blighted potatoes the English landlords continued to export wheat from their estates. Between 1846 and 1851 the potato famine raged in Ireland, and an estimated one million people died from starvation or disease brought on by hunger.

1850s

With an estimated average of 79 westerly situations per year, an increasing zonal flow replaced the easterlies during the 1850s; besides the already strong midsummer westerlies, the midwinter westerlies also became stronger. Continental types with frequent blocking had mainly dominated the circulation during the early 1850s, but a change to maritime types occurred following the 1855 cold winter. While cool summers in England were not conducive to viticulture, a rare outbreak of malaria in Scotland was indicative of local summer warmth.

Throughout the 1840s and 1850s, the population of Ireland was greatly reduced, first by famine, which lasted from 1845 to 1849, and then by migration. The population diminished from 8.5 million to around 3 million during the 1850s, a figure from which it has never really recovered; the total population of the island today is about 6.2 million.

1860s

The enhanced zonality in the circulation that began in the late 1850s continued into the 1860s. The associated advection of milder conditions into mainland Europe caused Alpine glaciers to recede and appeared to signal the close of the Little Ice Age. With an average of 98 westerly situations per year, the ongoing increasing zonal flow accelerated during the 1860s, with moderate to strong midwinter and midsummer westerlies.

1870s

Although midwinter westerlies were fairly strong and midsummer westerlies remained strong, there was a slight decline in the general zonal flow in the 1870s, with an average of 87 westerly situations per year. As a result, blocking, with quasi-stationary cyclonic weather types, dominated the circulation over the British Isles.

During this mostly wet cyclonic decade the frequent rain caused an agricultural crisis from which, as far as corn production is concerned, Britain has never really recovered. Despite some war-time incentives in the early 1940s, the decreased acreage under cultivation has remained and continues today, with agricultural land and green-field sites now under threat from burgeoning urban developments.

1880s

With an average of 85 westerly situations per year, there was a slight decrease in the zonal flow during the continental 1880s. Anticyclonic situations tended to increase, resulting in more frequent blocking; midwinter and midsummer westerlies remained fairly strong. Although the chill of the Little Ice Age was thought at the time to have ended, renewed cold that had developed in late 1879 persisted into the 1880s. A near approach to glaciation occurred in the Scottish Highlands, and glaciers re-advanced in the Alps. Very cold winters were a notable feature of the decade, and hundreds died of hypothermia in the London slums. The rather abrupt transition from very high to low solar activity following the major sunspot maximum in 1871 may have contributed to this cooling trend.

The resemblance between the continental decades of the 1880s, 1850s and 1810s formed the main evidence for the rediscovery by the German climatologist Eduard Brückner, in 1890, of the 35-year climatic cycle that had been first proposed by Francis Bacon in the early 17th century. However, due to the warming trend that had set in during the early 20th century, the anticipated cold wave in the 1920s did not materialise. A notable 13-year series of dry years began in 1882.

1890s

Although on average there were 88 westerly situations per year, low index patterns continued to dominate during the early 1890s, giving rise to notably dry anticyclonic conditions extending from Ireland to Siberia. The initially weak zonal circulation caused concern that the severe conditions of the Little Ice Age were about to return, especially with the experience of the very cold winter of 1895, when the Thames in London became partly frozen. However, midwinter and midsummer westerlies remained fairly strong, and eventually milder winters, heralding the early 20th-century warm period, began to occur from 1896 as high index situations associated with maritime types started to increasingly affect the British Isles.

EARLY 20TH-CENTURY WARMING: 1900 TO 1939

The warming that occurred in the first four decades of the 20th century reached a peak during the late 1930s. It is of interest that this period of warming coincided with an increasing transparency of the atmosphere as volcanic dust from the eruptions that occurred in the 19th century had gradually cleared out of the air. However, we must be cautious in assuming a simple relationship between volcanic influence and temperature trend, since renewed cooling from about 1940 began when there had not been any significant volcanic eruptions since 1912, and the cooling continued for another 20 years or so before there was any real increase of volcanic dust. Similarly, today, the notion of simply linking one cause and one effect – increasing carbon dioxide emissions and global warming – must be treated with caution.

The growing season lengthened by two weeks during this favourable period compared with that of the mid 19th century, with last spring frosts arriving earlier and first autumn freezes later. After 1925, Alpine glaciers receded from valley floors into the mountains.

1900s

During the 1900s there were, on average, 97 westerly situations per year. The zonal flow was initially normal, but together with strengthening midwinter westerlies it became stronger from 1903. This effect was linked with a marked change in the circulation from continental to maritime types during the early years of the decade. For instance, while 1901 was a continental easterly dry year, 1903 was a cyclonic maritime wet year. A well-marked series of wet years occurred from the late 1900s to 1919.

1910s

The cyclonic decade of the 1910s was exceptionally wet, with an average of 99 westerly situations per year. However, in 1911, the frequency of Atlantic blocking highs affecting the circulation over the British Isles was exceptionally high, and the warm dry summer of that year, the so-called 'Halcyon Summer', enjoyed by many, was one of the hottest summers on record. But there were downside effects to the extreme conditions. For instance, in London alone 2,500 children died of heat-related illnesses; widespread riots and strikes broke out, with the worst coinciding with the peak of the August heat wave; and chaos at docks and railway stations raised fears of food supplies as strikes threatened to paralyse the whole country.

1912: a very cool wet summer

This year saw one of the coolest wettest summers on record, with a wet June and one of the coolest Augusts recorded, 12.9 °C (55 °F). These exceptional conditions were linked with two factors: the depletion of solar radiation by a volcanic dust veil (skies were not normally blue even in fine weather), and a negative sea surface temperature anomaly in the western North Atlantic. During April and May an unusually large ice field was reported in the Labrador Current off the

Newfoundland Banks, and 395 icebergs were counted south of 48° N, compared with an average of 83. The icebergs also spread much further south than usual; on 14 April the *Titanic* struck one of these icebergs at 41° 46′ N and sank with the loss of many lives.

1915: First World War Flanders mud

In 1915 Atlantic depressions, associated with the polar front that was lying further south than usual, tracked more or less eastwards along latitude 50° N. The resulting exceptionally heavy rainfall over England and nearby mainland Europe, and the disruptive military operations, were major factors that led to the infamous mud in Flanders on the Western Front during the First World War. The negative precipitation anomaly that caused the extreme wet conditions may have been related to a lingering volcanic dust veil caused by the eruption of Katmai, Alaska, in 1912.

1918: a cool summer

As in 1912, the cool summer of 1918 was preceded by an unusually large amount of sea ice in the North Atlantic.

1920s

With a decadal average of 109 westerly situations per year (the highest on record) and strong midwinter and midsummer westerlies, an intense zonal flow prevailed during the maritime 1920s. A high incidence of severe storms and maritime types dominated the circulation during the early years of the decade.

1921: agricultural crisis

Weather-related agricultural problems during this mostly wet decade were compounded by the so-called 'Great Betrayal' when, in 1921, price guarantees for farmers were abolished by the government. Although the Agriculture Act had been passed in December 1920 to regulate cereal prices and maintain minimum pay for farm workers it was partly repealed in July 1921. As a result, the price of wheat fell by 48 per cent within one year and the minimum pay for farm workers was abandoned. The fall in wages caused great distress in the agricultural community, and many farm workers left the land for good to seek employment in the towns and cities.

1930s

With a decadal average of 98 westerly situations per year, a normal to high zonal flow prevailed in the maritime 1930s, a comparatively dry decade. The midwinter and midsummer westerlies continued to be generally strong, but the frequency of blocking situations affecting the circulation over the British Isles in the three years 1939–1941 was exceptionally high. Further afield, the 1930s is well known in climatic history for the long drought that, together with severe dust storms, caused the catastrophic Dust Bowl in the Great Plains of the United States. North America had experienced a prolonged period of westerlies during the decade, and Midwestern states in the rain shadow of the Rocky Mountains had little or no rain.

MID 20TH-CENTURY COOLING: 1940 TO 1979

Following the warming during the first four decades of the 20th century, cold winters set in during the early 1940s, resulting in the whole of Britain being covered with a thick blanket of snow for the first time since the end of the Little Ice Age. This was a timely reminder of how an unexpected bout of severe weather can disrupt transport, power supplies and communications even in more modern times. The rather abrupt transition from very high to low solar activity following major sunspot maxima in 1947 and 1957 may have contributed to this cooling trend.

1940s

With a decadal average of 95 westerly situations per year, the zonal flow during the 1940s can be generally termed normal; the midsummer westerlies certainly remained strong, and blocking situations were exceptional rare in 1945. However, the decade was notable for several exceptional features: marked variations in the westerlies; a sharp return to low index situations; a weak midwinter zonal flow; the highest decadal frequency of blizzards on record since 1880; and three consecutive severe winters, 1940, 1941 and 1942, an unparalleled sequence in the known climatic records at that time. There was a striking decrease in the frequency of blocking highs during the three years 1948–1950, during which period progressive situations were predominant.

1950s

Although with a decadal average of 90 westerly situations per year the overall zonal flow was normal, a sharp decline in the westerlies set in during the 1950s. This was the fourth such minimum in the more or less 200-year oscillation of the long-term wind record back to the mid 14th century. Nevertheless, midwinter westerlies remained fairly strong throughout the decade.

31 January 1953: the Great Storm

At the time of this storm, the associated storm surge and sea flood were events which were considered only to recur on average every 100 years or so, but perceptions have changed since then, and although sea defences have been reinforced, eastern coastal dwellers today are under a real threat, living on borrowed time. The 1953 sea flood is widely considered to have been the worst ever natural disaster to affect England, but statements of this kind need to be carefully weighed against comparable events in the historical record presented in this volume, together with current analysis showing that severe storms affecting the British Isles have become more frequent in recent decades. Today the UK Meteorological Office classifies a rise of just 60 cm (2 feet) as a surge event, and the Environment Agency issues flood warnings if the surge coincides with a high tide.

1960s

With a decadal average of 80 westerly situations per year, the late 20th-century decline in zonality generally accelerated during the 1960s, apart from 1961 (104 westerly days) and 1967 (102 westerly days). The decade also witnessed the coldest winters and the highest number of blizzards since the 1880s. Severe storms, on the other hand, were less frequent than usual. The adverse effects that can occur in very cold winters were well illustrated by those that developed during the 1963 severe winter, when, for instance, the demand for fuel, heating appliances, warm clothing and antifreeze strained productive capacity in the industries concerned and often defeated the suppliers. The expansion of demand in these activities was, however, more than offset by a contraction in other fields of work. In the economy as a whole the seasonal peak of unemployment during winter was far above normal.

1970s

With an average of 73 westerly situations per year, the mid 20th-century decline in zonal flow continued throughout the 1970s. An increased incidence of extremes and inter-annual variability was particularly pronounced during the decade. Further afield, it appears that 1975 marked the onset of the late 20th-century period of global warming. Earlier, it was even being suggested that due to the cooling trend in the 1960s and early 1970s the current interglacial was giving way to a new ice age. However, the very warm dry summer of 1976 gave a strong signal that perhaps the trend was being reversed (Fig. 47).

LATE 20TH-CENTURY WARMING:
1980 TO THE LATE 1990S

1980s

With an average of 72 westerly situations per year, the mid 20th-century decline in zonal flow continued into the 1980s. The exceptionally low values of 52 and 54 westerly days in 1980 and 1987, respectively, rank as the second and third lowest annual values in the record from 1861 to 2000. Following the cool years of 1985 and 1986, an upward trend in temperatures was detected over the British Isles during the latter part of the decade, bringing the region into step with the now evident period of global warming. From 1988 a series of mainly mild winters occurred due to markedly increased sea-surface temperatures in the waters surrounding the British Isles. The Baltic Sea, North Sea and waters to the south

FIG 47. Dried-up pond due to a prolonged drought. (Nigel Cattlin/FLPA)

and west of the British Isles had become warmer than usual to a considerable depth, while sea-surface temperature anomalies south of Iceland and Greenland remained negative. The increased sea-surface temperature gradient was transferred, in part, to the overlying atmosphere, causing the jet stream to flow along a path somewhat further north than normal. This, in turn, led to Atlantic depressions tracking north of the British Isles and persistent anticyclones near or just south of the region. This had been the predominant circulation pattern associated with the warm dry summers, both in this decade and up to 1991, especially those of 1989 and 1990.

1990s

The 1990s were the warmest decade on record. However, embedded in the overall warming trend there were some notable anomalies. Despite a high count of 102 westerly situations in 1990, the zonal flow over the British Isles continued at low ebb, with an average of only 76 westerly situations per year. Further afield, the Pinatubo (Philippines) volcanic eruption in June 1991 caused the greatest impact on global climate since the eruption of Krakatau in 1883; this effect included marked cooling in the northern hemisphere during 1992 and 1993. The situation which had prevailed during the late 1980s ended in the late summer of 1992 as the jet stream migrated to a more southerly track. This allowed depressions with less settled weather types to move east across or even south of the British Isles. An abrupt change in the circulation from high to low index ushered in the severe winter of 1996; during this year only 50½ westerly situations were recorded (the lowest annual value on record since 1861). The warmth of the 1990s attained a peak in 1998 when, for example, temperatures over England regularly rose to 12–15 °C (54–59 °F) in February. Since then, the late 20th-century warming trend seems to have stalled or even reversed, and present predictions of future climate are in a state of flux.

CHAPTER 10

Climatic Change: Taking the Long View

Climate is determined by a balance among numerous interacting processes in the oceans and the atmosphere and at the land surface ... If we are to assess the possibility and nature of man-made climatic change, we must understand how the physical processes produce the present climate and also how past changes of climate, clearly not man-made, have occurred.

Stephen Schneider & Lynne Mesirow,
The Genesis Strategy: Climate and Global Survival, 1976

GLOBAL WARMING?

W E LIVE AT A TIME OF LIVELY DEBATE ABOUT THE CLIMATE of our planet, with the subject of global warming at the top of the agenda. In the British Isles, for example, values of the CET series reached their highest levels on record during the late 20th century, with mild winters in the 1990s being a notable feature of this warming. However, temperature values at the turn of the century are suggesting that the warming trend may have stalled or even reversed. Also, taking a broader view, the recent exceptionally temperate conditions experienced in the British Isles have been offset by extremely cold winters and record snowfalls in other parts of the world such as North America, where no comparable trend of rising temperatures has, so far, been detected. Furthermore, satellite and radiosonde observations do not appear to signal any clear tendency towards either warming or cooling in the upper air.

Thus, the question arises as to whether the atmosphere of the earth is really warming and, if so, at what rate and to what extent. As we are still in the process of assembling an adequate database, both in space and time, this conundrum must remain unresolved for the time being.

Furthermore, the effects of any severe volcanic activity, not, so far, experienced in living memory, should not be overlooked when attempts are made to predict future climatic trends. For instance, during the expected thermal recovery following the most severe phase of the Little Ice Age in the late 17th century, widespread and persistent volcanic dust veils caused surface temperatures in the northern hemisphere, including the British Isles, to fall abruptly in the 1780s. Further volcanic events in the early 1800s resulted in the chill of the Little Ice Age continuing well into the 19th century.

Apart from speculating about future climate, one of the main challenges facing atmospheric scientists today is to attempt to unravel the extent to which human activities, such as the use of fossil fuels and changes in land use, are combining with natural influences in affecting the climate. When adjusted for unequal spatial reporting and urban heating, it appears that temperature levels over the earth's surface have increased by about 0.5 °C (0.9 °F) since the late 19th century. It has been suggested that an enhanced greenhouse effect is the primary process at work here, but since the warming has now been shown to be less intense and different in timing from that predicted by climate modellers there is an urgent need for further research to obtain a better understanding and knowledge of both human and natural effects on the climate.

CLIMATIC HISTORY OF THE EARTH DURING GEOLOGICAL TIMES

As a general background for an overall study of British climate, both temporal and spatial, the following review traces in broad terms the climatic history of the earth through geological times, when conditions were mostly warmer than they are today. More precisely, a mild non-glacial climate, characterised by low-lying lands, extensive seas and warm ice-free polar regions, has existed for nine-tenths of the time since the Cambrian, when the temperature difference between the equator and the poles was very small compared with that of today.

From a study of the rate of decay of radioactive elements in rocks, such as uranium and thorium, it has been estimated that the earth's crust solidified about 5,000 million years ago. However, the classic geological timescale that became recognised in the 19th century only referred to the interval of earth history from about 540 million years ago to the present, that is, the Phanerozoic ('exposed life') aeon, during which a chronology of events for only about the last 12 per cent of geological time had been determined. Based on classic principles laid down by the Danish geologist–priest Nicolaus Steno (1638–1686) and the English scientists Robert Hooke (1635–1703) and William Smith (1769–1839), the succession of fossil assemblages, preserved in sedimentary rocks, was used to derive a calendar of geological events, according to the relative ages of the strata. Owing to fossils being almost absent in rocks older than about 500 million years, comparatively little could be discovered about geological events in the previous 88 per cent of earth history, and it was correspondingly very difficult to determine palaeoclimatic conditions over this immensely long interval of time. However, following developments in radiometric dating methods during the 1950s, it finally became possible to determine, with absolute values, the ages of igneous and metamorphic rocks formed during these very ancient times.

The geological column is divided into eras, periods and epochs. The boundaries between these intervals represent relatively abrupt changes in environmental and climatic conditions over the earth's surface. Palaeoclimatic conditions during geological times can be determined on the assumption that climate-sensitive rocks, such as evaporates (salt and gypsum), red beds, dune sandstones, coal measures and tillites (fossilised boulder clay), were formed under particular climatic regimes similar to those of the present time in tropical, temperate and polar zones.

Pre-Cambrian era: 5,000 to 600 million years ago

Until recently, very little was known about the climate of the Pre-Cambrian era. However, tillite deposits, discovered in several parts of the world and dated by radiometric methods, indicate that a number of ice ages occurred, with particularly strong signals at about 2,300 million and 700 million years ago. Evidence of both glaciation and hot desert conditions has been found for this era in northern parts of the region now known as the British Isles.

Palaeozoic or Primary era: 600 to 230 million years ago

At the beginning of the Palaeozoic era, in the Cambrian period, there were several continental landmasses, widely scattered over the earth's surface. The British Isles region was covered by a shallow sea which gradually became deeper. The climate became equable, with warm water conditions and perhaps hot deserts in some of the land areas. Although the Cambrian period began cold it ended warm and equable, with similar conditions continuing into the early Ordovician period over the area now known as the British Isles.

During the Ordovician period a broad sea extended across the British Isles with a land area in central England and also in the northwest towards the end of the period. The seas were warm and clear and many volcanoes rose from the sea bed. The existence of glacial deposits in North Africa indicates that an ice age occurred towards the end of the period, about 450 million years ago, with Antarctic-type ice sheets over the present Sahara Desert, then part of Gondwanaland in the southern hemisphere. Following this glaciation, during the Silurian and Devonian periods, there was a long warm interval in the earth's climatic history.

The sea continued across the British Isles during the Silurian period, with land in central England and the northwest. Warm equable conditions prevailed, with deserts in some parts of the world.

After the Caledonian mountain-building movement in the Devonian period the British Isles region was mainly land, with sea only in the central valley of Scotland, southern England and the west Midlands. The climate was warm and semi-arid, but there is evidence of heavy rainstorms occurring in a wet season.

During the Lower Carboniferous period there was land in northern Scotland, Wales, Cornwall and East Anglia. Seas covered southern Scotland, most of Ireland and much of England. The climate was warm, and while the British Isles region was a semi-tropical area some regions of the world were desert.

During the Upper Carboniferous period uplift gave rise to land in northwestern Scotland and southern England, and shallow seas with great deltas. The climate of the British Isles region was semi-tropical, with great swamp forests. However, a cooling trend which set in during the latter part of the period continued into the Permian period and culminated in extensive glaciation over Gondwanaland about 300 million years ago, the Permo-Carboniferous Ice Age. Beds of tillites, several hundreds of metres thick, indicate that vast continental ice sheets covered areas now known as Australia, India, South America and South Africa. Intervening deposits, containing coal seams, show that a number of warm interglacials also occurred during Permo-Carboniferous times.

After the uplift of the Upper Carboniferous period, the British Isles region was mainly mountainous during the Permian period, with a large sea and lowland area lying across northern and central England, and in the southwest. While hot desert conditions prevailed in the British Isles, icecaps covered Gondwanaland.

Mesozoic or Secondary era: 230 to 63 million years ago

The warm dry climates that prevailed in the late Permian continued into the Triassic period, during which time the assembly of a single super-continent, Pangaea, was completed. Pangaea comprised two major subcontinents, Laurasia to the north and Gondwana to the south of the Tethys Sea, a central oceanic region of which the present Mediterranean Sea is a remnant. As first suggested by the English pioneer geologist Sir Charles Lyell (1797–1875), climatic changes associated with such a shift in the distribution of the continents and oceans would have been considerable.

The interior of Pangaea was situated in low and middle latitudes, beyond the reach of moisture-bearing maritime winds. Widespread deposits of evaporates, red beds and sandstones indicate that great deserts extended across northern Europe during this period, similar to the Sahara over North Africa today.

During the Triassic period desert basins lay between mountain ranges in the British Isles; towards the end of the period the Midland and southern basins joined. Although temperatures in the tropics during the Triassic were probably similar to those of today, values at higher latitudes in the northern hemisphere, then dominated by seas, were much warmer than at present. The temperature gradient between the equator and the pole has been estimated to have been only about half that of the present, which would have resulted in a weakened atmospheric circulation with lighter winds and less intense weather systems. However, the climate over the British Isles became wetter at the end of the Triassic period.

During the Jurassic period the climate was warm over the British Isles; there were mountains over Scotland, most of Ireland and eastern England and a fairly shallow sea covered southwest and central England. Most of England, apart from the southeast, was land in the Cretaceous period, and the climate continued to be mainly warm.

Following the fragmentation of Pangaea during the Jurassic and Cretaceous periods, broad seaways formed between the new continents. These allowed moisture-bearing winds to penetrate far inland, and the general aridity that had prevailed in the Triassic was replaced by more humid conditions. Also, the gradual northward drift of landmasses into higher latitudes of the northern hemisphere, displacing former oceans, led to an increase in the zonal temperature gradient, which resulted in a more vigorous atmospheric circulation. The climate of the Jurassic was generally mild, and there was no polar ice. While high ground was located in regions now known as Scotland, Ireland, East Anglia, the Pennines and southwest England, a fairly shallow sea covered central England with extensive warmth-demanding forests developing in surrounding low-lying areas. The Isle of Skye has become known as Scotland's Jurassic Island, because of the discovery of many dinosaur remains.

During much of the late Mesozoic era, the earth's climate had been warmer than at present, and no ice ages or polar icecaps developed in this era. However, towards the close of the Cretaceous period, about 70 million years ago, there is evidence of global cooling, which eventually culminated in the Pleistocene glaciation.

Cenozoic or Tertiary era: 63 to 1.5 million years ago

A long cooling trend, the so-called Cenozoic climatic decline, became a definite feature of the earth's climate around 55 million years ago. Australia broke contact with Antarctica in the mid Eocene, 45–48 million years ago, and as it drifted northwards a sea passage began to be opened up between the two continents. By 30 million years ago, a fully circumpolar ocean current system had become established in the southern hemisphere. Out of reach of warm ocean currents, Antarctica became thermally isolated and cold. Glaciation was initiated there during the Oligocene period, and by 25 million years ago sufficient snow had accumulated to form a thick South Polar icecap, which may have further enhanced the global cooling trend by its high reflectivity.

During the Eocene period the British Isles region was mainly land, apart from the southeast, and a tropical-type climate prevailed in southern England. The warm temperate climate during the Oligocene period was followed by cooling in the Miocene period; a cool temperate climate prevailed in the British Isles during the Pliocene period.

Pleistocene and Recent periods: the last 1.5 million years

The interval of about 1.5 million years from the beginning of the Pleistocene period, or ice age, to the present only represents a very small fraction of the earth's history. However, abundant evidence of ice sheets alternately advancing and receding over North America and northern Europe makes it a period of great interest, since remnants of these large-scale frozen layers can be seen today in the glaciers of Switzerland, Norway and Alaska. Although, as mentioned above, similar intervals of glaciation occurred throughout geological time, they are comparatively rare events. It has been suggested that ice ages occur with a periodicity of about 150 million years, the lack of evidence in the Jurassic being attributed to the absence of landmasses at either of the poles during that period.

In the early 20th century, the classic chronology of the Pleistocene ice age, devised by the German geographers Eduard Brückner and Albrecht Penck, was based on glacial deposits in Europe, which appeared to indicate that there had been four major episodes of glaciation: Günz, Mindel, Riss and Würm. However, this approach suffered from the drawback that each new advance of ice had removed earlier chronological evidence. New forms of field evidence, discovered in the 1960s, began to suggest that the traditional four-fold glacial sequence had greatly simplified the complexities of Pleistocene history. It is now believed that there may have been as many as 18 glacial advances during the past 1.8 million years, a periodicity which coincides with the 100,000-year cycle in the eccentricity of the earth's orbit and supports the hypothesis of variations in orbital parameters causing changes of climate.

This novel approach to glacial chronology is based on the concept that changes of climate in the Pleistocene caused fluctuations in the temperature and chemistry of the oceans that are reflected in the shells of microscopic organisms that float near the ocean bottom. Following the death of these tiny creatures, their shells sink and accumulate on the sea bed, where they can be abstracted and analysed in ocean cores. The expansion and contraction of ice sheets on land can be inferred from these shells in two ways. First, changes in the coiling and distribution of certain species provide a continuous record of colder and warmer intervals of ocean water. Second, since the oxygen dissolved in ocean water comprises two isotopes, oxygen-16 and oxygen-18, variations in the isotopic ratios contained in the shells reflect differences of evaporation rates at the sea surface. A higher ratio of the heavy oxygen-18 to oxygen-16 in the core record suggests a colder climate, while a lower ratio suggests warmer conditions.

According to current palaeoclimatic research, the onset of the latest ice age actually occurred about ten million years ago, when mountain glaciers began to expand in the northern hemisphere and a substantial growth took place in the Antarctic ice sheet. The regional glaciation of Antarctica reached its maximum five to seven million years ago, when the volume of the South Polar icecap was 50 per cent greater than at present. This event was accompanied by a eustatic fall of sea level that caused the Mediterranean Basin to dry out and become a great desert, with a highly reflective cover of evaporites.

By compounding the long-term trend of increasing land in low latitudes, and hence higher surface albedo values, the desiccation of the Mediterranean may have been a significant factor in the initiation of extensive and intense glaciation during the Pliocene and Pleistocene periods. Continental ice sheets appeared for the first time in the northern hemisphere about two million years ago, extending over lands adjacent to the North Atlantic Ocean, since when there has been a long and complex series of glacial and interglacial cycles with a periodicity of about 100,000 years, which may be partly related to changes in the earth's orbit. The penultimate and last glacial maxima occurred, with approximately equal intensity, 130,000 and 18,000 years ago. The intervening interglacial, the Eemian, reached its peak around 125,000 years ago.

In 2001 a prehistoric collection of flint tools was discovered during an archaeological dig at Pakefield, near Lowestoft (Suffolk), which revealed that ancient humans had lived in Britain 200,000 years earlier than previously believed. It had been thought that man first arrived north of the Alps and Pyrenees and then into Britain 450,000–500,000 years ago. But the dig uncovered pieces of worked flint that have been dated to 700,000 years ago. The tools appear to have been made by early man hammering sharp flakes off flint pebbles carried by a proto-river flowing across what is now East Anglia. The so-called 'pebble-bash people' lived about 200,000 years earlier than Boxgrove man, previously thought to have been the earliest known humans to have settled in this part of northern Europe. At the time the tools were made the climate of Britain was balmy and the environment included a wide range of animals and plants. Britain was then connected to mainland Europe, and sediments laid down by rivers at the time are found today along the coastline of north Suffolk and Norfolk. As the sediments were deposited, the remains of animals, plants and tools became embedded inside them. This is not the first time that East Anglia has been the site of internationally important discoveries. One of the most important Neanderthal sites in Europe was unearthed at Lynford in Thetford Forest (Norfolk) in 2002, and the remains of giant hippopotamus were discovered in a quarry at Norton Subcourse, near Loddon, in 2004.

The last glacial advance of the Pleistocene period, known as the Würm in Europe (Devensian in Britain, Midlandian in Ireland) and the Wisconsin in North America, began about 60,000–70,000 years ago. Continental ice sheets in the northern hemisphere attained their maximum extent about 18,000 years ago when an extensive layer of ice, hundreds of metres thick, covered northern and central parts of the British Isles. The sea level fell by about 100 m (330 feet) and sea-surface temperatures in the North Atlantic decreased by about 10 °C (18 °F) compared with their peak in the Eemian interglacial. Ice sheets over northern Europe and North America began to recede about 15,000–14,000 years ago, and widespread deglaciation occurred relatively rapidly during the following thousand years or so. After the recession of the ice sheets there was a particularly warm phase in west Europe, the Allerød period. This and other periods in postglacial and historic times are outlined in Chapter 9 and Part II.

The main course of the climatic history of the British Isles since the last ice age can be traced from a wide range of evidence, including the movement of glaciers in the Alps and Scandinavia, Arctic sea ice, rises and falls of former sea levels, ocean cores, flora and fauna, pollen analysis, peat stratigraphy, varves and radiocarbon dating.

In the last million years or so there has been a recurring pattern in which a glacial period, lasting about 100,000 years, is followed by a warmer, interglacial, period of 10,000–20,000 years' duration. The present interglacial period, the Holocene, has already lasted a little more than 10,000 years. It is salutary to realise that there have been interglacials shorter in length and, consequently, the possibility of a new glacial period in the offing cannot be ignored. However, due to the increased emissions by man of carbon dioxide and other greenhouse gases into the atmosphere, a warming trend has been speculated to continue for at least another century or so by some atmospheric scientists.

THE PRESENT CLIMATIC DILEMMA

The English physicist John Tyndall (1820–1893) discovered that of all the atmospheric gases, water vapour and carbon dioxide possess the greatest heat-trapping qualities – that is, the greenhouse effect. Tyndall was the first to suggest, in 1861, that variations of atmospheric carbon dioxide could be linked with changes of temperature, and in 1896 the Swedish chemist Svante Arrhenius (1859–1927) was the pioneer in investigating the effect that doubling atmospheric carbon dioxide would have on the earth's climate, one of the main concerns of atmospheric scientists today.

Today is therefore a critical time for the study of climatic change with, as mentioned earlier, a lively debate taking place between advocates and sceptics of global warming. On the one hand, atmospheric scientists at the Hadley Centre for Climate Prediction and Research, UK Meteorological Office, have become increasingly confident that recent warming is due, in part, to man-made emissions of greenhouse gases. To advance their ideas, numerical modelling experiments, taking into account physical and chemical atmospheric processes, are being undertaken to predict changes of climate. Maps and diagrams of temperature, precipitation, soil moisture content, sea-level change and sea ice for future years and seasons in the 21st century are simulated using climate models closely adapted to the 'business as usual' scenario proposed by the Intergovernmental Panel on Climate Change (IPCC) – that is, a situation in which it is assumed that the concentration of atmospheric carbon dioxide will more than double if mid-range economic growth occurs and no measures are taken to contain greenhouse-gas emissions. Under these conditions, a warming of 2–5 °C (4–9 °F) has been predicted over the British Isles for the 21st century, with, for example, warmer drier summers and milder wetter winters occurring during the 2080s, with less frost and fog than today. More extreme weather events, such as coastal storm surges, are also expected to be experienced.

On the other hand, sceptics have reservations about such future scenarios, which are based on data of contested validity. It is also argued that present-day climate models are still at an early stage of development and that they are being used to predict relatively precise effects against inadequate knowledge of natural climatic variability and scarcity of relevant observational material. Furthermore, the 'business as usual' scenario, assuming a doubling of greenhouse-gas emissions, is based on predicted socioeconomic premises (a doubling of population and a related increase in energy use) that lie outside the science on which the theory is based. Sceptics claim that to use climate models to forecast such particular conditions is assuming a capability they do not possess and, at the same time, neglects possible feedback mechanisms related to water vapour and clouds.

Thus, in summary, while many atmospheric scientists believe that increasing emissions of greenhouse gases into the atmosphere will lead to continual global warming at least during the next hundred years or so, others are less certain and point out that periodic changes of the earth's orbital situation could result in the first peak of the next glacial period occurring within the next few thousand years, with relatively abrupt climatic shifts towards an intermediate colder phase, similar to the Little Ice Age, occurring at any time from now on.

Finally, a crucial factor that, regrettably, is too often omitted in the debate on climatic change is the dynamical dimension which, by means of reconstructed and actual circulation patterns from the onset of the present interglacial 10,000 years ago to the modern epoch, provides a better knowledge and understanding of climate, past, present and future. In particular, this study should include the monitoring and analysis of the circulation over the key region of the British Isles by means of the Lamb weather types, with special attention paid to the behaviour of the westerlies. Initiated by Lamb in the Meteorological Office and continued by him in the Climatic Research Unit, this project in synoptic climatology has been shown to keep a finger not only on the pulse of British Isles climate but also more widely on the global circulation.

PART II

Chronology of Climatic History, 1st Century BC to AD 2000

We don't want to know what is past, tell us what is to come!' Yet, that it is only by study of the past and passing, that we can arrive at any knowledge of the future, is very manifest to every thinking mind.

Luke Howard, *Climate of London*, 1833

INTRODUCTION

A YEAR-BY-YEAR ACCOUNT is presented here of what is known about the weather and climate experienced in the British Isles during historical times. In addition to the yearly accounts, decadal divisions are shown in the chronology from the beginning of the 9th century, when the data became more discrete. Decades provide a convenient time lapse for comparative studies, short enough to allow daily, seasonal and yearly weather events to be meaningfully recorded while at the same time long enough for any significant trends in meteorological elements such as temperature, rainfall and circulation patterns to be identified. Decadal variations in such features are sometimes quite appreciable and well marked: some decades are warmer, others colder, some wetter, others drier. Although such variations may not comprise major long-term climatic changes, they can be considered as being linked to distinctive climatic fluctuations in the short term.

Wherever possible, each decade is classified according to its predominant weather type – that is, maritime, cyclonic, continental or anticyclonic – as inferred from the data available for the ten-year period. In general, the maritime type, and to some extent the cyclonic type, can be linked to high-index progressive westerly decades, whereas the continental type, and to some extent the anticyclonic type, can be linked to low-index blocked easterly decades.

Unless otherwise stated, temperature and rainfall extremes are given with reference to the Central England Temperature (CET) series from 1659 and the England and Wales Precipitation (EWP) series from 1766, respectively. The temperatures assigned to months and years refer to the mean values for those periods.

Exceptional events, such as severe storms, very cold winters and droughts, are marked with an asterisk. These are objectively defined according to the abnormal values of the particular elements involved (e.g. wind strength, temperature and rainfall).

Prior to 1752, events in Britain were recorded on the Old Style (OS) Julian calendar. Appropriate corrections have been applied for converting OS dates to the New Style (NS) Gregorian calendar; for example, OS dates in 14th-century records are converted to the NS calendar by adding 8 days.

Winters are identified by the year in which the January fell, and include data for the previous December.

EARLY ROMAN COOL PHASE:
1ST CENTURY BC TO AD 200

During the 1st century BC, some areas of Britain, in particular the southwest, south and southeast, had already established close trading links with the Roman Empire and were 'Romanised' before the later military operations and invasion. **55 BC** * Summer – 29–30 August: severe storm. Julius Caesar began his first expedition to the British Isles on 24 August, but on the fifth and sixth days his fleet, anchored off Dover, was pounded by a combination of severe easterly gales, high tides and a storm surge. Some of his ships were completely wrecked, while others lost their anchors, cables and rigging. Faced with this disastrous situation, Caesar abandoned his invasion attempt and returned to Gaul. **54 BC** * Summer – June to July: severe storms. The following summer Caesar planned a second attack on Britain. However, this time strong west to northwesterly winds in late June forced him to wait 25 days until 18–20 July for more favourable conditions. Then, having landed and penetrated some distance inland, he was forced back to the coast two days later due to another storm that caused further damage to his fleet, with the loss of 40 vessels. **44 BC** Volcanic dust veil (DVI estimated c.1000), Mount Etna eruption, sun dimmed, cooling effect, crops damaged and inferred failed harvests, famines in Rome and Egypt; these events were ominously connected at the time with Caesar's death. **AD 7 or 9** First recorded Thames flood, possibly due to a North Sea storm surge caused by northwesterly gales in the North Sea; great loss of life. **AD 8–10** Three successive severe winters in mainland Europe. **AD 15** Two Roman legions almost destroyed by a North Sea storm surge. **AD 18** So-called 'hurricane', Westminster destroyed. **AD 37–41** Abortive attempt to invade Britain; possibly a weather-related failure. **AD 38** Severe sea flood, English east coast and Thames estuary inundated, 10,000 believed drowned. **AD 43** Following the earlier unsuccessful attacks by Julius Caesar in 55 and 54 BC, this year marked the start of the Roman invasion of Britain proper, with a four-legion army led by Aulus Plautius. **AD 48** Thames flood, probably caused by heavy rainfall; great loss of life and much damage. **AD 60** Storm, strong winds, severe sea flood, exposed English and French coasts inundated; Roman forces suppressed British rebellion under Boudicca. **AD 68** Inferred gales and severe sea floods; Isle of Wight separated from

England. AD 69 Heavy thunderstorms; London partially destroyed by lightning.
AD 79 Inferred volcanic dust veil (estimated DVI 1000–2000), Vesuvius eruption. AD
80 Very cold winter – various chronicles record a year between AD 77 and 84;.
severe flood on the Severn. AD 96–98 Evacuation of Scotland. AD 125 Heavy
snowfall. AD 125–130 Inferred dry conditions – serious fire in London. AD 134 Very
cold winter – Thames frozen for two months. AD 139 Possible drought – Thames
dried up for two days. AD 153 Very cold winter – intense frost lasted three months,
Thames froze. c. AD 155 Inferred dry conditions – serious fire at Verulamium/
St Albans (Hertfordshire). AD 167 Smallpox epidemic ravages the Roman Empire.
AD 173 Very cold winter – intense frost lasted three months, Thames froze.

LATE ROMAN WARM PHASE: 3RD AND 4TH CENTURIES

220 Very cold winter – intense frost said to have lasted five months. 230 Cold winter
– Thames in London believed frozen for six weeks. 242 Heavy snowfall. 245 * Severe
storms. Inferred cyclonic situations, severe sea floods, inferred North Sea storm
surge, many thousands of acres inundated in Lincolnshire. 250 to 252 (or 230) Cold
winter – Thames frozen for nine weeks. 253 * Inferred severe storm. Inferred
cyclonic situation/storm-force gales, much damage, 900 houses blown down in
London alone. 272 Famine. 275 Start of Saxon raids in the Channel. 277 * Severe
storm. Inferred cyclonic situation/severe gales, people killed in London. 291 Cold
winter, many rivers frozen for six weeks. 296 Severe winter in mainland Europe. 298
Drought and famine in Wales; inferred easterly winds. 300 Famine in Scotland. 306
Famine in Scotland. 310 Famine. 329 (or 359) Very cold winter – heavy snowfall,
many rivers frozen for six weeks. 341 Heavy snowfall. 353 Severe floods in Cheshire,
5,000 people and many cattle believed drowned. 359 Very cold winter, sea frozen off
coasts, rivers frozen, intense frost for 14 weeks in Scotland. 362 Drought. 367 Romans
suffered a military disaster due to concerted sea-borne attacks by the Picts of Scotland
and Ireland. 369 Situation restored and town defences strengthened. 374 Drought.

DARK AGES COOL PHASE: 5TH TO 9TH CENTURIES

400–440 Bout of storminess, many sea floods and coastal changes in south
England, loss of life on Dutch coast. 401 Very cold winter in mainland Europe.
407 Roman forces withdrawn from Britain. 410 Cities authorised to provide their
own defence, marking the end of Roman Britain. 411 Very cold winter in
mainland Europe. 419 Severe sea floods in south England, Solent and

Southampton Water coasts devastated, Goodwin Sands partly submerged. **432** Very cold winter in mainland Europe. **439** Drought. ***c.*442** Disintegration of former Roman villas, but their estates continued to be cultivated. **443** Very cold winter in south Europe – unusually deep snow for half of the year, many people and cattle died due to the cold. ***c.*450** Germanic (Anglo-Saxon) tribes begin conquest and settlement of Britain. **462** Very cold winter in mainland Europe. **474** Cold winter – four-month period of frost and snow. **479** Thames flood extended 16 km (10 miles) above and below London. **480** Drought in Scotland. **484** Drought – dried-up springs and rivers. **508 (507 or 509)** Very cold winter – rivers frozen for two months. **520** * Inferred severe storm. Inferred cyclonic situation and storm-force southwesterly winds, Atlantic storm surge affected Cardigan Bay, severe sea floods affected west Wales and perhaps southwest England, including the legendary province of Lyonesse off Cornwall (see also November 1099), farmland lost to the sea. **525** Cold winter – Thames frozen for six weeks. **530** Severe floods in Humberside. **536** Volcanic dust veil (estimated DVI 4500), Rabaul (Papua New Guinea) major eruption, sunlight blocked for 12–18 months; the most severe and prolonged short-term northern hemispheric cooling (lasted over a decade) on record over the past two millennia; serious effects followed, including crop failures, famines and a decline in tree growth. **536** Bread famine in Ireland. Cold spring. **537–539** Continuing bread famine in Ireland. ***c.*542** Bubonic plague ravaged Europe. **545** Very cold winter. **548** * Severe storm. Inferred cyclonic situation and storm-force gales in southeast England, houses damaged in London, great loss of life. ***c.*550** Anglo-Saxons conquered eastern England. **554** Very cold winter – heavy snowfall. **566** Very cold winter in mainland Europe. * Severe storm. Inferred cyclonic situation, recorded storm affected south English coast. **575** Wet summer. Wet autumn. **577** Anglo-Saxon settlers reached the Bristol Channel. **579** Wet summer. Wet autumn. **580s** Series of disastrously wet years in mainland Europe. **584** Very mild winter in mainland Europe. **589** Drought – sea floods in northeast England. **590** Wet summer. Wet autumn. **593** Very cold winter in mainland Europe. **597** Augustine's mission to Kent.

7th century

Spread of Christianity in England; priories, abbeys and churches built. **604** Cold winter. **605** Very warm, drought, inferred blocking-high situations with easterly winds. Very cold winter in south Europe, trees and vines destroyed by frost. **613** Anglo-Saxon settlers reached Chester. **630** Thames flood. ***c.*650** Central England conquered by Anglo-Saxon settlers. **664–665** Drought. **670** Very cold winter in mainland Europe – many people and livestock killed. **676** Drought. **680–** * Drought. **682** Inferred blocking-high situations, a three-year drought centred on

681 (probably the so-called 'St Wilfred's Drought' in Sussex), one of the most severe droughts on record. **685** Blood-rain: precipitation usually caused by the presence of very fine sand or dust particles (sometimes of volcanic origin) in rain drops; particles can be carried long distances by upper winds; Vesuvius and Etna were both active in 685. **690** Very cold winter in mainland Europe. **695** Very cold winter – Thames frozen for six weeks, booths built on the river, early type of Frost Fair.

8th century

Viking conquest and settlement of England. **713** Dry year in Ireland. **717** Dry summer in Ireland. **719** Dry summer. **721** Very warm summer. **737** Drought. **738** Severe floods in Scotland, Glasgow inundated, over 400 families drowned. **741** Drought. **743** Drought. **744** Dry year in Ireland. **747** Dry year in Ireland. **748** Dry year in Ireland. **759** Autumn – October: intense frost to early March (760). **760** Very cold winter. Autumn – October: intense frost to February (761). **761** Very cold winter (uncertainty whether this severe season occurred in 761 or 760). **762** Very warm; drought. **763** Very warm dry summer – dried-up springs. **764** * Very cold winter. Inferred blocking-high situations, one of the most severe winters on record; inferred volcanic dust veil, major eruption(s); a peak in the Greenland Ice Sheet Project Two (GISP2) sulphate record (dated to within 2–3 years of 767) indicates that this very cold winter was probably connected with a volcanic aerosol event that left marked traces on Greenland. December (763) to April (about 120 days): very cold spell, heavy snowfall, intense frost, crops and trees damaged, many birds, animals and fish perished; frozen rivers in mainland Europe, such as the Danube, north Black Sea ice-bound out to 160 km (100 miles), ice thickness continually increased by frequent snowfall. A thaw in February caused this huge ice mass to break up into pieces that were driven south as large ice floes by northerly winds; some of the ice masses entered the Bosporus and crashed against the walls of Constantinople (Istanbul), causing serious damage; the chronicler Theophanes the Confessor witnessed this event as a child and later described how he had climbed on top of one of the ice masses and found it was possible to walk on a solid bridge of ice from Europe to Asia. Cold late spring. * Dry summer: drought. Inferred blocking-high situations (probably comparable to 1959 drought), widespread outbreak of fires caused by extreme dryness.

> *In the same year [764] many towns, monasteries and villages in various districts and kingdoms were suddenly devastated by fire; for instance, the calamity struck Stretburg [Cirencester (?)], Winchester, Southampton, the city of London, the city of York, and many other places.*
>
> Simeon of Durham

772 Droughts in Ireland and mainland Europe, inferred blocking-high situations with easterly winds. Warm summer. **775** Very warm dry spell after a long frost. **783** Drought. Very warm summer.

> *Summer was so very hot that very many men died of that heat.*
>
> Carolingian Annals

791 Intense frost in mainland Europe. **793** Warm summer. **794** Drought in mainland Europe (*Carolingian Annals*). **795** Severe winter in mainland Europe – heavy snowfall, many people and horses killed in northwest Pontus (Anatolia). **797** Drought, also in mainland Europe. **799** Stormy year; many shipwrecks off British coasts.

800s

801 * Very mild wet winter. Inferred cyclonic westerly situations. * 28 December (800) or 1 January: severe storm. Inferred cyclonic situation, storm-force southwesterly gales, much damage, many houses destroyed and many trees blown down. Late 801: extensive sea floods. **808** Very mild winter. **809** Floods in mainland Europe (*Carolingian Annals*).

810s

Continental (?). Two very cold winters in mainland Europe. Inferred warm dry summers due to absence of harvest failures. **811** Very cold winter. **815** Floods in mainland Europe. Very cold winter.

820s

Continental. Decade of famine caused mainly by cold winters and cool summers in mainland Europe. **820** Floods in mainland Europe. Cool wet summer in mainland Europe. **821** Cool wet summer in mainland Europe. Wet autumn in mainland Europe. **822** * Very cold winter. Inferred blocking-high situations, severe conditions extending from Ireland to central Europe, major rivers frozen including the Rhine, Danube, Elbe and Seine, settlements and bridges damaged when ice broke; inferred volcanic dust veil, major eruption(s); GISP2 sulphate peak dated 822–823 indicates that this very cold winter was connected with a volcanic aerosol event that left marked traces on Greenland. **822–823** Drought, inferred blocking-high situations. **823** Very cold winter in south Europe – inferred volcanic dust-veil effect, people and cattle died. **824** Drought in mainland Europe. Very cold winter – inferred volcanic dust-veil effect. **827** Very cold winter – Thames frozen for nine weeks.

830s

A mostly wet decade with further cold winters in mainland Europe. **836** Severe floods in north England and south Scotland, Tweed overflowed. **838** Warm summer. **839** Severe sea floods affected the Flemish coast and also possibly the English east coast, mass evacuation of people.

840s

Cyclonic (?). Variable weather conditions, with wetness being the chief cause of concern in mainland Europe. **841** Cool summer. **843** Cold winter. **845 (or 846)** Very cold winter. **846** * Very cold winter. Inferred blocking-high situations over the Norwegian Sea and Scandinavia, northeasterly winds prevailed throughout winter and spring until early May; according to Prudentius, Bishop of Troyes, villagers near his city were attacked by packs of hungry wolves. **849** Cold winter.

850s

Anticyclonic or continental. A mostly dry decade in mainland Europe, with several cold winters. **850** Warm summer. **852** Warm summer. **856** Very cold dry winter in mainland Europe (possibly also in Britain); inferred volcanic dust veil, major eruption(s); GISP2 sulphate peak dated to within 2–3 years of 854 indicates that this severe winter was connected with a volcanic aerosol fallout that left marked traces on Greenland. **859** Very cold winter in mainland Europe; reports of optical phenomena, inferred volcanic dust-veil effect; Adriatic frozen.

860s

Inferred maritime or cyclonic. A mostly warm wet decade in mainland Europe; summers favourable enough to encourage the northward spread of viticulture. **860** * Very cold winter. Inferred blocking-high situations, inferred volcanic dust veil, major eruption(s); GISP2 sulphate peak readings dated to within 2–3 years of 856 and 858 indicate that this severe winter was connected with a volcanic aerosol fallout that left marked traces on Greenland, reports of optical phenomena during previous autumn appear to confirm presence of volcanic dust veil; snow cover and frost in the Rhineland from November (859) until April (120–150 days), making it one of the longest winters on record; Adriatic Sea and Venetian lagoons frozen, traders and merchandise entered the city-port on ice. **862** Cold winter. **863** Very mild winter, chroniclers noted an almost complete absence of frost, suggesting that several weeks of frost were usually expected during 'normal' winters at that time.

870s

Continental (?). The early 870s at least appear to have been dry with further references to viticulture in England. **870** Warm summer. **871** Alfred the Great, King of Wessex, halted Danish advance in England. **872** Cold winter. Warm summer. **874** * Very cold winter. Inferred blocking-high situations, inferred volcanic dust veil, major eruption(s), GISP2 sulphate peak dated to within 2–3 years of 876 indicates that this severe winter was connected with a volcanic aerosol fallout that left marked traces on Greenland; early November (873) to late April: very cold, frozen rivers and water bodies, frozen Rhine bore riders; snow cover to late March (about 130 days); thaw and snow-melt followed by severe floods. Cold spring. Warm summer. **875** Very cold winter – early November (874) to late April: intense frost, severe floods followed thaw. **877** * Early 877: severe storm. Inferred cyclonic situation and storm-force gales, invading Danish fleet struck by storms in the Channel, 120 ships lost off Swanage. **878** May: Battle of Ethandun (probably Edington in Wiltshire), Danes defeated by Saxons under Alfred.

880s

Continental (?). **880** Cold winter. **881** Cold winter. **886** Cool summer. **887** Cold winter.

890s

892 Severe late frost, many vines destroyed and cattle perished. **894** Very mild winter. **898** Late frosts.

MEDIEVAL WARM EPOCH (LITTLE OPTIMUM): 900–1299

900s

Apart from the very cold winter of 908, there was a notable absence of extreme seasons during this decade. **908** Very cold winter – many rivers frozen for two months.

910s

913 Very cold winter in mainland Europe – inferred volcanic dust veil, major. eruption(s); GISP2 sulphate peak reading dated to within 2–3 years of 913–914 indicates that this severe winter was connected with a volcanic aerosol fallout that left marked traces on Greenland. **916 (or 918)** Inferred very cold winter in Ireland – 'great snow, cold and unusual frost', cattle perished. **917** Very cold winter in mainland Europe.

920s

921 Great storm in Ireland. Warm summer. **923** Very cold winter – Thames frozen for about three months. **(or 929)**. **928** Very cold winter in mainland Europe. Warm summer. **929** Very cold winter – Thames frozen for about three months. **(or 923)**.

930s

Continental. Several cold winters in mainland Europe. **932** So-called 'fire from heaven burnt' the Connaught mountains (west Ireland), many people burnt by the 'fire' (inferred heavy thunderstorm and lightning strikes); dried-up streams and lakes (inferred drought in Ireland). **934, 935** Intense frosts, frozen rivers and lakes in Ireland. **939, 940, 944** Inferred dry year in Ireland. **938** Very cold winter – intense frost: 27 December (937) to late April, crops damaged, people died from starvation.

940s

940 Very cold winter – GISP2 sulphate peak readings dated to within 2–3 years of 936, 938 and 939 indicate that this severe winter was connected with an aerosol fallout from one or more volcanic eruptions that left marked traces on Greenland. **944** * Severe storm. Inferred cyclonic situation, storm-force gales, much damage, 1,500 houses destroyed in London alone.

950s

950 Inferred dry year in Ireland. **955** Great frost and snow, cattle perished in Ireland. Warm summer. **956** Inferred dry year in Ireland. **959–960** A bolt of fire passed through Leinster (southeast Ireland), inferred heavy thunderstorm, people and cattle killed, houses burnt in Dublin.

960s

Maritime (?) **960** Snow and diseases in Ireland. **964** Very cold winter.

970s

970 Stormy. **971** An exceptionally gloomy year. Summer – 15 July (OS): so-called 'St Swithin's Storm', when the remains of the Anglo-Saxon bishop were reburied at Winchester; it is claimed that the saint manifested his displeasure of the move by causing a great storm that was followed by 40 wet days. However, such unfavourable conditions are not referred to in any of the contemporary accounts, and the story is probably a later invention to account for the English proverb that has become associated with St Swithin down the years. **974** Inclement weather in Ireland. Warm summer. **975** Very cold dry winter – western Baltic probably froze. **976** Very cold winter in north Europe. **977** Warm summer.

980s

Continental. **981** Inferred dry year in Ireland. * Inferred severe storm. Inferred cyclonic situation/storm-force gales, turrets and steeples destroyed in Ireland. Very cold winter. Very cold spring. **986** Dry year in Ireland. **987** Very warm dry year, onset of a notable series of droughts. **988** Drought. Cold winter – 27 December (987): start of a very cold spell said to have lasted four months. Warm summer. **989** Warm year, drought.

990s

Continental. Several 'good' years in mainland Europe; inferred favourable springs and summers. **991** Great whirlwind in Ireland. Very cold winter. Wet autumn (?) – crop failures, famine. **992** Drought. Very cold winter in south Europe. Very warm dry summer. **993** Drought. Very warm dry summer. **994** Drought. Third successive very warm dry summer – dried-up crops. **995** Heavy thunderstorm in Armagh (north Ireland). Very cold winter in mainland Europe. **998** Very cold winter – Thames frozen for over a month. * Autumn: inferred severe storm. Inferred cyclonic situation/storm-force winds, 'a warring of mighty winds', much damage including destruction of houses and woods in Ireland.

1000s

Cyclonic (?). **1006** Dry winter. Dry spring. **1008** Severe storms. **1009** * Severe storm. Inferred cyclonic situation/storm-force gales, many shipwrecks. Very warm dry summer in Ireland.

1010s

1011 Inferred dry year in Ireland. Very cold winter. **1012** Sea floods affected English coasts. **1013** Wet year. **1014** * 4–5 October: inferred severe storm. Inferred cyclonic situation, severe sea flood, so-called 'Mickle Sea Flood', probable storm surge, widespread floods, many towns inundated, people drowned. 10 October: further sea floods, many areas inundated. **1015** Severe sea floods with spring tides, great loss of life. **1015–1016** Severe sea floods, North Sea coasts. **1017** Famine year. Canute the Great ruled England, Denmark and Norway to 1035.

1020s

1020 Very cold winter. **1022** Very warm dry summer – people and animals died due to the excessive heat.

1030s

Maritime. Inferred warm decade due to the absence of cold winters, apart from

1033 and 1034, and bad harvests. **1033** Very cold winter in mainland Europe and also probably England. **1034** * Summer: inferred severe storms. Inferred cyclonic situation, sea floods. 30 June: out-of-season frost, crops and fruit damaged, famine followed (see also 1040 for possible duplication). **1035** Mild winter. **1036** Cold winter (?). **1039** * Severe storm. Inferred cyclonic situation.

1040s

Continental. Cold decade, several cold winters, various famines. **1040** Summer – sea floods; 30 June: out-of-season frost, crops and fruit damaged (see also 1034 for possible duplication). Autumn – food scarcity. **1041** Stormy year. **1042** Severe conditions; crops failed, many cattle died. Cool summer. * Autumn – 9 November: severe storm (?). Inferred cyclonic situation, severe sea floods affected North Sea coasts. **1043** Famine year. Cool summer. **1044** Famine year. Very cold winter. **1045** Very cold winter – heavy snow, many people and livestock killed. **1046** Winter – February: very cold; intense frost and snow, many people died, cattle, birds and fish perished. **1047** Famine year. * Very cold winter. One of the most severe winters on record, January to late March: heavy snowfall, intense frosts, rivers frozen, sea partly frozen, Skaggerak frozen. Summer – stormy, frequent thunderstorms. **1048** Famine year, many people and animals died. Very cold winter. **1049** Famine year, many people and animals died.

1050s

1051 Famine year. Cool summer. **1052** Stormy year. **1053** Winter – severe gales, much damage. **1054** Very cold winter. * 27 December (1053): severe storm. Inferred cyclonic situation, severe gales, much damage. **1056** Mild winter. Cool summer. **1057** Inferred dry year in Ireland.

1060s

1060 Cold winter. **1061** Very cold winter – Thames frozen for two months. **1063** Very cold winter – Thames frozen for 14 weeks. **1066** Inferred dry year in Ireland. Mild winter. Dry summer. * Autumn – September to early October: severe storms. William, Duke of Normandy, assembled his forces in north France during the dry summer and by late August was ready to invade England. However, as the fine weather gave way to a stormy spell with west to northwesterly gales in the Channel, his operation was delayed for over a month. Eventually, when conditions improved with favourable southerly winds in early October, William's forces set sail for southeast England and landed at Pevensey on 4 October. 20 October: Battle of Hastings. **1067** Very cold winter. **1068** Cold winter. **1069** 'The Harrying of the North' by William I. Very cold winter –

widespread famine, especially severe in the north, with heavy loss of life. Cool summer.

1070s

Continental. Several cold winters. **1070** Cold winter – January: intense frost with heavy snowfall over high ground in north England. **1072** Very cold winter. Autumn – 7 November: intense frost to April (1073). **1073** Cold winter. Spring – March: cold; April: cold. **1074** Very cold winter. **1075** Followed by a decade or so of dry years. **1077** * Very cold winter. Severe winter also in mainland Europe; 7 November (1076): intense frost to late April; as with the 764 severe winter, a substantial number of independent reports reflect the extreme conditions of this prolonged negative temperature anomaly. Early November (1076): snowfall, by mid-month major water bodies and rivers were frozen including the Bodensee, Elbe, Rhine, Danube, Rhone, Po and Tiber; severe frost and snow cover generally persisted until late March and even early April 1077 in some places, 120–140 days; the frozen Rhine was crossed on foot as late as April. Dry summer – widespread fires, towns and cities affected, including London. **1078** Drought. Very dry summer.

1080s

1081 * Winter – 31 December (1080) (or 1081): severe storm. Inferred cyclonic situation/severe gales. **1082** Famine year. **1083** * Late October to early November: severe storm. Inferred cyclonic situation, heavy rainfall, severe floods, great loss of life. **1085 (or 1086)** Very cold winter. **1086** Wet; many thunderstorms, people killed by lightning; widespread famine from England to Italy. **1087** Wet, rain-famine. **1088** Wet. Inferred cool wet summer – crops remained unripe for harvesting until late November, food shortages. **1089** Drought (?). Mild winter. Cool summer – another very late harvest.

1090s

Cyclonic. **1090** * November: severe storm. Inferred cyclonic situation/heavy rain, severe floods, London Bridge damaged. **1091** Inferred dry year in Ireland. Mild winter. Stormy autumn. * 11 October: severe storm. Inferred cyclonic situation/storm-force gales, much damage, 500 houses destroyed in London alone, church steeple at Winchcomb (Gloucestershire) destroyed by lightning. * 23 October: severe storm. Inferred cyclonic situation/storm-force gales, many houses, churches and Tower of London damaged, church steeple in Salisbury blown down. * November: severe storm. Inferred cyclonic situation, heavy rain, severe floods, London Bridge swept away, over 600 houses and many churches blown down, Tower of London damaged, loss of life. **1092** Wet year. * Winter: inferred severe storm. Inferred cyclonic situation/severe North Sea storm, high spring tides, inferred storm surge, severe sea floods, Kent estate of Earl Godwin of Wessex inundated, possible initial formation of the Goodwin Sands. Spring – severe frost. Cool summer. **1093** Wet year; heavy rain, rivers overflowed, severe floods. Very cold winter – frozen rivers bore horsemen and wagons, bridges destroyed by drifting ice in subsequent thaw, watermills swept away. Autumn – wet, river floods in north England. **1094** Wet year. Mild winter. Cool summer. **1095** Famine year; unseasonable storms; severe snowstorm in Ireland, many lives lost. Dry spring. Very warm summer. Autumn – 24 November to 2 December 1095: appeal made by Pope Urban (connection between the famine and the Crusade was obvious to many of his contemporaries). **1096** Famine year. **1097** Wet year.

> In all things a very sad year and over grievous from the tempests.
> *Anglo-Saxon Chronicle*

Mild winter. **1098** Wet year. Mild winter. Cool summer. **1099** * 17 November: severe storm. Inferred cyclonic situation, one of the most severe North Sea storms on record, storm-force gales combined with high tides produced a storm surge, severe floods, east coast pounded as far south as Kent; the Island of Lomea, formerly owned by Godwin, Earl of Wessex (traditional site of the Goodwin Sands), lost to the sea; exceptional swelling of tidal water in the Thames drove the flow westwards with such force that the river burst its banks, many riverside towns and villages inundated with a great loss of life; the Dutch coast was also inundated and 100,000 people were drowned; the legendary province of Lyonesse, lying off the Cornish coast between Land's End and the Scillies, was said to have been lost to the sea in a flood during November 1099.

1100S

Maritime (?). **1100** * Severe storm. Inferred cyclonic situation, severe sea floods, high spring tides, possible North Sea storm surge, much damage, Thames overflowed, many riverside towns and villages inundated. Very cold winter. **1102** Very warm dry summer. **1103** Wet year. * 18 August: severe storm. Inferred cyclonic situation/heavy rain, crops damaged, animals perished. **1105** Wet year. Winter – January: river floods in Wales. **1106** Winter – 1 February: heavy snowfall. Warm summer. **1108** Inferred dry year in Ireland. **1109** Stormy year. Cool summer.

1110S

1110 Spring – 12 May: severe night frost, fruit trees damaged. Cool summer. *
Summer: severe storms. Inferred cyclonic situations/heavy rain, crops damaged.
1111 Very cold winter. **1112** Inferred dry year in Ireland. **1113** Mostly very dry.
1114 Very dry year. * Drought. Inferred anticyclonic situation, one of the greatest
droughts on record, most severe in southeast England, Thames at an exceptionally
low level. Very dry winter. Spring – April: Thames almost dry. Very warm dry summer –
widespread crop and forest fires. Autumn – drought continued, 17 October: Thames
again low due to drought coinciding with an exceptionally low tide, people waded
across the river at London Bridge. **1115** Very cold winter – frost lasted about 10
weeks, frozen rivers, bridges damaged by ice; severe floods probably due to
subsequent thaw. **1116** Wet year. Very cold winter, frost and snow. It remains unclear
whether there were two successive severe winters in 1115 and 1116 or if the reports
for 1115 are misdated and actually refer to the following year. Cool wet summer – crops
failed. **1117** Wet year. Very mild dry winter – mildness indicated by early vegetative
growth in the Netherlands. Cool wet summer. **1118** Cool summer. **1119** Mild winter.

1120S

Continental (?). **1121** * 2 December (1120): inferred severe storm. Inferred
cyclonic situation/storm-force gales, heavy seas in the Channel, the royal vessel
White Ship wrecked, Henry I's son Prince William and all hands drowned. **1122**
Very mild wet winter. * 31 December (1121): severe storm. Inferred cyclonic
situation/storm-force gales. * Spring – 29 March: severe storm. Inferred cyclonic
situation/storm-force gales, much damage to shipping. * Autumn – 1 August:
severe storm. Inferred cyclonic situation/storm-force gales, much damage to
shipping. **1123** Mild winter. **1124** Wet year. Very cold winter in mainland Europe,
frozen rivers and water bodies in the Netherlands, people died from the cold.
Cool summer in mainland Europe. **1125** Very cold winter in mainland Europe
and, as in 1124, frozen rivers and water bodies in the Netherlands (England may
also have been affected), severe floods probably due to subsequent thaw. Cool
summer in mainland Europe. **1126** Very cold winter in mainland Europe, third
successive severe winter (England may also have been affected, at least in the
southeast), frozen mainland European rivers including the Po and Weser. **1128**
Very cold winter. **(or 1125)** Spring – late April: heavy snowfall. Warm summer.
1129 Warm dry summer – drought in Ireland.

1130S

Anticyclonic. **1130** Cold winter. Warm summer. **1132** Very cold winter. **1134** Storm
floods. Cold winter. * Autumn – 8 October: severe storm. Inferred cyclonic

situation with storm-force gales, severe sea floods affecting east coast, possible North Sea storm and storm surge. **1135** Inferred dry warm year, dried-up rivers and parched vegetation. **1136** Inferred dry year, dried-up rivers. Very warm dry summer. **1137** Inferred dry year. Warm summer. Owing to indefinite dating, it is not possible to determine if all three years, 1135, 1136 and 1137, were dry, or just one or two of them. **1138** Warm summer.

1140S

Cyclonic or maritime. **1140** Spring – 19 May: tornado at Wellesbourne (Warwickshire), large hailstones, one or two people killed, 40 houses damaged and a church roof carried away. **1141 (or 1140)** Very cold winter – heavy snowfall, Thames frozen at Oxford. **1143** Very cold winter – January: Meuse frozen; 1 January: Thames frozen. **1144** Mild winter. Autumn drought. **1146** Viticulture in Belgium badly affected by wet conditions. **1149** Dry winter – very cold winter in mainland Europe: sea frozen off the Dutch coast. Very warm summer – heavy rain at harvest time, crops badly damaged.

1150S

Maritime (?). **1150** * Very cold winter. Inferred blocking-high situation, intense frost from 17 December (1149) to late February or early March; Thames frozen, bore people, horses and carriages, and probably used by skaters on bones; sea frozen off the Low Countries out to 5 km (3 miles), congealed waves resembled towers of ice, frozen Rhine crossed on foot near Cologne; these effects are indicators of extremely low temperatures: inferred –25° to –30 °C (–13° to –22 °F) from well-documented comparable situations such as January 1709 and December 1788. **1151** River floods, inferred heavy rain. Very mild winter. Cool summer. **1152** Very cold winter – 1 January: heavy snowfall, lying snow to 9 February. Cool wet summer. **1154** Very cold winter in Denmark. **1156** Floods, inferred heavy rain. Very cold winter. Cool summer. **1157** Mild winter. Warm summer. **1158** Dry year; Thames ran dry, river crossed dry-shod in London. Mild winter.

1160S

1160 Very cold winter. **1162** * 23 February: severe storm (perhaps a doubling of the 1164 event). Inferred cyclonic situation, severe floods affected North Sea coasts of mainland Europe. **1163** Cold winter. **1164** * 23 February: severe storm. Inferred cyclonic situation, possible North Sea storm, severe gales in the North Sea, storm surge, severe floods affected northwest German coast, 20,000 believed drowned. **1165** Very cold winter. **1167** Very cold winter. **1168** Very cold winter. **1169** Cool summer.

1170S

Anticyclonic or continental. **1170** Fairly mild winter. Warm summer. * Autumn –
8 November: severe storm. Inferred cyclonic situation, possible North Sea storm,
severe sea floods affected the Netherlands. **1172** Very mild wet winter – westerly.
Very mild wet spring – westerly; early March: early phenological events, such as
trees leafing and birds nesting, recorded in mainland Europe. **1173** Very cold dry
winter. Very cold dry spring. Warm summer. **1174** Cool summer. **1176** * Severe
storm. Inferred cyclonic situation, possible North Sea storm, severe sea floods
affected Lincolnshire. Very cold winter – heavy snowfall, followed by intense
frost. **1177** Winter – December (1176): south Baltic Sea frozen. Warm dry summer.
1178 * Severe storm. Inferred cyclonic situation, severe sea floods in the
Netherlands, people drowned. Cold winter – early January: heavy snowfall, deep
drifts, floods followed thaw. **1179** Very cold winter. Cool summer.

1180S

Anticyclonic. **1180** Very cold winter. **1181** Land flood. **1182** Mild winter. **1184**
Warm summer. **1185** Warm summer. **1186** Very mild winter in mainland Europe
– January: very mild in the Baltic region. **1187** Mild dry winter – December (1186)
to January: very mild, early phenological events recorded in mainland Europe,
such as fruit trees in blossom, birds nesting. **1188** Warm summer. **1189** Warm
summer.

1190S

Maritime and cyclonic. **1190** Mild winter. **1191** Drought (?). Cool summer. **1192**
Mild winter in Denmark. **1193** Wet year; storms, thunderstorms and floods. **1196**
Cool summer. **1197** Cool summer. **1198** Mild winter. **1199** Land flood, inferred
heavy rainfall.

1200S

Continental (?). **1200** Cold winter. Wet spring – heavy rain, severe floods. Autumn
– November: four-day wet and windy spell; 7 November: thunderstorm. **1201** Wet
year. Spring – 20 May: start of wet spell to mid September. Wet summer – heavy
thunderstorms with hail; 2 and 17 July: heavy thunderstorms, heavy rain, flood
damage; 15 August: storm, severe floods, crops and property damaged. Autumn –
15 September: end of wet spell from 20 May. **1202** Wet year. Very cold winter.

*Ale was frozen within houses and cellars and sold by weight. Such a great snow
fell also therewith that beasts died in many places in great numbers.*

Raphael Holinshed

Very wet summer – August: frequent thunderstorms. **1203** Spring – April: floods. **1204** Late winter to spring – late January to May: drought with summer-like heat in France. **1205** Cold year; drought. * Very cold winter. Inferred blocking-high situations, one of the coldest winters on record, intense frost from late January to late March with possibly brief mild interludes (as were also known to have occurred in the 1709 very cold winter), five cold spells were distinguished of different intensity between November (1204) and April; frozen rivers in England including the Thames, frozen water bodies in the Netherlands, and it was also possible to walk across the frozen Danish Sound from Germany to Denmark. In England frost prevented ploughing, agricultural work was suspended for over two months, winter seed was destroyed and there was widespread famine. Spring – March: very cold; c.20 March: end of continuous frost. Very warm dry summer – 30 June and 4 August: thunderstorms. **1206** Cold winter – cold spell from 28 December (1205) to 25 March. Spring – 2 May: heavy snowfall in south Scotland. Warm dry summer in mainland Europe – 22 July: heavy thunderstorm. **1207** Winter – December (1206): wet. * 3 February: severe storm. Inferred cyclonic situation, storm-force gales, heavy snowfall, property damaged, trees blown down, many sheep and cattle lost in deep snow. Cold dry spring. Cool dry summer. Autumn – c.30 November: heavy rain. **1208** Drought. Warm dry summer in mainland Europe. **1209** Thames flood, Bermondsey inundated. Dry summer – drought, payments for deepening wells recorded in the Winchester manorial accounts.

1210S

Continental. **1210** Cold winter – very cold spell from January to c.21 February: frost and snow, frozen rivers including the Severn near Gloucester, trees destroyed, wildlife perished; late February: rapid thaw, ice disappeared within four days. Spring – April: cold; May: cold. **1211** Cold winter. Dry summer. Outbreak of fires due to drought led to an early attempt at fire precautions: building legislation came into effect in London the following year whereby roofs made of reeds, rushes, straw or stubble were forbidden. **1212** Dry summer – 17 July: dry southerly winds, the first Great Fire of London, many houses destroyed, over 1,000 people killed; August: cool. Autumn – September: cool, wet. **1213** Probably dry year; dried-up Wye crossed dry-shod. Cold winter – December (1212): gale. **1214** Cold winter. Dry summer – low water level in the Thames, people waded across the river in London. **1215** Magna Carta: King John made concessions to the English barons. * Autumn – 2 October: severe storm. Inferred cyclonic situation. **1216** Winter – December (1215): mild; February: inferred cyclonic situation, strong southwesterly gales, Atlantic storm surge affected Solway Firth, King Alexander's Scottish army struck by sea flood, 1,900 drowned.

* Spring – 28 May: severe storm. Inferred cyclonic situation, stormy conditions and severe northeasterly gales in southeast England, English fleet under King John forced to disperse off the Isle of Thanet, which allowed French forces under Prince Louis to land and occupy much of England. * Summer: severe storm (uncertainty whether the year is 1216 or 1218). Inferred cyclonic situation, severe floods, North Sea coasts of mainland Europe, 10,000 drowned. Autumn – 26 October: severe gales. **1217** Very cold winter. Warm summer. **1218** Mild winter. * Autumn – 24 November: severe storm (uncertainty as to whether year is 1216 or 1218). Inferred cyclonic situation, one of the most severe North Sea storms on record, inferred storm-force gales, severe sea floods affected German and Dutch coasts (also possibly English east coast), coastal defences of Frisia and Holland breached, formation of Zuider Zee initiated, many thousands drowned. **1219** Very cold winter. Wet summer (?). Wet autumn.

1220S

1220 Mild wet winter – January: wet; February: wet. Wet autumn. **1221** Winter – January: cold; February: storm flood. Dry summer – July: mostly dry; 12–13 July: inferred cyclonic situation, continuous rain; August: dry. * Autumn – 25 October 1221 (or 1220): severe storm. Inferred cyclonic situation, storm-force northeasterly gales, much damage in London. **1222** Dry year. Winter – January: stormy, sea floods; 15 February: heavy thunderstorm. Spring – March (or April): heavy snowfall, intense frost, trees badly damaged and did not leaf later in many places. Very warm dry summer – July: dry; August: dry. Wet autumn – 21 September: thunderstorms followed by a wet stormy spell to 9 February (1223). **1223** Wet: a year without a summer. Mild wet winter – December (1222): wet; January: wet; 9 February: end of wet stormy spell from late September 1222. * Late September (1222) to 9 February: wet stormy spell. Inferred cyclonic situations, storm-force gales, buildings damaged and trees blown down. Wet spring. June: thunderstorms and hail.

> *There were such inundations of rain and overflowings of waters continuing in every month of the year that it very greatly hindered the seasons and the fruits were very late in maturing: so much so that in the month of November there were hardly any crops to lay up hastily in the barns.*
>
> Matthew Paris, St Albans

Autumn – September: wet; October: wet. **1224** Mild dry winter – severe drought. * January: severe storm. Inferred cyclonic situation, storm-force gales, buildings and trees blown down. Wet autumn – September: wet; October: wet. * 25 October:

severe storm. Inferred cyclonic situation and storm-force gales, much damage.
1225 Very cold winter – sea frozen off the Norwegian coast. Very dry summer –
June: very dry; July: very dry. Wet autumn – September: wet; October: wet.
1226 Very cold wet winter. Summer crops perished in France due to drought.
Very warm dry autumn in France – an exceptional abundance of wine. **1227** Very
cold winter. Summer – late July: heavy thunderstorms, cattle and sheep killed.
Autumn – September: wet; October: wet. **1228** Winter – severe river floods. Warm
wet summer – heavy thunderstorms and rain, much damage, loss of life. Very wet
autumn – harvest damaged and heavy loss of crops. **1229** Very cold winter –
waters frozen, heavy snowfall. Spring – cold to March.

1230S

Maritime. **1230** Very cold winter – January: heavy snowfall. Summer – 1 July:
heavy thunderstorm in London. **1231** Very dry summer. Very dry autumn.
1232 Dry spring. Warm very dry summer – June: very dry; July: very dry. Autumn –
September: dry; October: dry; November: frequent thunderstorms. **1233** Winter –
17 February: gales in southeast England. Wet spring. Cool wet summer – heavy
rain, widespread floods. Very wet autumn – September: very wet; October: very
wet. **1234** * Very cold winter. December (1233): dry; January: dry; January to early
February: intense frost; 9 February: lying snow in England; accounts from over
40 sources indicate that a large-scale cold anomaly affected many parts of
Europe; olive, fig and nut trees, and vineyards damaged; however, despite
widespread reports of frost it appears that the cold was more intense and longer-
lasting in central and southern Europe, since rivers and water bodies in Austria
and Italy were frozen, including the Venetian lagoons, but the Rhine and Moselle
did not freeze. Summer – July: wet; 23 July: heavy thunderstorm and whirlwind.
Wet autumn. **1235** Very wet spring – Thames rose to exceptionally high levels.
Warm summer – June: dry; July: dry. **1236** Drought. Cold wet winter – January:
very wet; February: very wet; Thames flood, Westminster Palace inundated.

> *Incessant and torrential rain swept into the area, causing much flooding and*
> *hardship to local people. Monsoon-like rains poured from leaden skies through*
> *January, February and the first part of March. Livestock was lost and disease*
> *spread rapidly amongst animals. During the rest of March dry weather set in and*
> *between April and August the area basked in hot sunshine. A prolonged drought*
> *began, and even after the wet winter water soon became scarce and rivers fell to*
> *low levels, especially the Teme and the Avon.*
>
> Anon, Herefordshire and Worcestershire Records

Mild mainly dry spring – early March: very wet; April: inferred dry; May: dry. Very warm dry summer. * Summer: drought. Inferred blocking-high situation.

> *Also in the same summer, as people remarked, after an unusually wet winter, there was a continual drought with an almost intolerable heat continuing four or more months. So much so that marshes and lakes were dried up, watermills stood useless and profitless, and, the water being dried up, the earth gaped into cracks. Also the seed corn in many places barely grew as high as two feet.*
>
> Matthew Paris, St Albans

Very wet autumn – 13 October: heavy rain and floods. * 19 November: severe storm. Inferred cyclonic situation, one of the most severe North Sea storms on record, storm-force gales combined with high tides produced a storm surge, severe sea floods pounded east coast, sea rose continuously for two days and a night without ebbing, beaches swept away, great loss of life, houses destroyed, trees blown down, many sheep and cattle perished, Thames overflowed, Westminster Palace inundated, many shipwrecks.

> *Then on the morrow of St Martin [12 November (os)] and within the octave of the same there burst in astonishing floods of the sea, by night, suddenly, and a most mighty wind resounded, with great and unusual sea and river floods together, which especially in maritime places, deprived all ports of ships, tearing away their anchors, drowned a multitude of men, destroyed flocks of sheep and herds of cattle, plucked out trees by the roots, overturned dwellings, dispersed beaches at Wisbech and in neighbouring townships, and so by the sea shore and coast, countless men perished.*
>
> Matthew Paris, St Albans

1237 Mild winter. * 30 December (1236): severe storm. Inferred cyclonic situation, storm-force gales, houses and trees blown down. February: wet; 21 February: heavy rain, rivers overflowed including Thames, severe and widespread floods. Summer – c.8 June: heavy rain and hail. Autumn – 28 November: severe gales; 29–30 November: thunderstorm. **1238** Wet winter. Wet spring. Partly dry summer – June: very warm and dry; July: very warm and dry; August: wet.

> *The drought and heat were beyond measure and custom in two or more of the summer months.*
>
> Matthew Paris, St Albans

Very wet autumn. * 28 September: severe storm. Inferred cyclonic situation, storm-force gales, over 20 shipwrecks off Portsmouth alone. October: very wet; November: very wet. **1239** Mild wet winter – December (1238): severe floods; January: wet; February: wet. Wet spring – March: wet.

1240S

Anticyclonic. **1240** Winter – January: dry; February: dry. Spring – March: dry; April: wet; May: wet. Warm wet summer – June: wet; July: wet; August: wet. Wet autumn – September: wet; October: wet; November: wet. **1241** Very cold winter – many rivers frozen; December (1240): wet; 8 December: heavy snowfall. Mild dry spring – April: mild dry; May: mild dry. Warm dry summer – June: warm dry; July: warm dry; August: warm dry. Warm dry autumn – September: warm dry; October: warm dry. * April to October: drought. Inferred blocking-high situation, one of the most severe droughts on record, exceptional warm dry conditions (comparable to the 1959 drought).

> *Drought and intolerable heat dried up deep lakes and wide marshes, exhausted the rivers, desiccated the fishponds, and suspended the working of mills, verdure perished and herds pined away from hunger and thirst.*
>
> Matthew Paris, St Albans

1242 Cold winter – December (1241): very cold; heavy snowfall, frozen rivers. Spring – May: mild dry. Warm dry summer – June: warm dry; July; warm dry; August: warm dry. Autumn – September: warm dry; October: warm dry. * 26–27 November: severe storm. Inferred cyclonic situation, heavy rain and thunderstorms, sea and river floods, Thames overflowed, parts of London inundated, including Westminster and Lambeth, together with surrounding low-lying country up to 10 km (6 miles) from the river. **1243** Renewed drought. **1244** Warm summer – August: dry. Dry autumn – September: mostly dry; October; early November: dry; 20 November: drought broken by heavy thunderstorms. **1245** Drought. Dry summer.

> *There was a dry summer this year in Wales.*
>
> Oseney Annals

June: dry; July: dry; August: wet. Autumn – September: wet; October: wet. **1246** Inferred cold winter – December (1245): cold; 12–13 December: heavy snowfall in Ireland, lying snow to 1 January; heavy snowfall in central and east Europe, Black Sea frozen up to 5 km (3 miles) off coast. Spring – 2 May: intense frost with snow, fruit trees and crops damaged. Wet summer – June: wet; July: wet; 26–27 July: heavy thunderstorms with large hail, river floods, crops damaged, birds and beasts killed; August: wet. Autumn – September: wet; October: wet. **1247** Winter – 19–21 February: start of cold wet spell to 28 March. Wet spring – March: cold wet; April: cold wet; May: cold wet.

> *A long spell of bad weather followed [February]: unseasonable, wintry, stormy, cold and wet, so that both gardeners and farmers complained that spring had been transformed into winter by a backward movement, and they very much feared that they would be deceived in their hopes of crops, plants, fruit trees and corn. This disturbed weather lasted continuously up to the feast of the translation of St Benedict [18 July NS], scarcely a single fine day intervening.*
>
> Matthew Paris, St Albans

1248 Very dry summer. Dry autumn.

> *This year passed temperate and calm, filling the barns with abundance of corn, and making the presses flow with wine.*
>
> Matthew Paris, St Albans

Mild dry winter (?). Spring – March: mild dry (?). Very dry summer – June: very dry; July: very dry.

> *In many countries extremely destructive fires raged, reducing towns and cities to ashes, but were caused neither by heat nor drought[?] In England, indeed, not to mention other fires, the greater part of the borough of Newcastle-upon-Tyne, together with the bridge, was consumed by a raging fire.*
>
> Matthew Paris, St Albans

Autumn – November: very warm. * 26–27 November: severe storm. Inferred cyclonic situation/North Sea storm, storm-force gales, storm surge, severe sea floods, dykes breached in the Netherlands, land lost to sea in Schleswig. Matthew Paris commented on a storm surge which occurred at about the same time and questioned the reason for its exceptional effect, not knowing, understandably, the suction power of an intense North Sea depression to raise the sea level in this situation.

> *The sea exceeded its normal height by a long way and caused irreparable damage to those living near it ... the sea rose three times with a tremendous surge, without*

any appreciable decrease or ebb. Although it seemed likely that this was due to the force of the wind, which was blowing from the sea at the time with extreme violence, nevertheless because it often happened that the wind raged from the sea and yet the sea did not rise as violently as this, older people were astonished at this unheard novelty.

Matthew Paris, St Albans, December 1248

1249 Very mild wet winter.

The whole weather of winter was changed into spring so that neither snow nor frost covered the face of the earth, nor bound it in their customary manner, for two days together; trees were seen to be sprouting in February and young birds singing and sporting as though it were April.

Matthew Paris, St Albans

December (1248): very mild; late month: sea floods; January: very mild; 4 January: North Sea storm surge affected the Netherlands and northwest Germany; February: mostly mild, stormy, trees uprooted. * 11 February: severe storm. Inferred cyclonic situation, North Sea storm surge, severe sea floods, dykes breached in the Netherlands. 26–27 February: heavy snowfall; according to Matthew Paris a tournament planned at Northampton on 26 February was postponed because of bad weather. Spring – March: very mild; April: cold spell to mid May. Summer – June: wet, heavy rain and river floods, inferred cyclonic situations.

At the beginning of June such a huge deluge of rain fell, mostly around Abingdon, that willows and other trees and houses near the rivers and streams, and even sheepcotes and the sheep in them, salt-works and mills with bridges, and a chapel not far from Abingdon, were carried away. The green corn with its sprouting ears coming into flower was levelled to the ground so that the bread afterwards seemed to have been made from bran rather than wheat.

Matthew Paris, St Albans

July: dry (?). Autumn – 4 November: gales.

1250s

Continental (?). **1250** Autumn – stormy. * 8 October: severe storm. Inferred cyclonic situation, one of the most severe North Sea storms on record, storm-force gales, inferred storm surge, severe sea floods, southern North Sea coasts pounded, much damage, east and southeast English coasts, and also in the Netherlands, sea defences breached, marshes inundated, rivers overflowed due to their waters being held back by the large rise in sea level, Zuider Zee enlarged.

Daily in the first week of the waxing moon [from 8 October] the air began to be much disturbed by dense mist and violent winds. The winds began to tear off the branches and the leaves which were then withering on the trees and carry them a great distance through the air. And what was more damaging, the rough sea, rising above its usual level and the tide flowing twice in succession without any ebb, made such a horrible roaring noise that it resounded in places from it, to the amazement of the hearers, even the older ones. No one living now could remember seeing this before. In the darkness of the night the sea seemed to burn as if set on fire [perhaps due to so-called 'Fire of Sea', caused by bioluminescent plankton] and waves joined with waves as if in battle, so that the dexterity of the sailors could not come to the aid of their doomed ships. Even large and strongly built vessels foundered and sank. And if we remain silent concerning others, at one single port, namely Hartburn [possibly near Tynemouth], besides small and medium-sized boats, three fine ones were swallowed by rough seas. At an eastern port called Winchelsea, apart from sheds for salt-making, fishermen's buildings, bridges and mills, more than three hundred houses and several churches were destroyed in that place by the violent rise of the sea. Holland in England and Holland overseas, with Flanders and other low-lying places near the sea, suffered irreparable damage. Rivers flowing into the sea were forced back and overflowed, so that meadows, mills, and the neighbouring houses were destroyed, and the corn not yet stored in the barns was swept away from the flooded fields.

Matthew Paris, St Albans

1251 Very cold winter. * Spring – 21 March: inferred severe storm. Inferred cyclonic situation, one of the most severe North Sea storms on record, storm-force gales, storm surge, severe sea floods (sea rose 2 m/7 ft higher than previously known level), east coast pounded from Lincolnshire to Kent. * 26 May: severe storm. Inferred cyclonic situation, heavy thunderstorms, much damage, houses destroyed in Windsor. Summer – 3 June: out-of-season snowfall. Autumn – 24 September: heavy rain. * 6 October: inferred severe storm. Inferred cyclonic situation, severe sea floods. **1252** Dry. * Winter – 20–21 January: severe storm. Inferred cyclonic situation, severe gales, sea floods, much damage. February: dry. Very mild dry spring – March: mild dry, 20 March: start of drought. * 1252–1253: drought. Inferred blocking-high situations; 1252–1253: the two driest consecutive years on record.

During most of March, and the whole of April and May, the earth was parched by
the burning heat of the sun, the wind continually blowing from the east, north or
north-east ... unendurable heat so burnt up the surface of the earth that all the
herbage was withered, and the meadows refused all kinds of food to the cattle.

Matthew Paris, St Albans

April: mild dry; May: mild dry. Very warm dry summer – June: warm dry; July:
warm dry; August: wet. During the drought many people died from the excessive
heat and crops were ruined; the drought continued into June and July but was
partly broken by heavy rain in August.

The grass was so burned up in pastures and meadows that if a man took up some
of it in his hands it straight fell to powder, and so cattle were starved for lack of
meat. And because of the exceeding hot nights there was such abundance of fleas,
flies and gnats that people were vexed and brought in case to be weary of their
lives. And herewith chanced many diseases, as sweats, agues and other. In the
harvest time there occurred a great dearth and murrain amongst cattle, especially
in Norfolk, the Fens and other parts of the south.

Anon

Great heat and drought in the summer of this year so that people used to cross the
Shannon without wetting their feet: and the wheat was reaped twenty nights
before Lammas, and all the corn was reaped at that time; and the trees were
burning from the sun.

Irish Chronicles

Wet autumn – September: wet; October: wet, heavy rain and river floods.
1253 Dry. Cold winter. Spring – April: dry; May: dry. Summer – June: dry; July:
wet; August: wet, heavy rain, severe floods, rivers overflowed, much damage, but
only a temporary break in drought which did not make up for the previous
shortage as the rain quickly ran off hardened ground into the rivers and failed to
replenish deep springs. Partly wet autumn – heavy rain, rivers overflowed;
September: wet (?). * October: severe storm. Inferred cyclonic situation/storm-
force gales, North Sea storm surge, high tides, severe sea floods along the east
coast from Lincolnshire to the Thames estuary. 6 October: renewed drought, as
corn could not be ground at local mills, farmers were forced to make a day's
journey to have it done. **1254** A year without a summer. Very cold winter with
northeasterly winds January to March; 20–21 December (1253): heavy snowfall;
January: cold; February: cold. Cold spring – northeasterly winds; March: cold;

April: cold; May: cold. Cool summer – June: cool dry (?); July: cool very wet; 8 July: heavy hailstorm, much damage; August: cool wet (?). Wet autumn – stormy, sea floods, large areas inundated including several Fenland villages; September: cool wet (?); October: cool wet (?); November: cool wet (?). **1255** Cold winter – February: very wet; 21 February: start of wet stormy spell to March. Spring – late March: start of drought into early June.

> *The north wind blowing nearly the whole spring. And throughout the whole of the month of April, neither shower nor dew moistened the dry earth or gave it warmth. The air, however, parched by the blowing of the north and east winds, assumed the colour of citrons and generated sickness.*
>
> Matthew Paris, St Albans

Summer – early June: dry.

> *In this same summer there was a drought due to the east winds continuing, taking away the morning dew and suspending that of the evening, from mid March to the calends of June [8 June NS]; the grains of corn were seen lying in the dust whole, not decaying so as to germinate and perfect their increase.*
>
> Matthew Paris, St Albans

Mid to late June: wet.

> *The earth with its half-dead roots and seeds, felt beneficient rain and seasonable sweet refreshing ... dews decay was turned into living sap, and everything revived promising a harvest of fruit.*
>
> Matthew Paris, St Albans

c.13 July: thunderstorms, hail, floods. Autumn – 8 November: start of wet spell to 11 June (1256). **1256** Wet year. Cold wet winter. Summer – occasional heavy thunderstorms, floods. Very wet autumn – September: very wet; October: very wet; November: very wet. **1257** A year without a summer. Very wet winter – December (1256): very wet; January: very wet; February: wet. Wet spring – March: wet; April: wet; May: wet. Cool wet summer – June: wet; July: wet; August: wet. Wet autumn – September: wet; October: wet; November: warm wet. **1258** Wet; a year without a summer – volcanic dust veil (estimated DVI 1000), major eruption in the tropics. Wet winter – December (1257): mild wet; January: mild wet; February: wet; mid February into March: cold, northeasterly winds, snowfall, poor people suffered, farming halted, flocks lost.

*Not a single frost or fine day occurred nor was the surface of the lake hardened by
frost but continuous heavy rain and mist obscured the sky until early February
followed by a long spell of cold northerly winds.*

Anon

Cold very late spring – northerly winds; March: cold (?); April: cold (?); May:
cold (?). Wet summer – inferred volcanic dust-veil effect; June: cold (?) wet; July: wet.
* 1 July: severe storm. Inferred cyclonic situation, heavy rain, severe floods, crops
damaged, loss of life. Although crops ripened during a following brief warm
spell, they were badly beaten down later by heavy rain during August into
autumn. August: wet. Wet autumn – September: wet; October: wet; very late
harvest, some crops not gathered in until November, many thousands died of
famine. **1259** Winter – 6 December (1258): severe storm; 8 December:
thunderstorm, heavy rain. Very warm dry summer – August: dry. Autumn –
October: wet; November: wet.

1260s

Anticyclonic. **1260** Mild winter – December (1259): wet; January: wet. Late spring.
Mainly dry early summer – June: dry; July: dry; August: cool and showery;
3 August: heavy thunderstorm, hail. Autumn – September: cool; October: cool.
1261 Very cold winter – December (1260): mild dry; January: cold; February: cold;
frozen Thames, bore people, carriages and various entertainments (early type of
Frost Fair). **1262** Warm dry summer. **1263** Drought. Very cold winter – December
(1262): frozen Thames, bore people and carriages. 7 December (1262): severe
storm. Inferred cyclonic situation, severe gales, houses and trees damaged. Warm
dry summer – June: very dry; July: very dry. Wet autumn (?). * 9 October: inferred
severe storm. Inferred cyclonic situation/storm-force gales, 'hail and tempest',
Norwegian fleet battered at the Battle of Largs (Ayrshire). **1264** Spring – 15 March:
stormy in north Scotland; 20 May: gales in southeast England. **1265** Storms,
strong winds. Spring – 24 May: heavy thunderstorm. Autumn – November: river
floods, inferred heavy rain. **1266** Mild winter. Warm summer – June: dry; July:
dry. **1267** Drought in east England. Cold winter. Warm summer. **1268** * Severe
storm. Inferred cyclonic situation, Dunwich partly lost to the sea, river Blyth
partially silted up and ships hampered entering and leaving harbour. Very cold
winter, Thames froze in London; December (1267): cold (?); January: cold (?).
19–21 January: severe storms; February: cold (?). Spring – April: heavy
thunderstorm followed by a fortnight-long wet spell. Summer – June: dry; July:
dry; August: wet. Autumn – September: wet; October: wet. **1269** Very cold winter –
Skagerrak and Kattegat frozen; December (1268): cold (?). 2 December (1268): severe

ice storm. Inferred cyclonic situation, freezing rain, glazed frost ('black ice') on ground, hazardous walking and riding on slippery surfaces. 7 December (1268): Thames froze, shipping blocked, merchandise transported overland from Channel ports to London, situation continued to 9 February; January: cold (?); February: cold (?), wet; thaw with floods probably late February. Summer – June: dry; July: dry; August: wet. Autumn – September: wet; October: wet.

1270s

Cyclonic. **1270** Very cold winter – December (1269): cold; January: cold; Thames initially frozen upstream from London Bridge, river bore people and animals; ice later extended downstream, water traffic obstructed from entering the Thames, merchandise transported overland from Channel ports to London. February: cold but undated thaw, heavy rain, floods. Wet spring – March: river floods, inferred heavy rain; April: wet; May: wet. Wet summer (?) – heavy rain, crops damaged, Thames overflowed, severe floods, rain-famine. Autumn – November: cool. **1271** Drought. Cold winter – December (1270): cold; January: cold; February: cold. Spring – March: cold. Cool summer – June: dry (?); July: dry (?). * 11 July: severe storm. Inferred cyclonic situation, storm-force gales, heavy rain, trees blown down. Autumn – widespread gales, great damage; 18–19 September: heavy rain, river floods in Canterbury, much of the city swept away; November: cool (?). **1272** Cold winter (?) – December (1271): cold (?); January: cold (?); February: cold (?). Warm very dry summer – June: very dry; July: very dry; August: dry (?). Very dry autumn – September: dry; October: very dry; November: very dry. **1273** Winter – floods. Spring – March: very wet, river floods. * Late March: severe storm. Inferred cyclonic situation, storm-force gales, houses and trees blown down. Very wet summer – June: very wet; July: very wet. **1274–1275** Undated sea floods on Sussex coast. **1274** Spring – March: very cold; April: dry (?); May: dry (?). Very dry summer – June: very dry; July: very dry. **1275** Dry spring – May: dry (?). Cool summer – June: wet, floods; August: wet. Wet autumn – September: wet, storm surge, sea floods; October: wet; November: wet. **1276** Wet winter – very cold winter in mainland Europe; December (1275): wet; January: wet; February: wet. Spring – March: wet; April: dry; May: dry. Very warm dry summer – June: dry; July: dry. **1277** Cold winter – February: very wet. Spring – March: very wet, river floods; April: mild dry. Very dry summer – June: very dry; July: very dry. Autumn – c.16 October: heavy rain, floods in east England; sea floods on Lincolnshire coast. **1278** Mild winter. Dry summer – June: very dry; July: very dry. Autumn – November: very warm. **1279** Very mild winter – December (1278): very mild; January: very mild; February: very mild; 10 February: storm surge (?), sea floods, much damage in northwest England. Spring – March: very mild; May: heavy thunderstorms, buildings and trees damaged. Summer – June: dry; July: dry.

1280s

Maritime (?). **1280** Spring – April: river floods. * Summer – 9 August: severe storm. Inferred cyclonic situation, heavy rain, severe river floods, houses, mills and bridges submerged, crops swept away, people and cattle drowned. Autumn – 16 October: heavy snowfall; November: wet. **1281** Winter – December (1280): wet spell to 13 January; c.30 January: start of very cold spell to early March, heavy snowfall, farming activities suspended. Spring – early March: very cold; drought followed, Thames ran dry, crossed dry shod. **1282** * Very cold winter. Inferred blocking-high situation; December (1281): heavy snowfall; 1 January to 9 February: very cold, heavy snowfall, Thames froze, five arches of old London Bridge carried away due to ice pressure, other bridges, including one at Rochester similarly affected, frozen river crossed dry shod between Lambeth and Westminster, fish frozen dead in ponds, birds perished from hunger. Warm summer. * Autumn – November (?): severe storm. Inferred cyclonic situation, severe gales, severe sea floods, inferred North Sea storm surge, buildings and churches, including Spalding monastery, destroyed, many people drowned in coastal towns of east England including Boston, Great Yarmouth, Dunwich and Ipswich. 6 November: sea floods in north Wales. **1283** Mild dry winter, notably early vegetative growth in mainland Europe. Cool wet summer. Autumn – September: wet; October: wet. **1284** Warm dry summer – June: very dry; July: very dry; August wet (?). Wet autumn – October: warm; November: warm. **1285** * Early 1285: inferred severe storm. Inferred cyclonic situation, sea floods affected Fens and Humberside. Mild wet winter. Spring – March: mild wet. Very warm dry summer – June: very dry; July: very dry. **1286** Cold winter. * Spring – March: severe storm. Inferred cyclonic situation, east coast pounded by combined strong easterly winds and high tides, 100 m (330 ft) wide coastal strip washed away, coastal houses, churches and a small monastery lost to the sea. May: dry. Summer – June: dry; July: dry. Autumn – November: cold. **1287** Cold winter. * December (1286): severe storm. Inferred cyclonic situation, one of the most severe North Sea storms on record, storm-force northwesterly gales, storm surge, east coast pounded, much of Dunwich swept into the sea, onset of the port's decline. * 6–7 January: severe storm. Inferred cyclonic situation/storm-force gales/heavy rain, severe sea floods on east coast, many places inundated, included the Fens, Yarmouth, Dunwich and Ipswich. * 9 February: severe storm. Inferred cyclonic situation/storm-force northerly gales/North Sea storm surge/heavy rain, severe sea floods on east coast, many places inundated from the Humber and East Anglia to Kent and Sussex, where the last remnants of old

Winchelsea were engulfed, floods also in Norfolk, Horsey Gap probably breached, sea waters swept inland to Ingham, Potter Heigham and Hickling, rising to a level 30 cm (1 ft) above Hickling Priory altar, over 100 people drowned in Hickling alone; St Benet's Abbey, Holme, saved by its enclosing walls, Great Yarmouth flooded including its church, many shipwrecks. Dry spring – March: cold. Warm dry summer – June: dry; July: dry. **1288** Drought. Mild winter (?). * 15 December (1287): severe storm. Inferred cyclonic situation, one of the most severe North Sea storms on record, inferred storm-force gales, probable storm surge, severe sea floods, East Anglian coast badly breached, towns inundated, houses swept away, many hundreds drowned, cattle and freshwater fish perished; severe floods also inundated Holland, Zuider Zee further enlarged, many thousands drowned. * 24–29 December (1287): severe storms. Inferred cyclonic situations/storm-force gales, severe sea floods affected East Anglia, Yarmouth and neighbouring towns inundated, Norfolk Broads created. January: tidal floods in the Thames; February: sea floods affected English east coast. * 11 February: severe storm. Inferred cyclonic situation, northerly winds, North Sea storm surge, severe sea floods, dykes destroyed, Thanet, Romney and Winchelsea inundated; Thames estuary flood, villages distant from the river inundated but uncertainty as to whether this is the same event as February 1287. Very warm dry summer, followed by great loss of life.

> In the beginning of July, that is to say, on the feast of SS Processus and Martinian, there began an intolerable heat and an increasing great drought, which endured continually for five weeks, namely, to the feast of St Oswald, so that in the interval it did not rain at all.
>
> Oseney Annals

July to mid August: very warm dry, many people died from excessive heat. Autumn – 22 October: storms at sea off north England; November: cold. **1289** Very mild winter in mainland Europe; floods. Spring – March: cold. Very warm summer – June: very dry; 9 July to 5 August: mostly wet and windy. Wet autumn – November: warm; 7 November: sea floods.

1290s

Continental (?). **1290** Mild wet winter.

> Snow was not once seen to cover the earth but instead rain distilled almost day and night that its heaviness by day darkened the earth and the air.
>
> Oseney Annals

Uninterrupted transition from autumn (1289) into spring over mainland Europe, trees retained leaves until new foliage appeared, strawberries eaten at Christmas, vines in growth and blossomed mid January. 18 January: severe floods, much damage in Norwich. Wet spring – March: dry. Dry summer. Autumn – September: wet; October: wet. **1291** Spring – May: dry. Very warm summer – June: very dry; July: very dry; August: wet. Wet autumn – September: wet; October: wet. **1292** Winter – 2 December (1291): severe floods. Spring – March: cold. * 25 May: severe storm. Inferred cyclonic situation, gales, sea floods in north England. Summer – floods; August: wet. Wet autumn – 1 November: thunderstorm with violent winds, floods. **1293** Mild winter (?). * December (1292): inferred severe storm. Inferred cyclonic situation, North Sea storm surge, widespread floods in east England. 3–4 January: thunderstorm, gales, sea floods. * Spring – 22 April: severe storm. Inferred cyclonic situation/storm-force northerly winds, Channel and North Sea, ships took shelter at Scarborough (Yorkshire), snowfall, followed by thunderstorm and heavy rain into May. May: wet; snowfall. Warm summer – June: dry; July: wet; 26 July: prolonged thunderstorm; August: wet. **1294** Winter – December (1293): cold; January: cold. Spring – April: wet; 18 April: wind and snow in north England; May: wet; 21 May: heavy snowfall. Cool wet summer – July: wet; August: wet, river floods. Wet autumn – September: wet. * October: inferred severe storm. Inferred cyclonic situation, North Sea storm surge, severe floods in east and southeast England, Dunwich harbour breached, Rotherhithe, Bermondsey and Westminster inundated. **1295** Cold wet winter. * 26–27 January: severe storm. Inferred cyclonic situation, storm-force gales, heavy rain, winter-seed badly damaged. Spring – March: wet; 8–9 April: strong winds, heavy rain in north England. **1296** Drought. Mild winter. Spring – March: inferred heavy rain, river floods in north England; c.5 April: inferred heavy rain, river floods affected the Tweed. Warm summer – June: wet; July: wet. Autumn – October: wet; November: wet. **1297** Cold winter. Spring – 16 April: heavy thunderstorm, giant hail, fireballs. May: very dry. Warm very dry summer – June: very dry; July: very dry. Autumn – October: dry; November: dry. **1298** River floods. (**or 1297**). Spring – May: wet. Mainly dry summer – Oxford fires; June: very dry; July: very dry. **1299** Very cold winter – February: wet. Spring – March: wet. Summer – June: warm; July: warm.

LATE MIDDLE AGES RECESSION: 1300–1539

1300S

Continental (?). A dry decade. **1300** Cold winter. Cold spring. Very dry summer – June: very dry; July: very dry. Autumn – November: cold. **1301** Cold winter in

Scotland, mild in mainland Europe; December (1300): cold. Wet spring (?).
Summer – August: wet (?). Autumn – September: wet (?); October: wet (?). **1302** Sea
flood in Solway Firth. Mild winter. Spring – May: wet. Dry summer – fire
precautions taken in London; June: very dry; July: very dry. Autumn – October:
warm; November: warm. **1303** Dry. Very cold winter. Spring – May: dry. Warm
summer – June: dry; July: dry; August: wet. Wet autumn. **1304** Wet winter. Spring
– March: wet. Warm very dry summer – start of dry conditions that continued
into 1305; perhaps the time when the Rhine fell to a very low level and could be
crossed on foot in several places between Strasbourg and Basel. Autumn –
September: very dry. **1305** Winter – January: cold; February: cold dry. Spring –
March: cold dry; May: very dry. Very warm dry summer. * Summer to autumn:
drought. Inferred blocking-high situations.

> *In this year there was such burning heat and such a drought throughout the*
> *summer that the hay failed in most parts of the country and the beasts of the field*
> *died for want and a double heat oppressed mankind.*
>
> Matthew of Westminster

c.22 July to 22 August: very warm dry. Autumn – c.22 September to 22 October:
very warm dry. **1306** * Very cold winter. Late December (1305) to early February:
intense frost and snow prevented ploughing and other farm work; spring
ploughing usually began in early January in east England.

> *The fish died in the ponds, the birds in the woods, and the herds in the fields. And*
> *many of the birds of the air were so enfeebled that they were caught without nets*
> *or snares by the hands of men.*
>
> Matthew of Westminster

21 February to 21 April: intense frost.

> *The frost was broken up by a rainy southwest wind for three days. And when men*
> *thought that the winter was over, the air again gathered in clouds and the east*
> *wind blew assiduously, the frost returned.*
>
> Matthew of Westminster

Frozen rivers in mainland Europe, including the Seine, Rhine and Po; Skagerrak
and Kattegat also frozen; one of the most severe freezing events of the Baltic Sea
on record. Spring – March to 21 April: very cold. Very dry summer – June: very
dry; July: very dry. **1307** * Winter – 2 February: severe storm. Inferred cyclonic

situation, severe gales, North Sea storm surge and severe sea floods in east England. Spring – April: dry (?); May: dry (?). Summer – June: dry (?) July: dry (?). Very wet autumn – October: very wet; November: very wet. **1308** Winter – December (1307): wet. Spring – May: very dry. Summer – June: very dry; August: wet. Autumn – September: wet; October: wet. **1309** Very cold winter – entertainments on the frozen Thames (early type of Frost Fair); January: rapid thaw, river floods. Summer – June: very dry; July: very dry; August: wet. Autumn – September: wet (?); October: dry; November: dry.

1310S

Cyclonic summer (Fig. 48). **1310** Water shortage in London. Very cold winter – Thames froze, river bore people, London Bridge damaged by ice, shipping from the Baltic to the Channel disrupted by ice. Spring – May: dry. Cool summer – June: dry; July: dry. Autumn – October: dry; November: dry. **1311** Winter – January: cold (?). Spring – May: dry. Summer – June: dry; harvest: cool and stormy. **1312** Winter – January to early spring: dry. Spring – April: dry; May: dry. Summer – June: dry. **1313** Wet winter (?). Summer – June: dry; July: dry; August: wet; bad harvest, famine, many cattle perished. Wet autumn. **1314** Wet. Cold winter. Wet spring – April: cold. Cool wet summer – July: wet; August: wet; heavy rain, river floods,

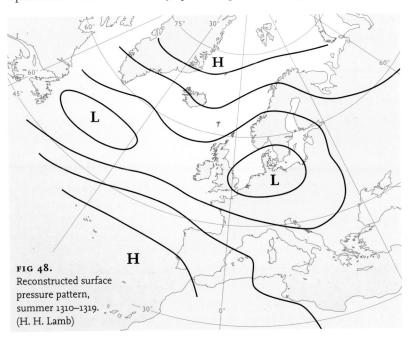

FIG 48.
Reconstructed surface pressure pattern, summer 1310–1319. (H. H. Lamb)

damaged crops, bread shortage, corn imported from France. Very wet autumn – floods. **1315** Very wet: a year without a summer; inferred volcanic dust veil lasted about five years, distant eruption, Kaharoa (New Zealand). Wet winter – December (1314) to January: cold and wet, river floods, occasional lying snow. Wet spring. Cool very wet summer – one of the worst summers on record, inferred volcanic dust-veil effect; July: very wet; August: very wet, widespread river floods, bad harvest, food shortage, great mortality, cattle plague, several famine years followed. Very wet autumn – river floods. **1316** Very wet year; river floods, Fens inundated, famine, cattle plague. Cold wet winter – December (1315): very wet, river floods. Wet spring – March: wet; May: wet; heavy rain hampered crop sowing. Cool wet summer – inferred volcanic dust-veil effect; river floods, very bad harvest. Wet autumn – September: wet; October: wet, river floods; November: floods. **1317** Wet year, river floods. Cold wet winter – frost, snow. Inferred cool wet summer – volcanic dust-veil effect; bad harvest. **1318** Cold winter – heavy snowfall in Ireland; depleted fodder stock, farm animals turned out of farms to forage, thousands perished in frozen pastures. Spring – March: sea floods coincided with North Sea storm surge in the Netherlands; May: cold wet. Warm dry summer – June: very dry; July: very dry; cattle plague, thousands of putrefying carcasses burnt or buried in mass graves, so-called 'Great Dying of Beasts' continued into the early 1320s. Wet autumn (?). **1319** Winter – floods; very cold in mainland Europe: frozen rivers and lakes in Italy and Switzerland. Summer – July: wet (?); August: very wet; wet harvest, cattle plague continued. Very wet autumn – September: very wet; October: very wet.

1320s

Continental (?). **1320** Summer – August: wet; bad harvest. Wet autumn. **1321** * Inferred severe storm. Inferred cyclonic situation, North Sea storm surge, severe sea floods, bridges and Fen causeway damaged. Winter – unfavourable conditions in Scotland, people suffered, many animals perished. Spring – April: wet; May: wet. Very warm summer – June: dry; July: dry. **1322** Winter – February: very cold. Spring – March: very cold; April: very cold. Summer – August: wet (?). Autumn – September: wet (?); October: wet (?). **1323** Very cold winter, also mainland Europe – one of the most severe freezing events of the Baltic on record; Adriatic Sea froze. Spring – April: wet (?) May: wet (?). Autumn – October: dry; November: dry. **1324** Sea floods affected Fens and Kent coast. Warm summer – August: wet (?). Autumn – September: wet (?); October: wet (?). **1325** Drought year; rivers in France so low that the transport of goods by boat was impossible. Mild winter (?) – floods. Very warm very dry summer – June: very dry; July: very dry; water shortage, dried-up springs, streams and rivers, low salty Thames, tidal water penetrated further upstream than usual. Autumn – November: cold dry. **1326** Drought, water shortage, Thames salty nearly all year. * Drought. Inferred blocking-high situations.

> *For in this year there was an unprecedented drought in Ireland: so that in winter there was not much rain, and in spring, summer and autumn there was none, and very great dryness and great heat, so that the brooks and great rivers (which always gave plenty of water) were almost dry.*
>
> Anon

> *There was a great drought throughout all England both in summer and in other times of the year, so that men led their animals for watering, in some parts of the country, for 3 or 4 leagues. Brooks and streams, wells and marshes, which previously had never dried up, everywhere became dry; the pond at Newport in Essex, in circuit nearly a league, was dry, so that all the fish perished. In the same way, the water at Havering Mere, formerly bearing great ships, was shrunk to such an extent that it was hardly possible for it to take a little vessel. And the river Thames for nearly the whole year was salt.*
>
> Annales Paulini

* Severe storm. Inferred cyclonic situation, severe gales, damage by cliff erosion at Dunwich. Cold dry winter – mainland Europe: very cold winter, pack ice in the Baltic and North Sea, Dutch coastal estuary waters frozen, frozen rivers including the Seine and Rhine, Bodensee partly frozen. Spring – March: cold dry. Warm very dry summer – June: very dry; July: very dry. **1327** Heavy rain, floods in north England. Winter – January: dry. Dry summer – June: dry; July: dry. Autumn – November: cold. **1328** Cold winter. * 22 January: severe storm. Inferred cyclonic situation/storm-force gales, severe sea floods in east England, Dunwich inundated, 400 houses and three churches lost to the sea, harbour entrance irrevocably blocked, river Blyth diverted northwards, port's trade effectively terminated, many merchants and citizens left, nearby village of Newton swept away. Spring – March: cold. Warm summer. **1329** Wet winter (?). Warm very dry summer – June: very dry; July: very dry. Autumn – November: cold. **1328** Cold winter. * 22 January: severe storm. Inferred cyclonic situation/storm-force gales, severe sea floods in east England, Dunwich inundated, 400 houses and three churches lost to the sea, harbour entrance irrevocably blocked, river Blyth diverted northwards, port's trade effectively terminated, many merchants and citizens left, nearby village of Newton swept away. Spring – March: cold. Warm summer. **1329** Wet winter (?). Warm very dry summer – June: very dry; July: very dry. Autumn – November: cold.

1330s

Westerly summers (Fig. 49). **1330** Cold winter. * January: inferred severe storm. Inferred cyclonic situation/North Sea storm, probable storm surge, severe sea floods affected Fens and Sussex; this event coincided with lesser storm damage in the Netherlands. Spring – March: cold; May: wet. Cool wet summer – bad harvest, famine. Cool wet autumn. **1331–1332** Severe floods, Sussex, Kent and east English coasts, lower reaches of the rivers flowing into the Wash and Humber overwhelmed. **1331** Early winter – very wet, floods. Dry spring – early March to mid June: very dry.

> *About this time there was such drought that for 15 weeks no rain at all fell upon the earth ... but suddenly a little before the day the tournament was to be held there fell so much rain that all the ground was thoroughly watered.*
>
> Annales Paulini

Very dry summer. **1332** Dry. Very dry spring. Warm dry summer – June: dry; July: dry. **1333** Dry. Dry winter (?). Spring – April: dry. Warm dry summer – June: very dry; July: very dry. **1334** Very cold winter. Warm dry summer. Autumn – November: cold; c.19 November: early start to winter. * 30 November to 1 December:

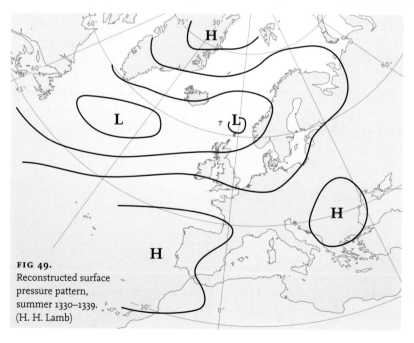

FIG 49.
Reconstructed surface pressure pattern, summer 1330–1339. (H. H. Lamb)

severe storm. Inferred cyclonic situation/North Sea storm/storm-force gales, storm surge, severe sea floods affected English east coast and Thames estuary, sea walls breached, many animals drowned, inundated low-lying agricultural land became infertile salt marshes; this event coincided with a major storm surge that affected the Netherlands. **1335** Very cold winter – many animals died of hunger; *c.*19 November (1334): start of cold spell with frost and snow to March; *c.*7 December (1334): severe snowstorm, westerly winds, heavy thunderstorm in northeast England. Spring – March: cold. Cool summer – August: very wet; floods affected east coast and probably the Fens, crops damaged. Autumn – September: very wet; October: dry; November: dry. **1336** Sea floods affected east England; this event coincided with lesser storm damage in the Netherlands. Mild winter (?) – heavy snowfall in Ireland (?). Warm dry summer – June: very dry; July: very dry. **1337** * Winter – January: mild; inferred severe storm. Inferred cyclonic situation, severe sea floods, extensive storm damage in east England. Spring – *c.*25 May: thunderstorm, heavy rain. Summer – June: dry (?), 25 June: thunderstorm, heavy rain; July: wet; August: very wet. Wet autumn – September: very wet; October: very wet; November: wet. **1338** Cold wet winter – December (1337): wet, floods. * January: wet; inferred severe storm. Inferred cyclonic situation, North Sea storm surge, severe sea floods, east England, sea defences breached, barns and crops inundated, sheep drowned; this event coincided with lesser storm damage in the Netherlands. Warm summer – June: dry (?); July: dry (?); August: very wet. Very wet autumn – September: very wet; October: wet; November: wet. **1339** Very cold wet winter – floods; December (1338) to February: intense frost.

> *In the beginning of December there came a very hard frost so that the whole of the saturated ground was completely frozen and the whole earth was seen to be like ice. This frost lasted 12 weeks whence the whole of the winter sowing was as if dead.*
>
> Anon

Spring – March: cold. Dry summer – August: wet (?). * 12 August: severe storm. Inferred cyclonic situation/heavy rain, severe river floods (Tyne). Wet autumn (?) – September: wet (?); October: wet.

1340S

Maritime or cyclonic; northwesterly-type summer (Fig. 50). **1340** Winter – early wet, late very cold dry; January: very cold; February: very cold with lying snow. Spring – March: very cold; May: dry. Warm dry summer – June: warm dry; July: warm dry. Autumn – 21 September: start of warm spell. **1341** Mild winter – January: sea floods on Sussex coast. **1342** Winter – 16 January: heavy thunderstorm, church tower

destroyed in London; February: cold. Spring – March: cold; April: cold; May: dry (?).
Mainly dry summer – June: dry; July: drought; August: wet. Warm wet autumn –
September: warm wet; October: warm wet. **1343** * Early 1343: inferred severe storm.
Inferred cyclonic situation, widespread sea floods in east England; this event
coincided with lesser storm damage in the Netherlands. Winter – December (1342):
mild; February to mid April: cold, lying snow for at least 10 days. Dry summer –
June: very dry; July: very dry; 9–13 July: very warm, severe thunderstorm heavy rain
(12 July); 14–21 July: cloudy, foggy at times. **1344** Sea floods on east coast. Mild wet (?)
winter. Warm dry summer – June: very dry; July: very dry. **1345** Cold wet winter (?).
Dry spring (?). Cool summer – June: dry; July: dry; August: wet. Wet autumn. **1346**
Wet winter – floods. Spring – May: wet; April: wet. Dry summer – June: dry; July:
dry. Dry autumn – October: dry; November: dry. **1347** * Severe storm. Inferred
cyclonic situation and storm-force gales, Dunwich further damaged, several
hundred more houses lost to the sea. Winter – floods. Spring – May: wet (?). Cool
summer – June: dry (?); July: dry (?); August: wet. Wet autumn – September: wet;
October: wet. **1348** Wet year, river floods. Winter – floods. Wet summer – June:
Black Death arrived in Britain; July: wet; August: wet. Wet autumn – floods. **1349**
Cold winter – December (1348): wet, floods; January: wet, floods; February: floods.
Cool wet summer. Wet autumn – September: wet, floods; October: wet, floods.

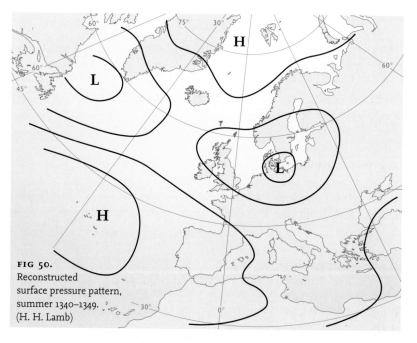

FIG 50.
Reconstructed
surface pressure pattern,
summer 1340–1349.
(H. H. Lamb)

1350S

Continental (?). **1350** Floods; fields still waterlogged from floods of 1349. Mild winter. Spring – April: wet (?); May: wet (?). Cool summer – June: dry; July: dry; August: wet. Autumn – September: cold (?) wet; October: wet. **1351** Cold winter (?) – severe floods. Spring – March: cold (?); April: wet (?); May: wet (?). Warm summer – severe floods. Autumn – October: dry; November: dry. **1352** Dry. Cold winter. Spring – April: dry; May: dry. Warm very dry summer – June: very dry; July: very dry. * Autumn – c.9 November: severe storm. Inferred cyclonic situation/storm-force gales, 'great tempest of wind', damaged houses and churches, mills overturned, trees uprooted. **1353** Mild dry winter. Dry spring – March: start of drought. * Spring to summer: drought. Inferred blocking-high situations; shortage of pasture due to dry conditions. Summer – July: culmination of drought. **1354** Very cold winter. Spring – March: cold, start of drought. * Spring to summer: drought. Inferred blocking-high situations. Warm summer – July: culmination of drought; late summer: very wet. Autumn – very wet. **1355** Very cold winter in mainland Europe: frozen rivers, including the Rhine, Po and Arno. Spring – May: dry. Wet summer – June: dry; July: wet; August: very wet. Autumn – September: very wet; October: very wet. **1356** Dry. Very dry spring. Cool partly wet summer – June: very dry; July: wet; August: wet. Autumn – September: wet; October: wet. **1357** Mild winter – January: wet (?); February: wet (?), sea floods in Sussex. Spring – March: wet (?); May: dry. Dry summer – June: dry; July: dry. **1358** River floods in north England. Mainly dry summer – June: dry; July: dry; late summer into autumn: heavy rain, exceptionally high river levels, many houses and settlements swept away in ensuing floods, late harvest. **1359** Very cold winter. Very cool summer – June: dry (?); July: dry (?); August: wet. Wet autumn – September: wet; October: wet.

1360S

Maritime and cyclonic. **1360** Plague year; about one quarter of the population died. Mild winter. Warm very dry summer – June: very dry; July: very dry. **1361** Cold winter. Very warm dry summer – June: very dry; July: very dry. **1362** Wet year. Mild winter. * 23–24 January: severe storm. Inferred deep depression in the North Sea, one of the most severe North Sea storms on record, storm-force southwesterly gales, particularly violent in south and east England, many buildings and churches damaged, towers, steeples and spires blown down (including Norwich Cathedral), many trees uprooted, Ravensburgh (or Ravenspur) east of Hull mostly destroyed, several other towns in Holderness (east Yorkshire) lost to the sea, Dunwich suffered further severe damage, great loss of life; widespread damage by winds; costly repairs to buildings reported in Winchester Bishopric

Account Rolls; most likely date of the severe flood, *Grote Mandrenke* or *Grosse Manndränke* ('Great Drowning of Men'), when storm-force northwesterly gales struck the German Bight; Frisian Islands and Danish coast flooded, 30 churches inundated, many properties destroyed, great loss of life, Rungholt (Nordfriesland), former prosperous German city, lost to the sea. Summer – June: very dry; July: very dry; August: wet, bad harvest. Wet autumn. **1363** Cold winter – 25 December (1362) to 27 March: intense frost. Spring – March: cold; April: wet; May: wet. Summer – June: wet; July: wet. **1364** Very cold winter, also in mainland Europe – major rivers and water bodies frozen including the Rhine, Rhone and Venetian lagoons. February: wet. Spring – March: very cold wet. **1365** Mild winter in mainland Europe. Cool fairly wet summer – August: wet. Wet autumn – September: wet; October: wet. **1366** Mild winter (?). Spring – May: dry. Very cool summer – June: dry; July: wet; August: wet. Wet autumn. **1367** Very cold winter – early winter: wet. Spring – March: wet. Wet summer. Wet autumn (?) – September: wet (?); October: wet (?). **1368** Mild winter – floods (?). Spring – April: dry (?); May: dry (?). Dry summer (?) – June: dry (?); July: dry (?); August: wet. Wet autumn. **1369** Storm surge. Winter – severe floods. Cool wet summer – severe floods, bad harvest. Wet autumn.

1370s

Anticyclonic. **1370** Wet year. Cold winter, wet (?). Cool wet summer – due to the 1369 bad harvest there was already a grain shortage, prices rose to famine level, 1370 became known as 'the great dear year'. Wet spring (?). Summer – June: dry (?); July: dry (?); August: wet. Autumn – September: wet; October: wet. **1371** Drought. Winter – December (1370): cold; February: cold dry. Spring – March: cold dry; April: cold dry. Summer – June: dry; July: warm dry; August: warm wet. Autumn – September: wet; October: wet. **1372** Cold winter. Cool summer – June: dry; July: dry; August: very wet. Wet autumn – September: very wet; October: wet. **1373** Spring – April: wet; May: wet. Summer – June: dry; July: dry; August: very wet. Wet autumn – November: warm. **1374** Mild wet winter. Mild spring. Cool summer – June: dry (?); July: dry (?). **1375** Drought; outbreak of fires probably explains the issue of further regulations the following year whereby vessels or tubs were to be placed outside every house. Cold winter. Warm dry summer – good harvest. Autumn – September: dry (?); October: warm dry (?). * 16 October: inferred severe storm. Inferred cyclonic situation and North Sea storm, inferred storm surge, severe floods affected the Netherlands, settlements inundated. November: warm (?). **1376** Further fire precautions issued in London. Mild winter. Wet spring (?). Dry summer (?) – August: warm (?). Dry autumn (?) – October: warm (?); November: warm (?). **1377** Very cold winter, dry (?). Dry spring

(?). Summer – June: dry (?); July: dry (?); August: very wet (?). Wet autumn (?) – September: very wet (?); October: very wet (?). **1378** * Severe storms. Inferred cyclonic situations/heavy rain, floods. Cool very dry summer – June: dry; July: dry. **1379** Cold winter. Summer – July: wet.

1380s

Anticyclonic. **1380** Mild wet winter. Spring – April: wet (?); May: wet (?). * 9 May: severe storm. Inferred cyclonic situation, severe sea floods, North Frisian Islands inundated, many people and cattle drowned. Summer – June: wet (?); July: wet. Wet autumn. **1381** Very cold winter – December (1380): very wet; January: very cold in mainland Europe; February: thaw, floods. Spring – April: wet (?); May: wet (?). **1382** Winter – February: dry. Spring – March: dry; April: dry. Warm very wet summer. Very wet autumn – September: very wet. **1383** Mild winter – December (1382): wet, 26–28 December: Thames in flood from Westminster to Windsor. Warm very dry summer. Very dry autumn – September: very dry. **1384** Mild dry winter. Dry spring. Warm very dry summer. Wet autumn – October: wet; November: wet. **1385** Wet winter – February: mild. Spring – March: mild; May: warm. Dry summer. Autumn – October: warm. Warm summer – June: dry; July: dry. **1386** Crops submerged; sea defences raised on Sussex coast. Winter – floods. Warm, dry (?) summer – June: dry (?); July: dry (?); August: wet. Wet autumn – September: wet. **1387** Cold snowy winter. Very warm summer, also mainland Europe, so-called 'Old Hot Summer' – exceptionally low water levels on the Rhine, people waded across the river at Cologne; July: warm; August: warm wet. Autumn – September: wet; October: wet; November: cold. **1388** Drought. Cold winter – January: snow. Spring – March: cold; April: dry; May: dry. Summer – June: dry; July: dry; August: wet. Autumn – September: wet; October: wet. **1389** Inferred volcanic dust veil, Iceland eruption. Cold winter. Summer – August: wet. Wet autumn – September: wet; October: wet.

1390s

Anticyclonic. **1390** Dry. Winter – February: dry. Spring – March: dry; April: dry. Warm, very dry (?) summer – June: very dry (?); July: very dry (?). **1391** Mild winter in mainland Europe. Very dry summer – June: very dry (?); July: very dry (?); August: wet; floods in north and east England. **1392** Cool summer in mainland Europe. **1393** Warm dry summer – June: warm; July: warm. **1394** Very cold winter in mainland Europe. Very dry summer – June: very dry: July: very dry. **1395** Mild wet spring. **1396** Very cold winter. Wet spring. Summer – June: wet (?); July: wet (?); August: wet. Wet autumn. **1397** Mild winter in mainland Europe. Very dry summer – June: very dry; July: very dry. Wet autumn. **1398** Mild winter in mainland Europe. Wet autumn. **1399** Drought. Very cold winter in mainland Europe – heavy snowfall, Rhine and Baltic Sea frozen; December (1398): dry. Summer – August: wet, early part: severe west coastal gales. Wet autumn – September: wet; October: wet.

1400S

Cyclonic. **1400** Probably a very wet year; serious river and sea floods, Humberside inundated. Cold winter. Very warm summer – July: wet; August: wet. Wet autumn – September: wet; October: wet. **1401** Winter – severe floods. Warm wet summer. Very wet autumn – floods; September: very wet; October: very wet. **1402** Very mild winter. Wet summer – June: stormy; August: very cool wet. Very wet autumn – severe floods; September: cool wet; 8 September: heavy rain, whirlwind reported in Wales; October: wet. **1403** Very cold winter. Spring – May: wet (?). Wet summer (?) – June: wet (?); July: wet (?). **1404** Very cold winter – also mainland Europe; Bodensee frozen. Cool wet summer. Wet autumn – September: wet; October: wet; November: warm. * 28 November: inferred severe storm. Inferred cyclonic situation and North Sea storm surge, severe sea floods affected Kent and the Netherlands, so-called 'St Elisabeth's Flood', coastal dunes and islands breached and washed away in Holland, many drowned; the flood takes its name from the feast of St Elisabeth of Hungary (19 November OS). **1405** Mild dry winter. Cool wet summer. **1406** Very cool wet (?) summer – rain and gales. **1407** Mild winter. Very dry summer (?) – June: very dry; July: very dry. **1408** River floods in north England. * Very cold winter. One of the most severe winters on record; December (1407) to March: intense frost, heavy snowfall, Thames froze, people walked dry-shod across the river; also mainland Europe: North Sea froze between Denmark and Norway, frozen lakes and rivers including the Danube, bridges in France destroyed by floating ice, vines and fruit trees frozen, watermills stopped, great shortage of bread and fuel, thousands of birds perished. Spring – March: very cold. Summer – August: very windy. Autumn – strong winds, crops damaged; September: floods. **1409** * Severe storm. Inferred cyclonic situation/North Sea storm/storm-force northerly gales, storm surge, St Andrews Cathedral (Fife) damaged. Very cold winter – intense frost, lasted 15 weeks; severe floods in Sussex. Cool wet summer – gales; July: wet.

1410S

Maritime. **1410** Very cold winter – intense frost lasted 14 weeks, frozen Thames bore people and riders; January: dry; February: dry. Dry spring – March: dry. Warm very dry summer – June: very dry; July: very dry. **1411** Very stormy winter with many gales. Cool summer. Autumn – 12 October: disturbed tides affected

the Thames, probable North Sea storm surge. **1412** Warm dry summer – June: dry; July: dry. **1413** Winter – January: very dry; February: very dry. Spring – March: very dry. * March: severe storm (?). Inferred cyclonic situation, storm surge. 18 April: Henry V's coronation: very wet, snowstorm; May: very dry. Very dry summer – June: very dry; July; very dry. * 19 August: severe storm. Inferred cyclonic situation/storm-force southerly gales, large amount of sand exposed during an extremely low tide was raised by the gales and wind-blown, Forvie (Aberdeenshire) buried in sand dunes still standing today up to 30 m (100ft) high. Autumn – November: cold. **1414** Cold winter – persistent easterly winds. Cold spring – easterly winds; March: cold; May: very dry. Very dry summer – June: very dry; July: very dry; August: stormy. Wet stormy autumn – November: wet. **1415** Mild very wet winter. Spring – March: wet; April: wet. Warm very dry summer – 19 August: English fleet under Henry V set sail for France from the Solent with favourable wind and weather conditions for Channel crossing. Very dry autumn – September: very dry; October: very dry; although the autumn was initially very dry, conditions became less settled in late October with frequent rain; 3 November: Battle of Agincourt. **1416** Mild wet stormy winter – January: strong winds; February: wet, stormy. Spring – March: wet, stormy; April: wet, stormy; May: very dry. Cool very dry summer – June: very dry; July: very dry; severe dryness prevented growth of pasture. **1417** Cold winter – stormy, continuous heavy snowfall. Spring – stormy, persistent snowfall. * April: severe storm. Inferred cyclonic situation/storm-force gales, shipwrecks in the Channel.
Warm very dry summer – June: very dry; July: very dry. **1418** Many references to destruction of crops. Cold winter. Warm very dry summer – storm, crops destroyed by hail, strong northeasterly winds; June: very dry; July: very dry. **1419** Cold winter – persistent cold northerly winds. Spring – March: cold, northerly winds; April: cold, northerly winds. Summer – June: very dry; July: very dry; August: wet. Autumn – September: wet; October: wet.

1420S

Maritime. Cyclonic-type winters (Fig. 51); westerly-type summers (Fig. 52). **1420** Very cold winter – 8 December (1419): heavy snowfall. * 26 April: severe storm. Inferred cyclonic situation, North Sea storm, severe sea floods in the Netherlands, 100,000 drowned. May: very dry. Very warm dry summer – June: very dry; July: very dry. **1421** Very mild winter in mainland Europe. Summer – August: very wet. Very wet autumn – heavy rain, crops damaged; September: very wet; October: very wet; November: very wet. * 27–28 November: severe storm, St Elisabeth's Flood. Inferred cyclonic situation, one of the most severe North Sea storms on record, storm-force gales, storm surge, severe sea floods, east English and Dutch coasts

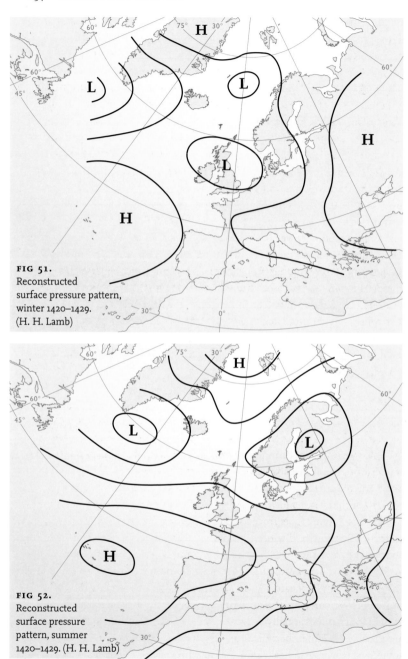

FIG 51.
Reconstructed
surface pressure pattern,
winter 1420–1429.
(H. H. Lamb)

FIG 52.
Reconstructed
surface pressure
pattern, summer
1420–1429. (H. H. Lamb)

pounded, many villages lost to the sea in the Netherlands where dykes were breached, many thousands drowned, Zuider Zee finally reached its 20th-century form. **1422** Severe floods, crops destroyed in Sussex. Spring – April: very dry; May: very dry. Very warm summer – July: dry; August: very dry. Autumn – September: very dry; October: very dry. **1423** Very cold winter – heavy snowfall; also mainland Europe: Baltic Sea partly frozen. Spring – May: very dry. Cool summer – June: very dry; July: very dry; August: wet. Very wet autumn. **1424** Cold wet stormy winter – continuous heavy rain, floods. Wet spring (?). Very warm dry summer – June: very dry; July: very dry. Very dry autumn. **1425** Floods, crops destroyed in Sussex. Mild winter – many storms. Spring – stormy especially in March. Warm wet summer – June: very wet; July: very wet (?); August: very wet. Mild wet autumn. **1426** Dry. Warm summer – June: wet (?); August: wet (?). **1427** Very wet year, river floods, bad harvest, famine. Cold winter. Spring – April: wet; May: wet. Wet summer – June: very wet, 20 June: floods in St Albans (Hertfordshire); July: very wet; August: very warm dry. Autumn – September: wet; November: dry. **1428** A year without a summer. Dry winter. Wet spring – March: very wet; April: very wet; May: wet. Very cool wet summer, severe floods; June: wet; July: wet, floods; August: wet. Very wet autumn. * 8–9 October: severe storm. Inferred cyclonic situation, heavy rain, severe floods and damaged crops. 1 November: thunderstorm; 4 November: rain and hail; 6–11 November: cold clear spell with hoar frost. **1429** Winter – February: cold. Spring – March: cold. Wet summer – floods, crops destroyed in Sussex. Wet autumn.

1430s

Complex cyclonic-type winters over mainland Europe. Cyclonic-type summers. Since, during the last thousand years, only the 1690s experienced so many cold winters or severe spells within the span of one decade, and with data becoming more plentiful, Lamb investigated the circulation patterns of the 1430s by means of reconstructed surface pressure charts (Figs 53–64). **1430** Mild winter – southerly–southeasterly, blocking highs over Scandinavia and west Russia, cold winter in mainland Europe; frozen rivers including the Danube. Warm summer. **1431** Stormy. Possibly cold winter, cyclonic. 8 December (1430): stormy; late December to early January: very wet. *25–27 January: severe storm. Inferred cyclonic situation, heavy rain and snow. Warm summer. Autumn – stormy; ships carrying wine from Bordeaux heavily damaged in the Channel; 24 November: stormy. **1432** Very cold winter – anticyclonic easterly; intense frost; also 'cold' rains in January and especially February. Warm summer – August: wet. Autumn – September: wet; 5 September: Bishop of Exeter enjoined prayers for the abatement of storms and heavy rain that had prevented the harvest being

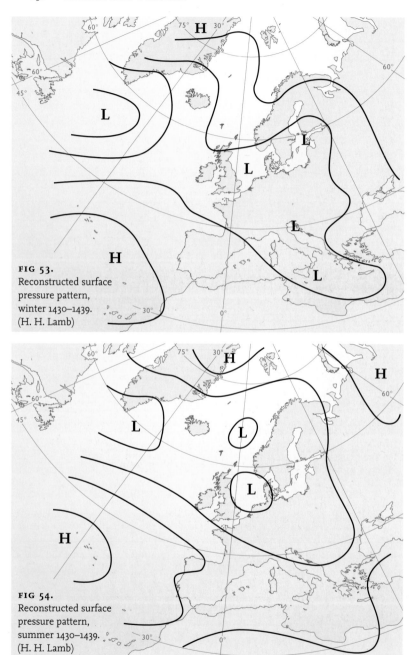

FIG 53.
Reconstructed surface pressure pattern, winter 1430–1439. (H. H. Lamb)

FIG 54.
Reconstructed surface pressure pattern, summer 1430–1439. (H. H. Lamb)

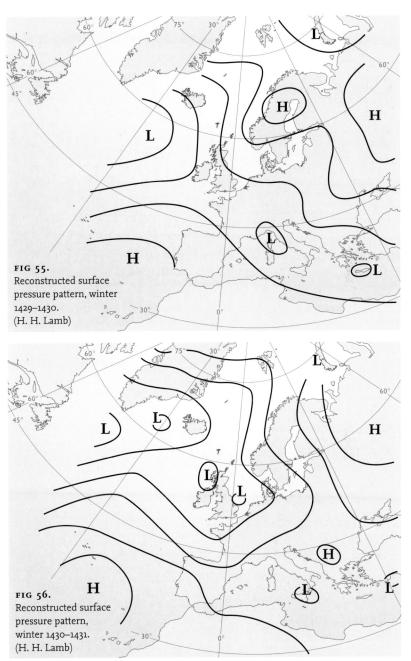

FIG 55.
Reconstructed surface
pressure pattern, winter
1429–1430.
(H. H. Lamb)

FIG 56.
Reconstructed surface
pressure pattern,
winter 1430–1431.
(H. H. Lamb)

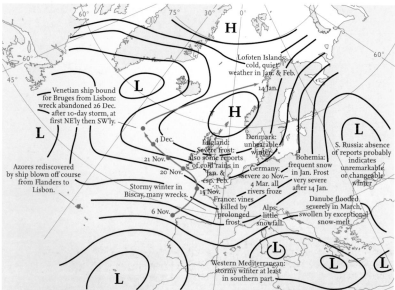

FIG 57. Reconstructed surface pressure pattern, winter 1431–1432, with plotted weather reports including tracks of two ships blown off course in the Atlantic. (H. H. Lamb)

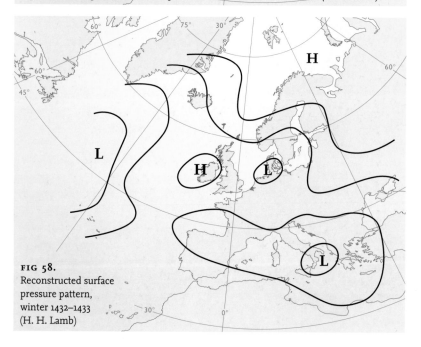

FIG 58.
Reconstructed surface
pressure pattern,
winter 1432–1433
(H. H. Lamb)

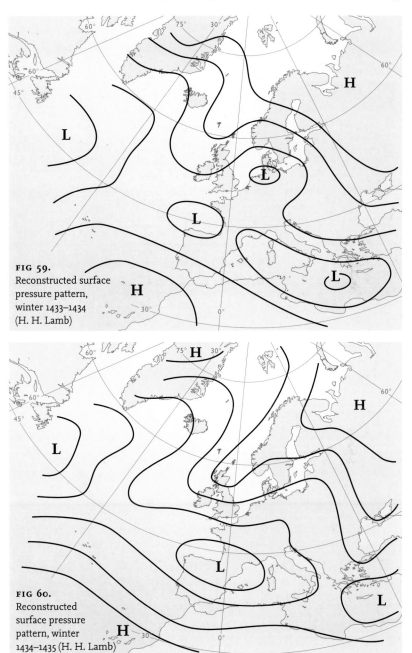

FIG 59.
Reconstructed surface pressure pattern, winter 1433–1434 (H. H. Lamb)

FIG 60.
Reconstructed surface pressure pattern, winter 1434–1435 (H. H. Lamb)

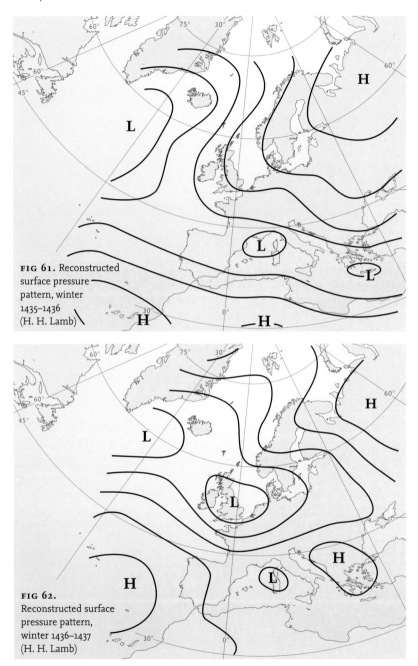

FIG 61. Reconstructed
surface pressure
pattern, winter
1435–1436
(H. H. Lamb)

FIG 62.
Reconstructed surface
pressure pattern,
winter 1436–1437
(H. H. Lamb)

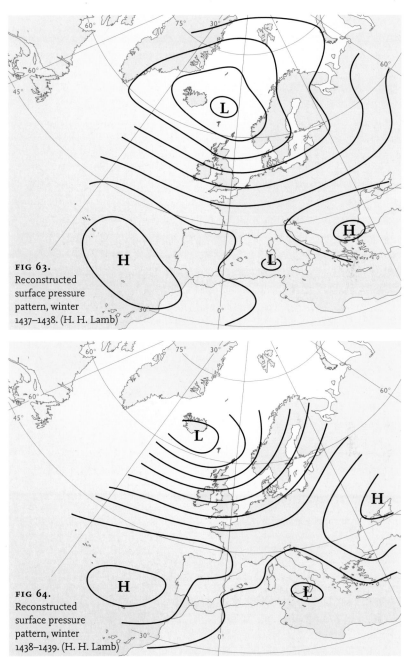

FIG 63.
Reconstructed
surface pressure
pattern, winter
1437–1438. (H. H. Lamb)

FIG 64.
Reconstructed
surface pressure
pattern, winter
1438–1439. (H. H. Lamb)

gathered in. **1433** Very cold winter – anticyclonic. Warm summer – July (?): a sudden strong cool wind, heavy hailstorm, crops destroyed. **1434** Very cold winter – cyclonic northeasterly. Thames frozen, river closed to shipping, merchandise unloaded at the estuary and transported by land to the city. Very warm summer. **1435** * Very cold winter. Very cold easterly-type winter; also severe in mainland Europe: frozen Belgian rivers and Bodensee; 3 December (1434) to 19 February: intense frost, Thames frozen at London and as far downstream as Gravesend; severe conditions intensified hardship of people already badly affected by the high price of grain. **1436** Cold winter – southeasterly. Very cool summer. **1437** Wet winter – cyclonic. Spring – floods. Cool wet summer – river floods. Autumn – 5 October: Bishop of Exeter enjoined prayers for cessation of storms and heavy rain which were damaging the harvest. **1438** Inferred mild wet winter – westerly. Late 1437 to early 1438: heavy snowfall and continuous rain, severe floods. Cool wet summer – severe storms, heavy rain, river floods, crops badly damaged, corn imported from Prussia to London by the lord mayor, but many elsewhere starved or were reduced to making bread substitutes from ivy leaves and fern roots.

1439 Wet, river floods, great scarcity, famine in Scotland. Inferred very wet stormy winter – westerly. * 2 (or 4) December (1438): severe storm. Inferred cyclonic situation/storm-force gales, great damage in London. Wet summer – river floods.

1440S

1440 Cold winter (?). Cool summer. **1441** Cold winter (?). Warm very dry summer. Very wet autumn – floods. **1442** Very warm dry summer. **1443** Very cold winter and parts of spring. Warm dry summer. Wet autumn – rain, floods, crops damaged. **1444** An exceptionally favourable year. **1445** Cool summer. **1446** Mild winter. Spring – April: very cold. * 19 April: severe storm. One of the worst North Sea storms on record, inferred deep depression over the North Sea, storm-force gales, probable storm surge, sea floods affected Danish, German and Dutch coasts, 100,000 drowned; very cold with thunderstorms and heavy snowfall in mainland Europe. May: very cold. **1447** Very cold winter – February: very cold. Very warm summer – Thames floods. **1448** Cold winter. Dry spring. * March: inferred severe storm. Inferred cyclonic situation, North Sea storm surge, Thames floods, Poplar and Stepney inundated. Cool dry summer.

1450S

1450 Mild winter. Autumn – 18 October: sea and river floods. **1451** Spring – March to April: freezing drought in the Netherlands. **1452–** Inferred volcanic dust veil (estimated DVI 3,000), submarine eruption, **1453** Kuwae (New Hebrides), indicated by peaks in the Greenland and Antarctica ice-core sulphate records, strong global cooling inferred during following three years. **1452** Very cold winter – heavy snowfall. Warm summer. **1453–1457** Tree growth stunted in Europe, inferred volcanic dust-veil effect. **1453** Favourable conditions for winter and spring crops; apart from Calais, English possessions in mainland Europe lost. Summer – June: reports of thick fog and red twilights in Constantinople, inferred volcanic dust-veil effect. **1456** Mild winter. **1457** Warm summer. **1458** Cold winter, also mainland Europe; rivers frozen. Warm summer.

1460s

1460 Cold winter (?) – very cold winter in mainland Europe; Baltic Sea frozen, Bodensee partly frozen, Hanseatic ports ice-bound. Wet summer. Wet autumn. **1461** Wet winter – floods; February: heavy snowfall, snowstorm-blizzard conditions. **1462** Mild winter in Germany. **1464** Drought. Cold winter. **1465** Pevensey Levels (Sussex) flooded. Very cold winter – frost and snow, many cattle perished. **1467** Storm surge. **1469** Very cold winter in mainland Europe; Zuider Zee frozen.

1470s

Anticyclonic. **1470** Cold winter – also mainland Europe; Bodensee frozen. * Autumn – November: inferred severe storm. Inferred cyclonic situation, sea floods, North Sea coasts, many thousands drowned. **1471** Spring – 21–23 March: severe gales affected Lincolnshire coast. **1473** Drought. Very warm summer. **1474** Drought. Mild winter in mainland Europe. Very warm summer. **1475** Very warm dry year. Sea floods, Humberside towns lost to the sea. **1477** Very warm dry year. Cold winter (?). Wet summer (?). **1478** Very mild winter in mainland Europe. **1479** Very warm dry year.

1480s

Maritime. **1480** Very cold winter in mainland Europe – frozen rivers including the Seine. **1481** Cold winter. * December (1480): severe storm. Inferred cyclonic situation, severe gales affected southwest England, four shipwrecks in Mount's Bay (Cornwall). Wet summer – floods. **1482** Very cold winter in Holland. Cool wet summer – floods. **1483** Mild winter in Germany. Autumn – October: heavy rain, severe river floods in the Severn and Wye, so-called 'Duke of Buckingham's Great Water'. **1485** River floods. **1488** Frost, heavy snowfall; river floods.

1490s

Cyclonic or frontal. **1490** Dry. Very cold winter in southern Europe – Adriatic Sea frozen off Venice. **1491** Cold winter – also mainland Europe; ice on the Rhine, frozen Swiss lakes. **1492** Cold winter. **1494** Very cold winter in mainland Europe –

frozen Venetian canals and lagoons. **1496** Cold winter – also in mainland Europe, Baltic frozen. 12 January: severe gales in the Netherlands. **1497** Spring – May: John Cabot sailed from Bristol to Newfoundland. Summer – August: Cabot returned to Bristol. **1498** Dry. **1499** River floods.

1500S

1500 Dense volcanic dust veil (DVI 1000), Java (Indonesia) eruption. Wet winter. Inferred cool wet summer. Autumn – late September to December: stormy and wet in Ireland. **1501** Inferred cool wet summer – bad grain harvest. **1502** Very cold winter – also mainland Europe. Inferred cool wet summer – bad grain harvest. **1503** Very cold winter in mainland Europe – Po frozen. Warm dry summer – bad grain harvest, especially in west England. **1504** Very cold winter. **1505** Sun dimmed by high-level haze over mainland Europe, inferred volcanic dust-veil effect. Wet summer. Wet autumn in Ireland. **1506** Very cold winter – January: frozen Thames (first time for over 70 years), river bore people, horses and carts. * 21 January to 5 February: severe storms. Inferred cyclonic situations, stormy conditions in the Channel and North Sea. Wet early summer, perhaps improved later – good harvest. **1507** Inferred dry year; great fire in Norwich. **1508** Very cold winter in mainland Europe. Inferred warm dry summer – good harvest. **1509** Inferred warm dry summer – good harvest. * 6 October: severe storm. Inferred cyclonic situation, North Sea storm, sea floods affected the coasts of Holland, Zealand and Friesland.

1510S

Dry anticyclonic winters, wet cyclonic summers. **1510** Inferred volcanic dust veil (DVI 300), Iceland eruptions. * Spring: severe storm. Inferred cyclonic situation/storm-force winds, floods, damaged houses and bridges, trees blown down. Inferred warm dry summer – good harvest. **1511** * Severe storm. Inferred cyclonic situation/storm-force winds, floods, damaged houses and bridges, trees blown down in Ireland. Very cold winter. **1512** Inferred cool wet summer – bad harvest. **1513** Very cold winter in mainland Europe – frozen rivers including Maas and Rhine. Variable summer – July: warm; later: cool wet. **1514** * Very cold winter. Polar continental airstream associated with blocking-high situations over north Europe; December (1513): very cold, easterly; frozen rivers including the Rhine and those in Belgium; January: very cold, easterly; Thames frozen, bore people and carriages; February: southerly. Inferred warm dry summer – good harvest. Autumn – November: floods. **1515** Mild winter in mainland Europe. Summer to autumn – late July to early September: wet with floods in mainland Europe. **1516** Very warm dry. Mild winter in Germany. Inferred warm dry summer – good

harvest. **1517** Very cold dry winter, also mainland Europe –
frozen Thames, Irish rivers and Swiss lakes. Dry spring. Very warm summer.
* September to May (1518): drought. Inferred blocking-high situations. **1518** Cold
dry winter. Dry spring – great drought from September (1517) to May. Inferred
warm dry summer – good harvest. **1519** Wet summer in Ireland. Wet autumn in
Ireland.

1520S

Cyclonic. **1520** Inferred cool wet summer – bad grain harvest. * 28 June: severe
storm. Inferred cyclonic situation. Autumn – 14 November: inferred heavy rain,
severe floods, bridge swept away in Sudbury (Suffolk). **1521** Summer – less bad
grain harvest, apart from west Britain and Ireland. **1522** Cold winter in Ireland.
1523 Early part: inclement in Ireland. Wet thundery summer in Ireland. * Early
November: severe storm. Inferred cyclonic situation, severe gales. **1524** Early part:
inclement in Ireland. Wet autumn in Ireland. **1525** Warm summer in Ireland.
1526 * January: severe storm. Inferred cyclonic situation. **1527** Wet year. Mild
winter in Germany – mid January: wet floods. Wet spring – April to June: very
wet, damaged crops. Wet summer – June: wet; July: wet; bad grain harvest, great
scarcity, many died. Wet autumn – September: wet; November: wet. **1528** Wet year.
Wet winter – December (1527): wet; January: river floods by mid to late month;
followed by dry spell into early April. Spring – late April into early to mid June:
wet, floods. Summer – July: dry; August: dry. Autumn – September: wet, bad grain
harvest. **1529** Mild winter in mainland Europe. Cool summer.

1530S

Cyclonic becoming anticyclonic. **1530** Mild dry winter – December (1529):
southwesterly; January: westerly; February: southwesterly. Warm spring. Warm
autumn. * 14–15 November: severe storm. Inferred cyclonic situation/North Sea
storm, storm-force gales, storm surge coincided with a spring tide, severe sea
floods, Essex and Kent coasts, and Isle of Thanet inundated, many houses and
trees blown down; even greater destruction in Holland, 50 towns and settlements
partly or completely destroyed, great loss of life and cattle (this event appears to
have had similar features to the 1953 storm). **1531** Mild winter in Germany. Warm
dry autumn. **1532** Mild winter in Germany. * 11–12 November: severe storm.
Northwesterly situation, inferred North Sea storm/storm-force southwest or
northwesterly gales, storm surge coincided with a neap tide, severe sea floods,
dykes breached, thousands drowned in Danish and Dutch coastal areas.
1534 Cold winter – Thames frozen in London. **1535** Inferred volcanic dust veil
(DVI 300), Etna eruption. Very cold winter – November (1534) to February: intense

frost, Thames frozen downstream of Gravesend. Wet summer – floods, bad grain harvest. **1536** Very cold winter in mainland Europe. **1537** Very cold winter – December (1536) to January: very cold spell, Thames frozen. Wet summer. **1538** Start of drought. * Drought: 1538–1539. Inferred blocking-high situations, droughts in two successive years, dry conditions continued into the 1540s. Mild winter. Very warm dry summer. **1539** Wet year; inferred volcanic dust veil (DVI 50), Popocatépetl (Mexico) eruption. Very warm dry summer – dried-up rivers.

LITTLE ICE AGE, PHASE I: 1540–1699

1540s

Continental. **1540** Very warm dry year, probably one of the warmest on record. Cold winter with snow in Ireland. Mild dry spring – February: dry, start of drought to September. * February to September: drought. Inferred blocking-high situations, only six occasions of rain in London, dried-up streams and wells, very low water level on the Thames, salty sea water flowed upstream of London Bridge, cattle perished due to lack of water; drought also in mainland Europe: many dried-up small rivers, very low water level on the Rhine, river could be walked across at several locations. Very warm dry summer – persistent anticyclonic situations extended northeast from the Azores high over west Europe; June: dry, anticyclonic southwesterly; July: anticyclonic southwesterly type; August: anticyclonic southwesterly type. Autumn – September; mostly dry. **1541** Dry year; early part: frost and snow in Ireland. Cold winter (?) – dry. Wet spring, followed by drought. * Drought. Inferred blocking-high situations; serious effects from the combined 1540 and 1541 droughts: dried-up small rivers, the Trent reduced to a runnel, very low water level on the Thames, salty sea water flowed upstream of London Bridge, thousands died from diarrhoea and dysentery, many cattle perished. **1542** Wet summer – river floods. **1543** Wet year. Wet summer – floods. **1544** Cold winter in mainland Europe. **1545** Dry year. Very cold winter. Cool wet summer – bad grain harvest. * 25 June (OS?): severe storm. Inferred cyclonic situation, storm-force gales, heavy hailstorms, buildings damaged and trees blown down. 28–29 July: overnight thunderstorms, light winds early on 29 July but they later suddenly increased to westerly in an inferred thundery trough; the loss of the English warship *Mary Rose* might be linked to this event: her lower gun ports had been left open, adverse conditions caused the ship to heel, rapidly flood and sink, 400 crew drowned. Autumn – September: warm dry in mainland Europe. **1546** Very cold winter – also mainland Europe: Flemish waterways, Rhine, Danish Belts and Sound frozen. **1547** Late 1547:

intense frost. **1548** Drought. Very cold winter in mainland Europe – French rivers frozen. * Early February: inferred severe storm. Inferred cyclonic situation, inferred storm-force gales in the Thames estuary, river barges sunk from London to Gravesend. **1549** Very cold winter in Denmark. Wet spring in southeast England.

1550s

1550 Inferred volcanic dust haze (DVI 70), Tala (Philippines) eruption. Inferred cool wet summer – bad grain harvest. **1551** Spring – 25 May (OS?): earthquake in Surrey, strong winds, severe floods, many cattle drowned at Saltney (Cheshire). Inferred wet summer – bad grain harvest. **1552** Winter – December (1551): tidal floods on the Thames flowed upstream as far as Millwall; January–February: two North Sea storm surges affected the Netherlands. **1553–1554** Volcanic dust veil (total DVI 1000), Pichincha (Ecuador) and Hekla. (Iceland) eruptions. **1553** Very cold winter in Holland. * 15–25 January: severe storms. Inferred cyclonic situations, strong mild southwesterly winds veered later to severe cold north to northwesterly gales, hail, snow and thunder, North Sea storm surges, severe sea floods. Summer – inferred blocking-high situations, spell of easterly winds; notable coloured sunsets observed over Scandinavia, inferred volcanic dust-veil effect. **1554** Dimmed sun reported over Europe, inferred volcanic dust-veil effect. Very cold winter. **1555** Wet year. Very cold winter – stormy and wet in Ireland; January to early March: heavy snowfall in Scotland; late February: end of cold spell in England. Wet summer – bad grain harvest, inferred volcanic dust-veil effect. * Autumn – early October: severe storm. Inferred cyclonic situation, one of the most severe North Sea storms on record, inferred severe northwesterly gales, exceptionally high spring tide, storm surge, severe floods, buildings adjacent to the Thames (including Westminster Palace and Westminster Hall) inundated, the storm surge had dammed the river already swollen by heavy rain. **1556** Dry year; springs and wells ran dry, wheat rose from 8 shillings to 53 shillings per quarter during drought, famine. Variable summer, partly wet but very dry in east England; bad grain harvest. **1557** Extensive dry fog, inferred volcanic dust-veil effect. Very cold winter. Summer – 14 August: heavy thunderstorms and tornadoes in Suffolk. **1558** Mild winter – January: cold dry spell. * 20 January: inferred severe storm. Inferred cyclonic situation, an abrupt change from cold to milder conditions (probably due to the passage of a warm front), four days of southwesterly gales, many shipwrecks off Dover. Very warm summer – 17 July: severe thunderstorm, squalls, giant hailstones, houses and churches blown down in Nottingham, heavy mud-laden water in the Trent carried 400 m (440 yd) downstream, uprooted trees, several people killed. **1559** Mild winter in Germany. Wet stormy autumn.

1560s

Cyclonic, later continental anticyclonic. **1560** Wet year. Cold winter. Inferred wet summer – bad grain harvest. **1561** Very cold winter. Summer – 14 June: thunderstorm in London, old St Paul's Cathedral steeple destroyed by lightning (topic for a contemporary ballad). **1562** Wet summer – bad grain harvest. **1563** Winter – partly cold; some rivers temporarily frozen including the Thames, Maas, Scheldt, Seine and Rhone; 19 January: severe thunderstorms, houses damaged in Leicester. Wet summer – 18 July: severe thunderstorms, people killed by lightning. **1564** Cold winter (?). Autumn – 30 September: tidal flood affected lower Thames valley, adjoining marshes inundated, many cattle drowned; October: wet; November: wet. **1565** Very cold winter – frozen rivers, including the Thames (Queen Elizabeth I is said to have walked on the frozen river), Severn and Wye; also severe in mainland Europe: frozen rivers and water bodies, including the Zuider Zee and Bodensee; December (1564): start of cold spell; early January: ice sports held on the frozen Thames by the Royal Court and other groups (probably one of the first occasions of such activity); 13–15 January: thaw, severe floods, bridges and houses swept away, many drowned, especially in Yorkshire, River Ouse bridge in York swept away; a notable fog (probably advection type) occurred during the following week. Spring – early March: thaw continued with severe floods comparable to 1947 inundation. Inferred wet summer – bad grain harvest. **1566** Inferred wet winter – December (1565): northwesterly type; January: westerly. * 2–3 January: severe storm. Inferred depression, severe gales, Thames floods (probably tidal), many drowned. February: northwesterly. Wet spring – floods. Dry summer – July: wet (?) mainland Europe: many rivers, including the Rhine and Danube, in flood. Dry autumn. **1567** Very cold winter – February: heavy snowfall, great losses of sheep, Richmond (Yorkshire). Dry summer. **1568** Very warm dry year. Winter – December (1567): probably mild; late winter: very cold. Spring – 28 March: stormy, many vessels sunk on the Thames. Dry summer. **1569** Inferred volcanic dust veil (DVI 10), Citaltépetl (Mexico) eruption. Cold winter. Wet spring. Autumn – 9 November: tornado at Ashley (Nottinghamshire), 55 m (60 yd) wide, lasted 7 minutes, 'everything' destroyed in its path.

1570s

Cyclonic. **1570** Wet year. Very cold winter – January: heavy snowfall, deep snow cover over high ground in north England (after the collapse of the 'Rising in the North', the rebels were last seen crossing the snowbound Cheviots). Wet stormy autumn. * 15 October: severe storm. Inferred depression over east England and North Sea, severe to storm-force gales combined with a high tide produced a storm surge, sea floods intensified by heavy rain from the Humber to the Strait of Dover, Thames estuary affected upstream as far as Erith, sea broke through in the Wash, dykes destroyed, Fens flooded, many trees and houses blown down, bridges swept away, widespread floods also in central, east and southeast England, many cattle and sheep perished, many shipwrecks. * 11–12 November: severe storm, 'All Saints Flood'. Inferred depression in the North Sea, one of the worst North Sea storms on record, storm-force northwesterly winds, storm surge, severe sea floods, coastal changes, much damage, towns and east coast inundated, Dutch sea defences breached, widespread floods, towns and cities inundated, including Amsterdam and Rotterdam, many thousands drowned. **1571** Very cold winter – late December (1570) to 12 February: severe spell, heavy snowfall, Derwentwater (Cumberland) frozen; mid February: thaw followed by floods. **1572** Cold winter – mid February to mid March: cold, snowfall. Spring – mid March: thaw, snow-melt. Autumn – 10 November: onset of very cold frosty spell. **1573** * Very cold dry winter. Easterly situation, blocking high over Scandinavia, low over the central Mediterranean, a cold northeasterly polar continental airstream affected Europe from west Russia to northeast Spain, frost from mid November (1572) to mid May, frost and snow for eight weeks, mid December (1572) to late January, December: very cold in mainland Europe, Bodensee frozen; January: cold in mainland Europe; February: cold dry in mainland Europe. Cold dry late spring – frost and snow to mid May, phenological events such as leafing and blossoming delayed until late May. Cool wet summer – bad grain harvest; 17 June: severe hailstorm, large hailstones, heavy rain, flash floods, houses damaged in Towcester (Northamptonshire). Wet autumn – September: cool wet in mainland Europe; very wet late harvest in Norfolk; 14 September: heavy rain; October: wet; cool in mainland Europe; early November: start of mild spell to late January (1574). **1574** Mild dry winter – late January: end of mild spell from early November (1573). Inferred wet autumn – 14 September: heavy rain, severe floods; 16 November: two high tides within one hour on the Thames, river overflowed, severe floods; 28–29 November: stormy, inferred storm-force southerly winds. **1575** Very cold winter – frozen rivers and water bodies including Derwentwater (Cumberland) and Scottish lochs; also severe winter in mainland Europe, Rhine frozen; 24 February: thaw followed by widespread severe floods. Spring – May: thaw, floods. Warm dry summer. **1576** Very mild winter in mainland Europe. Spring – 5 March: severe floods; 27 March: tornado (?), buildings and trees blown down. **1577** Wet summer (?) – wet June; July: cool wet in mainland Europe; 7 July: hail showers; 14 August: heavy thunderstorms, churches damaged, two killed at Bungay and Blythburgh (Suffolk). **1578** Cold winter (?) – south Baltic very cold. Inferred cold spring – April: cold in mainland Europe; May: cold in mainland Europe. Dry summer – late August: start of very warm mostly dry spell; lack of water in the Manchester conduit led to water rationing in the city. Autumn – late summer drought continued into early autumn – 6 October: first rain, long drought partly broken. **1579** Wet year. * Winter – 14–20 February; severe snowstorm-blizzard (topic for a contemporary ballad). Northerly situation, severe snowstorm-blizzard conditions, heavy snowfall, 30 cm (12 in), locally probably up to 60 cm (24 in), deep drifts, 1.4 m (4.5 ft) in London, even deeper drifts in rural areas, loss of life, cattle perished. 20 February: thaw, snow-melt, heavy rain, severe floods, Thames overflowed, Westminster inundated. Spring – March: wet; 14 and 30 April: heavy snowfall, 30 cm (12 in) in London; 4 May: heavy snowfall, 30 cm (12 in) in London. Summer – 6 June: floods preceded by a cool dry period; c.30 August: wet and windy. Very cool autumn – September to October: strong winds, heavy rain, severe floods, towns inundated; 19–23 October: heavy rain, high water level on Thames, six drowned on the Kew ferry.

1580s

Anticyclonic. **1580** Dry year. Very cold winter. Spring – April: severe sea floods, hundreds of houses inundated, people drowned in the Channel. Stormy summer – 23 June: heavy thunderstorms, hail showers. **1581** Winter – very cold in mainland Europe (?): Baltic Sea almost completely frozen. Dry autumn. **1582** Wet year. Dry winter – 31 December (1581): Trent ran dry at Alrewas (Staffordshire). Wet summer – 22 August: heavy thunderstorms, large hail. **1583** Mild winter. Spring – late spring to summer: severe drought, many cattle perished. Very warm dry summer. **1584** Very cold winter. **1585** Winter – positive pressure anomaly over the British Isles; mild winter in France and Germany; drought in mainland Europe. Spring – 21 March to 21 June: mild with occasional rain in southwest England. Very wet summer – floods, crops damaged. Wet autumn – 8 November: heavy rain followed by floods in west England. **1586** Volcanic dust veil (DVI 1000), Kelud (Java) eruption. Very cold wet winter – February: very cold. Very wet spring – March: very wet. Inferred wet summer – bad grain harvest, inferred volcanic dust-veil effect. Very wet autumn. * September: severe storms. Inferred cyclonic situations, westerly winds, heavy rain, severe floods. 9 October: Severn rose suddenly following heavy rain. * 18 October: severe storm. Inferred cyclonic situation, storm-force gales, widespread heavy damage both on land and at sea, buildings, chimneys, tiles and haystacks blown down. **1587** Floods, Derwent Bridge in Derby swept away. Very cold winter. Very cold spring – late March to May: dry in southwest England. Cool dry summer. Autumn – September: cool. **1588** * A year without a summer. Winter – 2–4 January: river floods due to heavy rain in Wales, Severn rose at Shrewsbury, western suburbs flooded; 8 January: Severn rose again but less than before. 11 May: start of long wet period with floods until November.

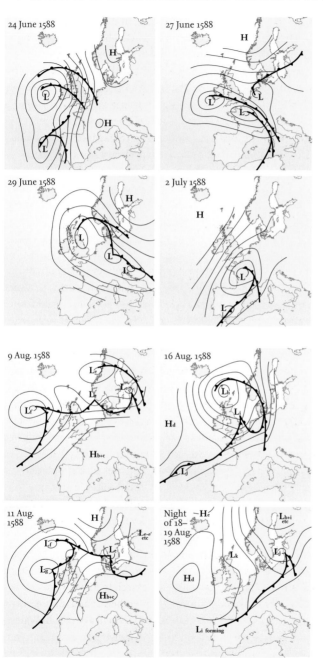

FIG 65. Synoptic weather maps, 24, 27 and 29 June, and 2 July 1588. (H. H. Lamb)

FIG 66. Synoptic weather maps, 9, 11, 16 and 18–19 August 1588. (H. H. Lamb)

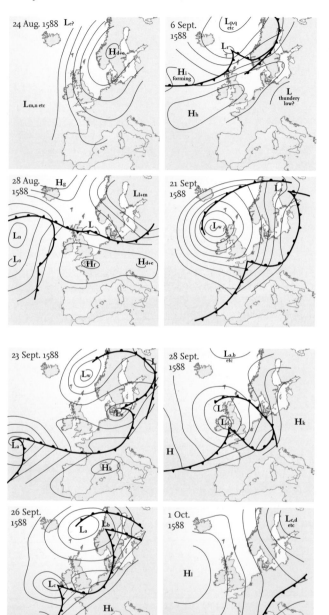

FIG 67. Synoptic weather maps, 24 and 28 August, 6 and 21 September 1588. (H. H. Lamb)

FIG 68. Synoptic weather maps, 23, 26 and 28 September, 1 October 1588. (H. H. Lamb)

Cool wet summer – June (Fig. 65 and 66): very wet; 5–17 June: cyclonic southwesterly, severe gales in the Channel battered Spanish Armada (9 June); 19–24 June: southerly; 25–30 June: cyclonic. July: very wet; 2 July: northeasterly, heavy rain; 8–14 July: cyclonic; 20 July: cyclonic southeasterly, heavy rain; 27 July: cyclonic northeasterly, heavy rain, floods; 29 July: northerly, severe floods in west England, Severn overflowed; 31 July: squally west to northwesterly winds, followed by mostly light westerly winds in the Channel until 8 August; after being defeated off Gravelines in the Strait of Dover, the Armada vessels were swept north by strong southwesterly winds into the North Sea; 9–11 August: southwesterly, inferred heavy rain, severe floods. * 14–18 August: severe storms. Inferred intense depression moved northeast across north Britain, southwest to westerly severe gales with hurricane-force winds off northeast Scottish coasts; 17 August: cyclonic westerly, northeasterly winds in the North Sea allowed the Armada to head west off north Scotland; 18 August: northerly. Late August: continued break-up of Armada vessels in severe southwesterly gales. Autumn – (Fig. 67 and 68) 2–11 September: anticyclonic spell allowed remaining Armada vessels to make some progress southwards. * 21 September: severe storm. Inferred depression moved northeast off the Hebrides, westerly situation, storm-force southwesterly winds, more Armada vessels wrecked on the Hebridean and Irish coasts. 1 October: northerly situation 3–8 October: anticyclonic situation; 26 October: cyclonic westerly situation. **1589** Very cold winter in Denmark and Germany – early February: very cold. Summer – mid June: heavy rain; 10 August: flood. Autumn – 21 November: early frosts.

1590S

1590 Dry year; volcanic dust veil (DVI 50), Colima (Mexico) eruption. Very cold winter – severe conditions continued into early April. Mostly dry spring – March: no rain for six weeks in southwest England; 9 April: end of cold spell; 9–29 April: mild, showery; 27 May: start of wet spell to 10 June. Summer – 10 June: end of wet spell; 11–16 June: probable dry spell; c.18 June to 1 August: mostly dry but interrupted by rain on 12 and 30 July. Autumn – early October: cold. **1591** Dry year. Cold dry winter – 30 December (1590): heavy snowfall, start of cold spell to mid April. Dry spring – 21–23 and 29 March: heavy snowfall; 5–6 April: heavy snowfall; 14 April: thaw, rain, swollen rivers; dry spell followed to 7 July. Very dry summer. * Summer to autumn: drought. Although a spell of strong westerly winds occurred during the summer, it brought little rain, and rivers such as the Trent, Aire and Calder almost ran dry; Thames also at a low level as it was possible to cross the river on horseback at London Bridge. Autumn – drought continued into early October; November: mild spell to 21 February (1592).

1592 Mostly mild winter – 21 February: end of mild spell from November (1591); 22 February: first snow of the winter – 23–25 February: intense frost and snow. Very mild spring. Summer – 1 June: renewal of drought from 1591 summer, dry conditions continued into late September. Autumn – c.12 September: strong southwesterly winds drove Thames estuary tidal waters back and the river became partly dry upstream; 15 September: Thames ran dry from London Bridge to Westminster; late September: end of drought from 1 June. **1593** Volcanic dust veil (DVI 1000), Ringgit (Java) eruption. Mild winter. Warm dry summer. Autumn – late part: generally wet and stormy; 8 October: windy with rain and hail; 25 November: start of wet spell into early January (1594). **1594** * Wet year; a year without a summer. Wet winter, mild in Denmark – 25 December (1593) to 4 January: Severn in flood due to previous wet spell. Wet spring – March: wet; 21 April: heavy rain; May: cold wet, floods. Very cool wet summer – inferred volcanic dust-veil effect; June to early August: cool and wet, floods, bad grain harvest.

> *June and July were very wet and wonderful cold like winter, that the 10 day of July [20 July NS] many did sit by the fire, it was so cold; and so was it in May and June; and scarce two fair days together all that time ... There were many great floods this summer, and about Michaelmas [29 September/9 October NS], through the abundance of rain that fell suddenly.*
>
> Simon Forman, Astrologer

Very wet autumn – September to early November: wet, severe floods. **1595** Wet year. Very cold winter, also severe in mainland Europe – frozen rivers and water bodies including the Thames, Rhine, Elbe, Moselle, Po and Venetian lagoons; late February: thaw, great snow-melt, severe ice floods along rivers in mainland Europe broke down even the strongest stone bridges. Cold spring – March: thaw, floods; April: cold. Wet summer – bad grain harvest. Autumn – early part: wet; early November to December: mild with strong west to northwesterly winds. **1596** Wet year. Winter – late January: wet, windy.

> *The rain lasts day and night and the country is waterlogged, roads are in such a state that it is impossible to travel by carriage or on horseback.*
>
> Anon, London, January 1596

20–27 January: Severn floods due to heavy rain. Spring – 14–15 April: heavy snowfall followed by floods; May: cool wet, floods. Very wet summer (Fig. 69), severe floods, widespread harvest failures, famine; June: cool wet; 11 July to 16 August: stormy, severe gales in Scotland, many shipwrecks off east coast. August: wet. Very wet

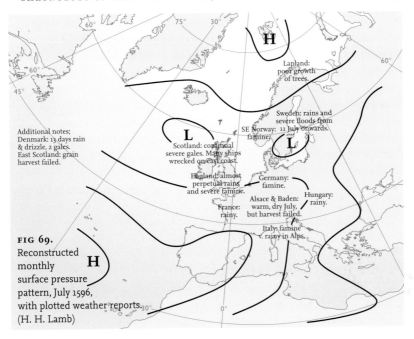

FIG 69.
Reconstructed
monthly
surface pressure
pattern, July 1596,
with plotted weather reports.
(H. H. Lamb)

autumn – heavy rain, floods. **1597** Wet year; volcanic dust veil (DVI 300), Hekla
(Iceland) eruption. Wet winter – December (1596): heavy rain, waterlogged
ground; January–February: cold wet, floods. Cold spring – March: cold dry; April:
wintry showers; May: cold dry. Cold summer – early part: wet; late summer:
improved conditions but bad grain harvest, famine. **1598** Volcanic dust veil (DVI
140), Öraefajökull and Grimsvötn (Iceland) eruptions. Spring – March: dry; 11–14
March: very mild; 15 March to 10 April: cold, hail and snow; April: frost and snow;
May: wet. Summer – early August: occasional rain. Autumn – October to early
December: occasional rain. **1599** Mixed winter, alternate frosts and thaws – mid
to late December (1598): very cold, Thames nearly frozen at London Bridge; c.28
December to 11 January: thaw; c.12–20 January: frost then thaw. Cold dry spring.
Very warm summer – June–July: mostly warm dry. * Autumn – early September:
severe storms. Inferred cyclonic situations, severe storms in the Channel.

1600s

Continental. **1600** Severe river floods, Trent changed course at Holme near
Newark (Nottinghamshire). Very cold winter – heavy snowfall in Ireland; mid to
late December (1599): stormy wet, floods. Very cold late spring – April: cold,
occasional snow; early May: cold dry, little vegetative growth; late May: start of

wet spell into early June. Summer – early June: wet spell, floods; 4 June: heavy snowfall; 11 June: start of warm spell; 26 June: heavy thunderstorm with hail in Norfolk. Autumn – 17 September: frost and snow in north England. **1601** Volcanic dust veil (DVI 1000), possibly Kamchatka (Asiatic Russia) eruption; reports from mainland Europe of the sun and moon remaining dim until late July 1602; start of a three-year famine in Ireland. Cold winter in Denmark. * 14 January: severe storm. One of the worst North Sea storms on record, inferred cyclonic situation/storm-force northerly winds, sea floods affected English east coast, coastal sand dunes breached at Eccles and Flattgates, near Horsey (Norfolk), sea water poured through an 800 m (880 yd) gap into the Hundred Stream and River Thurne. February: heavy snowfall; 11 February: storm, southeast England. Spring – early April: start of mostly dry spell into early autumn – 9 May: thunderstorm with hail in east England. Warm dry summer but cool in Ireland. Autumn – c. September: end of long dry spell from early April; October: wet in Ireland; November: intense frost in Ireland. **1602** Winter – very cold in Ireland; December: stormy in Ireland; January to early February: wet, Severn occasionally very high; 3 January: severe floods in north England, Aire very high; late February–March: mild dry. Spring – May: stormy in Ireland. Wet summer – inferred volcanic dust-veil effect; bad grain harvest, famine, thousands died in Ireland. Dry autumn – 8–9 October: frost, heavy snowfall. **1603** Exceptionally wet; famine in Ireland; return of plague, many thousands died. Mixed winter – 29–31 January: snow and rain; 1 February: start of very cold spell, but also floods on 1 and 16 February. Autumn – late November: very cold. **1604** * Winter – 14 January: severe storm. Inferred cyclonic situation, one of the most severe North Sea storms on record, storm-force northerly winds, storm surge probably coincided with high spring tide, coast breached at Eccles (Norfolk), 2,000 acres and 66 houses together with inhabitants lost to the sea, church ruined, village abandoned as floodwaters failed to recede; East Anglian coastline fundamentally changed. Dry spring. Dry summer – late June: cool; c. early July; start of dry spell; 13 August: thunderstorm with heavy rain and hail. Autumn – 3 September: end of dry spell, Avon ran dry in west England; 14–17 October: heavy snowfall in southwest and west England. **1605** Cold winter (?). Spring – May: wet. Summer – June: wet. **1606–1607** Volcanic dust veil (total DVI 550), Etna eruption. **1606** Dry year. Spring – 8–9 April: floods. Summer – 18 June: continuous rain for 24 hours in central and east England. **1607** Mild winter – January: heavy rain followed by floods, villages near Bristol inundated. * 30 January: severe storm. Cyclonic situation, inferred depression(s) moved northeast across the country to give a run of strong southwesterly winds, severe sea flood in the Bristol Channel probably caused by an Atlantic storm surge (when funnelled into the Bristol and English

Channels such a surge can cause devastating effects); the large volume of water funnelled into the English Channel and southern North Sea produced severe floods in the Norfolk Broads and Fens; sea came in so strongly in Romney Marsh that it did not seem possible that the area would ever be reclaimed; severe floods in the Bristol Channel apparently arrived suddenly in the early morning and extended along the coast for 32 km (20 miles) and in some places the water was 3.7 m (12 ft) deep, over 2,000 drowned, a board in the church at Kingston Seymour (Somerset) commemorates the event; however, according to the Barnstaple Church Register the place that was most affected by this 'mighty storm and tempest from the river' was Barnstaple (Devon), where, at least, damage costing £2,000 occurred.

> By reason of a great tempest, the sea brake in at divers places on the north side of this country, as at Barnstaple, where was much hurt done. At Bridgwater, two villages near thereabouts and our market town over flown, and report of 500 persons drowned, besides many sheep and other cattle. At Bristol it flooded so high that divers packs which were brought thither against Paul's fair, standing together in a common hall of the city for such purposes, stood three feet deep in water.
>
> Walter Yonge, lawyer diarist

* Spring – 12 April: inferred severe storm. Inferred cyclonic situation, severe sea floods, large areas inundated in east England, towns and villages flooded, thousands drowned, many sheep and cattle perished. 27 April: severe flood, 250 houses inundated in Coventry (Warwickshire). Very warm dry summer – many people died from heat-related illnesses. Autumn – October to November: wet (?); c.21 November: onset of cold spell (north England), frozen rivers including the tidal York Ouse, ice reported 1 m (3 ft) deep. **1608** * Very cold winter (topic for a contemporary ballad). Late autumn (1607): onset of very cold spell to late February, intense frost, snow.

> In 1607, about a fortnight before Xmas [4 January 1608 NS], began the hard frost which continued about 5 weeks; victuals were frozen so hard they would take no salt; the cold meat kept over night was so hard, that it could not be cut to be eaten.
>
> West Country diarist

Another old West Country document records that prices rose tremendously, hay was selling at 9 shillings per truss and cattle died for want of fodder. 15 January: Thames partly frozen, river frozen over above Westminster (18 January); also one of the most severe winters on record in mainland Europe: frozen rivers and water bodies including the Scheldt, Zuider Zee, Bodensee and Baltic Sea; 20 January:

Thames frozen, first recognised Frost Fair held on the river in London, other rivers and water bodies also frozen, including the Severn and Wye; frozen Lake District lakes bore large numbers of men and horses, loaded with corn; most mills frozen up so corn could not be ground; people froze to death, many trees killed, ships stranded by sea ice several miles out into the North Sea; c.24 February: thaw. Very cold spring – rivers remained partly frozen; 6 April: still unmelted ice; thaw followed by severe floods. Warm summer – late July to early August: very warm. * Summer – inferred severe storm. Inferred cyclonic situation/storm-force gales, severe sea floods, great loss of life, animals drowned, many houses damaged, Spurn Head peninsula breached, thousands of acres inundated, sandy shoreline between Great Yarmouth and Happisburgh (Norfolk) partly broken down and washed away by violent tides which allowed the sea to break through, many inland places damaged, including Postwick, Thorpe by Norwich, Trowse and Carrow; 2,000 people mustered the following year to repair Norfolk sea defences. Autumn – c.28 September: intense frost in north England. **1609** Wet year. Mild winter – mainland Europe: drought, positive pressure anomaly; late February to early April: cold dry in central and east England. Dry spring. Summer – early part: dry; late summer wet with floods.

1610s

Anticyclonic. **1610** Very cold winter – frozen Thames bore people and carriages; December (1609): cold dry; 5, 10 and 11 January: three floods in east England. Very warm dry summer. Autumn – late October to late February 1611: wet in east England. **1611** Wet winter – 10 January: heavy snowfall, lying snow to 30 January, 90 cm (3 ft) in north England; 12 January: start of wet spell into February, floods increased on 30 January, bridges destroyed in west England; late February to late May: dry spell. Dry spring – dry spell from late February to late May; 11 May: intense frost, thick ice in north England; unusually high tide at Easter caused floods in King's Lynn (Norfolk). Summer – late May to mid June: rain and showers ended drought from spring; July–August: heavy rain, floods. Autumn – 9–13 October: heavy snowfall followed by frost. **1612** Very cold winter in Germany – December (1611): 'hard', cold (?) weather. * January to at least August: drought. Inferred blocking-high situations. Dry spring – c. mid April: strong cold easterly (?) winds. Very warm dry summer – dried-up rivers in north England. Autumn – 30 November to 1 December: storms, strong winds, rain in north England. **1613** Wet year. Mild wet winter. Spring – March: start of wet spell to early August, severe floods. Very wet summer. * Autumn – 11 November: severe storm (topic for a contemporary ballad). Inferred depression over the North Sea, one of the greatest North Sea storms on record, storm-force northerly winds, storm surge, sea broke through at Wisbech (Cambridgeshire), much of the town inundated, sea floods also affected the Fens, Lincolnshire, Isle of Ely, Norfolk (five villages inundated, many drowned), Suffolk, Essex, Kent and Romney Marsh. **1614** Volcanic dust veil (DVI 1000), Indonesian eruption. Very cold dry winter – late February: start of mainly dry three- to four-month spell. Dry spring. Very warm dry summer – red sun reported in Austria, inferred volcanic dust-veil effect. Autumn – 3 September: start of wet spell in north England; November: 'foul', wet (?) weather. **1615** Dry year; drought affected much of Europe from England to Hungary. Very cold winter, heavy snowfall, rivers frozen – 15 December (1614): start of cold spell in west England; 26 January: heavy snowfall, roads and fields covered to tops of gates and hedges.

> *On the 16th of January [26 January NS] ... it began to snow and freeze, and so by interval snowing without any thaw till the 7th of March [17 March NS] following, at which time was such a heavy snow upon the earth as was not remembered by any man then living.*
>
> Francis Drake, FRS, Eboracum

16 January to 22 March: further snowfall. * Spring: severe river floods. Late March to early April: thaw, snow-melt, severe river floods, particularly in Yorkshire and Lincolnshire; Trent, Ouse, Aire and Calder overflowed, much damage, many bridges destroyed; one of the most severe river floods on record (comparable to 1947 floods).

> *It pleased God that at the thaw fell very little rain, nevertheless the flood was so great, that the Ouse [York] ran down [streets] with such violence as to force all the inhabitants of those streets to leave their houses ... Ten days this inundation continued at the height, and many bridges were driven down by it in the country, and much land over flown.*
>
> Francis Drake, FRS, Eboracum

4 April: start of a mostly dry spell to late August. Very warm dry summer.

> *After this storm followed such fair and dry weather, that in April the ground was as dusty as in any time of summer. This drought continued till the 20th of August [30 August NS] following without any rain at all; and made such a scarcity of hay, beans, and barley, that the former was sold at York for 30s and 40s, a wayne load, and at Leeds for four pounds.*
>
> Francis Drake, FRS, Eboracum

1616 Mild spring in north England. Very warm dry summer. * Autumn –
24–27 September: inferred severe storm. Inferred cyclonic situation with a
depression probably over south England, strong easterly winds over north
England, heavy rain, river floods on Aire and Calder. **1617** Wet year. Very mild
wet winter. * Winter: severe storms. Inferred cyclonic situations with
depressions probably over south England, easterly gales, new sea defences along
East Anglian coast almost swept away. December (1616) to mid February: very wet,
floods. Wet summer – June to mid July: wet, floods. Autumn – September: wet,
windy. **1618** Cold winter (?). Cold spring – c.7–16 March: snow. Summer – late
August: dry in north England; 30 August: start of wet spell to early September.
Autumn – c.12 September: end of wet spell. **1619** Cold winter (?) – frozen Danish
Sound. Dry spring. * Spring to autumn: drought. Inferred blocking-high
situations, dried-up springs, rivers and wells. Mostly dry summer. Dry autumn –
early November: end of drought.

1620s

Cyclonic and probably maritime. **1620** Very cold winter – Thames froze, Frost
Fair, frequent snowfall; 13-day spell of continuous snow in Scotland, many sheep
perished on Eskdalemuir. Summer – early part: very dry. Autumn – 26 November
to mid December: cold spell with snow; 29 November: Severn overflowed in
Worcestershire, many drowned. **1621** A year without a summer. Very cold winter
but with milder intervals – c.5 to 14–17 December (1620): cold spell, Thames
frozen; 9 December: severe flood on the Severn, at least 68 people drowned;
14–17 December: thaw, rain, floods; 27 December: renewed cold, frost, heavy snow
in east England; 31 December to 1 January: very cold with further snow in west
England; 4–15 January: mild wet spell in west England; 20 January: strong
westerly winds, rain in west England; 30 January: start of another very cold spell,
frozen rivers in north England; Thames frozen again, more intense than before,
Frost Fair; 21–23 February: end of cold spell, frost broke in north England. Cool
wet spring – early March: wet. Cool wet summer. Cool wet autumn.
* 22–24 October: inferred severe storm. Inferred cyclonic situation, continuous
rain followed by severe floods, much damage in north England.

> *On Thursday last there was the highest tide that hath been seen many a year for it
> ran all over Westminster Hall and did great harm.*
>
> Anon, London, 6 November 1621

> *The present year has been one long winter, cold and rainy to a remarkable extent.*
>
> Anon, London, 12 November 1621

1622 Sea floods, high tides breached coastal sand dunes in East Anglia. Very cold winter. Summer – c.25 June to 7 July: wet; bad grain harvest. Autumn – early November: wet, windy. **1623** Very cold winter – c.4–14 January: mild wet. Very cold spring – heavy snowfall; c. March to early June: drought. Very dry summer. Wet autumn. **1624** Dry year. Very cold winter – February: intense frost, heavy snowfall, Thames frozen, many died of the cold. Very cold spring, heavy snowfall; severe conditions continued into April; May: start of very warm dry spell into summer. Very warm dry summer – grass and hay very scant, water failed in many places. Mild autumn – mid September: end of warm dry spell. * October: severe storm. Inferred cyclonic situation/storm-force gales, many shipwrecks in the Downs. November: very wet. **1625** Severe sea floods, coastal dunes breached in East Anglia. Mild wet winter, apart from a late cold spell (20 February to 6 March). * Spring – 8 March: severe storm. Inferred intense depression moved into the North Sea, severe to storm-force westerly gales veered northwesterly on 9 March; storm surge, severe sea floods, marshes and low-lying coastal areas inundated in Yorkshire, Lincolnshire, Essex and Kent, flood damage along London's waterfront, Westminster Hall inundated; also much damage and loss of life in the Netherlands. Wet summer – mid June to 11 July: continuous rain. Autumn – September: volcanic dust veil (DVI 800), Katla (Iceland) eruption, ash fallout affected the Faroe Islands and Norway. **1626** Very warm wet summer. Dry autumn. **1627** Very cold winter in Denmark. Spring – late March: very wet in west England; early May: very wet in west England. Cool wet summer. Wet autumn. * 7 November: severe storm. Inferred cyclonic situation/storm-force gales, many shipwrecks off East Anglian coast. **1628** Wet year. Cold winter (?) – mid February: frost in west England. Very cold wet spring. Summer – cool to late July. Autumn – inferred heavy rain; floods. **1629** Winter – February: severe floods. Spring – 21 May: start of warm dry spell in southwest England. Autumn – early part: very wet in east England.

1630s

Anticyclonic probably continental. **1630** Mild very wet winter. * 14 January: severe storm. Inferred cyclonic situation, strong winds, rain in southwest England. Wet spring. Very dry summer – c.11 July: very warm spell in west England. **1631** Cold winter (?) – 11–26 December (1630): cold spell, frost, snow in west England. Summer – 7 July: heavy thunderstorm; 9 August: hailstorm in west England. * Autumn – late October: severe storm. Inferred cyclonic situation/storm-force winds, heavy rain, many shipwrecks. **1632** Winter – December (1631): volcanic dust veil (DVI 600), Vesuvius eruption; January: mild wet; 3 February: heavy thunderstorm at Weymouth (Dorset). Spring – 23 April: tide flowed twice in one hour at London

Bridge. Very wet summer. Wet autumn. **1633** Wet year; severe flood in Newcastle-upon-Tyne (Northumberland), many drowned. Very cold wet winter – frozen Thames; severe river floods in Cork, bridges and buildings damaged. Spring – April: cold wet. Wet summer – start of wet spell to c.24 November. Autumn – c.24 November: end of wet spell from summer. **1634** Dry year. Very cold wet winter – frozen rivers, including Thames and Trent; 20 January: start of dry spell to 20 March. Spring – 20 March: end of dry spell from late January; renewed dry conditions continued to 19 April in southwest and west England. Warm dry summer. * Summer to autumn: drought. Inferred blocking-high patterns, severe drought in summer continued into early autumn, burnt-up grass, dried-up springs. Warm dry autumn – October: warm dry, water levels too low for barges; 21–22 October: drought broken by a severe storm. * 21–22 October: severe storm. Cyclonic northwesterly and westerly situations, inferred storm-force west to northwesterly gales coincided with a high spring tide, North Sea storm surge, severe sea floods, German and Danish North Sea coasts badly affected, much damage, great loss of life. **1635** Dry year. Very cold winter with intervening thaws – late December (1634) to early January: short-lived cold spell, river Dee frozen; 15 January: renewed cold, heavy snowfall, Thames froze, Frost Fair; January: heavy snowfall, severe floods followed thaw; early February: renewed cold, heavy snowfall, severe floods followed thaw; 5 February: severe flood in Salisbury, water 30 cm (1 ft) deep in cathedral. Dry spring – March: cold; 3–7 March: heavy snowfall, snowstorm/blizzard conditions, deep drifts, 2 m (6–7 ft), locally over 6 m (20 ft), travel halted, shops closed in Chester; 4 April: hailstorm, large hailstones, 10 cm (4 in) circumference, Castletown (Isle of Man). Warm mostly dry summer. Dry autumn. **1636** Dry year. Mild winter in Germany. Mild early spring. * Early March to August: drought. Inferred blocking-high situations. May: volcanic dust veil (DVI 300), Hekla (Iceland) eruption, reports of notable sky glows in Scandinavia. Very warm dry summer. Autumn – September: severe drought-related effects, trees and vegetation despoiled of verdure as if in a severe winter. * 22 November: severe storm. Inferred cyclonic situation, southwesterly winds, heavy rain, severe flooding (west England), Bristol inundated, sea walls breached at Clevedon (Somerset), low-lying ground in many other nearby areas inundated but flood marks 30 cm (1 ft) lower than 1607 sea flood. **1637** Dry spring. Very warm dry summer. **1638** Volcanic dust veil (DVI 500), Roung (Java) eruption. Very cold winter – floods followed thaw. Very warm dry summer. Cool wet autumn. * 10 November: notable tornadoes. Tornadoes and thunderstorms moved across southwest England, widespread damage including Widecombe church (Dartmoor), lightning fireball exploded inside the building during a service, tower and roof demolished, 60 of the congregation killed or injured. **1639** Mild winter in Denmark. Cool wet summer.

1640s

Cyclonic. **1640** Volcanic dust veil (DVI 500), Komagatake (Japan) eruption. Winter –
December (1639): wet at times; January: wet at times; 4 February: very high water
levels; 22 February: heavy snowfall; 26–27 February: thaw, then wet to 6 March.
Very wet spring – 31 March to c.10 April: very cold, frost more severe than in
January; April: wet and stormy, floods; 3 April: heavy snow; May: wet at times.
Summer – 13–15 July: heavy thunderstorms, rain, hail, severe flood. Autumn – late
September: heavy rain, floods in southwest and west England. **1641** Dry year;
volcanic dust veil (DVI 1500), Indonesian eruptions. Very cold winter in Denmark
– 17 January to 14 February: wet. Mild wet spring – April: severe floods in the
Fens; 26 May: start of very warm spell to 8 June. Summer – 8 June: end of very
warm spell; late July to early August: renewed dry mainly very warm spell to
2 September. **1642** Mixed winter – early December (1641): frost, snowfall;
19 December: sudden thaw, snow-melt, rain in north England; January: wet. Wet
summer. Autumn – 21 November: start of wet spell into December. **1643** Very wet
winter – December (1642): wet. Spring – 2 May: start of dry spell. Very warm partly
wet summer – June: very wet in Ireland. * Autumn – 16 November: severe storm.
Inferred cyclonic situation, followed by unseasonably cold weather with snow.
1644 Cold winter – February: heavy snowfall. Spring – 25–26 May: heavy
thunderstorms, large hail. Summer – 20 June to 21 July: dry in southwest
England. Autumn – 1–16 December: wet spell. **1645** * Inferred severe storm.
Inferred cyclonic situation, storm surge, floods on east coast. Very cold winter in
Ireland – early December (1644): wet; January: early part: cold; 16–30 January:
thaw, wet, severe flood. Spring – mid March: wet and windy, floods in southwest
England; late May: dry spell in southwest England. Very warm dry summer.
1646 Volcanic dust veil (DVI 300), Makjan (Moluccas) eruption. Very cold winter
(Denmark) – 19 December (1645) to 25 January: cold spell with intervening thaws
(3 and 5 January); 25 January: thaw. Spring – 31 May: heavy thunderstorms, large
hailstones, funnel clouds. Variable summer – 2 July to 10 August: mainly very
warm, probably dry; 26 August: start of very warm, probably dry, spell to early
September. Autumn – 1–14 September: very warm spell in southwest England;
16 September to 12 October: wet spell, severe floods. **1647** Inferred wet summer –
bad grain harvest; 1–4 June: very warm spell. * Autumn – October: severe floods,
severe storm. Inferred cyclonic situation, coastal storm-force gales, many shipwrecks.
1648 Wet year. Mild wet winter. Very cool wet summer – bad grain harvest.

*A most exceeding wet year, neither frost nor snow all the winter for more than six
days in all ... prodigiously wet summer, very cold.*

John Evelyn

Autumn – 9 September: end of wet spell from late August followed by floods.
1649 Very cold winter – 25–27 January: wet spell; 28 January: flood; 31 January:
Thames frozen, Frost Fair; 9 February: stormy in southwest England. Spring –
11–13 April: wet spell; 22 May: start of dry spell to 5 June. Summer – 5 June: end of
dry spell; 1–22 July: dry; 11 August: start of mainly dry spell to 3 September.
Autumn – 3 September: end of mainly dry spell; late November: mostly wet spell.

1650s

Continental. **1650** Volcanic dust veil (DVI 500), Santorini (Aegean) eruption. Mixed
winter – early January: cold, frost, snow; 18–21 January: mild, thaw, severe floods.
Autumn – 13 September to 4 October: occasional rain. **1651** Dry year. Winter –
intense frosts in Denmark. Dry spring. Very warm dry summer. **1652** Dry year.
Mild winter – January: cold.

> *We found the ways very deep with snow, and exceeding cold.*
> John Evelyn, on a journey to Calais, 10 February 1652

20 February: windy, high water levels in southwest England. Very dry spring –
March: start of drought. * Spring to summer: drought. Very warm dry summer –
inferred blocking high over Scandinavia. 5 July: drought broken by heavy
thunderstorm.

> *After a drought of nearly four months, there fell this 25th day so violent a tempest*
> *of hail, rain, wind, thunder and lightning as no man alive had seen the like in this*
> *age. The hail was, in some places, four and five inches across, and brake all the*
> *glass about London.*
>
> John Evelyn, 5 July 1652

1653 Dry in south but very wet in north. Uncertain winter – early January:
reference to both storms with floods and frosts. Very warm summer. **1654** Dry.
Winter – positive pressure anomaly over the British Isles; mild winter in
Denmark; drought in mainland Europe. Very warm summer. * Autumn –
November: severe storm. Inferred cyclonic situation, storm-force gales in east
Scotland, trees blown down, ships in harbours swept out to sea. **1655** Very cold
winter – frozen rivers, including the Thames, Frost Fair. * February: severe
storms. Inferred cyclonic situations, severe storms in east Scotland, followed by
a long cold spell. Very wet summer in north England; August: wet, floods, crops
swept away in north England. **1656** Cold winter – December (1655): frozen Ouse
(Yorkshire) bore people. * 20 December: severe storm. Cyclonic easterly situation,

inferred depression over the Channel, severe to storm-force easterly gales affected Scottish east coast, heavy snowfall, severe sea floods, several piers damaged, houses damaged, many trees blown down, shipwrecks (vessels keeled due to weight of snow). Mid to late January: prolonged frost; 7 February: severe frost. Mainly cold spring – late March to April: cold, storms of snow and sleet, floods; 16 April: heavy snowfall; 11 May: snowstorm over high ground; mid May: start of warm dry spell. **1657** Uncertain winter – 30 December (1656): heavy snowfall. Very mild dry spring. Very warm summer – 31 August: heavy rain. **1658** * Very cold winter. Inferred blocking-high situations, one of the most severe winters on record; mid December (1657): start of very cold spell to late March, mostly north to northeasterly winds, heavy snowfall, one of the longest periods of lying snow on record (101 consecutive days); also severe in mainland Europe, frozen rivers and water bodies in Denmark, France, Germany and Italy. Very cold spring. Mixed summer – early part: cool; 12 June: heavy storm with hail and rain.

The season as cold as winter, the wind northerly near six months.
John Evelyn, 22 June 1658

July: very warm. * Late August: severe storm. Inferred cyclonic situation, severe to storm-force southwesterly gales, much damage, trees blown down, fruit destroyed. * Autumn – 13 September: severe storm. Inferred cyclonic situation, severe to storm-force gales in southeast England, chimney pots and roofs removed, trees blown down. **1659** Winter – December (1658): cold, much lying snow. * 26 December (1658): severe storm. Inferred cyclonic situation/severe easterly gales, heavy rain on east Scottish coast, sea floods, people drowned. January: average temperatures; February: average temperatures: 2 February: stormy in Scotland. Average spring temperatures – May: dry, inferred westerly. Cool summer – June: dry, inferred southwesterly. * 18 June: severe storm. Inferred cyclonic situation, severe gales, damage in Scotland. July: inferred settled conditions; August: wet, inferred cyclonic, frequent depressions over north England. * 10–11 August: severe storm. Inferred cyclonic situation, severe easterly gales, heavy rain, severe floods, crops damaged in Scotland. Cool autumn – September: wet. * 12–15 September: severe storms. Inferred cyclonic situation, gales, crops destroyed in Scotland.

1660s

Continental (?). **1660** Volcanic dust veil (DVI 2100), eruptions (Ecuador, Peru, Banda Sea and Iceland). Very cold winter. * 18 December (1659): inferred severe storm. Inferred cyclonic situation, storm-force gales in north England. January:

cold, heavy snowfall. Mild spring. * March: inferred severe storm. Inferred cyclonic situation/severe gale-force winds, North Sea storm surge, high tides and heavy rain in the Thames Basin combined to produce severe sea and river floods at London, sea floods also at Dover. 30 March: easterly winds, heavy rain, severe floods, houses and streets inundated in London (perhaps the same March storm as given above). Cool summer. Average autumn temperatures – 21–22 November: severe floods, Thames Valley. **1661** Very mild winter – 18 December (1660): storm, strong winds, rain in north England.

> It is strange what weather we have had all this winter – no cold at all, but the ways are dusty, and the flies fly up and down, and rose bushes are full of leaves, such a time of year as was never known in this world before.
>
> Samuel Pepys, 31 January 1661

January: notable red skies observed in Denmark, inferred volcanic dust-veil effect. * 27–28 February: severe storm. Cyclonic southwesterly/cyclonic situations, inferred storm-force gales, thunderstorm with hail in London. Wet spring with average temperatures; 1 March: northerly situation; late March to April: wet, floods; May to late June: mainly wet, floods. Cool wet summer – 3 June: heavy rain, floods, waters rose 1.2 m/4 ft in London; 16 August: roads in bad state; bad grain harvest. Very warm wet autumn. **1662** Wet year. Very mild winter – 18–23 December (1661): cold spell; January: mild wet;. Parliament ordered prayers for more seasonable conditions.

> It having hitherto been summer weather, that is, both as to warmth ... just as if it were the middle of May or June.
>
> Samuel Pepys, January 1662

February: mild; 24 February: rain; 27 February: heavy thunderstorm, hail. * 28 February: severe storm. Inferred cyclonic situation, severe to storm-force westerly gales, thunderstorms, rain, hail, buildings damaged, Ipswich church spire blown down, trees uprooted, several people killed in London alone.

> Every where [streets] full of brick-battes and tiles flung down by the extraordinary wind the last night, such as hath not been in memory before.
>
> Samuel Pepys, 28 February 1662

Average spring temperatures. Cool wet summer. Warm mostly dry autumn. **1663** * Very cold winter. December (1662): very cold; 7 December: heavy snowfall.

At my waking, I found the tops of the houses covered with snow, which is a rare sight, which I have not seen these three years.

Samuel Pepys, 7 December 1662

8–11 December: intense frost, Thames frozen, Frost Fair, skating introduced. * 12–14 December: severe storm. Inferred cyclonic situation/storm-force gales in east Scotland, partly built new Dysart harbour (Fife) destroyed, heavy building materials dispersed, large ship destroyed and blown out into the Firth of Forth. 15–21 December (1662): intense frost, heavy snowfall; 22–25 December: thaw, ice on water bodies broken up; 29 December: renewed cold; 1 January: cold; 25 January: muddy ground, mild (?); early February: frost; 23 February: thaw, heavy rain (27 February). Very cold wet spring. * 29–30 April: severe storm. Inferred cyclonic situation/severe northeasterly gales in east Scotland, two Newcastle ships wrecked off the Fife coast near St Andrews, 36 lives lost; probably the storm in which Nairn on the Moray Firth was endangered by blown sand. 15 May: very warm, thunderstorms. * 16 or 18 May: notable floods. Heavy thunderstorm, torrential rain, flash floods, bridges swept away, men, horses and cattle drowned. Very cool wet summer.

It is said there has not been one fair day these three months.

Samuel Pepys, 6 July 1663

Warm autumn – 7 September: severe frost; October: sea floods in London. * 29–30 October: severe storm. Cyclonic westerly situation (30 October), inferred severe west to northwesterly gales in the North Sea, sea floods affected German and probably other North Sea coasts. **1664** Volcanic dust veil (DVI 500), Pacaya eruption. Mild wet winter – 14–15 December (1663): wet, floods. * 16–17 December: severe storm. One of the most severe North Sea storms on record, inferred cyclonic situation/storm-force gales, storm surge, exceptionally high tides, severe floods, Thames estuary and London inundated.

There was last night the greatest tide that was ever remembered in England to have been in this river all Whitehall having been drowned.

Samuel Pepys, 17 December 1663

Wet spring, average temperatures. Warm wet summer – 6 July: heavy thunderstorm; 26 August: heavy thunderstorm. Cool wet autumn. **1665** Notable red twilights observed in London, inferred volcanic dust-veil effect. Very cold winter – Thames froze; late December (1664): reference to previous heavy rainfall;

7 January into late February: mostly cold and frosty, brief thaw with heavy rain (27 January to 1 February); 16 February: snowfall and intense frost (one of the coldest days then known in England). Very cold dry spring, created good breeding conditions for rats; plague outbreak later in year.

> *The last winter hath been as hard a winter as any have been these many years.*
> Samuel Pepys, 5 April 1665

Cool mostly dry summer – 12 July: tornado in Norfolk; late July: wet at times. Cool wet autumn – November: stormy, heavy rain, probably severe floods at Cley (Norfolk). * 17 November: severe storm. Inferred deep depression, exceptionally low pressure (c.931 mb), possibly the lowest unofficial value on record in London. * 24–25 November: severe storm. Inferred cyclonic situation/storm-force gales, heavy rain.

> *A night of as great a storm as was almost ever remembered.*
> Samuel Pepys, 24 November 1665

30 November: a wet and windy climax to a very stormy month, roads in bad state, English ships trapped in ice at Hamburg. **1666** Average winter temperatures – December (1665): very cold; 2–7 December: intense frost in London; 21 December: renewed frost; 28 December: Thames began to freeze, river blocked by ice (30 December), Frost Fair (?); plague much reduced; 1 January: river still frozen; 6–10 January: ice on Thames broken up by thaw, river traffic restarted. * 6 January: severe storm. Inferred cyclonic situation/storm-force northwesterly to northerly gales, exceptionally high tide, sea floods, inferred storm surge, coastal dunes swept away between Horsey and Waxham (Norfolk coast), extensive sea flood damage. * 3–4 February: severe storm. Inferred cyclonic situation/storm-force gales, heavy rain, houses blown down in London. Late February: start of dry spell into spring. Mostly dry spring, average temperatures. Very warm dry summer – almost dried up rivers; 6 July: start of mostly wet spell with occasional showers, severe hailstorms. * August to September: drought. Warm autumn – 12 September: Great Fire of London. Wet autumn – 13–14 September: easterly winds in final days of dry spell; 15 September: onset of unsettled conditions in south North Sea began breakdown of drought; 19 September: first significant rain for about three months dampened down fires in London. **1667** Inferred volcanic dust veil, Mount Tarumae (Japan) eruption. Very cold winter – so-called 'Double Winter' in mainland Europe, many rivers froze twice, but winter was not so severe in England; 7–8 December (1666): wet and

windy; January; mainly cold; 11 January: Thames ice-covered; 19 January: thaw.
* 3 February: severe storm. Inferred cyclonic situation/severe southeast to west
gales in east Scotland, houses and bridges damaged, severe floods followed thaw
of lying snow. 11 February: wet and misty, inferred advection of mild moist air
over cold ground. Very cold dry spring – March: very cold, probably one of the
coldest Marches on record; 16–25 March: heavy snowfall; late March to late April:
cold dry spell.

> The cold so intense that there was hardly a leaf on a tree.
>
> John Evelyn, 14 April 1667

Very warm mostly dry summer – July: parched ground, travel on streets
hampered by dust in London; 6 August: continuous rain brought end to dry
spell. Cool autumn – 23 and 29 November: heavy snowfall. **1668** Mild winter. Cool
spring – mid May into summer: mainly wet. Wet summer, average temperatures.
Warm dry autumn – October: many dried-up springs and wells in north England.
* Autumn: severe storm. Inferred cyclonic situation, severe sandstorm in East
Anglia, inferred storm-force southwesterly gales raised sand from Lakenheath
Warren (Suffolk) and carried it 8 km (5 miles) away to bury a village (then known
as Downham) and silt up the Little Ouse between Thetford and Brandon;
Downham later became known as Santon Downham to commemorate the event.
1669 Dry year. Cold winter – mainland Europe: drought, positive pressure
anomaly; December (1668): rain, severe flooding; 12–26 January: cold spell with
first frost of the winter. Cold spring – 21–30 March: mild; 30 March to 6 April:
cold spell, snow; 28 April: rain broke dry spell.

> The first day of rain we have had many a day, the streets as dusty as in summer.
>
> Samuel Pepys, 28 April 1669

Very warm summer. Warm autumn – September: dry. * 23 October: severe storm.
Inferred cyclonic situation/storm-force easterly to northeasterly gales on east
Scottish coast, sea floods, rain, thunder, trees blown down, many shipwrecks,
great loss of life both on land and at sea.

1670s

1670 Very cold winter – 24 December (1669): inferred anticyclonic situation, high
pressure, 1036 mb (30.6 in) at Bristol; c.27 December: start of cold dry spell to
13 January, almost dried-up rivers; 5 January: heavy snowfall; 14 January: thaw,
rain; February: renewed cold, heavy snowfall in north England; 22 February: thaw,

rain. Average spring temperatures – March: storm, strong southeasterly winds, heavy rain in Dublin; April: wet; 28 April: river floods at Oxford. Average summer temperatures. Warm autumn – floods in west Norfolk marshlands; 23 October: severe gales. **1671** Average winter temperatures; 25 December: thick fog in London.

> *This was the thickest and darkest fog on the Thames that was ever known in the memory of man.*
>
> John Evelyn

January: wet, stormy; 10 February: unseasonably mild winter up to this date, exceptionally wet and stormy; 14 February: start of cold spell into early March. Average spring temperatures; 8 March: cold dry season; 22 March: rain; 16 April: cold dry; 8 May: rain. Cool summer – 12 July to c.12 August: wet spell. Cool mostly wet autumn. * 22–23 September: severe storm. Inferred cyclonic situation/storm-force gales, over 70 shipwrecks off east coast. 27 September; severe floods; October: wet; 1 November: end of wet spell with floods. **1672** Very cold winter, positive pressure anomaly over the British Isles – drought in mainland Europe; December (1671): thick fog in London. * 19–21 December (1671): severe ice storm. Inferred cyclonic situation, freezing rain (probably warm frontal) fell on cold ground in southwest and central England, heavy deposits of glazed frost ('black ice'), many roads blocked by fallen trees which had collapsed under the weight of ice; this storm was followed by exceptionally mild conditions (probably warm sector) that allowed early blooming of bushes and flowers. 13 February: heavy snowfall. Average spring temperatures; 29 May: probable start of dry spell. Cool summer – dry spell to mid July; 17 July: rain broke dry spell; 9 August: start of wet spell to 21 October. Average autumn temperatures – September: wet; 21 October: end of wet spell; 6 November: return of wet conditions. **1673** Wet; volcanic dust veil (DVI 1000), Indonesia eruptions. Average winter temperatures – December (1672): mild wet; 30 December: thaw, rapid snow-melt, floods in north England. Cold spring – 30 March to mid April: cold spell, snow, rain, floods; c.15–22 April: dry; 23 April: wet; 21 May: cold dry period. Very wet summer, average temperatures – bad grain harvest; July: wet, floods; early August: wet. Very cool autumn – September: heavy out-of-season snowfall; 10 September: very wet; October: mostly wet. **1674** Cold year. Very cold winter – heavy snowfall in north England; December (1673): severe floods; January: very wet, severe floods in north England; late January: occasional snow and rain, floods; February: very cold, snow; 11 February: thaw (?), very wet, severe floods. Very cold spring – March: one of the four coldest Marches on record, 1.2 °C (34.2 °F). * c.18 March: notable snowstorm-blizzard conditions. So-called 'Thirteen Drifty Days', heavy snowfall, severe snowstorm-blizzard conditions continued almost every day for nearly a fortnight, deep drifts, many sheep, cattle and horses perished in south Scotland. 23–25 March: thaw, severe floods; 26–27 March: rain; 28–30 March: renewed cold, snow; 17–18 May: severe floods. Very cool summer, wet in north England – 3 June to 8 July: dry spell. Very cool autumn – September: mainly dry; 2–3 October: rain, end of dry spell; 30 November: heavy snowfall. **1675** A year without a summer. Winter – early part to late January: mild; late winter: cold, snow; December (1674): anticyclonic. * 31 December (1674): severe storm. Inferred cyclonic situation, storm-force gales in northeast Scotland, whole forests uprooted, gales may have raised and shifted sand along south coast of Moray Firth. January: westerly; 13 January: mild season, signs of early phenological events.

> *Warm dry calm Christmas [4 January], grass springing, herbs budding, birds singing...*
>
> Ralph Josselin, Earl's Colne, (Essex)

February: northwesterly. Cold wet spring – March: northeasterly; April: anticyclonic westerly; May: anticyclonic. Cool wet summer – an exceptional negative pressure anomaly, persistent cyclonic systems intensified over British Isles; June: cyclonic; July: cyclonic; August: cyclonic. Very cool dry autumn – 11 October: dry hard roads in Newcastle, mainly dry conditions continued to late December; rivers almost ran dry, barges hardly able to operate on the Thames. **1676** Very mild winter – December (1675): cyclonic westerly; 22 December: heavy snowfall, 45 cm (18 in), end of dry spell from autumn (1675); January: cyclonic westerly; 19 January: start of cold spell, snowfall; 22 January: heavy snowfall followed by several wet days; floods (28–29 January); February: mostly mild, cyclonic westerly; late February: dry in north England. Cold dry spring – March: cyclonic southwesterly; April: anticyclonic northeasterly; May: northwesterly. Very warm dry summer – 19 June to 1 July: very warm; 17–26 August: westerly gales. Very cool dry autumn. * Autumn: severe storm. Inferred cyclonic situation/severe northwesterly gales, sand raised and blown from coastal dunes on the Moray Firth, fields covered to a depth of 60 cm (2 ft) near Nairn. September to October: only occasional rain; 13 September: mainly dry conditions continued; October: wells dry; November: northwesterly; late November: start of very cold spell into the 1677 severe winter. **1677** Very cold winter – late November (1676) to early February (Fig. 70): very cold, occasional snow, hard frost, frozen rivers including the Thames (Frost Fair), Tees and Derwent; December (1676): very cold, anticyclonic; 20 December: heavy snowfall. This severe winter might

FIG 70. The frozen Thames at Southwark, December 1676.

have been the time of the 'Great Frost' over Exmoor, as described by R. D. Blackmore in his book *Lorna Doone*. 30–31 December: brief thaw; January: northwesterly; 3 January: renewed frost to 13 January.

> *The people pass over them [rivers] ... the Thames at London was so much frozen that huts were built ... carts and coaches went over.*
>
> Anthony Wood, Oxford

13 January: thaw, heavy rain, floods; 31 January to 10 February: renewed cold; February: northerly; 16–20 February: snow. Average spring temperatures – March: cyclonic southwesterly; 11–24 March: intense frost, snow in Wales; 15–19 March: heavy rain in Wales; 23 March: heavy snow; April: southwesterly; May: northwesterly; early month: wet, floods. Average summer temperatures; June: very wet; August: very warm. Variable autumn – September: cyclonic; September to 22 October: very warm dry. **1678** Variable winter – December (1677): anticyclonic; 3–8 December: frost; c.10 December: start of wet spell, floods (18 December); January: cyclonic northerly; 14–18 January: wet spell, floods; 27 January: heavy thunderstorm; February: northwesterly/northerly. Very cold spring – March: cyclonic westerly; April: northeasterly; May: cyclonic. Average summer temperatures – 12–28 July: dry spell; August: very warm. Very warm autumn –

early to mid September: very warm dry; October: mainly wet in north England; November: very mild dry. **1679** Very cold dry winter – December (1678): easterly; 15 December: snowfall in north England; 19–31 December: dry, frost; January: anticyclonic; early January: dry, low river levels; 11 January: easterly, heavy snowfall in London; 17–24 January: occasional heavy snowfall; February: easterly; occasional snowfall. Cold spring – March: northeasterly; occasional rain; April: westerly; May: anticyclonic; very warm. Very warm summer – 21–30 June: wet; August: very warm, showery. Cool wet autumn – September to October: wet, severe floods; mid November: low river levels.

1680s

Anticyclonic (?). **1680** Volcanic dust veil (DVI 1400), Indonesia eruptions (including Krakatau), notable red skies observed in mainland Europe. Cold winter in Ireland, Denmark and Germany – December (1679): westerly; 2 December: very mild season; January: cyclonic westerly; 8–9 January: heavy rain, river floods; late January: strong winds; February: cyclonic. Cold spring – March: northwesterly; April: westerly; May: southeasterly; 11 May: early phenological events, including leafing and flowering of bushes and trees. Cool wet summer – June: wet, floods; notable red skies observed in Denmark, inferred volcanic dust-veil effect; July: westerly; very warm, occasional heavy rain. Very warm dry autumn – September; dry; October: southwesterly, dry; November: southwesterly. **1681** Very cold dry winter – December (1680): anticyclonic; 11 December: start of cold spell, snow; January: dry, anticyclonic; February: cyclonic westerly. Cold dry spring – March: anticyclonic northerly; snow still lying at end of month; April: anticyclonic, dry; May: dry, anticyclonic. * Spring to summer: drought. Blocking-high situations.

> [A bad time for farmers], *especially in the latter end of May [early June] and beginning of June [mid June NS] grain was extremely dear ... cattle were reduced ... to eat the leaves of trees. The ground was never seen so russet in May. Boatmen reduced to penury for want of water.*
>
> Anthony Wood, Oxford

> *It still continued so great a drought as had never been known in England.*
>
> John Evelyn, 22 June 1681

Spring – April and May: anticyclonic. Cool dry summer – June: anticyclonic (?); July: anticyclonic; 14 July: end of a four-month dry easterly spell in Scotland; August: weak frontal zone over the British Isles, ridge extended from Azores high to central Europe. Very warm autumn – September: southwesterly type; November: start of mild dry spell into December. **1682** Mild winter, stormy, strong westerlies – December (1681): cyclonic westerly, 20–21 December: heavy rain ended mild dry spell; January: cyclonic westerly. * 26 January: severe storm. Inferred cyclonic situation, severe probably southwesterly gales, chimneys and roofs damaged in London. February: northwesterly. Cold spring – early March: heavy rain, floods (8 March); April: cyclonic southwesterly, wet; May: cyclonic westerly, wet to c.24 May, severe floods on rivers, including the Thames and Wear. * 14 May: severe storm. Inferred cyclonic situation, storm-force gales, trees uprooted. Very cool summer – 6–7 June: floods in north England; 11 June: stormy, gales. * 21 June: severe storm. Inferred cyclonic situation, so-called 'hurricane' reported, inferred storm-force gales. July: westerly. Cool autumn – September to c.20 October: dry at first, cool wet later. **1683** Average winter temperatures – December (1682): westerly, latter part: heavy rain, floods, 30 December: inferred strong gales in northeast England, churches damaged in Durham; January: mild dry, westerly; February: westerly. Mild spring – March: mild dry, southwesterly; April: mild very wet, westerly; May: cyclonic, very wet. Cool summer – June; latter part: wet; July: westerly; 13 August: floods in north England. Very cool autumn – 19 September: heavy rain in north England; September to December: cold, frozen rivers in north England; 7 October: intense frost, snowfall in east England; late November: start of very cold spell into 1684 severe winter. **1684** Dry year. * Very cold winter (Fig. 71, 72 and 73). Northeasterly situation; the coldest winter on record in England during the instrumental period, spell of intense frost said to be the longest on record, the Thames in London frozen from mid December to mid February with ice 25 cm (10 in) thick in places, passable on foot, bore coach traffic and supported a Frost Fair. However, at that time, the Thames was virtually dammed by the old London Bridge and the stagnant tideless flow above the bridge would have made the river more prone to freezing. Snow on the Mendip Hills over 1.8 m (6 ft) deep in places, people buried; some snow patches still remained at midsummer. Other English rivers frozen included the Trent and the Tees, on which a tent was erected and sheep roasted; the intense frost lasting over 50 days caused a cold drought with dried-up ponds, rivers and springs; plants and shrubs destroyed. December (1683): anticyclonic northerly; 15 December: start of severe frost; ground frozen to a depth of over 1 m (3 ft) in southwest England, frozen rivers and water bodies in Britain, Ireland and mainland Europe including the Thames (see above), Shannon (ice 2 m (7 ft) thick, bore carriages and cattle), Lee in Cork (bore carriages), Bodensee, Swiss lakes and Venetian lagoon; ice also formed on the northern fringe of the Adriatic Sea; January: anticyclonic easterly; mostly very cold, Thames still frozen.

I went across the Thames upon the ice, which was now become so incredibly thick as to bear not only whole streets of booths, in which they roasted meat and had divers shops of wares as in a town, but also coaches and carts and horses which passed over. So I went from Westminster Stairs to Lambeth and dined with my Lord Archbishop.

John Evelyn, 19 January 1684

20 January: frost gave a little but returned and continued to mid February; February: mostly very cold, anticyclonic northerly.

The frost still continuing more and more severe, the Thames before London was planted with booths in formal streets, as in a city or continual fair ... It was a severe judgement upon the land, for the trees were splitting as if lightning-struck, men and cattle perished in divers places, and the very seas were so locked up with ice that no vessels could stir out or come in. The fowl, fish, and birds, and all our exotic plants and greens, were universally perishing, many parks of deer were destroyed, and all sorts of fuel were so dear that there were great contributions to preserve the poor alive. Nor was this severe weather much less intense in most parts of Europe, even as far as Spain and the most southern tracts.

John Evelyn, 3 February 1684

15 February: a thaw began, breaking ice and severe floods destroyed bridges.

This traffic and festivity were continued until 5 February [15 February NS] when it began to thaw but froze again. My coach crossed from Lambeth to the horse-ferry at Millbank, Westminster. The booths were almost taken down.

John Evelyn

18 February: the thaw continued with the first rain for eight weeks; although the Thames remained partly frozen, ships were able to reach the Port of London by 21 February. The frost was followed by an early example of an urban smoke fog (smog); its effects were graphically described by the diarist:

London, by reason of the excessive coldness of the air hindering the ascent of the smoke, was so filled with this fuliginous steam of the sea-coal, that hardly could one see across the streets; and this filling the lungs with its gross particles, exceedingly obstructed the breath, so that as no one could scarcely breathe. There was no water to be had from the pipes and engines; nor could the brewers and divers other tradesmen work; and every moment was full of disastrous accidents.

John Evelyn

Dry backward spring – March: anticyclonic northeasterly; April: anticyclonic; latter part: start of drought to late August. * Late April to 20 August: drought. Blocking-high situations; 1684 was almost as dry as 1681, and comments by Evelyn were similar to those he made in 1681. May: cyclonic southwesterly; generally dry cool, some very warm weather about mid month. Very warm dry summer – June: very warm dry; July: southwesterly, mostly very warm dry; 20 August: rain broke drought.

> *Some small sprinkling of rain; the leaves dropping from the trees as in autumn [23 July NS] ... we now had rain after such a drought as no man living had known in England, to the great refreshing of the ground.*
>
> John Evelyn, London, 20 August 1684

> *This summer in general from the beginning of May till the latter end of August, was the hottest and driest that I ever remember; or (I think) any man else, being more like Spain for hot dry settled weather than England.*
>
> Sir John Wittewronge,
Rothamsted, Hertfordshire

Autumn – September: warm.

> *Most excessively hot, for we have not had above one or two considerable showers – and they storms – these eight or nine months. The trees lose their leaves like winter, and many of them are quite dead for want of refreshment.*
>
> John Evelyn, London, 3 September 1684

October: warm; November: cyclonic; early November: abrupt change to wintry conditions, frost, heavy snowfall.

> *Great snows and hard frosty weather the last week in October, most of the snow that fell the 30th [9 November NS] lying on the ground the 31st [10 November NS] ... so that it looked more like the end of December or January and was as cold weather as is usually in those months.*
>
> Sir John Wittewronge,
Rothamsted, Hertfordshire

1685 Very cold dry winter – December (1684): very cold, anticyclonic; January: very cold, anticyclonic, Thames froze, thawed and re-froze; 2 January: notable snowstorm-blizzard conditions, many perished in the snow.

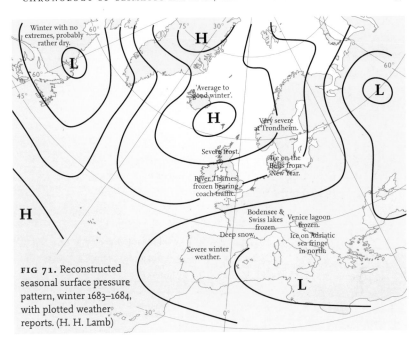

FIG 71. Reconstructed seasonal surface pressure pattern, winter 1683–1684, with plotted weather reports. (H. H. Lamb)

Text within map:

Winter with no extremes, probably rather dry.

'Average to good winter'.

Very severe at Trondheim.

Severe frost.

Ice on the Bells from New Year.

River Thames frozen bearing coach-traffic.

Bodensee & Swiss lakes frozen.

Venice lagoon frozen.

Deep snow.

Ice on Adriatic sea fringe in north.

Severe winter weather.

FIG 72. Frost Fair on the Thames in London, winter 1683–1684.

FIG 73. The frozen Thames above London Bridge with a Frost Fair, winter 1683–1684.

> *It proved so sharp weather, and so long and cruel frost, that the Thames was*
> *frozen across. The frost often dissolved and froze again.*
>
> John Evelyn, London,
11 January 1685

February: very cold, anticyclonic southerly; 5 February: start of dry spell.

> *A very dry February, very cold and calm, till the last three days, not one shower of rain*
> *from the 1st [11 February NS] to the last, and but one snow anything considerable, a*
> *very backward year for grass, blossoms etc and a very tedious long winter.*
>
> Sir John Wittewronge,
Rothamsted, Hertfordshire

Mild dry spring – March: anticyclonic; 16–17 March: rain temporarily broke dry spell; April: dry, southwesterly.

A very dry April as March and February had been before and indeed the whole
winter, there fell several snows but hardly any rain to speak of from Michaelmas
to Lady Day.

Sir John Wittewronge, Rothamsted, Hertfordshire

May: northwesterly.

The weather has been so long dry that by the 10th [20 May NS] all the small ponds
... were quite dry.

Sir John Wittewronge, Rothamsted, Hertfordshire

Very cool dry summer – June: northwesterly type; 30 June: end of dry spell; July:
cyclonic westerly; August: frequent showers but water levels still very low; rivers
almost dried-up, boatmen had no trade. Warm wet autumn – early September:
wet, floods in north England; November: warm very wet. * 20 November: severe
storm. Inferred cyclonic situation, severe gales, ships damaged in the Channel.
1686 Very mild winter.

This winter was so calm and warm that the anemones continued all winter in
flower till January 22 [1 February NS] primroses began to bloom the beginning of
January, the rose leaves continued on the trees: which all were wiped by the frosty
weather, beginning the 21st instant [1 February NS].

Sir John Wittewronge, Rothamsted, Hertfordshire

December (1685): mild wet, cyclonic westerly; 18 December: heavy rain, floods; January:
mild very wet, cyclonic southwesterly (?); early January: high water levels, severe
floods; February: dry, southwesterly; 8 February: start of dry spell.

An extraordinary dry February; there fell neither hail, snow, nor one shower of
rain from the beginning to the end of the month.

Sir John Wittewronge, Rothamsted, Hertfordshire

Very mild mainly wet spring – March: cyclonic; 14 March: end of dry spell; April:
anticyclonic westerly; May: cyclonic. Warm mostly dry summer – late June: wet,
thunderstorms, severe floods, houses and bridges swept away in north England;
July: westerly. Average autumn temperatures; November: mild. **1687** Mainly mild
winter, little or no frost or snow – December (1686): mild, westerly; 17–18
December: rain, floods.

This month of December was the warmest and calmest season for the time of the year that I remember (as was the last month) little or no frosts in either.

          Sir John Wittewronge, Rothamsted, Hertfordshire

January: mild, anticyclonic.

This month of January was mostly warm dry and open weather; no frosts worth speaking of no snow at all but not so clear as usually but many dark close days in it.

          Sir John Wittewronge, Rothamsted, Hertfordshire

18 January to 7 February: dry; February: mostly dry, anticyclonic.

This month of February was very dry for the most part only the 8th day [18 February NS] and night was a great rain, the rest calm, and dry and for the most part and warm, the latter end of the month the ways were dusty etc.

          Sir John Wittewronge, Rothamsted, Hertfordshire

Very cold backward spring – March: anticyclonic (?); 13 March: end of dry spell; April: northwesterly; May: cool and windy, probably westerly/northwesterly; c.18 May: start of wet spell. * 22 May: severe storm. Inferred cyclonic situation/ storm-force gales, strong winds held back Thames floodwaters, exceptionally low tide, river crossed on foot in several places. Summer – July: dry, anticyclonic.

This summer was very hot and dry for about six weeks, namely, from the middle of June [late June NS] until the latter end of July [early August ns], so that grass was very much burnt up, and many apples fell off the trees, etc.

          Sir John Wittewronge, Rothamsted, Hertfordshire

August: mostly cool. Cool wet autumn – c.10–24 September: very wet spell; 21/23 October: heavy rain; November: mostly warm, very wet, floods. **1688** Average winter temperatures – December (1687): wet, probably cyclonic; 5 December: heavy rain, floods in Dublin. * 11 December (1687): severe storm. Inferred cyclonic situation, east to southeasterly winds, heavy rain in Ireland, Dublin inundated. * 28 December (1687): severe storm. Inferred cyclonic situation, storm-force northeasterly gales in north and east England, 50 ships sunk or swept ashore. January: anticyclonic northwesterly (?); February: anticyclonic. Very cold dry backward spring – March: mostly very cold, southeasterly; April: cold, frequent snowfall, northwesterly; May: cyclonic. Very cool summer – July: westerly. Very cool autumn – October: northwesterly. * 30 October: severe storm

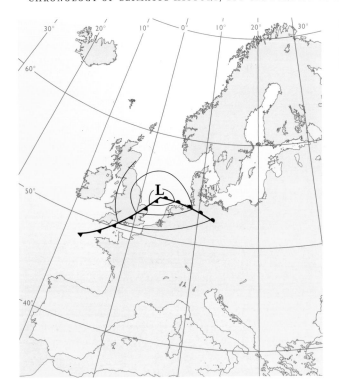

FIG 74. Synoptic weather map, 30 October 1688. (J. A. Kington)

(Fig. 74). Cyclonic westerly situation, southwesterly gales veering northwesterly, heavy seas in the southern North Sea forced William of Orange's invasion fleet back to their Dutch port; however, following an unsettled spell of about nine days, the wind turned easterly, which allowed him to sail across the southern North Sea into the Channel and land at Brixham (Devon). 17–19 November: storms in the Channel. **1689** Very cold winter – December (1688): cyclonic southeasterly (?); 20–24 December: stormy; late December to mid February: very cold spell, heavy snowfall, Thames partly frozen, Frost Fair; January: mostly anticyclonic.
* 21 January: severe storm. Inferred cyclonic situation, severe gales, churches and trees damaged. February: cyclonic westerly. Backward spring, mostly average temperatures – March: very wet, floods, cyclonic; April: cyclonic southwesterly (?); 11–13 April: heavy rain, floods; May: anticyclonic; 24–26 May: very warm, but turned cooler on 29 May. Very cool summer – July: westerly.

An extraordinary drought, threatening great wants as to the fruits of the earth.

John Evelyn, 3 July 1689

* 21 July: severe storm. Inferred cyclonic situation/severe to storm-force gales, rain, thunder, houses destroyed, trees uprooted, ships damaged, loss of life. Very cool autumn – October: wet; November: wet. * 15–26 November: severe storms. Inferred cyclonic systems over North Sea; 17–19 November: northwesterly situation, 20–26 November: northerly/cyclonic northerly situations, 22 November: inferred severe northerly gales, Danish–Norwegian fleet in distress off the Yorkshire coast.

1690s

Continental probably later partly cyclonic or maritime. **1690** Mild winter – December (1689): cyclonic westerly (?); January: cyclonic westerly; 1 January: lying snow, 30 cm (12 in); c.8 January: start of a mild wet spell, severe floods (c.16 January). * 21 January: severe storm. Inferred cyclonic situation/storm-force gales, snowstorm-blizzard conditions, houses and trees blown down, loss of life. February: cyclonic northwesterly; 5 February: mild wet spell continued. Very cold spring – March: cyclonic westerly; early March to early May: dry; April: anticyclonic westerly; May: anticyclonic northeasterly. Cool summer – July: anticyclonic/anticyclonic westerly; mid July: start of dry spell; 11 August: rain, end of dry spell; 23 August: start of cool wet spell into September. Cool autumn, several severe storms – probably severe floods at Cley (Norfolk); September: very wet stormy. **1691** Cold dry winter – December (1690): northerly; mostly cold; January: anticyclonic easterly; 18 January: cold spell continued; February: westerly. Cold wet spring – March: anticyclonic southeasterly; April: probably cyclonic westerly; May: anticyclonic northeasterly. Dry summer, average temperatures – June: very warm, occasional thunderstorms; July: anticyclonic westerly; August, very warm. Dry autumn.

An extraordinary dry and warm season [November] without frost, and like a new spring, such as had not been known for many years.

John Evelyn, London, 1691

1692 Cold year. Very cold winter – December (1691): dry, anticyclonic southerly; January: anticyclonic; 7 January: start of cold spell; February: northwesterly, cold; late February: occasional heavy snowfall with northeasterly gales in the Scottish Highlands. Cold very late spring – March: northwesterly/northerly; 2 March: northeasterly snowstorm-blizzard conditions in Scotland; April: anticyclonic westerly; early April: stormy, rain, snow; May: northerly; early May: cold, wet and windy. Very cool wet summer – June: wet; 9–12 June: strong stormy westerly winds. * 19 June: severe storm. Inferred cyclonic situation/severe gales, heavy rain, much damage, trees stripped of leaves by the strong winds and rain. July: cyclonic northwesterly; heavy rain, floods continued through July into August and September;. Very cool autumn – September: cool wet; c.26 September: start of cold mostly dry spell with northerly winds; October: frosts from 9 October, prevented fruit ripening; 27 October: end of mostly dry spell. **1693–1698** Volcanic dust veil (total DVI 3000–3500), several eruptions. **1693** A year without a summer; volcanic dust veil (DVI 800), Icelandic and Indonesian eruptions; volcanic dust fell in Scotland and on ships at sea (Hekla eruption in Iceland continued until August); first in a succession of six so-called 'ill years' in which wet summers and cold winters in Scotland prevented crops ripening and led to famine. Average winter temperatures – December (1692): anticyclonic westerly; January: anticyclonic northwesterly; early part: wet and stormy; February: northwesterly. Very cold wet spring – March: cold wet, frequent snow, northwesterly; 8 March: heavy snowfall. * 30 March to 3 April: severe storm. Inferred cyclonic situation, severe gales, buildings damaged. April: wet, cyclonic; May: northerly; early May: wet. Cool wet summer – inferred volcanic dust veil; July: northwesterly; August: very wet, bad grain harvest; failed harvests in mainland Europe, famine, millions died in France and neighbouring countries. Cool autumn – November: very wet. **1694** Cold; volcanic dust veil (DVI 900), Indonesian eruptions. Cold winter – December (1693): cold, northwesterly; January: cold, anticyclonic/anticyclonic easterly; snow (19 January); February: anticyclonic northwesterly/anticyclonic northerly; cold spell continued to 10 February followed by drought. Very cold dry spring – March: anticyclonic; rain on 2 March brought a brief break to the drought but dry conditions returned between 23 March and 10 April, after which the drought continued until at least 23 May; April: dry, westerly; May: mainly dry, anticyclonic easterly.

This is an extraordinary dry season, for there has been scarcely one shower since the beginning of April.

John Evelyn, 16 May 1694

Very cool summer – July: mainly dry, westerly; 29 July: rain ended more or less drought conditions from late February. * 11–19 August: severe storm. Inferred cyclonic situation/severe gales, crops damaged, heavy rain hampered harvest. c.30 August: start of dry spell. Very cool autumn – September; dry, coldest September (with 1807) on record, 10.5 °C (51 °F); 29 September: rain ended dry spell from c.30 August; October: westerly. * 29 October to 2 November: severe storm. Inferred cyclonic northwesterly/northerly situations, severe northwesterly gales in northeast Scotland, winds shifted coastal sand dunes inland from the south coast of the Moray Firth, farmland on the Culbin estate, near Nairn, buried up to 15 m (50 ft) deep in blown sand; area remained a wilderness of shifting sand dunes (known as the 'Scottish Sahara') until the Culbin Forest was planted in the 20th century. Early November: start of cold spell extending into the 1695 severe winter. **1695** A year without a summer, one of the coldest years on record; inferred volcanic dust-veil effect. * Very cold winter.

> *With long frost and snow [the winter], was, I think, the very sharpest I ever passed.*
>
> John Evelyn

Also severe in mainland Europe, many rivers and water bodies froze, including the Bodensee, with ice thick enough for the fully laden to cross it. December (1694): anticyclonic/anticyclonic southeasterly; 27 December: start of a mostly very cold spell for about a month with lying snow; January: anticyclonic easterly; Thames froze, Frost Fair; February: anticyclonic southeasterly; ground frozen until thaw on about 10 February, floods followed but frost and snow intermittently returned. Very cold spring, second-coldest spring on record (with 1770); odorous yellow fog reported in Ireland, inferred volcanic dust fallout;

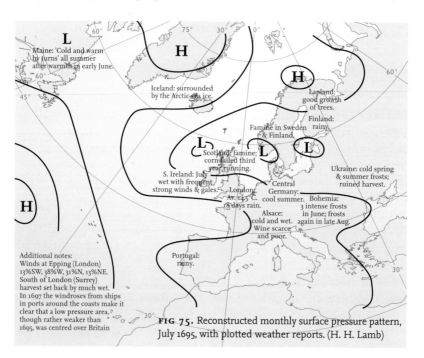

FIG 75. Reconstructed monthly surface pressure pattern, July 1695, with plotted weather reports. (H. H. Lamb)

March: northerly; cold, intermittent snow, 21 March to late April: northeasterly winds; April: northerly; early April: very cold, snow; c.21–24 April: southwesterly winds with rain, briefly interrupted long spell of severe wintry conditions; May: anticyclonic northeasterly; late May: mild wet. Very cool wet summer. Persistent yellow fog in Ireland, inferred volcanic dust fallout; bad grain harvest, famine; June; early part, dry, northeasterly winds; late June: end of dry spell; July: cyclonic westerly, one of the coldest Julys on record, 13.4 °C (56 °F) (Fig. 75); late August to early September: cool, northerly winds and night frosts (21 August).

Greater frosts were not always seen in winter.

John Evelyn, London

27 August: renewed wet spell. Very cool autumn – early September: end of wet spell from late August; 19–26 September: mostly northerly situations. * 22 September: severe storm. Cyclonic northeasterly situation, inferred small intense depression moved quickly east to northeast from the Channel into the southern North Sea, cyclonic storm-force gales, northeasterly over English east coast and westerly over south North Sea coasts, great damage in London, ship overturned in the Thames, 200 ships (mostly colliers) wrecked off the Norfolk coast, over 1,000 lives lost, many vessels stranded in the Channel, Dutch fleet driven back to The Downs. **1696** Severe flood, the so-called 'St Faith's Flood' in Norwich. Very cold early winter, later mild wet – December (1695): probably northerly; early part: cold, snow, followed by mild wet spell into February; January: cyclonic westerly; February: mild wet, westerly; forward vegetative growth in mainland Europe. Very cold spring – March: northerly, cold; snow and hail; April: northeasterly; May: cyclonic; very wet on 27 May. Cool wet summer – June: warm, occasional rain and thunderstorms; July: northwesterly; occasional rain and showers; August; severe shortage of food in Scotland. Very cool wet autumn. **1697** Dry year. Very cold winter, several mild interludes – December (1696): anticyclonic northerly; 8 December: inferred heavy rain, widespread floods; 11 December: start of cold spell with snow, mostly continued into February; 27–29 December: mild westerly interlude; January: anticyclonic; 6–8 January: mild wet interlude; 8 January: renewed cold northeasterly winds; 12–18 January: mild wet westerly interlude; 18 January: renewed cold northeasterly winds; February: anticyclonic southeasterly; cold spell continued. * 17–18 February: severe storm. Inferred cyclonic situation and severe gales in southwest England, buildings damaged, loss of life, 18 February: onset of mild westerly conditions. 21–23 February: final thaw. Average spring temperatures – March: anticyclonic northwesterly; April: anticyclonic. Very cool summer – 7 June: inferred heavy rain, severe flood due to a

bog-lake burst at Charleville (Co. Cork); July: cyclonic. Very cool autumn –
20–30 September: mainly cyclonic northwesterly situations. * 1–2 October: severe
storm. Cyclonic northwesterly/northerly situations, inferred depression over the
Hebrides probably moved southeast into the North Sea, severe northwesterly
gales over northwestern parts of the British Isles, settlement on North Uist
(Outer Hebrides) overwhelmed by blown sand, early snow over Welsh mountains
and possibly high ground further north; probable North Sea storm surge, severe
floods in the German Bight. Further storms and strong winds to mid October;
November: wintry conditions set in early. **1698** Cold; a year without a summer –
conditions possibly severe enough for incipient glaciation in the Scottish
Highlands. Very cold winter – December (1697): anticyclonic; 5 December:
Thames froze, ice 7.5 cm (3 in) thick; 1–17 December: occasional rain, sleet and
snow, lying snow, 20–30 cm (8–12 in); 19–22 December: thaw, snow, sleet and rain;
23–24 December: mild southwesterly; 25–31 December: easterly, occasional mist;
January: anticyclonic; return of cold conditions, heavy snowfall, deep drifts, rivers
froze.

Excessive cold weather and piercing winds.

John Evelyn, London, 12 January 1698

February: anticyclonic easterly; very cold, frequent snowfall, ice 20 cm
(8 in) on water bodies, frozen sea off Suffolk coast. Very cold backward spring –
March: cyclonic northwesterly; 8 March: rivers still frozen in southeast England;
April: very cold, anticyclonic westerly; May: very cold, anticyclonic northerly,
coldest May (with 1740) on record, 8.6 °C (47.5 °F); frequent snowfall, crops
damaged; 1 May: heavy snowfall, 15 cm (6 in) lying snow to 5 May in north England;
13 May: heavy snowfall, 25–30 cm (10–12 in). Very cool wet summer – June: wet;
July: cyclonic westerly; 21–25 July: wet spell; August: cool mostly wet,
northwesterly. * 9 August: severe storm. Inferred cyclonic situation, storm-force
probably westerly gales in southwest Ireland, flow of the Shannon halted for
three hours, people walked across the almost dry river bed. Very cool wet autumn
– September: wet; October: cool wet, cyclonic; November: wet and frosty by turns;
21/23 November: snow. **1699** Dry year. Cold wet winter – December (1698): cold
wet, cyclonic westerly. * 5 December (1698): severe storm. Inferred cyclonic
situation, severe southwesterly gales, property damaged in southwest Ireland.
* 27 December (1698): severe storm. Cyclonic situation, inferred severe southerly
to southeasterly gales in the North Sea, many shipwrecks off the south
Norwegian coast. January: occasional snow, westerly/northwesterly; strong
northwesterly storms on 3 and 8 January; February: cold, cyclonic; strong west to

northwesterly storms on 17 and 27 February. * 29 February: severe storm. Inferred cyclonic situation/storm-force gales, houses damaged, several people killed by fallen trees. Very cold spring – March: anticyclonic; April: northwesterly; 4–10 April: wet spell; May: mostly dry, anticyclonic. Warm dry summer – June: alternate wet and dry weeks; July: mostly dry, anticyclonic; 5 July: start of very warm spell to 2 August; 11 August: strong southwesterly storm. Cool autumn – September: dry; October: dry at first, wet spell later; November: mostly dry with light winds, probably anticyclonic; 26 November: start of foggy spell to 5 December in London.

WARM DRY INTERLUDE: 1700–1739

1700S

1700 Cool year; volcanic dust veil (DVI 100), Samoa (South Pacific) eruption. Cold winter – December (1699): mainly mild, cyclonic westerly; January: mainly mild, anticyclonic westerly.

There happened this week so thick a mist and fog that people lost their way in the streets, it being so intense that no light of candles or torches yielded any (or but very little) direction. I was in it and in danger. Robberies were committed between the very lights which were fixed between London and Kensington on both sides, and while coaches and travellers were passing. It began about four in the afternoon and was quite gone by eight, without any wind to disperse it. At the Thames they beat drums to direct the watermen to make the shore.

John Evelyn, London, 4 January 1700

February: mostly mild, occasional frosts, southwesterly.

The season, hitherto the most mild and gentle that ever, I think, was known, now altered into sharp and hard frosts for some days.

John Evelyn, Wotton, Surrey, 4 February, 1700

Very cold spring – March: mostly cold, northerly; April: cyclonic, mild, stormy, showers and thunderstorm (15–28 April); May: very cold, mostly wet. Very cool dry summer – 10–23 June: dry spell; July: cyclonic westerly; August: mostly wet. Very cool autumn. **1701** Mainly cold winter with some mild interludes – December (1700): cyclonic westerly; 12–18 December: cold spell, 25–31 December: mild spell; January: cyclonic westerly, changeable with both mild and cold spells, occasional heavy snowfall; 28 January: anticyclonic southeasterly situation, thaw. * 29 January:

severe storm. Southerly situation, inferred depression west of the British Isles with storm-force southerly gales, much damage both on land and at sea, buildings destroyed, many trees blown down, many shipwrecks in the Channel and southern North Sea, great loss of life. 30 January: cold southeasterly situation, severe frost; 31 January: southerly situation, less cold with rain; February: cyclonic westerly/westerly; 1–10 February: southeasterly situation, mild wet; mid February: renewed cold, occasional snowfall, strong storm (15–16 February). Very cold spring – March: northwesterly; cold, occasional snowfall; 12 March: start of mostly dry spell; April: cyclonic northwesterly; very cold, one of the coldest Aprils on record, 4.7 °C (40.5 °F); 27–28 April: end of dry spell. Warm summer – June: partly wet; July: very dry, anticyclonic; 31 July to 21 August: mostly wet; 22 August: start of mostly dry spell to 20 September; 27 August: hailstorm in Lincolnshire, large hailstones, animals killed, crops damaged. Average autumn temperatures – 20 September: end of dry spell from late August; October: occasional rain; 3–6 November: wet spell. **1702** * Early part of year: severe storms. Inferred cyclonic situation, storm-force gales, severe floods on North Sea coasts, many polders breached on the west coasts of Schleswig-Holstein and northwest Germany near Hamburg. Very mild wet winter – December (1701): westerly; c.11–18 December: wet spell; January: wet, westerly; February: westerly; 1–11 February: wet spell. * 13–14 February: severe storm. Inferred cyclonic situation/severe gales, large fall of pressure recorded in southeast England. Cold spring – March: westerly; early March: start of a dry spell; 12 March: strong storm; April: northwesterly/northerly; occasional rain; May: anticyclonic; early May: start of warm mostly dry spell into early summer. Very warm dry summer – 4 June: rain ended dry spell; July: westerly; August: very warm mainly dry. Average autumn temperatures – September: occasional rain or showers. * 22 October: severe storm. Cyclonic westerly situation, severe southwesterly gales perhaps veering later northwesterly over northeast Scotland and adjacent North Sea coasts, further heavy drifting of Moray Firth coastal sands extended affected area (see 1694 event), course of river Findhorn changed. **1703** Wet winter, average temperatures – very mild winter in mainland Europe; December (1702): cyclonic; alternating cold and mild spells with snow and rain, respectively; January: mild wet; February: mainly mild wet, southerly. Mild spring – March: changeable with both rain and snow, westerly; April: cyclonic southwesterly/westerly; late April: start of more favourable spring weather; May: wet, cyclonic southwesterly; wettest May for ten years in London. Wet summer, average temperatures – June: cool wet; July: wet, cyclonic westerly; 1–5 August: wet, followed by a mostly dry spell in north England. Very cool autumn – c.10 October: end of mostly dry spell in north England; 23 November: winds increased to severe gales during following two weeks, chimney pots damaged, several shipwrecks; 28–30 November: cyclonic southeasterly/southerly situations. **1704** Dry year. Probably a wet winter with mild to average temperatures – December (1703): dry, westerly/northwesterly; 1–6 December: cyclonic spell. * 7–8 December (1703): severe storm, 'The Great Storm'. Cyclonic southwesterly situations, intense depression moved northeast across Wales and south England into the North Sea, low may have originated four days earlier as a tropical cyclone off the eastern seaboard of North America that due to a strong jet stream tracked rapidly northeast across the North Atlantic; hurricane-force southwesterly winds, the storm was at its greatest intensity south of a line from Pembroke to Yarmouth, a 480 km (300-mile) swathe of destruction through Wales and south England, great damage, 800 to 900 houses destroyed, 400 windmills blown down, 100 churches stripped of covering lead, including Westminster Abbey, numerous spires and steeples shattered, many barns and stables demolished, Eddystone lighthouse off Plymouth Sound washed away with its designer Henry Winstanley, many shipwrecks especially in the Thames estuary, Downs, Goodwin Sands, Solent and Spithead, 300,000 trees damaged or uprooted, trees and grass in Kent covered by a salt deposit 32 km (20 miles) from the sea; an accompanying Atlantic storm surge funnelled up the Bristol Channel, port of Bristol and surrounding low lying ground flooded, great loss of life and damage accentuated by an abnormally high tide, water level rose 2.4 m (8 ft) above previous maximum at Bristol, 15,000 sheep drowned; an exceptionally high tide also in the Thames on 9 December caused severe river floods in London; 8,000–9,000 people killed by the storm, total storm damage assessed at £1–4 million; ten days later the author Daniel Defoe published an advertisement in a London newspaper requesting information about the storm, an overwhelming response, over 70 descriptions from correspondents in all parts of the country; due to Defoe's initiative, the 1703 storm is one of the most fully documented prior to the official instrumental period. February: northwesterly. Mild spring – March: mostly wet, southerly/southwesterly; April: mild, southwesterly; mid April to 22 June: dry; May: dry, anticyclonic northerly. Warm summer – Azores high frequently extended northeast over central Europe; 22 June: rain, ended dry spell from mid April; July: westerly. Very cool autumn – 5–31 October: dry, occasional frost, ploughing ceased due to dried-out ground. **1705** Dry year. Mainly cold dry winter – December (1704): cyclonic southeasterly; January: anticyclonic; February: anticyclonic. Cold spring.

Such fine weather as has hardly been known at this season without frost.
John Evelyn, London, 4 March 1705

11–26 March: mild, foggy in London; April: dry, anticyclonic westerly; May: dry, anticyclonic westerly. * April to July: drought. Four-month-long period of blocking-high situations, especially remarkable as such an extended dry season with burnt-up vegetation had not been experienced for many years. Dry summer, warm to average temperatures – June: warm dry.

> *The season excessively hot and dry, and for such a long time that all the country was burnt up.*
>
> John Evelyn, London, 28 June 1705

July: mostly dry, anticyclonic; August: while an anticyclonic situation continued over mainland Europe, more unsettled southwesterly conditions set in across the British Isles. * 22 August: severe storm. Inferred cyclonic situation, severe to storm-force gales affected south England, many shipwrecks in the Channel. Very cool autumn, dry at least from mid September to early October – October: westerly type, dry at first but a wet spell began in late October. **1706** Average winter temperatures – c.14–20 December (1705): very wet stormy; January: anticyclonic southeasterly. * 3 January: severe storm. Inferred cyclonic situation/heavy rain, floods, great damage. 10 January: very mild; 17 January to 7 February: cold, occasional snow.

> *The rain and a thaw upon a deep snow hindered me from going to church.*
>
> John Evelyn, Wotton, Surrey, 7 February 1706

Mostly mild spring – March: frequent northwesterly winds, wintry showers; April: mostly cold, occasional showers, thunder. Very warm dry summer – July: anticyclonic westerly. * 27–28 July: severe storm. Inferred cyclonic situation, heavy rain, occasional thunderstorms, southwesterly storm-force gales veered northwesterly, rivers overflowed, severe floods, corn damaged, hay carried away, bridges destroyed, trees uprooted, rain cleared and winds eased later on 28 July. Warm autumn. **1707** Dry; volcanic dust veil (DVI 750), Vesuvius, Santorini and Fujiyama eruptions. Average winter temperatures – January: anticyclonic. Mainly dry spring, average temperatures – c.23 March: start of very dry spell to late May. Very warm summer – July: very warm, westerly; 30 July: so-called 'Hot Tuesday', farm workers and horses died of heat stroke during harvest. Average autumn temperatures. * 1–2 November: severe storm. Inferred cyclonic situation/cyclonic storm-force gales, poor visibility, four British naval ships wrecked off Isles of Scilly, 2,000 sailors drowned, including their commander-in-chief, Admiral Sir Cloudesley Shovell, one of the worst British maritime disasters on record,

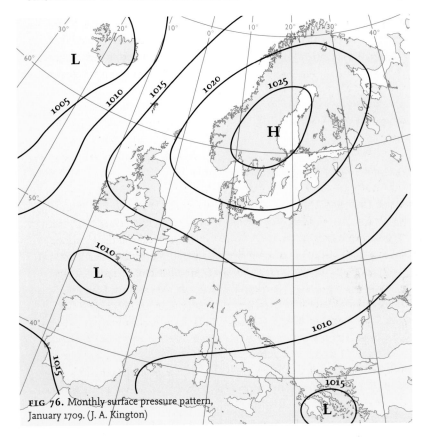

FIG 76. Monthly surface pressure pattern, January 1709. (J. A. Kington)

precipitated the search to determine longitude at sea, other vessels damaged with loss of life. **1708** Mild wet winter – January: cyclonic southeasterly; 4 February: heavy snowfall. Cool wet spring. Cool wet summer – bad grain harvest; July: westerly/cyclonic westerly. Warm cool autumn – September: warm, southwesterly. **1709** Wet. * Very cold winter. Blocking high over Scandinavia, a very cold easterly polar continental airstream affected much of Europe; although the frost lasted three months in England, the winter was less severe in Ireland and Scotland; frozen Thames crossed on foot but ice not strong enough for a Frost Fair, ice-covered sea along some beaches; frozen rivers and water bodies in mainland Europe, including the Rhine, Seine, Po and Danish rivers, Sound and Belts, Zuider Zee and Baltic Sea, Adriatic and Mediterranean shores ice-covered in places such as Venice, Genoa and Marseilles, many people, cattle, wild animals and trees killed. 26 December (1708) to 4 January: fog in London; January: very cold, southeasterly (Fig. 76).

On 26 December [6 January NS] last it began to freeze, and so continued with
snow every day more or less till about Thursday, the 6th instant [17 January NS],
when the snow ceased, which was then very deep; but it lay on the ground without
the least thaw, and continued freezing till the 9th [20 January NS] in the evening,
when there was a very great fog, when the weather began to give and the snow to
melt. It was very sharp, and the Thames was frozen over in several places, and
people walked upon the same.

Anon, London, 19 January 1709

Spring – April: cold; May: cold. Average summer temperatures – July: westerly.
Warm autumn.

1710S

Anticyclonic. **1710** Average winter temperatures – January: southerly, 30 January
to 4 February: fog in London. Average spring temperatures. Cool summer –
westerly/southwesterly. Warm autumn – 18 September to 13 October: warm dry
spell; 13 October: frost; early–mid November: mild wet spell; 24 November: cold,
frost. **1711** Very mild winter, frost-free to late January – 15–24 December (1710):
mild wet, stormy, heavy thunderstorm (15 December), packet boat sunk in the
Irish Sea (20–21 December); January: anticyclonic/anticyclonic southwesterly;
1–25 January: mild, river traffic active on ice-free Thames; 30 January to 1 February:
heavy snowfall; 11–15 February: frost, skating on London canals; 15–17 February:
partial thaw; 18–19 February: heavy snowfall; 20 February: snow followed by rain;
22–26 February: wet spell. Mild spring – March: mostly cold wet; 3–5 March: heavy
snowfall; 6 March: snow mostly gone; 13 March: rain; April: mostly cold wet; May:
occasional rain; 25–27 May: very warm. Average summer temperatures – June:
very warm mainly dry (early part); 7 June: stormy; 18 June: heavy thunderstorm;
25–30 June: occasional rain; July: mostly cool wet, west/northwesterly; August:
mostly wet. Warm autumn – 2 September: end of wet spell from 28 August;
c.6–15 September: dry spell; 16–24 September: mostly wet spell, occasional
thunderstorms; October: changeable; November: changeable. **1712** Volcanic dust
veil (DVI 200), Miyakeyama (Japan) eruption. Dry winter, average to mild
temperatures – December (1711): wet; January: anticyclonic/anticyclonic
northeasterly; 2–9 January: heavy snowfall, 10 January: end of cold spell, thaw,
snow-melt; February: dry. Average spring temperatures – March: mainly dry;
1–10 April: wet; c.12–18 April: some rain, then dry to late May. Very warm dry
summer – June: mostly dry; 27 June: thunderstorm, heavy rain, end of very warm
dry spell; July: westerly; c.6–12 July: mostly wet. Cool autumn – c.10 November:
start of wet spell which probably extended more or less into December.

* 29 November: severe storm. Inferred cyclonic situation/storm-force gales, houses damaged, trees blown down. **1713** Mild wet winter – December (1712): probable start of wet spell; 29–30 December: snowfall; January: probably mostly anticyclonic; 13–15 January: frost; 16 January: frost broken, followed by occasional rain; late January to April: notable wet spell.

> *I have never seen such a continuous of rainy weather; we have not had two fair days together these 10 weeks.*
>
> Anon, 27 February 1713

February: mild wet. * 5 February: severe storm. Inferred cyclonic situation, severe gales, damage in southeast England, tiles and chimney pots removed in London. * 26 February: severe storm. Inferred cyclonic situation, storm-force gales, east England, Norwich Cathedral spire blown down, other structural damage inferred. Very cold wet spring – inferred severe floods, Denver Sluice breached, Fens inundated; March: wet; April: mostly wet. Very cool summer – July: westerly. Average autumn temperatures. **1714** Dry year; one of the driest years on record, 280 mm (11 in) recorded in London, less than 50 per cent of the normal annual amount. Dry winter – December (1713): frequent fog in London; January: very dry, anticyclonic. * 12 February: severe storm. Inferred cyclonic situation/storm-force gales in north England, buildings damaged, trees blown down. Cold spring. * Summer: drought. July: very warm dry, anticyclonic westerly. Warm dry autumn – September: westerly type. **1715** Mild winter – January: anticyclonic southwesterly. Very mild spring – early April to late May: cold wet spell. Very cool wet summer – July: westerly/anticyclonic westerly. Very warm autumn – 22 November: end of dry spell, cold spell followed, frequent snow, Tees frozen for about two months. **1716** Dry year. Very cold winter, also in mainland Europe – large water bodies and rivers frozen including the Danish Sound, Zuider Zee and German rivers; 5 December (1715) to 20 February: very cold, heavy snowfall, deep lying snow, London streets almost impassable, Thames frozen for almost three months, Frost Fair; January: very cold, easterly; 25 January: Thames frozen so deep that an unusually high spring tide (North Sea storm surge) raised river ice 4 m (13 ft) but did not break nor apparently affect progress of the Fair; floods followed thaw; 4–8 February: fog (probably advection type) affected London. * 12 February: severe storm. Inferred cyclonic situation, severe gales, north England, houses damaged. Dry spring, average temperatures. Cool dry summer – June to mid September: dry spell; Thames fell so low that people walked across under London Bridge arches; July: northwesterly. Cool autumn – 25 September: strong southwesterly winds, incoming tide held up in Thames estuary for

24 hours, only a shallow narrow channel about 9 m (30 ft) wide mid river, people again walked across Thames under London Bridge arches. **1717** Volcanic dust veil (DVI 570), Vesuvius, Kirishima Yama (Japan) and Guatemala eruptions. Cold wet winter – January: probably anticyclonic; January–February: occasional fog in London. Very cold spring – late March to early June: mostly dry. Very cool showery summer – inferred volcanic dust-veil effect. Cool autumn. **1718** Cold winter – December (1717): mild stormy. * 24–25 December (1717): severe storm. Cyclonic westerly/northerly situations, primary depression over Scandinavia, associated cold front moved southeast followed by severe northwesterly gales, storm surge, sea floods affected southern North Sea coasts, including England, storm damage, great loss of life and livestock, especially on northwest German coast. 27–31 December (1717): anticyclonic spell; January: anticyclonic. Average spring temperatures. Very warm dry summer – July: anticyclonic westerly. Warm autumn. **1719** Dry. Average winter temperatures – January: anticyclonic southwesterly. Cold dry spring. Very warm dry summer. * Summer: drought. Inferred anticyclonic situation, fodder scarcity, dried-up ponds, farmers forced to buy water for cattle, many beasts slaughtered; July: anticyclonic.

> On this day [6 September] sometime was set apart for prayers to seek God on account of the great heat and extreme drought. Such a summer for heat in the months of May, June, July and August was hardly known in the memory of any man living. The pastures scorched, the pits and ponds dried up, the poor beasts of the fields pining for want of water ... the season is very threatening for man and beast. A sickly time both in the cities and in the country, fevers and deaths many.
>
> Anon, Guestwick Congregational Church Book, Norfolk

Wet autumn, average temperatures.

1720s

Fairly normal zonal flow (estimated 82 westerly situations on average per year in the period 1723–1729). **1720** Average winter temperatures; mild until about 11 February, followed by a month-long cold spell. Cold wet spring. Very cool wet summer – river floods. Cool autumn. **1721** Volcanic dust veil (DVI 250), Katla (Iceland) eruption; notable red sun observed for two months in mainland Europe. Average winter temperatures – December (1720): westerly gales. Very cold spring – March: frequent snow in north England. Very cool summer – inferred volcanic dust-veil effect; 19 July: inferred heavy rain, floods, Wear rose higher than in living memory. Average autumn temperatures. **1722** Mild winter. Average spring temperatures. Very cool summer. Very warm autumn – October: inferred

anticyclonic, occasional fog in London. **1723** Mild winter. Mild spring. Very dry summer, average temperatures – cattle suffered due to lack of water, burnt-up corn and little hay; July: wet, but fields still parched in generally dry conditions. Very warm autumn – 22 November: gales. **1724–1729** Volcanic dust veil (total DVI 420), Iceland eruptions. **1724** Very mild winter. Cold spring. Warm wet summer. Cool autumn – late October: dry, dried-up meres in Norfolk. **1725** A year without a summer; inferred volcanic dust-veil effect. Average winter temperatures.
* Mid January to late April: drought. Inferred anticyclonic situations, one of the driest spells then experienced in England. February: occasional fog in London. Average spring temperatures – April: dry spell ended mid to late month, rain in west Scotland (12 April) and south England (25 April); late April: general onset of wet spell into early September. Very cool wet summer – coldest summer on record, 13.1 °C (56 °F), inferred volcanic dust-veil effect; floods, rain was accompanied by cool conditions, resulting in poor late ripening of crops; June: wet, floods; July: wet; 9–12 July: brief dry interlude; 13 July: wet spell renewed and continued until 4 September with mostly southwest to westerly winds; late August: wet. Average autumn temperatures – 5 September: start of warmer drier spell after prolonged cool wet period since late April. **1726** Very cold late winter – January: cold; 12 January: heavy snowfall; 24–25 January: thaw, snow turned to sleet and rain. Mild spring – 19 March: Thames at exceptionally high level. Very warm summer. Warm autumn. **1727** Undated North Sea storm surge, floods in London. Average winter temperatures. Very mild wet spring – May to early June: very wet spell in north England. Very warm dry summer – early June: very wet; 18 June and 2 July: floods on Wear. Warm autumn. **1728** Cold wet winter. Very mild wet spring – 13 April: heavy hailstorm, corn damaged; 23 May: heavy rain, floods in Tyne basin. Very warm wet summer. Average autumn temperatures – September: fog on six days in London. **1729** Very cold dry winter. Very cold spring – 31 May: tornadoes, buildings and trees destroyed along their tracks through Sussex and Kent. Warm dry summer. Very warm wet autumn – September: one of the warmest Septembers on record, 16.6 °C (62 °F); November: whirlwind, much damage, roofs lifted off houses, trees uprooted, Barford St Martin (Wiltshire).

1730S

Cyclonic maritime; normal zonal flow (estimated 98 westerly situations on average per year); 1730–1733: volcanic dust veil (DVI 400), Vesuvius, Canary Islands, Etna and Jan Mayen eruptions. **1730** Dry year, first in a series of four exceptionally dry years lasting until June 1734. Mild mainly dry winter – 7 December (1729): inferred heavy rainfall, severe flood, 12 people drowned, Warrington (Lancashire); 12, 16–18 January: thick fog in London, many lives lost;

late February: wet, floods; 26 February: snow, sleet, hail in north England. Very mild wet spring – March: wet, occasional snow, later rain; early April: dry; late April to mid May: easterly wet spell. Dry summer, average temperatures. Very warm autumn – one of the warmest autumns on record; September: occasional rain or showers; late October: wet; November: occasional rain. **1731** Dry year, driest of the series of four years (1730–1733). Very cold dry winter – 1 December (1730): inferred heavy rain, severe floods; 17 December: very cold, Frost Fair in north England; 14–28 January: very cold spell, sleet, snow; 11–14 February: very cold spell, heavy snowfall in north England. Dry spring, average temperatures. Warm summer. Very warm dry autumn – one of the warmest autumns on record. **1732** Dry year. Mild dry winter. Mild wet spring – May: cold wet; 12 May: heavy snowfall in Edinburgh; 18 May: thaw, severe floods. Warm dry summer. Very warm dry autumn – September: North Sea storm surge. **1733** Very warm dry year; ninth warmest year (with 1834 and 1921) on record; widespread reports of dry fog, inferred volcanic dust-veil effect. Very mild dry winter. Very mild dry spring – May: dry, northeast winds. Very warm summer – July: very warm, local thunderstorms, exceptionally large hailstones, 20 cm (8 in) diameter on 25 July. Mostly cool dry autumn – many cattle slaughtered due to scarcity of grass; November warm: birds began building nests. **1734** Mild wet winter – 11 January: start of month-long mild spell, reports of early phenological events in north England. * 19 January: severe storm. Inferred cyclonic situation/severe gales, sea floods affected east coast, Wisbech inundated, many shipwrecks in the Channel. Late February: start of wet spell. Very mild wet spring – trees and hedges in full leaf in north England; May: frost. Warm summer – 24 July: heavy rain; 20–21 August: heavy rain. Cool dry autumn – October: Atlantic storm surge affected the Dee estuary; 12 October: heavy rain. **1735** Wet winter, mild to average temperatures – January: wet, floods. * 19 January: severe storm. Intense depression (945 mb or less), moved northeast over England, heavy rainfall, severe to storm-force west to southwesterly gales affected south Britain, the most violent winds since 1703, much damage in London, houses wrecked, trees blown down; northeasterly gales over north Britain on northern side of the low were probably even stronger. 16–17 February; westerly situation. Mild spring – 20 March: whirlwind, lead blown off church roofs, water blown out of a Norfolk river; April: partly dry; May: dry. Cool wet summer. * 19 July: severe storm. Inferred cyclonic situation, heavy rainfall, severe floods in the Thames valley, crops damaged. Roads in bad state until August due to frequent rain. Warm wet autumn. * 3–4 September: severe storm. Inferred cyclonic situation/severe gales, heavy rain, much damage to houses and trees. 18 September: severe floods, people, livestock and bridges swept away;

26 September: heavy hailstorm, report of hail 60 cm (2 ft) deep in Ayrshire.
1736 Very mild wet winter, some frosty spells (most severe 8–23 February) –
21 December (1735): wet, severe floods; February: wet; 19 February: heavy snowfall.
* 27 February: severe storm. One of the most severe North Sea storms on record,
inferred depression probably moved east across the country into the North Sea,
severe northwest to northerly gales affected east Britain and west North Sea
associated with a strong Arctic maritime air stream, heavy wintry showers, storm
surge, severe sea floods, east coast pounded from Lincolnshire to London,
Thames rose to its highest level for 50 years. Mild dry spring – 3 March: heavy
snowfall. Very warm wet summer – June: dry; July; frequent showers,
thunderstorms. * 23–26 July: severe storm. Inferred cyclonic situation, four-day
wet spell, continuous heavy rain, 127 mm (5 in), severe floods, much hay swept
away. Warm dry autumn. * 20 October: severe storm. Inferred cyclonic situation.
23–30 October: fog in London; November: very wet, stormy, floods. **1737** Very mild
winter. * 24–31 December (1736): severe storm. Inferred cyclonic situation, stormy
southwesterly winds, alternate periods of heavy rain, and heavy sleet and snow.
1–4 January: cyclonic north and northwesterly situations, snow showers,
4 January: high tide, Thames flood, Westminster Hall inundated. * 5 January:
severe storm. Anticyclonic northwesterly situation, inferred deep depression over
the North Sea, severe northerly gales over the North Sea, storm surge, high tide
and swollen Thames (due to previous two weeks of wet weather over the Thames
basin) combined to give severe floods in London, Westminster Hall inundated to
a depth of 60 cm (2 ft). * 20 January: severe storm. Inferred cyclonic
situation/heavy rain, severe floods in west England, many sheep drowned. Very
mild spring – began wet but turned dry in April. Warm wet summer – August:
one of the wettest Augusts on record. * 14 August: severe storm. Cyclonic
northeasterly situation, small intense depression moved northeast along the
Channel on an unusual southerly track for August, short-lived severe to storm-
force easterly gales buffeted southeast and east England, trees blown down, ships
sunk in the Thames, winds less strong over north Britain. Average autumn
temperatures. **1738** Dry year. Mild dry winter. * 12 December (1737): severe storm.
Inferred cyclonic situation, severe gales, southeast England, much damage.
17–19 January: strong winds, rain, hail, severe floods in north England. Mild
spring – May: very warm, showery. Warm wet summer. Dry autumn, average
temperatures. **1739** Wet year; inferred volcanic dust veil, Mount Tarumae (Japan)
eruption. Very mild wet winter but frost in January – 15 January: strong winds in
west England; 24–26 January: westerly situation. * 25 January: severe storm.
Cyclonic westerly situation, inferred deep depression moved rapidly east-
northeastwards over central Britain, severe west to southwest gales, buildings

damaged, trees blown down, many shipwrecks off Scottish coasts. February: mild.
Cold wet spring – March: strong cold probably northerly winds, fruit-tree
blossom damaged; April: cold northeasterly winds; May: cold northeasterly
winds. Mostly wet summer – cool to average temperatures. Very cool dry autumn.
* 22 September: severe storm. Inferred cyclonic situation, severe gales, southeast
England, much damage in London. 8 October: onset of cold easterly winds with
frequent frosts heralded 1740 severe winter; 12 October: snow; November: cool;
3–10 November: brief wet spell interrupted frosty conditions; 10 November:
easterly winds, renewed cold spell; 26 November to 4 January (1740): frequent
rain, longest break in the mainly dominant cold easterly winds of the severe
winter.

LITTLE ICE AGE, PHASE II: 1740–1772

1740s

Continental dry decade; fairly normal zonal flow (estimated 81 westerly situations
on average per year). **1740** Coldest year on record, with conditions possibly severe
enough for incipient glaciation in the Scottish Highlands. * Very cold winter.
The most severe winter since 1716 and one of the coldest on record – inferred
volcanic dust-veil effect; January: one of the driest Januarys on record; towards
the end of December (1739) and beginning of January the weather turned colder
and from 5 to 11 January 1740 it began to freeze at night with strong and
extremely cold east to northeasterly winds (probably associated with a blocking
high over Scandinavia); this was the severest part of the winter, London streets
became clogged with snow and ice, sea froze along English coasts and remained
ice-covered into March, –24 °C (–11 °F) in London on 14 January, Thames
completely frozen upstream from London Bridge, Frost Fair held on river,
floating ice and miniature icebergs froze together to produce a snow field rising
in places into huge heaps and hillocks, London Bridge and shipping damaged,
many vessels sank in collision with ice masses, cost of the damage to shipping
between the Medway and London bridges was computed to be £100,000; other
English rivers froze including the Yorkshire Ouse and Tyne, many birds perished,
plants damaged or destroyed. Also very cold winter in mainland Europe – frozen
rivers and water bodies including the Rhine, Po, Dutch canals, Zuider Zee,
Bodensee, Danish Sound and Swiss lakes; Baltic Sea completely ice-bound in one
of the most severe winter freezing events on record. * 9–11 January: severe storm.
Inferred depression over north France, easterly situation, severe easterly gales,
several cargo vessels sank due to sea ice on lower Thames, many lives lost, great

shortages followed for nearly two months as ice prevented ships entering the Port of London. February: cold; 2–4 February: rain and thaw interrupted long frost; large ice masses heaped up on the frozen Tyne; 28 February: cold spell ended, large ice masses floated down the Tyne the following day. Very cold dry backward spring – 5–8 March: second cold spell; 9 March: thaw, onset of southwesterly winds with light rain, finally ended the 1740 severe winter – c.11 March: rivers which had been blocked became clear of ice in north England; late April: drought in north England; May: cold, one of the coldest Mays on record, 8.6 °C (47.5 °F); 16 May: heavy snowfall. Very cool summer, early dry, late wet – 12 June: drought in north England; 24 July to c.26 August: wet; bad grain harvest. Very cool dry autumn – one of the coldest autumns on record. * 15–18 September: severe storm. Inferred depression over or near the British Isles, cyclonic southwesterly situation, severe southwesterly gales affected England and North Sea; 18 September: shipping greatly damaged when the southwesterly gales increased and backed to southerly storm-force with thundery squalls. October: one of the coldest Octobers on record, 5.3 °C (41.5 °F); 9 October: northerly winds brought unusually severe conditions with early night frosts and ice on many rivers; 12 October: stormy, snow, rain; 10 November: strong to gale-force northwesterly winds. * 12 November: severe storm. Deep depression moved northeast over southeast England, severe northerly gales with wintry precipitation moved south across the country giving snow showers in London (13 November), hurricane-force winds struck the city, one of Westminster Abbey's spires blown down, boarding school in Kensington destroyed and occupants killed, houses damaged, also people and shipping badly affected on the east and south English coasts. **1741** Dry year. Cold winter – c.8–21 December (1740): frosty; 21 December: frost broke. * 25 January: severe storm. Inferred cyclonic situation, severe west to southwesterly gales affected Scotland, widespread structural damage. Very cold dry backward spring – one of the driest springs on record; January to August scarcely half the rainfall usually recorded in that eight-month period. Warm dry summer – 12 June: start of warm dry spell; c.31 August/2 September: heavy rain ended dry spell from 12 June. Very warm autumn – 6–12 September: foggy (London); 16–30 September: cool wet spell, 114 mm (4.5 in) rain recorded. * 19 September: severe storm. Cyclonic situation, inferred primary depression north of Scotland, an intense secondary low moved rapidly northeast across central England, heavy rain, severe to storm-force southwesterly winds south of centre caused considerable structural damage both on land and at sea, tower and steeple of St Margaret and St Mary's Church, King's Lynn (Norfolk), blown down, probably sea flood at Cley (Norfolk), much damage to shipping in the Thames, Wash and Tyne, trees uprooted, southwesterly winds continued in London for several more days. **1742** Dry year. Cold dry winter – 8–17 December (1741): foggy, southeast England; January: mild; early February: renewed cold; 5 February: strong winds, west England. Very cold partly dry backward spring – March: one of the driest Marches on record; April: wet, nearly 50 mm (2 in) rainfall. Warm summer – c.24 June to 25 July: wet; c. mid August to mid September: longest dry spell of year; August: very dry, one of the driest Augusts on record. Very cool wet autumn. * 13–14 October: severe storm. Inferred cyclonic situation/severe gales, south Wales, sea broke through at Cardiff, many vessels cast away. **1743** Dry year. Very cold dry early winter, remainder mild dry – December (1742): cold dry; much ice in the Thames; 14 February: severe gales in southeast England. Dry spring, cold to average temperatures – 12 April: strong northerly winds, hail showers in northeast England. Warm dry summer – July: wet, followed by mostly dry conditions to October; 29 August: heavy hailstorm, crops damaged. Very warm dry autumn – September: one of the driest Septembers on record, rather foggy, London (inferred anticyclonic situation); October: rather foggy in London; 5 October: drought in north England. **1744** Volcanic dust veil (DVI 300), Cotopaxi (Ecuador) eruption. Cold dry winter, springs running low – late February: wet. Cold wet spring. Mostly dry summer, average temperatures – c.25 July: start of showery spell into mid September. Wet autumn, average temperatures – 17 September: end of showery spell followed by very wet spell into November. * October: severe storms. Inferred cyclonic situations, heavy rain, severe floods, several people drowned attempting to ford swollen rivers, three or four people drowned in the Coquet at Alnwick (Northumberland), new bridge at Weldon Mill (Northumberland) carried away by a severe flood on the Coquet. 1–23 November: mostly wet, heavy rain, floods. **1745** Dutch data indicate possible easterly annual wind component, inferred blocking. Cold dry winter – severe conditions to c.11 March. Cold wet very late spring – c.11 March: end of wintry period, rest of month mild initially wet; early April: cold dry; c.25 April: start of wet spell; 28 April: northeasterly winds; 7 May: heavy rain, floods; 19 May: start of wet spell into June. Very cool wet summer – June: mostly wet; 29 June to c.5 July: dry; 9 July to 14 August: very warm dry; 17 August: heavy rain 50 mm (2 in); 25–31 August: mostly dry. Warm autumn – 2–13 September: dry; 13–19 September: changeable; 19 September: start of dry spell; mid October to mid November: wet; 14–29 November: cool dry; 29 November to 1 December: gales; 30 November to 11 December: alternate frost and rain. **1746** Very cold winter – December (1745): mostly wet; late January: freezing fog in London; February: frost, some thaws to mid month followed by occasional snow and rain. Mainly cold dry very late spring – early March: occasional snow and rain; May: mostly warm, northeasterly winds. Mostly dry summer, average temperatures – June: partly wet and dry;

3 June: dry easterly winds in north England; July: mostly dry, very warm, 29 °C (85 °F) on 18 July; August: probably warm dry. Very cool autumn – September: probably dry; October: wet; November to late December: mild wet. **1747** Mild wet winter. Cold late spring. Very warm summer – June: mostly wet to 17 July; 17 July: start of very warm dry spell; August: one of the warmest driest Augusts on record. Warm dry autumn – October: storm surge in the North Sea, London floods. **1748** Very cold winter. * 11–12 December (1747): severe storm. Inferred cyclonic situation, severe gales, heavy snowfall, 60 cm (24 in), much damage in London, trees blown down, shipwrecks in the Thames and at sea, widespread severe floods followed subsequent thaw, Fen banks breached. January: wet; heavy snowfall, many sheep lost; c.22–23 January: thunderstorms; February: cold, possibly frequent snow. Very cold wet very late spring – March: cold, fourth year running that wintry conditions continued into March following a cold February; April: cold. Average summer temperatures – showery becoming mostly dry. Warm dry autumn – one of the driest autumns on record; 2 September to late October: warm dry; November: one of the driest Novembers on record. **1749** Wet winter, mild to average temperatures. * 27 December (1748): severe storm. Inferred cyclonic situation, storm-force southwesterly gales, much damage and loss of life both on land and at sea. January: storm surge in the North Sea, floods in London. Dry late spring, average temperatures. Cool dry summer – June: exceptionally cool, out-of-season snowfall; 4–5 June: heavy snowfall in Scotland, many cattle perished; 14 June: snowfall in north England; 26–27 June: snowfall, 5 cm (2 in) in north England. Warm dry autumn.

1750S

Normal zonal flow (estimated 91 westerly situations on average per year). **1750** Very mild dry winter, weak midwinter westerlies – January: southwesterly; Atlantic storm surge affected Cork. * 19 February: severe storm. Inferred cyclonic situation, severe gales in west England. Very mild dry early spring. Warm dry summer – several heavy thunderstorms. Dry autumn, average temperatures – September: dry, many springs ran dry, severe water shortage; late October: very cool, wintry conditions set in early. **1751** Wet year; volcanic dust veil (DVI 20), Vesuvius eruption. Cold winter, weak midwinter westerlies. * 11–12 December (1750): severe storm. Inferred cyclonic situation and severe gales, vessels damaged in the Thames, floods in west England. January: heavy snowfall, 69 cm (27 in) at Richmond (Yorkshire); early February: severe frost; mid month: end of severe frost in southern areas; 18 February: severe frost in north England, Tyne frozen; late February to late March: wet and windy. Cold wet late spring. * 9 March: severe storm. Cyclonic situation, severe southwesterly gales, much damage in

London and on the Thames. 12–22 March: wet; 12–29 May: heavy rain. Cool wet summer – early June: warm dry; late month: renewed wet spell lasting rest of summer. Very cool autumn. * 11 September: severe storm. Cyclonic northwesterly situation, severe northwesterly gales over the North Sea in rear of a cold front, one of the most severe North Sea storm surges of the 18th century, sea floods, Hamburg inundated, floodwater comparable in height to December 1717 disaster, but no reports of damage or loss of life, improved sea defences evidently held.
1752 Volcanic dust veil (DVI 1000), Little Sunda and possibly Tambora (Indonesia) eruptions. Cold wet winter, fairly weak midwinter westerlies – 2 December (1751): thunderstorms, wintry showers, floods; mid January: heavy snowfall, 60 cm (24 in); February: stormy. Cold late spring – March: stormy. * 26–28 March: severe storm. Inferred cyclonic situation, severe to storm-force gales, buildings badly damaged in London, west window of Westminster Abbey shattered, hundreds of trees blown down. Cool wet summer – inferred volcanic dust-veil effect. Warm autumn – 4–6 September: heavy rain, severe floods, Tyne and Wear overflowed; 19 September: heavy rain, severe floods in Wales, 10,000 sheep perished; mid October: first frosts. **1753** Cold wet winter, weak midwinter westerlies – December (1752): dry; February: early part: inferred cold; 17 February: thaw, severe floods on rivers in north England, Tyne, Wear and Tees overflowed, much damage, houses along Wear suddenly inundated to upper storeys before occupants had time to leave, also exceptionally high level on Tees with some stretches 4.6 m (15 ft) above previous high water mark. Mild dry spring – March: storm surge in the North Sea; 22 March: floods in the Thames, Whitehall inundated. Wet summer, average temperatures. Cool autumn – late October: cool. * 7 October: severe storm. Inferred cyclonic situation, severe coastal gales for some days, many shipwrecks. November: first frosts. **1754** Volcanic dust veil (DVI 300), Taal, Luzon (Philippines) eruption. Average winter temperatures, strong midwinter westerlies – December (1753): frost followed by heavy snowfall, severe floods; early February: end of a 16-day frost. Cold very late spring – March: 12-day frost with daily snowfall. Cool wet summer – inferred volcanic dust-veil effect. Warm dry autumn – September: dry, one of the driest Septembers on record. **1755** Volcanic dust veil (DVI 1200), Katla (Iceland) eruption. Very cold winter with milder interludes, positive pressure anomaly over the British Isles, weak midwinter westerlies – mainland Europe: drought; very cold late winter, frozen rivers and water bodies, including French rivers, Lake Geneva and Venetian lagoons. Cold spring – c.22 May: cold dry, north to northeasterly winds, north England. Wet summer, average temperatures. Very cool wet autumn – 1 November: great Lisbon earthquake; November to early 1756: notable red skies observed in mainland Europe, inferred volcanic dust-veil effect.
1756 A year without a summer. Mild dry winter, fairly strong midwinter

westerlies , vegetative growth all winter – January: mild; February: dry spell continued into mid March. Very cold wet spring – March: mostly cold; 16 March: end of winter dry spell; April: very wet, one of the wettest Aprils on record, severe floods, crops badly affected. Cool wet summer – inferred volcanic dust-veil effect; severe floods; failed harvest; extensive food riots. Cool dry autumn. * 6–7 October: severe storm. Cyclonic westerly situation, inferred deep depression moving east into North Sea, severe to storm-force west to northwesterly gales in rear of low, stone buildings damaged, many houses and trees blown down, vegetation blasted by blown sea salt, shipwrecks, North Sea storm surge produced an exceptionally high tide, northwest German and adjacent coasts pounded, but no reports of damage or loss of life, improved sea defences had evidently held. * 14 October: severe storm. Inferred cyclonic situation. **1757** Very cold dry winter, very weak midwinter westerlies – late December (1756): start of a very cold frosty spell that continued, apart from several breaks, for nearly six weeks; January: very cold; 7–8 January: two extremely cold days, –7.8 °C (18 °F) at Lyndon (Rutland). Cold wet spring – 15 March: storm, shipwrecks off Liverpool; late March: end of stormy spell. Very warm wet summer – July: very warm, 32 °C (90 °F) on 14 July; August: floods. Dry autumn, warm to average temperatures. **1758** Cold winter, weak midwinter westerlies – late December (1757): heavy snowfall, followed by about ten days of heavy rain. * 27 December (1757): severe storm. Inferred cyclonic situation, severe gales and heavy rain, shipping greatly damaged. Mild dry spring – May: mostly very warm dry, frequent northeasterly winds. Wet summer, average temperatures – June: wet; July: very cool, one of the coldest Julys on record. Very cool dry autumn. **1759** Volcanic dust veil (DVI 300), Jorullo (Mexico) eruption. Very mild dry winter, fairly strong midwinter westerlies – 2–3 December (1758): thick fog (London); January: mild very dry, one of the driest Januarys on record; early leafing of trees in Denmark.

> I believe it is as mild a time, considering the season of the year, as hath been known in the memory of man, everything having the appearance and carrying with it the face of April rather than of February (the bloom of trees only excepted). The meadows now are as verdant as sometimes in May; the birds chirping their melodious harmony, and the footwalks dry and pleasant.
>
> Thomas Turner, Diarist, East Hoathly, Sussex, 11 February 1759

Very mild wet early spring. Very warm wet summer. Warm dry autumn – 18 September: notable coloured twilight on a high-level dust layer observed at Augsburg, inferred volcanic dust-veil effect.

1760s

Fairly normal zonal flow (estimated 83 westerly situations on average per year).
1760 Volcanic dust veil (DVI 250), Makjan (Moluccas) eruption. Cold dry winter,
midwinter westerlies absent, short but severe frosts. * 15–16 February: severe
storms. Inferred cyclonic situation, severe to storm-force gales, much damage
both on land and at sea, House of Commons and Admiralty damaged, HMS
Ramillies driven aground off Bolt Head (Devon), 700 sailors drowned. Very mild dry
spring. Very warm dry summer. Warm wet autumn. **1761** Very mild dry winter,
strong midwinter westerlies. Very mild dry early spring. Warm summer, frequent
thunderstorms, heavy rain – 11–12 July: rivers swollen, flood damage at Rothbury
(Northumberland) on the Coquet. Warm very wet autumn – c.12 October: heavy
rain, Tees overflowed, Yarm (Durham) inundated; November: very wet, inferred
cyclonic, rivers continued at very high level, bridges swept away in north
England. **1762** Mild winter, strong midwinter westerlies. * 12 January: severe
storm. Inferred cyclonic situation, severe gales, possible North Sea storm surge,
buildings damaged in London, Thames overflowed, Millbank gardens inundated.
15 January: gales affected Hampshire and Dorset coasts. * 24 February: severe
storm. Inferred cyclonic situation and severe gales, much damage, 13 whales
driven ashore. Very mild dry spring – March: very cold. * 4 March: notable
snowstorm-blizzard conditions. Inferred cyclonic situation, prolonged
snowstorm-blizzard conditions for 18 days, heavy snowfall, deep drifts, 3.0–3.6 m
(10–12 ft), 50 people killed, many cattle perished. 2 April: heavy snowfall in east
Scotland. Very warm dry summer. Very cool wet autumn – October: wet.
* 3 October: severe storm. Inferred cyclonic situation and severe gales, many
fishing boats damaged off East Anglian coast, especially at Great Yarmouth.
28 October: snowfall. * 6 November: severe storm. Inferred cyclonic situation,
heavy rain, severe river floods, water levels rose 3.7 m (12 ft) in less than five
hours, great damage, especially in east England, including severe floods at
Chelmsford, Cambridge and Norwich (300 houses and some churches inundated).
1763 Volcanic dust veil (DVI 600), Etna and Moluccas eruptions. Very cold dry
winter, midwinter westerlies absent – 25 December (1762) to late January: easterly
situation, very cold, intense frost. * Mid January: notable rime frost. Rime frost
for several days, trees etc coated with a heavy deposit of rime. January: very cold,
intense frost, rivers frozen, including Thames, Severn and most rivers in
Northumberland; 4 January: skating on the Thames at Oxford; 7–10 January:
thaw; 11–27 January: renewed cold and skating on the Thames at Oxford. Average
spring temperatures, dry to average rainfall. Very wet summer, average
temperatures – one of the wettest summers on record, inferred volcanic dust-veil
effect; mid July: end of dry spell from spring and start of wet spell to 15 September;

19 August: heavy thunderstorms with damaging squally winds, trees blown down. Cool autumn with average rainfall – 15 September: end of very wet spell from mid July; c.20 November: return of wet conditions, frequent floods for two months, river valleys and low-lying areas inundated, Fen banks breached, livestock lost. **1764** Notable year for floods. Mild wet winter, normal midwinter westerlies. * 1–2 December (1763): severe storm. Inferred intense depression over the British Isles, continuous heavy rain, strong southeasterly winds backed east to northeasterly over northeast England, Tyne rose 1 m (3 ft) higher than previously recorded, very high tide on Wear; inferred storm-force gales over south England, houses damaged, people killed, trees blown down, Thames overflowed, shipwrecks. * 14 January (?): severe storm. Inferred cyclonic situation and storm-force easterly gales over Shetland, depression probably located over Britain, shipwreck in Sandwick bay and many more off the coasts of south Britain. Mid January: wet conditions began to abate but did not completely cease until mid February. Cold dry spring. Wet summer, average temperatures – 18 June: heavy thunderstorms, lightning destruction of churches and naval ship promoted the introduction of lightning conductors. Very cool dry autumn. **1765** Cold dry winter, weak midwinter westerlies. * 28 February; severe storm. Inferred cyclonic situation, strong winds, heavy snowfall, snowstorm/blizzard conditions, severe snow penetration. Wet spring, average temperatures – March: heavy snowfall, sleet and rain, large rise in river levels, Coquet left its old course below Warkworth (Northumberland) and forced its way between two sandy hills that had long obstructed a nearer exit to the sea; April: wet. Mostly cool dry summer – frequent northerly winds. Very cool autumn – October: wet. **1766–1771** Volcanic dust veils (total DVI 3400). **1766** Volcanic dust veil (DVI 2950), Hekla (Iceland), Mayon, Luzon (Philippines) and Vesuvius eruptions. Very cold winter, fairly weak midwinter westerlies – January: very dry; one of the driest Januarys on record; February: snowfall in east Scotland. Very cold spring – late March: snowfall in east Scotland. * 26 March: severe ice storm. Inferred cyclonic situation, heavy snowfall, freezing rain, heavy deposit of glazed frost ('black ice') formed on the surface, trees damaged probably due to weight of ice. April: lying snow in east Scotland; 18–26 April: snowfall in east Scotland; 13–15 May: snowfall in east Scotland. Wet summer, average temperatures. Warm dry autumn. **1767** Cold winter, very weak midwinter westerlies. * 1 January: probable line squall. Following fine conditions earlier in the day, a sudden change occurred during the evening with a short-lived spell of strong gusty winds, buildings damaged, vessels collided on the Thames, 27 people killed. Early January: frost, snow, navigation suspended on the Thames. * Early January: severe storm. Inferred cyclonic situation, heavy snowfall, 60 cm (24 in). 21 January: start of thaw; mild

wet conditions continued into February, severe floods for ten days, bridges damaged; after a dry week, renewed rain and floods were followed by stormy spell into March; 1–9 February: lying snow in east Scotland. Very cold spring – 12–22 March: snowfall in east Scotland; 1–4 May: snowfall in east Scotland; 5 May: snowfall; 13 May: heavy rain. Very cool wet summer. Warm autumn – late September: inferred anticyclonic situation; very warm, said to have been the most summer-like season of the year; 19–25 September: fog in London. **1768** First in a seven-year series of wet years; volcanic dust veil (DVI 900), Cotopaxi (Ecuador) eruption. Cold wet winter, absence of midwinter westerlies – 1–2 December (1767): snowfall in east Scotland; 25 December: start of very cold spell; early January: rivers frozen, including Thames and Tyne; 1–7 January: very cold easterly, heavy snowfall, 23 cm (9 in), hard frost, –8 °C (17.5 °F), roads blocked, many people killed; c.10–12 January: thaw; 14 January: southerly, snow gone; 26–27 January: southerly, heavy rain; February: mostly wet, stormy with heavy rain (7–11 February); 21–23 February: southerly, heavy rain, severe floods, bridges swept away in north England, last days of lying snow in east Scotland. Dry spring, average temperatures – March: dry; occasional snowfall in east Scotland; 24–29 March: east to northeasterly winds, blue mist (London smoke) at Selborne (Hampshire). Wet summer, average temperatures – June: wet; 9 June: start of a prolonged wet spell. * 14 June: severe storm. Inferred depression over Britain, westerly winds with heavy continuous rain affected central England, easterly gales over east Scotland.

The deluge began here on Monday last, and then rained near eight and forty hours without intermission. I have had a fire these three days. The best sun we have is made of Newcastle coal. My hay and I are drowned.

Horace Walpole, 15 June 1768

July: inferred easterly situation, very warm, occasional heavy thunderstorms. Very cool wet autumn. * 1 September: severe storm. Inferred depression moved northeast over south England, easterly winds with heavy rain, severe floods. 13 September: strong northerly winds, rain, river floods, bridge damaged at Selborne (Hampshire); 15–26 September: wet spell, heavy rain, severe flood on the Don (Aberdeenshire); 16 September: wind, rain, hail, roads almost impassable, Abbotsbury (Dorset); 17 September: waterlogged fields; 22 September: easterly, heavy rain in south England; 14 October: floods at Oxford; 22 November: southwesterly winds, unusually low pressure (952 mb), but little or no wind or rain at Selborne (Hampshire). **1769** Cold winter, weak midwinter westerlies – late November to early December (1768): wet spell. 1–2 December (1768): severe storm. Inferred cyclonic situation, strong southwesterly winds, heavy rain, severe floods, including Thames, thunderstorm with hail on 2 December. 11–15 December: cold frosty easterly spell. * 12 December (1768): severe storm. Inferred cyclonic situation with heavy rain, severe floods, many rivers overflowed, including Thames (record high level), Exeter stage coach carried away by floods at Staines. 14 December (1768): easterly winds, snowfall; 24–27 December: mostly southwesterly winds, mild dry spell; early January: inferred heavy snowfall, intense frost, Thames froze, roads blocked, many people died due to cold; 8 January: thaw; 15 January: storm, southeasterly winds; 1 February: southeast to southerly winds, skating on St James's Park canal, London; 12 February: north to northeasterly winds, snowfall, sleet and fog; 26 February: westerly winds, heavy rain. Dry spring, average temperatures – 11 March: heavy rain, snow-melt; 23 March to 8 April: northeasterly winds, occasional snow showers; late April to mid May: mainly dry, parched ground; 23–24 May: southwesterly winds, thunderstorms. Cool mostly wet summer – 21 June: southwest to westerly winds, heavy rain; July: one or two showers but dry ground; August: occasional showers. Very cool dry autumn – 9 September: notable red sky observed at Oxford, inferred volcanic dust-veil effect; late September to 27 October: mostly dry; 10–13 October: fog in London. * 4 November: severe storm. Inferred depression, severe to storm-force southerly gales affected south England and the Channel, nine men drowned off Gosport (Hampshire).

1770S

Very weak zonal flow (estimated 57 westerly situations on average per year). **1770** Volcanic dust veil (DVI 3400), Colima (Mexico) eruption. Mild dry winter, normal midwinter westerlies – 12–14 December (1769): heavy rain, floods; 8 January: northwesterly winds, keen frost, –4 °C (25 °F) at Selborne, 28 January: heavy rain; February: first part: stormy; 23 February: northeasterly winds, blue mist (London smoke) at Selborne. Very cold late spring, second-coldest spring on record (with 1695) – March: wet start followed by a cold northerly spell, 16–29 March: most severe part of the season, snow showers, slight frost, –2 °C (29 °F) at Selborne (23 March); April: cold; 5–9 April: lying snow; 21–22 April: snowfall; 2–4 May: snowfall, followed by warm showery spell. Cool wet summer (last in a series of five wet summers, 1766–1770) – inferred volcanic dust-veil effect; June: after a warm start turned mostly cool for rest of summer; July: occasional heavy showers. Cool wet autumn – late September: occasional showers, thunderstorms; mid October: start of very wet season to late December; 18 October: river floods. * 8–9 November: severe storm. Inferred cyclonic situation, heavy rain, severe river floods, Wear at Sunderland Bridge rose to height of three-storey houses, cellars flooded in Durham, great deal of damage, Tyne rose 3.7 m (12 ft) above neap tide, river swollen to an unprecedented level at Alnwick (Northumberland). 15 November: heavy rain; 175 mm (7 in) recorded in a three-week period, severe river floods, Fens and other low-lying areas inundated. * 19–25 November: severe storms. Inferred cyclonic situations, heavy rain, severe floods in east England, water levels in Norwich comparable to those of 6 November 1762 flood, distressed people relieved with money, coal and bread by a city subscription fund.

Can any thing get from Norwich to Blundeston? 200,000 acres are drowned in the Fens here, and cattle innumerable.

Mrs Henry Head, Cambridge, 25 November 1770

1771 Persistent snowfields in the Scottish Highlands. Very cold winter, fairly weak midwinter westerlies. * 18–19 December (1770): severe storm. Inferred cyclonic situation with severe gales in east England, structural damage reported in Great Yarmouth, shipping off east coast, especially colliers, damaged and wrecked, 200 seamen drowned. Late December (1770): end of a prolonged wet spell from mid October (1770), followed by short very mild thundery spell; 6–19 January: very cold, inferred northeasterly winds, occasional snow, keen frost, –4 °C (24 °F) recorded on 9 January, skating on Norfolk Broads; 19 January to 5 February: thaw; 6 February: renewed cold, 10–11 February: heavy snowfall in east England; 12 February: severe frost, –16 °C (4 °F), lowest temperature for 20 years at Lyndon (Rutland); 18–24 February: fog in London. Very cold dry late spring – heavy snowfall in northwest Scotland, lying snow lasted eight weeks in Skye, so-called 'Black Spring', many cattle died; March: very cold; 7–9 March: heavy snowfall in Norfolk; 12 March: snow followed by rain in Norfolk; 23–28 March: occasional snowfall, hard frost, –8.3 °C (17 °F) recorded overnight at Selborne (Hampshire) on 26 March; 15–17 April: very cold, wintry showers, hard frost, –10 °C (14 °F) at Selborne (22.00 h); early May: occasional thick fog in London. Cool wet summer – 16–17 June: storm, inferred gales, heavy rain; 21 July: heavy rain; 31 July: thunderstorm, heavy rain; August: wet. Cool wet autumn – 14 September: heavy rain; October: mostly wet. * 25 October: severe storm. Inferred cyclonic situation/strong southwesterly winds, heavy rain, floods. 6–7 November: heavy rain, floods, snowfall in Scotland. * 16–17 November: severe storm. Inferred cyclonic situation, heavy rain, severe river floods (so-called 'Ripon Flood'), rivers in north England in flood included Tyne, Wear and Tees, many bridges swept away, Tyne at Newcastle rose 1.8 m (6 ft) higher than in December 1763 flood, flood on Wear almost as severe, Tees at Barnard Castle (Durham) rose so high that the battlement on the Yorkshire side of the bridge was forced down, streets inundated, 4.6 m (15 ft) -deep waters in streets at Yarm (Durham). **1772** Volcanic dust veil (DVI 250), Gunung, Papandayan (Java) eruption. Mainly cold winter, very weak midwinter westerlies – December (1771): mild dry, later wet; January: very cold, snow, unstabled sheep and horses cut off by snow in Shetland; 9–21 January: deep snow cover, hard frost –12 °C (11 °F), Selborne (20 January); 23–27 January: thaw; late January: start of more changeable conditions; February: renewed cold; 1–2 February: frozen water bodies in Scotland, heavy snowfall (3–4 February), ground remained snow-covered; 27 February: lying snow, 50 cm (20 in) deep in east Scotland. Very cold late spring – snow cover to 12 March in east Scotland; 13–14 March: snow showers; April: cold; 18–19 April: renewed lying snow; 20 April: start of dry spell to 16 May, England; c.8 May: easterly spell in northeast England. Warm dry summer – 4–6 June: strong winds, rain, showers; 7–30 June: mostly dry; 1 August: heavy rain, first since early June. Very warm very wet autumn. * 24–25 September: severe storm. Inferred cyclonic situation/severe gales, widespread damage, including property in Oxford and London. 26–29 October: heavy rain; November: wet; roads in a bad state, Tees in flood on 10 November.

BRIEF WARM INTERLUDE: 1773–1781

1773 Average winter temperatures, fairly strong midwinter westerlies – 22–24 December (1772): frost; 26 December: thaw; 14 January: Tyne frozen for about 6 km (4 miles) below Newcastle. * 17–18 January: severe storm. Inferred cyclonic situation, exceptionally low pressure, inferred c.950 mb recorded at Kemnay (Aberdeenshire), heavy rain. * 20 January: severe storm. Inferred intense depression over the North Sea, storm-force north to northwesterly gales (east Scotland), 400 trees blown down at Kemnay (Aberdeenshire) alone. 3–10 February: cold frosty spell, occasional snowfall. * 26 February: severe storm. Inferred cyclonic situation, severe gales, heavy rain, much damage. Mild wet spring – March: dry; May: very wet, frequent showers, thunderstorms; one of the wettest Mays on record, severe river floods, Fens inundated. Warm summer, occasional thunderstorms – 13 August: heavy thunderstorm caused much damage in London. * 19 August: severe storm. Inferred cyclonic situation/storm-force gales, heavy rain, trees and crops damaged, buildings destroyed, two people drowned in London. Cool wet autumn – 1 September to early November: prolonged wet spell; 7 September: storm, heavy rain in northwest Scotland; 20 September: rain, gales in northwest Scotland. * 11 November: severe storm. Cyclonic situation, inferred intense depression, exceptionally low pressure recorded on several days, heavy

rain. 25 November: heavy snowfall. **1774** Last in series of wet years from 1768. Very cold wet winter, fairly weak midwinter westerlies – 8 December (1773): severe gales; late December: start of a cold spell with some mild wet interludes; 3 January: northwesterly winds, keen frost, –5 °C (23 °F), skating match held in Edinburgh; 9–11 January; north to northeasterly winds, heavy rain, sleet, snow, severe floods, lying snow; 14 January: southwest to westerly winds, heavy thundery rain; 18 January: northerly winds, heavy snowfall; January to early February: heavy snowfall, 35 cm (14 in) recorded in east Scotland; 1 February: southwesterly winds, heavy snowfall, crops damaged by extreme weather changes (10 February); 12 February: thaw in east Scotland; 20 February: storm, southwest to southerly gales. Mild spring – 9–10 March: southeast to easterly winds, heavy rain, snow, lying snow; 12 March: Thames flood, highest level on record at Teddington, mainly due to heavy rain but also partly tidal, Henley Bridge carried away. Warm wet summer. Cool autumn – October: warm dry, almost summer-like conditions allowed harvest to be finished; November: northwesterly, cool; 11 November: first snowfall; 20 November: start of cold spell with frequent snowfall to 9 December.
1775–1777 Volcanic dust veil (DVI 1000), Vulcano Is (near Sicily), Pacaya (Guatemala), Vesuvius and Etna eruptions. **1775** Mild winter, normal midwinter westerlies – late November to early December (1774): cold spell with snow; these conditions, together with reports of severe conditions from mainland Europe, caused concern about the forthcoming winter, but milder weather set in later; 14 December: heavy rain; January: mild wet; February: mild wet. * 1 February: severe storm. Inferred cyclonic situation/severe gales, heavy rain, much damage both on land and at sea, including the Thames, unusually high tides in the Channel on 2 February, much damage at Portsmouth and on the Isle of Wight. Very mild dry early spring – 9–11 March: heavy rain; 12 March: start of dry spell to early June; 26 March: heavy snowfall in east Scotland; 28–30 April: very warm spell, 26.7 °C (80 °F). Very warm summer – 15 June: heavy thunderstorm, 'knee-deep' hail, severe floods, much damage at Selborne (Hampshire). Wet autumn, average temperatures. * 19 October: severe storm. Inferred cyclonic situation/severe gales, heavy rain, shipping damaged in the Thames and at sea. 29 October: severe gales affected north England, many shipwrecks; 4 November: Edinburgh roads in bad state due to heavy rain. **1776** Very cold winter, midwinter westerlies absent – 1–21 December (1775): dry spell, ice on ponds (13 December); early January: partly wet; 7–31 January: very cold, widespread heavy snowfall, deep drifts, Thames frozen, 27–31 January: severe frost, –18 °C (0 °F) at Selborne (Hampshire), probably the most severe since 1740; early February: thaw, heavy rain (7 February), severe floods; 15 February: renewed cold, widespread heavy snowfall, roads blocked in Scotland, easterly gales in

Shetland; mid February: wet and windy spell to early March. Very mild dry early spring – 2 March: heavy snowfall in east Scotland; early March to early May: dry spell; late April: renewed cold; May: mostly cool dry northerly winds; 5 May: hail showers. Average summer temperatures – June: showery; July: drier; early August: very warm dry, parched ground, followed by wet spell. Mainly warm autumn – September: cool wet; October: warm dry, inferred anticyclonic situation; fog on 14 days in London; November; average temperatures and rainfall; fog on 11 days in London; 19 November: onset of brief mild wet spell; 22 November: snowfall in north England. **1777** Very cold dry winter, weak midwinter westerlies – December (1776): fog on 18 days in London; 4–12 December: mild moist conditions, inferred tropical maritime airstream; 12 December: high pressure, 1016 mb, at Selborne (Hampshire); late December to mid January: very cold spell, snowfall; 1–8 January: lying snow; 4–11 January: heavy snowfall in east Scotland, 10–13 cm (4–5 in), roads blocked; 10 January: thaw; February: renewed cold spell, snowfall; late February to early March: thaw, mild, floods. Mild spring – 8–10 March: snowfall in east Scotland; c.25 March: unusually out-of-season warm conditions, 20 °C (68 °F); 27 March to 10 April: renewed cold; April: cold, snow showers in east Scotland. Mainly cool wet summer – June: cool and wet at times in east Scotland; c.10 June to late July: wet; 7–8 July: very cool, heavy rain. * 29–30 July: severe storm. Inferred cyclonic situation, heavy rain, severe floods, roads and houses damaged, crops swept away, people drowned. Late summer – warmer drier conditions. Very warm autumn – late September: 23 °C (74 °F). * 30 October: severe storm. Inferred cyclonic situation/storm-force gales, heavy thundery rain, much damage both on land and at sea, houses blown down in London. October: partly wet; November: stormy, several shipwrecks off Shetland. **1778** Cold winter, normal midwinter westerlies – late December (1777) to early January: cold, occasional snow, Thames frozen at Kingston (Surrey); 26–28 January; lying snow. Cold late spring – mid to late April: snowfall in east Scotland; 21 April: snowstorm. Very warm dry summer – July: very warm; 5 and 14 July: 31 °C (88 °F) recorded in London; 20 July: heavy thunderstorms, much damage caused by lightning in London. Very cool dry autumn – late September: water shortage; October: ground too dry for sowing (19 October); 25 October: severe frost, winter-like weather, Thames frozen at Kingston (Surrey). **1779** Warm wet year; volcanic dust veil (DVI 650), Sakurashima (Japan) eruption. Very mild dry winter, positive pressure anomaly over the British Isles, fairly strong midwinter westerlies – mainland Europe: drought. * 31 December (1778) to 1 January: severe storm. Probably the worst storm since 1703 but unlike the latter this storm affected the whole country, inferred deep depression over the North Sea, severe to storm-force northerly gales, much damage both on land and at sea, buildings damaged, barns, mills and trees blown down, lead stripped off

St Andrew's Church (Norwich), many shipwrecks, snowstorms, deep drifts, very high seas at high tide breached sea wall and quay at Whitehaven (Cumberland). January: mild dry; February: very mild, one of the mildest Februarys on record, 7.9 °C (46 °F). Very mild dry early spring – mid April: mild; 15 April: 23 °C (73 °F) at Lyndon (Rutland); 17 April: rain much needed, dry spell had lasted almost four months; late April to early May: cold, showery; 24 April: storm, hail, trees damaged; 3 May: snow showers, locally heavy, 9 cm (3.5 in) snowfall in east Scotland; late May: very warm dry. Very warm summer – 2 June: waterspout at Kemnay (Aberdeenshire); 16 June: tornado at Kemnay (Aberdeenshire); 9 July: heavy thunderstorm, two people killed by lightning in east Scotland; 13 July: 26 °C (79 °F); 26 July: heavy thunderstorm, large hail, heavy rain in east Scotland; August: warm. Very warm wet autumn. * 16 October: severe storm. Inferred cyclonic situation, strong winds, heavy rain. Late November: occasional rain, snowfall.

1780s

Cyclonic and continental; very weak zonal flow (estimated 54 westerly situations on average per year). **1780** Dry year. Very cold winter, the most severe since 1740, midwinter westerlies absent – 2 December (1779): snowfall in east Scotland; 9 December: snow showers, drifts in east Scotland; 13 December: thunderstorms; 22 December: start of cold spell into February, snowfall, keen frost, –4 °C (25 °F) on 25 December; 8–9 January: light snowfall in east Scotland; 16 January: thaw, rain; 17–28 January: snowfall in east Scotland; February: cold, occasional snow, greatest depth of the winter in east Scotland. Very mild spring – March to June: strong westerly winds, ships had difficulty sailing down the Channel, occasional snowfall in east Scotland; 3 April: heavy snowfall in east Scotland. Very warm dry summer – August: fog on ten days in London. Average autumn temperatures. * 15 October: severe storm. Inferred cyclonic situation, depression (ex-tropical hurricane), inferred severe gales, much damage both on land and at sea, tornado reported in southwest London, trees blown down, buildings damaged, two people killed. 7 November: wintry weather, lying snow; mid November: ten-day cold spell, snowfall; 24 November: start of dry spell to 23 December. **1781** Dry year, weak zonal flow (75 westerly situations). Cold dry winter, weak midwinter westerlies – December (1780): dry, one of the driest Decembers on record, 13 mm (0.5 in); 21 December: level snow, no drifting; 23 December: no rain since 24 November; January: very blocked northerly; early month: cold dry, lying snow; 14–15 January: easterly situation, dry, very hard ground, millers complained about water shortage; 23–24 January: easterly/cyclonic situations, snowfall; 27–31 January: westerly situation, rapid thaw, wet windy spell, many shipwrecks in the Channel; 13 February: westerly situation, severe to storm-force southwesterly gales, great damage both on land and at sea, houses wrecked, trees blown down; 21 February: anticyclonic situation, snowfall. * 27 February: severe storm. Northwesterly situation, deep depression (below 964 mb) in the North Sea, inferred severe north to northwesterly gales. Very mild dry spring – March: anticyclonic; 13 March: Herschel discovered Uranus during this anticyclonic spell; 12 April: start of dry spell into autumn – May: dry. * Spring to autumn: drought. Mostly dry spell from spring to autumn. Very warm mostly dry summer, third successive very warm summer – June: cool. * 20 June: heavy rainfall (temporarily interrupted drought). Cyclonic easterly situation, heavy thunderstorms, torrential rain, hail, houses and bridges swept away, people drowned, crops damaged. Late June: renewed dry spell; July; very warm mostly dry; late month: very low water levels in springs and wells; 11–13 August: reports of severe water shortage; 30 August: heavy thunderstorms, rain. Very warm dry autumn – September, early part: wet, thunderstorms (15 September); c.26 September: cool northerly spell; October: one of the driest Octobers on record, 13 mm (0.5 in); 19–24 October: snow showers in east Scotland; 21 October: great concern over water shortage.

No drought equal to the present had been known since autumn 1740.

Gilbert White, Selborne (Hampshire)

1–2 November: westerly situation, heavy snowfall in east Scotland; 5 November: cyclonic situation broke drought from spring – 15 November: strong winds, heavy rain.

LATE 18TH-CENTURY RECESSION: 1782–1799

1782 Cold wet year; possibly severe enough for incipient glaciation in the Scottish Highlands; a disastrous year for harvests, especially in Scotland where it became known as 'Black Auchty Twa' (Black '82), weak zonal flow (76 westerly situations). Mild dry winter, normal midwinter westerlies – December (1781): blocked, southerly and cyclonic; January: generally mild, westerly situations; frost and snow in east Scotland; 15–20 January: mostly westerly situations, snow showers in east Scotland; 29 January: start of cold spell; February: first part: cold; 1–8 February: snowfall in east Scotland; 12 February: heavy snowfall; 14 February: lying snow, 20 cm (8 in) (fortnight total), snowstorms continued for another week in east Scotland; 21 February: snowfall followed by rapid thaw; 22 February: start of thaw, much rain, but still cold in east Scotland. Very cold wet spring – one of the wettest springs on record, 315 mm (12.4 in); March: both cold with northeasterly

winds and mild with southwesterly winds; 10 March: heavy snowfall in north
England; 11–25 March: heavy snowfall in east Scotland, deep drifts, roads blocked,
snow-covered houses and streets in Aberdeen; 11 March: strong winds, north England,
heavy rain carried off snow, Tyne raised higher than in living memory (apart from
1771 flood); 16 March: light snow showers; 26 March: southerly wind, thaw in east
Scotland; 21–22 March: continuous snow spread north over England; April: very
cold wet, one of the coldest Aprils on record, vegetation 6–8 weeks later than usual;
1 April: cyclonic situation, heavy rain, snow mostly gone but deep drifts over high
ground in east Scotland; 10–11 April: northerly cyclonic situations, heavy snowfall
in east Scotland; late April to 5 May, mostly easterly situations, snow showers in east
Scotland; May: very cold wet; heavy snowfall in Aberdeenshire. Cool wet summer,
widespread floods, disastrous harvests, especially in north Britain – 18 June: heavy
thunderstorms; July: cool wet; August: cool wet. * 16–17 August: severe storm.
Cyclonic northwesterly situation, inferred strong northwesterly winds, heavy rain
in northeast Scotland, floods on the Dee and Don, several bridges carried away,
crops damaged. * 29 August: probable heavy squall. Cyclonic situation, the *Royal
George*, 100-gun naval warship, heeled at Spithead probably due to a sudden heavy
squall, as the lower portholes were open the ship quickly filled with water and sank
in about 8 minutes, Admiral Kempenfelt and about 900 men, women and children
drowned. Very cool autumn, early intense frosts – 19–20 October: snowfall in east
Scotland; 29–31 October: snow showers in east Scotland; November: very cool, one
of the coldest Novembers on record, 2.3 °C (36 °F); 25 November: heavy snowfall in
east Scotland and many other inferred areas; 26 November: lying snow; late
November: corn still green and uncut in Scotland. **1783** Weak zonal flow (75½
westerly situations); volcanic dust veil (DVI 2900), Asama (Japan) and Eldeyjar, Laki
and Skaptar Jökull (Iceland) eruptions. Cold winter, strong midwinter westerlies –
28–29 December (1782): anticyclonic northwesterly situation, snowfall in east
Scotland; 2 January: anticyclonic situation, intense frost; 8–15 January: cyclonic
westerly situations, wet and windy; 16–17 January: north/northeasterly situations,
snowfall in east Scotland; 18–19 January: cyclonic northerly situation, heavy
snowfall, deep drifts, carriage travel suspended in east Scotland; 24–25 January:
cyclonic situation, thaw; 29–31 January: westerly situation, saturated ground;
2 February: lying snow in east Scotland; 7–10 February: cyclonic situation, heavy
rain, hail, thunder, floods; 23–25 February: cyclonic northerly situations, heavy
snowfall in east Scotland; 26–28 February: mild, snow-melt in east Scotland. Cold
dry spring – March: very cold; 1–3 March: snowfall in east Scotland; 4–5 March:
lying snow, 10–17.5 cm (4–7 in), Selborne (Hampshire); 5–9 March: cyclonic situation,
thaw, snow mostly gone, severe river floods, depression over the southern North
Sea on 6 March; 10 March to 27 May: mostly dry; 25 March: cyclonic situation,

heavy snow showers in east Scotland; 6–9 May: snow, hail showers in east Scotland; 23 May: northeasterly situation, snow showers in east Scotland. * 27–30 May: notable rainfall. Cyclonic northeasterly situations, four-day wet spell, 95.25 mm (3.75 in) recorded at Lyndon (Rutland), believed to have been the longest continuous wet spell since July 1736, but amounts varied elsewhere; for instance, much less was recorded at Selborne (Hampshire). Very warm summer – June to September: dense volcanic dust veil, reduced visibilities, dimmed sun and moon observed in mainland Europe (Fig. 77, 78 and 79); 23 June: start of a very warm dry spell, marred by a thick haze (fallout from the Skaptar Jökull volcanic eruption in Iceland) which persisted into late July; July: very warm, one of the warmest Julys on record, 18.8 °C (66 °F), local heavy thunderstorms, much damage by lightning (1–3 July) but some places continued to suffer from drought, notable red skies

FIG 77. Synoptic weather map, 30 June 1783, with plotted reports of fog or thick haze over England. (J. A. Kington)

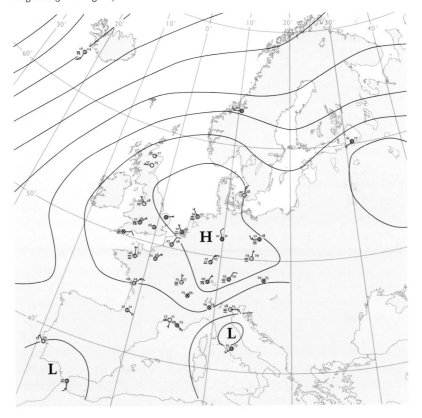

observed, volcanic dust-veil effect (11 July); 18 August: the Great Meteor, one of the largest meteors on record, was observed from Scotland to north France between about 21.00 and 22.00 h moving apparently slowly south or southeast. Mostly dry autumn, average temperatures – 26 September to 2 October: anticyclonic situation, fog in London; 8 October: northwesterly situation, lying snow in east Scotland; 12–15 November: northerly/cyclonic situations, stormy; snow showers in east Scotland; 25 November: anticyclonic situation, intense frost in east Scotland. **1784** Cold year; very weak zonal flow (60 westerly situations). Very cold dry winter, probably the most severe since 1740, very weak midwinter westerlies. * 23–26 December (1783): severe storms. On 23–24 December precipitation over the British Isles became wintry, deep depression over southwest England (25 December), associated frontal zone extended east over south England into northeast France, large area of snow and sleet in a cold

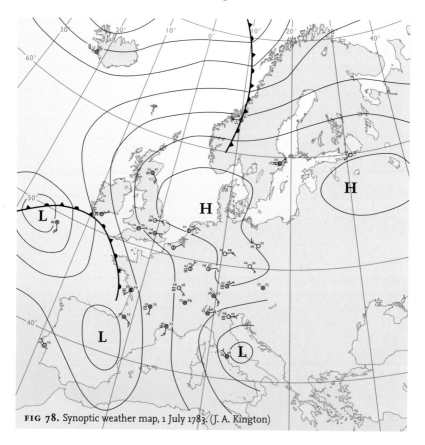

FIG 78. Synoptic weather map, 1 July 1783. (J. A. Kington)

east-southeasterly flow north of this system, while to the south there was rain and drizzle along the south coast in a mild southwesterly flow, by 26 December the low had moved over northeast France, and with the frontal zone lying along the south coast most of the country was now affected by a cold east-northeasterly flow giving occasional snow; at the same time, a further depression was located over central Scotland with storm-force easterly gales on its northern side; Scottish east coast badly affected, heavy snowfall, deep drifts, houses damaged, several shipwrecks. Late December (1783) to 20–21 February: mainly easterly winds, mostly very cold, frequent snow showers, deep lying snow, roads blocked, keen frost, – 3.1 °C (26.5 °F) recorded in east Scotland (31 December); 1 January: snowfall. * 2–3 January: severe storm. Depression moved northeast over western parts of the British Isles, mild Atlantic air began to spread into southwest England on 1 January and by the following day less cold conditions with continuous rain had extended

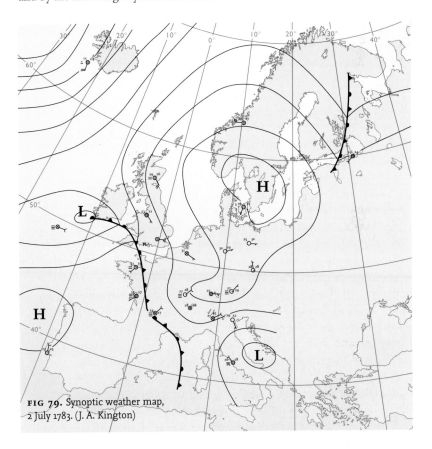

FIG 79. Synoptic weather map, 2 July 1783. (J. A. Kington)

over most of the country; this, together with a rapid thaw of lying snow, caused widespread flooding in south England; meanwhile, in the very cold air still over north Britain, severe to storm-force southeasterly gales accompanied by snowstorm-blizzard conditions occurred in east Scotland, lightning also reported, snow accumulated to depths not previously experienced, deep drifts, 5–6 m (16–20 ft), roads blocked, many people trapped in their homes for two days, houses unroofed in exposed country districts. 4 January: rain, light snowfall (8 January), showers, strong southwesterly gales (14 January), 19–20 January: northerly, heavy snowfall; 25–29 January: mainly northeasterly, heavy snowfall, drifts, roads blocked, severe frost, –14.5 °C (6 °F) at Totnes (Devon) on 24 January; early February: deep lying snow, houses completely buried, isolated people probably starved to death; 5 February: rain, rapid thaw, snow almost gone; 5–11 February: northerly, heavy snowfall in east Scotland, roads blocked, because of adverse winds few ships arrived at Aberdeen from the south, resulting coal shortage caused great distress; 6 February: Thames almost frozen over; 11–20 February: deep lying snow, 30 ships from America and mainland Europe forced to anchor off Gravesend, not being able to get any further upstream due to the great quantity of ice on the Thames (17 February), traffic crossed river on the ice; 21–22 February: mild, fog, snow-melt, floods; while most parts of Europe were affected by severe frost during January and February, it was stormy with floods in southern parts; when the frost finally broke low-lying regions adjacent to large rivers suffered greatly due to floods and ice. Very cold late spring – March: very cold; 1 March: snow showers, lying snow in east Scotland; 9–14 March: heavy snowfall, 30 cm (12 in) in east Scotland; 21 March: deep lying snow; 28 and 31 March: snowfall in east Scotland; 1 April, snowfall in east Scotland; 2–4 April: lying snow, local drifts, deep cover over high ground; 6–7 April: rain, snow-melt; 9–13 April: snowfall in east Scotland; 12–14 April: rain, hail, heavy snowfall, lying snow; 22–28 April: heavy snowfall in east Scotland; May: warmer conditions, welcome rain for crops. Very cool wet summer – inferred volcanic dust-veil effect; June: food shortages in Shetland, people starved. * 5 June: heavy hailstorms. Easterly situation, heavy hailstorms developed in a thundery trough over southwest England, damaged crops, windows broken, notable falls of hail, locally 60 cm (2 ft) deep; a most destructive and extensive hailstorm, 11 km (7 miles) long and 3.2 km (2 miles) wide, occurred in Somerset, with its storm centre 11 km (7 miles) west of Taunton it moved slowly northeast, severe flash floods.

It began with vast drops of rain, which were soon succeeded by round hail, and then by convex pieces of ice, which measured three inches [7.5 cm] in girth.

Gilbert White, Selborne (Hampshire)

July: two ships arrived in Shetland from London with free provisions for starving people. * 7 July: heavy thunderstorms. Shallow thundery lows over France, widespread heavy thunderstorms developed widely over England from Yorkshire to Devon, great damage, severe floods. 22 July: northwesterly gales, trees damaged; August: start of drought. * August 1784 to July 1785: drought. The driest period of any consecutive twelve months on record until the 1975–1976 drought. Cool dry autumn – early October: warm dry spell in Shetland; 23–25 October: cyclonic northwesterly/northerly, heavy snowfall; 18–22 November: snow showers in east Scotland. **1785** Cold year; extremely weak zonal flow (45 westerly situations, lowest on record); volcanic dust veil (DVI 2500), Vesuvius eruption. Very cold dry winter, very weak midwinter westerlies – early December (1784): start of cold frosty spell, occasional snow to early January; 2–6 December: heavy snowfall, 20 cm (8 in) in east Scotland. * 6–8 December (1784): severe storm. On 6 December an intense and deepening depression (969 mb) moved slowly northeast over England; heavy rain, inferred severe cyclonic gales, east coasts of north England and Scotland worst affected areas with storm-force onshore gales, over 100 shipwrecks; as the low moved away eastwards over the southern North Sea (7–8 December) a strong Arctic air flow spread south over the entire country, heavy snowfall, deep drifts, roads blocked, stage-coach travel badly affected. 9–10 December (1784): depression weakened and moved further away from the British Isles, winds decreased, skies cleared, sharp falls of temperature, very severe frosts on 10 December: –8.5 °C (16.7 °F) at Lyndon (Rutland), –18.3 °C (–1 °F) in frost hollow, Selborne (Hampshire); 21–23 December: snowfall in east Scotland; 31 December to 1 January: deep lying snow, travel halted, many areas; 8 January: heavy snowfall in east Scotland; heavy snowfall, hard frost, –6.7 °C (20 °F) on 10 January; 29–30 January: snowfall in east Scotland; late January: brief mild spell; 31 January to mid March: renewed cold spell, Thames frozen, bore traffic; 1 February: heavy snowfall in east Scotland; 3–4 February: snowfall in east Scotland; 17–23 February: heavy snowfall in east Scotland, greatest depth of the winter, roads blocked; 19–23 February: lying snow; 27–28 February: snow showers in east Scotland. Very cold dry spring – March: very cold, one of the coldest Marches on record, 1.2 °C (34 °F), northerly over British Isles (Fig. 80, 81 and 82). 8–9 March: anticyclonic easterly/easterly; heavy snowfall, east Scotland, deep drifts, several people killed. 21–22 March: snow showers, east Scotland. 27 March to 1 April: northeasterly/northerly; heavy snowfall in east Scotland; April: cold, blocking high off southwest Ireland, cold mostly northwesterly situations; 8–13 May: dry spell in south England. Wet summer, average temperatures – mid June to August: increasingly wet with rain or showers. Cool autumn. * 6 September: severe storm. Depression (below 984 mb), north England, inferred severe

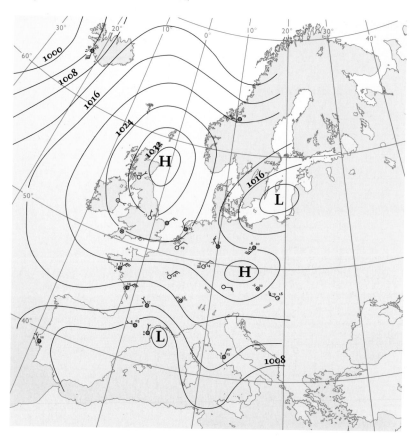

FIG 80. Synoptic weather map, 1 March 1785. Anticyclonic situation, first of three charts illustrating one of the coldest Marches in the Central England Temperature series. (J. A. Kington)

southwesterly gales, crops and trees damaged, widespread damage, including London, Portsmouth, Kent and Devon. 22 September: snow over high ground in east Scotland; 25 September: cyclonic; heavy rain; 25–30 October: mainly northwesterly; snowfall, snow showers, many areas, including east Scotland. * 31 October: severe storm. Cyclonic situation, depression (below 996 mb) over Scotland, heavy snowfall in east Scotland, deep drifts. 1 November: cyclonic situation, depression over north Ireland, tornado damage; early November: snowstorm, Shetland; late November: occasional snow, hail showers in east Scotland; 30 November: northerly situation, heavy snowfall in east Scotland. **1786** Cold year, weak zonal flow (77 westerly situations); volcanic dust veil

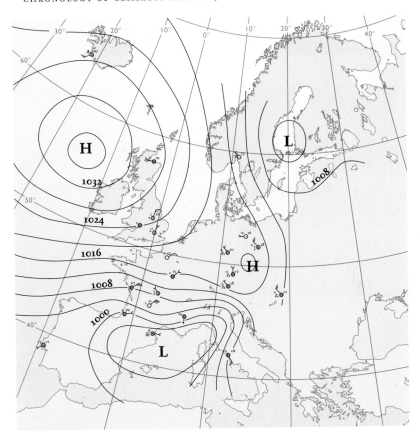

FIG 81. Synoptic weather map, 13 March 1785. Northeasterly situation, second of three charts illustrating one of the coldest Marches in the Central England Temperature series. (J. A. Kington)

(DVI 500), Pavlov (Alaska) eruption. Cold winter, normal midwinter westerlies – December (1785): changeable, much snow towards end in east Scotland; late December to early January: cold spell, occasional snow; 31 December: lying snow; 1–2 January: north/northeasterly situations, heavy snowfall, 90 cm (36 in), hard frost, –11 °C (12 °F), Dublin, upper Thames frozen in places; 4–16 January: cyclonic spell. * 4 January: severe storm. Cyclonic situation, southerly winds, severe snowstorms, deep drifts, lying snow, 15 cm (6 in), much damage both on land and at sea, roads blocked, houses damaged by blown snow (ceilings flooded), people froze to death. * 6 January: severe storm. Cyclonic situation, easterly gales in east Scotland, continuous rain, snow, many shipwrecks off east coast. 7–11 January:

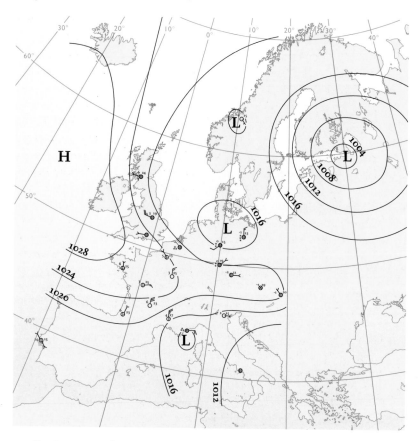

FIG 82. Synoptic weather map, 24 March 1785. Northerly situation, third of three charts illustrating one of the coldest Marches in the Central England Temperature series. (J. A. Kington)

cyclonic situation, thaw, severe river floods; 12–16 January: cyclonic situation, heavy snowfall, deep lying snow, 3 m (10 ft) drifts; 19–21 January: southwesterly situation, thaw; 21–31 January: mild, some days as warm as summer in east Scotland; February: changeable, alternate rain and snow in east Scotland; 7–8 February: west/northwesterly situations, heavy snowfall, 7.5 cm (3 in), Cambuslang (Lanarkshire); thunderstorm, rain, hail; 9–11 February: west to northwesterly situations, snow showers in east Scotland; 21–24 February: southeasterly situation, very cold; 25–28 February: easterly situation, moderate to heavy snowfall, 15 cm (6 in); late February to early March: very cold spell, longest frost of winter, strong easterly winds. Very cold dry late spring – March: very cold; 1–7 March: easterly situation, heavy snowfall, deep drifts, several people frozen to death (6–7 March); 10–12 March: westerly situation, rapid thaw; 15–25 March: cyclonic situation, snow showers in east Scotland (15–17 March); April: occasional snow showers in east Scotland; 2–6 May: cyclonic situation, occasional heavy showers, hail; 25–31 May: anticyclonic situation, onset of warmer conditions. Dry summer, average temperatures – June: mostly warm dry; 13 June: thunderstorm in south England; late June: cyclonic westerly situation, wet spell, first rain since 13 May in east Scotland, parched ground watered in Shetland; early July: wet spell continued; late July: warm dry; August: start of partly wet spell into autumn – strong winds, crops damaged, east Scotland (30–31 August). Very cool wet autumn – one of the coldest autumns on record, 7.5 °C (45.5 °F). * 14–15 September: severe storm. Cyclonic west/northwesterly situations, depression moved slowly east over north Scotland, severe westerly gales, probably hurricane-force gusts, especially over central and south England, and southern North Sea, much damage both on land and at sea, houses blown down, stage coaches overturned, trees uprooted, shipping damaged on Dutch coast, great loss of life. * 24–30 September: severe storms. Inferred cyclonic situations, severe westerly gales, Irish Sea coasts, Holyhead–Dublin packet-boat service suspended. 7 October: heavy rain. * 8 October: severe storm. Inferred cyclonic situation/severe gales, severe floods, high tides, extensive damage. October–November: northeasterly winds brought an early start to the cold season, Baltic almost ice-bound earlier than usual but concern about a forthcoming severe winter later proved unfounded. **1787** Mild to average winter temperatures, normal midwinter westerlies – December (1786): unsettled, more rain than snow in east Scotland. * 14 December (1786): severe storm. 15–23 December: occasional snow showers in east Scotland; January: mostly mild in east Scotland; 27–28 January: snow showers in east Scotland. Mild early spring – 2–3 March: storms from both west and east in east Scotland; 4 March: snow showers in east Scotland; April: turned colder, northeasterly winds in first three weeks halted growth; 13 April: snow showers in east Scotland; 20–21 April: rain, snow showers in east Scotland; 28–29 April: storm, snow showers in eastern Scotland; 1 May: lying snow, deep over high ground; 2 May: stormy, prolonged cold conditions had delayed grass growth in east Scotland (Fig. 83). Very cool summer – 5 June: stormy, rain, snow in east Scotland; 6–7 June: keen frost, trees blighted; 6 July: start of showery spell, heavy rain in northeast England; 24 July: river floods in Newcastle; 9 August: heavy thunderstorms. Cool autumn – 17 September, very low pressure; 21 September: storm in east Scotland. * 10–11 October: severe storms. Inferred cyclonic situation, gales, heavy rain, crops flattened in northeast England and east Scotland, severe flood on Wear.

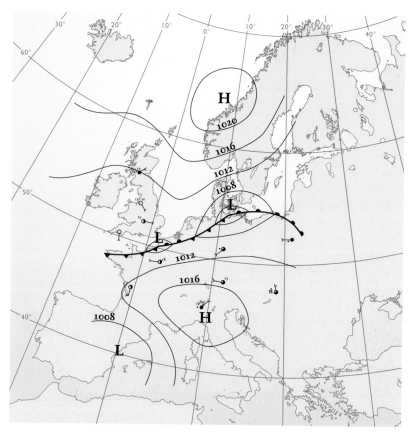

FIG 83. Synoptic weather map, 13 May 1787. Cyclonic easterly situation. (J. A. Kington)

Early November: mostly wet in east Scotland; 14–23 November: snowfall, snow showers in east Scotland. **1788** One of the driest years on record. Average winter temperatures, fairly weak midwinter westerlies. * 9 December (1787): severe storm. Inferred cyclonic situation, heavy rain, snow, thunderstorms, severe river floods, many items, including houses and cattle, swept away, several people drowned. 22–26 December: heavy snowfall, 30 cm (12 in), deep drifts; 30 December: deep lying snow; 31 December: thaw; 3 January: very mild, floods; late January: snowfall, heavy at times in east Scotland; 9 February: very wet ground badly affected farm work in east Scotland; late February: renewed occasional snowfall in east Scotland. Very mild dry spring – March: cold at first, easterly winds; 2 March: inferred northeasterly wind, smell of London smoke at Selborne (Hampshire);

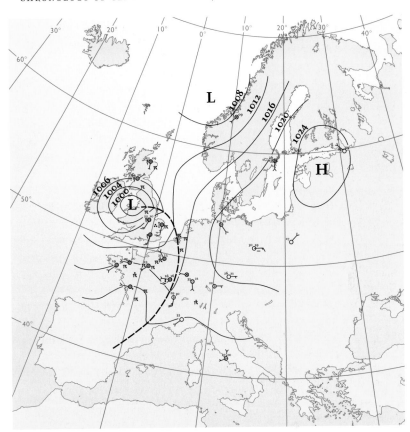

FIG 84. Synoptic weather map, 13 July 1788. Cyclonic situation, disastrous crop damage in France due to heavy thunderstorms and hailstorms associated with a cold front from the southern North Sea to the Pyrenees. (J. A. Kington)

4–6, 9 March: snowfall, 45 cm (18 in), deep drifts, roads blocked in east Scotland; 16 March: snowfall in east Scotland; 22–31 March: wet spell in east Scotland; 1 April: lying snow still over high ground in east Scotland; 3–5 April: snowfall in east Scotland; 15 April: hail, snow showers in east Scotland; May: mostly dry; 11 May: wintry showers in east Scotland; 18 May: heavy thunderstorm, houses damaged in London; 29 May: heavy thunderstorm, followed by 24-hour spell of continuous rain. Warm summer – June: mostly dry, frequent north to northeasterly winds.

The meadows have been parched to a January brown, and we have foddered our cattle for some time, as in winter.

Mrs Henry Head,
quoting William Cowper, 24 June 1788

* 28 June: severe flood, 'The Midsummer Flood'. Torrential, probably thundery, rain, lasting some hours in Suffolk, caused a notable inundation, locally known as 'The Midsummer Flood'. 13 July: heavy thunderstorms with hail (Fig. 84). August: dry. Mainly warm dry autumn – 4 September: heavy showers; 14 September: storm, inferred severe gales, trees damaged; 13–15 November: snow showers in east Scotland; 27 November: light snowfall, start of cold spell to mid January (1789). **1789** Very cold winter, third severe winter in the decade, fairly weak midwinter westerlies – late November (1788): start of a very cold spell (apart from a partial thaw from 24–25 December to mid January), winds mainly between north and east, heavy snowfall, large drifts, frozen rivers, including the Thames below London Bridge, Frost Fair on the river after a lapse of nearly half a century; December (1788): northerly, very dry, one of the driest Decembers on record, 13 mm (0.5 in); 10 December: concern over lack of rain; 11–18 December: snowfall in east Scotland; 14 December: navigation on the Thames interrupted due to low water level; 22 December: sea frozen off Brighton; 24–25 December: brief thaw; 26–27 December: renewed cold, heavy snowfall; January: several freeze–thaws; 2–9 January: mild, frequent rain, 13 January: renewed cold, heavy snowfall, deep drifts; 15 January: thaw, rapid snow-melt; 19 January: renewed cold, heavy snowfall; 21–22 January: thaw, snow-melt; 23 January: further snow; 24–31 January: mild, rain; 1–10 February: mild, snow gone on hills in east Scotland; 11–16 February: occasional snow showers; 17 February to 3 March: mild, occasional rain in east Scotland. The severe conditions during this winter caused much hardship, distress and unemployment; in London, the City authorities granted £1,500 to a fund for the relief of distress and suffering among the poor and unemployed, the Prince of Wales subscribed £1,000; however, in spite of such assistance many London families experienced great hardship and a large number of people perished from the cold and hunger. The 1789 winter was also severe in mainland Europe; frozen rivers and water bodies, including the Rhine, Danube, Po and Swiss lakes; Baltic Sea completely ice-bound in one of the most severe winter freezing events on record. Very cold late spring – March: very cold, northerly winds, frequent snow showers. * 9–16 March: notable snowfall. Heavy snowfall, 12.5 cm (5 in); heavier falls in east Scotland, 30 cm (12 in), 4.6 m (15 ft) drifts, roads blocked. 17–19 March: snow showers in east Scotland; 20–21 March: thaw; 22–31 March: renewed snowfall in east Scotland but unevenly distributed, for example,

although area 20 km (12 miles) around Aberdeen was badly affected, the snow was less deep beyond that limit and none at all in many places; similar effects in England, where some areas were buried in snow while other places had none; 1 April: mild wet; 1–4 April: renewed snowfall in east Scotland. Cool wet summer – June: cool; 30 June: constant easterly winds, no growth in garden during past ten days, tree foliage greatly damaged in east Scotland; 16–27 July: heavy rain, thunderstorms, waterspouts, whirlwinds, river floods, much damage, bridges swept away; 31 July: strong winds, heavy rain; 1 August: strong winds, crops damaged; 28 August to 3 September: further river floods, crops damaged in east Scotland. Very cool wet autumn – 19–20 September: Don overflowed, crops swept away; 1–15 October: wet easterly spell, crops damaged (east Scotland); 29–31 October: very cold, wintry showers (east Scotland). * 30–31 October: severe storm. Inferred cyclonic situation/severe gales, many shipwrecks, also shipping in the Thames and off east coast greatly damaged, great loss of life. 5–6 November: heavy rain, river floods, crops swept away (east Scotland); 6 November: snowfall over high ground; 6–7 November: storm, rain (east Scotland); 9–25 November: wet spell, north England and south Scotland, crops damaged.

1790s

Very weak zonal flow (estimated 55 westerly situations on average per year). **1790** Very mild winter, normal midwinter westerlies – 3 December (1789): thick fog (south England); 11–25 December: stormy, wet, occasional snowfall (east Scotland); 31 December: storm, floods on the Thames; January: fog on 22 days (London); 13 January: heavy rain; 5–23 February: mild spell, rapid vegetative growth (east Scotland). Dry early spring, average temperatures – 8–15 April: snow showers (east Scotland); 11 April: deep snow, 12.5 cm (5 in); 27 May: heavy thunderstorm, damage (London). Cool changeable summer, alternating warm dry and cool wet spells – 13 June: frost-damaged trees (east Scotland); 22 June: very warm, 31.7 °C (89 °F), heavy thunderstorms, people killed by lightning; 2 July: heavy thunderstorms; 10 July: ground frost; 14 July: heavy thunderstorms; 24 July: wheat crop badly affected by cool wet conditions; 28 July: heavy thunderstorm, hail 1 m (3 ft) deep, garden plants damaged (east Scotland); 30 July: heavy thunderstorm, extensive hail-covered ground as white as in a winter snowstorm (east Scotland); 23–24 August: storm (east Scotland). Average autumn temperatures. * 6 November: severe storm. Inferred cyclonic situation/severe gales, vessels overturned at Portsmouth, people drowned, heavy rain, river floods, crops beaten down, many items carried out to sea, including one man and 40 sheep (east Scotland). 20–21 November: heavy thunderstorms, property damaged by lightning, parish church, Calstock (Cornwall), destroyed. **1791** Mild wet winter, strong midwinter westerlies

– early December (1790): occasional heavy snowfall and snow showers in east Scotland. * 23 December (1790): severe storm. Inferred cyclonic situation/storm-force winds, heavy thunderstorms, much damage both on land and at sea, houses damaged, trees blown down, many shipwrecks, great loss of life. January: very stormy in Shetland, many ships believed wrecked; 4–18 January: stormy, wet, great losses at sea off east Scotland; 19–20 January: cyclonic situation, exceptionally low pressure (941 mb), windy and wet; 19–27 January: snowfall over high ground in east Scotland; 28 January to 1 February: strong winds, rain in east Scotland; February: stormy with storm surges and sea floods; 2 February: exceptional high tide (storm surge?) in London, much damage; 2–3 February: heavy snowfall in east Scotland; 5 February: snow gone in east Scotland; 10–22 February: wet and windy in east Scotland. * 26–28 February: notable snowfall. Northeasterly/northerly situations, heavy snowfall, roads partly blocked. Very mild dry early spring – March: stormy conditions, inferred strong northwesterly to northerly winds, North Sea. * 1–2 March: severe storm. Depression over the central North Sea, severe northwest to northerly gales, wintry showers over east Britain, probable storm surge, exceptionally high spring tides along English east coast, sea walls breached, many low-lying areas flooded, including London, Whitehall inundated. 5–18 March: lying snow still under hedges in places. * 21–22 March: severe storm. Depression over the east North Sea, severe north to northwesterly gales pounded British east coasts as far south as Norfolk. April: southwesterly; 3–8 May: snow showers in east Scotland. Variable summer, average temperatures – 1–6 June: summer-like warmth in east Scotland; 5 June: heavy thunderstorms, plants and crops damaged; 9 June: cold as winter, night frost in east Scotland; 12–15 June: notable sharp fall of temperature, wintry showers, night frosts and vegetation damaged.

> We are in close mourning for it [summer] in coals and ashes. It froze hard last night: I went out for a moment to look at my haymakers, and was starved. The contents of an English June are, hay and ice, orange-flowers and rheumatism! I am now cowering over the fire.
>
> Horace Walpole, 14 June 1791

Late June: very warm dry; July: wet; 14–15 August: heavy thunderstorms, hail damage. Average autumn temperatures – October: storm surges in the North Sea; 22 October: snow showers in east Scotland, heavy rain elsewhere, river floods, much damage; November: occasional snow showers and heavy snowfall over high ground from the Sussex Downs to east Scotland. **1792** Wet year. Very cold winter, very weak midwinter westerlies – 3–19 December (1791): snow showers, lying snow, travel badly affected in east Scotland; 1–3 January: thaw in east Scotland; 8–14 January: renewed snowfall in east Scotland; 16–22 January: snow showers; 23–24 January: thaw, river floods. * Winter: severe sea floods. Severe sea floods breached sand-dune barrier along the Norfolk coast, gaps occurred at Winterton, Horsey and Waxham, huge amount of sea water poured through nine breaches between Horsey and Waxham, widespread flooding extended beyond Hickling (5 km/3 miles inland), on uniting with fresh water contained in Hickling Broad, sea water destroyed fish and neighbouring farmland badly salt-contaminated. 27 January: inferred easterly gales, shipping affected sailing up Bristol Channel; 28 January: snowfall in east Scotland; 18–20 February: snowfall, snow showers; 25–26 February: rain. Mild very wet early spring – 6–9 March: snowfall, snow showers; 13–15 March: snowfall, snow showers in east Scotland; 1 April: storm, rain. * 5 April: severe storm. Inferred cyclonic situation/gales, heavy rain. * 13 April: heavy thunderstorms. Many areas affected, flash floods, Bromsgrove (Worcestershire) completely inundated, lightning strikes, much damage, many people injured and some killed. 21 April: snowfall in east Scotland; 1–4 May: snowfall in east Scotland; 9–10 May: snow showers in east Scotland. Wet summer, average temperatures – 24 June: thunderstorm, hail; 16 July: heavy thunderstorm, rain, severe floods in northeast England, Rede (Northumberland) rose nearly 4 m (13 ft), 0.3 m (1 ft) higher than 1771 flood, hundreds of acres of farmland inundated, also severe floods on Tyne, many streets inundated in Newcastle; 1 August: floods, crops destroyed; 28 August: heavy rain in northeast England, severe floods on Tyne, Tear, Derwent and Wear, low-lying ground inundated; frost in east Scotland, tree foliage turned brown and fell. Cool autumn – 15 September: snowfall in east Scotland; 20 November: heavy snow showers in east Scotland.

1793 Wet winter, average temperatures, normal midwinter westerlies – December (1792): exceptionally stormy, notable series of storms in the North Sea, inferred northwesterly to northerly severe gales, storm surges, floods. * 5 December (1792): severe storm. First in a series of notable storms during December 1792, a small but deep depression moved rapidly east across south England, cyclonic westerly gales. * 7–9 December (1792): severe storm. Depressions moved rapidly east across the British Isles into the North Sea, strong cyclonic winds, storm-force in places, much damage in south England and heavy snow in east Scotland. * 10–12 December (1792): severe storm. The most severe North Sea storm of the month, severe northwest to northerly gales, snow showers in east Scotland. 13 December: snowfall in east Scotland; 16 December: mild, renewed plant growth; * 19–23 December (1792): severe storm. A cold northerly airstream in a cyclonic circulation over the North Sea moved south over Britain; thunderstorm with violent gust, possible line squall, on 20 December, snowfall extended as far

south as Norfolk, strong northerly winds affected Scotland on 23 December.
January: cold with occasional rain, late January: snowfall in east Scotland;
February: stormy, occasional cold spells in east Scotland; 27 February: North Sea
storm surge. Very cold backward spring – 2–14 March: snowfall in east Scotland.
* 3 March: severe storm. Inferred cyclonic situation/severe gales, much damage.
26–30 March: wintry, snowfall in east Scotland; 1 April: heavy snowfall, people lost
in snow; 13–20 April: wintry showers; 29–31 May: heavy snowfall in east Scotland.
Dry summer, average temperatures – 3–11 June: dry hard ground; August: wet;
early part: warm with thunder, cool later in east Scotland. Dry autumn, average
temperatures – October: North Sea storm surge; 9 November: storm, heavy rain,
ship stranded off east Scotland, three men drowned; 16 November: storm,
shipwreck off east Scotland. **1794–1796** Volcanic dust veil (DVI 1000), Mexico,
Vesuvius, Aleutian and Kamchatka eruptions. **1794** Mild winter, fairly strong
midwinter westerlies – December (1793): wet; January: floods; 1 January: frost,
snow on hills in east Scotland; 9–19 January: mostly frost-free with early
vegetative growth in east Scotland. * 24–27 January: severe storm. Inferred
cyclonic situation, snowstorm-blizzard conditions, first snowfall of winter in
north Wales and Scotland, deep drifts, roads blocked and several shipwrecks off
Scottish east coast. 30 January: snowfall in east Scotland; 31 January: thaw, snow
nearly gone in east Scotland; February: southwesterly; 10–11 February: wet and
windy, some snowfall in east Scotland. Very mild early spring – 4–12 April: wet
and stormy in east Scotland; 3 May: dry, rain much needed in east Scotland;
8–10 May: thunderstorms, snow and hail in east Scotland. Very warm dry
summer – July: crops badly affected by lack of rain in north Wales and east
Scotland. Cool wet stormy autumn – 23 September: stormy and wet in east
Scotland; 26 September: snow-covered hills in east Scotland; October to
November: wet, storms, floods. * 6 October: severe storm. Inferred cyclonic
situation, coastal storm-force gales, hundreds of shipwrecks (Atlantic storm
surge in the Irish Sea sometime during October). * 4–7 November: severe storm.
Inferred cyclonic situation; heavy rain, strong easterly winds in east Scotland,
flood in Norwich on 6 November, low-lying parts of city badly affected, water
60–90 cm (2–3 ft) deep in many houses, people rescued by rowing boats,
subscription raised to relieve suffering of the inhabitants affected. * Mid
November: severe storm. Inferred cyclonic situation, strong easterly winds, rain,
hail showers, three shipwrecks off east Scotland. **1795** Dry year; volcanic dust veil
(DVI 1000), Aleutian eruptions. * Very cold winter. Inferred blocking-high
situations, absence of midwinter westerlies; 24 December (1794) to 8 February:
very cold spell; 25 December: lying snow in east Scotland; 30–31 December:
snowfall in east Scotland; January: one of the coldest Januarys on record: 3.1 °C

(26.4 °F); 14–22 January: snow showers, deep snow in east Scotland; 16–17 January: heavy snowfall in north Wales; 23 January: sea believed frozen 90 m (100 yd) from beach at Eccles (Norfolk); 25 January: coldest night of month, –20 °C (–4 °F) in London; 26–28 January: heavy snowfall; frozen rivers and water bodies, including the Thames, Dee, Trent and Zuider Zee; 1–6 February: heavy snowfall, travel halted in east Scotland; 8 February: partial thaw, severe floods, bridges damaged; 10–14 February: renewed cold, heavy snowfall, colliers frozen in port in east Scotland. * Mid February: thaw, severe floods. On 11 February, ice on the Tees at Stockton (Durham), frozen for five weeks, broke up, the river rose higher than ever before remembered, 20 cm (8 in) more than the 1771 river flood; severe floods following the thaw also occurred in Norwich, where the inhabitants of the low-lying parts of the city again suffered great distress in the second major inundation to affect Norwich within three months; Thames also in flood. 21 February: southerly wind, colliers finally arrived in east Scotland with much-needed coal; late February: still cold in places with occasional snowfall in east Britain. Cold dry late spring – early March: occasional snowfall continued in east Scotland; 17 March: inferred thaw, floods in Norfolk; 26 March: hills still snow-covered in east Scotland; 8–9 April: heavy rain, heavy snow-melt in Scottish hills, Don rose 2 m (7 ft), river floods in east Scotland; 25–30 April: cyclonic westerly situations; May: particularly stormy in the North Sea area, inferred strong northwest to northerly gales. * 6–12 May: severe storms. Initially mainly anticyclonic northerly situations, depressions moved southeast over the North Sea, storms affected east British coasts. 8–16 May: mainly northerly situations, wintry showers, heavy snowfall, 30 cm (12 in) in east Scotland. 25–28 May: anticyclonic northeasterly situations; wintry showers in east Scotland. Cool summer – June: exceptional frosts; 19 June: out-of-season snowfall in London; July: cool; 31 July: heavy rain, crops damaged, many mills in north Wales stopped working due to grain scarcity. Very warm autumn – September: very warm dry. * 17–18 November: severe storm, the 'Christian Storm'. Inferred cyclonic situation, storm named after Rear Admiral Sir Hugh Christian, Commander of the British fleet comprising 200 transports that had set sail from Portsmouth for the West Indies; however, due to increasing southwesterly gales, the fleet was forced back to port, but not before seven vessels had been wrecked off Chesil Beach, over 200 men and women drowned. **1796** Dry year. Very mild wet winter, fairly strong midwinter westerlies – January: very mild, one of the warmest Januarys on record; 15 January: stormy, strong northwesterly winds in north Wales; 24–25 January: stormy, strong west to southwesterly winds in north Wales; 29 January: Atlantic storm surge affected Bristol Channel; February: floods. Dry early spring, average temperatures. Cool dry summer – 18 August: heavy rain, swollen rivers in north England. Cool dry autumn. **1797** Very cold dry winter, normal midwinter westerlies – December (1796): North Sea storm surge; 24–25 December: very severe frost, –21 °C (–6 °F) in London; Thames frozen; 11 January: easterly wind, snowfall in north Wales; 31 January: stormy, strong westerly winds in north Wales; 16–28 February: daily fog in London. Cold wet spring. Warm wet summer. Very cool wet autumn – September–October: floods. **1798** Wet winter, average temperatures, normal midwinter westerlies. 11 January: snowfall in north Wales; 29 January: strong southwesterly winds in north Wales; 31 January: snow showers in north Wales. Very mild dry early spring. Very warm summer. Cool wet autumn – September: wet; North Sea storm surge; October: storm surge in the Channel. **1799** Cool year; a year without a summer – conditions possibly severe enough for incipient glaciation in the Scottish Highlands; volcanic dust veil (DVI 600), Fuego (Guatemala) eruption. Very cold winter, average rainfall, fairly weak midwinter westerlies – late December (1798) to early January: severe frost; January: very cold, –6.7 °C (20 °F) in north Wales; 30 January: heavy snowfall in north Wales; February: heavy snowfall spread from the east, snowstorm-blizzard conditions, deep snow cover; North Sea storm surge coincided with river floods due to snow-melt. Very cold dry late spring. Very cool wet summer – inferred volcanic dust-veil effect; 22 June: start of wet spell to 17 November (only eight days without rain); bad harvest in north Wales. Very cool wet autumn – October: floods; November: early part: continuous rain; 17 November: end of wet spell from 22 June.

LITTLE ICE AGE, PHASE III: 1800–1899

1800s

Continental; very weak zonal flow (estimated 47 westerly situations on average per year). **1800** Very cold dry winter, absent midwinter westerlies partly replaced by an easterly flow – Thames frozen; December (1799): one of the driest Decembers on record with 1780 and 1788, 13 mm (0.5 in); 31 December: very severe frost, –19 °C (–3 °F) in Norfolk;. January: early part: stormy, snowfall in Shetland, many shipwrecks, heavy loss of life; 9–21 January: easterly to northeasterly situations, frequent snowfall in north Wales; 22–23 January: rapid thaw, severe floods. Mild wet spring – April: cyclonic southwesterly. Very warm dry summer – one of the driest summers on record, 74 mm (2.9 in). * 23 June to 19 August: drought. Inferred blocking-high situations; because of the very warm dry conditions trees lost their leaves in London during August, no rain had fallen in the city for over eight weeks from 23 June until 19 August when an early morning thunderstorm ended the drought; the severity of the drought was commented upon by several contemporary observers.

Such a long course of dry weather as we have had this summer is hardly
remembered by any person living; from the 20th May to the 20th August, a period of
three months, no rain fell which had any effect on the ground. Just about the end of
this month [August] the pasture is beginning to recover its verdure.

Anon, Edinburgh

About the middle of August, reports were received of uncommon insects on the
corn; owing to the immense numbers of these insects, the ears of corn appeared
black in many fields. It was said that similar insects affected the corn in 1781,
which also was a warm dry summer. The newspapers abounded with reports of
conflagrations of forest in different and distant places, which though not
occasioned, were certainly much prompted by the extraordinary dryness of the
season. The French newspapers say that the Black Forest has been burning for
several weeks, and that the loss sustained is immense. The conflagration of
Radnor Forest in Wales, having raged for five weeks and destroyed about four
miles in extent, was extinguished by late rains.

James Meek, Cambuslang (Lanarkshire)

On 19–20 August, first-hand evidence of the conflagrations that occurred during
the summer drought was provided by the weather diarist John Andrews of
Modbury (Devon), who recorded that many acres of nearby moorland which had
been on fire for some time now seemed to be extinguished by the rain that had
fallen overnight; the drought was generally followed by more or less continuous
rain that damaged crops. Wet autumn, average temperatures. * 8 November:
severe storm. Inferred cyclonic situation/severe gales, hail and snow, much
damage, especially in London. **1801** Mild winter, fairly strong midwinter
westerlies – 4 January: strong westerly winds in north Wales; 24 January: strong
northerly winds in north Wales; 25 January: southeasterly, snowfall in north
Wales; 26 January: thaw. Very mild early spring. Very warm dry summer. Wet
autumn, average temperatures – 19 October: North Sea storm surge; 2 and 21
November: severe gales, ships driven ashore at Scarborough (Yorkshire). **1802** Dry
year. Very cold winter, fairly weak midwinter westerlies – 2 January: snowfall in
north Wales; 5–6 January: heavy snowfall in north Wales; 16 January: southerly,
rapid thaw in north Wales. * 21 January: severe storm. Inferred cyclonic situation,
storm-force westerly gales, severe damage, trees uprooted in northwest England
and north Wales. Mild dry spring. Cool wet summer. Dry autumn, average
temperatures. * Autumn: severe storm. Inferred intense depression in North Sea,
severe sea floods struck the Norfolk coast, spring tide and inferred severe
northwesterly gales combined to produce a North Sea storm surge, a large

amount of sea water flowed through a partially repaired breach between Waxham and Horsey (Norfolk). **1803–1805** Volcanic dust veil (DVI 1100), Cotopaxi (Ecuador) and Vesuvius eruptions. **1803** Cold winter, absent midwinter westerlies replaced by an easterly flow – 12 January: storm, shipwrecks, many drowned; 17–20 January: easterly winds, snowfall in north Wales; 24–28 January: snowfall followed by thaw in north Wales. Mild dry early spring. Warm dry summer. Very cool dry autumn. **1804** Mild wet winter, fairly weak midwinter westerlies. * 25 December (1803): severe storm. Inferred cyclonic situation, severe to storm-force gales, great damage, loss of life in London and on the Sussex coast. 7–8 January: heavy snowfall, notable change of wind direction from west-northwest to east-southeast in north Wales; 8 January: stormy in Shetland; 9 January: rapid thaw in north Wales; 20 January: storm, strong northwesterly winds in north Wales. Wet early spring, average temperatures. Warm summer. Very warm autumn – 25 November: snowfall, travel halted in Shetland. **1805** Cold year. Cold dry winter, absent midwinter westerlies replaced by an easterly flow. * Winter: severe storm. Inferred cyclonic situation/storm-force gales, many shipwrecks, great loss of life, 200 drowned in one ship alone, 80 buried on Chesil Beach (Dorset). 2 December (1804): snowfall in Shetland; January: inferred frequent snowfall; 3–4 January: southerly winds, thaw, snow nearly gone in north Wales; 14 and 20 January: southerly, renewed snowfall in north Wales; 22–23 January: easterly, heavy snowfall in north Wales; 30–31 January: northeasterly, further snowfall in north Wales. Dry spring, average temperatures. Wet summer, average temperatures – repairs completed to breaches in sand dunes between Winterton and Happisburgh along Norfolk coast caused by recent sea floods; July: northwesterly. Cool dry autumn – 25–28 October: southeasterly situations. **1806** Wet winter, average temperatures, strong midwinter westerlies. * 10 January: severe storm. Inferred cyclonic situation, severe west to northwesterly gales, thunderstorms, several people killed by lightning, many shipwrecks, numerous vessels from Liverpool sunk off the north Welsh coast. 12 January: northwesterly, snowstorms in north Wales. * 15–17 January: severe storm. Inferred cyclonic situation, strong westerly winds, rain, sleet, snow, thunderstorms and flooding in north Wales, loss of life in Plymouth and London. 26–27 January: heavy snowfall, southeasterly winds in north Wales. Dry spring, average temperatures – March: cold; 27 May: storm, shipwreck, loss of life off Sunderland. Warm wet summer – July: very wet, 150 mm (6 in); heavy thunderstorms, people killed by lightning. Very warm autumn – 2 November: storm off Plymouth and Exmouth. **1807–** Volcanic dust veil (DVI 1500), Salvador, Gunung Merapi (Java), Sao Jorge **1810** (Azores) and Etna eruptions. **1807** Dry year. Mild winter, normal midwinter westerlies – 14 January: snowfall, south to southeasterly winds in north Wales; 21–22 January: snowfall in north Wales; 11 February: heavy snowfall, roads blocked. * 18 February: severe storm. Inferred cyclonic situation, inferred severe gales affected English south coast, 40 ships went missing from their anchorage off Deal (Kent). Cold late spring. Very warm dry summer – circulation dominated by an extension of the Azores high. Very cool autumn – September: one of the coldest Septembers on record, 10.5 °C (51 °F); 5 September: cold northeasterly wind, heavy rain, large swell in the Tyne at Newcastle, a small island, King's Meadows, entirely under water the following morning and in a broad but confined part of the North Tyne (near Haughton paper mill), the river rose at least 4.6 m (15 ft) above its usual level; 12 September: intense frost, many trees lost their leaves; 12 November: heavy snow, sleet in northeast England. * 16 November: severe storm. Inferred cyclonic situation/severe easterly gales, sea probably broke through over land, many ships forced ashore, several shipwrecks off Whitby (Yorkshire). 30 November: North Sea storm surge. **1808** Very cold dry winter, frequent snow, fairly strong midwinter westerlies – 17–21 December (1807): daily fog in London; January: occasional snowfall in north Wales. * 14 January: severe storm. Inferred cyclonic situation/storm-force northwesterly gales, much damage both on land and at sea, houses washed away, several shipwrecks, Margate pier (Kent) partly wrecked, Harwich port (Essex) damaged. February: very cold; 11–12 February: inferred northwesterly situation, heavy snowfall in east England, travel dislocated several days; 15 February: severe frost, –13 °C (9 °F) in Ipswich. Cold dry very late spring – March: cold; April: floods; 6 May: notable coloured twilight observed in London, inferred volcanic dust-veil effect. Very warm summer – 13 July: so-called 'Hot Wednesday', 33–37 °C (91–99 °F) in southeast and east England (non-standard readings); 15 July: heavy thunderstorms, damaging hail (St Swithin's day). Very cool autumn. **1809** Cold wet winter, absent midwinter westerlies replaced by an easterly flow – very cold winter in north Europe. December (1808): onset of cold period; 24 December to 2 January: daily fog in London; January: cold; fog on seven days in London; 1–6 January: east to southeasterly situation, heavy snowfall, deep drifts in north Wales; 6 January: rapid thaw in north Wales. * 19 January: severe ice storm. Inferred cyclonic situations, cold easterly airstream over the British Isles between a blocking high over Scandinavia and low pressure to the west; although the eastward movement of a mild Atlantic airstream was impeded at the surface, it overran the cold air and produced precipitation that fell as freezing rain and formed a thick deposit of glazed frost or clear ice ('black ice') on surface objects; the weight of the ice may have brought down trees and grounded disabled birds coated with ice; Thames in flood, bridges carried away at Eton, Deptford and Lewisham; snowfall in other areas of the country including north Wales. 24 January: snowfall in north Wales; 25–26 January:

inferred warm front, southeasterly winds veered west, rapid thaw in north Wales, temperature rose to 8 °C (46 °F) in Scotland after a snowstorm ended a cold spell with easterly winds from December (1808). * 28–29 January: severe storm. Inferred cyclonic situation, severe southerly gales, thaw caused severe flooding in many places; for example, in Norwich the lower parts of the city were inundated, houses 2 m (6–7 ft) under water, rescue rowing boats plied streets, nearby water meadows badly flooded, the Fens appeared like an open sea, damage estimated at a million pounds. February: thaw-melt floods. Dry spring, average temperatures – April: depression over mainland Europe, northeasterly flow over the North Sea; 1–2 April: notable red skies observed in London, inferred volcanic dust-veil effect; 26 April: Thames flood. Very cool wet summer – June: out-of-season snowfall in Scotland; 12 August: heavy rain, swollen rivers in north England. Cool dry autumn – September: floods; October: fog on 11 days in London.

1810s

Continental; weak zonal flow (estimated 64 westerly situations on average per year). **1810** Cold year. Cold dry winter, normal midwinter westerlies – January: fog on ten days in London; 17 January: snowfall in north Wales. Cold spring. Cool summer. Wet autumn, average temperatures – October: fog on five days in London; 30 October: snowfall. * 2 November: severe storm. Inferred cyclonic situation/storm-force gales affected English east coast, beaches strewn with wrecks and bodies from Wells to Great Yarmouth (Norfolk). * 10 November: severe storm. Inferred deep depression, severe east to southeasterly gales, severe sea floods, North Sea waters driven up against English east coast, river flow held up, wind-blown tide flowed inland at Boston (Lincolnshire), sea banks breached, many houses flooded, Fens inundated, buildings damaged in Oxford. **1811–1818** Volcanic dust veils (total DVI 4400), several eruptions. **1811** Cold wet winter, weak midwinter westerlies – 19 December (1810): stormy, severe gales in the Channel, HMS *Satellite* sank with all hands; early January: very cold, intense frost, Thames only ice-free in centre, people walked along banks firmly set with ice and snow from Battersea Bridge to Hungerford Stairs; 2–5 January: easterly, snowfall; 18 January: snowfall in north Wales; 27–30 January: heavy snowfall, deep drifts; February: mostly mild; 1–2 February: rapid thaw; 3 and 8 February: notable red skies observed in London, inferred volcanic dust-veil effect. Very mild wet spring – unusually forward vegetative growth; March: very mild, anticyclonic southwesterly; April: southerly; 29 April to 20 May: wet spell in southwest England; May: southwesterly. * 12 May: notable tornado. Tornado, 460 m (500 yd) wide, track 8 or 10 km (5 or 6 miles) long, serpentine-shaped cloud reported at Bonsall (Peak District), large trees uprooted and carried away 18–27 m (20–30 yd), twisted tops of other trees carried 45–90 m (50–100 yd), cows lifted from one field to another were injured by their fall. Cool summer – mid June to December: notable red skies observed in London, inferred volcanic dust-veil effect; 27 July to 2 August: short very warm spell. Very warm autumn – September: fog on seven days in London; 1–19 September: warm dry spell; 12, 15 and 19 October: notable red twilights observed in London, inferred volcanic dust-veil effect. **1812** Wet year; volcanic dust veil (DVI 600), Soufrière (St Vincent), Awu, Great Sangihe (Celebes) eruptions. Average winter temperatures, fairly weak midwinter westerlies – 26–31 December (1811): cold spell, snow; 3 January: snowfall in north Wales; 21–25 February: strong winds, occasional rain. Very cold wet backward spring – March: very cold; 19–23 March: heavy snowfall, 30 cm (12 in), deep drifts with northeasterly gales in Edinburgh; skating on 27 March followed by a rapid thaw. 16–18 April: cold spell, snow with north to northeasterly winds; 8 May: notable coloured twilight, similar skies reported in London to late October, inferred volcanic dust-veil effect. Very cool wet summer – inferred volcanic dust-veil effect. Cool autumn – 19–21 October: storms, houses subsided into the Channel, North Sea storm surge (21 October), severe floods on east coast and in London; 7–13 November: foggy spell. **1813** A year without a summer. Cold dry winter, fairly weak midwinter westerlies – 7–18 December (1812): cold spell; 19–20 December: thaw; 13 January: snowfall over high ground in north Wales; 24–31 January: thaw in north Wales; February: wet, stormy. Mild spring – 31 May: notable red twilight observed in London, similar skies reported to end of year, J. M. W. Turner's sunset painting, inferred volcanic dust-veil effect. Very cool dry summer – June: northerly; July: northwesterly; August: dry, northwesterly. Very cool autumn. **1814** Cold year. * Very cold winter. Inferred blocking-high situation, absent midwinter westerlies partly replaced by an easterly flow; 27 December (1813) to 5 January: inferred anticyclonic situation, exceptionally thick smoke fog (smog) formed in London with visibilities less than 20 m (22 yd), coach travel and mail services disrupted, impossible to see across streets, many accidents, candles burnt in shops and counting-houses, heavy coal-tar pollution produced smarting effect on eyes, fog later extended over southeast and central England, finally dispersed by strengthening easterly winds on 5 January. January: inferred anticyclonic easterly situation, very cold, one of the coldest snowiest Januarys on record; strong northeasterly winds, heavy snowfall, snowstorm-blizzard conditions, snow-covered ground for five weeks with 5 m (15 ft) drifts in places, roads blocked, deepest snow for 40 years; 25–27 January: temporary thaw allowed mail to arrive in north Wales but Thames still frozen solid enough in London at the end of January for a Frost Fair to be held from 1 to 4 February (the last such event recorded in the City), temperatures had fallen to −11 °C (13 °F); frozen rivers

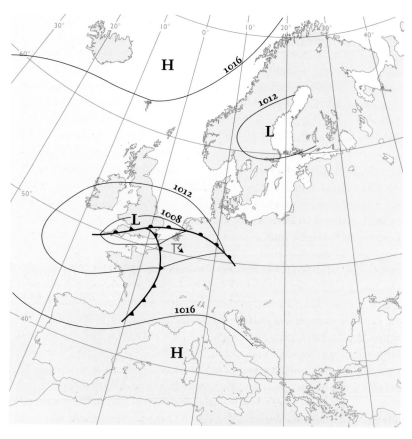

FIG 85. Synoptic weather map, 17 June 1815, Battle of Waterloo. (J. A. Kington)

elsewhere included the Tyne, Trent and Tweed. 5 February: inferred cyclonic southerly; wind shifted to the south, light snowfall, sleet, thousands of people still on the apparently firm central footpath on the frozen Thames, but the precipitation turned to rain in the evening, loud cracks occurred, some printing-press booths drifted away, two men drowned when a drifting floe overturned, high tide at 0200 h on 6 February added to the thaw, and one hour later the Thames was in motion with crashing ice floes, several more booths carried away, large moving ice fragments caused considerable damage to barges and lighters, bringing the last Frost Fair to a disastrous end; 6–13 February: thaw, ice broke up on the Tyne (6 February), severe floods, some brief very mild spells with mostly south to westerly winds. Very cold late spring – 1–12 March: frost, occasional snowfall; 20 March: rising temperatures more or less ended severe wintry conditions. Very cool dry summer – mostly cool showery conditions continued to late June, although temperatures rose briefly to 27 °C (80 °F) on 14–15 June with thunderstorms. Very cool autumn – September: anticyclonic; 5 November to 1 January (1815): notable red skies observed in London, inferred volcanic dust-veil effect; 27 November: heavy snowfall. **1815** Dry year; volcanic dust veil (DVI 3000), Tambora (Indonesia) eruption. Average winter temperatures, very weak midwinter westerlies. * 15–20 December (1814): severe storms. Inferred cyclonic situations/storm-force south to southwesterly gales, heavy rain, swollen rivers, cross-Channel traffic mostly suspended, several ships driven ashore at Ramsgate (Kent), great destruction of shipping as far north as Newcastle (Northumberland), severe damage in many urban areas (including Newcastle, Stafford and Jarrow) and coastal districts. 28 December (1814): heavy snowfall; January: frequent snow; 8 January: northwesterly, snowfall in north Wales; 19–21 January: northeasterly, heavy snowfall; 27–29 January: easterly, snowfall in north Wales. Mild wet spring – March: mostly mild; 10 March: heavy snowfall; 31 March: 23 °C (73 °F) in Suffolk; 1–9 April: very mild east to southeasterly spell; 14 April: snow showers; 15 May to December: remarkable sunsets reported in London, inferred volcanic dust-veil effect. Cool dry summer – 14 June: heavy thunderstorms; 17 June: cyclonic situation (Fig. 85), heavy rain; heavy thundery rain in Belgium made the ground muddy; this delayed Napoleon's attack and allowed more troops to join Wellington's army before the Battle of Waterloo. Cool autumn – 16 November: heavy snowfall. **1816** 'The Year Without a Summer'. Very cold winter, normal midwinter westerlies – 17–28 December (1815): frequent heavy snowfall. * 30 December (1815): severe storm. Inferred cyclonic situation, rapid thaw, heavy rain, severe floods in the Tyne (but not as great as in 1771), livestock lost, much damage in northeast England, including Durham, Darlington, Sunderland and Hexham, and along the Tees and Wear. 19–21 January: south to southeasterly situations, snow in north Wales; February: very cold; 6 February: heavy snowfall, deep drifts; 9 February: –16 °C (4 °F) in Suffolk; 16 February: rapid thaw, snow almost gone. Very cold late spring – 25–31 March: very cold northeasterly spell; 14 April: heavy snowfall; 11–12 May: wintry showers. Very cool wet summer – inferred volcanic dust-veil effect; June: northwesterly; July: very cool, cyclonic northwesterly, one of the two coldest Julys (with 1695) on record, 13.4 °C (56 °F); 18 July: heavy thunderstorm, rain, hail following a week of continuous rain (no such exceptionally wet conditions had occurred since 1799); 18–25 July: wet spell in north Wales; 30 July: winter snowdrifts still on Helvellyn (Lake District). * 31 July: severe storm. Inferred cyclonic situation, heavy rain, crops flattened, village lanes and ditches so full of water that boats could have been rowed along them.

During the whole of this singular summer the atmosphere has been particularly clear. This evening I observed from the Tower a range of lofty hills [Pennines] stretching eastwards and apparently forming two divisions, which I had never seen before.

David Pennant, Downing (Flintshire)

August: northwesterly; 12 August: heavy rain. * 31 August: severe storm. Inferred cyclonic situation, so-called 'hurricane' reported, many colliers wrecked off the Norfolk coast between Blakeney and Mundesley, also reports of further shipwrecks in the North Sea and Channel. Very cool autumn – 1 September: snow on Cader Idris (Snowdonia); 2 September: snowfall, keen frost, ice on water bodies; 28 September to 2 October: wet spell; 7 October: low-lying fields inundated due to heavy rain, all hopes dashed for a favourable end to the harvest; 10 November: early snowfall, 5 cm (2 in). **1817** Wet year; volcanic dust veil (DVI 300), Roung (Java) eruption. Mild wet winter, fairly strong midwinter westerlies – 25 December (1816): report of conditions being 'more like May than December'; 15–16 January: heavy snowfall; 17–18 January: thaw. * 26–27 January: severe storm. Inferred cyclonic situation, storm-force gales, trees blown down. February: wet, stormy. Very cold spring – March: very cold; 19 March: snowfall, drifts; April: one of the driest Aprils on record with 1912 and 1938, 8 mm (0.3 in), blocking high off southwest Ireland. Very cool wet summer – 18–24 June: very warm spell, 28 °C (82 °F) recorded on 20 June, thunderstorms (21/23 June); July: wet. * 1 July: severe storm. Inferred cyclonic situation, low pressure recorded (981 mb), heavy rain in north Wales. Dry autumn, average temperatures – September: fog on seven days in London. **1818** Cold wet winter, very strong midwinter westerlies – 3 January: snowfall in north Wales; 4 January: rapid thaw in north Wales. * 12–16 January: severe storms. Cyclonic westerly situations, series of depressions moved northeast over the British Isles, heavy rain, severe southwesterly gales, locally storm-force; 15 January: buildings badly damaged in Edinburgh, trees blown down in north Scotland, Hamburg inundated. Cold wet spring – March: wet. * 4, 7–8 and 22–23 March: three severe storms. 4 March: very cold, snow, overnight storm, severe gales, thunderstorms, several shipwrecks in the Channel; 7–8 March: severe gales, showers; 22–23 March: severe gales, trees damaged. 10 April: heavy rain, severe flood; 17–21 April: cold easterly spell; 22–25 April: wet spell, floods; mid May: start of a warm mostly dry easterly spell. Very warm dry summer – claimed to have been the longest, warmest and driest in living memory; early June: easterly spell continued, very warm with occasional thunderstorms; 16–20 June: showery southwesterly spell; 21 June to late July: renewed very warm mostly dry conditions; 29 June to January (1819): notable coloured twilights observed in

London, inferred volcanic dust-veil effect; 18 July: heavy, probably thundery, rain in north England; 24 July: 32 °C (90 °F) at Thwaite (Suffolk); August: warm mostly dry. Very warm autumn – 5 September: end of dry conditions; November: one of the warmest Novembers on record, 9.5 °C (49 °F). **1819** Wet year. Average winter temperatures, fairly strong midwinter westerlies – December (1818): mild; January: mild, occasional rain, 15 January: stormy, travel dislocated by heavy-going roads; 25 January: low pressure (967 mb), strong southerly winds in north Wales. Very mild wet spring – 23–29 April: cold easterly spell. Warm dry summer – June: occasional thunderstorms; 22–31 July: very warm spell, occasional thunderstorms. Very cool dry autumn – 8–12 October: very warm spell, 24 °C (76 °F); 17–31 October: cold spell, occasional snow. * 23 October: severe storm. Inferred cyclonic situation, storm-force gales, snowfall, houses damaged, trees uprooted in London.

1820s

Weak zonal flow (60 estimated westerly situations on average per year).
1820 * Very cold winter. 9–14 December (1819): severe frost; 23 December: very mild, heavy overnight rain; 1–23 January: mainly anticyclonic, very cold spell, occasional snowfall; 6 January: Thames shipping blocked by ice; 13–15 January: severe frost, –19 °C (–3 °F); 17 January: Thames shipping still blocked by ice; 18–22 January: heavy snowfall, deep drifts, roads blocked; 23–24 January: thaw, floods; severe conditions and high pressure readings during January (1040 mb on 9 January) featured in contemporary newspapers. 19–21 February: heavy snowfall, 15 cm (6 in); 23 February: snow almost gone. Average spring temperatures – March: very cold. * 2 March: severe storm. Inferred depression in the North Sea; severe to storm-force northwesterly gales, North Sea storm surge, severe sea floods pounded English east coast, including King's Lynn and Norfolk marshland, some of highest flood levels on record, severe damage (such destruction had not been experienced for 41 years, since the storm of 31 December 1778 to 1 January 1779). 11–13 March: brief cold spell, southeasterly winds, some snow but soon melted; late May: very warm. Variable summer – late June: very warm; July: heavy thunderstorm with hail, hundreds of acres of crops destroyed in Norfolk. Very cool dry autumn. **1821** Wet year; volcanic dust veil (DVI 300), Iceland eruption. Dry winter, average temperatures, weak midwinter westerlies – 16–17 December (1820): heavy snowfall, 17.5 cm (7 in); late December: dry northeasterly winds; 5–6 January: snowfall; 7–8 January: thaw; February: very dry. Wet spring, average temperatures – 26 May: wintry showers, snow and thunder; 27 May: brief snowfall in London (latest known date for the capital). Very cool summer – 13–26 June: cool east to northeasterly spell, local frosts; July and August: notable coloured sunsets

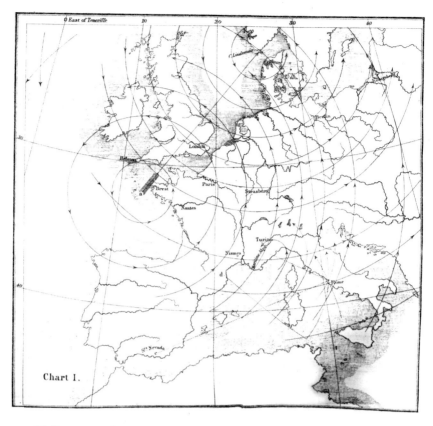

FIG 86. Synoptic weather map, 24 December 1821, by Heinrich Brandes. (H. W. Dove)

observed in London, inferred volcanic dust-veil effect; 15–25 August: very warm spell; 18 August: dimmed sun, inferred volcanic dust-veil effect. Very warm wet autumn – November: heavy rain, floods; 3–4 November: stormy, grounds damaged; 26/30 November: stormy. **1822–1824** Volcanic dust veil (total DVI 2200), widespread eruptions. **1822** Warm year. Very mild wet winter, normal midwinter westerlies – December (1821): very wet; widespread river floods including Thames at Henley, Maidenhead and Kingston. * 24–26 December (1821): severe storm (Fig. 86). Large depression off northwest France moved northeast across southeast England and the North Sea to south Norway; deepest known low (946 mb recorded in London) over the British Isles during the instrumental period; 24 December: inferred heavy rain; 25 December: severe river floods, including one of the highest known on the Trent; severe Thames floods during late

December, in which waters reached halfway up Kingston market-place buildings, may also have been caused by the heavy rain of this storm; 26 December: rain, snow, overnight frost in inferred cold sector of low. This cyclonic situation was later discussed by Heinrich Brandes in 1826 and published by Heinrich Dove as one of the earliest-known synoptic weather charts (see Chapter 6). Late December (1821): countryside in a depressed state due to recent heavy rain and severe floods; early January: further severe floods; 4 January: northerly situation, snowfall in north Wales; 7 January: start of dry mild spell. * 31 January to 2 February: severe storm. Inferred cyclonic situation/severe southwesterly gales, heavy rainfall, severe floods on rivers, including Tyne, Tees and Wear (river rose 3.7 m/12 ft above its normal height), adjacent low-lying land inundated. * 5 February: severe storm. Inferred cyclonic situation, severe gales, much damage. 17 February: early leafing and flowering events. Very mild wet spring – March: very mild, westerly. * 6 March: severe storm. Westerly situation, severe southwesterly gales, Thames tidal flow held back for several hours, islands appeared in the river between London and Southwark bridges. * 22 March: severe storm. Inferred cyclonic situation, severe northwest to northerly gales, many shipwrecks in the Thames. 28 March: 21 °C (70 °F) in Suffolk; mid May: very warm. Very warm summer – June: very warm, occasional thunderstorms, Azores high extended northeast over Europe; July: very wet in north Wales; 3 July: wet in north England; August: dry very warm. Very warm autumn – 16 October to 30 November: mostly warm wet; November: notable coloured skies observed, inferred volcanic dust-veil effect.

1823 Possibly severe enough conditions for incipient glaciation in the Scottish Highlands. Very cold winter, absent midwinter westerlies partly replaced by an easterly flow – 8–14 December (1822): onset of cold spell; 30 December: much ice on the Thames at Greenwich; January–February: heavy snowfall, severe snowstorms in northeast England; January: frequent snow in north Wales; 15 January: southwesterly winds set in over west Europe; 30 January: snow gone in north Wales; February: stormy. * 2 February: severe storm. Large depression moved northeast over west Europe (probably across north France), stormy conditions, inferred strong winds and heavy rain from Edinburgh to Genoa, heavy thunderstorm, rain, hail at Nice. Like 24 December 1821, this cyclonic situation was reconstructed by Heinrich Brandes as part of his historic synoptic weather chart series, published in 1826. 8 February: heavy snowfall, snowstorm, deep drifts, blocked roads, partially opened later in north England by tunnels cut through the drifts. Average spring temperatures – March: cold, snow, rain; March to September: notable coloured sunsets observed in London, inferred volcanic dust-veil effect; late April through most of May: warm. Very cool wet summer – 29 June: start of wet spell to 15 August; mid August to late September: more favourable conditions. Cool autumn – 31 October: severe gales, much damage; early November: Thames flood at Windsor. **1824** Wet year. Mild winter, strong midwinter westerlies. * 17 December (1823): severe storm. Inferred cyclonic situation, severe gales, much damage. Cold wet backward spring. * 3 March: severe storm. Inferred cyclonic situation, severe gales, much damage. Cool wet summer – 14 July: severe hailstorm, crops destroyed; 22 August to late September: dry very warm. Wet stormy autumn – 9–12 October: wet spell, river floods. * 10 October: severe storm. Inferred cyclonic situation, strong winds, heavy rain, extensive river floods, including Wear inundation, river rose to an exceptionally high level, much damage. * 23 November: severe storm, 'The Great Gale or Outrage'. One of the worst storms on record; inferred cyclonic situation, severe to storm-force southwesterly gales affected many areas, especially southwest English coasts, combination of gales and a spring tide produced an Atlantic storm surge, Chesil Beach (Dorset) breached, East Fleet village mostly destroyed, 50–60 people drowned, 95-ton sloop *Ebenezer* swept over the bank into the Fleet, water in Abbotsbury decoy meadows nearly 7 m (23 ft) deep, Hurst Spit on the West Solent shifted 37 m (40 yd), much damage, including the Plymouth and Lyme Regis breakwaters, and Weymouth Esplanade, many shipwrecks in the Channel. **1825** Warm dry year. Mild winter, fairly strong midwinter westerlies – 4–5 December (1824): moderate snowfall, 6.3 mm (2.5 in). * 24–25 December (1824): severe storm. Inferred cyclonic situation/inferred severe southwesterly gales, a so-called 'perfect hurricane' reported with brief 'calm' intervals for several days; snow, sleet, rain and frost followed each other with remarkable rapidity; river floods, including Tyne, riverside villages inundated. January: very mild in north Wales; 25–31 January: anticyclonic westerly situations; February: fog on six days in London. * 2 February: severe storm. Inferred depression over the North Sea, one of the most severe storms of the 19th century, northwesterly situation, exceptionally high tide, overnight severe northwesterly gales probably caused a North Sea storm surge, Tyne rose above Newcastle Quayside with floating boats, riverside houses flooded; northwest German coastlands also inundated. 4 February: northerly situation, snowfall. Mild wet spring – 2 March: heavy snowfall; 14–22 May: cold easterly spell. Warm dry summer – late June to July: very warm dry; July: one of the driest Julys on record; 18–19 July: 32–36 °C (90–97 °F) at Thwaite (Suffolk); 5 August: storm, severe gales, much damage. Very warm wet autumn – 11–12 October: stormy; 20–21 October: light snowfall, heavy falls over high ground; 1–5 November: stormy, severe gales, heavy rain; 7 November: snowstorm. **1826** Dry year; volcanic dust veil (DVI 300), Kelud (Java) eruption. Average winter temperatures, weak midwinter westerlies – 29–30 December (1825): light snowfall, 5 cm (2 in); January: very cold dry; 6–7 January:

easterly, snowfall in north Wales; 10 January: west-northwesterly, snow-covered ground, snowfall in north Wales; 13 January: much ice on Thames at Greenwich; 16–17 January: Thames partly frozen over; February: mostly mild; onset of long drought. * February to September: drought. Inferred mainly anticyclonic situations. Mild dry early spring – 10 March: 19.4 °C (67 °F) at Gordon Castle (Morayshire). Very warm dry summer – one of the warmest summers on record; June: 32 °C (90 °F) recorded; 21 July: rain, one of the few wet days during the summer, parched ground in east Britain from Aberdeenshire to Suffolk, cattle suffered.

> *Dry summer the driest that has been known for a number of years ... meadows not fit to mow ... beasts foddered in the middle of summer to keep them alive ... wheat crops very good all others very bad.*
>
> John Hoyte, Craxton (Leicestershire)

4 August: severe storm, floods in London; 25 August: fall of blood-rain in London, a rare atmospheric phenomenon due to dust particles (possibly originating from the Sahara) transported aloft by southeasterly winds and precipitated as red-coloured raindrops. Average autumn temperatures – September: end of drought. **1827** Cold dry winter, frost and snow, fairly weak midwinter westerlies – 2–5 January: snow; 6–10 January: mild wet; 11–13 January: snow, rain. * 14 January: severe storm. Inferred cyclonic situation/storm-force gales, trees blown down, buildings damaged, followed by heavy snowfall on 15 January. 19–27 January: light snowfall, 5 cm (2 in); 28–31 January: southwesterly winds, mild, thaw; February: very cold; 9–20 February: severe northeasterly spell, Thames and other water bodies frozen, including Diss Mere (Norfolk); skating, stalls and booths erected, 1,500 people on the ice (20 February); 22–28 February: less cold westerly spell. Very mild wet spring – March: changeable, occasional rain, a little snow. Dry summer, average temperatures – 5 June: unusually cool southwesterly wind, fruit trees damaged, otherwise June and July generally warm mostly dry; August: severe floods, north England, much damage in Glendale Ward (Northumberland). Very warm wet autumn. **1828** Warm wet year. Very mild wet winter, weak midwinter westerlies – 7–11 January: cold northeasterly spell, occasional snow. * 12–13 January: severe storm. Inferred cyclonic situation, severe probably southwesterly gales, many shipwrecks, including 13 vessels at Plymouth. 15–16 January: snowfall; 17 January: rain, severe floods; 18–30 January: mild dry spell; 9–14 February: heavy snowfall, deep drifts. Very mild wet early spring. Warm wet summer – 24 June to 8 July: very warm spell; 9 July: reported pressure fall heralded forthcoming wet spell; 10–14 July: heavy rain, river floods, roads

impassable, many towns inundated, crops damaged in north England; early
August: heavy rain, river floods, streets inundated in York on 3 August, severe
gales, houses and trees damaged.

> *Such floods as never was known by the oldest men living, hundreds of acres of hay*
> *swam away particularly by the Trent.*
> John Hoyte, Croxton (Leicestershire), 9–10 August 1828

15 August: end of wet spell. Very warm dry autumn. **1829** Cold year; volcanic
dust veil (DVI 300), Kamchatka (eastern Russia) eruption. Dry winter, mostly
average temperatures, cold in east England, midwinter westerlies absent, partly
replaced by an easterly flow – 1 December (1828): continuous rain in north
England, Tyne exceptionally swollen; late January: cold, frost, ice on Thames,
snowfall in north Wales; February: snow. Cold spring, average rainfall – March:
cold. Cool wet summer – inferred volcanic dust-veil effect; June: wet;
Horticultural Fête at Chiswick washed out by a heavy thunderstorm; 16 June:
start of a cool wet spell; July: very wet, occasional thunderstorms; cold with night
frosts in Scotland; 24 July: easterly situation, heavy rain, thunderstorms, swollen
rivers in north England and north Wales, flood-threatening situation on Tyne
(25 July); August: very wet. * 2–4 August: severe storm. Anticyclonic northwesterly
situation turned cyclonic northerly as a depression over the Norwegian Sea
moved south across northeast Scotland into the southern North Sea, severe
north to northeasterly gales affected northeast and central Scotland, and east
England, heavy rainfall especially in the northeast Scottish Highlands, severe
river floods between Moray and Angus ('Moray floods'), stone bridges and houses
swept away, many shipwrecks, great loss of life, coastline altered at river mouths.
27–28 August: storms, heavy rain, showers, further floods in same areas of
northeast Scotland as during 2–4 August storm. Very cool stormy autumn –
6–7 October: brief snowfall (earliest known date). * 13–14 October: severe storm.
Cyclonic/northerly situations, depression over the North Sea moved slowly
south, heavy rain, severe northeasterly gales affected east Scotland and
northeast England, swollen rivers, including the Tees and Tyne, severe river
floods, waters penetrated cellars of Newcastle Quayside and Close (highest Tyne
flood since 30 December 1815), many shipwrecks. * 25 November: severe storm.
Strong easterly flow between high pressure over Scandinavia and north of
Scotland and a depression over France, heavy snowfall, 15 cm (6 in), severe
easterly gales pounded North Sea coasts, many shipwrecks; this may have been
the storm in which the Spurn Head lighthouse tower (later abandoned) was
undermined.

1830s

Continental; very weak zonal flow (estimated 56 westerly situations on average per year). **1830** * Very cold winter. December (1829): anticyclonic, 18–31 December: cold spell, occasional snow; 18 December: 7.5 cm (3 in); 24–25 December: rivers frozen; 29 December: much ice on the Thames; January: anticyclonic; 1–2 January: cold spell continued; 4–5 January: thaw; 10–21 January: renewed cold, heavy snowfall; 20–21 January: severe east to southeasterly gales, 15 vessels driven ashore in northeast England; 22 January: still much ice in the Thames; 23 January: newspaper accounts of exceptionally severe conditions in France, Germany and Spain; Bodensee completely frozen; one of the most severe winter freezing events of the Baltic Sea on record; 27 January: snowfall in north Wales; 29–30 January: snowfall; February: slack pressure gradient, severe frosts; 2–7 February: light snowfall, 5 cm (2 in), Thames blocked by ice at Greenwich; 7–8 February: southerly wind, rapid thaw, floods, ice blocking Thames at Greenwich drifted out to sea (10 February); 24 February: mild, ice on ponds (frozen for nearly ten weeks) began to break up. Very mild wet spring – March: very mild; 26 March: 22 °C (71 °F) at Suffolk; 2–4 April: snowfall. Mostly very cool wet summer – 25–26 June: heavy thunderstorm, rain, severe river floods; 24–29 July: very warm; 26 August: snowstorm over Cairngorm Mountains. Average autumn temperatures and rainfall – September: cool wet; October: warm dry. **1831–1833** Volcanic dust veil (total DVI 1400), widespread eruptions, reports of an unusual 'dry fog', blue-green sun and moon, and a notable coloured sunset painted by Turner. **1831** Wet year. Cold winter, very weak midwinter westerlies – 12 December: snow; 23–29 December: cold spell, hard frost, –12 °C (11 °F) at Greenwich (25 December), heavy snowfall (27–28 December); 30–31 December: thaw, rain, snow gone; 13 January: mild, but thick ice still on ponds; 24 January to 6 February: cold spell, occasional snowfall; 7 February: rapid thaw, snow-melt aided by strong southwesterly winds, severe river floods, Tyne and its tributaries rose to unusually high levels, Newcastle Quayside and many other lower parts of the city inundated (9 February); 10 February: 16 °C (61 °F) at Thwaite (Suffolk). Very mild wet spring – 24 March: snowstorm followed by sleet; 29 March to 3 April: cold northeasterly spell; 6–9 May: cold frosty spell, snowstorm (6 May), tree leaves, fruit blossom and vegetables badly damaged; 16 May to 4 June: easterly spell, local thunderstorms. Very warm unsettled summer – alternate wet and very warm dry days, abundant vegetation growth; 1 June: notable coloured skies observed, inferred volcanic dust-veil effect; 5 June: wind shifted westerly after three-week easterly spell; 1–9 July: very warm spell; 2–5 August: notable 'dry fog' observed, inferred volcanic dust-veil effect; frequent thunderstorms; 17 August: widespread heavy thunderstorms. Very warm wet autumn. **1832** Dry winter, average temperatures, fairly weak midwinter westerlies – 6 January: light snowfall; 28 January: river floods; February: very dry; 22–25 February: persistent fog in London. Mild spring – 13 May: heavy snowfall. Warm wet summer – 22–29 August: wet spell, occasional thunderstorms, heavy thunderstorm at Barnard Castle (Durham), Tees rose to a great level (25 August). Warm autumn. **1833** Wet winter, average temperatures, very weak midwinter westerlies – 31 December (1832): light snowfall; February: very wet stormy; one of the wettest Februarys on record, 150 mm (6 in) at Thwaite (Suffolk), severe floods. Mild dry spring – March: cold; 23 and 26 March: heavy snowfall; 18 April: end of cold spell; May: very mild dry, one of the warmest Mays on record, 15.1 °C (59 °F), onset of warmer conditions in early May produced a rapid change in the countryside.

Vegetation flashed all at once into beauty. The appearance of barren winter was changed to the verdure of summer in one week from 2 May.
Orlando Whistlecraft, Thwaite (Suffolk)

26–30 May: cool dry northeasterly spell. Cool stormy summer. * 2 June: severe storm. Inferred cyclonic situation, severe to storm-force gales, buildings damaged, boats wrecked on the Thames, people killed, trees blown down, vegetation blighted, withered leaves turned brown. 11–12 June: stormy, southwesterly gales, crops damaged; 20 June: heavy rain, 35 mm (1.4 in) during less than two hours at Thwaite (Suffolk). * 31 August: severe storm. Inferred depression in the North Sea, severe north to northwesterly gales, heavy rain for 36 hours, much damage both on land and at sea, many trees blown down, leaves discoloured as if scorched by fire, over 70 shipwrecks off east coast. Average autumn temperatures – September: wet; 9 November: first snowfall. * 19 November: severe storm. Inferred cyclonic situation/severe gales in northwest England, buildings damaged in Liverpool, several shipwrecks on the Mersey, 13 people drowned off Formby (Lancashire). **1834** Very warm year, ninth-warmest year (with 1733 and 1921) on record. Very mild wet winter, fairly strong midwinter westerlies – December (1833): westerly. * 31 December (1833): severe storm. Inferred cyclonic situation, severe gales, heavy rain, many ships broke moorings, several barges sunk in the Thames. January: southwesterly; 10 January: Tyne swollen by heavy rain. * 27–28 January: severe storm. Inferred cyclonic situation, heavy rain, river floods in northeast England, Tyne overflowed at Newcastle, Quayside and Close flooded on evening high tide, area below Blaydon (Durham) inundated. 28 January: start of mild dry spell; February: anticyclonic southwesterly. Mostly mild dry spring – 8–25 April: cold easterly spell, snow showers (10–12 April); May: southwesterly; 20–31 May: warm dry. Very warm

summer – 11–17 July: very warm dry spell; 17 July: marked effects of drought in countryside, cattle driven daily miles for water, occasional heavy thunderstorms but rain soon vanished in dry soil; 25 August: heavy rain ended drought. Very warm dry autumn – September: anticyclonic southwesterly; 30 September to 6 October: fog in London; 20–22 November: brief cool spell, light snow, sleet (21 November). **1835** Volcanic dust veil (DVI 4000), several eruptions including Coseguina (Nicaragua). Mild dry winter, normal midwinter westerlies – 31 December (1834): very mild, only light showers, ponds and springs failed; January: one of the mildest Januarys on record; 1–8 January: cold spell; 9 January: thaw, heavy rain ended drought; 16 January: storm, heavy rain followed by snowstorm; 16–22 January: cold spell, occasional snowfall, 5 °C (23 °F) on 18 January; 22 January: rapid thaw; 23–31 January: mild dry; February: stormy. Mild wet spring – March: wet stormy; 15–17 April: cold spell, snow sleet showers; 26–27 April: cold northerly spell, light snowfall. Very warm dry summer – Turner's sunset painting, inferred volcanic dust-veil effect; 10 June: heavy thunderstorm at Newcastle (Staffordshire), Derwent overflowed; July: very warm dry; August: very warm mostly dry; 21–26 August: occasional showers, thunderstorms in west England. Wet autumn, average temperatures.
* 24–26 October: severe storm. Inferred cyclonic situation, strong winds, heavy rain, river floods in northeast England, Tweed rose 3 m (10 ft) in three hours on 26 October. 18 November: storm, depression moved east over northern North Sea into the Baltic, northwesterly to westerly gales, widespread showers; 20–21 November: heavy rain, river floods in northeast England, Tyne rose suddenly and overflowed. **1836** Cold dry winter, probably severe enough for Thames to have been frozen if the old London Bridge had not been demolished in 1831, normal midwinter westerlies – 19–26 December (1835): cold spell, snowstorm (19 December), ponds frozen with ice 10 cm (4 in) thick; 27–29 December: thaw; 1–2 January: renewed cold, snow showers; 11–12 January: light snowfall, 7.5 cm (3 in); 29–30 January: light snowfall; February: stormy; 2 February: heavy snowfall.
* 17 February: severe storm. Inferred cyclonic situation, north to northeasterly gales, probable North Sea storm surge, heavy snow sleet showers, floods in northeast England, Tyne overflowed. 25–26 February: storm-force gales in northeast England, ships badly damaged off Scarborough (Yorkshire). Wet early spring, average temperatures – March: wet stormy; 31 March to 1 April: cold, light snowfall, 5 cm (2 in); 1 May: stormy, snow showers; 4–10 May: easterly spell, wet turning dry; 21–30 May: cold dry northeasterly spell. Average summer temperatures – above and below normal in England and Scotland respectively; 1–5 July: very warm dry spell, 29 °C (85 °F) on 5 July; 29 July: heavy thunderstorms, rain in northeast England, severe floods on the Tyne and its tributaries. Very cool

wet autumn – September: very cool; 2 September: stormy, heavy rain. * 28–31
October: notable early snowfall. Inferred northerly situation, heavy snowfall, 30
cm (12 in), heavier falls in north Britain, 100–130 cm (40–50 in) in Edinburgh;
thaw arrived five or six days later. * 23 November: severe storm. Depression
moved northeast over England, severe westerly gales, heavy showers. * 27–29
November: severe storms. Inferred cyclonic situation, depressions moved
northeast over the British Isles, storm-force west to southwesterly gales, much
damage, houses unroofed, trees blown down. **1837** Wet winter, average
temperatures, weak midwinter westerlies – 23–31 December (1836): cold, frequent
snow. * 25–27 December (1836): severe storm. Inferred depression over the
Channel or north France, severe east-northeasterly gales, very heavy snowfall,
150–450 cm (60–180 in), deep drifts up to 15 m (50 ft), snowstorm-blizzard
conditions, eight people killed, roads blocked, business and communication by
post or otherwise suspended for several days; 27 December: Lewes avalanche (the
only one on record in lowland England), snow accumulated on top of South
Downs suddenly swept down and buried cottages below, 15 people trapped under
heavy snow, eight lives lost. 6–10 January: thaw, very mild spell, south to
southwesterly winds, but snow remained in drifts and under hedges; heavy rain
in northeast England, severe damaging river floods on the Tyne and Wear;
12 January: renewed cold, snowstorm; 28–30 January: heavy snowfall, 30 cm (12 in).
Very cold dry late spring – one of the coldest springs on record; March: very cold,
northerly; 17–31 March: cold spell, occasional snow; April: very cold, one of the
coldest Aprils on record; 3–4 April: snow showers; 10 and 22 May: wintry showers;
27–30 May: warm dry spell. Very warm summer – June: warm showery conditions,
rapid vegetative growth; July: very warm; 28–30 July: heavy thundery rain; August:
warm mostly dry. Cool dry autumn – September: anticyclonic northerly; 23–29
September: cool mostly dry easterly spell. * 6 October: notable tornado. Inferred
cyclonic situation, severe tornado at Kilburn (Yorkshire), terrifying roar of wind,
everything destroyed in its path, trees uprooted, hedges torn out and crops
ruined. **1838** Cold year. Very cold dry winter, absent midwinter westerlies partly
replaced by an easterly flow – blocking high over Scandinavia dominated
circulation. * 20 December (1837): severe storm. Inferred depression over central
England, heavy rain, strong westerly winds; northeast England: strong
northeasterly winds, severe river floods, particularly on the Wear and Brownie
(Durham). Late December (1837): notably mild dry Christmas, birds sang as if it
were spring; 24–31 December: mild moist, south to southwesterly winds; January:
very cold, Thames and Trent frozen; 4 January to 27 February: very cold spell;
6 January: first winter snowfall in north England, continued to end of month,
Tyne frozen up to 8 km (5 miles) below Newcastle, many skaters (such an intense

frost had not occurred since 1814), −12.5 °C (9.5 °F) at Newcastle on 20 January, −16.1 °C (3 °F) at Ryton, −21 °C (−6 °F) in Norfolk, lowest temperature of the 19th century recorded in London, −16.1 °C (3 °F) at Greenwich; 27 January: Thames frozen at Greenwich; February: very cold; 3 February: thaw with northwesterly wind, became more rapid in sunshine on 5 February, but rain with south to southeasterly winds on 6 February preceded a renewal of cold easterly winds on 7 February. * February: severe storm. Inferred cyclonic situation, severe northeasterly gales in northern North Sea, Otterswick beach in Orkney scoured by sea action, ancient forest floor exposed. 12 February: −12 °C (11 °F) in Suffolk; 24 February: heavy snowfall in northeast England. Very cold dry spring – 5 March: thaw with rain; 8 March: snow gone; 15–30 April: stormy, cold northwesterly gales; May: warm early, night frosts later. Cool wet summer. Cool autumn – September: fog on 11 days in London. * 7 September: severe storm. Depression over north England moved northeast into northern North Sea, severe to storm-force north to northeasterly gales pounded northeast English and east Scottish coasts, storm made famous by the wreck of SS *Forfarshire* and rescue of its passengers by the Longstone (Farne Island) lighthouse keeper, William Darling, and his daughter, Grace. * 11 October: severe storm. Inferred cyclonic situation/storm-force winds, 2,000 ships sought refuge in Great Yarmouth Roads off the Norfolk coast. 13 October: snow showers. * 28 October: severe storm. Inferred cyclonic situation/storm-force gales, houses damaged in London, carriages blown off Great Western Railway track, 21 men drowned in the Bristol Channel. * 28 November: severe storm. Inferred deep depression (941 mb), central Ireland, east-southeasterly gales in north Ireland. **1839** Wet year. Dry winter, average temperatures, strong midwinter westerlies – 25 December (1838): snowfall. * 6–7 January: severe storm, 'The Night of the Big Wind'. Inferred cyclonic situation, one of the most intense depressions on record and the most severe storm on record to have affected Ireland (those of 1703 and 1987 had less impact in Ireland than in England); an exceptionally deep depression (930 mb) moved east-northeast north of Ireland across north Scotland into the North Sea, cyclonic southwesterly situation, severe southwesterly gales, particularly over Ireland, south Scotland and north England, whirlwind and tornado activity reported, over 400 people killed, great damage, thousands of trees blown down in Ireland, over 20 per cent of the housing in Dublin damaged, considerable structural damage in south Scotland and north England, many shipwrecks, Menai Bridge damaged. Very cold dry spring – March: very cold; 6–8 March: northeasterly spell, snowfall, drifts; April: blocking high west of Norway; 14–15 May: northerly wind, snow, sleet, hail showers. Very cool wet summer – 18 June: easterly wind, showers, thunder, heavy rain, floods in north England; 22–30 July:

southwesterly wet spell. Wet autumn, average temperatures – 14–15 September: inferred cyclonic situation, stormy, southwesterly winds, heavy squally showers; heavy rain; severe river floods in northeast England; 5 October: stormy, westerly winds; 24 October: stormy, southeasterly winds, rain, possibly the stormy conditions in which ten ships were driven ashore on Chesil Beach (Dorset), nine were wrecked while the tenth, a craft of 500 tons, was swept over the bank by the sea from the West Bay and floated away little the worse for wear into the smooth waters of Portland Roads; 26–31 October: cool east to northeasterly winds, occasional showers; November: mostly mild wet; 1–3 November: strong northeasterly winds, heavy showers; 26–27 November: cold north to northeasterly winds, wintry showers.

1840s

Maritime; weak zonal flow (estimated 63 westerly situations on average per year). **1840** Dry year. Wet winter, average temperatures, fairly strong midwinter westerlies – December (1839): mild wet; 1–7 December: fog in London; 8 February: snowfall; 17 February to 6 March: cold easterly spell, occasional snowfall. Dry spring, average temperatures – 21–27 March: cold spell, snow showers; April: mild, warmest April then on record. Very cool dry summer – July: warm; occasional showers; late July: drought affected countryside, dried-up ponds and rivers; August: very warm; 11–19 August: showery. Very cool autumn – 21–26 September: wet westerly spell. * 17 November: severe storm. Inferred cyclonic situation/severe gales, many shipwrecks and loss of life on the coast, much damage in London, main losses on the Thames: 20–30 vessels severely damaged, 18 coal-bearing barges sunk and 100 watermen boats holed. Late November: portents of a severe winter, snow, sleet, west England (18 November), severe frost, west England (26–28 November); thick fog in London (27–29 November). **1841** Very cold winter, very weak midwinter westerlies – 11–25 December (1840): very cold easterly spell, occasional snowfall; January: very cold with milder spells, heavy snowfall; 3 January: westerly wind, overnight heavy thunderstorm, rain, severe snowstorm, deep snow; 4 January: northerly wind, snowstorm, 13 or 15 cm (5 or 6 in); 5–6 January: snowfall; 9 January: severe frost, –16 °C (4 °F) at Thwaite (Suffolk); 10–11 January: snowfall, 17 cm (7 in); 12–16 January: thaw, heavy rain, severe floods, Till valley (Wiltshire) flood disaster, over 70 houses destroyed, 200 people made homeless; 17–18 January: westerly winds, decreasing snow cover; 19–20 January: northerly wind, snow showers; 22–30 January: mild westerly spell, occasional rain; 31 January: northerly wind, rain, snow; February: cold, heavy snowfall; 1–5 February: heavy snowfall; 11–12 February: thaw, end of cold spell. Very mild early spring – late April to May: warm; 23–29 May: very warm, 30 °C (86 °F) at Thwaite (Suffolk) on 28 May. Very cool wet summer, 1–3 June: very warm;

8–12 June: cool northeasterly spell, ice on ponds; late June to July: wet; 1–25 August: wet; 26–31 August: very warm. Cool wet autumn – 3–4 September: heavy thunderstorms, showers, severe floods; late September: start of wet spell, river floods. * 4–7 October: severe storms. Inferred depression over England, heavy rain, 69 mm (2.7 in) in northeast England, severe river floods, including Tyne, Newcastle, many Quayside cellars inundated, Derwent rose to then known greatest height (apart from 1771), occasional heavy showers, easterly wind turned westerly over central England. 18 October: storm, westerly gales, branches broken off trees; 15–17 November: light snowfall, hard frost, –7 °C (20 °F) in west England on 17 November; 18 November: thaw, inferred freezing rain, glazed frost ('black ice'); 19 November: thaw continued, rain, snow gone in Cheltenham (Gloucestershire) but remained over high ground in the West Country. **1842** Cold winter, very weak midwinter westerlies. * 29 December (1841): severe storm. Inferred cyclonic situation/storm-force winds, much damage, trees uprooted in London, many barges sunk on the Thames. January: very cold; 13–14 January: heavy snowfall, drifts; 26 January: notable snowstorm in south Durham. Mild spring – 10 March: storm, gales; April: easterly spell; 2 May: end of easterly spell. Very warm dry summer – June: very warm; 7–13 June: very warm easterly spell, 30.6 °C (87 °F) at Thwaite (Suffolk) on 12 and 14 June. * 21 July: notable tornado. Tornado hit Birkenhead (Cheshire) from the southeast, about 73 m (80 yd) in width, lasted about three minutes, everything bent ahead of it, houses shaken, people thrown to the ground. 28 July: storm, gales; August: very warm; 10 August: heavy thunderstorms, rain, hail; 14–23 August: very warm, 31–32 °C (88–90 °F) at Thwaite (Suffolk). Very cool wet autumn – 19–20 October: cold, hoar frost in west England. * 21–23 October: severe storm. Inferred cyclonic situation/storm-force gales, much damage, great loss of life, many shipwrecks off south and east English coasts. 26 October: snowstorm, snow cover over high ground in west England; 22–23 November: continuous snowfall. **1843** Mild winter, fairly strong midwinter westerlies – January: mild; floods in Wales; 8 January: snowfall, 30 cm (12 in); 11–12 January: light snowfall, 5 cm (2 in) in west England. * 13 January: severe storm. Inferred cyclonic situation, deep depression (below 950 mb) moved east-northeast across north Ireland and south Scotland, inferred storm-force southwesterly gales, violent gusts, south of centre, heavy rain, showers, snow disappeared, numerous coastal disasters including those at the Goodwin Sands, Plymouth, Devonport, Boscastle and New Brighton. 14 January: cold southwesterly wind, rain, snow; 15 January: dry, snow-covered ground in west England; 2 February: start of cold spell, frequent snow; 4 February: storm, inferred severe northwesterly gales, much damage. Wet spring, average temperatures – 1–10 March: cold spell continued, snow patches and deep drifts over high ground; 10–13 April: snow showers; 14–30 April: mild, occasional rain, showers in west England; May: mild wet in west England. Very cool wet summer – June: cool wet; July: wet; August: heavy thunderstorms, severe hailstorms; 9–19 August: very warm, 29–32 °C (84–90 °F); 9 August: heavy thunderstorms, large hailstones, torrential rain, flash floods, crops destroyed, trees uprooted in Norfolk (this event led to the formation of the former Norwich Union insurance company); 21 August: end of summer heat. Cool autumn – floods in Wales.

1844 Dry year. Mild dry winter, normal midwinter westerlies – December (1843): mild dry; 9 January: snowfall; 20 January: storm, shipwreck, Goodwin Sands; 28–30 January: stormy, westerly winds; 31 January: snow showers; February: very cold wet; 2–4 February: heavy snowfall; 7–8 February: black frost, brief thaw; 21–26 February: rain, snow, heavy falls in north England. Mild dry early spring – 12–13 March: snow showers; 25 March: start of a 13-week drought; May: dry, one of the driest Mays on record; 25–31 May: north to northeasterly spell. Very cool summer – 23–24 June: end of drought, heavy thunderstorms in west England, very warm, 33.3 °C (92 °F) at Thwaite (Suffolk); 4 July: 12-hour period of rain in East Anglia after no significant falls for over 14 weeks; 20–29 July: very warm, 27–29 °C (80–85 °F). * 3 August: severe storm. Inferred depression, storm-force southwesterly gales, violent gusts in southwest and west England, and south Wales, loss of life. Average autumn temperatures – 2–6 November: wet easterly spell, floods. **1845** Cold year, conditions possibly severe enough for incipient glaciation in the Scottish Highlands; volcanic dust veil (DVI 250), Hekla (Iceland) eruption; exceptionally cool wet weather in Ireland led to a potato blight that in turn caused the Irish famine, 1846–1849, one million people died and another million emigrated. Very cold dry winter, weak midwinter westerlies – 1–15 December (1844): cold easterly spell, keen frost, –6 °C (22 °F) on 6 December; 26–31 December: slight thaw, fog, rime frost; 2 January: northerly wind, overnight snowstorm. * 25–26 January: severe storm. Inferred cyclonic situation, storm-force southwesterly gales, shipwrecks in the Channel and off East Anglia. 27–29 January: snowfall; February: very cold, frequent snowfall; 12 February: hard frost, –10 °C (14 °F) at Thwaite (Suffolk); 23–24 February: lying snow; 25 February: strong winds, rain. Very cold spring – March: northerly; 1 March: heavy snowfall; 4–6 March: snow showers; 13–17 March: very cold northeasterly spell, occasional snow, severe frost, –15 °C (5 °F) at Thwaite (Suffolk) on 14 March; 21 March: heavy snowfall; 21–23 March: thaw, floods; May: very cold. Mostly very cool wet summer – inferred volcanic dust-veil effect; poor grain harvests in Britain and potato crop failure in Ireland combined to create widespread famine and death in Ireland; June: very warm; 11–15 June: very warm east to southeasterly spell; 10 July: end of very warm conditions; 18–20 August: northwesterly, heavy rain, river floods in north England. Cool autumn – floods in north England; 2 September to early October: notable coloured sunsets observed, inferred volcanic dust veil; 17 September: stormy, southwesterly type, strong southerly winds, showers in southwest England; 3 October: heavy rain, severe floods on the Tyne, Tweed and Wear, crops swept away. **1846–1850** Volcanic dust veil (total DVI 1800), several eruptions. **1846** Warm year. Very mild winter, normal midwinter westerlies – 24 December (1845): cold, severe northerly gales, ice-covered ponds, two shipwrecks off Bideford (Devon), 40 people drowned in Cardigan Bay; January: floods; 9 February: light snowfall; late February: mild spell, 18 °C (64 °F) at Thwaite (Suffolk) on 28 February. Mild wet very early spring – 4 April: northerly winds, snow, hailstorms; 21 May: start of warm dry spell into the summer. Very warm dry summer – many people died of heat-related illnesses in England; June: anticyclonic southwesterly, very warm, one of the warmest Junes on record, 18.2 °C (65 °F); 1–18 June: very warm dry spell, 30–32 °C (86–89.5 °F) at Thwaite (Suffolk); 24 June: heavy thunderstorms, very warm, 35 °C (95 °F) in London; July: very warm, thunderstorm (5 July), 34 °C (93 °F) at Thwaite (Suffolk); August: floods in Wales. * 1 August: notable hailstorms. Easterly situation, heavy thunderstorms and violent hailstorms formed on another very warm day, 33 °C (91 °F) at Thwaite (Suffolk), glass in the Buckingham Palace picture gallery destroyed and gallery flooded, 7,000 panes of glass broken in the Houses of Parliament, and a glass arcade in Regent Street smashed beyond repair by large hailstones, many buildings severely damaged by lightning, Windsor and Ditton Parks also badly affected. 7–8 August: cyclonic easterly type, heavy thunderstorms, torrential rain, severe river floods, bridges carried away in Tees valley, river rose 4.3 m (14 ft) above its usual level at Barnard Castle (Durham), heavy thunderstorms, flash floods in west England, Frome and Avon overflowed at Bristol; 15 August: hailstorm at Camberwell (Surrey), large hail caused great damage, this event ended spell of summer storms. Very warm autumn – late September: end of very warm dry spell from late May; c.22 September to 21 November: stormy spell, severe gales. * 20–21 October: severe storm. Deep Atlantic depression (below 970 mb, possibly an ex-tropical hurricane) moved east over the British Isles, severe southwest to westerly gales affected southwest Ireland, southwest England and Channel coasts. 23–24 October and 20 November: storms, severe coastal gales, many shipwrecks. **1847** Very cold dry winter, absent midwinter westerlies replaced by an easterly flow – 1–18 December (1846): cold spell, occasional snow; 19–21 December: westerly winds, thaw; 23–24 December: snowfall; 30–31 December: southwesterly winds, thaw; 20–21 January: easterly winds, heavy snowfall; 23–24 January: thaw, rain; 1–3 February: northeasterly winds, heavy snowfall; 8–9 February: ground still snow-covered, London streets snow-filled;

26–28 February: easterly winds, snowfall. Wet late spring, average temperatures –
9–10 March: northerly winds, snow, hail showers; 1–3 April: snow showers;
13–18 April: cold easterly spell; late May: very warm. Warm dry summer – June:
ridge from Azores high extended northeast over south British Isles, 1–3 June: very
warm; 11–14 July: very warm, 32 °C (89 °F) at Thwaite (Suffolk) on 14 July; 16 July:
heavy probably thundery rain, river floods, bridges destroyed, Bodmin Moor
(Cornwall); 30 July to 2 August: very warm. Warm autumn – 16–17 September:
stormy, strong westerly winds, heavy rain. **1848** Wet year. Wet winter, average
temperatures, midwinter westerlies absent – 5–7 December (1847): stormy, severe
westerly gales, frequent rain, showers, several shipwrecks; 16 December: southerly
winds, heavy rain, showers; 19 December: heavy rain in north England, severe
flood on Wear, ships swept out of Sunderland harbour (Durham); 19–29 December:
cold easterly spell; January: very cold; 31 December to 1 January: snowfall;
2–3 January: southerly winds, thaw, snow gone; 18–19 January: lying snow;
28–29 January: snowfall; 30–31 January: thaw, snow gone; February: mild very wet.
Very mild wet spring – March: floods; 16–21 March: wet, severe floods; 30 March
to 6 April: very mild; May: very warm dry, 27–29 °C (80–84 °F) at Thwaite (Suffolk);
29 May: heavy thunderstorms, floods in northeast England. Very cool wet
summer – July: heavy thunderstorms. Cool wet autumn, floods in north England
– 12–20 October: cold northeasterly; 18 October: snowstorm. **1849** Very mild
winter, normal midwinter westerlies – 1–6 January: cold easterly, light snowfall
(5 January); 7–9 January: thaw, snow nearly gone. * 10 January: severe storm.
Depression moved east across Scotland, severe easterly gales north of centre over
north Scotland, Peterhead (Aberdeenshire) harbour defences washed away by
easterly gales/heavy seas; southwest to westerly gales over remaining parts of
British Isles, continuous rain in central England. * 24–26 January: severe floods.
Severe flooding in north Scotland, probably due to heavy rainfall, much damage
in Inverness, Loch Ness rose 4.3 m (14 ft), highest level then on record; strong
westerly winds over central England. Wet spring, average temperatures –
18–19 April: snowstorm-blizzard conditions, deep drifts; 1–8 May: cold easterly,
heavy rain, thunder (2–3 May). Cool dry summer – 7–12 July: very warm, thunderstorm,
heavy rain in Newcastle, much damage (8 July). Average autumn temperatures –
17–28 September: cool easterly, strong cold winds in northeast England
(17–18 September); 25–28 November: frost, frozen ponds; 29–30 November: thaw.

1850s

Continental, later maritime; weak to fairly normal zonal circulation (estimated
79 westerly situations on average per year); dry decade. **1850** Average winter
temperatures, very weak midwinter westerlies. * 7 December (1849): severe storm.

Inferred cyclonic situation, severe gales, six vessels lost on Gunfleet Sands off the Essex coast and 20 men drowned off the Tyne (Northumberland). * 28 December (1849): severe storm. Deep depression (below 995 mb) moved southeast over the North Sea, northwesterly to northerly gales pounded east coasts of Scotland and England, Spurn Head peninsula breached, probably due to a North Sea storm surge. January: very cold, occasional snow; 10–22 January: east to northeasterly spell, occasional snowfall. * 5–6 February: severe storm. Inferred cyclonic situation, severe to storm-force westerly gales, chimney pots removed, trees blown down. Cold spring – March: anticyclonic northwesterly; 24–29 March: very cold spell, frozen ponds, occasional snow showers. * 30 March: severe storm. Inferred cyclonic situation, easterly gales, inferred shipwrecks, 200 lives lost (drowned?), near Margate. 1–18 April: showery spell. * 18 April: notable tornado. Tornado carried off roofs, blew down chimneys and trees in Dublin, heavy thunderstorm with large hailstones also occurred in the city. Average summer temperatures/rainfall – 1–5 June: very warm easterly (west England); 15–17 July: heavy thunderstorms; late August: cool spell, snowfall over Cairngorms nearly down to Braemar, thunderstorm in central England; 22 August: morning frost in south England. Cool dry autumn. * 6 October: severe storm. Inferred depression, severe westerly gales, showers, much damage, vessels driven ashore in the Thames, heavy shipping losses at Liverpool. 17–26 November: mild wet westerly in west England; 28 November to 1 December: cold northwesterly in west England. **1851** Very mild winter, strong midwinter westerlies – 18–21 December (1850): cold spell, occasional snow, snow-covered high ground, frozen pools; heavy snowfall, 30 cm (12 in) on 19 December; January: mild wet; early part: stormy, southwesterly gales. Cold spring – May: mostly dry, ridge extended northeast over British Isles from the Canary Islands. Cool thundery summer – June: occasional rain, showers; 21 June: thunderstorm in west England; July: mostly dry; 1 and 24 July: thunderstorms in west England; 17 August: heavy thunderstorm, heavy rain in Durham. Cool dry autumn – 11–14 September: morning fogs in London. * 25 September: severe storm. Inferred cyclonic situation/storm-force gales, many shipwrecks. November: northerly; 4 November: moderate snowfall, 10 cm (4 in), tree branches broken; 16–20 November: cold spell, frozen ponds, snow showers; 22–24 November: thaw, rain; 28–29 November: renewed frost. **1852** Wet year, several floods; volcanic dust veil (DVI 550), several eruptions including Etna. Mild wet winter, very strong midwinter westerlies – 1–3 December (1851): thaw; January: very mild in north England, strawberries gathered at Tynemouth (Northumberland), apple trees in bloom at Wallsend (Northumberland); 9–10 January: light snowfall, 5 cm (2 in); 11 January: rain, snow gone; 15 January: stormy, thunderstorm, hail; 16 January: Wear in flood.

* 2 February: severe storm. Inferred cyclonic situation, westerly winds, heavy rain in north England, Bilberry reservoir embankment earth dam at Holmsforth (near Huddersfield) collapsed, flood surge released, 90 people drowned. 16–17 February: stormy, westerly gales. Dry spring, average temperatures – 21–31 May: cold northerly, heavy thunderstorms, hailstorms (31 May). Warm wet summer – July: one of the warmest Julys on record in north England and Scotland; 1–24 July: very warm, occasional thunderstorms; 5 July: heavy thundery rain, floods in northeast England; August: very wet, rainy spell continued into September and October; 11 August: stormy, high seas, English south coast; 17 August: heavy thunderstorm, torrential rain, English south coast. Very wet autumn, average temperatures – one of the wettest autumns on record. * 18 September (?): severe storm. Inferred depression, severe cyclonic gales, heavy rain, high seas in the Channel, flooding in the Thames and Severn, especially the latter where the entire valley was inundated with floating uprooted trees, crops and drowned animals; Thames bank towing path at Putney under 2m (6 ft) of water, Great Western Railway between Paddington and Hanwell (Middlesex) flooded for over 6 km (4 miles). * 26–30 October: severe storms. Inferred cyclonic situation/storm-force gales, many shipwrecks, great loss of life on northeast English coast, occasional rain in west England. November: cyclonic; one of the wettest Novembers on record; North Sea storm surge, sea floods coincided with Thames river floods, London inundated; 17–18 November: notable flood, so-called 'Duke of Wellington's Flood', occurred during one of the highest Thames floods on record, Wellington's funeral cortège disrupted by floodwaters at Maidenhead (Berkshire); Oxford described as standing in a sea of water. **1853** Mild wet winter, normal midwinter westerlies – 11 December (1852): Tyne rose to an exceptional height due to prolonged rainfall, river transformed into one large sheet of water from Hodhaugh to Newburn, flood damage on the Wear but not as bad as on the Tyne; 16–17 December: stormy night, southwesterly winds, rain, showers, new railway bridge at Haltwhistle on the Alston branch of the Newcastle & Carlisle Railway swept away due to the Tyne flood. * 25–27 December (1852): severe storms. Inferred depression, north Britain, extremely low pressure (948 mb) recorded at Culloden (Inverness) on 27 December, severe mostly southwesterly gales, much damage to property, trees blown down, severe shipping losses at Liverpool and other ports and coastal towns, lighthouse and south pier damaged at Maryport (Cumberland); Chesil Beach (Dorset) was damaged during such a storm in 1852. January: mild; 23–27 January: cold northerly, snow showers; February: North Sea storm surge; 4 February: start of cold spell, occasional snowfall, 17–19 February: hard to severe frost, –14 °C (6.5 °F) at Thwaite (Suffolk) on 19 February; 22–24 February: thaw, rain. * 26 February: severe storm. Inferred cyclonic situation,

severe westerly gales, many shipwrecks, large number of vessels ran ashore along the east coast from Northumberland to the Goodwin Sands, stormy conditions increased during following days with severe snowstorms. Very cold dry spring – 1 March: snowstorms, lying snow; 17–23 March: snow showers; 27 March: milder conditions; 20 April: snow-covered hills in west England; 22–26 April: cold northerly, severe floods (25 April); 5–17 May: cold wet north to northeasterly, lying snow (10 May); 20–27 May: warm dry north to northeasterly. Very cool wet summer. Cool autumn, average rainfall – 25 September: inferred trough, strong southerly winds, showers in west England, severe northwesterly gales affected other areas, many shipwrecks; 24 November: heavy rain, snow over high ground in west England. **1854** Dry year. Cold dry winter, normal midwinter westerlies – 16–31 December (1853): cold, frequent snowfall, keen frost, –6 °C (21 °F) in north England, temperatures continued to fall in England until 7 January; early January: cold spell continued, heavy snowfall. * 3–6 January: severe storm. Inferred depression over the Channel and/or north France, severe easterly gales, heavy snowstorm-blizzard conditions, deep drifts, hard frost, –10 °C (13 °F) at Greenwich, much damage, ice floes impeded navigation on the Thames, 50 ships driven ashore at Gorleston-on-Sea (Norfolk), including the vessel *Abraham*, which foundered with the loss of all hands only a short distance offshore; 258 vessels were wrecked or damaged and 467 people drowned in January. 7–8 January: rapid thaw; February: North Sea storm surge; 18 February: northwesterly, moderate snowfall, 10 cm (4 in), many vessels driven ashore on northwest coasts (18–19 February). Mild dry spring – 10–20 April: dry easterly. Very cool dry summer – July and August: mostly very warm, occasional showers, thunder. Very warm dry autumn – 19–24 October: storms, shipwrecks off northeast England; 22–23 October: snow showers, snow-covered high ground in west England; November: stormy, 131 vessels wrecked or damaged; 12–16 November: track of severe storm from the Mediterranean to the Black Sea reconstructed by the French meteorologist Urbain Le Verrier, following the destruction of the French fleet at Balaklava on 14 November. **1855–1858** Volcanic dust veil (total DVI 1250), several eruptions including Vesuvius and Cotopaxi (Ecuador). **1855** Very cold dry winter, very weak midwinter westerlies – heavy snowfall; ships ice-bound for 12 weeks at King's Lynn (Norfolk), crews walked along the frozen tidal Ouse to reach their vessels; 27 December (1854): snowfall, hills snow-covered in west England; January: very dry, one of the driest Januarys on record. * 1 January: severe storm. Northwesterly situation, inferred depression over the North Sea, severe west to northwesterly gales, exceptionally high tide on the northwest German coast. 17–22 January: cold snowy spell in west England. * 20 January: severe storm. Cyclonic situation, severe north to northeasterly gales affected east England, inferred shipwrecks,

28 lives lost, probably drowned off Margate. February: very cold, one of the coldest Februarys on record, −1.7 °C (28.9 °F), making it colder than February 1740; Thames would probably have been sufficiently frozen for a Frost Fair if the old London Bridge had still been in place; 1–22 February: very cold mostly easterly spell, frequent snowfall, historic cricket match played on the ice at Ely on 12 February, −17 °C (2 °F) at Cheltenham (Gloucestershire) on 17–18 February, Tyne entirely frozen above Scotswood; 24–25 February: southerly winds, thaw, rain, slippery ground probably due to a deposit of glazed frost ('black ice'). Very cold dry spring – March: cold, occasional snow showers. * May: severe storm. Inferred cyclonic situation/severe gales, shipwreck on the Manacles, Cornwall, 191 lives lost. 1–5 May: cold easterly, hard frost, −8 °C (17 °F), wintry showers (3 May); 24–26 May: mild, southerly winds. Wet summer, average temperatures – June: warm, occasional thunderstorms; 23 July: heavy thunderstorms, severe river floods in northeast England, much damage in the Tees valley (Durham), bridge carried away at Newbiggin (Northumberland). Cool autumn – 29–30 October: stormy, many shipwrecks off northeast and east English coasts; November: notable coloured twilights, inferred volcanic dust-veil effect; over 300 shipwrecks off British coasts in October and November. **1856** Dry winter, average temperatures, weak midwinter westerlies – December (1855): notable coloured twilights observed, inferred volcanic dust-veil effect; exceptionally wide and abrupt changes of temperature; 6–13 December: very cold, light snowfall, hard frost, −9 °C (16 °F) in west England (13 December); 14–17 December: mild, 6 °C (42 °F) in west England (15 December); 19–22 December: hard frost, Tweed riverbed (Berwick) almost dry for several hours, apparently due to a sudden onset of frosty conditions upstream on 19 December; −12 °C (11 °F) in west England on 22 December; 23–27 December: another sudden temperature change, mild southwesterly, occasional rain, west England; January: further temperature fluctuations; 1–9 January: mild moist spell; 10–15 January: cold spell, hard frost, −11 °C (13 °F) in west England on 13 January; 16–21 January: mild wet spell, 4 °C (39 °F) on 17 January; 27–30 January: cold, wintry showers, hard frost, −7 °C (20 °F) on 30 January. Very cold spring – 18–19 May: stormy and wet, inferred severe gales. Average summer temperatures and rainfall – late July to mid August: very warm, 11 August: 32 °C (89 °F) at Thwaite (Suffolk). Cool autumn – 27–28 September: easterly wet spell, severe river floods (28 September), Northumberland and Durham, much damage, Tyne 2.4 m (8 ft) above its usual level at Hexham (Northumberland), one of the highest floods in living memory; 2–16 October: wet spell; 17 October to 18 November: dry spell, occasional fog; November: notable coloured twilights observed to February 1857, inferred volcanic dust-veil effect; 25–26 November: snow, rain; 27–30 November: hard frost,

–7 °C (20 °F) in west England on 30 November. **1857** Dry year. Average winter temperatures, weak midwinter westerlies – December (1856): like December 1855, another notable month for an exceptionally wide range of temperatures; 1–2 December: very cold, hard frost, –11 °C (12 °F) in west England on 2 December; 3–12 December: thaw, mild, wet, west England; 3–4 December: very cold other areas, moderate snowfall, 10 cm (4 in), severe frost, –13 °C (9 °F); 5 December: thaw, wet; 7 December: very mild, 16.7 °C (62 °F) at Thwaite (Suffolk); 8 December: severe floods on Tyne, Wear and Tees due to rapid frost melt-thaw; 25–29 December: very cold, hills lightly snow-covered; 28 December: hard frost, –11 °C (12.5 °F) at Thwaite (Suffolk); 30–31 December: westerly, thaw, very mild, 6.7 °C (44 °F) at Cheltenham (Gloucestershire); 3 January: stormy, strong southwesterly winds, heavy rain; 5–6 January: very cold, keen frost, –3.3 °C (26 °F) at Cheltenham, snowfall; 15–20 January: mild, wet, brief snowfall in west England (20 January); 23–25 January: rain, sleet, snow; 29–31 January: hard frost, –11 °C (12 °F) at Cheltenham, snowfall; 2–5 February: snowfall; 6–7 February: mild southwesterly, thaw, 8.3 °C (47 °F) at Cheltenham; 10–28 February: mostly mild, occasional frosty interludes. Average spring temperatures – 8–9 March: westerly, light snow showers; 22 March: easterly, lying snow; 24–30 April: cold southeasterly, sleet, snow (26 April); 1–9 May: dry northeasterly; 25–26 May: stormy, southerly, heavy showers. Very warm summer – frequently 32 °C (90 °F) at Thwaite (Suffolk), many heat-related deaths; June: very warm, occasional thunderstorms, showers; July: warm, occasional showers; 6–14 August: frequent showers, thunderstorms; 15–30 August: warm dry. Very warm autumn – September: warm frequent showers, thunderstorm; 2–3 November: stormy, wet. **1858** Dry year. Mild dry winter, positive pressure anomaly over the British Isles, normal midwinter westerlies – December (1857): mild; February: drought in mainland Europe: Bodensee at one of its lowest water levels on record; 1–2 February: snow showers; 14 February: snowfall; late February: cold easterly. Mostly cold late spring – 1–12 March: cold mainly easterly; heavy snowfall, deep drifts (1–2 March); gales, much damage (8 March); heavy snowfall (10 March), hard frost, –9 °C (16 °F) at Cheltenham, Gloucestershire (11 March); late March: renewed mild spell; 7–8 and 12 April: snow, sleet and rain. Warm dry summer – many heat-related deaths; 1 June to late September: very warm, heavy thunderstorms; 1–16 June: warm; very warm, 33 °C (92 °F) at Thwaite (Suffolk) on 16 June; 25 July: gales, fruit blown off trees. Dry autumn, average temperatures – 20 October: stormy, shipwrecks off Great Yarmouth, lives lost; 24–25 November: stormy, cold easterly. **1859** Dry year. Very mild dry winter, strong midwinter westerlies – December (1858): mild; January: mild; 23 January: stormy, gales, rain in southwest and west England; 30 January: snowstorm. Mild very early spring – 7–8 March: hail, snow showers;

30 March: snowfall; 16–17 April: snow showers. Very warm summer – occasional thunderstorms, many heat-related deaths; July: mostly very warm, Azores high extended northeast over British Isles; 16–18 July: 31–33 °C (88–92 °F); August: July high pressure moved a little south, light westerly flow over British Isles. Cool wet autumn – 22 October: snow shower, hard frost, –6.7 °C (20 °F) at Cheltenham. * 25–26 October: severe storm, 'Royal Charter storm'. Depression (below 990 mb) on 25 October moved northeast from the Southwest Approaches over England and Wales, early on 26 October severe gale- to hurricane-force northeast to northerly winds over the Irish Sea caused the wreck of the Royal Charter off the north coast of Anglesey with the loss of 500 lives; another ship, the Great Eastern, narrowly escaped being destroyed at Holyhead, and Stephenson's viaduct at Penmaenmawr was swept away; on the southern flank of the depression strong to gale-force westerly winds with heavy rain occurred over south England, chain pier at Brighton destroyed, 195 shipwrecks off British coasts. These and other related disasters led to the introduction of gale warnings by the newly formed British Meteorological Office. * 1 November: severe storm. Inferred depression, severe gales, heavy rain, widespread damage, lives lost in London, shipwrecks off East Anglia and in the Thames. 30 November: lying snow.

1860s

Maritime and anticyclonic; normal zonal flow (98 westerly situations on average per year). **1860–1862** Volcanic dust veils (total DVI 1500), several eruptions including Iceland, Vesuvius and Molucca Islands. **1860** A year without a summer; conditions possibly severe enough for incipient glaciation in the Scottish Highlands. Very cold wet winter, normal midwinter westerlies – December (1859): heavy snowfall; 4 December: rain, snow; 19 December: severe frost, –17 °C (2 °F) at Thwaite (Suffolk); 20–21 December: stormy, less cold, snow, rain; January: wet; 6 February: snow showers; 11–13 February: heavy snowfall, deep drifts, hard frost, –6.7 °C (20 °F) at Cheltenham (13 February); unsettled cyclonic conditions set in during late winter; late February: gales caused much damage. * 27–28 February: severe storm. Inferred depression, severe to storm-force westerly gales, much damage in London, boats capsized in the Thames, two men drowned after being blown into the Deptford canal, shipwrecks off Portsmouth (Hampshire) and St David's Head (Pembroke). Cold wet late spring – further damaging gales; 8 and 10 March: light snowfall. * 18 April: severe storm. Inferred cyclonic situation/storm-force gales, storm lasted 70 hours. 24 April: stormy spell lasted 66 hours, further gales followed; 12 May: heavy rain and floods. * 26–28 May: severe storm. Inferred deep depression, one of the worst and longest-lasting storms on record (90 hours), storm-force westerly gales, many trees blown down, many shipwrecks, great loss of life including 200 Great Yarmouth and Lowestoft fishermen, snowstorm-blizzard conditions in London, heavy snowfall over the north Pennines, roads blocked, drifts over 1 m (4 ft) on 28 May. Very cool wet summer – cyclonic and northwesterly situations, inferred volcanic dust-veil effect; June: cyclonic, very cool wet, one of the coldest wettest Junes on record; heavy thunderstorms; July: northwesterly; August: cyclonic westerly; 16–19 August: stormy; storm-force westerly winds at Weston Super Mare (Somerset) on 18 August. Very cool autumn – 17 November: snowfall; 25–30 November: wet spell.

1861 Strong zonal flow (108 westerly days); volcanic dust veil (DVI 800), Makjan (Moluccas) eruption. Cold winter, weak midwinter westerlies – 1–8 December (1860): wet spell, lake embankments breached in London; 15–31 December: severe frost, occasional snow, very severe frost, –20 °C (–4 °F) at Cheltenham (25 December); 30 December: rain, thaw, fog in west England; January: renewed cold, severe frost, occasional snow; 6–8 January: snowfall, locally heavy, 30 cm (12 in) in Norfolk; 8 January: very severe frost, –18 °C (–1 °F) at Thwaite (Suffolk); 9–10 January: severe frost at Thwaite (Suffolk); 14–15 January: easterly situation, snowfall in west England and Wales; 20–31 January: mild, 7 °C (45 °F) at Cheltenham (25 January); 6–7 February: westerly/cyclonic situations, stormy, heavy rain, snowfall.
* 9 February: severe storm. Easterly situation, inferred depression over the Channel and/or north France, northeasterly gales, shipwrecks off Hartlepool (Durham), after five launches Whitby (Yorkshire) lifeboat capsized on the sixth attempt, 12 of the 13-man crew drowned. * 21 February: severe storm. Cyclonic southwesterly situation, intense depression (below 980 mb) moved northeast over the British Isles, severe to storm-force mostly southwesterly gales, extensive damage, including a wing of the Crystal Palace in London, Chichester (West Sussex) cathedral spire blown down, 'ancestral trees' uprooted in Warwickshire and Gloucestershire. Dry early spring, average temperatures – 11–12 March: stormy, rain, heavy snowfall; 17 March: stormy, rain, snow showers; 21–22 March: cyclonic westerly situation, heavy snowfall; April: cold; 27 April: anticyclonic northeasterly situation, rain, sleet, snow. * 23 May: severe storm. Westerly situation, inferred severe to storm-force southwesterly gales, over 140 shipwrecks. Average summer temperatures/rainfall – August: very warm dry, 32 °C (90 °F) at Thwaite (Suffolk) on 12 August. Average autumn temperatures – September: mostly dry very warm; October: very warm dry. * 2 November: severe storm. Inferred depression over the North Sea, severe to storm-force northerly gales, several shipwrecks off east England, snow over high ground in west England. 9–13 November: cyclonic spell, gales, heavy rain, vessels damaged on the Thames, shipwrecks off East Anglia (10 November); 14–18 November: cold northerly spell, heavy snowfall, snow showers (16–17 November), hard frost, –9 °C (16 °F) at

Cheltenham on 18 November; 20–30 November: mild, 9.4 °C (49 °F) at Cheltenham on 30 November. **1862** Strong zonal flow (106 westerly days). Mild dry winter, fairly weak midwinter westerlies – 14 January: wet, snow on hills in west England; 19 January: southerly situation, heavy snowfall; 21 January: easterly situation, snowfall in west England; 22 January: cyclonic situation, lying snow; 24 January: cyclonic situation, storm, heavy rain; 7–9 February: anticyclonic situation, snowfall, hard frost, –9.4 °C (15 °F) at Cheltenham; 19–20 February: southerly situation, stormy, rain, showers. Very mild wet spring – March: southerly; 5 March: westerly situation, snow, rain; 17 March: cyclonic situation, snow, rain; 21 March: anticyclonic northerly situation, heavy snowfall; April: westerly; May: southerly; 6 May: southeasterly situation, very warm, 29 °C (84 °F), warmest day of the year at Thwaite (Suffolk). Very cool summer – June: cool wet. Very cool autumn. * 19 October: severe storm. Depression over the British Isles, severe westerly gales, widespread damage, severe floods in London, many vessels damaged in the Thames, shipwrecks off south and east English coasts. 26 November: lying snow. **1863** Strong zonal flow (115 westerly days). Very mild winter – 1–4 December (1862): southeasterly situation, inferred severe gales, scouring tides, major shift of east coastal sand dunes landwards, remains of the submerged village of Eccles (Norfolk) temporarily exposed. * 18–20 December (1862): severe storm. Westerly/northwesterly/northerly situations, severe northwesterly gales, damage both on land and at sea, shipwrecks off Liverpool and in the North Sea, over 50 lives lost. * 26–27 December (1862): severe storm. Depression over southern Norway, northwesterly gales, locally severe, pounded exposed Scottish and English east coasts, exceptional scouring tides along northeast Norfolk coast, sand dunes severely damaged and breached, remains of the submerged village of Eccles again temporarily exposed. Strong midwinter westerlies; January: frequent heavy snowfall; 23 January: cyclonic westerly, stormy; 1, 3 and 8 February: heavy snowfall. Mild dry early spring – 7–11 March: heavy snowfall; 6–9 April: cyclonic westerly spell, 7 April: heavy snowfall. Cool summer – June: very warm, showery; July and August: very warm dry. Average autumn temperatures. * 23 September: heavy rainfall. Depression over the British Isles, heavy rainfall, 60 mm (2.4 in) recorded in two hours at Edinburgh. **1864** Dry year; normal zonal flow (97 westerly situations). Dry winter, average temperatures, weak midwinter westerlies. * 1–3 December (1863): severe storm. Cyclonic situation, severe to storm-force gales pounded England and northwest France, hardly a house undamaged in Norwich, over 140 drowned off the Norfolk coast. Late December (1863): frequent heavy snowfall mainly in north England and Scotland; January: further heavy snowfall; 8–11 February: lying snow; 16 February: cyclonic westerly, snow showers, lying snow; 18–23 February: anticyclonic easterly situations, snow showers, lying snow. Mild spring – March: Dale Dyke earth embankment reservoir above Sheffield collapsed, flood surged into the city, 250 people drowned, much damage; 7–9 March: heavy snowfall; 10–11 March: cyclonic westerly situation, snowstorms; 26–30 March: heavy snowfall; 1–5 April: snowfall; 14–20 May: very warm anticyclonic spell: 16 May: heavy thunderstorm, torrential rain, local streams flooded in southwest Northumberland; 18 May: 27 °C (80 °F) at Thwaite (Suffolk); 20 May: heavy thunderstorm. Very cool dry summer – 4 July to 21 August: dry spell, very warm at times, 27 °C (81 °F) at Thwaite (Suffolk) on 20–21 July; 5 August: very warm anticyclonic westerly situation, 30 °C (86 °F) at Thwaite (Suffolk). Average autumn temperatures. **1865** Weak zonal flow (67 westerly situations). Cold winter, normal midwinter westerlies – late December (1864): cold; 16–19 December: easterly spell, heavy snowfall, 15–30 cm (6–12 in); 31 December: heavy snowfall in northeast Scotland; 2 January: snowfall; 25–31 January: heavy snowfall, 20–25 cm (8–10 in), 2.4–4.6 m (8–15 ft) drifts; February: frost, snow continued; 12–13 February: moderate snowfall, 7.5 cm (3 in) in southwest England; 15 February: hard frost, –12 °C (11 °F) at Thwaite (Suffolk); 16–17 February: heavy snowfall, 20 cm (8 in); 20 February: heavy snowfall, 90 cm (36 in), 3 m (10 ft) drifts, roads blocked in northeast Scotland. Mild spring – March: northerly situation; 22–27 March: heavy snowfall, snowstorms; April: very mild dry, one of the warmest Aprils on record, 10.6 °C (51 °F) (April 2007 warmest); 27 April: 24 °C (75 °F) at Thwaite (Suffolk); May: very warm dry; 22–23 May: 27 °C (80 °F) at Thwaite (Suffolk). Warm wet summer – June: very warm dry; 23 June: 29 °C (84.5 °F) at Thwaite (Suffolk); July: very warm, frequent heavy thunderstorms; August: sultry, frequent heavy thunderstorms; 27 August: start of dry spell. Very warm autumn – September to early October: very warm dry spell, no rain recorded in east England for six weeks; 8 October: heavy thunderstorms followed by unsettled spell with heavy rain to end of month. * 25 October: severe storm. Cyclonic situation, inferred depression over the British Isles, cyclonic storm-force gales, trees blown down. * 22 November: severe storm. Cyclonic situation, deep depression over the British Isles, extremely low pressure, 945 mb recorded at Dolgellau (Merioneth), inferred severe gales, buildings damaged in London, trees blown down, boats swamped in the Thames, shipwrecks off southwest England and south Wales. **1866** Strong zonal flow (105 westerly situations). Very mild wet winter, strong midwinter westerlies – 27 December (1865): renewed unsettled spell; 29–31 December: heavy snowfall in Scotland. * 31 December (1865): severe storm. Cyclonic westerly situation, deep depression (945 mb) moved northeast over the northern Hebrides, severe gales, widespread thunderstorms. * 10–11 January: notable snowstorm-blizzard conditions. Westerly situation, very dense heavy snowfall, 20–38 cm (8–15 in), snowstorm-blizzard conditions, 4.5 m

(15 ft) drifts, transport disrupted, widespread damage to trees and telegraph poles, great loss of life on coasts, many sheep buried in snow. Late February: occasional heavy snowfall. Cold dry spring – early March: cold with frost, lying snow (2 March); 6–9 March: snowfall, very heavy in Scotland, 100 cm (40 in) in Perthshire; 13 March: lying snow; 6 April: heavy snowfall, 15 cm (6 in) in southwest Scotland; May: cool showery; 1 May: snow over Yorkshire Wolds. Average summer temperatures/ rainfall – June and July: very warm, occasional heavy thunderstorms. Warm wet autumn – November: stormy, heavy rainfall, severe river floods affected Horsey and Hickling (Norfolk). **1867** Fairly normal zonal flow (80 westerly situations). Variable wet snowy winter, very weak midwinter westerlies – 30–31 December (1866); heavy snowfall, deep drifts, roads blocked; January: mostly very cold, heavy snowfall; 1–2 January: cyclonic north/northeasterly situation, heavy snowfall, 20 cm (8 in), snowstorm, 6 m (20 ft) drifts, railways dislocated, severe frost, −12 °C (10 °F) at Thwaite (Suffolk) on 2 January; 10 January: cyclonic northerly situation, heavy snowfall, roads and railways blocked, Dover, Deal and Brighton cut off; 12 January: northerly situation, snowstorm in northwest England and southeast Scotland; 14 January: severe frost, −13 °C (8 °F) at Thwaite (Suffolk); 15–16 January: anticyclonic north/northeasterly situation, heavy snowfall, 23 cm (9 in), 1–2.5 m (3–8 ft) drifts; 22–23 January: southwesterly situation, heavy snowfall, 75 cm (30 in), 6 m (20 ft) drifts in eastern Scotland, railways blocked; 23–24 January: thaw; February: mild. Cold wet spring – 4–20 March: easterly spell; 8 and 11 March: snowstorms, lying snow; 12–13 March: snowstorms; 18–20 March: heavy snowfall, 30 cm (12 in), snowstorms; 22 March: snowfall to 1000 h, lying snow; 23–26 March: milder; May: warm early and late, but third week cold with much snow. Unsettled summer, average temperatures and rainfall. * 26 July: heavy rainfall. Northeasterly situation, heavy rainfall, 93.2 mm (3.67 in) recorded at Greenwich Observatory, largest 24-hour total on record in England. 19–20 August: cyclonic situation, very warm conditions followed by heavy thunderstorms. Cool dry autumn. **1868–** Volcanic dust veil (total DVI 1000), Mauna Loa, Vesuvius, Etna, Iceland, **1870** Mexico and Salvador eruptions. **1868** Warm dry year; strong zonal flow (109 westerly situations). Mild winter, normal midwinter westerlies – 6–8 December (1867): brief northerly spell, snow and rain; 22 January: storm in Wales, many vessels damaged off coast; 23 January: light snowfall. * 24–25 January: severe storm. Cyclonic westerly situation, severe southwesterly gales affected Scotland and north England, and exposed coasts of Ireland, Wales and southwest England, stone buildings in Edinburgh blown down by unusually strong winds possibly due to mountain lee wave effect downwind of the Southern Uplands, severe floods in north England. Very mild spring – 3 March: heavy snowfall; 8 March: heavy rain, heavy snowfall in north England and Scotland; May: southwesterly;

2 May to 21 September: mostly very warm; 19 May: southeasterly situation, 32 °C (90 °F) at Tonbridge (Kent), earliest known date for this high temperature in England. Very warm dry summer – over 30 °C (86 °F) on many days, many people died from heat-related illnesses; 13–30 June: very warm spell; July: very warm, 5–18 July: very warm spell, 34 °C (94 °F) at Thwaite (Suffolk) on 16 July; 22 July: anticyclonic situation, 38.1 °C (100.5 °F) at Tonbridge (Kent), highest temperature on record in the British Isles (cf. 10 August 2003: 38.1 °C/100.6 °F at Kew); 21 July to 5 August: very warm spell, 2 August: 36.7 °C (98 °F); 22 August: gales, shipwrecks on the Mersey and off southwest England. Cold autumn – 21 September: end of very warm dry spell from 2 May; 5–7 November: northwest/northerly situations, heavy snowfall. **1869** Normal zonal flow (93 westerly situations). Very mild wet winter, fairly weak midwinter westerlies – December (1868): southwesterly; very mild wet, notable coloured sunsets observed, inferred volcanic dust-veil effect; 2 January: heavy snowfall in north England; February: very mild, one of the mildest Februarys on record; 1 February: severe gales; 4–12 February: westerly spell; 6 February: gales in the Channel, many vessels damaged; 8 February: snow-melt, heavy rain in northeast England, severe flood on the Tyne and tributaries, Newcastle Quayside inundated; 10 February: heavy snowfall in northeast England; 27–28 February: northwesterly situation, heavy snowfall, 45 cm (18 in) at Portree (Isle of Skye). Cold wet spring – 11–14 March: mainly northeasterly situation, snowfall; 19 March: cyclonic situation, Cornish coast strewn with wreckage; 26–29 March: northerly turning easterly situation, heavy snowfall, 15–18 cm (6–7 in); 5–15 April: very warm spell; 12 April: 25 °C (77 °F) at Thwaite (Suffolk). Dry summer, average temperatures. * 15–16 June: severe storm. Cyclonic/anticyclonic northerly situations, depression (below 995 mb) moved east-southeast over north England, severe northeasterly gales occurred in its rear, east coast of Scotland and northeast coast of England badly affected, many shipwrecks, great loss of life. July: very warm dry; mid July to late September: notable coloured sunsets observed, inferred volcanic dust-veil effect; 23–28 August: very warm spell, maximum 32.8 °C (91 °F). * 28–29 August: notable temperature fall. Very large and rapid drop of temperature associated with an anticyclonic northeasterly situation: 28 August: 33 °C (91 °F); 29 August: 11 °C (52 °F) recorded at Garendon (Leicestershire). Warm autumn – early October: very warm dry; 26–30 October: cold northerly spell; 27–28 October: heavy snowfall; 29 November: light snowfall, 5 cm (2 in).

1870s

Cyclonic; normal zonal flow (87 westerly situations on average per year). **1870** Fairly dry continental year; weak zonal flow (69 westerly situations). Cold winter, weak midwinter westerlies – early December (1869): snow, hard frost, –9 °C (16 °F) at Thwaite (Suffolk) on 3 December; 6–7 December: severe gales; 16–17 December: cyclonic westerly situations, severe gales, heavy rain, thunderstorm; 25–27 December: heavy snowfall, 13–25 cm (5–10 in), 4 m (13 ft) drifts; 29 December: hard frost, –11 °C (13 °F) at Thwaite (Suffolk); January: frequent snowfall; 27 January: severe gales in north England; early February: frequent snowfall; mid February: severe easterly gales in a broad continental flow extending from Denmark to northwest Spain; 25–26 February: heavy snowfall, 25 cm (10 in) in Scotland. Mild dry spring – 12–13 March: heavy snowfall, 20–25 cm (8–10 in); 28 March: snow showers. Very warm dry summer, occasional heavy thunderstorms – June: very warm dry; 16 June: heavy thunderstorm, large hail in north Dorset; July: very warm dry; 9 July: heavy thunderstorm in Yorkshire. Cool autumn. * 12 October: severe storm. Cyclonic situation, storm-force gales, many shipwrecks. 19 October: cyclonic southwesterly situation, tornado damage in Devon and Somerset; 13 November: cyclonic northwesterly situation, heavy rain, severe floods at Tyne Dock (Northumberland), 100 families evacuated from inundated houses. **1871** Weak zonal flow (77 westerly situations). Very cold winter, one of the most severe winter freezing events of the Baltic on record, very weak midwinter westerlies – 8–9 December (1870): snowfall; 9 December: severe floods at Tyne Dock (Northumberland), heavy snow and rain had caused a large accumulation of snow and water upriver and a sudden thaw produced a rapid and powerful surge of surface water; 21–31 December: anticyclonic easterly situations; 21–23 December: heavy snowfall, blizzards, severe frost, –13 °C (8 °F) at Malton (Yorkshire); 24 December: heavy snowfall, severe frost, upper reaches of Tyne frozen, skating at Newcastle; 25 December: severe frost, –16 °C (3 °F) at Thwaite (Suffolk); 26 December: heavy snowfall, serious railway accident at Hatfield (Hertfordshire), eight killed; 27–31 December: severe frost, heavy snowfall, 20 cm (8 in); January: very cold occasional snow; 1–2 January: lying snow, hard frost, –10 °C (14 °F) at Thwaite (Suffolk), heavy snowfall, 55 cm (22 in) in Perthshire, branches broken off trees; 9 January: heavy snowfall, 30 cm (12 in); 12 and 21 January: heavy snowfall, 20 cm (8 in) in Wales; 24–25 January: heavy snowfall; 29 January: lying snow; February: mainly mild; 5 February: thaw, end of very cold spell. * 10 February: severe storm. Cyclonic situation/storm-force gales, many shipwrecks off English east coast. Very mild early spring – 11 March: lying snow; 14–16 March: heavy snowfall, 30 cm (12 in); 18–27 March: very mild, 17–19 °C (63–66.5 °F) at Thwaite (Suffolk); 12–29 April: cyclonic spell; 19 April: thunderstorm with heavy rain at Durham, river floods in north England. Unsettled summer, average temperatures and rainfall – 6–14 August: very warm anticyclonic spell, 31 °C (88 °F) at Thwaite (Suffolk) on 13 August. Very cool autumn

– 1–16 September: very warm spell, 26 °C (79 °F) at Thwaite (Suffolk) on
1 September; heavy thunderstorm (6 September); 21–22 September: stormy;
November: cold, continuous frost, –6 °C (22 °F) at Thwaite (Suffolk) on
14 November; 17–30 November: occasional heavy snowfall, 15 cm (6 in). **1872** One
of the wettest years on record; strong zonal flow (101 westerly situations). Very
mild wet winter, normal midwinter westerlies – 1–12 December (1871): cold spell,
severe frost, –14 °C (7 °F) at Thwaite (Suffolk) on 8 December; 13–31 December:
mild; January: mild wet; 6 January: heavy thunderstorm, Thwaite (Suffolk);
19 January: inferred deep depression over north Britain, extremely low pressure
(947 mb) at Sumburgh (Shetland). * 23–26 January: severe storms. Cyclonic
situation, very low pressures recorded, widespread severe gales, shipping
damaged in the Thames (24 January). February: very mild; 18–19 February:
cyclonic westerly situation, gales; 24 February: cyclonic southerly situation, heavy
rain, swollen rivers in north England. Wet very early spring, average temperatures
– 19–22 March: north/northeasterly situations, heavy snowfall, 20 cm (8 in);
28 March: stormy, frequent thunderstorms; May: warm; occasional heavy
showers, thunderstorms. Warm wet summer – June: very warm; 29 °C (84 °F) at
Thwaite (Suffolk) on 17 June; 18 June: southerly situation, heavy thunderstorm,
rain, floods in north England; 27–28 June: thunderstorms; July: very warm;
29–32 °C (85–89 °F) at Thwaite (Suffolk) on 5, 21, 25 and 26 July; frequent heavy
rain, thunder. Wet autumn, average temperatures – 1–13 September: very warm
humid; 14 September: onset of cool wet spell; 21 September: northwesterly
situation, brief snowfall; 23 September: cyclonic situation, slight frost, –2 °C
(29 °F) in London, earliest known date for this low temperature; October: very
wet; 21 October: cyclonic situation, 27-hour rainy period; November: very wet;
12–16 November: east-northeasterly spell, snowstorms (13 November).
1873 Normal zonal flow (94 westerly situations). Wet winter, average temperatures,
fairly strong midwinter westerlies – December (1872): mild stormy.
* 8–9 December (1872): severe storm. Westerly cyclonic situations, severe to
storm-force gales, snowstorms (8 December), heavy rain, buildings damaged,
including Oxford colleges, houses blown down in London, many barges sunk in
the Thames, trees uprooted. 16–17 December (1872): cyclonic situation,
snowstorms; 1–18 January: mild stormy; 19 January: start of cold spell; 30 January
to 2 February: easterly spell, heavy snowfall, 15–30 cm (6–12 in), Dartmoor cut off;
23–25 February: heavy snowfall, 15–18 cm (6–7 in) in Cumbria. Cold spring –
March: mostly mild dry; 1 and 16 March: heavy snowfall. Showery summer,
average temperatures – July: very warm dry; 33 °C (91 °F) at Thwaite (Suffolk) on
23 July; August: very warm dry. Very cool dry autumn. **1874** Strong zonal flow
(111 westerly situations). Very mild dry winter, very strong midwinter westerlies –

4 December (1873): heavy snowfall, 15 cm (6 in) in Kent. * 7–13 December (1873): notable fog. Anticyclonic situation, hard frosts and dense fogs, thick smoke fog (smog) formed in London and persisted throughout the week of the annual Cattle Show, great inconvenience caused, followed by a 40 per cent increase in the death rate due to respiratory diseases. * 16 December (1873): severe storm. Westerly situation, storm-force winds in north England, many buildings severely damaged, ten people killed. January: mild dry. Mild dry early spring – March: North Sea storm surge; 1–2 March: heavy snowfall, roads blocked; 9 March: heavy snowfall, 30 cm (12 in) in west Scotland; 24–25 March: heavy snowfall, 18 cm (7 in). Dry summer, average temperatures – July and August: very warm dry; 20 July: 33 °C (92 °F) at Thwaite (Suffolk); many deaths due to heat-related illnesses in July. Warm wet autumn – October: North Sea storm surge; 20–24 October: stormy; 11 November: anticyclonic northerly, heavy snowfall; 29 November to 11 December: stormy. **1875** Continental easterly year; decline in zonal flow, fairly normal zonal flow (81 westerly situations); notable volcanic dust veil (DVI 1000), Iceland eruption. Cold wet winter, normal midwinter westerlies – December (1874): very cold, occasional heavy snowfall, severe frost, –14.5 °C (6 °F) at Thwaite (Suffolk) on 30 December; January: very mild wet; 1 January: southerly, severe rime frost, –13 °C (8 °F) at Thwaite (Suffolk); 2 January: westerly, thaw; 5 January: westerly situation, fresh ice flowed down the Tyne; 21 January: heavy snowfall, large drifts; February: frequent frost; 20–25 February: heavy snowfall, large drifts. Mild dry spring – March: North Sea storm surge; April: haze observed up to great heights, inferred volcanic dust-veil effect. Wet summer, average temperatures – July: wet; 7 August to 20 September: very warm dry. Warm wet autumn. * 26 September: severe storm. Cyclonic southwesterly situation, storm-force gales in north England, severe damage, shipwrecks in the Mersey. October: very wet, floods; November: very wet, floods; 9–14 November: cyclonic spell. * 14 November: severe storm. Cyclonic situation, depression over the British Isles, storm-force cyclonic gales affected south England, heavy rain in north England, severe floods. **1876** Weak zonal flow (75 westerly situations). Average winter temperatures/rainfall, normal midwinter westerlies – December (1875): frost and snow to 18 December; 1–6 December: mostly northeasterly situations, occasional heavy snowfall, 15–20 cm (6–8 in); 21 January: snowstorm-blizzard conditions, two trains collided near Peterborough (Northamptonshire), 14 people killed; 13 and 24–25 February: heavy snowfall, 20–30 cm (8–12 in); late February: very mild. Very cold wet spring – 8–12 March: heavy snowfall, 9 March: inferred depression over north Scotland, extremely low pressure (946 mb) recorded at Wick; 17–22 March: heavy snowfall, 15 cm (6 in) in Scotland, deep drifts, railways blocked; 10–14 April: cyclonic and northerly situations, heavy snowfall, locally 60 cm (24 in), deep drifts

over high ground; May: cold dry. Very warm dry summer, deaths from heatstroke – 20 June to 21 August: very warm dry, 32 °C (90 °F) on 14 August; 31 August: gales, Channel crossings delayed. Warm wet autumn – September: very wet; 28 September: waterspout off Isle of Wight; October: very warm; 14 October: tornado, property damaged in Nantwich (Cheshire); November: mild wet.

1877 Increase in zonal flow, strong (115 westerly situations); wettest year in a series of nine consecutive wet years, 1875–1883. Very mild wet winter, normal midwinter westerlies – December (1876): mild wet; 22–26 December: heavy snowfall.
* 30 December (1876) to 1 January: severe storm. Cyclonic situation, gales affected southwest England, strong winds and floods in London, heavy snowfall in the Scottish Highlands. January: stormy, very mild wet, floods; North Sea storm surge; 6 January: severe gales, heavy seas, much damage along English south coast. * 30 January: severe storm. Cyclonic northwesterly situation, severe northwesterly gales, many fishing boats lost in the North Sea, over 100 seamen drowned. 10 February: heavy snowfall, 15 cm (6 in) in the Scottish Highlands; 18 February: end of prolonged mild wet spell; 28 February: keen frost, –6 °C (22 °F) in Thwaite (Suffolk). Very cold wet spring – March: cold, stormy; April: cold; 11 April: heavy snow in Scotland. Wet summer, average temperatures – June: very warm dry, Azores high extended over much of Europe; July and August: showery with thunder. Cool wet autumn – October: North Sea storm surge. * 14–15 October: severe storm. Cyclonic southwest to westerly situation, inferred storm-force southwesterly gales, much damage both on land and at sea, many trees and telegraph poles blown down. November: mild mainly wet; 11 November: cyclonic southerly situation, extremely low pressure (940 mb) at Monach Lighthouse (Outer Hebrides), inferred deep depression over northwest Scotland. * 24–25 November: severe storm. Cyclonic/northwesterly situations, storm-force gales pounded English southeast coast, many shipwrecks, several vessels ran aground on the Goodwin Sands. **1878–1881** Notable volcanic dust veil (total DVI 1250), several eruptions including Cotopaxi (Ecuador). **1878** Decline in zonal flow, weak (69 westerly situations). Very mild winter, normal midwinter westerlies. Mild wet early spring. * 24 March: severe storm. Northerly situation, small depression (possibly a polar low) moved south along the east coast from north of Scotland, line squalls with severe northwesterly to northerly gales moved rapidly south over the country, one of these intense wind systems caused a major naval disaster: HM training ship *Eurydice*, caught unawares with ports open, capsized off the Isle of Wight with the loss of all hands (a fine sunny day had suddenly changed unexpectedly into wintry conditions). 24–25, 28 March: heavy snowfall in southwest England; May: mild wet, severe floods (7–8 May). Warm wet summer – 21 June to 22 July: very warm mostly dry spell, thunderstorms, hail, flash floods

on 16, 23 and 30 June. Cool wet autumn – October: warm; 24 October: severe tornado struck Walmer, near Deal (Kent), width 140–210 m (450–700 ft), everything destroyed along its track over 1.6 km (1 mile); November: very wet; 12–17 November: cyclonic northerly situations. * 12 November: severe storm. Cyclonic northerly situation, inferred storm-force gales, severe snowstorm, heavy snowfall, 40 cm (16 in) over north England and Scotland, trees blown down. 15 November: cyclonic northerly situation, severe floods in Norwich, combined effect of rapid snow-melt, heavy rain, gales and high tides, hundreds of city inhabitants forced to flee in boats, several lives lost. **1879** A year without a summer – very cold wet year, one of the coldest years on record; conditions possibly severe enough for incipient glaciation in the Scottish Highlands; fairly normal zonal flow (81 westerly situations). Very cold wet winter, absent midwinter westerlies replaced by an easterly flow – severe spell, comparable to the 1690s, comprising weeks of sub-freezing temperatures in December (1878) and January; December (1878): very cold dry; 7–8 December: heavy snowfall, 30 cm (12 in), severe snowstorm in northeast England, trees damaged; 12–14 December: heavy snowfall, 15 cm (6 in) in Devon; heavy snow on 15, 17 and 25 December: hard frost, –10 °C (13.5 °F) at Thwaite (Suffolk); January: very cold; 1–2 January: heavy snowfall; 12 January: hard frost, –7 °C (19.5 °F) at Thwaite (Suffolk); 7 February: end of very cold spell. Very cold late spring – 12–13 March: heavy snowfall, 15 cm (6 in); 11–12 April: heavy snowfall, 15 cm (6 in) in Scotland; May: cold, northeast flow over south Britain between high over east Atlantic and low over southeast Europe; 27 May: thundery rain, cyclonic northerly situation with a depression over the Channel, start of a wet spell. Very cool wet summer, one of the coldest wettest summers on record – inferred volcanic dust-veil effect; June: very wet, one of the wettest Junes on record; 21 July: severe flooding; August: stormy. * 3 August: severe storm. Cyclonic easterly situation, heavy thunderstorms, large hailstones, roofs smashed in London, whirlwind or tornado, hail, heavy rain, floods in east England. Very cool dry autumn – 24 September: severe floods in east England; 3 October: start of mostly dry spell to end of year; 13 November: start of cold spell; 20–21 November: heavy snowfall, 20 cm (8 in) in south and west England.

1880s

Continental; normal zonal flow (85 westerly situations on average per year). **1880** Weak zonal flow (75 westerly situations); wet over England but dry over Scotland. * Very cold winter. Fairly weak midwinter westerlies; severe conditions extended across France, Switzerland and Italy to north Africa, heavy snow in Paris, frozen rivers in France, Zuider Zee frozen, Bodensee partly frozen.

December (1879): anticyclonic southwesterly type; initially very cold, less severe later; 2 December: severe frost, −13 °C (9 °F) at Thwaite (Suffolk); 4 December: anticyclonic situation, very severe frost, −30.5 °C (−23 °F) unofficial minimum record at Blackadder (Berwickshire), people froze to death, many trees killed; 7 December: severe frost, −15 °C (5 °F) at Thwaite (Suffolk). * 28 December (1879): severe storm, Tay Bridge disaster. Deep depression (below 975 mb) moved northeast late on 28 December along the northwest coast of Scotland, severe west to southwesterly gales south of the centre, trees blown down, buildings damaged, newly opened railway bridge over the Firth of Tay collapsed, train crossing the bridge at the time blown into the Firth, 75 people drowned. January: dry, anticyclonic; one of the driest Januarys on record; severe frosts, mostly dry in east England; February: mostly very mild in east England. Dry early spring, average temperatures – March: mostly very mild; late May: end of drought in east England; 26 May: 31 °C (87 °F) in London. Wet summer, average temperatures – August: very warm dry, easterly spell in east England. Cool wet autumn – 11 September: end of very warm spell in east England; October: cool very wet. * 19–20 October: notable early snowfall. Northerly/cyclonic northeasterly situations, heavy snowfall, 20–30 cm (8–12 in) in southeast England. November: mild partly wet. **1881** Continuing weak zonal flow (79 westerly situations). Very cold wet winter, midwinter westerlies absent – December (1880): mild partly wet; January: very cold to 28 January. * 18–19 January: severe storm and snowstorm-blizzard, 'The Great Victorian Blizzard' (Fig. 87). Cyclonic easterly situation, deep depression (below 974 mb) moved from Biscay into the eastern Channel and then turned south over France; one of the worst snowstorm-blizzard situations on record to affect south and central England, heavy snowfall, 30–40 cm (12–16 in), even heavier locally, 60 cm (24 in) in Hampshire and on the Isle of Wight; 120 cm (48 in) over Dartmoor, severe easterly gales, deep snowdrifts, 3–5 m (10–15 ft), much destruction both on land and at sea, traffic paralysed in south England for three days, Oxford temporarily isolated, trains buried, many shipwrecks in the Channel, Gorleston lifeboat attempted to rescue people from a stricken ship but all drowned (18 January), commerce brought to a standstill, London deprived of its milk supply due to rail disruption, about 100 people died in blizzards, many others had to be dug out of their homes, countless birds perished. 20 January: secondary depression moved east along Channel, snowfall doubled in the Isle of Wight, where over 60 cm (24 in) had already fallen in the main storm (18/19 January); 21–22 January: severe frost, −14 °C (7 °F) at Thwaite (Suffolk); 26 January: −16 °C (3.5 °F) at Thwaite (Suffolk); 28 January: end of very cold spell; 7 February: heavy snowfall in northeast England. Backward spring – 4–6 March: heavy snowfall, 40–60 cm (16–24 in), snowstorm in east Scotland, roads and railways

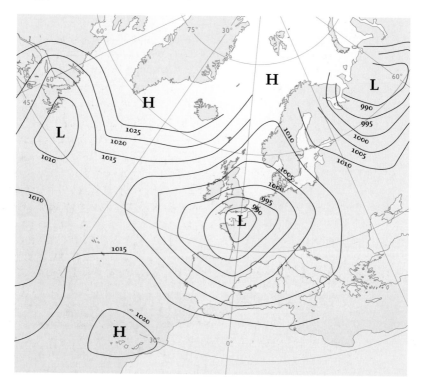

FIG 87. Surface pressure chart, 19 January 1881, showing the cyclonic easterly situation that caused 'The Great Victorian Blizzard'. (Wetterzentrale)

blocked, drifts over 4 m (13 ft) in Scotland. Variable summer – 9 June: hard frost; July: very warm, 36–38 °C (97–101 °F), many heat-related deaths; early August: very warm spell continued; 9 August: start of cool wet spell to early September. Average autumn temperatures – October: cool. * 13–15 October: severe storm. Westerly/cyclonic northerly situations, deep depression (960 mb) moved northeast across north Ireland and south Scotland into the North Sea, storm-force east to northeasterly gales affected east Scotland ahead of low, followed by widespread severe westerly gales, at least 46 people killed, over 100 shipwrecks, great loss of life at sea, including 129 in the Eyemouth (Berwick) fishing fleet disaster, much damage on land, especially in south Scotland and north England, great destruction of trees in Scotland, also hundreds blown down in England. November: very warm dry; 26–27 November: severe storm, southwesterly/cyclonic westerly situations, inferred severe gales. **1882** Wet cyclonic year, increasing zonal flow, normal (89 westerly situations). Very mild winter, fairly strong midwinter

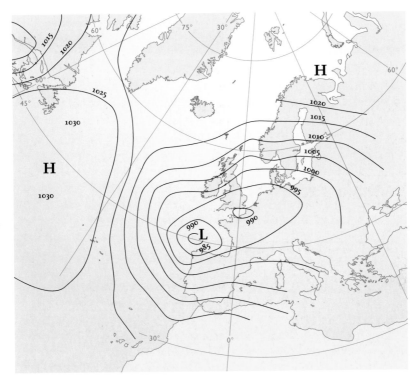

FIG 88. Surface pressure chart, 6 December 1882, showing the cyclonic easterly situation that caused 'The Border Blizzard'. (Wetterzentrale)

westerlies – notable season for frequent gales; 17–20 December (1881): cyclonic/westerly situations, gales; January: mild dry; notable for anticyclonic situations, 1047 mb recorded on 18 January; 14 February: end of mild dry spell; rain, snow (15 February). Very mild wet early spring – early March: wet, windy; 7–20 March: warm dry spell; 22–23 March: cold storms. * 29 April: severe storm. Cyclonic situation, intense secondary depression (below 995 mb) off southwest Ireland, inferred storm-force southwesterly gales, spring foliage wind-damaged, more trees blown down in London parks than in any previously known storm. Very cool wet summer – 26 July to 21 August: very warm dry spell; 22–23 August: severe storm, cyclonic westerly situation. Cool very wet autumn – September: cool; 12 September: heavy rain. * 24 October: severe storm. Cyclonic situation, primary depression south of Iceland, secondary low (below 990 mb) over northeast England, severe damaging southwesterly gales in east England, strong northwesterly winds in southwest England and Wales, heavy snowfall,

20 cm (8 in) in central England. * 28 October: severe storm, 'Black Saturday'. Northeasterly situation, large depression (992 mb) covered much of west Europe, storm-force northeasterly gales, many shipwrecks off English east coast, many vessels driven aground, great loss of life. November: mild mostly dry in east England; 15 November: heavy snowfall in central England. **1883** Wet year, strong zonal flow (106 westerly situations); volcanic dust veil (DVI 1000), Krakatau eruption (26–27 August), various atmospheric phenomena observed for the first time, such as Bishop's ring and noctilucent clouds, inferred volcanic dust-veil effect. Mild wet winter, normal midwinter westerlies – early December (1882): frost, fog. * 4–8 December (1882): severe snowstorm-blizzard conditions, 'The Border Blizzard' (Fig. 88). Cyclonic easterly situation, slow-moving depression (below 990 mb) over the eastern Channel, snowstorm-blizzard conditions, strong northeasterly winds, south Scotland, north and central England worst affected, heavy snowfall, 80–100 cm (32–40 in) in Berwickshire, drifts 6 m (20 ft), roads blocked, trees damaged. Very cold dry spring – March: one of the coldest Marches on record, 1.9 °C (35.4 °F), only 1785 (1.2 °C/34.2 °F) and probably 1674 and 1667 colder; temperatures about normal during first five days of March but following severe storm on 6 March very cold with frequent frost, snow and mostly northeasterly winds to end of month. * 6 March: severe storm. Northerly situation, inferred storm-force northerly gales over north Britain and the North Sea, great loss of life, including over 130 Hull fishing fleet seamen. * 10–11 March: severe storms. Anticyclonic/northerly situations, northerly gales, unusually high spring tides along east coast in places such as the Humber and Boston, possible North Sea storm surge, sea floods in the Fens. 16–18 March: heavy snowfall, 20 cm (8 in); 11–13 May: heavy rain, river floods including the Severn. Very cool summer. Wet autumn, average temperatures – dust-laden skies indicated by various optical phenomena observed over Europe, inferred volcanic dust-veil effect. * 1–2 September: severe storm. Cyclonic situation, intense depression off southwest Ireland (ex-tropical hurricane) moved northeast over the British Isles, severe gales, heavy rain over west and south England, extensive damage, one of the lowest tides on record in the Thames (2 September), possibly due to extreme pressure changes over the North Sea. 9 September: anticyclonic westerly situation, notable red sunsets observed, inferred volcanic dust-veil effect; 26 September: cyclonic situation, severe gales; 17–18 October: westerly situation, severe southwesterly gales. **1883–1890** Volcanic dust veils (total DVI 1500), various eruptions. **1884** Dry year, normal zonal flow (98 westerly situations); various atmospheric phenomena observed such as unusual sky and cloud colours, blue suns, green moons, Bishop's ring, inferred volcanic dust-veil effect. Very mild winter, very strong midwinter westerlies. * 12 December (1883): severe storm.

Northwesterly situation, storm-force gales, considerable structural damage, Lincoln Cathedral damaged, mill chimneys blown down in north England, five people killed. 19–27 January: one of the stormiest spells on record. * 26 January: severe storm. Westerly situation, very deep depression moved east across Scotland and then turned sharply north, 925.6 mb at Ochtertyre (Perthshire), lowest pressure on record in the British Isles; mostly westerly severe gales, heavy snowfall, 30 cm (12 in) in northwest Scotland, deep drifts, buildings damaged, many trees blown down, over a million on one estate alone in southwest Scotland. Dry early spring, average temperatures. Warm dry summer – June: ridge from Azores high extended northeast over British Isles; 11 August: very warm, 35 °C (95 °F) at Norwich. Dry autumn, average temperatures – 30 November: heavy snowfall. **1885** Decline in zonal flow, fairly normal zonal flow (83 westerly situations). Mild wet winter, very weak midwinter westerlies – 12–14 January: heavy snowfall, 25 cm (10 in); 21 February: heavy snow, 25 cm (10 in) in east Scotland. Very cold spring – 21–22 March: heavy snowfall, 15–20 cm (6–8 in), trees damaged. Very cool dry summer – June: noctilucent clouds observed, inferred volcanic dust-veil effect. Very cool wet autumn – 25 September: northerly situation, heavy snowfall in Scottish and Welsh mountains; snowflakes recorded in London. **1886** Normal zonal flow (92 westerly situations); volcanic dust veil (total DVI 1300), Etna, New Zealand and Tonga eruptions. Very cold generally dry winter but occasional heavy snowfall, fairly weak midwinter westerlies – 5–6 January: heavy snowfall, 25–30 cm (10–12 in), start of cold spell to 18 March; 13 January: northwesterly situation, gales, thunderstorms; 19 January: heavy snowfall, 15 cm (6 in) in Isle of Man and Wales; 25–26 January: heavy snowfall, 15 cm (6 in) mainly in west Britain; 28 February to 2 March: heavy snowfall, 60 cm (24 in), railways dislocated. Cold wet spring – 15–16 March: heavy snowfall, 15 cm (6 in) in Scotland and north England; 18 March: end of cold spell from 5 January. * 30 March: severe storm. Westerly situation, inferred storm-force southwesterly gales, damage in northwest England, buildings blown down in Liverpool, tram overturned in Wigan (Lancashire), many shipwrecks. 9–10 April: heavy snowfall; May to early June: thick haze, dimmed coloured sun observed in Italy, inferred volcanic dust-veil effect. * 11–15 May: notably late snowfall and severe river floods. Depression moved across south England (12 May), heavy rain, and out-of-season heavy snowfall over high ground, 25 cm (10 in) in Cumbria, severe river floods (14–15 May) followed three days of heavy rain, Severn and Trent rose 5.5–6 m (18–19 ft) above normal seasonal levels. Dry summer, average temperatures – reddish-yellow sky afterglows observed, inferred volcanic dust-veil effect. Very warm wet autumn – early October: very warm spell with thunderstorms. * 14–16 October: severe storm. Small intense depression (969 mb) moved southeast across Ireland, Wales and England, severe westerly gales, heavy rain, river floods, bridges swept away, widespread damage, electric railway swept away at Brighton (Sussex), many trees blown down in Ireland, south and central England, great loss of life at sea, especially off coasts of southwest England and south Wales. 26–27 October: anticyclonic/easterly situations, heavy snowfall-blizzard conditions. **1887** Dry anticyclonic continental year (one of the driest years of the 19th century); weak zonal flow (73 westerly situations). Cold winter, normal midwinter westerlies. * 8–9 December (1886): severe storm. Deep depression (927 mb) moved east across north Ireland/north England, severe to storm-force gales, southwesterly over south Britain, east to southeasterly over north Scotland, many shipwrecks, Southport and St Anne's lifeboats in Lancashire lost (27 out of 29 crew members drowned). 26 December (1886): cyclonic situation, heavy snowfall, 30 cm (12 in), drifts 2.5 m (8 ft), trees and telegraph wires damaged; 3–5 January: cyclonic westerly/cyclonic situations, heavy snowfall, 15–20 cm (6–8 in) in London; 7 January: depression over Bristol Channel, heavy snowfall, 20–35 cm (8–14 in). * 2 February to August: drought. Very cold dry late spring – March: occasional heavy snowfall, 15–45 cm (6–18 in). Very warm dry summer – dried-up pastures in July and August. Very cool autumn, average rainfall – October: northwesterly. * 29–31 October: severe storm. Cyclonic westerly situation, inferred severe southwesterly gales, 17 people killed off south English coast. **1888–1890** Volcanic dust veil (total DVI 1100), Japanese and Aleutian eruptions. **1888** Continuing weak zonal flow (71 westerly situations). Very cold dry winter, fairly weak midwinter westerlies – one of the most severe winter freezing events of the Baltic on record; 27 December (1887): anticyclonic northeasterly situation, heavy snowfall, 30 cm (12 in), 4–5 m (13–16 ft) drifts; 13–14 February: cyclonic situation, heavy snowfall, 60 cm (24 in); 19 February: northeasterly situation, heavy snowfall, 20 cm (8 in), deep drifts, railways dislocated;. Very cold wet late spring. * 9–11 March: severe storm. Cyclonic situation, severe gales, many lives lost. 11–14 March: cyclonic situation, heavy snowfall, 25–40 cm (10–16 in) in north England and Scotland, railways blocked; 18–20 March: anticyclonic easterly situation, snowstorm (19 March), Channel crossings delayed. Very cool wet summer. * 10 June: notable out-of-season snowfall. Westerly situation, heavy snowfall, 15 cm (6 in) in the Scottish Highlands. July: cyclonic. * 7–12 July: notable out-of-season snowfall. Mainly northwesterly situations, heaviest amount of snow over high ground in Scotland, north Ireland, north England and Wales. 15 July: cyclonic easterly situation, thunderstorms, large hailstones, 7 cm (2.8 in) diameter, fell in Gloucester. Cool autumn – 16 November: cyclonic westerly situation, inferred strong southwesterly gales in north England, buildings damaged; 28 November:

cyclonic situation, inferred severe gales, Staithes (Yorkshire) lifeboat capsized in rescue of fishermen. **1889** Dry anticyclonic or continental year, continuing weak zonal flow (79 westerly situations). Dry winter, average temperatures, normal midwinter westerlies – frequent but mostly light snowfall; early December (1888): mild spell, plants still in growth; 2–4 February: northwest/northerly situations, severe storm, loss of life on coast, shipwreck off Dungeness; 10–11 February: cyclonic northerly situations, heavy snowfall, 20–30 cm (8–12 in). Wet spring, average temperatures – 3–4 March: heavy snowfall, 20–30 cm (8–12 in). Showery summer, average temperatures and rainfall. Cool dry autumn – 24 November: westerly situation, inferred severe southwesterly gales, sea wall severely damaged at Sandgate (Kent), main roads impassable.

1890s

Anticyclonic, later maritime; normal zonal flow (88 westerly situations on average per year). **1890** Strong zonal flow (103 westerly situations). Average winter temperatures, very strong midwinter westerlies – 17–27 January: heavy storms, south and west English coasts; February: very dry; one of the driest Februarys on record. Early spring, average temperatures. Cool wet summer – 8 July: cyclonic situation, heavy snowfall in the Scottish Highlands, 20 cm (8 in) at Ben Nevis Observatory. Warm dry autumn. * 7 November: severe storm. Cyclonic situation, severe southwesterly gales, much damage including London, Birmingham and Liverpool. 25–28 November: northeasterly situation turning anticyclonic, heavy snowfall, 30–60 cm (12–24 in), keen frost, –4 °C (25 °F) at Kew on 28 November, trees damaged. **1891** Normal zonal flow (94 westerly situations). Very cold dry winter, normal midwinter westerlies – December (1890): very cold, –0.8 °C (30.6 °F), one of the coldest Decembers on record, rivers frozen; 14 December: anticyclonic situation, keen frost, coldest December day on record in London, –6 °C (21 °F); 18–20 December: cyclonic (19 December), heavy snowfall, 20–45 cm (8–18 in); January: very severe conditions, many thousands skated on the frozen Fen rivers and Norfolk Broads, Thames almost blocked by ice between Westminster and London Bridge; 23 January: cyclonic westerly situation, end of skating season; 24 January: Norwich–Yarmouth river traffic opened up on the Yare after five weeks being suspended; February: average temperatures; very dry, no rain fell over much of England, spring flowers in bloom, farmers well ahead with sowing. Very cold spring – early March: wet, otherwise wintry. * 9–13 March: severe storm, snowstorm-blizzard conditions. Deep depression (below 980 mb) moved east along the Channel, severe easterly gales, heavy snowfall, snowstorm-blizzard conditions affected south and southwest England, and Wales, 30–60 cm (12–24 in), 150 cm (60 in) on Dartmoor, deep drifts, over 6,000 sheep perished in

Devon and Cornwall, transport disrupted, trains buried in deep drifts in southwest England, more than 200 lives and 60 ships lost in the Channel, over 500,000 trees blown down, lanes in Devon remained blocked by snow until late March and traces of snow lasted until June on higher parts of Dartmoor and Exmoor. 13 May: very mild, 23 °C (73 °F) at Norwich. * 17–18 May: notable late-season snowstorm. Cyclonic northerly situation, remarkable fall in temperature, 3 °C (37 °F) at Norwich, heavy snowfall, 15–18 cm (6–7 in) in Norfolk, widespread drifting. Very cool wet summer – 24–26 August: storm, westerly situation, heavy rain in northwest England, 250 mm (10 in) in two days at Seathwaite (Lake District). Wet autumn, average temperatures. * 20–21 September: severe storm. Cyclonic and northerly situations, severe conditions in central and north England, loss of life. * 13–14 October: severe storm. Southerly/cyclonic westerly situations, deep depression (below 960 mb) northwest of Scotland (14 October), severe to storm-force south to southwesterly gales, many trees blown down in London, Windsor and Richmond parks, extremely low pressure (947 mb) recorded at Cawdor Castle (northeast Scotland) on 14 October indicates the formation of a secondary low with destructive winds south of its centre; English south and southwest coasts particularly badly affected. **1892** Fairly normal zonal flow (81 westerly situations). Cold winter, normal midwinter westerlies – 5–10 January: heavy snowfall, 20–30 cm (8–12 in) mostly in the Scottish Highlands. * 28 January: notable floods. Westerly situation, inferred heavy rain, severe floods in Strathglass, Bonar Bridge and Strathspey areas (northeast Scotland), Bonar Bridge destroyed, Strathspey railway partly washed away. 15–20 February: mostly cyclonic northeasterly situations, widespread heavy snowfall, 20 cm (8 in). Very cold dry spring – March: very cold; 10 March: northerly situation with depression off northeast England, heavy snowfall, 15 cm (6 in) in Manchester; 15–16 April: northerly situation, depression over northwest Ireland moved southeast across England, heavy snowfall, 20–30 cm (8–12 in), railways dislocated. Very cool summer – August: dry early, wet later. Very cool wet autumn – 21 October: cyclonic northerly situation, heavy snowfall. **1893** Dry year, normal zonal flow (91 westerly situations). Cold winter, weak midwinter westerlies – 4–5 December (1892): northwesterly situation, heavy snowfall, 15 cm (6 in) in Manchester; 5–6 January: anticyclonic/southeasterly situations, heavy snowfall, 30 cm (12 in); 25–26 February: cyclonic northeasterly/cyclonic situations, heavy snowfall, 20 cm (8 in). Very mild dry spring – one of the warmest springs on record; 1 March: start of drought. * Spring and summer: drought. Blocking-high situations, one of the most severe and longest droughts on record in England, less than a third of the normal rainfall recorded in south England from March to June; a spell of over 60 days without rain was recorded during the spring in a narrow strip along the

coasts of Kent and Sussex. April: anticyclonic; 20 April: early heat wave, 28 °C
(82 °F) in London. Very warm mostly dry summer – 2 July: anticyclonic situation,
'cloudburst' (probably heavy thunderstorm) over the Cheviots, bridges washed
away; 8 July: cyclonic southerly situation, thunderstorms, large hailstones, 5 cm
(2 in) in diameter, whirlwinds in north England, storm off Skegness (Lincolnshire),
lives lost. Cool autumn – 23 September: northerly situation, wintry showers in
Edinburgh (possibly earliest known date). * 16–20 November: severe storm. Deep
depression (below 970 mb) moved slowly east across Ireland and Scotland, severe
northwesterly gales in rear of low, severe damage both on land and at sea (17
November), people drowned off northern coasts, temperatures fell by 10 °C (18 °F)
over England as winds veered from north to northeasterly (18 November), heavy
snowfall in east Britain, deep drifts 1.5 m (5 ft), trains halted at Cambridge
(19 November), many trees blown down, 298 shipwrecks and 293 people drowned
on east coast alone. **1894** Normal zonal flow, 93 westerly situations. Mild wet
winter, fairly strong midwinter westerlies. * 3–5 January: severe storm. Easterly
situation, severe northeasterly gales, heavy snowfall, 15–20 cm (6–8 in), traffic
disrupted, great loss of life off east coast. * 12 January: severe storm. Cyclonic
southwesterly situation, severe southwesterly gales, inferred heavy rain,
widespread loss of life, especially in the Great Yarmouth fishing fleet. February:
very stormy. * 10–13 February: severe storm. Deepening depression (975 mb) on
11 February, 945 mb (12 February over Oslo) moved east across north Britain,
severe southwest to westerly gales, especially on 11 and 12 February, buildings
damaged, severe stormy conditions, particularly in Norfolk. Mild early spring.
Very cool wet summer. Average autumn temperatures – 12–13 November:
persistent gales for at least 48 hours; 14–17 November: heavy rain, 81.8 mm (3.22
in). **1895 or 1896** Volcanic dust veil (DVI 1300), southern hemisphere eruption?
1895 Fairly dry year, weak zonal flow (69 westerly situations). * Very cold winter.
Blocking-high situation, absent midwinter westerlies replaced by an easterly
flow, the most protracted severe spell since 1814. * 21–22 December (1894): severe
storm. Westerly/cyclonic northwesterly situations, storm-force winds, heavy seas
pounded English east coast, high tides, probable storm surge, much damage both
on land and at sea, city trams blown over in north England, serious rail accident
on 21 December near Crewe (Cheshire), express train ran into a goods wagon
blown onto opposite line, 14 people killed, 60 injured. 29 December (1894):
northwesterly situation, severe gales, high tides, sea defences damaged in East
Anglia; 31 December: northerly situation, heavy snowfall, 15 cm (6 in); January:
very cold, cyclonic northerly; 12–13 January: heavy snowfall, 15–30 cm (6–12 in),
drifts 60 cm (2 ft); 23 January: northerly situation, severe northwesterly to
northerly gales, heavy squally snow showers, heavy seas, North Sea storm surge,

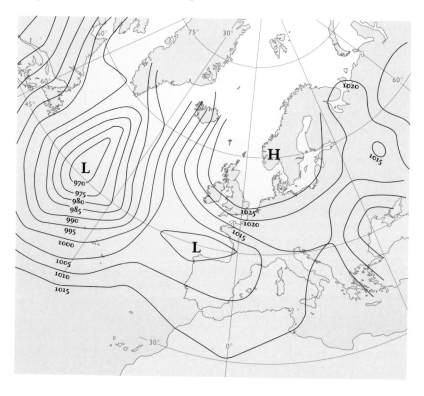

FIG 89. Surface pressure chart, 15 February 1895, showing an anticyclonic southeasterly situation with a blocking high over Norway. (Wetterzentrale)

abandoned Eccles church tower (Norfolk) finally collapsed; 27–28 January: cyclonic/northerly situations, heavy snowfall, 15 cm (6 in). February: very cold, one of the coldest Februarys on record, blocking-high situation, persistent easterly spell brought some of the coldest weather on record to the British Isles; frozen rivers and water bodies, thousands of birds perished, soup kitchens set up to alleviate suffering of poor people, ice 26 cm (10 in) thick on the Norfolk Broads, Thames river traffic suspended in early February, ice floes on the river up to 2 m (6–7 ft) thick; 6–10 February: heavy snowfall, 30 cm (12 in) mainly in southwest Scotland, northwest England and the Isle of Man, locally heavier including 45 cm (18 in) in the Lake District and 75 cm (30 in) in southwest Scotland; 11 February: −27.2 °C (−17 °F) at Braemar (Aberdeenshire), lowest temperature then on record in the British Isles (now equalled in 1982 and 1995); 9–17 February: Thames more or less blocked by ice floe, 2 m (6–7 ft) thick, impossible for full-powered

FIG 90. Roehampton Lane, Putney Heath, Great Frost of 1895. (J. A. Kington)

FIG 91. Putney Heath, Great Frost of 1895. (J. A. Kington)

FIG 92. Wimbledon Common, Great Frost of 1895. (J. A. Kington)

FIG 93. Penn
Ponds, Richmond
Park, Great Frost
of 1895.
(J. A. Kington)

FIG 94. Penn Ponds, Richmond Park, Great Frost of 1895. (J. A. Kington)

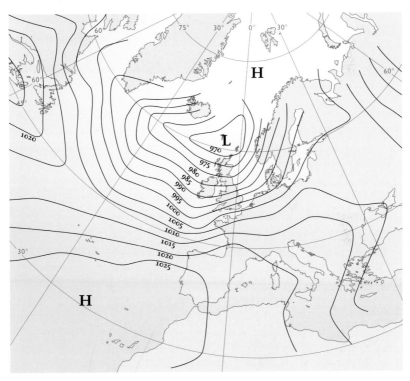

FIG 95. Surface pressure chart, 24 March 1895, showing the cyclonic westerly situation in which a secondary low developed. (Wetterzentrale)

steamers to force their way up and down the river except with the tide, ice-skating on frozen lakes and rivers, including the Fens and the Thames, special trains laid on for skaters to Lake Windermere and Loch Lomond. Severe floods followed the thaw that finally brought the severe conditions to an end, water levels in the Thames rose 30 cm (1 ft) higher than previously recorded. Dry spring, cold in east England. * 24 March: severe storm. Cyclonic westerly situation (Fig. 95), with a deep primary low north of Scotland, an intense secondary depression (978 mb) over southeast Ireland moved northeast across Wales and England to north Norfolk, severe to storm-force southwesterly gales, destructive storm centre, 50–80 km (30–50 miles) wide, passed over central/east England, including Cambridge, one of the worst storms on record to affect this area, stone buildings demolished, factory chimneys and church steeples blown down, wrecked houses in Norwich, Peterborough Cathedral damaged, leaden roof of Banqueting Hall, Whitehall, completely rolled up, thousands of trees blown down, 14 people killed, many hundreds injured. Wet summer – 10 August: southerly; heavy thunderstorms, torrential rain, tornado in Yorkshire, property damaged, trees blown down, Atlantic tidal wave in Mount's Bay (Cornwall), ships in harbour violently disturbed. Warm autumn – September: anticyclonic southwesterly; 24 September: 30 °C (86 °F) in London (notable late date for this high temperature). * 20–29 October: notably early snowfall. Mostly northeast/northerly spell, early snowfall, 10–15 cm (4–6 in). **1896** Dry year, fairly normal zonal flow (83 westerly situations). Mild dry winter, normal midwinter westerlies. Very mild dry spring. Warm dry summer. Very cool wet autumn – 10–11 October: heavy snowfall, 13 cm (5 in) in north Britain. **1897** Fairly normal zonal flow (80 westerly situations). Wet winter, average temperatures, absent midwinter westerlies replaced by easterly flow – 22–23 January: heavy snowfall, 20–30 cm (8–12 in), deep drifts, roads blocked, areas cut off in East Anglia; 30 January: heavy snowfall, 30 cm (12 in). Cool wet early spring – March: southwesterly. Warm showery summer – 24 June: shallow depression (below 1015 mb) in east Channel, heavy thunderstorms, hail damaged crops and glass, Queen Victoria's Diamond Jubilee events ruined. Warm dry autumn – November: warm dry; notable late blooming of plants; 27 November: very stormy, westerly situation, storm-force gales, trees blown down, buildings damaged, sand dunes damaged and breached along Norfolk coast, 11 shipwrecks, over 40 drowned off the coast from Great Yarmouth to King's Lynn. * 28–30 November: severe storm. One of the most severe North Sea storms on record, deepening intense depression (below 975 mb) over north Scotland on 28 November moved southeast into the North Sea, storm-force northwesterly gales, storm surge, severe sea floods on so-called 'Black Monday' (29 November), North Sea defences badly breached, great damage along the east coast from Norfolk to Essex, including an extensive breach in the coastal sand dunes at the Horsey–Hundred Stream Gap (Norfolk), thousands of acres of salt marshes formed in Norfolk, sea defences on north bank of the Thames estuary also breached, shipwrecks all round the British coasts, trees and telegraph poles blown down, much structural damage. **1898** Strong zonal flow (109 westerly situations). Very mild winter, fairly strong midwinter westerlies – 20–22 February: heavy snowfall in southwest England, 30–40 cm (12–16 in), locally 60 cm (24 in), trees damaged. Cold spring – 24–26 March: strong northeasterly flow, heavy snowfall, 13 cm (5 in). Dry summer, average temperatures. Very warm autumn – November: changeable; 22–23 November: heavy snowfall, 30 cm (12 in). **1899** Fairly normal zonal flow (81 westerly situations). Very mild wet stormy winter, normal midwinter westerlies. * 1–2 January: severe storm. Cyclonic situation, trough over the British Isles, severe to storm-force southwesterly gales, Holyhead Railway partly washed away, shipwrecks off coasts of south England and Wales, depression (below 975 mb) over north Britain on 2 January moved southeast to affect mainland Europe. * 12 January: severe storm. Cyclonic westerly situation, depression north of Scotland, severe to storm-force southwesterly gales (more destructive than those on 1–2 January), Holyhead Railway again damaged, Channel ferries cancelled. 21 January: cyclonic situation, depression off northwest Ireland, severe southwesterly gales; 11 February: southwesterly storm. Cold wet spring – 18 March: anticyclonic northeasterly situation, heavy snowfall, 20 cm (8 in); 21–22 March: cyclonic northerly situation, heavy snowfall, 15 cm (6 in) in the Scottish Highlands. * 7 April: severe storm. Cyclonic situation, severe southwesterly gales, much damage on Welsh and southwest English coasts. May: cold; ground frost occurred until end of the month. Very warm dry summer – drought conditions, frequent fires on commons. Warm autumn – 1 October: cyclonic situation, tornado in Wiltshire, 90 m (100 yd) wide, moved along a 32 km (20 mile) track, much damage to buildings and trees; 8 November: westerly storm, troop-ships damaged carrying British forces to South Africa.

EARLY 20TH-CENTURY WARMING: 1900–1939

1900S

Continental becoming maritime; normal zonal flow (97 westerly situations on average per year). **1900** Normal zonal flow (93 westerly situations). Cold wet winter, fairly weak midwinter westerlies – 11–12 December (1899): cyclonic situation (12 December), heavy snowfall, 25 cm (10 in). * 29 December (1899):

severe storm. Cyclonic situation, deep intense depression over the Irish Sea, extremely low pressure (950 mb) recorded on the Lleyn Peninsula (Caernarvon), widespread severe cyclonic gales, storm-force in the Channel, South Goodwin lightship driven from moorings, ship blown ashore off Dungeness (Kent). February: cold; 2–3 February: easterly/cyclonic easterly situations, heavy snowfall, 20–30 cm (8–12 in); 8–10 February: heavy snowfall, 30 cm (12 in), drifts 1 m (3 ft); 13–14 February: heavy snowfall. * 15 February: severe snowstorm. Depression (below 985 mb) off southwest Ireland, strong south to southeasterly flow over the British Isles, heavy snowfall in north England, deep drifts, roads and railways blocked, loss of life. Cold dry spring. Warm summer, average rainfall – July: very warm. * 12 July: severe flood. Cyclonic situation, weak pressure gradient, shallow depression (below 1010 mb) over the east Channel; heavy thunderstorm, torrential rainfall, 95 mm (3.8 in) in 75 minutes at Ilkley (Yorkshire), floodwaters surged down steep hillsides above town, buildings destroyed, roads and bridges washed away, large boulders and hundreds of tons of debris deposited in main street. 16–25 July: 32 °C (89 °F) in London; 27 July: heavy thunderstorms associated with a shallow depression. Warm autumn.

1901 Dry continental easterly year, weak zonal flow (61 westerly situations). Mild winter, fairly weak midwinter westerlies – December (1900): very mild wet. * 30 December (1900): severe storm. Cyclonic situation, intense depression (below 1000 mb) moved rapidly across Ireland and north England, severe southwesterly gales on its southern flank in the Southwest Approaches and Channel, hurricane-force gusts on exposed coasts of Wales and south England, exceptionally heavy rain, up to 90 mm (3.6 in), severe floods, many buildings damaged, thousands of trees blown down, several shipwrecks in the Southwest Approaches and Channel, over 200 people killed. 1–2 January: cyclonic westerly/westerly situations, further severe floods followed heavy rain on 30 December; 31 January: northerly situation: cyclonic northerly situation, heavy snowfall, 25–30 cm (10–12 in). Average spring temperatures – 21 March: anticyclonic easterly situation, heavy snowfall in southwest England, 45 cm (18 in), drifts 3 m (10 ft); 29 March: westerly situation, heavy snowfall in north Wales, 150–200 cm (60–80 in) over mountains, many sheep killed. * 30–31 March: severe snowstorm. Deep Atlantic depression, below 980 mb (30 March) moved northeast over Scotland, cyclonic gales, snowstorm-blizzard conditions with drifts in Scotland, north England and Wales, heavy snowfall, 150–200 cm (60–80 in) in the Welsh mountains. Warm dry summer. Dry autumn, average temperatures – October: hard dried-out land. * 12–13 November: severe storm. Cyclonic situation, depression (below 990 mb) over the Southwest Approaches moved east into the Channel, severe gales, several shipwrecks in the Southwest

Approaches and Channel, over 200 drowned. **1902** Normal zonal flow (92 westerly situations); volcanic dust veil (total DVI 1000), Mont Pelée (Martinique), Soufrière (St Vincent) and Santa Maria (Guatemala) eruptions. Cold winter, fairly strong midwinter westerlies. * 12–14 December (1901): severe storm and snowstorm. Cyclonic easterly/cyclonic northeasterly situations, deep depression (below 985 mb) moved slowly east over the Channel into north France, northeasterly gales, snowstorm-blizzard conditions, heavy snowfall, 40 cm (16 in), deep drifts, roads and railways blocked, telegraph poles brought down. 18 December (1901): cyclonic northerly situation, heavy snowfall, 15–30 cm (6–12 in) in north England and south Scotland; 31 January: anticyclonic situation, 1053.6 mb at Aberdeen, highest pressure on record in the British Isles; February: cold; 7 February: cyclonic situation, heavy snowfall, 30 cm (12 in). Cold spring – May: very cold, one of the coldest Mays on record, cold northwesterly flow over the British Isles between high pressure west of Portugal and low pressure over Scandinavia. Very cool showery summer – inferred volcanic dust-veil effect; 1 July: northerly situation, heavy rainfall, 83 mm (3.25 in) in Ipswich during two hours. Warm dry autumn. **1903** Maritime cyclonic. Very wet year, strong zonal flow (111 westerly situations). Very mild winter, normal midwinter westerlies – 4 December (1902): anticyclonic situation, heavy snowfall, 15 cm (6 in); February: very mild; one of the mildest Februarys on record; 21 February: Saharan dust fallout affected south England and Wales. * 26–27 February: severe storm. Westerly/cyclonic situations, deep depression (960 mb) moved northeast over Scotland into the North Sea, storm-force, locally hurricane-force, southwesterly gales, many trees blown down, buildings damaged, train overturned on the Leven viaduct, near Ulverston (Lancashire), many people injured; stronger more damaging winds in Ireland, most severe storm since 'The Night of the Big Wind' (January 1839), extensive damage in Dublin, over 3,000 trees blown down in Phoenix Park alone. Wet very early spring, average temperatures. Very cool wet summer – inferred volcanic dust-veil effect; 10 June: easterly situation, start of very wet spell. * 13–15 June: heavy rain and severe floods. Mainly northeasterly situation, slow-moving depression produced a three-day spell of continuous heavy rain (one of the longest spells of continuous rain on record); owing to the unusual circular track of the low its rainy sector affected central England for three days giving continuous rain; widespread severe floods in the Thames Valley reached almost the highest level on record. Warm wet autumn – 10 September: cyclonic situation, depression moved rapidly east over Ireland and England, its strong winds had a remarkable effect on vegetation along the English south coast, scorched brown shrivelled-up leaves on trees even several kilometres inland leeward of the South Downs; October: very wet, 218 mm (8.6 in), wettest October on record as well as the wettest of any month in the year on record, severe flooding; 30 November: northerly situation, heavy snowfall. **1904** Normal zonal flow (99 westerly situations). Wet winter, average temperatures, normal midwinter westerlies – 17 February: cyclonic situation, heavy snowfall, 18 cm (7 in) in Scotland; 26 February: cyclonic situation, heavy snowfall, 15 cm (6 in) in Scotland and north England; 29 February to 1 March: anticyclonic easterly (1 March), heavy snowfall, 15 cm (6 in). Average spring temperatures. Dry summer, average temperatures – July: light southwesterly flow over British Isles, high pressure over mainland Europe. Cool dry autumn. * 8–9 November: severe storm. Northwesterly/cyclonic westerly situations, depression over the south Scandinavia–Baltic region, inferred strong to storm-force northwesterly gales over the British Isles. 20–23 November: mainly northerly situations, heavy snowfall, 30–45 cm (12–18 in), deep drifts, 5m (16 ft) in the Lake District. **1905** Strong zonal flow (113 westerly situations). Dry winter, average temperatures, normal midwinter westerlies – 21–27 December (1904): anticyclonic spell, infamous so-called 'Black Christmas' due to thick fog. * 6–7 January: severe storm. Westerly situation, inferred severe gales, exceptionally high tide in the North Sea, probable storm surge, severe sea floods, great damage to cliffs and coastal defences in East Anglia, lives lost at sea. 15–16 January: southerly/cyclonic southerly situations, heavy snowfall in northwest England, lives lost at sea. Wet early spring, average temperatures. Warm summer, average rainfall – 20–29 August: cyclonic spell; 24–26 August: exceptionally heavy rainfall, 250 mm (10 in) in east Ireland. Very cool autumn – October: very cool, one of the coldest Octobers on record; 2–5 November: cyclonic spell, including depression (below 990 mb), probably stormy conditions in the Channel, railway steamer *Hilda* wrecked off St Malo, 128 people drowned. **1906–1907** Volcanic dust veil (DVI 110), Vesuvius and Aleutians eruptions. **1906** Strong zonal flow (118 westerly situations). Mild winter, average rainfall, fairly strong midwinter westerlies – 6 January: gales in the North Sea and Channel; 7 February: heavy snowfall, 15 cm (6 in); 8 February: widespread thunderstorms and tornadoes, associated with a line squall, moved southeast. Cold spring. * 12–13 March: severe storm. Northerly/westerly situations, depression (980 mb) moved northeast over the British Isles, severe northerly gales affected exposed coasts, probable North Sea storm surge, sea floods affected north Norfolk and North Sea German coasts. Warm dry summer – 31 August to 3 September: southerly situation, late summer heat wave, 32 °C (90 °F) on four successive days, including an overall September maximum, 35.6 °C (96 °F), on 1 and 2 September. Very warm wet autumn. **1907–1909** Notable twilight phenomena observed, inferred volcanic dust-veil effect. **1907** Strong zonal flow (103 westerly situations); volcanic dust veil (DVI 150), Shtyubelya Sopka–Ksudatch (Kamchatka) eruption. Cool dry winter, normal midwinter westerlies – 5 December (1906):

northwesterly gales in Scotland. * 25–28 December (1906): severe snowstorm-blizzard conditions. Mainly cyclonic northerly situations, slow-moving complex cyclonic system east of Britain, heavy snowfall affected all areas except parts of southwest England, particularly heavy falls occurred in northeast England, and south and east Scotland, 60 cm (24 in), deep drifts, roads blocked, Aberdeen cut off for three days, telegraph wires brought down, blocked signals caused a serious rail collision near Arbroath (Angus) involving two passenger trains, 22 people killed. 23 January: anticyclonic situation, ridge of an intense anticyclone over east Europe (1060 mb) extended west across the British Isles. * 20 February: severe storm. Northerly situation (Fig. 96), very deep depression in the North Sea (935 mb), severe to storm-force northwest to westerly gales, SS *Berlin* wrecked off the Hook of Holland. Wet spring, average temperatures. 18 March: cyclonic westerly situation (Fig. 97), liners *Jebba* and *Suevic* wrecked off the coasts of Cornwall and Devon in strong winds and fog. 7 April: cyclonic situation, heavy

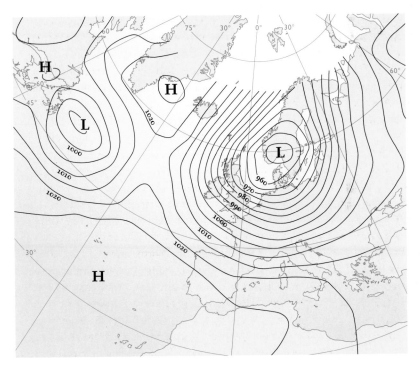

FIG 96. Surface pressure chart, 20 February 1907, showing the northerly situation in which the SS *Berlin* was wrecked off the Hook of Holland. (Wetterzentrale)

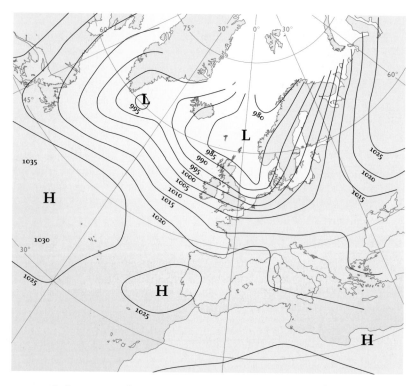

FIG 97. Surface pressure chart, 18 March 1907, showing the cyclonic westerly situation in which the liners *Jebba* and *Suevic* were wrecked off the coasts of Cornwall and Devon. (Wetterzentrale)

snowfall, 15 cm (6 in). Very cool summer, average rainfall – 22 July: easterly situation, heavy thunderstorms, deep fall of hailstones, widespread damage; 2 August: heavy thunderstorms, tornado at Guildford. Warm autumn – 25 September: warmest day of the year, 25.5 °C (78 °F) in London, notably late date for this high temperature. **1908** Normal zonal flow (91 westerly situations). Average winter temperature and rainfall, normal midwinter westerlies. * 13–14 December (1907): severe storm. Cyclonic/cyclonic northerly situations; inferred severe gales; shipwrecks, heavy loss of life off Scilly Isles. 8 January: heavy snowfall. * 22 February: severe storm. Westerly situation, depression (below 965 mb) centred between Scotland and Iceland, severe to storm-force southwesterly gales, locally hurricane-force, severe damage, buildings damaged, many trees blown down, loss of life both on land and at sea, lightship sank off Grimsby (Lincolnshire). 27–29 February: mainly cyclonic northwesterly situation, heavy

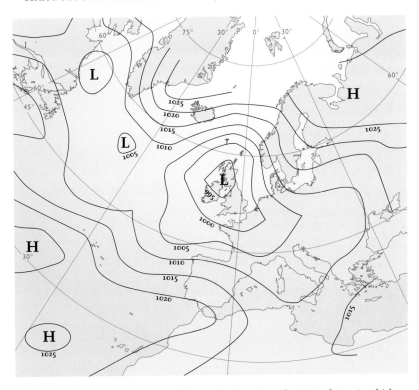

FIG 98. Surface pressure chart, 25 April 1908, showing the cyclonic circulation in which the secondary low was embedded that caused severe snowstorms. (Wetterzentrale)

snowfall, 20–45 cm (8–18 in). Cold wet late spring – 3 March: cyclonic situation, heavy snowfall; April: very cold, 19 April (Good Friday): northerly situation, snow and hail showers, 22 April (Easter Monday): northerly situation, further snow. * 23–26 April: notably late severe snowstorm (Fig. 98). Cyclonic situation, secondary depression moved southeast from Ireland into the Channel and then northeast over the Thames estuary, snowstorm-blizzard conditions, heavy snowfall, 60–75 cm (24–30 in), one of the heaviest spring snowfalls on record, roads and railways blocked, trees damaged, during a severe snowstorm on 25 April the American liner *St Paul* accidentally rammed the Royal Navy cruiser HMS *Gladiator* in the Solent, 30 lives lost. 28 April: thaw, snow-melt, severe flooding in the Thames. Cool summer, average rainfall – 3 June: localised heavy thundery rain; 12 July: thundery conditions. Very warm dry autumn – late September to early October: warm spell, 25 °C (77 °F) in Norwich. **1909** Normal

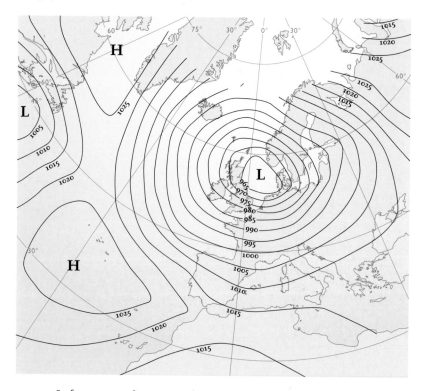

FIG 99. Surface pressure chart, 3 December 1909, showing the northwesterly situation in which many ships were wrecked off British coasts. (Wetterzentrale)

zonal flow (85 westerly situations). Cold dry winter, positive pressure anomaly over the British Isles, normal midwinter westerlies – mainland Europe: drought; 10 December (1908): increasing number of skaters at Great Yarmouth during the previous two or three weeks; 26–29 December: easterly flow, heavy snowfall, 20–25 cm (8–10 in), road traffic dislocated; 15–16 January: heavy snowfall in Scotland, railway blocked at Rannoch (Perthshire). Cold wet late spring. * 1–10 March: severe snowstorm. Mainly cyclonic northeasterly situations, heavy snowfall, 20–40 cm (8–16 in), deep drifts, 1.5 m (5 ft), southeast England worst affected, 50–70 cm (20–28 in), damaged trees and shrubs. Very cool wet summer – inferred volcanic dust-veil effect; June: very cool, one of the three coldest Junes on record, 11.8 °C (53 °F). Cool autumn – 14 October: line squall; 26 October: cyclonic easterly situation, depression (below 985 mb) southwest of the British Isles, Broadstairs (Kent) inundated following heavy rain, 150 mm (6 in), during previous three days.

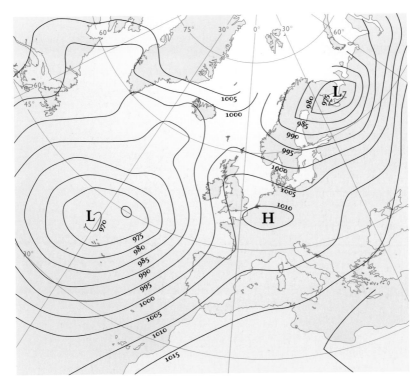

FIG 100. Surface pressure chart, 21 December 1909, showing the anticyclonic situation that affected south England with snowfall elsewhere. (Wetterzentrale)

1910S

Cyclonic maritime; normal zonal circulation (99 westerly situations on average per year). **1910** Cyclonic year, fairly normal zonal flow (82 westerly situations). Mild wet winter, fairly strong midwinter and midsummer westerlies.

* 2–3 December (1909): severe storm (Fig. 99). Cyclonic/northwesterly situations, deep intense depression (948 mb) moved east across Ireland and north England into the North Sea, severe westerly gales, many shipwrecks, including the Isle of Man mail boat *Ellan Vannin*, which foundered with all hands off the mouth of the Mersey. 19–21 December (1909) (Fig. 100): heavy snowfall, 25–30 cm (10–12 in), apart from south England which was affected by fine anticyclonic conditions, elsewhere snow-blocked roads. 26 and 28 January: heavy snowfall, 30 cm (12 in) in Scotland and north England, roads and railways blocked. January: cold, frost and snow; February: wet. Average spring temperatures – 6 April: easterly situation, depression moved abnormally southwest over England and Wales. Cool wet summer – inferred volcanic dust-veil effect; 5 June: widespread heavy thunderstorms; 9 June: further widespread heavy thunderstorms from Wales to southeast England, hailstones in large heaps 60–90 cm (2–3 ft) deep; 17 June: severe floods in mainland Europe, 1,000 drowned in Hungary alone. Very cool autumn, average rainfall – 13–14 October: anticyclonic northeast/easterly situations, inferred severe gales pounded east coast, many shipwrecks in the North Sea, 43 drowned. **1911** Dry year, strong zonal flow (105 westerly situations). Very mild winter, average rainfall, fairly weak midwinter westerlies – December (1910): wet, North Sea high tides, severe sea floods, heavy material losses in the Fens; 16 December: deep depression (971 mb) off west Scotland, inferred severe southwesterly gales in the Channel; 12 January: northerly situation, snowfall, minor shipping losses; February: cold dry. Mild dry spring – 4–6 April: anticyclonic east/northeasterly situation, heavy snowfall, 23 cm (9 in), deep drifts; May: mainly dry; 6 May: start of a mostly dry spell into early autumn. * Early May to 13 September: drought. Mainly anticyclonic situations; besides very warm conditions, the drought from early May intensified in July, August and early September; the anticyclonic situations gave rise to mostly fine conditions over much of the country. 31 May: Great 'Derby Day' thunderstorms, 17 people and four horses killed at Epsom (Surrey). Very warm dry summer – so-called 'Halcyon Summer', one of the warmest summers on record; July: very warm, ridge of Azores high extended northeast over British Isles; 22 July: anticyclonic westerly situation, warmest July day then on record, 36.0 °C (96.8 °F) at Epsom (Surrey) (cf. 19 July 2006, 36.3 °C/97.3 °F at Charlwood, Surrey); 29–30 July: cyclonic easterly/cyclonic southerly situations, heavy thunderstorms, hail; August: one of the warmest Augusts on record, Azores ridge shifted a little south to allow a light southwesterly flow over the British Isles; 9–10 August: anticyclonic situation, very warm, 37.8 °C (100 °F) at Greenwich (highest official temperature on record). Warm autumn – 12 September: rain, associated with a depression that moved northeast from Dorset to the Wash, ended the long drought from early May. **1912** A year without a summer, strong zonal flow (103 westerly situations); volcanic dust veil (DVI 150), Katmai (Alaska) eruption. Very mild wet winter, midwinter westerlies absent – 8 January: westerly situation, heavy snowfall, 25 cm (10 in) in Scotland. * 17–18 January: severe storm and heavy snowfall. Southeasterly situation, storm-force southeasterly gales over the North Sea and inferred parts of Britain, heavy snowfall, apart from south England, 30 cm (12 in), locally 60 cm (24 in), deep drifts, 2 m (7 ft), traffic dislocated, trees blown down. Very mild spring, average rainfall – April: very dry; one of the driest Aprils on record. Very cool wet summer – one of the coolest wettest summers on record, including a wet June and one of the coolest Augusts on record, 12.9 °C (55 °F),

inferred volcanic dust-veil effect. August: cyclonic westerly. * 25–26 August: heavy rainstorm. During 25–26 August a small but well-developed depression (below 995 mb) moved slowly north from off east Kent across East Anglia into the North Sea, rain set in over southeast England late on 25 August, heavy falls over East Anglia early on 26 August continued until the following morning, in the Norwich area the downpour produced over 200 mm (8 in) of rain; the effect of this exceptionally intense and prolonged downpour was made even worse by northwesterly gales that raised high tides on the east coast, which in turn held up floodwaters in the river valleys and overwhelmed the natural and man-made defences of the region; remarkably, only three people died as a result of the disaster, due, unfortunately, to the rescue operation that followed rather than the initial effect; widespread serious floods occurred in East Anglia, particularly in Norwich, where water levels reached their highest on record, 3,600 buildings damaged or destroyed, 15,000 people made homeless, 40 bridges swept away, widespread dislocation of road and rail traffic; Norwich was cut off by road, rail and river and most of the Fens remained under water during the following winter. 31 August: anticyclonic conditions that extended northeast over the British Isles ended the summer rains and brought about a dry period that persisted in many areas until 28 September. Very cool autumn, average rainfall – September: anticyclonic; 29–30 November: cyclonic/northerly situations, depression moved east over south England, heavy snowfall, 20–25 cm (8–10 in).
1913 Strong zonal flow (120 westerly situations). Very mild wet winter, very weak midwinter westerlies – December (1912): very mild; 26 December: cyclonic situation, storm. * 11–13 January: severe snowstorm. Cyclonic southwest/southeasterly situations, slow-moving trough extended southeast over British Isles, heavy snowfall especially in south Scotland and north England, 30–60 cm (12–24 in), 90 cm (36 in) in places, deep drifts, 3 m (10 ft), rail and postal services disrupted. Mild wet early spring – 22–23 March: cyclonic situation, coastal storms. * 11–12 April: severe storm. Cyclonic/northerly situations, heavy snowfall, 30–45 cm (12–18 in), many trees brought down, rail traffic disrupted. 10–28 May: warm dry spell. Cool mainly dry summer – June: dry; July: northwesterly type; 15 July (St Swithin's Day): northerly situation, heavy rain, 75 mm (3 in) in Mayfield (Sussex); August: northwesterly. Very warm autumn, average rainfall – 13 October: anticyclonic southerly situation, tornado moved from south Wales to Shropshire, trees damaged. * 27 October: notable tornado event. Southerly situation, one of the most severe tornado events on record, stormy thundery conditions in west England; tornado developed out of a heavy thunderstorm which moved from Devon to Cheshire, maximum width 300 m (1,000 ft), travelled 160 km (100 miles) from Barry to Chester at about 56 km/h

(35 mph), five people killed. **1914** Strong zonal flow (113 westerly situations). Very mild dry winter, fairly weak midwinter westerlies. Very mild wet early spring – 15–16 March: westerly situation, coastal storms; 20 March: cyclonic situation, heavy snowfall, 15 cm (6 in). Average summer temperatures and rainfall – 14 June: anticyclonic northeasterly situation, slack pressure gradient, heavy thunderstorms, flash floods and hail damage. Warm dry autumn – 30 October: easterly situation (Fig. 101), storm-force gales and heavy seas pounded the northeast and east English coasts, Hospital Ship *Rohilla* wrecked on rocks off Whitby (Yorkshire); also probably the storm-force conditions in which the beach of the submerged village of Eccles (Norfolk) was exposed and heavily scoured by strong tides. 15 November: cyclonic situation, heavy snowfall, 10–18 cm (4–7 in) in Scotland and north England. **1915** Weak zonal flow (70 westerly situations). Mild

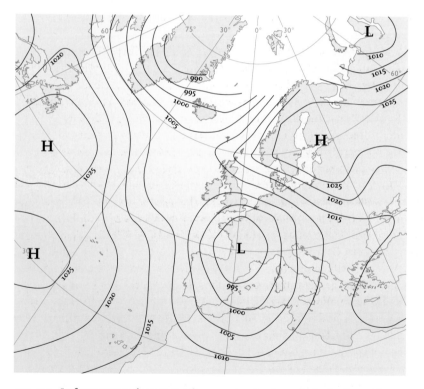

FIG 101. Surface pressure chart, 30 October 1914, showing the easterly situation with storm-force gales over the English northeast coast in which the Hospital Ship *Rohilla* was wrecked off Whitby, Yorkshire. (Wetterzentrale)

wet winter, one of the wettest winters on record, fairly weak midwinter westerlies – December (1914): very wet; one of the wettest Decembers on record; 9 December: cyclonic situation, heavy rain over southeast England associated with a depression that moved northeast through the Strait of Dover; 28 December: cyclonic situation, depression (987 mb) south of Ireland, heavy snowfall, 18 cm (7 in), many trees damaged by weight of snow. 22 January: cyclonic northerly situation, heavy snowfall, 30 cm (12 in), trees and telephone wires damaged; 22 February: cyclonic situation, heavy snowfall, 15–18 cm (6–7 in). Dry late spring, average temperatures – 18–19 March: northerly situation, heavy snowfall, 10–20 cm (4–8 in), deep drifts, 3 m (10 ft) over high ground; 13 May: cyclonic easterly situation, heavy snowfall, 30 cm (12 in) over high ground. Cool unsettled summer with both wet and dry spells. Very cool dry autumn – 25–26 September: cyclonic situation, depression moved slowly north from northeast England on a track between 80 and 160 km (50 and 100 miles) off the North Sea coast when, about 64 km (40 miles) east of Peterhead, it turned sharply east, heavy rain, over 125 mm (5 in) at stations east of Inverness, including the remarkable total of 200.9 mm (7.91 in) at Dalcross Castle. October: southeasterly; 12 November: cyclonic easterly situation, deep depression (below 975 mb) moved east across south Ireland and England, severe cyclonic gales, heavy rain and snow. **1916** Wet year, normal zonal flow (92 westerly situations). Very mild wet winter, very strong midwinter westerlies – December (1915): mild, cyclonic westerly; January: very mild dry; westerly; warmest January on record, 7.5 °C (45.5 °F); 1 January: cyclonic westerly situation, coastal storms; 6–7 February: westerly situation, heavy snowfall, 30–35 cm (12–14 in) in Scotland and northeast England. * 16 February: severe storm. Cyclonic westerly situation, deepening depression (970 mb) moved east-southeast over north Scotland into the North Sea; severe westerly gales affected Ireland, England and the Channel. 22–26 February: heavy snowfall, 20 cm (8 in), deep drifts, 3.5 m (11 ft). Cold wet spring – March: very cold; frequent snow. * 27–28 March: severe storm. Cyclonic situation (Fig. 102), severe gales with near hurricane-force gusts, much damage, many trees and buildings blown down, snowstorm-blizzard conditions, heavy snowfall, 13–25 cm (5–10 in), deep drifts, 12 m (40 ft) over high ground, many upland villages cut off, isolated farms buried in deep drifts, roads and railways blocked, many shipwrecks. Very cool changeable summer with both dry and wet spells – June: one of the three coldest Junes on record, 11.8 °C (53 °F). Warm wet autumn – 4–14 October: westerly spell; 11 October: heavy rain, 200 mm (8 in) at Loch Hourn in the Western Highlands, heaviest 24-hour total on record in Scotland; 16 October: tornado, 90 m (100 yd) wide, considerable damage in Essex. **1917** Cold year, normal zonal flow (93 westerly situations). Very cold dry winter but less severe in Scotland – many English rivers frozen for the first time since 1895;

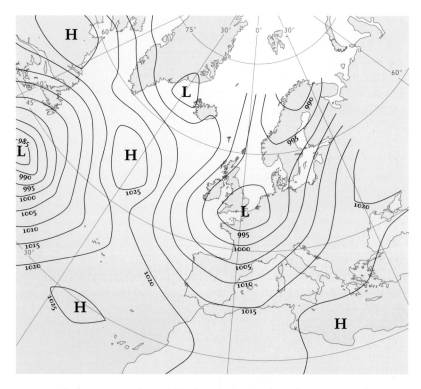

FIG 102. Surface pressure chart, 28 March 1916, showing the cyclonic situation that caused a spring snowstorm. (Wetterzentrale)

absent midwinter westerlies replaced by an easterly flow – 17–18 December (1916): northeasterly/cyclonic situations, heavy snowfall, 17 cm (7 in) in Scotland; 16 January: heavy snowfall, 30 cm (12 in); 25–26 January: east/southeasterly situations, heavy snowfall, 35 cm (14 in), Chesil Beach (Dorset) damaged. Very cold late spring – one of the coldest springs on record; 10 March: cyclonic southerly situation, heavy snowfall in Scotland, snowstorm-blizzard conditions in the Grampians; April: northeasterly winds, heavy snowstorms in north and west Britain; 29 March to 5 April: cyclonic/northerly situations. * 1–3 April: severe snowstorm-blizzard conditions. Cyclonic situation, one of the most severe snowstorms on record in Ireland, deep drifts, 3 m (10 ft) on west coast; also heavy snowfall in Scotland and north England with blizzards over high ground. April: cold. Warm wet summer – 16 June: heavy rainfall, over 100 mm (4 in) in London. * 28 June: severe rainstorm. Northerly situation, small depression (below 1008 mb) moved slowly east along the Channel, heavy rain, 243 mm (9.56 in) at Bruton

(Somerset), second-highest rain-day total on record. 29 July to 3 August: mainly northerly situations, heavy rainfall in southeast England, total fall for the six days over 200 mm (8 in) in Kent, one station in Canterbury recorded 250 mm (10 in). Warm autumn. **1918** Strong zonal flow (117 westerly situations). Mild winter, normal midwinter westerlies – 19 December (1917): heavy snowfall, 15 cm (6 in) in Scotland; January: frequent snow, severe frosts in Scotland, Dee and parts of Loch Lomond frozen; 7 January: northerly situation, heavy snowfall in north Scotland, deep drifts, 12 m (39 ft) in Orkney, Highland Railway blocked in Sutherland and Caithness; 15–16 January: cyclonic/westerly situations, heavy snowfall, 15 cm (6 in), many sheep lost in deep drifts in the Welsh mountains; February: very mild; 28 February to 2 March: heavy snowfall, 15 cm (6 in). Mild dry early spring – 19–20 April: northerly/cyclonic situations, heavy snowfall, 18 cm (7 in) in northwest England. Cool summer. 16 July: cyclonic situation, heavy hailstorm; 17 July: heavy thundery rain occurred along parallel bands running southwest to northeast across England. Very cool wet autumn – September: very wet, one of the wettest Septembers on record. **1919** Cold year; global influenza epidemic reached Europe; normal zonal flow (95 westerly situations), notably late and early snowfall. Wet winter, average temperatures with both cold and mild spells; very weak midwinter westerlies – 19 December (1918): cyclonic situation, depression over the Irish Sea moved east, heavy snowfall; 22 December: cyclonic situation, depression off Scottish east coast, heavy snowfall, 30 cm (12 in) in north England with deep drifts; 3–4 January: cyclonic situation, heavy snowfall, 30 cm (12 in) in central and north England; 27–28 January: cyclonic westerly/northeasterly situations, heavy snowfall, 25–30 cm (10–12 in) in central and north England. Wet spring – March: very cold wet; frequent snow; 29 March: cyclonic northerly situation, heavy snowfall, 30 cm (12 in); 2 April: minimum –15 °C (5 °F). * 27–28 April: notably late snowfall. Cyclonic northerly situation, widespread snowfall, heaviest in southeast and east England, 20–35 cm (8–14 in), deep drifts, 1.8 m (6 ft), communications disrupted, fruit trees damaged. Cool dry summer – July: northwesterly type, Azores high extended northeast over British Isles. Very cool mostly dry autumn. * 19–20 September: notably early snowfall. Northerly situation, snowfall in Scottish and Welsh mountains, and also over high ground in England as far south as Dartmoor, 10 cm (4 in), sleet showers in London, earliest known date for such widespread wintry precipitation, late summer flowers and vegetables damaged by frosts. * 11–12 November: severe snowstorms. Cyclonic northerly situation, widespread snowstorms, particularly severe in north England and Scotland, 20 cm (8 in) in Edinburgh, 40 cm (16 in) in Balmoral. 14 November: easterly situation, exceptionally cold, –23.3 °C (–10 °F) at Braemar (coldest November day on record).

1920s

Westerly maritime; strong zonal flow (109 westerly situations on average per year). **1920** Strong zonal flow (119 westerly situations). Very mild wet winter, strong midwinter westerlies – 2 December (1919): westerly situation, storm-force gales; 11 January: cyclonic westerly situation, severe gales. * 26–27 January: severe storm. Westerly/southwesterly situations, large depression over the east Atlantic, severe southerly gales with hurricane-force gusts over Ireland, Scotland and west England, southerly gales affected the English east coast. 19–20 February: easterly situation (20 February), heavy snowfall, 20 cm (8 in). Very mild wet early spring – 15 March: cyclonic situation, heavy snowfall, 30 cm (12 in). * 12–15 April: severe storm. Cyclonic situation, hurricane-force winds over high ground at 900 m (3,000 ft). * 29 May: severe flood. Heavy thunderstorms developed in a slack cyclonic situation over England, torrential rainfall, 117 mm (4.6 in) in 2½ hours at Louth (Lincolnshire), flood debris dammed river bridge in the Lincoln Wolds, when the 'dam' finally broke a torrent of water 200 m (220 yd) wide swept through the town, 22 people drowned, 1,000 made homeless, record flood level engraved on a town building. Very cool summer, average rainfall. Warm dry autumn. * 1–4 October: severe floods. Cyclonic/southerly situations, heavy rain, 180 mm (7 in), severe floods in mountains above Balmoral and Ballater (Aberdeenshire). **1921** Very warm dry year, ninth warmest year (with 1733 and 1834) on record, very strong zonal flow (124 westerly situations); one of the driest years on record, occurring remarkably within a series of wet years. Very mild winter, very strong midwinter westerlies – 11–12 December (1920): anticyclonic southeasterly/easterly situations, heavy snowfall, 35 cm (14 in); January: westerly, wet; 16–17 and 24 January: westerly/cyclonic situations, heavy snowfall, 20 cm (8 in) in Scotland. Very mild dry very early spring – 14–15 April: northerly situation, widespread heavy snowfall; 17–18 April: cyclonic/northerly situations, heavy snowfall in east Britain; 24 April: anticyclonic situation, end of unsettled conditions that had prevailed in March and much of April; a long spell of mostly warm dry weather followed. Very warm dry anticyclonic summer. * Late spring to autumn: drought. Inferred blocking-high patterns. 17 July: anticyclonic situation, Thames at Teddington fell to only about one-quarter of its normal monthly level. Very warm dry autumn – October: parched ground in Norfolk, River Waveney reduced to a mere trickle, brown dried-up fields, hardened ground prevented ploughing, farmers reduced to cutting branches off trees and hedges as fodder for cattle; 6 October: 29 °C (84 °F) in London (notably late date for a temperature over 27 °C (80 °F). * 6 November: severe storm. Cyclonic situation, one of the most severe North Sea storms on record, depression in the North Sea, storm-force northwesterly gales, much damage, many lives lost. **1922** Wet year, strong zonal flow (107 westerly situations). Very mild wet winter, very weak midwinter westerlies – 27 December (1921): westerly situation, gales; 3–5 January: northerly situation, snowstorm in north Scotland; 15 January: cyclonic westerly situation, depression intensified over northwest Britain, widespread gales and snowstorms, particularly severe in Scotland; 27–28 January: Historic snowstorm in the USA, 'Knickerbocker Storm': very heavy snowfall, 51 cm (20 in), in the northeast States, most severe snowstorm on record in Washington DC. Cold late spring – 8 March: cyclonic situation, severe gales; 19–22 March: northerly/anticyclonic situations, heavy snowfall in Scotland, Wales and west England, severe snowstorm-blizzard conditions over high ground in south Wales and southwest England; May: very mild; late May: exceptionally warm spell, 33 °C (91 °F) in London on 22 May. Very cool wet summer – 4 July: cyclonic situation, gales. Very cool dry autumn. **1923** Wet year, very strong zonal flow (129 westerly situations, highest annual value on record). Very mild wet winter, strong midwinter westerly – February: very wet; one of the wettest Februarys on record; 21 February: westerly situation, heavy snowfall, 30 cm (12 in) in central and north England, and Scotland. Cold spring – 15 May: cyclonic situation, heavy snowfall in the Scottish Highlands, Pennines, Cotswolds and parts of south England. Mostly dry summer, average temperatures – June: northwesterly. * 8 July: severe floods. Light southwesterly gradient, inferred heavy thundery rain, severe floods in north Scotland, 550 m (600 yd) section of railway track swept away by a water torrent at Carrbridge (Inverness). 9–10 July: anticyclonic southerly/easterly situations, heavy persistent thunderstorms overnight; 11–13 July: anticyclonic situation, very warm, 32 °C (90 °F). Very cool wet autumn – 12 October: cyclonic situation, storm, Dover and Sandgate Castle (Kent) damaged. * 15 November: severe storm. Cyclonic situation, depression (below 980 mb) over Scotland, southwesterly gales affected north England, heavy rain, severe river floods, Mersey overflowed, Sale (Cheshire) inundated, floodwater 3 m (10 ft) deep in Sale Priory; severe snowstorm and heavy snowfall, 75 cm (30 in) at Braemar (Aberdeenshire). **1924** One of the wettest years on record, normal zonal flow (94 westerly situations). Average winter temperatures/rainfall, fairly weak midwinter westerlies – 25 December (1923): westerly situation, heavy snowfall, 20 cm (8 in) in Scotland and north England, 60–90 cm (24–36 in) in Aberdeenshire; January: mild wet; 8–9 January: cyclonic southeasterly/easterly situations, widespread heavy snowfall, 15 cm (6 in) in London; February: cold dry; 29 February: northwesterly situation, heavy snowfall in north Scotland, severe blizzard, trains snowbound, many roads blocked. Cold wet late spring – 9–15 April: cyclonic spell; 11 April: heavy snowfall, 20 cm (8 in) in Shetland, deep drifts, 2 m (7 ft). Very cool wet summer. * 31 May to 1 June: severe floods. Cyclonic situation, inferred heavy rain, Worcestershire Agricultural Show washed out. * 18–19 August: severe floods. Cyclonic situation, heavy rain, 239 mm

(9.4 in) at Cannington, Quantock Hills (Somerset), third-largest daily total on record, severe floods. Warm wet autumn – 27 November: cyclonic situation, storm-force gales. **1925** Normal zonal flow (97 westerly situations). Very mild wet southwesterly winter, fairly strong midwinter westerlies – 21 February: cyclonic situation, widespread heavy snowfall, 15 cm (6 in). Wet spring, average temperatures. Warm dry summer – June: anticyclonic, very dry, one of the driest Junes on record, 11 June: hottest day, 31 °C (87 °F). Very cool autumn – 28 November: northerly situation, heavy snowfall, 20–25 cm (8–10 in). **1926** Strong zonal flow (118 westerly situations). Wet winter, mostly mild but two cold spells, weak midwinter westerlies – 6 December (1925): start of cold spell, keen frost, skating in London; 30 December: westerly situation, inferred milder conditions, gales; 13–16 January: anticyclonic easterly/cyclonic situations, renewed cold, heavy snowfall, 30 cm (12 in). Mild spring. * 14–15 May: notable late snowfall. Northerly situation, heavy snowfall, 10–15 cm (4–6 in). Warm summer, average rainfall. Cool wet autumn – 19 September: 32 °C (90 °F) in London, unusually late date for this high temperature. * 25–29 October: notable early snowfall. Cyclonic/easterly situations, widespread heavy snowfall, 30 cm (12 in) in Scotland. 5 November: cyclonic westerly situation, severe southwesterly gales. **1927** Wet year, sixth in series of consecutive wet years since 1921 and wettest year since 1903, normal zonal flow (91 westerly situations). Mild winter but some cold spells, fairly strong midwinter westerlies – 4–5 January: northerly/westerly situations, heavy snowfall; 20 January: cyclonic westerly situation, heavy snowfall, 14 cm (5–6 in). * 28 January: severe storm. Westerly situation, deep depression (950 mb) north of Scotland moved northeast, storm-force southwesterly gales affected Scotland and north England, widespread damage especially in Glasgow with hurricane-force gusts, 11 people killed, over 100 injured; 15 further deaths elsewhere in Scotland. 2 February: heavy snowfall, 20 cm (8 in). Mild spring – 25–27 April, cyclonic northwesterly/northwesterly situations, polar low over Iceland moved southeast, heavy snowfall in north England and Scotland; 27 April: hurricane-force winds, blizzards, deep drifts, 3m (10 ft) in Shetland. Cool wet summer – June: wet; July: wet; 11 July: northerly situation, heavy thunderstorms, rail traffic disrupted; August: wet. Wet autumn, average temperatures – September: wet. * 29 September to 2 October: notably early snowfall. Westerly/cyclonic situations, light snowfall, 5–10 cm (2–4 in) in the Lake District and Scotland. * 28–29 October: severe storm. Cyclonic southwesterly/cyclonic situations, depression (below 980 mb) moved northeast over the Irish west coast and Scotland into the North Sea, storm-force southwesterly gales affected west Ireland, north Wales and northwest England, Atlantic storm surge, severe floods affected coasts of north Wales and northwest England, sea defences breached, coastal cottages collapsed, railway lines washed away, Fleetwood

(Lancashire) inundated, five people drowned, houses damaged, 400 made homeless, trees blown down, ten drowned off Co. Mayo. 7–11 November: northerly situation, heavy snowfall (11 November). **1928** Strong zonal flow (117 westerly situations), fairly strong midwinter westerlies; high incidence of severe storms. Mild wet winter. * 5 December (1927): severe snowstorm. Southerly situation, depression over the southwest entrance to the Channel moved slowly east into north France; cold easterly airstream over England with temperatures near or a little below freezing point, heavy precipitation; mild southwesterly airstream with temperatures of 8–10 °C (46–50 °F) was located on the southeast side of the low; on meeting the barrier of cold dense air in the easterly flow, the mild air was forced to rise and its temperature was soon reduced to below freezing point; frozen precipitation falling through the cold easterly produced heavy snowfall, 15 cm (6 in) and deep drifts; snowfall was heaviest in south England, near centre of low, and many places were isolated for days owing to blocked roads; supplies for cut-off inhabitants were dropped for the first time by aircraft. 21 December: southerly situation, ice storm, freezing rain, glazed frost ('black ice'), many road accidents, train services badly disrupted. * 24–27 December (1927): severe storm and snowstorm-blizzard conditions, 'The 1927 Christmas Blizzard'. Cyclonic/easterly situations, from 25 to 27 December an intense depression moved southeast from Ireland into the Channel and then across France to the Mediterranean; as temperatures fell on Christmas Day, rain turned to heavy snow and by midnight roads were blocked and rail traffic disrupted, snowstorm-blizzard conditions continued all night and most of 26 December with easterly winds, heavy snowfall, 15 cm (6 in) and 50–60 cm (20–24 in) over the Chilterns and North Downs, deep drifts, 4.5 m (15 ft), locally up to 6 m (20 ft) in further exposed places such as Salisbury Plain, hundreds of roads blocked, vehicles buried, telephone wires and tree branches broken by weight of snow, St Albans isolated, many villages completely cut off, houses buried in drifts, provisions again dropped by air; the pattern of the snow storm was remarkable, being most severe with deepest snow on Dartmoor, Salisbury Plain, North Downs and the Alton–Basingstoke district, whereas practically no snow fell in Oxford and mostly rain in east Kent and the South Downs; a sudden local thaw caused severe floods, particularly in the Canterbury and Maidstone districts. 29 December (1927): anticyclonic easterly situation, renewed frost, as the thaw had not lasted long, delays in communication continued owing to the great depth of snow. 31 December to 1 January: cyclonic/southerly situations, rapid general thaw, heavy rain, severe floods, particularly along the Thames; 3 January: the severe conditions continued to ease but deep drifts, 2 m (6–7 ft), remained on roads in Hampshire as late as 21 January. * 6–7 January: severe storm, 'The Chelsea Floods'. One of the most severe North Sea storms on record, cyclonic westerly/westerly situations, deep depression (below 980 mb) over Scotland moved rapidly southeast into the North Sea, severe to storm-force northwesterly gales, resulting storm surge coincided with an exceptionally high spring tide and an unusually large run-off in the Thames basin (due to heavy rain and melting snow), these factors combined to cause one of the most severe floods on record in the Thames, water level rose nearly 2 m (6 ft) above the predicted height, riverside buildings flooded including the Tate Gallery, water flowed into the normally dry moats of the Tower of London, many river embankments breached from the City to Hammersmith, 14 people drowned in basements of their houses. * 10–12 February: severe storms. Cyclonic westerly situations, inferred severe southwesterly gales, property destroyed, lives lost. Mild spring – 7–14 March: easterly spell, heavy snow (10–12 March), 15–20 cm (6–8 in), roads blocked by drifts, snow as far south as the Isles of Scilly. Cool summer, average rainfall. * 28 June: severe floods. Westerly situation, heavy rainfall, 200 mm (8 in) in the Welsh mountains, extensive floods at Blaenau Ffestiniog (Merioneth). 6–26 July: very warm dry, 15 July: 33 °C (91 °F); 20 July: unexpected squall line moved rapidly up the Channel associated with a localised storm surge, many people drowned. Mild wet autumn – 22 October: cyclonic westerly situation, tornado in London, buildings damaged; 10–25 November: severe storms, westerly/cyclonic situations, deep primary depression north of Scotland, series of intense secondary lows moved east over England into the south North Sea, gales and hurricane-force gusts; 10 November: cloudy with occasional rain and southwesterly winds, cyclonic activity increased and centres of the lows passed nearer to the British Isles, until on 15 November the first severe gales were experienced in the Channel, Rye (Sussex) lifeboat capsized with the loss of 17 hands, a southerly gale had developed overnight and the lifeboat had been launched to help a vessel in distress off Dungeness (Kent). * 16–18 November: severe storm. One of the worst North Sea storms on record, cyclonic/cyclonic westerly situations, an intense secondary depression (968 mb) moved rapidly east-northeast over the British Isles into the North Sea, severe southwest to westerly gales in southern districts with hurricane-force gusts, much damage both on land and at sea, cross-Channel ferries suspended, conditions temporarily improved in the rear of the low but the general situation remained unsettled with an alternation of stormy and fine weather conditions. * 23–25 November: severe storm. Cyclonic westerly situation, further gales struck early on 23 November as an even deeper and more intense depression moved rapidly east over north Britain (950.7 mb at Edinburgh), severe southwest to westerly gales, locally hurricane-force, occurred south of the low's centre, and again much damage both on land and at sea, and cross-Channel services suspended. **1929** Continental; normal zonal flow (91 westerly situations) but absent midwinter westerlies. Very cold dry winter – 1 January: anticyclonic situation, historic cricket match played at Hambledon (Hampshire); 9 January: anticyclonic southerly situation, heavy snowfall, 15 cm (6 in) in Scotland; 15–17 January: northerly/westerly situations, widespread heavy snowfall, 30 cm (12 in), especially in northeast Scotland. February: southerly; blocking high over central and north Europe gave rise to exceptionally cold weather in mainland Europe: rivers and water bodies frozen, including the Rhine, Danube, Baltic Sea and Zuider Zee; initially the blocking high did not affect the British Isles, which remained under the control of Atlantic depressions, but on 11 February a slight alteration in the circulation allowed easterly winds to reach the country, advecting cold conditions from north Europe; this was the beginning of a very cold spell which lasted to the beginning of March, during which time many places recorded their lowest temperatures since 1895 and the Thames was frozen in some reaches; 11–12 February: southeasterly situation, secondary depression over southwest British Isles on 11 February, heavy snowfall in southwest England, Wales and Scotland; 15 February: coldest day of the severe spell, –18.3 °C (–1 °F) at Ross-on-Wye (Herefordshire); 16 February: cyclonic southeasterly situation, heavy snowfall in Scotland, Wales and southwest England, continuous snow fell in very large flakes for 12 hours, exceptional depths of undrifted snow, 120 cm (4 ft) at Dean Prior in southeast Dartmoor (Devon), probably the deepest daily total on record at a location below 300 m (1,000 ft), many roads blocked; 26 February: heavy snowfall in central and east Scotland, many roads blocked; many skaters in the Lake District during this cold spell, conditions were ideal as there was little snow cover on the smooth ice surface, frozen Lake Windermere was said to have borne 50,000 people, skating continued until a thaw set in during March. Average spring temperatures – 10 March: although maximum temperatures in the Lake District reached 21 °C (70 °F), skating continued in calm sunny conditions on thick ice preserved by cold nights; the cold spell ended when an anticyclone extended over the British Isles from mainland Europe giving fine calm conditions; although the nights remained almost as cold as before, strong sunshine by day warmed the air, resulting in a large diurnal range of temperature; 28 March: 25 °C (77 °F) at Wakefield (Yorkshire); 7 May: cyclonic situation, storm-force winds. Cool dry summer – 20 July: anticyclonic southwesterly situation, a probable squall line moved rapidly east along the Channel, unexpected high waves, lives lost off southeast English coast. Very warm wet autumn – September: anticyclonic westerly; November: very wet; 11 November: cyclonic westerly situation, severe southwesterly gales, heavy rain, 200 mm (8 in) in Glamorgan, severe floods in the Rhondda Valley and Pontypridd, hundreds of houses inundated with coal-slurried water.

1930S

Maritime; normal zonal circulation (98 westerly situations on average per year).
1930 Wet cyclonic year, strong zonal flow (115 westerly situations). Mild wet
winter, fairly strong midwinter westerlies – December (1929): very wet. * 5–7
December (1929): severe storm. Deep depression (below 950 mb) off western
coasts of the British Isles moved slowly northeast, southwest to westerly severe
gales, hurricane-force over exposed southwestern parts of the British Isles and
Channel, severe to hurricane-force gales continued until 10 December, many
shipwrecks, lives lost. January: very mild wet; 11 January: westerly situation, heavy
snowfall, 15–20 cm (6–8 in) in Scotland. * 12 January: severe storm. Depression
northwest of Scotland, storm-force southwesterly gales over south Britain, one of
the most destructive storms to affect England and the Channel, many trees
blown down, many shipwrecks, great loss of life. February: mostly cold dry;
6 February: northeasterly situation, heavy snowfall, 20–25 cm (8–10 in) in
Scotland and north England. Wet spring, average temperatures – 15 March:
cyclonic situation, widespread heavy snowfall, 20 cm (8 in); 19–20 March: cyclonic
northerly/westerly situations, widespread heavy snowfall, 15–30 cm (6–12 in). Wet
summer, average temperatures – 20–23 July: mainly cyclonic northerly situations,
four-day spell of continuous rain, almost 300 mm (12 in) at Castleton, North York
Moors, severe flood in Esk. Mild wet autumn – rain-damaged crops. **1931** Wet
year, fairly normal zonal flow (80 westerly situations). Wet winter, average
temperatures, normal midwinter westerlies – 18 January: northwesterly situation,
heavy snowfall, 15–25 cm (6–10 in) in Scotland; 31 January: cyclonic situation,
heavy snowfall, 15–25 cm (6–10 in) in Scotland; 16 February: cyclonic
northwesterly situation, heavy snowfall, 30 cm (12 in) in Scotland. Cold wet spring
– March: southeasterly; 1–2 March: northerly/anticyclonic situations, widespread
heavy snowfall, 45 cm (18 in) in Orkney, deep drifts, 1 m (3 ft) in east Scotland;
9–10 March: easterly/northerly situations, widespread heavy snowfall, 20 cm
(8 in). Cool wet summer. * 14 June: severe storm. Cyclonic situation, heavy
thunderstorms, destructive tornado at Erdington near Birmingham, heavy rain,
63 mm (2.5 in) in less than 40 minutes at Cannock (Staffordshire), 100 mm (4 in)
over high ground in northwest England, severe floods, roads and bridges
destroyed, hundreds of livestock drowned. 3–5 August: anticyclonic/anticyclonic
easterly situations, heavy thunderstorms, flash floods in London. Cool autumn –
November: exceptional prevalence of south to southeasterly winds, mild very wet,
apart from north Scotland and east England; 2 November: southwesterly situation,
heavy rain, 244 mm (9.6 in) in two days, floods at Brecon. * 9–11 November: severe
storm. Deep depression (below 965 mb) moved northeast over northwestern
coasts of the British Isles, severe south to southwesterly gales coincided with an

exceptionally high tide, Isle of Wight briefly split in two between Yarmouth and Freshwater Bay by the gale-driven high tide, heavy seas in the Channel, sea floods, waves 12 m (40 ft) high broke over houses in Sandgate (Kent), streets flooded in Portsmouth (Hampshire), buildings damaged along the English south coast from Cornwall to Kent. **1932** Strong zonal flow (106 westerly situations). Mild dry winter, strong midwinter westerlies – 29 December (1931): northerly situation, widespread heavy snowfall, 20 cm (8 in); February: cold; drought, no rain recorded in normally wet Borrowdale (Cumberland). Cold wet spring – 6–7 March: westerly/cyclonic westerly situations, widespread heavy snowfall, 13 cm (5 in); May: very wet, widespread floods. Warm dry summer – 18–20 August: 32 °C (90 °F) exceeded on three consecutive days, 37 °C (99 °F) at Greenwich on 19 and 20 August. Cool wet autumn – 23–25 November: westerly situation, heavy snowfall, 15 cm (6 in) in Scotland. **1933** Dry continental easterly year, weak zonal flow (78 westerly situations). Average winter temperatures and rainfall, some cold spells, fairly weak midwinter westerlies – February: cold intrusion with snow and rain. * 23–26 February: severe snowstorm/blizzard conditions (Fig. 103). Cyclonic/cyclonic southeasterly situations, as a depression slowed down off southwest Ireland, a band of heavy rain became stationary over England, Wales and Ireland, precipitation turned to wet snow as it engaged with a cold easterly flow which had covered the region some days previously; although little snow fell over south England, severe snowstorm-blizzard conditions affected most other parts of the country, 60–90 cm (24–36 in), deep drifts, 4 m (13 ft), London–South Wales trains badly delayed, deep snowfall in the Dublin mountains, newspaper headlines on 26 February: 'Isolated towns and villages, 20,000 people cut off, impassable roads, many sports fixtures abandoned, hundreds of cars in snowdrifts.' Very mild spring, average rainfall – April: warm, chestnut trees in blossom by the end of the month, about four weeks before the usual date. Very warm dry mostly anticyclonic summer – following a brief cold northerly outbreak, 26–28 June, the summer was marked by a prolonged warm dry spell which was partly broken on 27 August when heavy rain in a southerly situation affected Ireland, Scotland and northwest England; however, dry conditions soon returned and dominated the weather into September. Dry autumn. * 25–28 October: notable early snowfall. Northerly/cyclonic northerly situations, widespread light snowfall, 5–10 cm (2–4 in) over Dartmoor and Lincolnshire. **1934** Strong zonal flow (113 westerly situations). Cold dry winter, strong midwinter westerlies – 26–27 February: northerly situation, heavy snowfall in Scotland and north England, 60 cm (24 in) in Yorkshire. Wet spring, average temperatures – 10–20 March: cyclonic spell; 16–17 March: heavy snowfall, 30 cm (12 in) in Scotland; 7–9 April: cyclonic northeasterly situation, heavy snowfall, 20 cm (8 in) in Scotland. Very warm dry

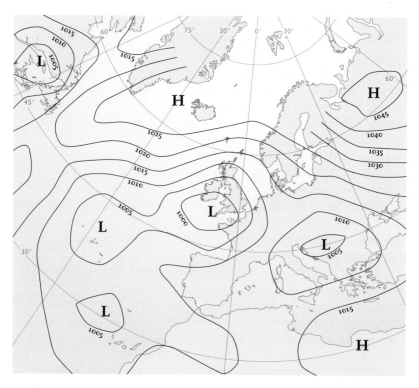

FIG 103. Surface pressure chart, 24 February 1933, showing the cyclonic southeasterly situation that caused the severe snowstorm-blizzard conditions that affected many parts of England. (Wetterzentrale)

summer. Very warm dry autumn. * 30–31 October: notable early snowfall. Cyclonic northerly situation, heavy snowfall in Scotland, 20 cm (8 in) in West Linton (Borders). **1935** Wet year, strong zonal flow (103 westerly situations). Very mild wet winter, fairly weak midwinter westerlies – December (1934): very mild, 8.1 °C (46.6 °F), one of the warmest Decembers on record; 27–29 January: heavy snowfall, 22 cm (9 in) in northeast England. Average spring temperatures – 10–11 March: depression over Biscay, sleet, heavy snowfall, 16 cm (6 in) in southwest and south England; 4–5 April: heavy snowfall, 20 cm (8 in) in Scotland; May: cold; mid month: record May frosts, –12 °C (10 °F) in Rickmansworth frost hollow (Hertfordshire), fruit blossom damaged after opening in very warm anticyclonic conditions on 6 May, large commercial orchard crop losses. * 16–17 May: notable late snow. Cyclonic northerly situation, heavy snowfall, most areas including, exceptionally, the Isles of Scilly, 15 cm (6 in), 60–90 cm (24–36 in) over Pennines, 1 m (3 ft) drifts, roads blocked, worst May snowstorm for 60 years in Birmingham. Very warm dry summer. Warm wet autumn. * 15–17 September: severe storm. Westerly/cyclonic situations, severe gales (exceptionally strong winds for early autumn) with hurricane-force gusts. 30 November: cyclonic westerly, heavy snowfall, 15 cm (6 in) in Scotland. **1936** Normal zonal flow (96 westerly situations). Wet winter, average temperatures, fairly weak midwinter westerlies – 4 December (1935): westerly situation, heavy snowfall, 20 cm (8 in) in south Scotland; 22 December: heavy snowfall, 20 cm (8 in) in central Scotland; 19–20 January: cyclonic situation (20 January), heavy snowfall, 25–30 cm (10–12 in) in Scotland, and north and central England, villages isolated in Scotland, road and rail traffic severely disrupted. Dry spring, average temperatures. Wet summer, average temperatures. Warm autumn. * 17–19 October: severe storm. Cyclonic/cyclonic northwesterly situations, deep depression (965 mb) north of Shetland on 17 October moved east into south Norway, severe westerly gales pounded north Scottish coasts; although gales ceased over the British Isles by 18 October, northwest to northerly gales continued on 19 October over the Hebrides, Irish Sea and North Sea. * 26–27 October: severe storm. Westerly situation (similar to previous storm, 17–19 October, but more severe westerly gales), widespread hurricane-force gusts affected Scotland and north England. * 30 November to 1 December: severe sea floods. Northwesterly situation, severe gales affected east coast, severe sea floods. **1937** Cyclonic year, normal zonal flow (86 westerly situations). Very mild wet winter, fairly weak midwinter westerlies – 4–6 December (1936): westerly/cyclonic/northerly situations, heavy snowfall, roads blocked in west and north Scotland. * 16–22 January: severe storms. Intense cyclonic activity over the Atlantic, southeasterly gales generally affected the British Isles; 17–19 January: cyclonic westerly situations, period of strongest winds, secondary depression (985 mb) over southwest Ireland moved across the British Isles into the North Sea, many shipwrecks, Channel ferries delayed. 29–31 January, heavy snowfall, 15 cm (6 in) in north England and Scotland, 45 cm (18 in) in Aberdeenshire. * 27 February to 1 March: severe snowstorm-blizzard conditions. Short cyclonic northerly spell, heavy snowfall in Scotland, north England and Wales, northerly winds, snowstorm-blizzard conditions (the term *blizzard* officially used for the first time by the UK Meteorological Office to describe this type of heavy snowfall event), heavy snowfall, 30 cm (12 in), locally 50 cm (20 in), deep drifts, 1.5–4 m (5–13 ft), roads blocked, trees and telegraph poles brought down. Wet spring, average temperatures – 4–9 March: easterly spell; 6–7 March: snowstorm, heavy snow, 25 cm (10 in), telegraph poles brought down. * 11–13 March: severe snowstorm. Cyclonic situation, heavy snowfall in north Ireland, south Scotland and north England, deep drifts, 3 m (10 ft), five people killed, Belfast milk supply had to be brought in from Scotland. Warm dry summer – June: tornado affected southern outskirts of Birmingham causing structural damage. Dry autumn, average temperatures. **1938** Very strong zonal flow (124 westerly situations). Mild wet winter, strong midwinter westerlies – 7–11 December (1937): cyclonic easterly situations, widespread heavy snowfall, 30 cm (12 in), many roads blocked; January: very mild wet; 14 January: westerly situation, inferred severe southwesterly gales, widespread damage; February: dry mild at first, cold later; 1 February: westerly situation, deep depression (below 965 mb) north of the British Isles, strong westerly gradient over the country, extremely low pressure, 948 mb, recorded at Deerness (Orkney). * 11–13 February: severe storm. Anticyclonic northwesterly/northerly situations, strong northerly flow over the North Sea, severe northerly gales, severe sea flood, much damage along the East Anglian coast from the Wash to Southwold (Suffolk), new sandbank defences breached at Horsey (Norfolk), 3 m (9 ft) -deep torrent of water poured through a 640 m (700 yd) gap, 50 sq km (20 sq miles) of marshes inundated, three villages marooned, floodwater continued to rise for four days, freshwater rivers affected several kilometres inland; although mainly forgotten and overshadowed by the 1953 disaster, this East Anglian 1938 inundation was both greater and longer-lasting; it had been caused by the bank across the exit of Old Hundred River into the sea being weakened during the coastal gales of 1936. 13–17 February: mostly easterly situation, heavy snowfall, 2.5 m (8 ft) drifts in Kent. Very mild dry spring – March: very mild; one of the mildest Marches on record, 9.1 °C (48.4 °F); April, blocking high west of Ireland. * Spring: drought. Inferred anticyclonic situations, no rainfall recorded at a number of stations in England and Wales during March and April (one of the driest Aprils on record), standpipes set up in several towns by August. Average summer temperatures/rainfall. * 1–3 June: severe storm. Cyclonic situation, small intense depression moved northeast over England, severe westerly gales in the Channel, snow over high ground in north England and at low levels in north Scotland; exceptionally severe gales for the time of year overnight on 1–2 June. 1–12 August: exceptionally heavy thundery spell, widespread damage including that caused by a tornado in Scotland on 11 August. Very warm wet autumn. * 4 October: severe storm. Cyclonic situation, deep depression (below 970 mb) north of the British Isles, strong westerly flow over the country. November: one of the warmest Novembers on record, 9.4 °C (48.9 °F); 5 November: westerly situation, 21 °C (70 °F) at Cambridge, one of the warmest November days on record. * 23–24 November: severe storm. Cyclonic/westerly situations, deep depression (960 mb) moved east across northern parts of the British Isles, severe westerly gales, unusually strong over inland England, heavy snowfall, 15 cm (6 in) in south Scotland. **1939** Weak zonal circulation (77 westerly situations). Mostly mild wet winter, weak midwinter westerlies. * 15–19 December (1938): severe storm. Southerly situation on 15 December, south to southeasterly gales affected western parts of the British Isles, but advancing mild Atlantic air halted as a blocking anticyclone over mainland Europe intensified; frosty conditions set in on 17 December in a southeasterly situation as strong to gale-force easterly winds began to affect southeast England, heavy snowfall, 30 cm (12 in) on 19 December, cold air advancing westward across England introduced a generally frosty spell which continued into early January. 21–22 December (1938): anticyclonic easterly/northeasterly situations, widespread heavy snowfall, 30 cm (12 in), roads blocked; 26 December: westerly situation, heavy snowfall, 20–30 cm (8–12 in) in south England; 1 January: cyclonic situation, heavy snowfall, 20 cm (8 in) in north England; 10 January: cyclonic westerly, heavy snowfall, 20 cm (8 in); 25–26 January: cyclonic/cyclonic northeasterly, heavy snowfall, 30 cm (12 in), locally 60 cm (24 in), deep drifts, 3.5 m (11 ft) over high ground in southwest England. Mild spring. Wet summer, average temperatures. Very warm wet autumn.

MID 20TH-CENTURY COOLING: 1940–1979

1940S

Normal zonal circulation (95 westerly situations on average per year). **1940** Weak zonal flow (71 westerly situations). * Very cold winter. Blocking-high situation, absent midwinter westerlies replaced by an easterly flow – also severe winter in mainland Europe. December (1939) to February: prolonged frosty spell with frequent snow, skating at Christmas, snow-covered slopes and frozen ponds provided many sledging and sliding grounds for country children and evacuees to enjoy in wartime Britain, severe conditions continued for six weeks until mid February, by which time the sea was frozen along the English south and southeast coasts with ice extending for hundreds of metres offshore; Thames frozen for 13 km (8 miles) between Teddington and Sunbury, London reservoirs frozen with ice 30 cm (1 ft) thick; record amount of ice in the Baltic. 16–17 January: northerly/anticyclonic northerly situations, widespread heavy snowfall, 30 cm (12 in), deep drifts in Kent. * 26–29 January: severe ice storm. Southerly/southeasterly situations, a cold southeasterly airstream prevailed over the British Isles between a blocking high over Scandinavia and low pressure to the west; although the eastward movement of mild Atlantic air was halted at the surface, it overran the cold air aloft and produced a three-day severe ice storm comprising a prolonged fall of freezing rain over a broad band of the country from southern counties across west England to north Wales which formed a treacherous layer of glazed frost or clear ice ('black ice') over 2.5 cm (1 in) thick on roads and pavements, doors froze solid, trees and telephone wires were brought down by the sheer weight of ice, thousands of birds and small animals perished; elsewhere there was heavy snowfall, 30–60 cm (12–24 in), locally 60–120 cm (24–48 in), deep drifts, isolated villages and snowbound trains. Very mild spring, average rainfall. Warm dry summer – 19–24 August: northerly spell, 24 August: ground frost, –3 °C (27 °F) in London, earliest known date for such a frost in recent times. Warm wet autumn. **1941** Weak zonal flow (76 westerly situations). Very cold winter with frequent snow – absent midwinter westerlies replaced by an easterly flow, above normal amount of ice in the Baltic; 30–31 December (1940): cyclonic/cyclonic easterly situations, heavy snowfall, 15 cm (6 in); frequent sub-zero temperatures, widespread skating in Scotland; 18–20 January: cyclonic southeasterly/cyclonic situations, heavy snowfall, 30–60 cm (12–24 in) in Scotland, and north and central England, deep drifts, 3 to 4.5 m (10–15 ft); 2 February: cyclonic northeasterly situation, heavy snowfall, 20 cm (8 in) in southwest England; 4–5 February: anticyclonic/westerly situations, heavy snowfall in Wales and Scotland. * 18–20 February: severe snowstorm-blizzard conditions. Cyclonic easterly/cyclonic northerly situations, depression over southeast England moved north off northeast England, northerly winds, severe snowstorm-blizzard conditions, heavy snowfall, 75–100 cm (30–40 in), deep drifts in southeast Scotland and northeast England, Durham cut off for three days, six trains carrying 1,000 passengers buried in drifts, smaller falls of snow in central and east England. Very cold wet spring – one of the coldest springs on record; March: northeasterly winds, frequent snow, rain; 26–27 March: cyclonic/southerly situations, severe snowstorm, heavy snowfall, locally 90 cm (36 in), deep drifts, 9 m (30 ft) in north Scotland, worst snowstorm since the 1880 winter; 30–31 March: cyclonic southerly situation (31 March), depression off west Scotland, heavy snowfall, 25 cm (10 in) in west Scotland. Warm summer, average rainfall. Very warm dry autumn. **1942** Normal zonal flow (96 westerly situations). Very cold mostly dry winter with occasional snow, very weak midwinter westerlies – coldest winter in England since 1895 (third successive severe winter); Baltic Sea completely ice-bound, one of its most severe winter freezing events on record; January: southwesterly flow over north Britain. * 19–20 January: severe snowstorms. Southerly situation, strong southerly flow over the British Isles with a blocking high over Scandinavia, severe snowstorms affected all areas, heavy snowfall, 30–60 cm (12–24 in), roads and railways blocked, food dropped by aircraft to a snowbound train south of Wick (Caithness). 28 January: frozen sea reported off north Norfolk by an RAF aircraft; another plane returning to base in north Norfolk on 28–29 January encountered a severe snowstorm; 2 February: cyclonic situation, heavy snowfall, 15–30 cm (6–12 in) in north England and southeast Scotland; 5 February: anticyclonic situation, heavy snowfall in east Scotland and England, deep drifts, 5 m (16 ft), villages cut off in Aberdeenshire. Mild wet spring – 4–7 March: heavy snowfall, 30 cm (12 in), 1 m (3 ft) drifts in north England, many roads blocked. Warm dry summer. Dry autumn, average temperatures. **1943** Strong zonal flow (117 westerly situations). Very mild wet winter, fairly weak midwinter westerlies – December (1942): intense cyclonic conditions over the Atlantic; 31 January: cyclonic situation, heavy snowfall, 18 cm (7 in) in the Ochil Hills (Scotland). Very mild dry spring – 7 April: northwesterly situation, stormy. * 8–9 May: notable late snowfall. Cyclonic/northerly situations, depression (975 mb) off northeast England moved north, heavy snowfall, 15–20 cm (6–8 in) in Scotland, north England, Isle of Man and north Ireland, deep drifts, 2 m (7 ft) in the Scottish Highlands. Warm dry summer. Warm autumn. **1944** Normal zonal flow (95 westerly situations). Mild dry winter, very strong midwinter westerlies – 18–19 December (1943): southwesterly/westerly situations, heavy snowfall, 15 cm (6 in) in Scotland; 26–27 February: northerly/cyclonic northeasterly, heavy snowfall, 30 cm (12 in) in Scotland, and north and central England, deep drifts in north Scotland. Very mild dry spring – 1 March: northwesterly situation, heavy snowfall, 30 cm (12 in) in Scotland, severe snowstorm, deep drifts, 9 m (30 ft) in north Scotland, blocked traffic, some parts of the country cut off for about a week. Warm summer, average rainfall – 4–6 June: cyclonic westerly/northwesterly situations, west to northwesterly gales ('D-Day gales'), storm-force gusts affected western coasts; August: inferred warm dry; high pressure extended from the Azores to Russia. Cool wet autumn. **1945** Fairly normal zonal flow (82 westerly situations). Average winter rainfall, weak midwinter westerlies – December (1944): very cold; 10–11 December: cyclonic westerly/cyclonic situations, heavy snowfall, 20–30 cm (8–12 in), locally 75 cm (30 in) in Scotland and north England, deep drifts in north Scotland, roads blocked. * 25–28 December (1944): notable fog. Anticyclonic situation, dense fog in London, visibility virtually nil on Christmas Day and from midday on 26 December to the early morning of 27 December. January: mostly very cold, frequent snow; 9–10 January: northerly situation, heavy snowfall, 60 cm (24 in) in northeast England. * 18–19 January: severe storm. Cyclonic/northerly situations, deep depression (below 975 mb) over south Scotland moved east to northeast into the Kattegat, severe southwesterly gales south of centre over England and Wales on 18 January veered northwesterly the following day across all parts of the British Isles. 19–30 January: sub-zero temperatures widely recorded, sea ice formed in Folkestone harbour, good skating conditions in the Fens and on Loch

Lomond; 25 January: easterly situation, heavy snowfall, 60 cm (24 in) in southwest England and south Wales, 75 cm (30 in) in Cardiff, one of the largest snow depths on record for a low-level station; 29–30 January: heavy snowfall, 25 cm (10 in) in north England and south Scotland, deep drifts, 6 m (20 ft) in north Scotland, many trains trapped; 30 January: cyclonic westerly situation, thaw with rain and snow ended cold spell from early January; February: very mild wet, one of the mildest Februarys on record. Very mild spring – May: southwesterly. Warm summer, average rainfall. Very warm dry autumn – November: one of the driest Novembers on record. **1946** Wet year, strong zonal flow (107 westerly situations). Mild wet winter, normal midwinter westerlies – 18–19 December (1945): extremely low pressure (949 mb) recorded at Valentia (Co. Kerry); 20 February: northerly situation, heavy snowfall, 45 cm (18 in), deep drifts, 1.5 m (5 ft) in northeast Scotland, many roads blocked; 26 February: northeasterly situation, heavy snowfall, 20 cm (8 in) in central Scotland and south England. Mild spring – 2 March: easterly flow over eastern Britain, heavy snowfall, 25 cm (10 in), deep drifts, 3 m (10 ft) in east Scotland, and east and south England, troops deployed to free villages in Kent; 4 March: easterly situation, widespread heavy snowfall, 15–20 cm (6–8 in). Cool wet summer – 2–4 July: heavy thunderstorms, large hail, flash floods. Very warm wet autumn – 6 November: anticyclonic situation, warmest November day on record, 21.7 °C (71 °F) at Prestatyn (Flintshire). **1947** Normal zonal flow (85 westerly situations). * Very cold winter. Blocking-high situations, weak midwinter westerlies – one of the snowiest winters of the 20th century; 16–20 December (1946): anticyclonic situation heralded an early start to the winter; 19 December: heavy snowfall; 28–29 December: westerly/anticyclonic westerly situations, heavy snowfall, 30 cm (12 in); January: very cold, most of the country snow-covered from mid January to mid March; 21 January: start of cold frosty spell to 16 March, frequent heavy snowfall, easterly winds, large numbers of livestock lost; 23 January: anticyclonic easterly, heavy snowfall, 27 cm (11 in) in southeast England, deep drifts, villages isolated; 25 January: anticyclonic easterly situation, widespread snowstorm-blizzard conditions. * 28–29 January: severe snowstorm-blizzard conditions. Anticyclonic easterly/easterly situations, very cold continental southeasterly airstream over the British Isles, heavy snowfall in south England, worst snowstorm-blizzard conditions since 1891, 3 m (10 ft) drifts, roads blocked, railways disrupted, severe blizzard over Exmoor, heavy snowfall, 18 cm (7 in) in the Isles of Scilly, shipping halted in the Channel. February: prevalence of north and east winds, no precipitation recorded at Glenquoich in the wettest part of the Scottish Highlands; one of the coldest snowiest Februarys on record, –1.9 °C (28.6 °F). * February: severe snowstorm-blizzard conditions. Snowstorm-blizzard conditions throughout February, widespread heavy snowfall,

30 cm (12 in), roads and railways disrupted. Mild spring – March: one of the wettest Marches on record, this combined with melting of deep snow caused the most severe floods of the 20th century. * 4–6 March: severe snowstorm-blizzard conditions. Cyclonic easterly/cyclonic northeasterly situations, depression over southwest England moved east into north France, east to northeasterly winds, widespread heavy snowfall, 30 cm (12 in), locally 55 cm (22 in) or more, such as in Clwyd (northeast Wales), 150 cm (60 in), 3m (10 ft) drifts over high ground, roads and railways badly disrupted. * 10–11 March: severe river floods. Cyclonic southeasterly/easterly situations, mild moist airstream moved across southwest England, rapid thaw, widespread floods from Somerset to Kent late on 11 March. 12–13 March: advancing warm front caused very heavy snowfall, 45–85 cm (18–34 in) in north England and south Scotland, deep drifts, 8 m (26 ft), farms and villages isolated. * 16 March: severe storm and river floods. Cyclonic situation, depression over Ireland, severe southwesterly gales with hurricane-force gusts, extensive damage, heavy rain, lower Trent valley flooded when the river met spring tides in the Humber, Fens severely inundated when dykes were breached; as floods in the Fens continued to rise, rescue and repair support for the region was pledged by government on 24 March. 22 March: southerly situation, thaw extended to all areas, most widespread severe river floods on record continued to affect low-lying ground into mid May. April: westerly; 12 May: start of a long, mainly warm, anticyclonic spell, renewed in July after breaks in June. Very warm dry anticyclonic summer – persistent high pressure extending northeast from the Azores high led to a prolonged warm spell; June: anticyclonic southwesterly; July: anticyclonic southwesterly; August: very warm dry, anticyclonic, one of the warmest Augusts on record, 18.6 °C (65.5 °F); no rain recorded in much of west Scotland. Very warm dry autumn – September: anticyclonic westerly; 18–19 November: small depression moved rapidly across southwest England and the Channel, heavy snowfall, 15 cm (6 in) in Wales, southwest and central England. **1948** Strong zonal flow (107 westerly situations). Very mild wet winter – 29 December (1947): cyclonic northwesterly situation, heavy snowfall, 15 cm (6 in) in Scotland, Wales, and central and north England; January: very wet, westerly; one of the wettest Januarys on record; 17–18 January: cyclonic westerly/westerly situations, heavy snowfall, 15–23 cm (6–9 in) in central Scotland, deep drifts, 2 m (7 ft), many roads blocked; 20–22 January: cyclonic situation, widespread heavy snowfall, 35 cm (14 in), 1 m (3 ft) drifts in Hampstead (London). Very mild dry spring – March: anticyclonic southwesterly; 9 March: westerly situation, 22.3 °C (72.1 °F) at Kinloss and Forres in northeast Scotland (föhn effect). Cool wet summer – 17 July: end of three-week spell of out-of-season cold northerly winds; 28–29 July: anticyclonic southeasterly situation, warmest night on record,

minimum temperature 23.3 °C (74 °F); day temperatures in London over 32 °C (90 °F) on three successive days (28–30 July). * 12 August: severe flood. Cyclonic situation, trough extended west over England from a depression (below 1005 mb) over the North Sea, continuous heavy rainfall, over 150 mm (6 in) in 24 hours over the uplands of Berwickshire, extensive flood damage in the Tweed valley, bridges, roads and railways damaged, landslides blocked roads and railways, seven mainline railway bridges destroyed over the Eye Water, valleys covered with 2 m (6–7 ft) -thick layer of mud and boulders. Very warm dry autumn. * 22 November to 1 December: notable fog. Anticyclonic southerly situation, formation of a persistent dense fog that spread from the Thames estuary westwards to the Welsh Borders and northwards to Lancashire and Yorkshire, many smoke fog (smog) deaths in London; by 28 November the fog had extended in a 1,900 km (1,200 mile) belt from Wales to Finland, nearly all shipping halted, aircraft grounded at many airports including London, Paris, Copenhagen, Stockholm and Helsinki, Berlin Airlift halted, several train collisions, London bus services temporarily suspended; when the fog finally dispersed on 1 December, due to an increasing southwesterly wind, the liners *Queen Elizabeth*, *Queen Mary* and *Aquitania* sailed out of Southampton in convoy. **1949** Third-warmest year on record, 10.6 °C (51 °F), strong zonal flow (115 westerly situations). Very mild dry winter, strong midwinter westerlies – mainland Europe: drought, positive pressure anomaly; 2 December (1948): southerly situation, exceptionally warm, 15–16 °C (59–61 °F) in northwest Scotland, 18.3 °C (65 °F) at Achnashellach (Ross and Cromarty), highest December temperature on record in the British Isles; 30 December: cyclonic westerly, widespread heavy snowfall, 30 cm (12 in). Mild spring. * 9–10 February: severe storm. Westerly situation, secondary depression (below 995 mb) over the Irish Sea (9 February) moved east across England into the North Sea, westerly gales, exposed British south coasts pounded by severe gales. 1 March: northerly situation, sea floods, small salt marsh formed in north Norfolk; 7 March: cyclonic situation, widespread heavy snowfall, 15 cm (6 in), roads blocked; mid April: southerly winds, very warm spell; 16 April: cyclonic southerly situation, 27 °C (80 °F) and above over much of England, 29.4 °C (85 °F) in London, highest April temperature on record. Very warm dry summer – 14 June: start of mainly dry spell; 7 August: cyclonic situation, widespread heavy rain interrupted generally fine conditions, 89 mm (3.5 in) in Ayrshire; 31 August: end of mainly dry spell. Very warm wet autumn – September: southeasterly; October: southwesterly. * 23–26 October: severe storm. Cyclonic situation, two depressions moved east across the British Isles into the North Sea, southwesterly gales veered northwest to northerly, storm-driven high tides caused much damage on the Danish coast.

1950s

Normal zonal circulation (90 westerly situations on average per year). **1950** Wet year, strong zonal flow (117 westerly situations). Very mild wet winter, fairly weak midwinter westerlies – 8–10 December (1949): cyclonic northerly/northerly situations, heavy snowfall, 30 cm (12 in) in northeast Scotland, north England and Wales, 2 m (7 ft) drifts; 30–31 January: cyclonic southerly/cyclonic situations, widespread heavy snowfall, 15–23 cm (6–9 in), 1 m (3 ft) drifts; glazed frost ('black ice') preceded thaw in south England on 30 January. Mild spring. * 25–26 April: severe late snowstorm-blizzard conditions. Northerly/cyclonic northerly situations, heavy snowfall, 40–45 cm (16–18 in) in Wales and south England, snowstorm-blizzard conditions, many trees and telephone lines damaged, traffic disrupted; although south London was badly affected, northern districts of the capital had little snow. * 21 May: notable tornadoes. Cyclonic situation, heavy thunderstorms, tornadoes, one tornado tracked northeastwards for almost 160 km (100 miles) from Buckinghamshire to Norfolk, its trail of damage included 50 unroofed houses in Linslade (Bedfordshire), two other tornadoes probably followed parallel tracks at about the same time. Warm wet summer – June: Azores high extended northeast over mainland Europe. Cool wet autumn. **1951** Wet year, normal zonal flow (92 westerly situations). Cold wet winter, normal midwinter westerlies – 3–4 December (1950): northerly situation, heavy snowfall, 15–23 cm (6–9 in) in north England and Scotland, locally 50 cm (20 in); 14–15 December: cyclonic/northerly situations, heavy snowfall, 25–40 cm (10–16 in), 4.5 m (15 ft) drifts on the Isle of Wight; 30 December: cyclonic situation, depression over northwest Ireland moved slowly southeast, heavy snowfall, 33 cm (13 in) in north England and Wales; 1–2 January: cyclonic situation, heavy snowfall, 22–30 cm (9–12 in), snowfall associated with a depression over Wales on 1 January that moved slowly north as another low tracked along the Channel on 2 January; 10 January: cyclonic situation, depression moved northeast over Scotland, heavy snowfall, 25 cm (10 in) in Scotland. * 4 February: severe storm. Cyclonic situation, complex deep depression (below 944 mb) over Ireland moved slowly north across the Hebrides, extremely low pressure (942 mb) recorded at Midleton (Co. Cork), lowest February pressure on record in the British Isles, cyclonic gales. 15–17 February: cyclonic southerly situation (16 February), heavy snowfall, 20 cm (8 in) in north Scotland, road and rail traffic disrupted. Very cold wet spring – 10–12 March: cyclonic easterly situation, heavy snowfall, 30 cm (12 in) in northeast Scotland. Average summer temperatures and rainfall – June and July: dry; August: wet, stormy. Very warm wet autumn. **1952** Weak zonal flow (75 westerly situations). Average winter temperatures/rainfall, fairly strong midwinter westerlies – 9 December (1951): cyclonic westerly, heavy snowfall, 20 cm (8 in) in Scotland;

27–31 December: cyclonic/cyclonic westerly situation, stormy spell, severe gales.
* 30 December (1951): severe storm. Cyclonic westerly situation, deep depression
(below 960 mb) moved east over north Scotland, severe gales with hurricane-
force gusts, widespread damage in north Scotland, several people killed, probably
the most severe storm to affect Scotland since 28 January 1927. 9 January: westerly
situation, heavy snowfall, 30 cm (12 in) in north Scotland; 15 January: westerly
situation, hurricane-force winds caused extensive damage in north Scotland,
Orkney and Shetland; 27–28 January: cyclonic westerly situation, heavy snowfall in
Scotland, north England and north Wales, 40 people injured, at least six killed in
Glasgow. Very mild wet spring – 29–30 March: heavy snowfall, 27 cm (11 in) south
of a line from Devon to Lincolnshire, deep drifts, 2 m (7 ft), over 300 roads
blocked, many villages cut off (probably the worst snowstorm to affect south
England in March since 1916); April: very mild, one of the warmest Aprils on
record; mid May: very warm anticyclonic spell; 19 May: 30 °C (86 °F) in London,
heavy heat thunderstorms, tornado moved unusually south, over 100 houses
damaged, many trees blown down. Warm generally dry summer – July: blocking
high caused Atlantic lows to be steered away from Britain to south Scandinavia;
August: low pressure over Scandinavia extended west to north of Scotland,
disturbed westerly flow now affected Britain; 1–15 August: notable cyclonic spell;
6 August: heavy thundery rain, floods in London. * 15–16 August: severe storm
and floods. Cyclonic/northeasterly situations, depression over Brittany moved
slowly northeast into southwest England, centred over Exmoor on 15 August
giving heavy rainfall, 230 mm (9.1 in), severe floods, Lynmouth inundated,
massive surge of water in the small basin of the Lyn rivers (nearly twice as great
as the highest recorded in the Thames), 34 people killed, nearly 100 buildings
destroyed. Very cool wet autumn – November: very cold, frequent snow, including
27 and 29 November: heavy snowfall in Wales, central south England and East
Anglia, 15–20 cm (6–8 in), deep drifts, 3 m (10 ft). **1953** Normal to strong zonal flow
(100 westerly situations). Dry winter, average temperatures, normal midwinter
westerlies – December (1952): anticyclone established over British Isles during
first week. * 5–10 December (1952): notable fog. Anticyclonic situation, dense fog
formed in London, began as a normal water fog but rapidly developed into an
urban smoke fog (smog) due to pollution in a light easterly drift (worst direction
at that time for industrial pollutants to be added into the London air), visibility
less than 11 m (12 yd) for three days, over 5,000 people died, fog began to disperse
in a westerly situation on 9 December (this event led to the introduction of the
Clean Air Act in 1956). 14–15 December (1952): north/northwesterly situations,
heavy snowfall, 20–30 cm (8–12 in) in west and north Scotland, northwest
England and north Wales, deep drifts, 4.5 m (15 ft) on the Isle of Skye, farms and

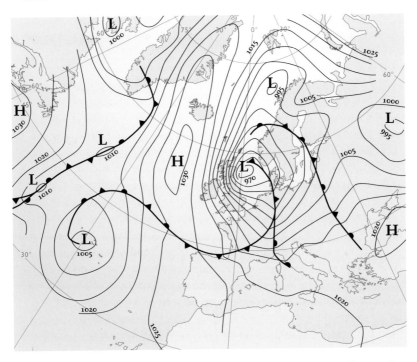

FIG 104. Synoptic weather map, 1200 h, 31 January 1953. Northerly situation showing the strong pressure gradient in rear of the severe North Sea storm. (H. H. Lamb)

villages cut off in Orkney and Shetland. * 17 December (1952): severe storm. Cyclonic northerly situation, deep depression (below 960 mb) off northeast Scotland moved southeast into the North Sea, severe to storm-force northwest to northerly gales with hurricane-force gusts affected Scotland and northeast England, buildings damaged. 5–6 January: northwesterly/cyclonic northerly situations, heavy snowfall, 15 cm (6 in). * 31 January to 1 February: severe storm (Fig. 104). One of the most severe North Sea storms on record, northerly and anticyclonic northerly situations, deep depression (below 968 mb) over north Scotland moved southeast into the North Sea, strong pressure gradient developed in its rear resulted in storm-force north to northwesterly gales with hurricane-force gusts; the ferryboat *Princess Victoria* foundered in the North Channel on 31 January, 133 lives lost. A severe North Sea storm surge (most destructive of recent times) pounded the English east coast from the Tees to the Strait of Dover, as well as the Dutch coast, the vertical rise of the tide above the predicted value was between 1.8 and 2.4 m (6–8 ft), locally 3.4 m (11 ft) from the Wash to the Strait of Dover, the storm surge was associated with exceptionally powerful storm waves; coastal defences, both natural sand dunes and sea walls, breached in many places, sea water advanced further inshore than normal, widespread severe floods, great damage, over 300 lives lost in England (1,500 in the Netherlands), 24,000 houses flooded, 40,000 people evacuated, 640 sq km (250 sq miles) of farmland in east England salt-contaminated. * 8–13 February: severe snowstorm-blizzard conditions. Widespread snowstorm-blizzard conditions occurred when a mild maritime airstream became engaged with a cold continental airstream; 8–9 February: westerly situation, heavy snowfall, 15–27 cm (6–11 in) in Scotland and northeast England; 10 February: cyclonic situation, deep depression moved east over south Britain, widespread heavy snowfall, 30–40 cm (12–16 in), deep drifts, 3.5 m (11 ft); 11–12 February: northeasterly situation: many roads blocked, villages and towns cut off. Mid February to mid March: mild dry spell allowed areas to recover from snow-melt floods. Mild spring. Average summer temperatures and rainfall – 1–5 June: northerly situation; 2 June: (Coronation Day), northerly winds, frequent showers; 18 July: cyclonic situation, heavy thunderstorms, widespread damage in south Britain. Very warm dry autumn. **1954** Strong zonal flow (119 westerly situations). Dry winter, average temperatures, weak midwinter westerlies – 25–26 January: trough of low pressure, heavy snowfall in west Britain and south England; February: cold, skating on frozen Norfolk Broads; 7–10 February: mostly cyclonic situations, heavy snowfall in northeast Britain; 28 February to 2 March: northerly/cyclonic situations, heavy snowfall, 15 cm (6 in). Average spring temperatures. Very cool wet summer – 6 June: cyclonic situation, onset of a series of depressions moving across the British Isles ended a changeable thundery period and started a cool wet spell that continued into late August; 25 August: start of a week-long dry spell between the summer and autumn rains. Very warm wet autumn – 17 September: westerly situation, first snowfall, Cairngorm Mountains snow-covered down to 760 m (2,500 ft); 17–19 October: cyclonic westerly situation, very wet spell affected Scotland and northwest England, crops destroyed, traffic dislocated by floods and landslides; 29 October: cyclonic westerly situation, renewed flooding in the same areas as ten days before, roads and buildings damaged; 8 November: westerly situation, heavy rain, severe floods in Ireland. * 26–30 November: severe storms. Cyclonic spell, severe south to southwesterly gales in the Channel, Chesil Beach (Dorset) breached (26 November), South Goodwin lightship capsized with loss of crew (27 November), extremely low pressure (947 mb) recorded at Midleton (Co. Cork) on 30 November. **1955** Weak zonal flow (74 westerly situations). Average winter temperatures/ rainfall, weak midwinter westerlies – 4 December (1954): cyclonic westerly situation, inferred severe southwesterly gales, Chesil Beach (Dorset) again

breached; 8 December: cyclonic situation, heavy snowfall, 35–55 cm (14–22 in) in
Scotland, heavy thunderstorm, tornado in London; 20–24 December:
northwesterly situation. * 21–23 December (1954): severe storms. Northwesterly
situation, depression (970 mb) north of Scotland on 21 December moved
southeast into south Scandinavia, severe to storm-force west to northwesterly
gales with hurricane-force gusts affected Scotland and northeast England; a
second depression on 23 December followed a similar track, storm-force
northwesterly gales over the North Sea produced the highest storm surge since
1953, but, fortunately, as the gales this time did not coincide with a spring tide
there were no severe floods. 2–6 January: easterly situation; 4 January: depression
in the Channel, strong easterly winds, heavy snowfall, 20 cm (8 in), snowstorm-
blizzard conditions, deep drifts, villages cut off on Dartmoor and Exmoor.
* 14–18 January: severe snowstorm-blizzard conditions. Depression moved east
along the Channel (13–14 January), heavy snowfall, 15 cm (6 in) in south England,
snowstorm-blizzard conditions; 17 January: northerly situation, severe conditions
with northeasterly winds moved north, heavy snowfall, 30–60 cm (12–24 in) in
north England and northeast Scotland, 90–95 cm (36–38 in) on the Grampian
Mountains, deep drifts, 9 m (30 ft), road and rail traffic blocked, a combined
operation, 'Snowdrop', was mounted by the Air Ministry and Admiralty to relieve
snowbound areas in north Britain by air. 8 February: cyclonic westerly situation,
heavy snowfall in north Britain, aircraft again dropped food supplies to isolated
communities; 16–20 February: northerly/cyclonic situations, snowstorm-blizzard
conditions in north Scotland spread south to south England, heavy snowfall,
35–50 cm (14–20 in), locally 90 cm (36 in), deep drifts, 6 m (20 ft), roads blocked,
many villages isolated, snowstorm-blizzard conditions from northwest England
to East Anglia (18–20 February), heavy snowfall, 25–50 cm (10–20 in) in north
Norfolk, deep drifts, 3 m (10 ft); 23 February: easterly situation, widespread heavy
snowfall, roads blocked, upland villages cut off. Cold wet spring – 6 March:
anticyclonic northeasterly situation, widespread heavy snowfall, 15 cm (6 in);
20 March: heavy snowfall; 14–21 May: northerly/cyclonic situations. * 17 May:
notable late snowfall. Cyclonic situation, widespread heavy snowfall, high-level
roads blocked in the Pennines, Peak District and south Wales, 2–3 hours' snowfall
in London. Very warm dry mostly anticyclonic summer – July: dry; 5 July: start of
a prolonged dry anticyclonic spell into late August. * 18 July: notable heavy
rainfall. Anticyclonic situation, heavy thundery rain, 280 mm (11 in) in
Martinstown (Dorset), flash floods, one of the heaviest daily total rainfalls on
record in England (a notable event in an otherwise dry month). August: dry;
31 August: westerly situation, dry anticyclonic spell initially broke down in
western areas with the onset of westerly winds; the dry spell broke down later in

the east on about 5 September. Warm dry autumn. **1956** A year without a summer; fairly normal zonal flow (80 westerly situations). Cold wet winter, normal midwinter westerlies – 8 December (1955): anticyclonic situation, widespread heavy snowfall; 20 December: cyclonic situation, depression moved east across south England, heavy snowfall, 30 cm (12 in) in Yorkshire; 9–10 January: cyclonic situation (10 January), widespread heavy snowfall, 30–40 cm (12–16 in), many roads blocked, villages isolated; 31 January: easterly situation, start of a four-week frosty spell with onset of a very cold easterly flow, notable temperature fall, maximum temperatures in London 8 °C (46 °F) on 30 January, –4 °C (25 °F) on 1 February; February: anticyclonic, ridge extended southwest over the British Isles from high pressure over north Russia; very cold, frequent snow, exceptionally heavy in southwest England; 1–2 February: anticyclonic easterly situation, heavy snowfall, 18–33 cm (7–13 in); 16 February: cyclonic northwesterly situation, heavy snowfall, 25 cm (10 in) in north England, deep drifts, 4.5 m (15 ft); 19–21 February: northeasterly/easterly situations, heavy snowfall, 25 cm (10 in), deep drifts, 3.5 m (11 ft) in east Kent, traffic halted. Dry spring, average temperatures – 30 March: Bezymjannaja (Kamchatka) eruption, unusual sky effects observed during the following six months, for example, rare stratospheric clouds reported in southwest England on 3–4 April, inferred volcanic dust-veil effect; 26 April: northeasterly situation, heavy snowfall, 15 cm (6 in) in north England, deep drifts over high ground, roads blocked. * Very cool wet summer. Inferred volcanic dust-veil effect; westerly/northwesterly types dominated circulation over the British Isles; June: northwesterly; July: weak westerly. * 29 July: severe storm. Cyclonic situation, depression (below 980 mb) moved northeast over central England into the North Sea, severe to storm-force southerly gales affected south England, Wales and the Channel, gales later turned northeasterly, many shipwrecks, great loss of life, landslides and floods, widespread damage, many trees blown down in south Britain. August: northwesterly, one of the coolest wettest Augusts on record; 6 August: heavy thunderstorms, hailstones in piles 1.8 m (6 ft) deep blocked streets in Tunbridge Wells (Kent). Warm dry autumn. **1957** Normal zonal flow (95 westerly situations). Very mild wet winter, fairly strong midwinter westerlies – 25–26 December (1956): cyclonic situation, widespread heavy snowfall, 10–20 cm (4–8 in), locally 25 cm (10 in), deep drifts, 2.5 m (8 ft) over high ground, blocked road and rail traffic, villages isolated; 18–19 February: cyclonic northerly/cyclonic situations, heavy snowfall, 30–40 cm (12–16 in) in central and north England. Very mild dry spring – March: southwesterly, very mild, one of the mildest Marches on record, 9.2 °C (49 °F). Warm wet summer – 28 June: start of very warm spell to 6 July; 29 June: anticyclonic southwesterly situation, very warm: 35.5 °C (96 °F) in London. * 23–25 August: severe storm. Cyclonic westerly situation, depression west of Ireland moved slowly northeast to north of Scotland, severe unusually strong westerly gales for the time of year, widespread damage. Warm autumn. * 4 November: severe storm. Cyclonic situation, inferred storm-force gales, newly built houses blown down in Hatfield (Hertfordshire). **1958** Weak zonal flow (75 westerly situations). Mild wet winter, normal midwinter westerlies – 10–11 December (1957): cyclonic southerly/cyclonic situations, heavy snowfall, 20 cm (8 in) in central and north England, and south and central Scotland, deep drifts, 2 m (7 ft) over high ground; 18–19 January: northwesterly situation, heavy snowfall, 15 cm (6 in) in Scotland and north England; 22–24 January: cyclonic northerly/cyclonic situations, widespread heavy snowfall, 30 cm (12 in), 57 cm (23 in) in Shoeburyness (Essex); 27 January: southerly situation, unusually warm, 18.3 °C (65 °F) on north Welsh coast, highest January temperature on record in the British Isles; 8 February: cyclonic situation, heavy snowfall, 20 cm (8 in) in Scotland, Wales, and central and north England, main roads blocked in Scotland, many rural districts isolated; 24 February: cyclonic situation, heavy snowfall, 15 cm (6 in), many roads blocked, 50 London Transport country buses trapped in drifts, heavier snowfall, 40 cm (16 in) in north England, deep drifts, 4.5 m (15 ft); 26 February: northerly situation, heavy snowfall, 23 cm (9 in) in East Anglia, roads blocked, Norwich cut off, helicopters deployed to supply isolated villages. Cold spring – 6–10 March: northerly situation; 8 March: heavy snowfall, 70 cm (28 in) in Scotland and northeast England, deep drifts, 1.5 m (5 ft) on North York Moors, traffic halted, villages isolated, light snowfall in many other areas; 5 April: cyclonic northeasterly, heavy snowfall, 15 cm (6 in) in south Scotland and north England, light snowfall in many other areas. Wet summer, average temperatures. Very warm autumn – 5 September: southeasterly situation, heavy thunderstorms, tornadoes, large hailstones weighing nearly 200 g (6½ oz) at Horsham (Sussex). **1959** Very warm year, eighth-warmest year (with 2004) on record, weak zonal flow (77 westerly situations). Average winter temperatures and rainfall, fairly weak midwinter westerlies – 1–15 January: mostly northerly situations: occasional heavy snowfall mainly in Scotland, deep drifts, 6 m (20 ft) in north Scotland, isolated villages in Caithness, Orkney and Shetland; heavy snowfall extended south to southwest and central England on 11 January: 23 cm (9 in) on Dartmoor; 28 February: southwesterly situation, 19 °C (66 °F) in Greenwich, highest February temperature on record at this station. Very mild spring. * 5 May to 10 October 1959: drought. A prolonged spell of dry, later warm, anticyclonic conditions to 23 June which was renewed on 4 July; drought then persisted (apart from occasional thunderstorms in July and August) to 10 October. Very warm dry summer – 4 July: anticyclonic southwesterly situation, renewal of dry anticyclonic conditions after a stormy interlude from 23 June.

Very warm dry autumn – 3 October: southerly situation, 29 °C (84 °F) in London; 10 October: cyclonic situation, drought broken by the first general fall of rain over England for several months.

1960s

Continental and cyclonic; fairly normal zonal flow (80 westerly situations on average per year). **1960** Weak zonal flow (76 westerly situations). Mild wet winter, very weak midwinter westerlies – 12–13 January: northerly/cyclonic situations, small depression moved south across Scotland, north England and Wales, heavy snowfall, 30 cm (12 in) in southeast England and East Anglia; 15 January: northeasterly situation, heavy snowfall, 25–30 cm (10–12 in) in south and southeast England; 18–19 January: cyclonic northwesterly/cyclonic situations, heavy snowfall, 50 cm (20 in) in Scotland, 1 m (3 ft) drifts in east Scotland, main-line railway closed; 10–11 February: northerly/cyclonic northerly situations, widespread heavy snowfall, 20 cm (8 in), deep drifts, 2 m (7 ft), roads blocked; 14–16 February: northerly situation, widespread heavy snowfall, 20 cm (8 in), locally 60 cm (24 in), roads blocked. Very mild dry spring. Wet summer, average temperatures – 1 and 3 July: anticyclonic northerly/anticyclonic situations, out-of-season night frosts, –1 °C (30 °F) in Norfolk; 4 July: start of wet spell to 6 September. Warm wet autumn – 7–11 September: short dry spell between the summer and autumn rains, late September to late October: severe river floods in west England. * 28 September to 8 October: severe storms and river floods. Mainly easterly/cyclonic situations, three depressions moved in rapid succession over the Channel, heavy rain, river floods in southwest England, Devon designated a disaster area, Lynmouth again affected but another flood disaster averted due to the new defences holding; 7 October: heavy thunderstorms, torrential rain, in south, central and east England, over 180 mm (7.2 in) in 90 minutes at Horncastle (Lincolnshire), town inundated with a raging torrent, houses and shops badly damaged, one man drowned. 18 October to 4 November: mostly cyclonic/easterly situations. * 21 and 26 October: severe storm and river floods. 21 October: cyclonic easterly situation, heavy rain, river floods in southwest England, 120 houses inundated in Sidmouth (Devon); 26 October: cyclonic situation, further heavy rain, river floods in Somerset and Devon, Exeter flooded for the fourth time in short succession. **1961** Strong zonal flow (104 westerly situations). Mild wet winter, weak midwinter westerlies – December (1960): westerly; January: southwesterly; February: southwesterly. Very mild dry spring – March: anticyclonic westerly, very mild dry; April: southerly, very mild, one of the warmest Aprils on record; May: anticyclonic. Cool dry summer. Very warm autumn, average rainfall – September: southwesterly. * 16–17 September:

severe storm. Cyclonic southerly/westerly situations, deep depression, 956 mb (ex-tropical cyclone) off west Ireland moved northeast into the Norwegian Sea, severe to storm-force southwesterly gales with hurricane-force gusts in west Ireland; elsewhere in Ireland at least 16 people killed, many houses damaged, communication and power services disrupted, thousands of trees blown down, shipping badly affected; southwesterly gales also affected north Scotland.

1962 Fairly normal zonal flow (82 westerly situations). Average winter temperatures/rainfall, strong midwinter westerlies – December (1961): southerly, 4 December: cyclonic situation, deepening Atlantic depression, heavy snowfall, 15 cm (6 in) in Scotland and north England; 18 December: start of cold spell into early January; 30–31 December: cyclonic northeasterly/cyclonic northerly situations, shallow depression over Biscay moved northeast across north France to south Denmark, heavy snowfall, 40 cm (16 in) in central and south England, 1 m (3 ft) drifts; January: westerly; 12–13 January: cyclonic/westerly situations, intense depression moved across Scotland, heavy snowfall, 27 cm (11 in) in Scotland and north England, 1.5 m (5 ft) drifts; February: anticyclonic westerly. * 16–17 February: severe storm. Northwesterly/anticyclonic northwesterly situations, deep depression (below 960 mb) moved southeast into Scandinavia, severe westerly gales affected northeast England and Scotland; 16 February: widespread damage, especially in Sheffield where exceptionally strong winds occurred due to a lee wave effect east of the Pennines, large amount of structural damage, 100 houses destroyed; 17 February: severe northwesterly gales in North Sea coincided with high tide, North Sea storm surge, sea defences breached in Holland, Denmark and northwest Germany, 340 drowned. 26–27 February: easterly situation, heavy snowfall, 20 cm (8 in) in east and south England, deep drifts, traffic dislocated. Very cold late spring, one of the coldest springs on record, exceptionally late leafing and blossoming phenological events – 1–3 March: anticyclonic northerly/northerly situations, widespread heavy snowfall, 40 cm (16 in); April: anticyclonic westerly; May: northwesterly. Very cool dry summer – 1–3 June: anticyclonic northerly/anticyclonic situations, record June frosts, –6 °C (22 °F) at Santon Downham (Norfolk). Dry autumn, average temperatures – 16–18 November: cyclonic/northerly situations, depression moved southeast across Britain to north France, widespread heavy snow, 30 cm (12 in), deep drifts, 3 m (10 ft) in south Wales. **1963–1968** Volcanic dust veil (DVI c.1,100), various eruptions. **1963** Weak zonal flow (70 westerly situations); volcanic dust veil (DVI 800), Mt Agung (Bali) eruption. * Very cold winter. Coldest winter in England since 1740, absent midwinter westerlies replaced by southeasterly flow associated with a blocking high over south Norway, also very cold in mainland Europe: frozen rivers and water bodies, including the Rhine, Zuider Zee and Bodensee.

December (1962): anticyclonic westerly, very cold. * 3–6 December (1962): notable
fog. Anticyclonic southerly situation, dense fog in London, similar to that of
December 1952, 750 people died. 22 December (1962): following mild foggy days,
frost set in during evening, start of so-called 'Big Freeze' to 4 March when
temperatures at several stations remained below 3 °C (37 °F), ground continuously
snow-covered for nearly ten weeks from 26 December. * 26–29 December (1962):
severe snowstorm-blizzard conditions. Northeasterly situation, widespread heavy
snowfall, 30–45 cm (12–18 in), 50–75 cm (20–30 in) in southeast England,
snowstorm-blizzard conditions, deep drifts, 6 m (20 ft), 1.75 m (6 ft) drifts in
London, over 200 roads blocked, villages and towns isolated, many power cuts,
food supplies airlifted by helicopter, five people died, thousands of cattle and
sheep starved to death. January: anticyclonic northeasterly, very cold, coldest
January since 1795. * 1–4 January: severe snowstorm-blizzard conditions. Worst
snowstorm-blizzard conditions since January 1881, easterly/cyclonic situations,
depression on 3 January moved north from France, associated snowstorm-
blizzard conditions over the Channel moved north across south England, heavy
snowfall, 45 cm (18 in), deep drifts, 6 m (20 ft) in southwest England, food
supplies airlifted by helicopter to isolated communities in Devon and Cornwall.
14 January: anticyclonic northerly situation, heavy snowfall, 18 cm (7 in) in north
England and Scotland, start of severe frosty spell, many rivers and harbours
frozen; 16–20 January: anticyclonic/easterly situations, heavy snowfall, 30 cm
(12 in), snowstorm-blizzard conditions, Scotland isolated from England, very
severe frost, –22.3 °C (–8 °F) at Braemar (Aberdeenshire), frozen sea off the
Kentish coast, ice floes in the Thames (London); February: southeasterly.
* 4–9 February: severe snowstorm-blizzard conditions. Mostly cyclonic
south/southeasterly situations, heavy snowfall, 50–60 cm (20–24 in), severe
snowstorm-blizzard conditions with hurricane-force winds, southwest England
and Wales worst affected, very heavy snowfall, 150–160 cm (60–64 in) in south
Wales, deep drifts, 6 m (20 ft), villages and farms isolated. 14–17 February:
southeasterly/anticyclonic easterly situations, heavy snowfall in north England
and Scotland; 24 February to 3 March: mostly anticyclonic/southerly situations, a
succession of dry sunny days brought a gradual end to the two-month period of
lying snow in the south, but severe night frosts continued until 3 March. Mild
wet spring – March: southerly/southwesterly; 4 March: end of cold spell from
22 December; April: southwesterly; May: cyclonic southwesterly. Cool summer,
average rainfall. Very warm autumn – autumn 1963 to January 1965: inferred
volcanic dust veil, notable coloured sunsets; November: cyclonic southwesterly.
1964 Normal zonal flow (97 westerly situations). Dry winter, average temperatures
– one of the driest winters on record; December (1963): anticyclonic

southeasterly; January: anticyclonic southwesterly; 12–13 January: anticyclonic easterly situation, heavy snowfall, 25 cm (10 in); February: anticyclonic southwesterly. Mild wet spring – March: southeasterly; 15 March: widespread heavy snowfall, 15–30 cm (6–12 in), deep drifts, 2 m (7 ft) in Scotland; April: cyclonic southwesterly; May: southwesterly. Dry summer, average temperatures. Warm dry autumn. * 9 October: severe storm. Cyclonic situation; although mainland Britain escaped the full brunt of this storm, the Channel Islands experienced stronger gales than in the 1987 storm. **1965** Weak zonal flow (76 westerly situations). Average winter temperatures/rainfall – December (1964): westerly; January: westerly; 20 January: cyclonic situation, widespread heavy snowfall, 25–30 cm (10–12 in); 28 January: easterly situation, heavy snowfall, 15–27 cm (6–11 in) in north England; February: anticyclonic northerly. Wet spring, average temperatures – March: cyclonic southerly: 1 March: easterly situation, heavy snowfall, 30 cm (12 in) in southwest and north England, 3–4 March: cyclonic/cyclonic easterly situations, heavy snowfall, 20–30 cm (8–12 in) in south Britain, deep drifts, 3 m (10 ft); 21–22 March: southeasterly situation (22 March), depression from Atlantic moved slowly north, heavy snowfall, 35 cm (14 in) in central and north England; 27 March to 2 April: exceptionally warm spell; 29 March: 25 °C (77 °F) in east England, 14 °C (24 °F) degrees above average; April: westerly; May: cyclonic. Very cool summer, average rainfall. Cool autumn. * 1 November: severe storm. Cyclonic situation, deep depression (below 964 mb) moved east across Scotland into the North Sea, heavy rain, storm-force westerly gales with hurricane-force gusts, five cooling towers at the Ferrybridge power station near Doncaster (Yorkshire) collapsed. 22 November: northerly situation, widespread heavy snowfall, 15 cm (6 in); 26–29 November: cyclonic situation, heavy snowfall, 30–40 cm (12–16 in) in north England and north Wales, deep drifts, 3 m (10 ft), many villages isolated. **1966** Wet year, weak zonal flow (73 westerly situations); volcanic dust veil (DVI 200), Awu, Great Sangihe (Celebes) eruption. Mild wet winter with some cold spells – December (1965): cyclonic westerly; 26 December: northerly situation; 28/29 December: anticyclonic/ westerly situations, heavy snowfall, 25 cm (10 in) in north Britain; January: southerly; 10 January: southeasterly situation, heavy snowfall, 15–40 cm (6–16 in) in south Britain; 15 January: anticyclonic northeasterly situation, heavy snowfall, 30 cm (12 in) in east England; 20 January: cyclonic easterly situation, depression moved east along the Channel, heavy snowfall, 25 cm (10 in) in south England; February: southerly; 14 February: anticyclonic easterly situation, heavy snowfall, 15 cm (6 in) in northeast England. Mild wet spring – March: anticyclonic westerly; April: cyclonic southeasterly; 1–2 April: cyclonic situation (1 April), shallow depression over southwest Ireland moved east into the southern North Sea,

heavy snowfall, 30–40 cm (12–16 in) in northwest England and north Wales, deep drifts, 1.5 m (5 ft); 14–15 April: easterly situation, heavy snowfall, 20 cm (8 in) in south England; May: cyclonic southwesterly. Cool wet summer – inferred volcanic dust-veil effect. Warm autumn – October: cyclonic; November: heavy rain, the collapse of a rain-saturated spoil tip buried the village school at Aberfan (Glamorgan), 144 killed including 116 children; 28 November: northwesterly situation, widespread heavy snowfall, 15 cm (6 in). **1967** Strong zonal flow (102 westerly situations, like 1961, a relatively high value during a general decline in the zonal flow). Very mild wet winter – December (1966): westerly. * 1 December (1966): severe storm. Cyclonic situation, exceptionally deep depression (943 mb) over Ireland moved east into the North Sea, widespread severe gales, heavy rain and snow in north Britain, veering northwest to northerly winds (2 December) brought snow showers as far south as London. January: southwesterly; 6–7 January: northwesterly/cyclonic situations, small depression moved south over Britain, heavy snowstorm in southeast England; February: southwesterly.
* 22–23 February: severe storm. Cyclonic situation (22 February), depression (below 970 mb) moved northeast across north England into the North Sea, widespread northwesterly gales and snow in rear of low over north Britain, gales also over the North Sea, storm surge, but as it was at about the time of a low tide there were no severe coastal floods. Mild wet spring – March: westerly. * 6–7 March: severe storm. Westerly/southwesterly situations, deep depression (below 980 mb) moved northeast off northwest Scotland, severe southwesterly gales with hurricane-force gusts in Scotland, 233 km/h (145 mph, 126 knots) gust in the Cairngorm Mountains, the highest gust speed then on record. April: anticyclonic northwesterly; May: very wet, cyclonic; wettest May since 1729. Warm dry summer. Warm wet autumn. * 4–5 September: severe storms. Westerly situation (4 September), severe westerly gales, buildings damaged, loss of life in north England, wind-driven sea encroached inland at Morecambe Bay (Lancashire), sea floods at Blackpool; cyclonic situation (5 September), intense depression (below 975 mb) moved northeast across Scotland, severe gales, hurricane-force gusts pounded exposed coastal districts, heavy rainfall, 75 mm (3 in) at Tiree (Hebrides) during first five days of the month. **1968** Wet year, weak zonal flow (64 westerly situations); volcanic dust veil (DVI 200), Fernandina (Galápagos) eruption. Cold winter, average rainfall – December (1967): northwesterly; 7–8 December: northerly/cyclonic northerly situations, polar low over north Ireland moved southeast, moderate to heavy snowfall, 10–30 cm (4–12 in), locally 50 cm (20 in), many roads blocked; January: anticyclonic westerly; 3 January: cyclonic situation, heavy snowfall in north Scotland, transport halted. * 8–9 January: severe storm and snowstorm-blizzard conditions. Westerly situation (8 January), deep

depression (below 1000 mb) moved southeast across southwest England into France, heavy snowfall, 30 cm (12 in) in Wales, and central and east England, snowstorm-blizzard conditions, deep drifts, 1.5 m (5 ft), traffic disrupted. * 14–15 January: severe storm. Westerly/cyclonic westerly situations, intense depression (below 960 mb) moved east across Scotland, severe southwesterly gales affected Scotland and north England with hurricane-force gusts, extensive damage, especially in Glasgow where 20 people died; severe floods in south England, westerly gales intensified overflow of rivers already swollen by snow-melt. February: cyclonic; 4–6 February: westerly/cyclonic situations, heavy snowfall, 15 cm (6 in), locally 30–45 cm (12–18 in) in Scotland, and north and central England. Wet spring, average temperatures – March: westerly; 17 March: westerly situation, deep depression off north Scotland, heavy snowfall, 15 cm (6 in), deep drifts, many roads blocked; April: cyclonic southerly; 2 April: northerly situation, heavy snowfall, 20 cm (8 in) in Scotland, deep drifts, 2 m (7 ft). Wet summer, average temperatures. * 10–11 July: severe storm and floods. Cyclonic easterly/cyclonic northerly situations, deepening depression moved northeast over south England, widespread heavy rain, 125 mm (5 in) in 90 minutes, extensive storm and flood damage, west and central England worst affected areas, several main bridges washed away, seven people killed. Very warm wet autumn. * 14–16 September: severe storm and floods. Cyclonic easterly/easterly/cyclonic northeasterly situations, an intense trough on 14 September was associated with a deepening depression off southwest England, heavy thunderstorms with torrential rain; continuous heavy rain, 150–200 mm (60–80 in) and severe river floods occurred in southeast and east England, particularly in Esher, Molesey, Walton, Weybridge and Guildford (so-called River Mole floods), London inaccessible from the south and southwest for two days; in East Anglia the Waveney valley was inundated, Bungay (Suffolk) cut off, the main-line railway at Diss (Norfolk) collapsed, homes and factories flooded, schools closed, troops employed to help evacuate families from their homes, and roads blocked: the worst floods since 1953. **1969** Very weak zonal flow (56 westerly situations). Cold winter, average rainfall – December (1968): cyclonic southerly; 24–27 December: cyclonic/northerly situations, heavy snowfall especially in east England, 50 cm (20 in) in Norfolk; January: cyclonic southwesterly, mild wet; February: cyclonic northerly; cold heavy snowfall. * 7 February: severe storm. Northerly situation, polar low off Norway moved south into the North Sea, heavy snowfall in its rear swept south over the British Isles on strong northerly winds, gust of 219 km/h (136 mph, 118 knots) at Kirkwall (Orkney), second-highest wind speed on record at a low-level station; moderate to heavy snowfall, 10–15 cm (4–6 in), 30 cm (12 in) in Kent, deep drifts, roads blocked, villages isolated,

followed by overnight severe frosts, –13 °C (8 °F) at Manchester on 8 February.
9–10 February: northerly/anticyclonic northwesterly situations, heavy snowfall in
west Scotland; 13–15 February: northerly/cyclonic/easterly situations, heavy
snowfall, 15 cm (6 in) in Scotland, Wales and north England, Whitby (Yorkshire)
and neighbouring villages isolated; 19–20 February: easterly/cyclonic easterly
situations, widespread heavy snowfall, 15–25 cm (6–10 in), locally 35 cm (14 in),
deep drifts, villages isolated in Kent. Very cold wet spring – March: anticyclonic
southeasterly, coldest March in many parts of the British Isles since 1962;
12–14 March: cyclonic situation, heavy snowfall in north England, Wales and
Scotland, 20 cm (8 in) over high ground, many villages isolated in east Scotland,
deep drifts, roads blocked. * 16–18 March: severe ice storm. Easterly/cyclonic
easterly situations, heavy freezing rain in central and north England, thick
deposits of glazed ice, structural and vegetation damage, telegraph and power
lines brought down, Orkney lifeboat and crew lost in severe easterly gales, Emley
Moor TV mast (near Huddersfield) collapsed on 19 March, probably due to the
weight of ice. Warm summer, average rainfall. Very warm dry autumn.
* 28–29 September: severe storm. Cyclonic westerly/anticyclonic situations,
deepening depression over the Atlantic moved east to north of Scotland (28
September), southwesterly gales increased and veered to severe northwesterly
gales, hurricane-force gusts affected Scotland, North Sea storm surge, severe sea
floods, Hull (Yorkshire) inundated with 1 m (3 ft) depth of water; conversely,
following the storm, pent-up tidal waters in the Humber strongly receded and
ferries were unable to operate due to the low water level in the estuary. October:
one of the warmest Octobers on record, 13 °C (55 °F). 15–17 November:
cyclonic/northwesterly situations, heavy snowfall in north Wales, north England
and Scotland, 20 cm (8 in) over high ground; 28–29 November: northerly
situation, polar low in the North Sea, northerly winds, heavy snowfall, 15 cm (6 in)
in northeast and east England.

1970s

Weak zonal flow (73 westerly situations on average per year). **1970** Fairly normal
zonal flow (81 westerly situations). Cold wet winter – 19–20 December (1969):
westerly situation, snowstorm-blizzard conditions, heavy snowfall in north Wales,
northwest England and southwest Scotland, 30 cm (12 in) over the Scottish
mountains; January: southerly; 16–18 January: cyclonic/southeasterly/southerly
situations, heavy snowfall, 15–30 cm (6–12 in) in Scotland and north England,
deep drifts in the Grampian Mountains; February: cyclonic northwesterly.
* 12 February: severe storm and snowstorm. Cyclonic easterly, deep depression
(below 984 mb) moved east along the Channel, heavy snowfall, 20 cm (8 in) in

south Britain, deep drifts, 2 m (7 ft), many roads blocked, power lines brought down in south Wales; severe cyclonic gales, hurricane-force gusts along south English coast. 17–18 February: cyclonic/westerly situations, widespread heavy snowfall, 20 cm (8 in), deep drifts in north Britain. Cold spring – March: northwesterly. * 3–4 March: severe storm and snowstorm. Northerly/cyclonic situations, depression (below 988 mb) off northwest Scotland moved southeast over Britain, widespread heavy snowfall, 15 cm (6 in), locally 30–35 cm (12–14 in), deep drifts, 3 m (10 ft), power lines brought down, communications disrupted, greatest nationwide snow cover since 1947. April: northwesterly; May: anticyclonic westerly. Warm dry summer. Very warm wet autumn. **1971** Weak zonal flow (63 westerly situations); volcanic dust veil (DVI 250), Mt Hudson (Chile) eruption. Mild dry winter – December (1970): anticyclonic; 26–27 December: easterly situation, polar low moved southwest over south England, widespread heavy snowfall, 20 cm (8 in); 29 December: cyclonic easterly situation, heavy snow in south England, deep drifts over high ground, many roads blocked; January: southwesterly; 10 January: anticyclonic southerly situation, out-of-season warmth, 18.3 °C (65 °F) on north Welsh coast, highest January temperature on record in the British Isles, temperatures above 16 °C (61 °F) widely recorded in the lee of high ground due to a föhn effect; 31 January: northeasterly situation, heavy snowfall, 15 cm (6 in) in Wales and west England. Average spring temperatures – March: anticyclonic westerly/anticyclonic northwesterly type; 4 March: anticyclonic situation, easterly winds affected south England, heavy snowfall, 15 cm (6 in) in southeast England; April: anticyclonic; 26 April: easterly situation, heavy snowfall, 13 cm (5 in) in south Wales and south England, traffic disrupted; May: cyclonic. Cool wet summer – inferred volcanic dust-veil effect. Very warm dry autumn – 13 October: anticyclonic northeasterly, small depression moved east along the Channel, early out-of-season snowfall in central England and south Wales. **1972** Weak zonal flow (75 westerly situations). Cold winter – December (1971): anticyclonic westerly; January: southerly; 17–18 January: cyclonic situation (17 January), heavy snowfall, 20 cm (8 in) in Scotland and north England, 40 cm (16 in) over the Scottish Highlands, roads blocked; February: southerly; 31 January to 2 February: southeast/southerly situations, widespread heavy snowfall, 20–25 cm (8–10 in). Mild wet spring – March: cyclonic westerly; 27–28 March: northwesterly situation, heavy snowfall, 20 cm (8 in) in north Britain, roads blocked; April: westerly; May: cyclonic. Very cool dry summer – June: one of the three coldest Junes on record, 11.8 °C (53 °F). Dry autumn, average temperatures – September: anticyclonic. * 12–13 November: severe storm. Cyclonic/cyclonic northerly situations, deepening intense depression moved rapidly east over north Ireland and England into mainland Europe, severe to storm-force westerly veering northerly gales, heavy rainfall, over 25 mm (1 in), many trees blown down, buildings damaged, 50 people killed in Britain, Holland and Germany. 17–19 November: northerly/anticyclonic/cyclonic southerly situations, widespread heavy snowfall, 20 cm (8 in). **1973** Weak zonal flow (67 westerly situations). Mild dry winter – December (1972): southwesterly; January: southwesterly; 19–21 January: cyclonic/southerly situations, heavy snowfall, 25 cm (10 in) in north Britain, 1 m (3 ft) drifts over high ground, many roads blocked; February: westerly; 12–15 February: westerly/cyclonic situations, heavy snowfall, 20 cm (8 in) in Scotland, and north and southwest England, deep drifts, 2 m (7 ft) over high ground, many roads blocked; 23–26 February: northwesterly/cyclonic northerly situations, widespread heavy snowfall, 25 cm (10 in) in the Grampian Mountains. Average spring temperatures. * 2–3 April: severe storm. Cyclonic/anticyclonic westerly situations, deep depression (972 mb) moved rapidly east across the British Isles into mainland Europe, severe to storm-force cyclonic gales, rain and snow with local hail and thunder, heavy snowfall, 18 cm (7 in) in south Scotland and north England, roads blocked, many trees blown down, buildings damaged. 27–28 April: cyclonic/cyclonic northerly situations, heavy snowfall, 15 cm (6 in) in Shetland, deep drifts, livestock perished; 1 May: northwesterly situation, heavy snowfall, 23 cm (9 in) in northeast Scotland. Warm summer. * 6 July: heavy rainfall. Cyclonic situation, shallow depression (below 1012 mb) over France on 5 July moved slowly north, local heavy thunderstorms formed in its cyclonic circulation, these produced exceptionally heavy rainfall in southeast England, including 117 mm (4.6 in) in 2¾ hours at Chessington (Surrey) and 118 mm (4.6 in) in 2½ hours, including 51 mm (2.0 in) in 45 minutes, at Surbiton (Greater London). Dry autumn, average temperatures – 6 November: start of stormy period to 17 December, series of north to northwesterly storms over the North Sea, storm surges and severe floods affected coasts of the German Bight and adjacent areas, comparable situation to December 1792 but storms and floods had been more severe in the earlier period. **1974** Normal zonal flow (96 westerly situations); volcanic dust veil (DVI 200), Fuego (Guatemala) eruption. Very mild wet winter – December (1973): westerly; 17 December: end of stormy period over the North Sea; 18–19 December: westerly/southeasterly situations, heavy snowfall in north Britain, 30 cm (12 in) over high ground, deep drifts; January: southwesterly; another stormy period, this time centred on western British Isles. * 11–12 and 27–28 January: severe storms. Southwesterly situations, severe to storm-force south to southwesterly gales with hurricane-force gusts over Ireland, severe Atlantic storm surge, floods with high tides affected Co. Cork and Co. Sligo, many trees blown down, roads blocked, buildings damaged. * 17 January: heavy rain. Westerly situation, heavy rain, 238 mm (9.37 in) at Sloy Main Adit

(Dumbartonshire), highest daily rainfall total on record in Scotland. February: cyclonic westerly/cyclonic southwesterly; 6 February: cyclonic situation, heavy snowfall, 15–20 cm (6–8 in) in north Britain. Dry spring, average temperatures – March: southeasterly; 1 March: cyclonic situation, heavy snowfall, 20 cm (8 in) in north Britain; 9–12 March: easterly situation, heavy snowfall, 16 cm (6 in) in Wales and south England; April: anticyclonic easterly; May: cyclonic. Cool summer – inferred volcanic dust-veil effect. Very cool wet autumn – October: very cool, northwesterly, one of the coldest Octobers on record. * 6–7 October: notable early out-of-season snowfall. Cyclonic/cyclonic northerly situations, depression over northwest Scotland moved southeast across the country, snowfall in Scotland, and briefly east England, in northerly airstream of the low's cold sector. 20–21 November: cyclonic situation, heavy snowfall, 18 cm (7 in) in north Wales.

1975 Weak zonal flow (69 westerly situations). Very mild winter, one of the mildest winters on record – December (1974): westerly, mildest December since 1934; January: westerly/southwesterly, mild; February: anticyclonic southerly. Cold wet spring – March: wet, northerly; 27–30 March: cyclonic northeasterly/ northerly situations, heavy snowfall, 25 cm (10 in) in central Scotland, lighter snowfall elsewhere; April: wet, northwesterly; 8 April: northerly situation, heavy snowfall, 15 cm (6 in) in Scotland and southeast England, locally 47 cm (19 in), 1 m (3 ft) drifts in the Scottish Highlands, roads blocked, many power failures; May: dry, anticyclonic northerly; start of drought to August 1976. * May 1975 to August 1976: drought. The most severe drought on record: all the included months, apart from September 1975, were either dry or had average rainfall. Very warm dry summer. * 2 June: notable out-of-season snowfall. Cyclonic situation, depression moved southeast across Scotland into the North Sea, unusually wintry conditions for June, widespread snowfall in north Britain, generally moderate amounts but heavy over high ground: 5 cm (2 in) in northwest England but 15 cm (6 in) over the Grampian Mountains, snow and sleet as far south as London and the English south coast (one of the latest out-of-season dates for wintry precipitation in the capital). * 14 August: heavy rainfall. Heavy thunderstorms and torrential rain, 171 mm (7 in) in London, flash floods, 100 houses and Underground station inundated at Hampstead Heath, one man drowned. Dry autumn, mostly average temperatures – September: westerly. **1976** Very weak zonal flow (58 westerly situations). Very mild dry winter – December (1975): anticyclonic westerly/ northwesterly; January: westerly. * 2–3 January: severe storm. Cyclonic/ northwesterly situations, deepening depression moved rapidly east across north Britain into the Baltic, severe to storm-force gales, with hurricane-force gusts, buildings damaged, power supplies and transport disrupted, many trees blown down, over 600 in Norwich alone, 60 people killed, including 28 in the British

Isles; more damage and loss of life in this storm than in any other since 1953.
24–26 January: northerly/northwesterly situations, heavy snowfall, 25 cm (10 in) in
Scotland and east England; 30 January: easterly situation, widespread heavy
snowfall, deep drifts, 2.5 m (8 ft) in southwest England; February: southerly; 10–11
February: westerly/northwesterly situations, widespread heavy snowfall, 23 cm
(9 in) in the Scottish Highlands, many roads blocked. Average spring
temperatures, near or above normal rainfall in north Britain but below average
elsewhere – March: anticyclonic; 21–22 March: southerly situation (21 March),
heavy snowfall, 20 cm (8 in) in southwest and northwest England, north Wales
and Scotland, deep drifts, 2.5 m (8 ft) in southeast Scotland; April: anticyclonic;
31 March to 1 April: cyclonic westerly/cyclonic situations, heavy snow, 30 cm (12 in)
in north Britain; 1 m (3 ft) drifts in Shetland; May: southwesterly/westerly. Very
warm dry summer, one of the warmest driest summers on record, which
culminated the 16-month drought – widespread heath fires in south England;
June: ridge extended northeast over the British Isles from the Azores high,
23 June to 7 July: notable heat wave comprised the climax of the warmest summer
on record during the past 300 years, temperature exceeded 32 °C (90 °F) on 15
successive days, including 33.2 °C (92 °F) on 3 July, one of the warmest days on
record; August: end of drought from May 1975; 3 August: very warm, 33.2 °C
(92 °F), also one of the warmest days on record. Very wet cool autumn. * 14–15
October: severe storm. Cyclonic situation, deep depression (965 mb) over the
Southwest Approaches moved northeast across England into the North Sea, heavy
rain, storm-force cyclonic gales, locally hurricane force, 159 km/h (99 mph) gust at
Prawle Point (south Devon), Channel ferry services disrupted, six people killed.
29 November: westerly situation, widespread heavy snowfall, 30 cm (12 in) over
high ground. **1977** Weak zonal flow (70 westerly situations). Cold, apart from
south England, wet winter – December (1976): cyclonic; 6–7 December:
southwesterly/cyclonic situations, heavy thunderstorms in southwest England,
tornado damage; 17–21 December: southeasterly/easterly situations, heavy
snowfall in central and north England; 29–30 December: cyclonic southerly
situation (30 December), heavy snowfall, 20–30 cm (8–12 in) in north England and
Scotland; January: cyclonic southwesterly, 12–13 January: cyclonic situation,
widespread heavy snowfall, 20–30 cm (8–12 in), several people killed, roads
blocked; February: cyclonic southerly; 11–12 February: cyclonic situation, heavy
snowfall, 30 cm (12 in) in north Britain. Average spring temperatures/rainfall –
March: southwesterly; April: northwesterly; cold; 3–10 April: mainly northerly
situations, wintry showers, keen night frosts, –4 °C (21 °F) on 6 April, fruit
blossom damaged; May: northeasterly. Cool dry summer – 4–7 July: anticyclonic
easterly situation, very warm, especially in north Britain, 29 °C (84 °F) in Glasgow

on 6 and 7 July, highest July value for the city since 1868. Very warm autumn – October: southwesterly; 21 November: northerly situation, heavy snowfall, 33 cm (13 in) in north Britain, 1 m (3 ft) drifts in Shetland. **1978** Weak zonal flow (78 westerly situations). Wet winter, average temperatures – December (1977): southwesterly; 6–8 December: cyclonic easterly/cyclonic situations, heavy snowfall, 20 cm (8 in) in north Britain, drifts 75 cm (2.5 ft); January: westerly; 3 January: northwesterly situation, deepening depression moved rapidly east across the country into the North Sea, heavy rain, gales, tornado damage at Newmarket (Suffolk). * 10–12 January: severe storm. Westerly/cyclonic/anticyclonic situations, rapidly deepening depression (below 980 mb) moved east across England, heavy snowfall, 40 cm (16 in) in north Britain on 10 January, severe to storm-force north to northeasterly gales with hurricane-force gusts in rear of the low, North Sea storm surge, widespread damage and sea floods in eastern areas, especially along exposed coasts of Norfolk and Kent, Wisbech and King's Lynn inundated, Hunstanton pier mostly swept away, Margate pier destroyed; although the spring tide was higher than in 1953, only one life was lost because of improved sea defences. 19 January: cyclonic situation, snowfall in Scotland, and north and east England, 20 cm (8 in) over high ground, lighter amounts elsewhere. * 27–30 January: severe storm and snowstorm-blizzard conditions, 'The Great Highland Blizzard'. Cyclonic/cyclonic northerly/anticyclonic conditions, deep depression, below 965 mb (27 January), moved slowly east over Ireland and north England; as it continued eastwards into the North Sea strong north to northeasterly winds affected the whole country, severe gales over the Scottish Highlands caused severe snowstorm-blizzard conditions, heavy snowfall, 65–90 cm (26–36 in), deep drifts, 10 m (33 ft), power lines and trees broken down, communications disrupted, over 200 vehicles and three trains stranded, six people killed, livestock and wildlife badly affected, following the blizzard 300 people rescued by helicopter from remote sites; worst blizzard in north Scotland since January 1955. February: southeasterly; 11 February: cyclonic easterly situation, coldest night of the winter in East Anglia; 12–14 February: northeast/northerly situations, heavy snowfall, 25–45 cm (10–18 in) in northeast England and south Scotland, 50–80 cm (20–32 in) over high ground; 14–15 February: anticyclonic situation (15 February), severe night frosts, −16 to −19 °C (3 to −2 °F) in Scotland. * 16–20 February: severe snowstorm-blizzard conditions. Mostly easterly situations, Atlantic fronts moving northeast towards southwest England (15–16 February) became slow-moving, snowstorm-blizzard conditions, easterly gales (18–19 February), southwest England and south Wales worst affected areas, heavy snowfall, 34 cm (13 in), 85 cm (34 in) over high ground, deep drifts, 10 m (33 ft) over Exmoor, traffic halted, power lines and telephone cables brought down, many towns and villages isolated, supplies airlifted by helicopter, three people killed, many livestock perished. Cold mostly dry spring – March: westerly; April: easterly, very cold, coldest April for over 40 years; 9–10 April: northerly situation, heavy snowfall, 20 cm (8 in) in northeast Scotland and southeast England; May: anticyclonic northeasterly. Very cool summer – 20 June to 8 July: several northwesterly situations, wet spell. Very mild dry autumn – driest autumn for at least 150 years; October: very dry, one of the driest Octobers on record; 13 October: very warm, 22 °C (72 °F) in Norwich; 24 November: start of cold spell, cold front moved southeast across country, occasional northerly winds, local snow showers; 28–30 November: anticyclonic situation, widespread night frosts.

1979 Weak zonal flow (75 westerly situations). Very cold wet winter, coldest since 1963 – December (1978): southeasterly. * 26–28 December (1978): severe river floods. Cyclonic/southeasterly situations, slow-moving fronts over north Britain, prolonged heavy rain in north Ireland, Wales and north England, widespread river floods. * 28–30 December (1978): severe snowstorm-blizzard conditions. Cyclonic/cyclonic easterly situations, fronts over north Britain began to move slowly south on 28 December, cold easterly winds set in over Scotland with heavy snowfall, colder conditions with marked temperature falls gradually extended south to all areas; late on 30 December a depression moved east along the Channel into south England, heavy snowfall, easterly gales, snowstorm-blizzard conditions affected this area, traffic disrupted, heavy snowfall also in Scotland, north and east England, 50 cm (20 in) over high ground, deep drifts, 3.5 m (11 ft), roads blocked; previously flooded areas in Yorkshire became skating rinks on 31 December. January: cyclonic; very cold, frequent snowfall, third-coldest 20th-century January on record, after 1940 and 1963, in England and Wales, Norfolk Broads frozen; late January: severe frost, –15 °C (5 °F) in Norwich; 1–2 January: anticyclonic situation, heavy snowfall, 25 cm (10 in), locally 60 cm (24 in) in north England, roads blocked; 9–10 January: westerly/cyclonic situations, heavy snowfall, 40 cm (16 in) in north England; 23–24 January: cyclonic northeasterly/ northerly situations, heavy snowfall, 15 cm (6 in); February: southeasterly; cold, frequent snowfall; 9–10 February: easterly situation, heavy snowfall, 20 cm (8 in) in southwest England and Wales. * 13–14 February: severe storm. Cyclonic easterly/easterly situations, depression moved east along the Channel into mainland Europe, severe easterly gales, exceptionally high seas, damaging waves pounded south coast, Chesil Bank (Dorset) breached, Portland isolated as an island, widespread snowfall in south England. * 14–16 February: severe snowstorm-blizzard conditions. Easterly situation, snowstorm-blizzard conditions, heavy snowfall, 30 cm (12 in), locally 60 cm (24 in), 1 m (3 ft) drifts in east England and Scotland, 100 major roads closed, Sheffield, Leeds and East

Anglian towns (including Norwich, Lowestoft and Felixstowe) cut off; planned helicopter tour of 'Arctic' Norfolk by Denis Howell (newly appointed snow minister) cancelled due to unfavourable weather conditions. Very cold wet spring – one of the coldest wettest springs on record; March: cyclonic westerly; 5 March: ice on Diss Mere (Norfolk) finally disappeared (its surface had been totally or partly frozen from 31 December 1978); 16–21 March: cyclonic situations, widespread heavy snowfall, 30 cm (12 in), locally 45 cm (18 in), Newcastle upon Tyne isolated; 24 March: anticyclonic southerly situation, depression moved rapidly northeast across Ireland, heavy snow, 30 cm (12 in) in northwest Scotland; April: cyclonic northwesterly; May: cyclonic westerly. Cool dry summer.
* 13–14 August: severe storm. Southwesterly/cyclonic situations, depression (13 August) deepened southwest of Ireland, on 14 August this now intense low (below 984 mb) moved northeast across the British Isles, heavy rain, severe gales affected much of the country, storm-force winds and heavy seas over the Irish Sea; Fastnet Yacht Race disaster, 300 yachts sailed into exposed conditions off the Irish south coast, only 85 yachts completed race, 136 crew members rescued but 15 drowned. Mostly average autumn temperatures and rainfall.

LATE 20TH-CENTURY WARMING: 1980–1999

1980s

Weak zonal flow (72 westerly situations on average per year). **1980** Very weak zonal flow (52 westerly situations); volcanic dust veil (DVI 500), Mount St Helens (Washington State, USA) eruption. Mild wet winter – December (1979): westerly.
* 4–5 December (1979): severe storm. Westerly/cyclonic westerly situations, deep depression north of Scotland, severe northwesterly gales pounded coasts of north Ireland and north Scotland; North Sea storm surge caused severe sea floods along the Norwegian coast. February: southwesterly. Dry cool spring, apart from mild northwest Britain – March: cyclonic. * 27 March: severe storm. Cyclonic situation, deep depression (below 988 mb) moved northeast across England, severe to storm-force southeasterly gales over the North Sea, Alexander Kielland platform disaster, former oil rig capsized, 123 workers killed. April: anticyclonic northwesterly; May: anticyclonic easterly; late May to June: notably brilliant sunrises and sunsets observed in the northern hemisphere, inferred volcanic dust-veil effect. Cool wet summer – June: very wet, one of the wettest Junes on record; Bishop's ring observed in England, inferred volcanic dust-veil effect. Cool autumn, average rainfall – October: very cool wet; November: cold spells early and late in month; 6 November: easterly situation, light snowfall,

6 cm (2.4 in) in the Channel Islands, earliest snowfall on record. **1981** Warm year; weak zonal flow (60 westerly situations). Mild dry winter – December (1980): westerly; January: westerly/northwesterly; February: anticyclonic westerly/anticyclonic southwesterly. Very mild wet spring – March: cyclonic southwesterly; April: anticyclonic easterly. * 24–26 April: notable late snowfall. Cyclonic/cyclonic northeasterly situations, depression (below 1000 mb) on 24 April moved slowly southeast across England, heavy snowfall in south Scotland, north Ireland and north England, further heavy snowfall followed on 25 and 26 April, blizzards occurred in northeasterly gales, snow extended south across parts of Wales, central and southwest England, deep snowdrifts, especially over high ground such as the Pennines and Mendips, 60 cm (24 in) in the Derbyshire hills, hundreds of spring lambs lost, power and telephone lines brought down. May: cyclonic. Cool dry summer – 6 August: thundery trough extended north across England from a shallow depression over France, heavy thunderstorms and rain in south, central and northwest England, late morning 'night darkness' with torrential rain and flash floods in London, record-breaking downpour, 109 mm (4.3 in) in Manchester. Cool wet autumn – October: very cool wet, one of the coldest Octobers on record; 21 November: westerly situation, mild disturbed southwesterly flow, several tornadoes (greatest outbreak on record in the British Isles). * 23–25 November: severe storm. Deepening depression (963 mb) north of Scotland on 23 November moved rapidly east into south Scandinavia, severe northwesterly gales with hurricane-force gusts affected north Britain and the North Sea, wind damage on Scottish coasts. **1982** Cool year; normal zonal flow (85 westerly situations); volcanic dust veil (DVI 800), El Chichón (Mexico) eruption, an already negative temperature anomaly was intensified by this event. Very cold winter – December (1981): cyclonic, coldest December in many parts for over a century; 6–7 December: northwesterly situation, very cold spell, rain followed by sleet and snow. * 8–11 December (1981): severe snowstorms. Rain turned to heavy snow on 8 December as a front moved south across central and south Britain, lying snow 20 cm (8 in) deep in many places, a depression that moved east on 11 December over north France brought further heavy snowfall to similar areas, additional 15–20 cm (6–8 in) of lying snow; exceptional fall of temperature in rear of the low caused by the deep snow cover and clear skies. 12 December (1981): anticyclonic situation, severe day maximum frost, –12 °C (10 °F) in Shawbury (Shropshire) followed by a very severe night minimum frost, –25 °C (–13 °F), a record low for any month in England; January: southwesterly. * 7–10 January: severe snowstorm. Late on 7 January a band of snow advanced into southwest England and extended to many other south and central areas the following day in a cyclonic easterly situation, more or less continuous heavy snowfall for 36–48

hours, 30–40 cm (12–16 in) in south Wales, west, central and south England, locally 60–80 cm (24–32 in) in heavier falls, deep drifts, road and rail traffic severely disrupted; 10 January: after the snow, an anticyclonic situation with light winds, clear skies and snow cover allowed very severe frosts to occur; the lowest temperature on record in Britain, –27.2 °C (–17 °F), was again equalled at Braemar (Aberdeenshire). February: southerly/southwesterly. Mild dry spring – March: westerly; April: anticyclonic; May: cyclonic westerly/cyclonic southwesterly. Warm summer – variable rainfall but very dry in Scotland; June: very wet, one of the wettest Junes on record; 18 June: cyclonic situation, heavy thunderstorm in northeast Bristol, flash floods, deep drifts of large hailstones. Very warm wet autumn – 21 September: cyclonic situation, intense secondary depression (below 992 mb) moved rapidly east across central Britain, heavy rain, hail and strong squally winds occurred as its cold front moved across south England; tornadoes in several places, including Bicester (four people injured) and Thaxted.

1983 Weak zonal flow (77 westerly situations). Mild winter – a notable incidence of severe storms in the Atlantic–European sector; December (1982): westerly. 20 December (1982): severe storm. Cyclonic westerly situation, exceptionally deep intense depression (932 mb) moved northeast over north Britain, lowest pressures recorded since December 1886 (927 mb), severe southwesterly gales and floods, considerable disruption, at least nine people killed. January: very mild, westerly; one of the mildest Januarys on record in England. * 18 January: severe storm. Northwesterly situation, depression (959 mb) over the Baltic, strong west to northwesterly winds affected the British Isles, gales in the North Sea. * 31 January to 1 February: severe storm. Cyclonic situation, deep depression (below 955 mb) over north Scotland moved east into the North Sea, widespread severe west to northwesterly gales, particularly severe over the North Sea, exceptionally high tides along east coast caused flooding in places but improved sea defences after the 1953 and 1978 storms mainly held and no lives were lost on the coast although four or five people were killed inland, Spurn Head peninsula (Yorkshire) damaged. February: anticyclonic. Cold wet spring – March: westerly; April: cyclonic; 1 April (Good Friday): northeasterly situation, snowfall in northeast and central England, snow spread south the following day, London and southeast England under snow on 3 April, heavy snowfall, 20 cm (8 in) on the South Downs, thaw on 4 April, meltwater caused flooding; 22 April: cyclonic situation, tornado damage in central England; May: cyclonic. Very warm dry summer – 5 June: anticyclonic northeasterly situation, thundery low over France, severe thunderstorms in south England, damaging large hailstones, 3–4 cm (1.5 in) diameter; 7 June: southeasterly situation, severe thunderstorms in Manchester and on Merseyside, damaging large hailstones, 3–4 cm (1.5 in) diameter; July: warm dry, one of the warmest Julys on record, 19.5 °C (67 °F), blocking high extended northeast over Europe, Atlantic disturbances steered north into the Iceland–Svalbard region. Dry autumn, mostly near average temperatures. **1984** Weak zonal flow (67 westerly situations). Mild wet winter – December (1983): southwesterly; January: westerly; snowfall in Norfolk. * 2 January: severe storm. Westerly situation, deep depression (below 972 mb) moved east off north Scotland, severe westerly gales, frequent snow showers in north Britain. * 13 January: severe storm. Cyclonic situation, very deep depression (below 948 mb) moved east across Scotland into the North Sea, near gale northwesterly winds in its rear moved southeast across Britain, widespread snow showers in Scotland, north Ireland and north England. Cold spring, dry in north and west Britain; driest spring on record in Glasgow; March: anticyclonic easterly; April: anticyclonic; May: northerly; cold northeasterly flow over British Isles between low over central Europe and ridge west of Azores. Very warm dry summer – 8 July: southerly situation, trough moved northeast over the country, scattered thunderstorms, York Minster badly damaged by lightning. Wet autumn, average temperatures – 30 November: cyclonic southerly situation, heavy rainfall, 267 mm (10.5 in) in 24 hours at Aberdeen. **1985** Cool year, weak zonal flow (63 westerly situations). Cold dry winter – December (1984): southwesterly; January: cyclonic; February: anticyclonic southerly. Cold wet spring – March: westerly; April: westerly. Very cool wet summer. Cool dry autumn, apart from Scotland, one of the driest autumns on record in England. **1986** Cool year, normal to strong zonal flow (100 westerly situations). Cold winter, variable rainfall – December (1985): southwesterly; January: westerly; February: very cold easterly; notable absence of westerlies, one of the coldest Februarys on record; festive ice-skating championships held at Welney Washes in the Fens. Very cold wet spring – March: southwesterly. * 20 March: severe storm. Cyclonic southwesterly situation, deep depression (below 976 mb) moved northeast off northwest Scotland, severe gales in the Scottish Highlands, hurricane-force gust in the Cairngorm Mountains, 246 km/h (153 mph, 133 knots), the highest gust speed on record in Britain. * 24 March: severe storm. Cyclonic situation, deep depression (below 968 mb) moved east across central Britain, heavy snowfall in north England, rain and severe westerly gales to the south, widespread storm-force gusts. April: cyclonic; May: cyclonic southwesterly. Cool wet summer. * 25 August: severe storm. Cyclonic situation, intense depression (below 996 mb), ex-tropical hurricane, moved east-northeast across England, widespread gales and heavy rainfall, generally 50–75 mm (2–3 in), 95 mm (3.8 in) in north Ireland, widespread floods. Variable autumn rainfall, average temperatures; September: cool; October: warm, westerly; November:

warm, westerly. **1987** Very weak zonal flow (54 westerly situations). Cold winter, despite mild December (1986) – early January: notable change of circulation patterns, mild westerly situations that had prevailed since mid October (1986) gave way to one of the coldest spells on record in many areas; December (1986): mild, westerly; January: anticyclonic easterly. * 12–14 January: severe snowstorm-blizzard conditions. Easterly situation, blocking high over Scandinavia, strong easterly flow over the British Isles, severe snowstorm-blizzard conditions, heavy snowfall, 50–60 cm (20–24 in) in east and southeast England, deep drifts, roads blocked, helicopter emergency hospital airlift, severe frost, –12 °C (10.4 °F) in south Britain, probably one of the coldest spells in the region since January 1740. February: southwesterly. Wet spring, average temperatures – March: westerly/southwesterly; April: very mild, cyclonic southwesterly; one of the warmest Aprils on record; May: anticyclonic northwesterly/anticyclonic northerly. Cool wet summer – July: northwesterly; late July: occasional heavy thunderstorms and rain in east England; 22 August: cyclonic situation, heavy thunderstorms, large hail, extensive damage in central and east England. Cool autumn, wet, apart from Scotland – September: westerly; October: very wet. * 15–16 October: severe storm. Cyclonic situation, depression, moved north from Biscay, explosive deepening on 15 October as it approached south Devon (first recorded report of the sting jet phenomenon), with a central pressure below 960 mb the low moved rapidly northeast over England, severe to storm-force gales, south and east of the depression, occurred in the early hours of 16 October, widespread severe damage, hurricane-force gusts in many inland places, commercial activity in London ceased for 24 hours, 18 people killed, many buildings damaged, power supplies and transport systems severely disrupted, 15 million trees blown down; the most violent and destructive storm to affect southeast England since 1703. **1988** Weak zonal flow (71 westerly situations). Very mild wet winter – December (1987): anticyclonic southwesterly; January: southwesterly; February: cyclonic northwesterly. * 9 February: severe storm. Cyclonic situation, very deep depression (below 948 mb) moved east across north Scotland, westerly gales, severe in places with hurricane-force gusts, buildings damaged, trees blown down, especially in northwest England, at least six people killed. Mild wet spring – March: westerly/northwesterly. * 3–4 March: severe storm. Northerly situation, depression (below 988 mb) north of Scotland moved southeast into the Skaggerak, severe northerly gales pounded British east coasts, Spurn Head peninsula breached by powerful wave action, lighthouse isolated. May: cyclonic southeasterly; 1 May: southeasterly situation, heavy thunderstorms in central and northwest England, 12 people killed by lightning strikes; 9 May: anticyclonic situation, heavy rain, 90 mm (3.5 in) in 24 hours in southeast England; 17–19 May: northerly situation, 19 May: heavy rain, 193 mm (7.6 in) in two hours in Halifax (Yorkshire), severe floods. Cool wet summer, warmer in Scotland, drier in southeast England. Cool dry autumn. **1989** Very warm year, seventh-warmest year (with 2003) on record; normal zonal flow (94 westerly situations). Very mild winter, very dry apart from northwest Britain, second-warmest winter on record – December (1988): westerly; January: very mild, westerly/southwesterly; February: westerly. * 13 February: severe storm. Westerly situation, depression (below 980 mb) north of Scotland, severe westerly to northwesterly gales in north Scotland, widespread damage both on land and at sea, large buildings unroofed, hurricane-force gusts including 233 km/h (145 mph, 126 knots) at Kinnaird Head lighthouse, Fraserburgh (Aberdeenshire), highest gust on record at a low-level station in the British Isles. 25 February: cyclonic situation, complex depression over British Isles, one centre southwest of Ireland moved east along the Channel, extremely low pressure (949 mb) recorded at Portland (Dorset), lowest pressure on record in south England since before 1870. Very mild wet spring – March: westerly; April: cyclonic; early April: notable change in circulation, with the long spell of very mild situations being replaced by cold easterly conditions associated with blocking high over Scandinavia (first such spell since mid October 1988); May: very dry, anticyclonic, probably driest May in London for 300 years. Very warm dry summer apart from northwest Britain. Very warm dry autumn – November: stormy. * 8 November: severe storm. Cyclonic situation, depression (below 988 mb) moved northeast across England, severe westerly gales with hurricane-force gusts affected south England, the Channel and south North Sea, strongest winds in London since October 1987, inferred hurricane-force winds in the south North Sea, oil rig overturned and sank.

1990s

Weak zonal flow (76 westerly situations on average per year). **1990** Very warm year, second warmest (with 1999) on record, 10.6 °C (51 °F); strong zonal flow (102 westerly situations). Very mild wet winter – the stormy period from November (1989) continued into April; December (1989): southerly. * 16–17 December (1989): severe storm. Southeasterly/cyclonic situations, very deep depression (below 944 mb) off southwest Ireland moved northeast across Ireland and Scotland into the North Sea, severe to storm-force gales, mainly south to southwesterly in direction but east to northeasterly over north Scotland, hurricane-force gusts buffeted Cornish coast, heavy rainfall, heavy seas, very high waves broke over exposed coasts, at least nine people drowned, fishing boat and crew lost in the Firth of Clyde. * January and February: severe stormy period. Besides the British Isles

(109 people killed), this was also an exceptionally stormy period in mainland Europe (over 120 people killed in France, Germany and the Netherlands). January: mild, southwesterly; 25 January to 27 February: series of depressions moved northeast across the British Isles (the most sustained spell of strong westerly winds on record). * 25 January: severe storm, 'The Burns Night Storm'. Cyclonic situation, deepening depression (below 950 mb) over Ireland moved northeast across north England and south Scotland, severe southwesterly gales south of centre with hurricane-force gusts buffeting English coasts; heavy rain, gales most intense over south Britain (a much larger area than the October 1987 storm), transport systems badly disrupted, widespread damage estimated at £2 billion, as the storm struck during daytime working hours many more people were killed (47) than in the October 1987 storm, 3 million trees blown down, heavy snowfall in parts of Scotland north of low centre. February: very mild, westerly/southwesterly; one of the mildest Februarys on record. * 3 February: severe storm. Westerly situation, secondary depression (below 992 mb) moved east along the Channel, heavy rain over England north of the centre briefly turned to snow in places, especially over high ground, severe flooding, severe gales affected France and Germany, 20 people killed. * 26–27 February: severe storm. Cyclonic/westerly situations, deep depression (948 mb) moved east across Scotland into the North Sea, stormy conditions affected most of the British Isles, severe northwesterly gales with hurricane-force gusts caused a storm surge that struck the coasts of north Wales and northwest England, sea defences breached, severe damage, at least 14 people killed. Very mild spring, dry apart from Scotland away from east coast; March: anticyclonic westerly, start of long dry spell to mid September; April: westerly/northwesterly; May: very dry, anticyclonic easterly; driest May of the 20th century in southeast England. Very warm dry summer apart from north Scotland; 3 August: anticyclonic situation, very warm, 37.1 °C (98.8 °F) at Cheltenham. Very warm autumn – mid September: end of long dry spell from March, lowest rainfall on record in England and Wales since 1727; October: southwesterly. **1991** Weak zonal flow (71 westerly situations); volcanic dust veil (DVI 1,000 estimate), Pinatubo (Philippines) eruption in June, notable coloured sunrises and sunsets observed, inferred volcanic dust-veil effect. Cold winter, average rainfall. * 7–9 December (1990): severe storm and snowstorm. Cyclonic situation, depression formed over central Britain on 7 December, an exceptionally large fall of pressure (40 mb in 36 hours) over south England, heavy rain turned to snow west and north of the centre as the low drifted south, heavy snowfall, 40 cm (16 in) on 8 December, northeasterly winds reached gale force in places. February: early part cold, frequent snowfall. Very mild dry spring – 16–21 April: mostly northerly situations, wintry showers of snow and sleet with hail and

thunder in east Britain; 21 February: widespread keen night frosts, −4.4 °C (24 °F) at East Hoathly (East Sussex). Warm summer, average rainfall. * 2–4 June: notable out-of-season snowfall. Shallow polar low (below 1012 mb) formed off east Britain on 2 June, overnight rain moved southeast across Scotland and north England with snow over high ground, snow showers occurred over Scotland and the Lake District on 3 and 4 June. Very warm dry autumn. * 16–17 October: severe storm. Westerly/northwesterly situations, deep depression moved slowly east north of Scotland, severe westerly veering northerly gales with hurricane-force gusts in north Britain. * 18–19 November: severe storm. Cyclonic/cyclonic northeasterly situations, depression over central Britain on 18 November moved slowly southeast, widespread heavy rain, strong to gale-force northeasterly winds in wake of low. **1992** Normal zonal flow (95 westerly situations). Mild dry winter – 1–3 January: westerly situation, severe westerly gales with hurricane-force gusts in Scotland; 10 January to 2 February: anticyclonic situations; 26 January: extremely high pressure recorded at Cynwyd (Merioneth), 1049 mb, highest value observed in England and Wales over past 60 years. Very mild wet spring – May: very mild, one of the warmest Mays on record (only May 1833 was significantly warmer); 13–31 May: dry spell, blocking high mostly located northeast of Britain; 14 May: southerly situation, 28.9 °C (84 °F) at Edinburgh, equalling May maximum record for Scotland; late spring: unprecedented warmth for the season, series of eight consecutive days above 25 °C (77 °F) in London. Warm wet summer – August: west/southwesterly. Cool wet autumn – November: westerly. **1993** Weak zonal flow (72 westerly situations). Mild dry winter – 4–28 January: westerly situations, prolonged unsettled spell, frequent damaging gales. * 10 January: severe Atlantic storm. Westerly situation, intense deep depression, below 916 mb (lowest value on record for north hemispheric temperate latitudes), south of Iceland moved northeast, inferred severe westerly gales affected north Ireland and Scotland, heavy wet snowfall, transport and power supplies widely disrupted. Very mild wet spring. * 13–14 May: notable late snowfall. Cyclonic situation, Arctic maritime airstream moved south across Scotland and Ireland but the development of a depression over England prevented the cold air progressing further south, heavy rain and snowfall over high ground in central and south Scotland, north England and north Wales, 30 cm (12 in) in the Southern Uplands. Cool summer, average rainfall – inferred volcanic dust-veil effect. * 8–9 July: notable fall of temperature. Westerly/cyclonic northwesterly situations, depression north of Scotland moved east, notable fall of temperature occurred over the British Isles as a cold front moved southeast, exceptionally cool in south England, 7.5 °C (45.5 °F), 13 °C (23 °F) below the seasonal average. Very cool autumn, average rainfall. **1994** Normal zonal flow (92 westerly situations). Mild wet winter, strong westerlies – December (1993): westerly, heavy rain and severe floods in mainland Europe, Cologne inundated. Mild wet spring – March: westerly. Very warm dry summer – July: bridge of high pressure extended northeast over Europe from the Azores high, Atlantic disturbances steered north over the Iceland–Svalbard region; 24 July: anticyclonic southeasterly situation, very warm, 33 °C (91 °F) at Lakenheath (Suffolk), widespread heavy thunderstorms, heavy rain, 75 mm (3 in) at Oxford. Very warm autumn, average rainfall – 14–15 September: cyclonic easterly/cyclonic northeasterly situations, deepening depression (below 996 mb) over the Channel moved northeast over south England into the North Sea, widespread heavy thundery rain, generally 25–50 mm (1–2 in), locally much heavier, 77 mm (3.1 in) in 36 hours at Wittering (Cambridgeshire), flooding in central and east England; November: very warm, southwesterly, warmest November on record, 10.2 °C (50.4 °F). **1995** Very warm year (sixth-warmest year on record), weak zonal flow (67 westerly situations). Very mild wet winter – January: heavy rain, severe floods, west mainland Europe, Cologne inundated. * 17 January: severe storm. Cyclonic southerly situation, deep intense depression (941 mb) moved rapidly northeast off northwest Ireland, widespread heavy rain, severe to storm-force southwesterly gales, hurricane-force gusts in exposed places; westerly winds in low's cold sector brought showers, hail, thunder and snowfall over high ground. February: very mild, westerly, one of the mildest Februarys on record. Mild dry spring. * 28 March: severe storm and snowstorm. Cyclonic situation, depression (below 996 mb) moved southeast over the British Isles, heavy snowfall, 35 cm (14 in) in north England, transport disrupted, power lines brought down. May: notable temperature fluctuations; 1–6 May: anticyclonic spell, exceptionally warm, 27 °C (80 °F) recorded on every day; 8–14 May: northerly/northeasterly situations, cold spell, heavy snow showers in Scotland and north England, widespread night frosts, including south England; 22–24 May: southerly/cyclonic situations, brief warm spell, 25 °C (77 °F). Very warm dry summer – 1–2 June: very cool northerly spell, night frosts; July: very warm; ridge from the Azores high extended northeast over central Europe; August: very warm dry (probably the warmest and one of the driest Augusts on record). Very warm autumn, average rainfall. **1996** Very weak zonal flow (50½ westerly situations); one of the driest years on record in England and Wales. Cold winter, average rainfall – December (1995): cold. * 24–26 December (1995): severe storm and snowstorm. Cyclonic/northerly situations, depression off northeast Scotland on 24 December moved southeast into the North Sea, cold air spread to all areas, heavy snowfall in Scotland and northeast England, 35 cm (14 in) in Shetland, snow flurries further south, northeasterly gales over Scotland on 25 December, blown snow caused large drifts, especially in Shetland. 27–28 December (1995): anticyclonic conditions, light winds, clear skies, exceptionally low temperatures, especially over the Scottish snowfields; 30 December: easterly situation, –27.2 °C (–17 °F) at Altnaharra (Sutherland), equalled previous lowest temperature on record in Britain at Braemar (Aberdeenshire). * 23–24 January: severe ice storm. Easterly situation, low pressure over France, freezing rain over England and Wales developed into an ice storm, trees and power lines damaged by heavy deposits of glazed frost, many falls and accidents on pavements and roads due to 'black ice'. February: heavy rain and severe floods in mainland Europe, Cologne inundated. * 5–6 February: severe snowstorm. Southwesterly/cyclonic situations, quasi-stationary occlusion lay north–south over west Britain on 5 February, heavy snowfall, 50 cm (20 in) in southwest England, Wales and southwest Scotland, extended over north and central England the following morning, strong southerly winds, deep drifts in the Southern Uplands. Cold dry spring – May: very cold, one of the coldest Mays on record, 1–2 May: northeasterly situation, depression off southwest England moved east into northwest France, northeasterly flow with slow-moving fronts affected the British Isles, heavy snowfall over high ground in north England and south Scotland. Warm dry summer – 22–23 July: cyclonic situation, thunderstorms on 23 July ended warm anticyclonic spell from 14 July; 6–7 August: cyclonic situation, depression (below 1004 mb) over the Irish Sea moved slowly northeast into the North Sea, thunderstorms over England and Wales, fall of soft hail, several centimetres deep in Sheffield (Yorkshire); 27–29 August: northerly situations, strong north to northwesterly winds (29 August) affected east England with gale-force gusts, heavy rain, 75 mm (3 in) at Lowestoft (Suffolk), wettest place in the British Isles. Warm autumn, average rainfall. **1997** Very warm year (fifth-warmest year on record), very weak zonal flow (59 westerly situations). Dry winter, average temperatures – 19–31 December (1996): mostly easterly situations, very cold spell, frequent severe night frosts, –13 °C (9 °F) at Aviemore (Inverness) on 25 December; 27–31 December: occasional snow with heavier falls in east and southeast England, 25 cm (10 in) on North Downs; January: very dry, one of the driest Januarys on record; February: very mild, one of the mildest Februarys on record. * 13 February: severe storm. Cyclonic situation, trough extended southeast over the British Isles from depression south of Iceland, severe to storm-force northwesterly gales with hurricane-force gusts, local damage in south Britain. Very mild dry spring – March: very mild (third-warmest March on record); 17 May: southeasterly situation, widespread heavy thunderstorms with large hail, flash floods and tornadoes. Very warm wet summer – June: very wet (one of the wettest Junes on record); July: heavy rain and severe floods in mainland Europe; August: very warm (second-warmest August on record). Very warm autumn, average rainfall – November: very warm (one of the warmest Novembers on record); short very warm spell, 21 °C (70 °F). **1998** One of the warmest years on record, weak zonal flow (77 westerly situations). Very mild winter, average rainfall. * 24 December (1997): severe storm. Cyclonic southwesterly situation, intense secondary depression (below 980 mb) moved northeast across Scotland, severe to storm-force southwesterly gales with hurricane-force gusts in exposed places, widespread rain, many buildings damaged, thousands of trees blown down, power supplies disrupted, six people killed. * 4 January: severe storm. Westerly situation, intense secondary depression (below 964 mb) moved east across Ireland and north England, severe to storm-force westerly gales affected Wales and south England with hurricane-force gusts in exposed places, power supplies and transport disrupted, widespread structural damage, river and coastal floods. 7 January: cyclonic southwesterly situation, tornado in Selsey (Sussex), hundreds of houses damaged; February: very mild dry (one of the warmest driest Februarys on record); 8–26 February: warmth of the 1990s attained a peak with temperatures regularly rising to 12–15 °C (54–59 °F) over England and Wales, the warmth accompanied by clear skies, bright sunshine and moderate breezes. Very mild wet spring. * 8–9 April: severe river floods. Cyclonic situation, a cold northeasterly flow over Scotland extended south and intensified while a slow-moving front lay west–southwest to east–northeast across Wales and central England, heavy rain, 50–60 mm (2–3 in), locally over 100 mm (4 in), occasional hail and thunderstorms, severe river floods, six people killed, buildings damaged; because of inadequate flood warnings a new alarm service was established under a reorganised Environment Agency. Average summer temperatures and rainfall but occasionally quite wet; June: very wet. * 11–12 July: severe storm. Cyclonic situation, deepening depression (below 988 mb) moved rapidly east to northeast across the British Isles, severe southwesterly gales south of centre with storm-force gusts in exposed places, a band of heavy rain, 50 mm (2 in) in south and central England, moved north across the rest of Britain on 12 July. Very mild wet autumn – September: a notable series of three ex-hurricanes, Charley, Danielle and Karl, gave unsettled conditions over the British Isles on 2–3, 6–9 and 30 September, respectively; October: very wet. * 20–31 October: severe storms and river floods. Mostly westerly situations, deep depressions affected the British Isles on most days, frequent prolonged rainfall, heaviest over high ground in western districts, especially Wales, 319 mm (12.8 in) at Treherbert in the Rhondda Valley (Glamorgan) in eight days, severe river floods followed in south Wales valleys, and on the Severn and Wye. * 24 October:

severe storm. Deep depression (below 968 mb) moved northeast over Scotland, widespread severe cyclonic gales with hurricane-force gusts in exposed places. * 9 November: severe Atlantic storm. Cyclonic southerly situation, intense depression between Scotland and Iceland (ex-tropical hurricane Mitch), severe westerly gales affected Scotland with hurricane-force gusts, buildings damaged, one person killed. **1999** Very warm year, second-warmest (with 1990) year on record, 10.6 °C (51 °F), weak zonal flow (76 westerly situations). Very mild wet winter. * 26–27 December (1998): severe storm. Westerly/cyclonic westerly situations, deep intense depression (below 956 mb) moved northeast off north Britain, widespread gales, particularly severe with hurricane-force gusts in north Ireland, central and south Scotland, and north England, buildings damaged, trees and telegraph poles blown down, power supplies and transport disrupted, five people killed. * 4 January: severe storm. Cyclonic southwesterly situation, deep intense depression (below 968 mb) off north Scotland, severe westerly gales in Ireland and Scotland, severe coastal floods in southwest Scotland, structural damage. 13–20 January: westerly situations, unsettled spell, frequent heavy rainfall, 40 mm (1.6 in) in southwest England, extensive floods on 18 and 19 January, especially in west and central England, and south Wales. Very mild wet spring. * 3–6 March: heavy snowfall. Cyclonic/cyclonic northerly situations, depression (972 mb) over east Scotland moved slowly east into the North Sea, northerly flow became established over the British Isles in the following three days, widespread heavy snowfall, 25 cm (10 in) in Sheffield (Yorkshire) on 6 March, heaviest falls over high ground in north England, subsequent heavy rain and snow-melt over the North York Moors caused severe floods in the Derwent. April: wet mild (one of the warmest Aprils on record). Very warm summer, average rainfall. Very warm autumn, average rainfall – September: very warm; 1–11 September: mostly anticyclonic southwesterly situations, warm spell, 30.4 °C (86.7 °F) at Gravesend (Kent) on 11 September, highest value so late in the season since 1947. * 18 September: severe storm. Southerly situation, deep slow-moving depression (952 mb) off west Ireland, strong to gale-force southerly winds, heavy rain, western parts of the British Isles, 92 mm (3.6 in) in Newport (Monmouth), river floods. * 24 October: severe storm. Cyclonic situation, complex depression moved slowly east across south Britain, severe southwesterly gales in the Channel with hurricane-force gusts, heavy rain and coastal flooding.

FURTHER OUTLOOK – UNSETTLED: 2000 TO...?

2000 Weak zonal flow (77½ westerly situations). Very mild wet winter.
* 24–25 December (1999): severe storm. Cyclonic southwesterly/cyclonic
situations, a large complex area of low pressure north of the British Isles,
extremely low pressures recorded over Scotland, 944 mb at Lerwick (Shetland)
and 946 mb at Aberdeen, widespread severe southwest to westerly gales,
hurricane-force gusts buffeted southwest England, three people killed, unusually
high tides caused severe sea floods along English south coast, especially in
Hampshire and Sussex. However, the country escaped the two destructive storms
that struck mainland Europe on 26 and 28 December; the first affected north
France and Germany, and the second the French west coast, Spanish north coast
and the Mediterranean, 120 people killed. Very mild wet spring. Warm dry
summer. Very warm wet autumn – October: very wet, wettest October since 1903;
7–12 October: very wet spell, heavy rain, widespread floods with southeast
England being the worst affected area following heavy thunderstorms and rain
on 10 and 11 October; 28 October: tornado caused damage along a 3 km (2 mile)
-wide track at Bognor Regis (Sussex). * 30 October: severe storm. Cyclonic
situation, an intense deep secondary depression, 950 mb (new October low-
pressure record value for England), moved east over central Britain, severe
westerly gales with hurricane-force gusts in exposed places, widespread heavy
rain, 40–60 mm (c.2 in), severe floods, extensive structural damage, road and rail
traffic disrupted, thousands of trees blown down.

Glossary

adiabatic: An atmospheric process that occurs without a transfer of heat between the system, such as a parcel of air, and its surroundings; in this process compression and expansion result in warming and cooling of the system, respectively.

advection: A process by which a property of an air mass, such as its warmth or humidity, is transferred by movement, usually in the horizontal direction.

albedo: A measure of the reflecting power of a surface, being that percentage of the incident radiation which is reflected by a surface; values of albedo (per cent) range from 10 for wet earth to 80 for fresh snow.

analogue: In meteorology, a past synoptic situation which resembles the current situation over an appreciable area. The sequence of weather which followed an analogue has sometimes been used as the basis of a weather forecast.

anomaly: In meteorology, this term usually signifies the departure of an element, such as pressure or temperature, from its long-period average value for the place concerned.

anticyclone: An area of high pressure around which the wind blows clockwise in the northern hemisphere and anticlockwise in the southern hemisphere.

Anticyclonic type: One of the main weather types defined by Dr D. Justin Schove to affect the British Isles.

Azores high: Part of the subtropical anticyclonic belt of the northern hemisphere. On average, the Azores high is centred on about 35° N in summer with a ridge extending across north France and north Germany; in winter it is centred on about 30° N with a ridge extending across south Spain.

backing: A change of the wind in an anticlockwise direction, in either hemisphere.

baroclinic: A baroclinic atmosphere is one where surfaces of constant pressure intersect surfaces of constant density. The atmosphere is always more or less baroclinic but baroclinicity becomes especially marked, implying major atmospheric instability, in frontal zones.

blocking: A term applied in synoptic meteorology to a situation during which the normal mobile mid-latitude zonal flow is interrupted for at least a few days by more or less stationary pressure systems.

bomb: In meteorology, this term applies to a situation in which the pressure at the centre of a depression falls at an exceptionally rapid rate, causing a narrow band of very strong winds, a so-called sting jet, to descend from about 5 km (3 miles) to the surface where it can cause great structural damage, major disruption of power supplies and uprooting of trees.

boundary layer: In the surface boundary layer of the atmosphere, up to about 1000 m (330 ft), airflow is mainly controlled by the presence of the earth's surface; within an overlying layer, the planetary boundary layer, up to about 600 m (2,000 ft), effects on airflow by the surface still remain significant.

CET: The temperature record for Central England, developed by Professor Gordon Manley, and now updated by the Meteorological Office; the series extends to the present on a monthly basis from 1659 and a daily basis from 1772.

circulation type: A synoptic configuration of atmospheric flow which is similar to one of the pre-defined patterns given, for example, in the Lamb British Isles Weather Type classification.

Continental type: One of the main weather types defined by Dr D. Justin Schove to affect the British Isles.

CRU: Climatic Research Unit, founded by Professor Hubert Lamb at the University of East Anglia, Norwich, in 1971.

cyclone: An area of low pressure around which winds blow anti-clockwise in the northern hemisphere and clockwise in the southern hemisphere; a cyclone of middle and high latitudes is called a depression.

Cyclonic type: One of the main weather types defined by Dr D. Justin Schove to affect the British Isles.

depression: A depression, or low, is a pressure system of closed isobars with low pressure at its centre; the wind circulation in the northern hemisphere is anticlockwise.

DVI: The Dust Veil Index is a numerical indicator devised by Professor Hubert Lamb to assess the impact of volcanic eruptions on weather and climate, as well as to allow a chronology of eruptions and their magnitudes to be constructed back to AD 1500. The formulae used to compute the DVI are scaled so that the Krakatau eruption of 1883 produces a value of 1,000 units.

electrometeor: A visible or audible manifestation of atmospheric electricity, such as lightning or thunder.

EWP: The precipitation record for England and Wales, updated by the Climatic Research Unit, that extends from 1755 to the present on a seasonal and annual basis.

frontal type: The two main frontal types, warm and cold, mark the transition zone between two distinct air masses.

GISP2: The Greenland Ice Sheet Project 2 (GISP2) comprises an investigation of an ice core over 3,000 m (10,000 ft) deep through the ice sheet into the underlying bedrock; the analysis of the core provides a proxy record of palaeoenvironmental changes over thousands of years.

hydrometeor: A meteor comprising an ensemble of liquid or solid water particles, such as rain or hail, falling through or suspended in the atmosphere, blown by the wind from the earth's surface, or deposited on objects on the ground or in the free air.

Ice Age (or Pleistocene Period): The most recent period of continental glaciation when much of Europe and North America was covered with ice. It began over a million years ago and ended about 10,000 years ago; the present ice sheets of Greenland and Antarctica are relics of this episode in earth history.

Icelandic low: The subpolar mean low pressure area centred near Iceland that represents an aggregate of many actual depressions.

insolation: The incoming solar radiation that reaches the earth and the atmosphere.

inversion: A feature at a point or layer of the atmosphere at which the temperature increases with increasing height.

isobar: A line drawn on a synoptic weather map through points of equal pressure.

isopleth: A line drawn on a map through points having the same value of a certain element such as pressure or temperature.

jet stream: A flow of very strong winds concentrated within a narrow band generally near the tropopause; it is normally some thousands of kilometres in length and a few kilometres in depth.

katabatic flow: A local downslope wind that occurs during a night with clear skies and a weak pressure gradient.

Lamb classification: The classification of British Isles weather types devised by Professor Hubert Lamb comprising seven main types: Anticyclonic, Cyclonic, Westerly, Northwesterly, Northerly, Easterly and Southerly.

lithometeor: A meteor comprising an ensemble of particles, such as in haze or smoke, most of which are solid and non-aqueous; the particles are more or less suspended in the air, or lifted by the wind from the ground.

Maritime type: One of the main weather types defined by Dr D. Justin Schove to affect the British Isles.

meridional: A type of airflow pattern in which the north to south or south to north wind component is well marked.

meteor: In meteorology, a phenomenon, other than a cloud, observed in the atmosphere or on the surface of the earth, which comprises a precipitation, a suspension or a deposit of liquid or solid particles, or an optical or electrical manifestation.

North Atlantic Oscillation: A measure of the pressure gradient between the Azores and Iceland, where a high value indicates strong zonal flow, that is, a vigorous mid-latitude westerly flow over the North Atlantic sector, and vice versa.

orographic: A term used to describe the lifting of air over a topographic barrier; clouds that form in this lifting process are called orographic clouds.

phenology: A branch of natural history devoted to the observation and recording of annually recurring events in nature such as the leafing and flowering of plants, migration of birds and behaviour of insects.

photometeor: A luminous phenomenon, such as a halo or corona, produced by the reflection, refraction, diffraction or interference of light from the sun or moon.

polar front: The main weather front that separates polar and tropical air masses and on which most of the travelling mid-latitude depressions develop.

polar-front jet stream: The jet stream associated with the polar front in middle and high latitudes that is usually located at altitudes between 9 and 12 km (30,000 and 39,000 ft).

progression: A term used to describe the dominant westerly movement of mid-latitude pressure systems.

radiation: One of the ways by which heat flows between two bodies. In meteorology, the two main forms of radiation are solar (short-wave) and terrestrial (long-wave); the former, also called insolation, has its maximum intensity within the visible range, whereas the latter, in the infrared range, is invisible.

radiosonde: A balloon-borne apparatus comprising sensitive elements and a radio transmitter that measure and send observations of pressure, temperature and humidity to a ground-based receiving station.

recession: In climatology, a deterioration of conditions, typically cooler and wetter, over a period of years.

singularity: A regular seasonal episode.

sinusoidal: Descriptive of a curve having the form of a sine wave with periodic maxima and minima values.

stationary (see blocking)

sting jet (see bomb)

stratosphere: The layer of the atmosphere above the troposphere and below the mesosphere, between 10 km and 50 km (6 and 30 miles).

synoptic chart: Weather map that shows pressure systems such as depressions and anticyclones, and fronts over a widespread area.

synoptic meteorology: The branch of meteorology which deals with weather analysis and forecasting by means of synoptic weather maps and the circulation patterns depicted on these charts.

tropopause: The boundary between the troposphere and the stratosphere. It lies at about 10 km (6 miles) above the ground.

troposphere: The layer of the atmosphere that extends from the earth's surface up to the tropopause at about 10 km (6 miles) above the ground.

veering: A change of the wind in a clockwise direction, in either hemisphere.

zonal flow: A west to east airflow.

zonal index: In general there is a broad westerly airflow over the temperate belt in which the British Isles region is situated. The strength of this circumpolar circulation depends on the mean pressure difference between two latitudes, 30° N and 55° N, which is termed the zonal index.

Bibliography

Badt, K. (1950). *John Constable's Clouds* (translated from the German by S. Godman). Routledge & Kegan Paul, London.

Bailey, M. (1992). Per impetum maris: natural disaster and economic decline in eastern England, 1275–1350. In Campbell, B. M. S., ed., *Before the Black Death: Studies in the 'Crisis' of the Early Fourteenth Century*. Manchester University Press, Manchester.

Betin, V. V. & Preobrazenskij, J. V. (1962). *The severity of winters in Europe and the state of the ice cover in the Baltic.* Gidrometeoizdat, Leningrad. [In Russian.]

Bleeker, W., Alaka, M. A., Beaufils, R. & Bessemoulin, J. (1956). *International Cloud Atlas: Abridged Atlas.* World Meteorological Organization, Geneva.

Blythe, R. (1966). Introduction and notes to *Emma*, by Jane Austen. Penguin, London.

Bonacina, L. C. W. (1937). Constable as a painter of weather. *Quarterly Journal of the Royal Meteorological Society*, **63**, 483–490.

Bonacina, L. C. W. (1938). Turner's Portrayal of Weather. *Quarterly Journal of the Royal Meteorological Society*, **64**, 601–611.

Bowen, D. (1969). *Britain's Weather: its Workings, Lore and Forecasting.* David & Charles, Newton Abbot.

Brandon, P. F. (1971). Agriculture and the effects of floods and weather at Barnhorne, Sussex, during the Late Middle Ages. *Sussex Archæological Collections*, **109**, 69–93.

Brazell, J. H. (1968). *London Weather*. Meteorological Office MO 783. HMSO, London.

Brezowsky, H., Flohn, H. & Hess, P. (1951). Some remarks on the climatology of blocking action. *Tellus*, **3**, 191–194.

Brooks, C. E. P. (1970). *Climate Through the Ages: a Study of the Climatic Factors and Their Variations* (republication of the second edition, 1949). Dover, New York.

Brooks, C. E. P. & Glasspoole, J. (1928). *British Floods and Droughts*. Ernest Benn, London.

Buisman, J. (1995). *Duizend Jaar Weer, Wind en Water in de Lage Landen, Deel 1 Tot 1300*, ed. A. F. V. van Engelen. Van Wijnen, Franeker.

Burt, S. (2007). The lowest of the lows: extremes of barometric pressure in the British Isles. Part 1 – the deepest depressions. *Weather*, **62**, 4–14.

Cave, C. J. P. (1926). *Clouds and Weather Phenomena*. Cambridge University Press, Cambridge.

Clarke, G. A. (1920). *Clouds*. Constable, London.

Clayden, A. W. (1903). *Cloud Studies*, John Murray, London.

Cozens-Hardy, B., ed. (1950). *The Diary of Sylas Neville: 1767–1788*. Geoffrey Cumberlege, Oxford University Press, London.

Crombie, A. C. (1969). *Augustine to Galileo. Volume I, Science in the Middle Ages; 5th–13th Centuries*. Penguin, Harmondsworth.

Crossley. A. F. (1960). *Handbook of Aviation Meteorology*. Air Ministry, Meteorological Office. HMSO, London.

Davis, N. E. (1972). Classified central-England temperatures and England and Wales rainfall. *Meteorological Magazine*, **101**, 205–217.

De Lisle, Squire (unpublished MS). Diary of Charles March Phillips, 1811–1855.

De Lisle, Squire (unpublished MS). Diary of Laura De Lisle, 1840–1872.

Dove, H. W. (1862). *The Law of Storms*. Longman, Green, Longman, Roberts, & Green, London.

Draper, W. (1973). *Chiswick*. Anne Bingley, London.

Dublin Census Office (1856). *The Census of Ireland, 1851*. HMSO, Dublin.

East, W. G. (1965). *The Geography behind History*. Nelson, London.

Eden, P. (2003). *The Daily Telegraph Book of the Weather: Past and Future Climate Changes Explained*. Continuum, London.

Eden, P. (2005). *Change in the Weather*. Continuum, London.

Fagan, B. (2002). *The Little Ice Age: How Climate Made History 1300–1850*. Basic Books, New York.

Firstbrook, P. (1997). *The Voyage of the* Matthew*: John Cabot and the Discovery of North America*. BBC Books, London.

Fish, M., McCaskill, I. & Hudson, P. (2007). *Storm-Force*. Great Northern Books, Ilkley.

Francis, P., ed. (1963). *John Evelyn's Diary*. Folio Society, London.

Gottschalk, M. K. E. (1971). *Stormvloeden en Rivieroverstromingen in Nederland: Deel I – De Periode voor 1400.* Van Gorcum, Assen.

Goudie, G. (1889). *The Diary of the Reverend John Mill.* University Press, Edinburgh.

Gram-Jensen, I. (1985). *Sea Floods: Contributions to the Climatic History of Denmark.* Climatological Papers 13. Danish Meteorological Institute, Copenhagen.

Gribbin, J. (1983). *Future Weather: The Causes and Effects of Climatic Change.* Pelican, Harmondsworth.

Hammersley, A. (1968). *Weather and Life.* Blandford Press, London.

Harcourt-Williams, M. & Stevenson, J., eds. (1999). *Observations of Weather: the Weather Diary of Sir John Wittewronge of Rothamsted 1684–89.* Hertfordshire Record Society, Hertford.

Harris, B. (2008). The potential impact of super-volcanic eruptions on the earth's atmosphere. *Weather*, **63**, 221–225.

Holford, I. (1976). *British Weather Disasters.* David & Charles, Newton Abbot.

Hoskins, W. G. (1964). Harvest fluctuations and English economic history, 1480–1619. *Agricultural History Review*, **2**, 28–46.

Howard, L. (unpublished MS). Meteorological Register, conducted by J. Gibson (Howard's Assistant). Stratford, Essex.

Huckstep, N. J., Mortimer, R., Farmer, G. *et al.* (1982). *The Reconstruction of European Climate on Decadal and Shorter Time Scales.* Climatic Research Unit, University of East Anglia, Norwich.

Hulme, M. & Barrow, E., eds. (1997). *Climates of the British Isles: Present, Past and Future.* Routledge, London.

Huntley, I. D. (1957). The Thames in winter. *Weather*, **12**, 373–376.

Jankovi V. (2000). *Reading the Skies: A Cultural History of English Weather, 1650–1820.* The University of Chicago Press, Chicago.

Jeffery, R. W. (1933). Was it wet or fine? Being an account of English weather from chronicles, diaries and registers. Unpublished MS. Meteorological Office Library, Exeter.

Jenkins, G., Perry, M. & Prior, J. (2007). *The Climate of the United Kingdom and Recent Trends.* Meteorological Office Hadley Centre, Exeter.

Johnson, W. (1970). *Gilbert White's Journals.* David & Charles, Newton Abbot.

Joll, E. (1967). *Agnew's 150th Anniversary Loan Exhibition of Paintings and Watercolours by J. M. W. Turner, R.A.* Agnew, London.

Jones, E. L. (1964). *Seasons and Prices: The Role of the Weather in English Agricultural History.* George Allen & Unwin, London.

Jones, P. D., Ogilvie, A. E. J. & Wigley, T. M. L. (1984). *Riverflow Data for the United Kingdom: Reconstructed Data back to 1844 and Historical Data back to 1556.* CRURP 8. Climatic Research Unit, University of East Anglia, Norwich.

Khrgian, A. K. (1959). *Meteorology: a Historical Survey, Vol. I* (translated from the Russian by R. Hardin). Gimiz, Gidrometeorolicheskoe Izdatel'stvo, Leningrad/Israel program for scientific translations, Jerusalem, 1970.

Kington, B. D. (1980). Searches for historical weather data: appeals and responses. *Weather*, **35**, 124–134.

Kington, J. A. (1969). The classification and nomenclature of clouds: a review in the light of modern dynamical and physical theory. Unpublished MSc thesis, University of London.

Kington, J. A. (1974). An application of phenological data to historical climatology. *Weather*, **29**, 320–328.

Kington, J. A. (1988). *The Weather of the 1780s over Europe*. Cambridge University Press, Cambridge.

Kington, J. A. (1988). *The Weather Journals of a Rutland Squire: Thomas Barker of Lyndon Hall*. Rutland Record Society, Oakham.

Kington, J. A. (1992). Weather patterns over Europe in 1816. In Harington, C. R., ed., *The Year Without a Summer? World Climate in 1816*. Canadian Museum of Nature, Ottawa, 358–371.

Kington, J. A. (1994). Synoptic weather mapping, 1675–1715. In Frenzel, B., Pfister, C., & Glaser, B., eds, *Climatic Trends and Anomalies in Europe 1675–1715*. Gustav Fischer Verlag, Stuttgart, 389–399.

Kington, J. A. (1995). The value of the Journal to Stella to historical climatology. Jonathan Swift, 1667–1745: an Interdisciplinary Commemoration. Trinity College, Dublin.

Kington, J. A. (1995). The severe winter of 1694/95. *Weather*, **50**, 160–163.

Kington, J. A. (1997). The severe winter of 1696/97. *Weather*, **52**, 386–391.

Kington, J. A. (1997). Observing and measuring the weather: a brief history. In Hulme, M. & Barrow, E., eds, *Climates of the British Isles: Present, Past and Future*. Routledge, London, 137–152.

Kington, J. A. (1998). The great storm of 1–2 October 1697. *Weather*, **53**, 424–428.

Lamb, H. H. (1964). *The English Climate*. English Universities Press, London.

Lamb, H. H. (1966). *The Changing Climate*. Methuen, London.

Lamb, H. H. (1970). Volcanic dust in the atmosphere; with a chronology and assessment of its meteorological significance. *Philosophical Transactions of the Royal Society (A)*, **266**, 425–533.

Lamb, H. H. (1972). *British Isles Weather Types and a Register of the Daily Sequence of Circulation Patterns, 1861–1971*. Geophysical Memoirs 116. HMSO, London.

Lamb, H. H. (1977). *Climate: Present, Past and Future, Volume 2: Climatic History and the Future*. Methuen, London.

Lamb, H. H. (1977). Supplementary volcanic dust veil index assessments. *Climate Monitor*, **6**, 57–67.

Lamb, H. H. (1982). *Climate, History and the Modern World*, 2nd edn. Routledge, London.

Lamb, H. H. (1983). Update of the chronology of assessments of the volcanic dust veil index. *Climate Monitor*, **12**, 79–90.

Lamb, H. H. (1994). British Isles daily wind and weather patterns 1588, 1781–86, 1972–1991 and shorter early sequences (in 1532, 1570 and other years, notably 1688, 1689, 1703, 1717, 1783–4, 1791, 1792, 1795, 1822, 1825, 1829, 1845, 1846, 1849, 1850, 1854–5). *Climate Monitor*, **20**, 47–71.

Lamb, H. H. & Frydendahl, K. (1991). *Historic Storms of the North Sea, British Isles and Northwest Europe*. Cambridge University Press, Cambridge.

Lamb, H. H. & Johnson, A. I. (1966). *Secular Variations of the Atmospheric Circulation since 1750*. Geophysical Memoirs 110, Met.O. 711e. Meteorological Office, HMSO, London.

Lamb, H. H., Lewis, R. P. W. & Woodroffe, A. (1966). Atmospheric circulation and the main climatic variables between 8000 and 0 BC: meteorological evidence. *Proceedings of the International Symposium on World Climate 8000 to 0 BC.* Royal Meteorological Society, London, 174–217.

Lamb, H. H. & Weiss, I. (1979). *On Recent Changes of the Wind and Wave Regime of the North Sea and the Outlook*. Fachliche Mitteilungen, GeophysBDBw Nr. 194, Traben–Trarbach.

Lane, F. W. (1967). *The Elements Rage: the Extremes of Natural Violence*. Readers Union/David & Charles, London.

Law, F. M., Black, A. R., Scarrott, A. R., Miller, J. B. & Bayliss, A. C. (n.d.). Chronology of British Hydrological Events. www.dundee.ac.uk/geography/cbhe.

Lawrence, E. N. (1956). British summers of the past. *Weather*, **11**, 223–227.

Lawrence, E. N. (1972). The earliest known journal of the weather. *Weather*, **27**, 494–501.

Le Roy Ladurie, E. (1971). *Times of Feast, Times of Famine: A History of Climate since the Year 1000*. Doubleday, New York.

Ley, W. C. (1894). *Cloudland: a Study on the Structure and Characters of Clouds*. Stanford, London.

Long, C. (1974). The oldest European weather diary? *Weather*, **29**, 233–237.

Ludlam, F. H. (1966). *The Cyclone Problem: a History of Models of the Cyclonic Storm*. Imperial College of Science and Technology, London.

Ludlam, F. H. & Scorer, R. S. (1957). *Cloud Study: a Pictorial Guide*. John Murray, London.

McCormick, M., Dutton, P. E. & Mayewski, P. A. (2007). Volcanoes and the climate forcing of Carolingian Europe, AD. 750–950. *Speculum*, **82**, 865–895.

McIntosh, D. H. (1963). *Meteorological Glossary*. Meteorological Office MO 729, AP 827. HMSO, London.

Manley, G. (1950). On British climatic fluctuations since Queen Elizabeth's day. *Weather*, **5**, 312–318.

Manley, G. (1952). *Climate and the British Scene*. New Naturalist 22. Collins, London.

Manley, G. (1970). The climate of the British Isles. In Wallén, C. C., ed., *World Survey of Climatology, Volume 5: Climates of Northern and Western Europe*. Elsevier, Amsterdam, 81–133.

Manley, G. (1974). Central England temperatures: monthly means 1659 to 1973. *Quarterly Journal of the Royal Meteorological Society*, **100**, 389–405.

Markham, S. F. (1942). *Climate and the Energy of Nations*. Oxford University Press, Oxford.

Mason, B. J. (1962). *Clouds, Rain and Rainmaking*. Cambridge University Press, Cambridge.

Murray, R. & Lewis, R. P. W. (1966). Some aspects of the synoptic climatology of the British Isles as measures by simple indices. *Meteorological Magazine*, **95**, 193–203.

Ogilvie, A. & Farmer, G. (1997). Documenting the medieval climate. In Hulme, M., & Barrow, E. eds, *Climates of the British Isles: Present, Past and Future*, Routledge, London, 112–133.

Ogley, B., Davison, M. & Currie, I. (1993). *The Norfolk and Suffolk Weather Book*. Froglets Publications, Westerham.

Ormerod, E. A. (1878). Pre-instrumental meteorology, contained in extracts from the Saxon Chronicle and Holinshed's Chronicles of England, Scotland, and Ireland. Unpublished MS.

Pearce, F. (1989). *Climate and Man: From the Ice Ages to the Global Greenhouse*. Vision Books, London.

Pearson, M., ed. (1994). *More Frost and Snow: the Diary of Janet Burnet 1758–1795*. Canongate Academic, Edinburgh.

Pestell, R. & Stannard, D. (1995). *Eccles-Juxta-Mare: a Lost Village Discovered*. Steeple Publishing, Eccles-on-Sea, Norfolk.

Pfister, C. (1999). *Wetternachhersage: 500 Jahre Klimavariationen Naturkatastrophen (1496–1995)*. Paul Haupt, Berne.

Pfister, C., Kington, J. A., Kleinlogel, G., Schule, H. & Siffert, E. (1994). High resolution spatio-temporal reconstructions of past climate from direct meteorological observations and proxy data. In Frenzel, B., Pfister, C., &

Glaser, B., eds, *Climatic Trends and Anomalies in Europe 1675–1715*. Gustav Fischer Verlag, Stuttgart, 329–375.

Pfister, C., Schwarz-Zanetti, G. & Wegmann, M. (1998). The most severe winters of the fourteenth century in central Europe compared to some analogues in the more recent past. In Wishman, E., Frenzel, B., & Weiss, M. M., eds, *Documentary Climatic Evidence for 1750–1850 and the Fourteenth Century*. Gustav Fischer Verlag, Stuttgart, 45–61.

Pfister, C., Weingartner, R. & Luterbacher, J. (2006). Hydrological winter droughts over the last 450 years in the Upper Rhine basin: a methodological approach. *Hydrological Sciences–Journal–des Sciences Hydrologique*, **51**, 966–985.

Pribyl, K. & Pfister, C. (2009). The beginning of the grain harvest in Norfolk as a proxy for mean April–July temperatures, c. 1270 AD – 1430 AD. Geophysical Research Abstracts, **11**.

Roberts, S. (1991). *Analysis of a Welsh Weather Diary of 1793–1835*. Department of Geography, University of Sheffield.

Roth, G. D. (1981). *Collins Guide to the Weather* (translated by E. M. Yates). Collins, London.

Rothwell, J. (2007). An 18th-century temperature series for the East Midlands 1748–1784. *The International Journal of Meteorology*, **32**, 303–316.

Royal Meteorological Society (1965–2000). Weather Log, April 1965–December 2000.

Ruskin, J. (1843). *Modern Painters*. Smith, Elder & Co., London.

Sainty, J. E. (1939). Past history of sea flooding and cause of the 1938 flood. *Transactions of the Norfolk and Norwich Naturalists Society*, **14**, 334–345.

Salter, M. & de Carle, S. (1921). *The Rainfall of the British Isles*. University of London Press, London.

Sargent, P. (2010). A moment in time 98: year without a summer, 1816. *Eastern Daily Press*, 30 January 2010, Norwich.

Schneider, S. H. & Mesirow, L. E. (1976). *The Genesis Strategy: Climate and Global Survival*, Plenum, New York.

Schove, D. J. (1951). Hail in history, AD 1630–1680. *Weather*, **6**, 17–21.

Schove, D. J. (1953). Climatic fluctuations in Europe in the late historical period. Unpublished MSc thesis, London University.

Schove, D. J. (1966). Fire and drought. *Weather*, **21**, 311–314.

Schove, D. J. (unpublished MS). The Little Ice Age in Scandinavia and Scotland.

Schove, D. J. (n.d.). Miscellaneous articles and papers in his bequest to the Climatic Research Unit, University of East Anglia, Norwich.

Schove, D. J. & Reynolds, D. (1973). Weather in Scotland, 1659–1660: the diary of Andrew Hay. *Annals of Science*, **30**, 165–177.

Shaw, N. (1923). *Forecasting Weather*. Constable, London.

Shaw, N. (1934). *The Drama of Weather*. Cambridge University Press, Cambridge.

Siegenthaler, D. (1994). Climatic trends and anomalies in England 1675 to 1715. In Frenzel, B., Pfister, C., & Glaser, B., eds, *Climatic Trends and Anomalies in Europe 1675–1715*. Gustav Fischer Verlag, Stuttgart, 133–149.

Smith, L. P. (1968). *Seasonable Weather*. George Allen & Unwin, London.

Steers, J. A. (1953). *The Sea Coast*. New Naturalist 25. Collins, London.

Stothers, R. B. (2000). Climatic and demographic consequences of the massive volcanic eruption of 1258. *Climatic Change*, **45**, 361–374.

Stratton, J.M. & Houghton Brown, J. (1978). *Agricultural Records* AD. *220–1977*, 2nd edn. John Baker, London.

Stringer, C. (2006). *Homo Britannicus: the Incredible Story of Human Life in Britain.* Allen Lane, London.

Svensmark, H. & Calder, N. (2008). *The Chilling Stars: a Cosmic View of Climate Change*. Icon Books, Cambridge.

Thornes, J. E. (1999). *John Constable's Skies: a Fusion of Art and Science*. University of Birmingham Press, Birmingham.

Titow, J. (1959–1960). Evidence of weather in the account rolls of the Bishopric of Winchester 1209–1350. *Economic History Review, 2nd Series*, **12**, 360–407.

Trevelyan, G. M. (1966). *Illustrated English Social History*. Penguin, Harmondsworth.

Vaisey, D. (1985). *The Diary of Thomas Turner 1754–1765*. Oxford University Press, Oxford.

van der Zee, H. & van der Zee, B. (1988). *1688: Revolution in the Family*. Penguin, London.

van Engelen, A. F. V., Buisman, J. & Ijnsen, F. (2001). A millennium of weather, winds and water in the Low Countries, in Jones, P. D., Ogilvie, A. E. J., Davies, T. D. & Briffa, K. R., eds, *History and Climate: Memories of the Future?* Kluwer Academic/Plenum, New York, 101–124.

Wanner, H., Brázdil, R., Frich, P. & Pfister, C. (1994). Synoptic interpretation of monthly weather maps for the late Maunder Minimum (1675–1704). In Frenzel, B., Pfister, C., & Glaser, B., eds, *Climatic Trends and Anomalies in Europe 1675–1715*. Gustav Fischer Verlag, Stuttgart, 401–424.

Wanner, H., Pfister, C., Brázdil, R. *et al.* (1995). Wintertime European circulation patterns during the Late Maunder Minimum cooling period (1675–1704). *Theoretical and Applied Climatology*, **51**, 167–175.

Werner, T. H. & Stringer, E. (1975). The Cloud Watchers: An Exhibition of Instruments, Publications, Paintings and Watercolours concerning Art and Meteorology c.1770–1830. Herbert Art Gallery and Museum, Jordan Well, Coventry.

Wheeler, D. & Mayes, J., eds. (1997). *Regional Climates of the British Isles.* Routledge, London.

Whillis, J. (1950). Mr. Pepys' weather. *Weather,* **5,** 96–99.

Whistlecraft, O. (1840). *The Climate of England.* Longman, Orme, Brown, Green and Longmans, London.

Whistlecraft, O. (1883). *Variations of Seasons in the Eastern Parts of England, as Observed at Thwaite, Suffolk.* Jarrold, London.

Wild, R. (1998–2007). A review of heavy snowfalls/blizzards/snowstorms/snow-falls greater than 13 cm in Great Britain between 1861 and 1996: parts 1–7. *International Journal of Meteorology,* **23,** 3–19; **24,** 19–32; **26,** 92–100; **29,** 17–26; **30,** 43–50, 363–367; **32,** 325–334.

Willis, J. H. (1944). *Weatherwise: England's Weather Through the Past Thirty Years.* George Allen & Unwin, London.

Woodward, A. & Penn, R. (2007). *The Wrong Kind of Snow.* Hodder & Stoughton, London.

Index

The New Naturalist Library